SEEKING WHAT IS RIGHT

SEEKING WHAT IS RIGHT

The Old Testament and the Good Life

Iain Provan

BAYLOR UNIVERSITY PRESS

Cover design by Kasey McBeath
Cover photograph by Nick Fewings/Unsplash
Book design by Baylor University Press

Hardcover ISBN: 978-1-4813-1288-2

Library of Congress Control Number: 2020022029

NATIONAL
ENDOWMENT
FOR THE
HUMANITIES

Seeking What Is Right has been made possible in part by a major grant from the National Endowment for the Humanities: NEH CARES. Any views, findings, conclusions, or recommendations expressed in this book do not necessarily represent those of the National Endowment for the Humanities.

Printed in the United States of America on acid-free paper with a minimum of thirty percent recycled content.

For
Gideon
Harriet
Malachy
And anyone else who shows up.

Contents

Acknowledgments

I have numerous people to thank for their help and support in the writing of this book. My wonderful wife Lynette provided constant encouragement and constructive criticism, as well as contributing substantially to the form and content of chapters 18 and 19 in particular. My research assistant Conor Wilkerson spent a lot of time proofreading the text, checking references for me, and generating indices. A number of other people then read the whole manuscript and offered helpful comments on it: immediate family members and my friends Ed Gerber, Ivan DeSilva, and Sandeep Jadhav. Various others read sections of the book and greatly helped me in shaping their content and argument: Margaret Cottle, Ross Hastings, Earl Phillips, John Stackhouse, and Sarah Williams. I am also grateful to the Regent College library staff for their support throughout the project and to Regent College more generally for having an excellent sabbatical policy that allows its faculty to devote dedicated periods to research and writing. The folks at Baylor University Press were their usual, supportive, splendid, professional selves. Finally, I must thank the Alexander von Humboldt Foundation in Germany for the funding that allowed me to spend a sabbatical term in Erfurt in the winter semester of 2019 to work on this book and also Christoph and Ursula Bultmann for the warm welcome they gave us there. The book is dedicated to my three wonderful grandchildren and to any others that may come along later. I hope that they may read it with profit when they are older.

Iain Provan
Epiphany 2020

ix

Abbreviations

Unless noted in the list below, all the abbreviations in this book follow the form in the *Society of Biblical Literature Handbook of Style*, 2nd ed. (Atlanta: SBL, 2014).

AJP	*American Journal of Physics*
BHP	British History in Perspective
CalC	Calvin's Commentaries
CBP	Commons Briefing Papers
CSSH	*Comparative Studies in Society and History*
CTAW	Christianities in the Trans-Atlantic World
CTHP	*Cambridge Texts in the History of Philosophy*
CTHPT	Cambridge Texts in the History of Political Thought
DHWC	Documentary History of Western Civilization
GBWW	Great Books of the Western World
HASt	Historical Association Studies
HE	*Human Ecology*
Hist	*Historian (London)*
HN	*Human Nature*
HS	Hellenic Studies
ITI	International Themes and Issues
JPSSDS	JPS Scholar of Distinction Series
MAPS	Memoir of the American Philosophical Society
MART	Mediaeval Academy Reprints for Teaching
NSEH	New Studies in European History
PHE	Penguin History of Europe
PSQ	*Political Science Quarterly*
RLMCMS	Religion and Law in Medieval Christian and Muslim Societies

SCEH	Studies in Central European Histories
SCES	Sixteenth Century Essays and Studies
SCI	*Scripta Classica Israelica*
SMRT	Studies in Medieval and Reformation Traditions
SSoc	*Science & Society*
Transf	*Transformation*
VIFRUF	Vorlesungen des Interdisziplinären Forums Religion der Universität Erfurt
ZIBBC	*Zondervan Illustrated Bible Backgrounds Commentary*

I

FOUNDATIONS

1

The Good Life and How to Recognize It

A Short Introduction

What's bad and what's good? What should we love and what should we hate? What is life for, and what am I? What is life? What is death? What kind of force is it that directs everything?[1]

Pierre Bezukhov (*in* War and Peace)

Bezukhov is having a difficult time. An immature, aimless young man, he has recently come into a great fortune, making him a very eligible bachelor. Too weak to resist the schemes of the Kuragin family, he has been maneuvered into a marriage with Hélène Kuragin, a beautiful but unintelligent woman whom he does not love. This unsatisfactory marriage has led in turn to a duel with his friend Fedya Dolokhov, who has been rumored to be having an affair with Hélène. After a violent row between Pierre and Hélène as a result of this duel, the couple have agreed to separate, and Pierre has left Moscow for St. Petersburg. On the road, he finds himself in the midst of an existential crisis, in which he asks the fundamental questions described in the epigraph just above. His understanding of life, upon which he has never before reflected, has been shaken, and he is looking for answers. Some of these answers concern the nature of the good life: "What's bad and what's good? What should we love and what should we hate?"

Many of us have asked similar questions at one point or another in our lives. We aspire to be good rather than evil. Indeed, an advertisement for a fairly recent book proposes that "everyone wants to think of himself or herself as good [now]."[2] I am not convinced that this second claim is true—so let us stick with the more modest notion of *aspiration* for the moment. Many or perhaps even most of us aspire to be good rather than evil. Consistent with this claim, recent polls taken in the United States (to focus just on one country) reveal that "the most popular New Year's resolution" for both 2017 and 2018 was "being a better person."[3]

But what does "being good" *involve*? We want to be "better people"—but "what does it actually mean to be 'good'?" asks the journalist reporting on the polls. We want to think of ourselves as good, perhaps—"But what does a good life look like?" asks the website advertising the book. These are important questions. We shall not get very far in our quest for goodness if we cannot identify, objectively speaking, what it is. So what is bad and what is good? What should we love and what should we hate? And to these two questions of Pierre Bezukhov we should add a third: how do we *know*?

THE CHARACTER AND ACTIONS OF GOD

Very different answers, connected with very different understandings of the nature of reality, have been offered to these three questions over the course of history. My purpose in this chapter is to elucidate the answers provided in the Christian Bible, in part by contrasting them with some of the alternatives. This is because the point of this whole book is to help readers of the Bible read it more deeply and accurately "for life"—and I need to begin with a solid foundation for this project. Let me state my thesis for this chapter right at its beginning. The heart of the biblical response to our three questions is this: that goodness looks like God, and that God reveals himself to us so that we begin to recognize and pursue it. We shall reflect on the first theme in the current section, and on the second in our next section, before discussing some competing opinions.

THE RICH YOUNG RULER

Our starting point lies in the sharp response that Jesus Christ gives to a certain young man in the gospels who asks him (in Mark and Luke's version of the story), "Good Teacher, what must I do to inherit eternal life?" (Mark 10:17; Luke 18:18).[4] Judging from his response, Jesus senses in the question a confusion in the young man concerning what the standard of goodness is—human or divine. Jesus is keen to clarify: "No one is good—except God alone" (Mark 10:18; Luke 18:19). In other words, we should ultimately measure "good" not by what an apparently good human teacher has to say—the young man does not of course fully understand who Jesus is—but by the character and actions of God. It turns out in this story, subsequently, that goodness involves radical generosity to the poor (Mark 10:21; Luke 18:22), just as God himself generously "causes his sun to rise on the evil and the good, and sends rain on the righteous and the unrighteous," indiscriminately giving good gifts to his children (Matt. 5:45). Unfortunately, the rich young ruler is not prepared for such a definition of the good and goes away sad, because he has great wealth (Matt. 19:22). He had thought of himself as a good person, and indeed as someone who was *eager* to be a good person. Yet he had underestimated what real goodness would require of him. If we, likewise, really wish to know what it means to be good, then in the words of Matthew 5:48 it is this: "Be perfect . . . as your heavenly Father is perfect."

Godlike Goodness

The remainder of the gospel tradition then unpacks for us what this Godlike goodness looks like in our own lives, as Jesus encourages his hearers to let others "see your good deeds and glorify your Father in heaven" (Matt. 5:16). It is important to attend to this teaching, it turns out, because "every good tree bears good fruit, but a bad tree bears bad fruit . . . Every tree that does not bear good fruit is cut down and thrown into the fire" (Matt. 7:17, 19). Conversely, the person who listens to Jesus' teaching may expect to hear these words from his master at the end of time: "Well done, good and faithful servant!" (Matt. 25:21). The *good* life that is described in such ways in the gospels is also the subject of much interest in the remainder of the New Testament (NT), where it is further characterized as the *holy* life. Holiness is simply goodness by another name. Writing to the Christians in Rome, for example, the apostle Paul reminds them that "just as you used to offer yourselves as slaves to impurity and to ever-increasing wickedness, so now offer yourselves as slaves to righteousness leading to holiness" (Rom. 6:19). In 2 Corinthians 7:1 he exhorts his fellow Christians, "Let us purify ourselves from everything that contaminates body and spirit, perfecting holiness out of reverence for God." The Christians in Ephesus are told "to put on the new self, created to be like God in true righteousness and holiness" (Eph. 4:24), and the author of the letter to the Hebrews urges his readers to "make every effort to live in peace with everyone and to be holy; without holiness no one will see the Lord" (Heb. 12:14). All Christians are called, like the Roman ones, "to be his holy people" (Rom. 1:7). They aim to be so "by persistence in doing good" (Rom. 2:7), clinging "to what is good" (12:9), overcoming "evil with good" (12:21), and abounding "in every good work" (2 Cor. 9:8).

THE REVELATION OF GOD

Goodness looks like God. His character and actions *define* the good, and by opposition also the bad—what we should we love and what we should hate. But how do we *know* the good? How do we discern what it is? The Bible teaches us that God reveals himself to us so that we begin to understand who he is and what goodness looks like. We are not left in the dark; God shines his light upon us so that we can see our way.

The Bible itself plays a central role in this divine revelation, not least because it describes the life, teaching, death, and resurrection of Jesus Christ, who turns out (unbeknownst to the rich young ruler) to have been God Incarnate on earth (John 1:1–18). This means that although "no one has ever seen God" in heaven, humanity has in fact encountered him on earth: "the one and only Son, who is himself God and is in closest relationship with the Father, has made him known" (John 1:18). So although we still know what we know about God only "in part," we understand more than enough to get on with our lives under God's rule, in the expectation that one day we shall "know fully, even as [we are] fully known" (1 Cor. 13:12). In the interim we are called to "grow" in our faith and "in the knowledge of God" (2 Cor. 10:15; Col. 1:10), and indeed in our goodness (holiness), so that we "become in every respect the mature body of him who is the head, that is, Christ. From him the whole body, joined and held together by every supporting ligament, grows and builds itself up in love, as each part does its work" (Eph. 4:15–16). Holy Scripture is given to us to help us in this quest: "All Scripture is God-breathed and is useful for teaching, rebuking, correcting, and training in righteousness, so that the servant of God may be thoroughly equipped for every good work" (2 Tim. 3:16–17). Reading it, reflecting on it, and wrestling with it, we learn what it means to be like Christ, becoming like him just as we become like the Father (e.g., Phil. 2:1–11; 1 Thess. 1:6). Seeking what is right, we learn "not [to] imitate what is evil but what is good" (3 John 11), in line with God's command: "Be holy, because I am holy" (1 Pet. 1:16).

WRONG PATHS

These biblical ideas concerning the nature of the good and how we discover it stand in significant contrast to other ways of thinking about these important matters. Most of us grow up in some kind of family or tribe, and in our younger years we are inevitably inducted into the worldview of our elders and the ethical codes connected with it. We accept, unquestioningly, what we are told about what is true and false, and right and wrong, and we may well continue to measure our lives against those standards in our adulthood. Biblical faith forbids us, however, from endowing these inherited norms with absolute authority in our lives. Sometimes it is necessary to *reject* what our tradition has told us about truth and virtue and follow instead a different path. Sometimes we need to choose *between* the ways of the kingdom of God and those of our family or tribe. Jesus himself did so (Matt. 12:46–50):

While Jesus was still talking to the crowd, his mother and brothers stood outside, wanting to speak to him. Someone told him, "Your mother and brothers are standing outside, wanting to speak to you." He replied to him, "Who is my mother, and who are my brothers?" Pointing to his disciples, he said, "Here are my mother and my brothers. For whoever does the will of my Father in heaven is my brother and sister and mother."

Earlier in the same gospel, and in connection with the same reality, Jesus announces that he has come to turn "a man against his father, a daughter against her mother, a daughter-in-law against her mother-in-law—a man's enemies will be the members of his own household" (10:35–36).

Then again, each of us inhabits as an adult a general culture that possesses its own norms of conduct and will usually enforce at least some of these by using sanctions of various kinds (e.g., imprisonment). Biblical faith certainly teaches both a general respect for such prevailing culture and a general duty of obedience to societal law (1 Pet. 2:13–17):

Submit yourselves for the Lord's sake to every human authority: whether to the emperor, as the supreme authority, or to governors, who are sent by him to punish those who do wrong and to commend those who do right . . . Show proper respect to everyone, love the family of believers, fear God, honor the emperor.

Yet biblical faith forbids Christ-followers from taking the lead in what to believe and how to live from the culture at large, which may well be dominated by very wrong beliefs and woefully twisted values. "Do not conform to the pattern of this world, but be transformed by the renewing of your mind," Paul urges the Christians in Rome. "Then you will be able to test and approve what God's will is—his good, pleasing, and perfect will" (Rom. 12:2). The general culture to which they are not to conform is graphically described by Peter as being marked by "living in debauchery, lust, drunkenness, orgies, carousing, and detestable idolatry" (1 Pet. 4:3). Even though the pagans may be "surprised that you do not join them in their reckless, wild living, and . . . heap abuse on you," Christians must hold firm to what is true and good. This may involve disobeying the authorities, as the apostles do in Acts 5:29, since "we must obey God rather than human beings."

What is bad and what is good? What should we love and what should we hate? And how do we know? Goodness is not defined in the end by family, tribe, culture, or state. All human claims about such matters must be assessed in the light of the goodness of God. And when we want to know more about what this looks like, we do not *consult* as our ultimate authority our family, tribe, culture, or state. In seeking what is right, we turn to God's revelation of himself, which casts light on the path that we should "walk in obedience to his commands" (2 John 6).

REVELATION AND NATURE

It is also true that what is good and right is not defined by what is "natural" to human beings at some more fundamental level underneath family, tribe, culture, and state. We ought not to depend on any consultation with "Nature" (as some call it) in deciding how to live. This is a particularly important truth to affirm in the light of the general importance historically of the concept of "natural law" in ethical reflection, and of the great weight given in particular, in much contemporary ethical discourse, to "what is natural" to individuals. We need to spend a little time, therefore, specifically on the business of revelation and nature.

The Bible itself teaches us that Creation (as Christians should call it) does reveal to those with eyes to see *certain* truths about God the Creator and about how we should live in his world. Paul proposes in Romans 1:20–22, for example, that "since the creation of the world God's invisible qualities—his eternal power and divine nature—have been clearly seen, being understood from what has been made." This means "that people are without excuse" when they turn away from God and worship idols—"images made to look like a mortal human being and birds and animals and reptiles." Creation supplies sufficient information about the nature of reality to make human beings culpable for their wrongdoing. It can also tell them something about how they *ought* to be living instead: "Look at the birds of the air," Jesus exhorts his listeners in Matthew 6:26–27, and learn something about dealing with anxiety.

The point about this general revelation of God in Creation, however, is that it is not *sufficient* for our lives. It teaches us a limited number of truths about God and therefore about goodness—but nowhere near everything that we need. We require in addition the *special revelation* of God in Christ and in Scripture. One of the reasons that this special revelation is important is that we are all more than capable of misinterpreting the truth that is found in God's general revelation; if we are instead to comprehend it accurately we need the corrective eye surgery that special revelation supplies. This is precisely because we are born into families, tribes, cultures, and states that have already lost hold (to a greater or lesser extent) of what is true and good. Before we are even conscious of our own governing beliefs and values, we find ourselves among people who, "although they knew God . . . neither glorified him as God nor gave thanks to him, but their thinking became futile and their foolish hearts were darkened" (Rom. 1:21). "They exchanged the truth about God for a lie and worshiped and served created things rather than the Creator," falling into terrible sin (Rom. 1:25 and the following verses). Inducted into these groups, we naturally "see" through distorted lenses.

In biblical faith, then, Creation is not the source to which we should mainly turn for revelation concerning God and the godly life. It has a role to play, and for that reason reflection on the "natural law" that all human beings are said to know something about, even if they do not always act upon it, has certainly formed some part of Christian discourse on theology and ethics throughout the ages. Thomas Aquinas (1225–1274) is commonly regarded as having provided the classical articulation of this Christian version of natural law.[5] Yet the role that "the natural" plays in orthodox Christian thinking about what is true and good has inevitably been limited. Indeed, we are often explicitly exhorted in Scripture not to do what is natural to us but to choose a different path. Paul urges the Christians in Rome, for example, to "clothe yourselves with the Lord Jesus Christ, and do not think about how to gratify the desires of the flesh" (Rom. 13:14).

This has certainly not been the approach of many modern thinkers in their deployment of arguments from "the natural." Here, even when traces of a Christian worldview survive in some of the other language associated with the argument, the word "natural" loses almost all connection with substantive biblical notions of God and Creation. What is "natural" now is only that which is "normal," perhaps "inborn" (not learnt)—"having a specified character by nature," or "occurring in conformity with the ordinary course of nature."[6] What is immediately evident even at the definitional level is that "God-designed" or "God-ordained" are not the ideas immediately evoked by the word natural in present English usage. In such usage, if God is to be found anywhere it is instead in the realm of the "supernatural," which *Merriam-Webster* defines as "relating to an order of existence beyond the visible observable universe" and "departing from what is usual or normal especially so as to appear to transcend the laws of nature."[7]

So it is that when many modern people employ the word "natural" when speaking about ethics, they quite consciously intend "not to bring God into it." Specifically, they are announcing their intention of deriving their moral code from that which accords with nature *rather than* from what religious faith or custom has hitherto taught. What is good is *determined* in relation to what is "normal," which may indeed come down to what is instinctive or innate. Moreover, humanity suffers no impediment in its quest to *interpret* the world of the natural in order to learn about this good. The Bible may well claim that human "thinking" has become "futile" as our "foolish hearts" are "darkened" by evil—that even as we claim to be "wise" we have become "fools" who need remedial assistance in order to arrive at the truth (Rom. 1:21–22). The modern readers of nature are vastly more optimistic, however, about our capacity to see and to think straight. They either believe implicitly or state explicitly that the truths that nature reveals are "evident" to the observant enquirer.

NATURE AND ETHICS

This post-Christian and unbiblical way of thinking about the nature of the good and how we come to know about it has been widely embraced in the modern period for various reasons. Intellectual coherence is not, however, one of these. Indeed, a number of quite serious questions immediately arise that require our critical attention. Is it really true that what is instinctive to us, even from birth, represents a sure guide to what is *right*? To the contrary, are there not instincts that each one of us possesses that absolutely need to be ignored in pursuit of what is right—instincts relating to some sexual behavior, for example? Does it help, then, to discover that many people share these same instincts—that certain desires are innate to groups rather than simply individuals? It is not easy to see how this helps at all. How exactly do we get from a proposition that something is "natural" to groups of people—cannibalism, for instance—to the proposition that it is right (at least for those groups of people) to behave in a certain way? Would it help, finally, if we were to discover somehow that all human beings possess a "natural tendency" in a certain direction? If all human beings were discovered to be selfish by nature, for example, would selfishness thereby become "right" and generosity "wrong"? But of course the task of discovering empirically what might be "natural" to all human beings is in any case fraught with challenges, which is why, historically, those making claims about what is "naturally" the case for humanity in general have so often taken refuge in grand assertions rather than presenting compelling evidence. Since I shall be interacting to various extents throughout the book with some of the larger and more public of these claims, it seems appropriate to introduce them briefly here. Two derive from France and two from the United States of America, and we shall consider them, and the questions that they beg, in chronological order.

The American Declaration of Independence (1776)

Published at the beginning of the Revolutionary War against Great Britain, the American Declaration of Independence, in its preface, considers first the general case in which it is "necessary for one people to dissolve the political bands which have connected them with another and to assume among the powers of the earth, the separate and equal station to which the laws of Nature and of Nature's God entitle them." It proceeds then to speak explicitly of self-evident truths: "that all men are created equal, that they are endowed by their Creator with certain unalienable rights, that among these are life, liberty, and the pursuit of happiness." It is to secure these rights that government is created by way of "the consent of the governed." Any people, faced with a government that has failed to do this job, has the right to "alter or to abolish it, and to institute new government." A "long train of abuses" evidencing "absolute despotism" is then recorded—a "history of repeated injuries and usurpations" on the part of the British king George III that have as their object "the establishment of an absolute tyranny over these states." Such a king, "whose character is thus marked by every act which may define a tyrant, is unfit to be the ruler of a free people." Therefore, the colonies are "absolved from all allegiance to the British crown."[8]

We note here, then, a grand assertion about "the laws of Nature" (and her God) "entitling" the rebellious colonists to certain things—but how and why? We also read of certain rights being "self-evident"—but to whom? Certainly the great majority of people throughout history have not believed that "all men are created equal," for example—and this includes the citizens of the ancient republic of Athens, which played such an important role in forming modern American republican consciousness. It was not clear at all to the Athenians of (say) the fifth century BC, any more than it was to those ancient people who created the Hindu caste system in India, that "all men are created equal," possessing an inalienable right to liberty. And plainly many in the American colonies in the eighteenth century did not truly believe it either, since they were just as happy as the Athenians to run their economies on the basis of slave labor.

THE DECLARATION OF THE RIGHTS OF MAN AND THE CITIZEN (1789)

Adopted by France's National Assembly in the midst of the French Revolution, this declaration speaks in its own preface of "the natural, unalienable, and sacred rights of man" in the light of which all "acts of . . . legislative power, and those of executive power" must be assessed. It goes on to say that "[m]en are born and remain free and equal in rights. Social distinctions may be based only on considerations of the common good" (Article I). Moreover, the "aim of all political association is the preservation of the natural and imprescriptible rights of man . . . liberty, property, safety, and resistance to oppression" (Article II). Further, the "source of all sovereignty lies essentially in the Nation. No corporate body, nor individual may exercise any authority that does not expressly emanate from it" (Article III). "Law is the expression of the general will. All citizens have the right to take part, personally, or through their representatives, in its making" (Article VI). And so on.[9] But whence do these "natural, unalienable, and sacred rights of man" derive, and why in fact should they form the context in which all "acts of . . . legislative power" and "executive power" must be assessed? Is it really true that "men are born and remain free and equal in rights"? Does that include women, and if not, why not?

The Declaration of the Rights of Woman and the Female Citizen (1791)

What is self-evident to whom concerning natural human rights quickly became an issue in eighteenth-century France, specifically with respect to women. Only a few months after the publication of the Declaration of the Rights of Man and the Citizen, the National Assembly declined even to discuss a women's petition on the subject of female equality. Later, in 1790, the Marquis of Condorcet—following through on his conviction that natural right and not social utility should determine law (for which reason he, at least, opposed the slave trade and slavery)—attempted once again to get the discussion going. "Either no individual in mankind has true rights," he asserted, "or all have the same ones; and whoever votes against the right of another, whatever be his religion, his color, or his sex, has from that moment abjured his own rights."[10] His words, too, fell on deaf ears. All of this is the prelude to the Declaration of the Rights of Woman and the Female Citizen, published in 1791 by the playwright and activist Olympe de Gouges (1748–1793).[11] In this declaration she outlined various basic rights that should be extended to women, including the right to participate fully in the making of law and at all levels of government. We gain some sense of the hostile context in which she made these demands, however, from the newspaper that reported her death in 1793.[12] "[She] believed her delusions were inspired by *nature* [my emphasis]," announced *Le Moniteur Universel*. "She wanted to be a Statesman; it would seem that the law has punished this plotter for having forgotten *the virtues suitable to her own sex* [my emphasis]."[13] She was not the only woman to suffer for such "forgetfulness" during this period in France, in which women generally were instructed in no uncertain terms to return home and leave public affairs to the men.[14] What was considered to be self-evidently "natural" by some was viewed as decidedly and self-evidently "unnatural" by others.

The Declaration of Sentiments (1848)

The same issues came to the fore in the United States in 1848 with the publication in that country of a Declaration of Sentiments concerning women's rights. Its author was Elizabeth Cady Stanton (1815–1902), who modeled it on de Gouges' work in France, ensuring that it also mimicked the style of an earlier founding document—in this case, the American Declaration of Independence. In "Sentiments" too, then, the language of self-evident natural rights is prominent, but with a twist: "we hold these truths to be self-evident: that all men *and women* are created equal" (my emphasis).[15] This declaration then proceeds to criticize not the government of King George III but that of *men in general* for failing to uphold in its various practices this principle of equality and instead engaging in "absolute despotism."[16] A list of abuses follows. Man has never permitted woman "to exercise her inalienable right to the elective franchise. He has compelled her to submit to laws, in the formation of which she had no voice." Moreover, "[h]e has withheld from her rights which are given to the most ignorant and degraded men—both natives and foreigners . . . [h]e has made her, if married, in the eye of the law, civilly dead." All of this and more, the document proposes, represents an "entire disfranchisement of one-half the people of this country, their social and religious degradation." In response, the declaration demands "immediate admission to all the rights and privileges which belong to them as citizens of these United States." So what is self-evident to whom, and how does identifying what is natural provide a foundation in any case for claims about rights?

FACTS AND VALUES

One is reminded in all of this, first, of a comment by Jean-Jacques Rousseau (1712–1778): "The philosophers who have examined the foundations of society have all felt it necessary to go back to the state of nature, but none of them has succeeded in getting there."[17] Indeed. The identification of what is "natural" to human beings is immersed in difficulty. One recalls, secondly, a comment by Rousseau's contemporary David Hume (1711–1776): "In every system of morality, which I have hitherto met with, I have always remarked, that the author proceeds for some time in the ordinary way of reasoning . . . and then he suddenly surprises me by moving from propositions with the usual copula 'is' (or 'is not') to ones that are connected by 'ought' (or 'ought not')."[18] This is a problem: to note that something "is" is not at all to demonstrate what "ought" to be. We cannot move simply from fact to value.

The summation of it all, then, is that the kinds of appeal to "nature" that modern people often make in constructing their view of what is good are not only inconsistent with biblical faith but also problematic on their own terms. The first of these realities should of course provide a sufficient reason, all by itself, for Christians to avoid invoking similar "natural law" arguments in their own moral discourse. I have spent some time describing the second reality, however, just in case any further ammunition is needed in the constant battle that must be joined with false ideas concerning "the good," if true ones are to prevail. This has not always been a battle that has been well-fought in Christian history. To the contrary, Christians have often resorted just as readily as everyone else to confident appeals concerning what is "self-evidently" natural.

We shall see this powerfully illustrated in both chapters 12 and 13 of this book, for example, with respect to nineteenth-century arguments concerning both slavery and women. Black Africans, it was claimed, are by nature incompetent, utterly dependent, docile, testy, and lazy. It is natural, it was asserted, for a woman to be delicate, dependent, and weak. Firm conclusions followed concerning the right ways of organizing society, in which of course (some) white men were to be in charge. In truth these statements tell us nothing at all about "black African" or "female nature," objectively and generally speaking. They inform us only about the prejudices, rooted in limited experience, of people who either did not travel very much outside their own narrow cultures or did not care to learn from others when they did. They therefore did not come to realize that what they believed to be "self-evident" about "nature" was in reality far from it. But even if the people making these statements had in fact been telling "the truth" about "African" or "female" nature, how would this have determined what was good and right in society? Let us grant for the sake of argument for a moment—even though it should not be granted—that it has been demonstrated that women are by nature "dependent." How does the fact of "dependency" then become a fate that determines the roles that a woman is permitted to play in society, rather than simply the starting point on a journey that may well lead to independence if society itself is willing to facilitate and support it? The "is" of description does not lead on inevitably to a particular "ought." It only appears to do so to people who have not given sufficient thought to the matter.

CONCLUSION

Looking back on this first chapter, then, we may encapsulate its argument as follows. Many people aspire to be good. However, this begs the question "what does 'good' mean?" In biblical faith, "good" means "being like God in character and action"; its synonym is "holy." How do we know what this goodness looks like? God reveals himself to us, so that we can discover enough about what is right to enable us to walk on life's journey successfully. The good is not defined in the end by family, tribe, culture, or state—or by our perceptions concerning what is natural to some or all human beings—and we do not come to sure knowledge of the good by consulting such authorities. Goodness is defined by God, and we come to know what it looks like by attending to God's special revelation in Christ and in the Holy Scripture whose central character he is. All human claims about the nature of the good life, then, must be measured against the moral vision that is articulated in Scripture. This brings us immediately to our next two, associated questions, which we shall discuss in chapters 2 and 3: what do we mean by "Scripture," and how should we read it "for life"?

DISCUSSION QUESTIONS

1. Do you think of yourself as a good person? How do you know?
2. What role should our feelings or convictions concerning what is "natural" have to play in our understanding of what is "right"?
3. What role should the opinions of our families, tribes, cultures, and states have to play in our understanding of what is "right"?

2

The Twenty-Five Percent Bible
Scripture and the Good Life

You are a chosen people, a royal priesthood, a holy nation . . . Once you were not a people, but now you are the people of God; once you had not received mercy, but now you have received mercy.

1 Peter 2:9–10

If all human claims about the nature of the good life must be measured against the moral vision articulated in Scripture, then what do we mean by "Scripture," and how should we read it in pursuit of holiness? To some readers, the first part of this question (at least) will come as something of a surprise. Is it not obvious that Scripture comprises the Old Testament (OT), which runs from Genesis to Malachi, and the NT, which runs from Matthew to Revelation? Is it not the case that it is all these books, fundamentally (leaving aside some minor differences concerning the "Apocrypha"), that the Christian Church has historically held to comprise the Christian Bible?[1] Yes, this is true. Quite near the beginning of the Church's history, however, the status of the OT as Christian Scripture was already being questioned, and as we shall see, such ideas are by no means completely absent from contemporary thinking in the Church. Our immediate task in the present chapter, therefore, is to rehearse all the very good arguments as to why the OT must be retained by Christians as Holy Scripture equivalent in status to the NT. However, even when the OT has been granted such status *in theory*, it has quite often been read in ways that have effectively disabled it *in practice* from functioning as authoritatively as it might. Our second task in this chapter, therefore, is to think hard about what kind of reading does and does not allow OT Scripture to function with *an authority that is equivalent* to that of the NT. For it is my conviction that the OT *must* be able to do this if we are to comprehend as fully as we require the nature of the good life that God calls us to live.

ON UNHITCHING OUR WAGONS

In April 2018 Andy Stanley, the senior pastor of North Point Community Church in Atlanta, Georgia, preached a well-publicized sermon concerning the Bible and the Christian life.[2] In it he urged his listeners to decouple the OT from their Christian faith. He acknowledged that these "Jewish scriptures," as he called them, are certainly an important "back story" for "the main story" of Christian Scripture—they represent a divinely inspired description of "God on the move through an ancient, ancient time." However, the OT was not regarded in the early Church as "the go-to source regarding *any* [his emphasis] behavior in the church." Those early Church leaders "unhitched the church from the worldview, the value system, and the regulations of the Jewish Scriptures," including the Ten Commandments; "they unhitched the church from the entire thing . . . everything's different, everything's new." We should follow their example: "Jesus' new covenant, His covenant with the nations, His covenant with you, His covenant with us, can stand on its own two nail-scarred resurrection feet. It does not need propping up by the Jewish scriptures." According to Stanley, the people of God in the NT are entirely distinct from the people of God in the OT, and our Bible is entirely distinct from theirs.

This is a very particular view of the role that the Bible ought to play in forming our understanding of the good life and guiding us to live it. Essentially Stanley proposes cutting out of our God-provided guidebook about 75 percent of its content and suggests that we should focus only on the remaining 25 percent. What are we to make of this proposal? My own belief is that it is seriously wrongheaded. In fact, to regard the OT as anything less than Scripture that is *actively relevant* to the Church is to step outside the bounds of historic, orthodox Christian faith. It is to step aside from following Christ and his apostles. In the next four sections of this chapter I shall try to demonstrate that this is so.[3]

JESUS AND THE OLD TESTAMENT

Consider first how Jesus himself regarded the OT and how he taught his followers to regard it. In the Gospels we find him again and again basing his teaching or arguments on this literature (e.g., Mark 14:27; Matt. 11:10), which he refers to on a number of occasions as "the Law and the Prophets" (e.g., Luke 16:16) or close variants. He specifically references the Ten Commandments in responding to the rich young ruler encountered already in our chapter 1 (Matt. 19:16–21). "What good thing must I do to get eternal life?" this man asks Jesus, and Jesus tells him to keep "the commandments," specifying five of them along with the general instruction "love your neighbor as yourself," which is drawn from Leviticus 19:18. The Ten Commandments are high-order illustrations, it seems, of what it means to "love the Lord your God with all your heart and with all your soul and with all your strength and with all your mind" and to "love your neighbor as yourself" (Luke 10:25–37).

After the resurrection, Jesus rebukes two of his confused and downhearted disciples precisely for failing to take these same OT Scriptures sufficiently seriously when trying to understand their present experience (Luke 24:25–27). The central importance of the OT Scriptures is emphasized again shortly afterwards, in Luke 24:44, when Jesus advises all the core disciples and others that "[e]verything must be fulfilled that is written about me in the Law of Moses, the Prophets, and the Psalms." If the disciples, after the resurrection, wish to understand what is happening in the world and in their lives, they must attend to these OT Scriptures. If they, and we, are to understand Christ, it is to these Scriptures that they must go. Jesus himself sends them to that resource.

THE APOSTLES AND THE OLD TESTAMENT

The earliest Church took this advice very seriously, not only post-resurrection but also post-Pentecost; we would of course expect disciples of Jesus to follow his lead on all things. Their perspective is particularly clear in 2 Timothy 3:16–17, which we already considered in chapter 1: "All Scripture is God-breathed and is useful for teaching, rebuking, correcting, and training in righteousness, so that the servant of God may be thoroughly equipped for every good work." The point that I need to emphasize here, though, is that *the primary reference in this text is to the OT*. When Paul was writing to Timothy in the first century AD, the NT did not yet exist. We see immediately, therefore, how impossible it is for Christians embracing apostolic faith to believe that these "Jewish scriptures" are (in Stanley's words) merely a "divinely inspired back story"—that they are not at the same time a "go-to source regarding . . . behavior in the church." The OT is, instead, inspired Scripture that is designed *precisely* so that it is *useful* to the Church in "teaching, rebuking, correcting, and training in righteousness." It is the very canon (or measuring stick) of Christian faith and practice in the first century. "I believe everything that is in accordance with the Law and that is written in the Prophets," affirms the apostle Paul to the Roman procurator Marcus Antonius Felix (Acts 24:14)—and his other letters to the Christian churches in the first-century Roman world illustrate the seriousness with which he took this idea.

As an example of the importance of OT Scripture to Paul, notice how he applies the Ten Commandments to the various ethical situations with which he is confronted in the emerging churches; this is particularly important in light of Stanley's advice that Christians should not obey these Commandments. Paul exhorts the Christians in Rome to love each other and thereby to keep "the commandments," specifying a number of them as well as referring (like Jesus) to the general instruction "love your neighbor as yourself" (Rom. 13:9–10). Earlier in this same letter he has already alluded to those Commandments that deal with worshipping other gods and making images of them, stealing, and adultery, and he has also referred to coveting in the course of a brief reflection that leads him to assert that "the law is holy, and the commandment is holy, righteous, and good."[4] Writing again to the Ephesian church, Paul reminds children that they should obey their parents in line with the Commandment "'Honor your father and mother'—which is the first commandment with a promise—'so that it may go well with you and that you may enjoy long life on the earth'" (Eph. 6:2–3).

For Paul and the other apostles, it was impossible to speak of Christ without speaking of him "in accordance with the Scriptures" of Israel that already existed—Scriptures in which "prophets, though human, spoke *from* God [my emphasis] as they were carried along by the Holy Spirit" (2 Pet. 1:20–21). These were Scriptures that the Church "at its origin received . . . as the sole authoritative witness . . . These Scriptures taught the church what to believe about God: who God was; how to understand God's relationship to creation, Israel, and the nations; how to worship God; and *what manner of life was enjoined* [my emphasis] in grace and in judgment."[5] They were "the very words of God" (Rom. 3:2) that Jesus did not come to abolish but to fulfill (Matt. 5:17). As such, they remained entirely relevant to the new "chosen people . . . royal priesthood . . . holy nation," just as they had once been to the old one—the people who had once been "not a people, but [were] now . . . the people of God" (see the epigraph to this chapter).

THE EARLY CHURCH AND THE OLD TESTAMENT

The generations of Christian leaders who came immediately after the apostolic age are typically known collectively as "the Church Fathers," and the age in which they lived as "the patristic period." Unsurprisingly, they followed the apostolic example when it came to the status of the OT as active Christian Scripture (albeit they did not always read it well—we shall return to this matter shortly). They held stubbornly to the belief that it was the Scripture of Israel that gave the Church its fundamental orientation to reality and that their reception of this literature as *their* Scripture was intrinsically bound up with their acceptance of Jesus Christ as Savior and Lord. They could not have the one without the other. Consider, for example, the two surviving defenses of the Christian faith written in the middle of the second century AD by Justin Martyr (c. 100–165). In both of these the OT is central: "Justin ... appealed to the Scriptures (the Old Testament) as a prophetic witness for the Messiah, Jesus Christ ... The Old Testament in Justin is without question recognized as the Scripture of the Christians."[6] Not a single one of the Church Fathers from Justin down to Augustine (354–430) believed that it was possible or desirable to "unhitch" the OT from their Christian faith.[7] Not a single one of them believed that the old Scriptures were merely "Jewish scriptures" describing "God on the move through ancient, ancient times," rather than active Christian Scripture providing a "go-to source regarding ... behavior in the church."

They maintained their position even though a serious challenge to it had already been mounted in the second century by Marcion of Sinope, who is the first self-identifying Christian known to us to have rejected the OT as Christian Scripture in its entirety.[8] That is to say, it is not as if the Fathers had never been presented with alternative possibilities. For Marcion, the God of the OT (the creator God) has nothing in common with the God of the NT (the savior God), the latter of whom is the true God. The OT prophets speak on behalf of the deficient Creator God, and not about Christ. "The law of the Creator God" that we find in the OT is moreover to be disregarded by Christians as "morally inferior, foolish, and absurd" in relation to NT ethical teaching.[9] Views like these were generally held by the "Gnostics" of the first few centuries AD, with whom Marcion is typically linked. These were "Christians" who nevertheless "accommodated widespread ideas of Hellenistic late antiquity" in their philosophy, which was strongly influenced in particular by Platonic thought.[10] Like Marcion, the Gnostics too appealed to the NT alone—to the 25 percent Bible—as their authority for faith and life. They especially liked the letters of Paul, who in their estimation "alone knew the truth ... [since] to him the mystery was manifested by revelation."[11]

A BATTLE AND A WAR

To sum up the first part of this chapter, then, the Christian Church was born already "with a Bible in its hands."[12] It was the OT—the "sole authoritative witness" in the beginning—to which the Church looked for its fundamental guidance regarding both faith and life. This Holy Scripture was in due course enlarged to including the writings of the apostles and those in apostolic circles. It was not *replaced* by these new writings, which were always rightly regarded as an important superstructure built on a prior foundation. Recognizing this, the postapostolic Church rejected early attempts to "unhitch" the OT from Christian faith. Its leaders understood that Marcion's ideas represented a fundamental assault on apostolic faith and ultimately on the lordship of Christ, who gave us the whole Bible as the canon of our faith and life.

If, in the process, the orthodox party in the early Church won its immediate battle with "Marcionism," it has become clear in the intervening centuries that the war in the Church over the place of the OT has never truly come to an end. Marcionism keeps on being resurrected. So it is that many modern Christians appear to believe exactly the kind of thing that Andy Stanley teaches about OT Scripture: that it really has very little to do with us. It is Jewish Scripture, and when we read it, we are essentially reading somebody else's mail. In fact, with respect to its moral guidance, modern Christians often appear to agree with Marcion that the OT is ethically inferior to the NT and that the latter proclaims a "higher moral standard" than the former. It is as if the OT had nothing to say about generosity to the poor before Jesus commended it to the rich young ruler. It is as if Abraham or Elijah (for example) had never been held up by the NT itself as models of faith and virtue whom Christians should imitate (Heb. 11:8–12; Jas. 5:13–18). It is as if the ethical teaching of the NT were, well, *new*—despite all the protestations of its authors to the contrary.

Against all such Marcionism we must insist that it is the whole Bible that Christians must continue to regard as Scripture. Both of its Testaments communicate together "the very words of God" to the Church, intended to shape both its faith and its practice—words to which Jesus Christ himself directs our attention.

OF DOGS AND FOXES

If Christ-followers are obliged by the terms of their discipleship to regard the OT as age-old Scripture that continues to function authoritatively in our lives, then how are we to read it? This is our next important question. For it is one thing to agree that the OT is authoritative Christian Scripture, and another to ensure that our way of reading it allows it actually to *function* authoritatively. We shall take as our starting point in discussing this question a treatise written by a famous Christian of the second century AD, who himself battled the Gnostics and Marcion: Bishop Irenaeus of Lyons in Roman Gaul (c. AD 130–202). The treatise is *Against Heresies*, and it was written around AD 180. It is useful to us not only because of the effort that Irenaeus expends in demonstrating the evident heresy involved in the Gnostic and Marcionite position but because of his astute commentary on the way in which the heresy is bound up with an inadequate approach to biblical interpretation (or "hermeneutics").[13]

RIGHT READING

There is one God who is the creator of all, Irenaeus affirms, and one Son of God who became the incarnation of the divine Word. There is also one Scripture that testifies to all of this, and we should expect to be able to identify in it, as in all other works of literature, a "hypothesis." He means by this "the gist of the literary work"; we would nowadays shorten this simply to "thesis." We should also be able to find an "economy"—the "structure or plot that allows us to discern the flow of the narrative."[14] Here Irenaeus articulates an important truth about the nature of Christian Scripture: that although its individual forms are various (narrative, law, poetry, and so on), all of these are embedded in an overarching story from Genesis to Revelation. Discovering this story's thesis, structure, and plot will then permit us to read well the various parts of the literary corpus in their proper context within the whole work, in the expectation that "all Scripture, which has been given to us by [the one] God . . . [is] perfectly consistent."[15] In this process, aspects that might initially appear, when read outside their given context, to be "morally inferior, foolish, and absurd" will gradually reveal their proper place in the developing account and so be understood according to their true significance.

The Gnostics, in Irenaeus' estimation, have made a complete mess of the whole business. They have failed to identify the true thesis of Scripture, and in consequence they have constructed false economies in describing its structure and plot. They are in any case quite uninterested in the hard work of thinking about texts in contexts. For instance, they judge the OT law "to be dissimilar and contrary to the doctrine of the Gospel" while not applying themselves "to investigate the causes of the difference of each covenant."[16] The important point for Irenaeus, by contrast, is that the Israelites were the Israelites and not the Church. Certainly "[God] elected the patriarchs on account of their salvation"; however, "he formed the nation as he taught the unteachable to give obedience to God."[17] The background to this not-well-expressed thought lies in Paul's comments in Galatians 3:24 about the law being a "schoolmaster" (KJV) to bring people to Christ. Rather than striving for a coherent reading, the Gnostics prefer to collect "a set of expressions and names scattered here and there [in Scripture] . . . [and] twist them . . . from a natural to a non-natural sense. In so doing, they act like those who bring forward any kind of hypothesis they fancy."[18] The correct way to read Scripture, conversely, is to take all the biblical verses that the heretics have scattered and to restore each to its proper position within the cumulative biblical narrative, read from beginning to end, so that the entire scriptural mosaic once again portrays a king rather than a dog or a fox.[19]

LITERAL READING

This "natural" reading of biblical texts within their larger context, taking account of the overall movement of the biblical Story from the beginning to the end and assuming that we should find within it a consistent, coherent message, might better be referred to as "literal" reading. Of course, this word has been much misunderstood and abused in the history of biblical interpretation, but this should not prevent us from using it properly.[20]

When we pursue the literal interpretation of any text, what we hope to discern is what the author meant to say—what his or her "communicative intent" was. We arrive at such a determination by studying not only the words employed but also the *manner* in which they are employed. Are they functioning metaphorically, for example, as in Jesus' statement, "I am the door"? This involves not only consideration of the *historical* and *cultural* circumstances in which the text first appeared (e.g., what were the literary conventions of the time?) but also attentiveness to its *literary* and *canonical* context—since words mean what they mean not only in sentences but also in paragraphs, sections of books, whole books, and whole collections of books. Reading "literally" *requires* such attentiveness to context; otherwise we may entirely misunderstand what an author means to say. The "literal sense" of a text cannot be grasped merely by looking at words in small units of text, one by one, and with the help of a dictionary. This is essentially the kind of thing that Irenaeus accuses the Gnostics of doing. But by itself this "one-by-one" approach will not help us at all to grasp what Jesus means, for example, in referring to himself as a door.

The literal sense of Scripture was, for the Church Fathers, its foundational sense, and it was strongly recommended to Christian Bible-readers by other bishops besides Irenaeus. Augustine, for example, says this:

> Whoever takes another meaning out of Scripture than the writer intended, goes astray . . . He is to be corrected . . . and to be shown how much better it is not to quit the straight road, lest, if he get into a habit of going astray, he may sometimes take crossroads, or even go in the wrong direction altogether.[21]

It is precisely reading the whole Bible in this way that allows each Testament to possess exactly the same authority as Scripture in the Church. In each case we read with the expectation that, in attending to the literal sense intended by its human authors, we shall also hear what God wants to say to us in the Bible about what to believe and how to live.

PLUMBING THE DEPTHS

Over against this right way of reading Scripture, which enables us to find the right direction in our journey through life, we must now set the first of two wrong ways—each of which is also represented, unfortunately, among the Church Fathers and then among their heirs throughout Church History. This is "allegorical" or "spiritual" reading, first invented by the Greeks in order to domesticate the ancient tales of Homer that had become unpalatable in many ways to the sophisticated people of Athens.[22] It was subsequently embraced with varying degrees of critical reflection by many early Christian leaders in the postapostolic period who were the beneficiaries of Graeco-Roman education. In this way of approaching the Bible, the Christian reader—while claiming to be led by the Holy Spirit— consciously moves *beyond* the natural (or "plain") sense of a biblical passage that we might reasonably attribute to the ancient human author, in the process essentially *abandoning* it in favor of another kind of textual meaning. The most important (spiritual) meaning of the text is to be found, allegedly, not on its surface but hidden in its depths. That is where God speaks, according to the allegorizers, no matter what the human authors may have intended to communicate.

When this hermeneutical approach is applied extensively to the NT as well as to the OT, it naturally threatens to undermine the authority of Scripture altogether. For if there is indeed in Scripture a significant gap between what a human author means to say (his "communicative intent") and what God intends to say, how are we to gain reliable access through Scripture to what God is saying? How are we to have any chance of recognizing when we are simply "reading into" the text our own concerns and prejudices rather than hearing the word of God— those moments when we are merely misusing Scripture in order to legitimate our own agendas and programs? For allegorizing occurs, according to some of its modern advocates (in a surprisingly candid moment) "when the literal meaning of a text is seen to run in a wrong or unhelpful direction . . . [when] the reader is unhappy with the literal meaning."[23] The problem is, of course, that "wrong or unhelpful" are measured here in terms of an authority that lies outside the text. The text itself, read "naturally" or "literally," no longer possesses such authority.

And yet we find a strong commitment to allegorical reading among many of the Church Fathers. In practice this applies much more to their reading of the OT than of the NT. In practice, then, it was the authority of OT Scripture that was mainly undermined in the patristic period by allegorical reading. For now the Christian was no longer reading for guidance concerning faith and life, in the same literal way, *first* the Law and the Prophets *and then* the apostles. Now the Christian began with a NT already wedded to Graeco-Roman culture in various ways and then looked *back* on the OT, using nonliteral interpretation to solve any consequential problems that arose. The OT text read in this way was naturally incapable, then, of challenging any aspect of the amalgam of NT and Graeco-Roman culture that was being imposed upon it. So it remains to this day. Scripture cannot challenge, in particular, interpretations of the NT that are quite implausible when one reads the NT texts primarily in the context of preceding OT Scripture.

This strong commitment to allegorizing among the Fathers was often accompanied, indeed, by a correspondingly strong disparagement of readers of OT Scripture who remain rooted in the literal. They often charge the latter with holding to a "Judaizing" interpretation. Clement of Alexandria was apparently the first to use this language, in his now almost completely lost work *Against the Judaizers*.[24] Origen then picks up the idea, accusing those "who do not wish to think that 'the law is spiritual'" of failing to take heed of "the leaven of the Pharisees."[25] Later, Gregory of Nyssa, in *Against Eunomius*, "argues that if a Christian 'judaizes' by relying on the bare text of Scripture . . . incorrect theology will be the result."[26] A particular example of this Judaizing is provided by the Council of Laodicea in 364: "Christians must not judaize by resting on the Sabbath, but must work on that day, rather honouring the Lord's Day . . . if any shall be found to be judaizers, let them be anathema from Christ."[27] One of the notable victims of this kind of rhetoric in the patristic period was Theodore of Mopsuestia (c. 350–428), who was very committed to the literal reading of Scripture and who was therefore accused of having a Jewish creed by the Second Council of Constantinople in 553, which condemned his "detestable" writings as containing "unbelievable folly and . . . disgraceful utterances."[28]

It is ugly rhetoric, reeking of implicit or overt antisemitism. It functions in the service of evasion, for "to call a Christian practice 'judaizing' is to label it, not to explain it," and it is certainly not to explain what is actually *wrong* with it.[29] The idea is simply to avoid having to engage in sustained and reasoned argument with opponents about right hermeneutics by way of imputing strong guilt through association.

HEROIC READING

Under such a "spiritual reading" regime, there is a clear and always present danger that the Bible-reader will, in the words of Augustine above, "go in the wrong direction altogether"—not only morally, but also hermeneutically. Examples of this happening in the history of biblical interpretation are legion, as interpreters have imposed their own worldview and values on OT texts while believing that they were telling their audiences "what they really mean." One of the ways in which this has manifested itself is in the imposition of what I call "heroic readings" on OT narrative.

Here is what Bishop Ambrose of Milan (339–397) has to say about Jacob, for instance, in his exegetical work *Jacob and the Happy Life*. Jacob was a wise man, alleges Ambrose, living a happy life because he pursued reason and possessed a clear conscience (since "the happiness of life does not lie in bodily pleasure, but in a conscience pure of every stain of sin").[30] Christians should likewise pursue reason and possess a clear conscience. This is a rather astonishing interpretation of the story of Jacob, in which the "hero" created by the interpreter bears virtually no relation to the person described in the biblical text. Whence does it arise? It arises from an unexamined cultural assumption that biblical characters, especially when they are identified as important to God's redemptive plan in some way, function ever and only as paradigms for our imitation, and as little else. But Jacob read "literally" is a disturbing figure: a cheat of epic proportions, and not a very religious one at that. The solution is simple: do not read him literally! Instead, create a hero of the faith, somehow—a hero who turns out (not coincidentally) to be as a much a Stoic as anything else.

But what if God has providentially designed biblical narrative so as *not* to be entirely "heroic" in nature? What if, as readers in need of God's guidance in our lives, we need to change our perspective and realize that our biblical stories, in realistically reflecting both light and darkness in biblical characters, force us indeed to *search* for what is to be imitated and what it is to be avoided? What if we are supposed to learn from Jacob not only how to live but also how not to live? This does appear to be how the apostles read OT narratives: they are "useful" to us both in modelling holiness *and* in modelling its opposite—as in the case, for example, of the Israelites who fell in the wilderness (Heb. 3:12–4:11; cf. 1 Cor. 10). If we stick to literal reading, then we have the possibility of discerning which is which, and very much to our own benefit. However, if we are already convinced that we "know" what "ought to be in the Holy Bible," and we are prepared to read it nonliterally in order to find only "holy persons" in its pages, then of course we shall inevitably miss what Scripture truly wants to say to us.

Even Irenaeus, who deserves praise in general for his reading of the whole Bible sequentially from beginning to end, must be criticized on this particular point. Faced with the scandalous story of Lot and his two daughters in Genesis 19, for example, he cannot prevent himself from reading the daughters as representing the Church and the synagogue—the Christianity and Judaism of his own time.[31] Nothing about this OT passage in itself, of course, encourages the reader to make such a connection, nor anything in the NT. There is in fact *no* good reason to make it, beyond that of rescuing a relative of a major OT figure, Abraham, from scandal. Even the most astute Bible-readers can go badly astray when they depart from their commitment to the literal sense of the text.

CONCLUSION

In the interests of maximal clarity, then, we may offer this summary of the cumulative argument of chapters 1 and 2. If we aspire to live a good life, then we must necessarily be able to identify what goodness looks like. Biblical faith proposes that "good" means "being like God in character and action" and that we come to understand its dimensions primarily by attending to God's special revelation in Christ and in the Holy Scripture whose central character he is. The Holy Scripture in question comprises two Testaments rather than one, and anyone who takes the teaching of Jesus Christ and his apostles seriously—identifying with the community of Christ-follower who were once "not my people" but have now *become* "my people"—is obliged to take the first of these Testaments just as seriously as the second when seeking guidance for life's journey. The Old Testament is the major part of the literature by which we must ultimately measure what the good life looks like—the 75 percent of the primary source material that we absolutely must consult as foundational Scripture, just as the early Christians did, when we want to know what to believe and how to live. We are then obliged to take the NT equally seriously as crucially important, subsequent Scripture—the 25 percent of the primary source material relating to faith and life that everywhere builds on what has gone before, and which we shall not properly understand if we limit ourselves to reading only from its pages. To take both of these Testaments "seriously" is to read them both literally, rather than in some other manner. It is to read them with attention to the "communicative intent" of their content within the unfolding literary and canonical context, whose overall thesis and structure/plot we must constantly keep in mind. In other words, everything must find its right place in the biblical Story, to which I shall hereafter refer as "Story" in recognition of the Christian conviction of its ultimate truth vis-à-vis all other stories.

A particularly important requirement in respect of this right reading of Scripture is that we are able correctly to discern the continuities and discontinuities between our two Testaments—the ways in which (in Irenaeus' terms) the Israelites were the Israelites and not the Church. It is to this question that we now turn in chapter 3.

DISCUSSION QUESTIONS

1. What do you consider to be the strong points of Andy Stanley's arguments (toward the beginning of this chapter) concerning a Christian approach to the OT, and why?
2. Leaving aside the question of strength, what do you find *attractive* about Stanley's position, and why? Why do you think that *others* find it attractive?
3. Does God ever say anything to us through Scripture that is not according to its literal sense? How do we know in such cases that it is really God's voice, and not just our own imagination?

3

In the Beginning
Design, Sin, and Redundancy

Moses permitted you to divorce your wives because your hearts were hard. But it was not this way from the beginning.

Matthew 19:8

In July 2019 thousands of people with Christian backgrounds gathered in Nashville, Tennessee, to participate in *Revive 2019*, which was advertised as "the largest annual Messianic conference" (in the world, one assumes). Its organizers were "excited to be able to play a part in the future of the Hebraic movement."[1] Who are these organizers? Typically they have been raised in Christian denominations that take the Bible very seriously in their pursuit of the good life. At some point they have then realized with fresh force that in the OT we are told that the holy God wants his people to keep the Sabbath, not eat certain foods, and so on—and they have asked themselves why they are not obeying him. For as the text quoted in our epigraph to chapter 2 tells us, Gentiles (non-Jews) were once "not my people," but now they *are*. In due course this has produced the "Hebrew Roots" movement, which recommends to Gentiles who regard Jesus Christ as the Messiah the adoption of the entire OT law (or, in its original Hb. terminology, "Torah"). Therefore, "Hebrew Roots" people observe the OT food laws, the Sabbath, and festivals like Passover and Tabernacles—but they do not celebrate Christmas or Easter. The men may have undergone adult circumcision and have circumcised their male children. For they are convinced that God did not intend for the appearance of Jesus (or Yeshua, as they call him) to make the rules and instructions of the OT invalid. In their view, it is a misunderstanding of the NT to argue that he did. The NT is, in reality, simply a kind of extension of Torah. To take the Bible seriously means, then, observing Torah in the way that the Messiah Yeshua did.[2]

Clearly these "Hebrew Roots" people take the inspired OT Scriptures very seriously in deciding what to believe and how to live. In this respect they have grasped the nature, as well as the purpose of these Scriptures really well. From the point of view of orthodox Christian faith, however, their perspective on the OT, and therefore on the nature of the good life, is problematic.

THE BIBLE AS STORY

At the heart of the problem lies another faulty hermeneutic that we must now add to the ones identified in chapter 2—another "wrong path" in biblical interpretation that we have not yet discussed. Christian Scripture (as we saw in that previous chapter) presents itself to us as an overarching Story containing other, embedded forms of literature (such as prophecy). It moves from a beginning in Genesis, through a long middle, to an end in Revelation. If we are going to read Scripture well, then, we need to understand that the Bible is not only *inspired* by God but also *shaped* by God in a particular way, such that we must always understand the parts within the context of the entire, unfolding whole—just as Irenaeus long ago insisted. We must specifically read the story of Israel and Israel's Torah within this larger context. This is what the Hebrew Roots movement fails adequately to do.

CREATION AND FALL

What then is the overall nature of this great Story? It begins when God creates everything that makes up the reality of our cosmos (Gen. 1–2)—a world created to a great extent by making distinctions, the most fundamental of which is between God and Creation. Creation is "other than" God, and it is not divine—that is why in biblical faith worship is not to be offered to anything *in* Creation. At the same time, Creation is *sacred*—a kind of temple in which God has chosen to make himself known to his creatures. It is, therefore, a place that is to be revered and protected out of love and respect not only for the Creator but also for Creation itself. It is essentially a *good* place, as Genesis and other Scriptures tell us, where God's blessing is experienced by his creatures. It is a wonderful place, created in such a way as to be exactly the right place (for the time being)—a beautiful place—for the flourishing of all that God has made.[3]

Among these creatures are human beings; and just as Creation as a whole is God's temple, so humans are the images of God that ancient people used to place in *their* temples (Gen. 1:26–27). We are God's image bearers, made a little lower than God himself and "crowned . . . with glory and honor" (Ps. 8). As such, we are created to play a crucial role in the cosmos, which is both to rule as monarchs (Gen. 1:26) and also "to serve [Creation] and keep/guard it" (2:15) just as the priests later serve and keep the tabernacle (Numbers 3:7–8, where we find the same Hb. language). It is *holy* work, this work of looking after God's garden as his tenants—for as Psalm 24:1 reminds us, "The earth is the LORD's [Yahweh's] and everything in it." As we do this work, we look forward in hope to something even better—to immortality. This hope is represented in the Genesis narrative by the tree of life; to eat from it, we are told, is to live forever (Gen. 3:22). This is a Story that, right from the beginning, is going somewhere. We are on a journey, and God has embarked on this journey with us. And at the end of the journey, something even better awaits us: a new cosmos, continuous with but also different from the one that we know now.

A problem has arisen, however: moral evil has entered the good world that God has created. Scripture understands its point of entry in the first instance in terms of misdirected moral freedom: humanity comes to distrust God and to lust after autonomy (Gen. 3). We cease to depend for moral guidance on the God who reveals his will to us, and we resort instead to other ways of deciding what is right and wrong. So it is that we follow "a way that appears to be right, but in the end . . . leads to death" (Prov. 14:12). The consequence is significant dysfunction in the world; in many ways, life is no longer good but is marked now by evil. Created to cooperate under God in the ruling of Creation, we seek instead dominion as gods over each other. Disabled in this way as image bearers of God, we are also unable to rule over Creation as we ought (Gen. 1:26–28). In various ways and to various extents, in all three areas just described—our relationships with God, each other, and the rest of Creation—biblical faith teaches that all human beings have departed from the good pathway that the Creator God has designed us to follow. In the words of the apostle Paul, "all have sinned and fall short of the glory of God" (Rom. 3:23)—and we are no longer engaged in the wholehearted pursuit of what is good.

The Redemptive Plan

However, the wonderful thing is that our Creator has developed a redemptive plan that is designed to put everything right. Early in the Story he makes a long-term commitment to Creation to continue to bless all of it (Gen. 9). It is expressed in the form of "an everlasting covenant . . . [with] all living creatures of every kind on the earth" (Gen. 9:16). To this covenant is added in Genesis 12 a covenant with Abraham that has implications specifically for *all human beings*. Abraham's family will be blessed by God so that all the nations will be blessed by God. Abraham is given a land in which this blessing can be worked out, so that Abraham may do *in a particular place* what all human beings are called to do *on the earth*. The people of God—the descendants of Abraham—are called out by God for a mission, and the mission is cosmic in its implications, involving the fulfilment of God's promise to bless his Creation. This is a Story that is still going somewhere. There is still *hope* in this Story that God will fulfil the plans he had in mind in creating the cosmos in the first place. God, in biblical perspective, is determined to see his Creation flourish.

It is the promise to Abraham in this covenant that God then *remembers*, in the book of Exodus, which leads on thereafter to a further covenant with the Israelites at Mount Sinai. This Sinai covenant focuses much more closely than its predecessors on the *one* nation, Israel. But Israel is still called, in this covenant, to a much larger task: "Although the whole earth is mine," God tells them, "you will be for me a kingdom of priests and a holy nation" (Exod. 19:5–6). The whole earth remains God's domain, and the task of God's people, as a "kingdom of priests," is still to mediate God's blessing to it. That is what priests do. Then in 2 Samuel 7 God makes a covenant with King David—a covenant with an individual Israelite, who is promised an everlasting royal house. So covenant "narrows down" in certain ways as we move along in the OT part of the Story: from all living creatures, to all human beings, then to one people-group, and ultimately to one person. The narrowing down, however, is still with an eye to the larger agenda, which is the blessing of all Creation. Ultimately in the biblical Story the monarchy of ancient Israel fails and is swept away; but hope remains, because God has committed himself to the descendants of David (e.g., Isa. 11:1–5).

We see this hope fully expressed in the prophetic literature of the OT. The prophets presuppose the three broken relationships of Creation as described in Genesis 3: the human relationship with God, with other human beings, and with the rest of Creation. But they look ahead to a time when all three relationships will be healed—to three transformations. Beyond the healing, they anticipate an entirely new order of being in the cosmos. The forces of cosmic darkness will be defeated, and all the suffering they have initiated will be abolished. Creation itself will be transformed, and as an aspect of that transformation, immortality (which seemed to be lost in Gen. 3) will be gifted to human beings after all. God's journey with Creation, begun "in the beginning," will be completed. There will be redemption of what has gone wrong, but there will also be the fulfilment of the plan that would have been enacted (it seems) if *nothing* had gone wrong. And this will involve, among other things, an end to all suffering.

It is this prophetic vision whose fulfilment begins in earnest in the person of Jesus of Nazareth, whom the apostle Paul describes in 2 Timothy 1:10 as having "destroyed death and ... brought life and immortality to light through the gospel." And we, his followers—both Jew and Gentile, integrated into one body which is the Church—now wait for this kingdom fully to arrive in the future. As we wait, we too are called to mission. For we are called not only to live the good life in this world—the life that God intends—but also to urge other people to turn from their sins and follow God's plan for their lives.

THE LOCATION OF ISRAEL IN THE STORY

This great biblical Story makes it abundantly clear, then, that God's choice of the descendants of Abraham and Sarah—the ancient people of Israel—as his primary mission partner in the world was a temporary one. It lasted only until the coming of the One who made a new covenant with all his followers that fulfilled all the older ones (Luke 22:20; 1 Cor. 11:23–25; Heb. 8:1–13). With the coming of Christ, the day of blessing on all peoples foretold in Genesis 12 arrived (Acts 3:25; Gal. 3:7–9; Eph. 2:11–13), and God's primary mission-partner in the world is no longer one particular people-group, but a universal Church comprising both Jew and Gentile. The Gentiles in this scenario are therefore "no longer foreigners and strangers, but fellow citizens with God's people and also members of his household, built on the foundation of the apostles and prophets, with Christ Jesus himself as the chief cornerstone" (Eph. 2:19–20). It is this universal Church, and not the particular people-group Israel, that has now rightly taken on the mantle of "a chosen people, a royal priesthood, a holy nation, God's special possession" (1 Pet. 2:9–10); and it is as this new "Israel"—the present "Israel of God" (Gal. 6:16)—that it reads the OT along with the NT Scriptures as its canonical rule in respect of faith and life.

This reading of the biblical Story is often dismissed nowadays by people who are hostile to it as "supersessionism" or "replacement theology." The hostility appears to derive in the main from a belief that this reading is to blame for Christian mistreatment of Jews throughout history. It is typically accompanied by an insistence that the Jewish people remain the chosen people of God, existing on a kind of parallel track with the Church throughout history and until the end of time. There is however no warrant at all in Christian Scripture for this latter idea. This is not in the slightest degree to diminish the importance of the Jewish people to God in the history of the world after Pentecost. They remain just as important, and just as beloved, as any other people group. As to the brutal treatment of Jews by Christians historically, we shall return to that dark topic in chapters 4 (briefly) and 14 (extensively). All that needs to be said at this point is that, to the extent that this brutal treatment has indeed been bound up with notions of one people "superseding" another, this has always involved a very grievous misunderstanding of the meaning and significance of the "replacement" in question—as if it implied some intrinsic lack of worth and value in Jews, or some innate inferiority in their religious practices, such that Christians in their "chosenness" were justified in their intolerance and oppression of the "unchosen." This is entirely to miss the biblical point and in consequence to commit evil. The Church, comprising both Jew and Gentile, has in fact "replaced" the OT people of God because at the heart of the mission of God in the world after Pentecost is the proclamation of Jesus as the Messiah. Obviously, non-Christian Jews cannot participate in this procla-mation, since they do not believe that Jesus *is* the Messiah. The "chosenness" of the new "Israel of God" (the Church) has nothing to do with God's blessing and love, or lack of it, but everything to do with *task*. It is more than regrettable that this has so often been misunderstood in the Church—but we cannot and should not respond to that misunderstanding by abandoning clear biblical teaching con-cerning the distinctive roles of Israel and the Church in different phases of the great Story.

DESIGN PARAMETERS

As we read the OT in this way, we need to recognize that, just as Israel has a particular "location" in Scripture, so too does Israel's Torah. It sits within a Story in which certain things have been true from the beginning (see the epigraph to this chapter). God has already designed Creation as a whole to function in cer-tain "very good" ways; right and wrong already exist (as Gen. 2–3 make clear). In that sense there is already "law" in the cosmos before we get to Moses—and it applies to both Jew and Gentile, who have both departed from it. The apostle Paul writes about this in Romans 1–3, summarizing our human predicament as follows: "There is no difference between Jew and Gentile, for all have sinned and fall short of the glory of God" (Rom. 3:22–23).

This set of divine "design parameters" in Creation that all human beings have in some measure set aside has often been referred to in the history of discussions about the good life as "natural law." The reader will not be surprised to hear, in the light of what I have written in chapter 1, that I shall avoid using this terminology in advancing my own argument in the remainder of this book. This language has the capacity, I believe, to take us significantly off track in our contemporary reflections about the good life. When I describe principles of conduct that are everywhere and always right, then, I shall instead refer in the interest of clarity to "creational law." This is moral law that is certainly writ large in Creation and in the human heart, as natural-law theorists claim. Against modern appropria-tions of the theory, however, Scripture teaches us that this law is perceived (to borrow biblical language from elsewhere) only as in "a glass, darkly" (1 Cor. 13:13, KJV), not least because it has been obscured by sin. If we are to say much about it, therefore, we shall not get very far by looking deep within ourselves, nor by conducting ambitious studies to discover what is generally "natural" in the human condition. We shall need instead to attend to the Triune God who reveals himself to us in Christian Scripture, the focal point of which is Jesus Christ. It is in the Story told by this Scripture that we shall discover who we are and what we are called to be.

If, according to this Story, God has already designed Creation as a whole to function in certain right ways, what is Mosaic Torah designed to do? How are we best to understand *this* important part of Scripture in the context of the whole? Mosaic Torah is designed, I propose, to guide and to preserve ancient Israel in its temporary role as God's primary mission partner in the world in the time before the life, death, and resurrection of Christ. It sets out to do this in various ways, as it touches on all kinds of aspects of life in the ancient Near East (ANE). As we shall see, this does not mean that it cannot greatly help Christians in their own quest for the good. It does mean, however, that we must think very carefully about *how* it can rightly do so.

CREATIONAL LAW AND TORAH

Some of this Torah material is explicitly regarded in the biblical Story as creational law deriving from the Creator God whose character does not change through time. It speaks directly to the design parameters of Creation—to the moral ideals that the people of God must attend to (and all human beings *should* attend to) in pursuit of what is good. Insofar as Torah reflects the moral vision of the kingdom of God in this way—the ideals that we are summoned to as people who desire to "be perfect . . . as your heavenly Father is perfect" (Matt. 5:48)—we would expect it to be of relevance to Jesus-followers, Jew and Gentile, and not only to ancient Israelites. This is why it is not surprising to see various of the Ten Commandments, for example, so regularly cited in the NT (as we saw in chapter 2); for it is always and everywhere right to worship God and not idols, to honor our fathers and mothers, and to refrain from murder, adultery, stealing, offering false testimony against our neighbor, or coveting his possessions. We shall come back to the Sabbath commandment in chapter 10. In the terms set out by Matthew 5:17–18, at least the great majority of these commandments clearly do *not* come under the rubric of those parts of Torah that have been "fulfilled" in the coming of Christ; these commandments remain until "everything is accomplished."

LAND AND EARTH

The Creator God does not change in his character. However, the great biblical Story does move ever onwards, and change *is* built into *this* Story. God chooses first an OT people, and then later a broader, NT people. They are not the same, and God does not address them in exactly the same way. So it is not surprising that even the great principles of the Ten Commandments, as they "touch down" in ancient Israelite society, are directed to some degree specifically to *that* OT people of God, and not necessarily to the later one. For example, the commandment that a child should honor both father and mother is connected in both Exodus 20 and Deuteronomy 5 to living long "in the land the LORD your God is giving you." The intention appears to be to connect creational law to the land of Canaan specifically. It is significant that when Paul promotes this same principle in writing to the church in Ephesus, however, he interprets the Hebrew word for "land" in a broader sense: "so that it may go well with you and that you may enjoy long life on the earth." Creational law is now addressed to a people of God who no longer dwell together in one particular land. We shall return to this text in the course of our reflections in chapter 14.

WIFE AND DONKEY

Similarly, the OT commandment that no one should covet his neighbor's possessions (Exod. 20:21; Deut. 5:17) includes among these possessions the categories of wife, slaves, ox, and donkey. The principle is applied thereby to ordinary ANE social reality back in those ancient times: "here are some of the most obvious possessions of your neighbor that you might covet." It is not easy to see how this social reality is consistent, however, with the ideals of the larger biblical Story, which begins by telling us that all human beings, male and female, are made in God's image and designed for joint governance over the earth (including the animals). Genesis 1 does not lead us to expect that we shall see women and slaves turning up on a list of male possessions that includes oxen and donkeys. And it is significant in this regard that when the commandment against coveting is repeated in the NT, these examples are not repeated along with it (Rom. 7:7; 13:9).

We shall return to this matter of slaves and women in chapters 12 and 13. For the moment, we may simply note that the particular shape given to the commandment against coveting in the Ten Commandments has everything to do with its ancient context, even if the principle involved transcends that context.

THE TEN COMMANDMENTS

If we are clearly led in such ways to expect that Mosaic Torah will *at least to some extent* comprise God's creational law applied to the ancient Israelite context, then of course it is right and proper to move out beyond the Ten Commandments and look for other examples where this might be so.

It is important here to understand—in case our particular Christian tradition makes us nervous about this move—that although the Ten Commandments are highly regarded in Scripture, they are not understood as a kind of self-sufficient summary of all that is really important in God's creational law. We recall from chapter 1 Jesus' conversation with the rich young ruler in Matthew 19:16–21, where Jesus does commend the Commandments to him as high-order illustrations of what it means to love God and neighbor. He affirms that he has kept them all, but something is still lacking (19:20). It turns out, we recall, that he is short on generosity to the poor (19:21). As we consider the Ten Commandments again in the light of this NT passage, one of the truths we notice about them is that they mainly tell us about some of the things that good people should *not* do to their neighbors—but they do not tell us about everything that a good person *should* do. In other words, they do indeed *illustrate*, but they do not *exhaust the description of* the good life in the OT. For example, we are often told elsewhere in the OT that we should be generous (Ps. 112:5; Prov. 11:25; 22:9); but generosity is not commanded in the Ten Commandments (which is precisely the issue in Matt. 19). We are likewise told in the Ten Commandments that adultery is wrong, but there is more to sexual sin than simply adultery. So it is that in Job 31:1, when Job is talking about loving one's female neighbor properly, he does not stop at adultery: "I made a covenant with my eyes not to look lustfully at a young woman" (cf. Matt. 5:27–30). We cannot be guided in our quest for the good, then, by the Ten Commandments alone. We need to read them, too, within their broader context.

FIELDS AND TREES

The brief example I want to provide here, in relation to this pursuit of creational law outside the Ten Commandments that we are now pondering, involves fields and trees. In Deuteronomy 24:19–22 we read the following:

> When you are harvesting in your field and you overlook a sheaf, do not go back to get it. Leave it for the foreigner, the fatherless, and the widow, so that the LORD your God may bless you in all the work of your hands. When you beat the olives from your trees, do not go over the branches a second time. Leave what remains for the foreigner, the fatherless, and the widow. When you harvest the grapes in your vineyard, do not go over the vines again. Leave what remains for the foreigner, the fatherless, and the widow. Remember that you were slaves in Egypt. That is why I command you to do this.

Unquestionably this is a law deeply embedded in the ancient Israelite context, in which that people once escaped from slavery in Egypt. The latter experience should give them empathy toward the vulnerable ("the foreigner, the fatherless, and the widow"), and allow them to share in harvest. Yet at the same time we have already been told in Deuteronomy 10:17–18 that God himself, "the great God, mighty and awesome, who shows no partiality and accepts no bribes," is the one who "defends the cause of the fatherless and the widow, and loves the foreigner residing among you, giving them food and clothing." To look after the vulnerable is to be like God—both in the OT and NT: "Religion that God our Father accepts as pure and faultless is this: to look after orphans and widows in their distress and to keep oneself from being polluted by the world" (Jas. 1:27). It is an aspect of the way that things ought to be, as everyone operates as his brother's (or sister's) keeper (Gen. 4:9). This being so, we should consider the specific injunctions in Deuteronomy 24. We may not personally possess wheat fields, olive trees, or vines, but the principle at work here is clear enough: we should not seek profit maximization in respect of what we own but instead should allow the poor and vulnerable to share in our wealth.

HARDNESS OF HEART

As we engage intelligently with Mosaic Torah, then, we certainly encounter creational law within it, albeit touching down explicitly in the particular circumstances of ancient Israelite history. It is always and everywhere right—including in ancient Israel—that people should honor their parents, avoid adultery, and look after widows and orphans (and so on). We also encounter another kind of law, however, that relates to the particular circumstances of ancient history. This is law that is specifically framed as a response to evil. Its purpose is not to inculcate moral ideals—to encourage us to live in accordance with God's creational law. It is designed instead to prevent the effects of the Fall from spreading further than they otherwise might.

JESUS ON DIVORCE

An important passage here is Matthew 19:3–9, part of which is cited in the epigraph to this chapter. Here some Pharisees ask Jesus, "Is it lawful for a man to divorce his wife?" They already know that the law of Moses allows "a man [to] give his wife a certificate of divorce and send her away" (19:7). Jesus' response is very significant: "Moses permitted you to divorce your wives because your hearts were hard. But it was not this way from the beginning" (19:8). His answer makes it clear, moreover, that what God ordained in Creation, in the beginning, remains the basis for the good life in the present: "Haven't you read . . . that at the beginning the Creator 'made them male and female,' and said, 'For this reason a man will leave his father and mother and be united to his wife, and the two will become one flesh'? So they are no longer two, but one flesh. Therefore what God has joined together, let no one separate" (19:4–6). We need to read Moses against the background of "the beginning."

That is to say: there is material in Mosaic Torah that does not come under the heading of creational law but exists only because of the hardness of the human heart, which renders us unwilling to follow in God's ways. The purpose of this material is not the inculcation of holiness—for holiness in this case involves commitment to a lifelong marriage. Rather, its purpose is the limitation of vice—in this case, the male desire to be rid of a spouse with as little trouble as possible.

Concessions and Civil Peace

All law takes account of evil in this way, in the midst of promoting good, and indeed it *must* do so—otherwise its ability to do good will be very limited. All law must in fact involve concessions to the very evils that it seeks to restrain. The Jewish scholar Leon Kass puts it this way:

> The emergence of law . . . [is] a response to the evils that lurk in the hearts of men. To control these evils, law must not only accept their unavoidable existence; it must also offer them concessions and, moreover, even enlist their aid in support of civil peace.[4]

All law, in other words, must attend to the "ifs" of the fallen world that we so often find illustrated in Mosaic Torah—for example, "if anyone schemes and kills someone deliberately" (Exod. 21:14). Evil has already damaged society here, even though there is a nearby commandment that explicitly forbids murder (Exod. 20:13). Exodus 21:14 is not concerned with the ideal in such circumstances but only with what must be done in response to the evil: "that person is to be taken from my altar and put to death." If there were no murders, such a violent response would be unnecessary.

Stiff-Neck Law

For the sake of having a shorthand, I shall refer to this kind of Torah as stiff-neck law—guidance that is designed for a stiff-necked or stubborn people (Exod. 32:9). Is this kind of Torah of relevance to Jesus-followers? In terms of our pursuit of moral *ideals*, the answer must obviously be "no"; this kind of Torah does not concern *ideals*. Yet the NT people of God, like our forebears, must necessarily be involved in the business of restraining evil as well as pursuing the good, and it is possible that such stiff-neck law might offer us helpful models for doing this, once every allowance is made for the very different location in the Story in which we find ourselves. A reading of the whole Story will be necessary, however, in order to make a wise judgment in any particular case. We shall return to this kind of question especially in chapter 8. For the moment, let me suggest only that in some circumstances stiff-neck Torah might be of indirect relevance to Christians. After all, marriage breakdown (e.g.) is not something that only happened in ancient history; it is sadly very much a modern phenomenon. It is surely better to regulate it in our modern context than not to do so, so that the damage it can cause might possibly be less than otherwise. Should we generally regulate "breakdowns" such as this, in our very different contexts historically and culturally, in ways that differ from how Mosaic Torah attempts to do so in the ANE context? In many cases the answer to this question is going to be "yes"—but it is certainly worth consulting the wisdom of the biblical past in considering how to proceed in the present.

REDUNDANCY IN TORAH

Granted the possibility that at least some stiff-neck law might be of continuing relevance to Christians, we are obliged by Scriptural teaching itself to conclude that this is certainly not the case in much of the remainder of OT Torah. The reason is not only that its purpose was always limited (as in stiff-neck law) but also that it has already been entirely accomplished.

CIRCUMCISION

For example, in his letter to the church in Galatia we find the apostle Paul adamant that physical circumcision is not a practice in which Gentile Christians ought to indulge—in fact, that to accept circumcision is to misunderstand the Gospel (Gal. 5:2–12). These are strong words, but their theological logic is quite obvious. Circumcision in ancient Israel was intended to distinguish the covenant people of God from the Gentiles. It was a physical reminder of the separation between Jew and Gentile that was wholly necessary, as a temporary measure, if God's plan of redemption for the cosmos was ultimately to be carried through— since this plan necessitated the survival of God's chosen and separate OT people until the Messiah would arrive. This distinction between Jew and Gentile is not rooted in Creation, however—as is, for example, the distinction between a human being and an animal (Gen. 2:24–26). After the coming of Jesus, therefore, it is entirely unnecessary. Indeed, it misses the point of the redemptive Story, which was always to reconcile *all* human beings to each other and to their Creator—and this the Church, comprising both Jew and Gentile, is already embodying, as it waits for the final consummation of God's plan.

Food Laws

The OT food laws possessed the same purpose—to separate Jew from Gentile. Unsurprisingly, then, Paul is also adamant about the wrong-headedness of maintaining these rules in the new situation of the Church—it makes absolutely no sense to do so. This is why he so strongly opposes Peter in Antioch, as he reports in Galatians 2:11–14. Peter should have known better than to "separate himself from the Gentiles because he was afraid of those who belonged to the circumcision group," ceasing his previous practice of eating with the Gentiles (v. 12). After all, he had earlier personally received a vision from God urging him that in the post-Pentecost period of the great biblical Story he should not "call anything impure that God has made clean" (Acts 10:15). Paul returns to the same theme in Romans 14:14: "I am convinced, being fully persuaded in the Lord Jesus, that nothing is unclean in itself"—that the distinctions in OT Torah between "clean" and "unclean" in respect of food, important for ancient Israel in their own context in the biblical Story, do not reflect creational law. Creational law itself requires, nevertheless, sensitivity toward the Christian believer who cannot quite bring himself to the correct conclusion on the matter of clean and unclean: "Do not let what you know is good be spoken of as evil. For the kingdom of God is not a matter of eating and drinking, but of righteousness, peace and joy in the Holy Spirit" (14:16–17).

Sacrifice

Finally, by way of example, OT sacrifice has already accomplished what it was intended to accomplish, and this, too, is something that the NT people of God should not continue. Jesus, the great high priest, has now entered the true tabernacle of Yahweh that Moses' tabernacle only foreshadowed. He "did not enter by means of the blood of goats and calves; but he entered the Most Holy Place once for all by his own blood, thus obtaining eternal redemption." It is his blood that cleanses "our consciences from acts that lead to death, so that we may serve the living God"—a sacrifice that was made "once to take away the sins of many." In these respects, at least, Torah "is only a shadow of the good things that are coming—not the realities themselves." The reality has now appeared—and "sacrifice for sin is no longer necessary" (Heb. 8:1–10:18).

ROOT AND BRANCH

It is evident that Jesus-followers, then, in taking the OT seriously in deciding what to believe and how to live, must at the same time pay serious attention to the ways in which our "Hebrew roots" do and do not develop in the biblical Story into long-lasting branches. And this the "Hebrew Roots" movement unfortunately fails to do. This is apparently because its members have difficulty in believing that what God once said to his OT people does not entirely represent what he wants to say to his NT people. It is particularly bizarre in this context that rules that clearly once applied to Israelites and not to Gentiles at all—and indeed were designed to separate Israelites, and later Jews, from Gentiles—are now being embraced by Yeshua-followers who have never been Jews in the first place. The justification offered for this move is stranger still: that somehow the "Hebrew Roots" movement represents the return of the ten lost tribes of northern Israel to their national identity under the Davidic Judean king (Christ).

This is not the only curiosity in this ideology that readers interested in further study might pursue. Another striking one is that members of the movement tend to go well beyond the demands of OT Torah in their practice, adopting Jewish traditions—even while refraining from becoming Jewish—such as keeping commandments that are not explicitly stated or detailed in the OT, wearing Jewish clothing, and learning the Talmud. Their conviction appears to be that what certain groups of contemporary Jews practice is in fact the most authentic version of proper Torah observance—the closest approximation to how Yeshua would have lived—and thus worthy of their own imitation.

If, then, the error in the "Stanley option" discussed in chapter 2 is that it vastly *underestimates* the continuity between the OT and the NT people of God, the error in the "Roots option" discussed in chapters 2 and 3 is that it greatly *overestimates* it. The actual situation is in fact much more complicated than either option allows. Both continuity and discontinuity exist, and we must be careful to give due attention to both.

HEROIC PHINEHAS

From the point of view of our pursuit of the good life, it matters quite considerably whether we do this—and whether, as a result, we get the balance between continuity and discontinuity right. I suppose that any serious Christian would want to keep the Sabbath, for example, if keeping the Sabbath is one aspect of pursuing the good life that God intends us to live. Arriving at a settled conviction concerning the question of continuity and discontinuity in the case of the fourth Commandment, however—which is never explicitly cited in the NT as having relevance for the life of the post-Pentecost people of God—is a necessary step on the way to knowing whether we should in fact keep the Sabbath or not. Similarly, I imagine that any serious Christian would wish to dedicate a "tithe" (tenth) of his or her income to God, in line with Leviticus 27:30–33, if indeed that is what God requires of us. But again, reflection on the question of continuity and discontinuity is a necessary step on the way to resolving that matter.

It is not only on the question of Mosaic Torah that we need such clarity. The same kind of issue arises when we read OT narrative, which is also given to help us know how to be good. But how are we to read it? In Numbers 25:6–13, for example, Aaron's zealous grandson Phinehas seeks to cleanse the Israelite camp of idolatry by driving his spear through an Israelite man and right into the stomach of his Midianite wife (or lover—it is not clear). As such Phinehas was a popular figure among many of the English Protestants of the seventeenth century whom we shall describe in more detail in chapter 9. In 1641 Samuel Fairclough, a minister in Suffolk, referenced his example in calling for the execution of King Charles I's close advisor, the Earl of Strafford. In 1644 Edmund Staunton did so again in calling for the execution of the Archbishop of Canterbury, William Laud. The decisiveness of Phinehas' actions, they thought, was exactly what was lacking among the contemporary powers in dealing with idolatry (i.e., with Roman Catholicism) in England. Thomas Brooks referred to the same passage in a sermon shortly before the execution of the king himself in 1649.[5] But what reason is there, in fact, to think that Christians after Pentecost should behave as Phinehas did before it? Is the continuity between the OT and the NT people of God such that we should take Phinehas as our role model in opposing idolatry? Or is it not?

EXAMINING THE SCRIPTURES

One of the things that becomes still clearer than before as a result of our reflections in this chapter is that the very shape of the God-inspired Scriptures forces us to *search* them in order to gain wisdom regarding how we should live. I used the same word in chapter 2 precisely in relation to the "heroic reading" of biblical *narrative* in general (of which the reading of Phinehas described above is only one particular example). It is also true, however, that the way in which *Torah* is presented to us in Scripture forces us into a search within it for creational law. That is, we are not provided by God in Christian Scripture simply with a book of rules for life that, if we keep them one by one, will make us holy. We are instead provided with an overarching Story with various literary genres embedded in it that demands our serious and thoughtful engagement if we are properly to understand what holiness looks like. The very way in which this literature has been put together, then, requires of us that we do not simply *read* the Scriptures but that, like the Berean Jews in Acts 17:11, we *examine* them "every day" in pursuit of the truth. The Greek verb here (*anakrinō*) has the sense of questioning, discerning, and arriving at a judgment. What holiness involves, in biblical faith, is not simply "self-evident." The God-ordained nature of Scripture requires that we ascertain what is right by way of a process of reading, questioning, discerning, and arriving at a judgment.

LOOKING AHEAD

The remainder of this book aims further to help serious, Christian Bible-readers to navigate these questions of continuity and discontinuity intelligently and faithfully, as they attempt to "read themselves into" the great biblical Story and thereby discover what the good life looks like. How, exactly, is the OT "useful" to us in this "seeking for what is right"? In the course of these three foundational chapters the outline of an answer to this question has already begun to emerge: we should obey commandments like "do not covet," for example, but there is no requirement that we should circumcise our male children, or keep the ancient food laws, or offer sacrifices. What further progress can we make in discerning how the OT should shape our Christian lives ethically, socially, and indeed politically—for we all live public, as well as private lives?

There are many ways in which we might proceed. My chosen framework in this book is a historical one. I have personally found it helpful as I have reflected on such questions over many years to look at how Christians before me have handled them. It creates an initial historical "distance" between myself and the topic at hand that helps to clarify my thinking about what counts as good and bad Scripture reading—and what this means for the contemporary Church in its own wrestling with the ethics of God's kingdom in the light of Scripture. In chapters 4 through 15 of this book, therefore, I explore how different Christian groups or entities throughout history have identified themselves with the "Israel" of the OT and have sought in their Bible reading to stand in continuity with this ancient people of God.

This requires that I offer a brief account of (mainly Western) history as I proceed—which I hope may itself be of some help to readers who do not know much about this subject as they begin. However, I am not aiming at comprehensiveness in this historical description. My intention is only to provide the reader with an overall sense of the context in which our Christian forebears wrestled with the particular issue that I have chosen for examination in each case. In each chapter, then, I update the historical timeline before pausing at a particular moment in it to examine an illustrative example (on occasion, two examples) of biblical hermeneutics "at work." Having examined how our predecessors applied the OT to their lives in a particular moment, I then offer some suggestions about how we modern Christians should assess their decisions, as people who read the whole Story "from the beginning"—OT first, followed by the NT. In chapter 16, finally, I offer a number of conclusions that we might draw from the whole exercise; in chapters 17 and 18 I then apply the summary paradigm of right reading that is described in chapter 16 to a number of contemporary ethical issues not discussed earlier in the book, in order to discover what light it can shed on how we should handle them. Chapter 19 reflects on the contemporary cultural landscape in which we wrestle with these issues and the challenges that arise as we do so. Chapter 20 concludes the volume by developing the biblical metaphor of "exile" for our life in such a context, discussing the disciplines that we need to cultivate in order to live well in it.

I hope in this process not only to suggest what the Bible teaches about the good life across a whole range of issues but also to make proposals about how we should and should not read Scripture in arriving at these and other conclusions—what the parameters of the search for what is right look like. I hope thereby to help readers to engage well with the Bible in approaching other aspects of the good life that, by the very nature of a relatively brief book, we cannot explicitly address here. The discussion questions listed at the end of most chapters (as in chapters 1–3) are already designed in part to get readers thinking about this wider realm of inquiry.

DISCUSSION QUESTIONS

1. What did you learn from the summary of the great Story of Scripture in this chapter that was new to you?
2. The fourth of the Ten Commandments enjoins the keeping of Sabbath (Exod. 20:1–17). On the basis of what you have read in chapters 1–3, do you think it likely that Christians should observe the Sabbath? Why or why not?
3. Read Leviticus 27:30–33, which is about dedicating a "tithe" (tenth) of one's agricultural produce to God. On the basis of what you have read in chapters 1–3, do you think it likely that this rule applies to Christians? Why or why not?

(Do not worry if you find questions 2 and 3 hard to answer; we are coming back to these issues in later chapters.)

II

EXPLORATIONS

4

The Emperor's New Clothes
Constantine as Biblical Hero

Finding in the New Testament no pattern of a Christian polity, [the Christian] will turn for it to the portrayal of the People of God in the Old Testament.[1]

S. L. Greenslade

On July 25, 306 AD, in York, England, Constantine, the son of a "senior" Roman emperor (titled "Augustus"), was himself proclaimed "Augustus" by his dead father's army.[2] Some years later (in 312), he marched on Italy and confronted a rival emperor, Maxentius, at the site of the old Milvian Bridge over the Tiber River in Rome. This battle, on October 28, 312, resulted in Maxentius' death and Constantine's supremacy over the western half of the Roman Empire. Since in what follows there will be many references to "the West" and "the East" in this empire, as well as to the "Western" and "Eastern" Church, it is wise to pause to offer an explanation. "East" refers to everything east of a notional line that runs between Greece and Italy and down through Roman North Africa, such that Egypt (e.g., Alexandria) and Syria (e.g., Antioch) are in the East while modern Tunisia and Algeria (e.g., the locations of ancient Carthage and Hippo) are in the West. Rome itself is in the West, therefore, while Constantinople (as it will shortly become) is in the East.

In the aftermath of the Battle of the Milvian Bridge, Constantine met his brother-in-law Licinius in Milan (313), and they agreed to divide the entire Empire between them. It was an unstable arrangement, however, fluctuating between war and uneasy peace, and Constantine finally defeated Licinius in battle (324) and had him executed (325). He took as his first name "Victor" and ruled a unified realm until his death on May 22, 337.

THE CHRISTIANIZATION OF THE EMPIRE

The story of Constantine told briefly in this way does not yet suggest its monumental significance for the history of the Christian Church—and for Christian reading of the Bible in relation to individual and community ethics, as well as to affairs of state. We must add some detail.

First, who was the man who arrived at the gates of Rome in 312 to fight Maxentius? He was the son of parents who had raised him to venerate a single great god—as various emperors before him, in the third century, had done.[3] As Peter Leithart explains, "The paganism of the third and fourth century was increasingly monotheistic, or at least henotheistic (believing in a chief, though not exclusive, high God)."[4] In Constantine's case, this god was Sol Invictus (the Unconquered Sun), identified with the sun god Apollo, who had allegedly appeared to Constantine in a vision in 310.[5] However, he had already been influenced by a Christian scholar, Lactantius, who had been tutor to Constantine's son Crispus at the imperial court since the same year—and Christians had for some time equated the sun with Christ, the Light of the World.[6] Lactantius was in the process of writing his *Divine Institutes*, in which he argued that monotheism had been the original religion of Rome before being replaced by the false idea of many gods and that "only through Christianity is true wisdom attainable."[7] It was for this reason, he proposed, that the Roman state should protect religious freedom (and specifically Christian freedom)—something that Constantine's father had already done. Lactantius now suggested that Constantine, if he wished his reign to flourish, should do the same.

TOLERATION OF RELIGION

This helps to explain the agreement made by Constantine and Licinius in Milan in AD 313 concerning imperial policy toward religion. Its effect was to allow Christians, along with everyone else, the liberty, prospectively, to follow whichever kind of religion they thought best—to worship Divinity as they saw fit. Retrospectively, all the church property seized during the earlier persecution of Christians under the emperor Diocletian (who had died in 311) was to be returned. The aim of the policy was to generate divine favor, on the one hand, and public tranquility, on the other. Nothing should any longer be done that risked the anger of God. The legal and social framework that subsequently emerged in pursuit of the protection of these new Christian rights helped to change forever the nature of the Church's relationship with the Roman Empire, and indeed its successors in both the East and the West. The rights of other citizens were already protected by "powerful patrons who might interpret [for them] both existing law and new laws."[8] Now Christian clergy—exempted from "compulsory public services so that they, like the priests of other religions, might devote their energies solely to the propagation of faith and to prayer"[9]—became such "patrons" of the Church. Bishops were authorized, among other things, to hear legal cases and to free slaves within their domains. Roman religion had always essentially been an affair of the state, and so it remained. But whereas Christians during the preceding three hundred years had frequently been persecuted as "traitors" to this state, they now found themselves absorbed fully into it by an emperor who was anxious above all to avoid any offence against Heaven that might adversely affect his rule.

CONSTANTINE THE CHRISTIAN

Constantine did not just tolerate the Christians, however. At some point, still uncertain to scholars, he began to identify as one. Looking back on his life, he emphasized the events surrounding his victory at the Milvian Bridge as a turning point; this was the moment when he understood the Christian God as the sovereign Lord who brings victory and came to grasp his own role as the vehicle of this God's will.[10] Yet the fact remains that the name taken by Constantine after the battle, "Invictus," refers directly to his previous patron Sol Invictus. Furthermore, the triumphal arch erected in Rome in 315 to celebrate the victory identified this same god as the one responsible for it, and Constantine's coinage throughout the intervening period also continued to reflect this same patronage.[11] It is only later that Sol begins to disappear from the coinage, as Constantine begins publicly to recognize Christ[12]—not least in his adoption (perhaps around 320) of the *labarum*, a military standard that displayed the "Chi-Rho" Christian symbol.[13] By the year of Constantine's victory over Licinius (325) he had replaced "Invictus" with a new name, "Victor," which more clearly indicated his new faith.[14] He was also presiding over the famous Council of Nicea, which sought to restore unity to a Christian Church riven by the Arian heresy and in succeeding generations came to set the standard for orthodox Christian belief ("Nicene orthodoxy").[15] Later, on his deathbed, Constantine was baptized as a Christian (337).

Only a few decades later, the emperor Theodosius I (ruled 379–395) made Nicene Christianity the official religion of the Roman state (380). Constantine had not been interested in effecting "the triumph of Christianity throughout his lands ... [and so] he allowed worship to continue in all its forms."[16] He was, in a certain sense, a pluralist—if we mean by this that he was generally unwilling to use state power to suppress forms of religion of which he increasingly disapproved.[17] Theodosius certainly did not share these qualms: he closed down pagan temples all across the empire. In his own eyes this was a decision vindicated by his

subsequent victory in 394 over the usurper Flavius Eugenius, who had enlisted
pagan support in his bid to control the Western Empire. Like Constantine, Theodosius simply assumed in the old Roman way that victory in battle was a sure
sign of the favor of one's chosen god(s)—an idea with a lot of mileage ahead of it
in the story of Church and State that we have now begun to tell.

The death of Eugenius dashed any remaining pagan hope that the Chris-
tianization of the empire might be halted and perhaps reversed. After Theodosius I, indeed, the Christianized Empire became increasingly intolerant of "Jews,
pagans, and heretics"—the standard "triple pattern" that quickly emerges in
Roman legal statutes of the fifth and sixth centuries when their authors are referring to the enemies of true religion (i.e., Nicene orthodoxy).[18] By the time we get
to the first year of Justinian's reign (527) we find a law being announced whereby
"it shall be possible for all to perceive [in social consequences] . . . that even what
pertains to the human advantages is withheld from those who do not worship
God rightfully." This law goes on to clarify that "[w]e call heretic everyone who is
not devoted to the Catholic Church and to our orthodox and holy Faith."[19] Here
was an emperor determined to remove "all traces of pagan philosophy and practice" from his empire—and to gain "total mastery" of his realm along Christian
lines.[20] The religion that under Constantine had looked for toleration had quickly
become, in gaining control of the empire, intolerant.

THE FATE OF THE JEWS

It is important to attend to one of the targets of Christian intolerance in
particular—not least because we shall be returning to their story in a focused
way later in the book. The life of Jews in the preceding pagan Roman Empire
had not generally been harsh. Its emperors had been inclined on the whole to
tolerate what they typically saw as a foreign religion that was certainly inferior
to their own but nevertheless possessed longstanding legal status in the Roman
world—even in spite of the fact that Jews (perversely) would not worship the
Roman gods. "It is right and just," affirmed the emperor Claudius (41–54), "that
the Jews should preserve their ancestral customs without any hindrance in the
entire world ruled by us"—such as the Sabbath, for example (which we shall discuss in chapter 10).[21] There had been notable exceptions to the tolerant emperors,
of course, such as Domitian (81–96), but there had also been notable friends to
the Jewish community. Perhaps the most surprising of these was the bloodthirsty,
tyrannical Caracalla (211–217), whose *Constitutio Antoniniana* (212) had given the
Jews Roman civil rights. Alexander Severus (222–235), who had a synagogue
in Rome named after him, was another, and so was the Christian-persecuting
Diocletian (284–305).

The point is not that there had been widespread philosemitism (i.e., positive attitudes toward Jews) among pagans in the Roman Empire prior to the Christian conversion of Constantine, but only that the levels of antisemitism had not been high. All minority religious groups within the majority religious culture were of course in principle vulnerable to suspicion and attack, and where there was not "[t]he active good will, or at least the acquiescence" of the majority toward a minority, serious trouble could evidently follow.[22] It happens, however, that it was Christians rather than Jews, in the main, who had hitherto endured most of the trouble.

Forbidden by No Law

All of this began to change in some ways with the conversion of Constantine, and then markedly with the creation of the Christian empire under Theodosius I. The negativity that many Christians had previously harbored toward Jews and Judaism—illustrated by my comments on "Judaizing" in chapter 2—now began to take political shape.[23] Augustine would shortly provide a highly influential summary of the theology behind the politics (especially in his treatise *Against the Jews*), restating and expanding what some of the preceding Church Fathers had already said. To wit: the Jews had rejected Christ and were responsible for his death, resulting in the loss of the Jerusalem temple, their scattering throughout the world, and their loss of status as the chosen people. They were the enemies of the Church, and Christians must be protected from them. They would be saved in the end, however, and in the meantime should be tolerated as servants in Christian society, not least "because they bore witness to the origins of Christianity and thus vouched for its truth."[24] Theodosius' own policy toward the Jews was considerably friendlier than that of some of the Christian bishops in the Empire who already held such views, and he made it his business to remind all Christians that even now "the sect of the Jews [was] forbidden by no law."[25] The direction in which the *general culture* was moving is however indicated, first, by the very fact that the emperor felt it necessary to forbid the Christian burning of synagogues and, secondly, by the intense pressure on Jews to convert to Christianity, which "at times degenerated into anti-Jewish riots, persecutions, and conversions by force."[26]

A further indication of the gradually worsening situation of the Jews within Christendom is that the attacks on synagogues by Christian mobs during the reign of Theodosius II (408–450) "became so frequent . . . that most of [his] imperial edicts were concerned with this problem."[27] That he, too, defended Jewish rights is significant, but so is that fact that during his reign it was "forbidden to build new synagogues or to enlarge those already in existence."[28] As Peter Shafer notes, "The overall deterioration in the situation brought about by the violent actions of the Church was now effectively condoned, at least in law."[29]

PERMITTED TO LIVE

So it is that in the centuries immediately following the fifth century we find a situation in which, officially, the Jews remained a legally protected minority in Christendom, benefiting still from their previous status under pagan Roman law. For example, at the end of the sixth century in the West Pope Gregory the Great (reigned 590–604) still maintained that "as [the Hebrews] are permitted to live by the Roman laws, justice allows that they should manage their affairs as they see fit."[30] They had a legitimate place in Christian society. However, if the Jews were indeed "permitted to live," it was now in the main very much as second-class citizens. Earlier in the sixth century the emperor Justinian's view had been that "the Jews and the heretics should be content with merely 'staying alive.'"[31] They should not expect much as "outsiders" in Christian society. It is consistent with this sentiment that his Justinian Code of law (534) "adopts practically none of the laws concerning the protection of synagogues from the Codex Theodosianus, even though the frequency of Christian attacks [against the synagogues] had certainly not diminished."[32] Indeed, he "took the legislation on Jews enacted by his Christian predecessors and made it tougher" on the former.[33] This was particularly important for what happened after the sixth century, since Justinian's "codification of legislation on Jewish matters served as the basis for all future legal practice and remained in force until after the Middle Ages."[34] While later law continued to protect Jews, then, to a greater or a lesser extent it also continued to discriminate against them; and while Christian bishops often (but certainly not always) sought to offer their own protection in word and deed, they did so in a climate typically very much shaped by a "stream of invective and pejorative language that denigrated Judaism," reinforced the distaste of Christians in general for Jews, and could lead to violence.[35]

CHURCH AND STATE IN EARLY CHRISTIANITY

The beginnings of the remarkable and fateful process by which Christianity moved from the margins of the life of the Roman state to its center lie with Constantine's conversion—and new questions inevitably and immediately arose for Christians as a result of it, aside from how they should treat the Jews. One of the more important of these questions, and the one that we shall shortly examine, concerned biblical interpretation: how should Christians now interpret their Bibles—and specifically, the OT? Before answering this question, we need some further background.

The Apostolic Church

In the period prior to Constantine, the Roman Empire had typically been regarded in the Church simply as a datum with which Christians, one way or another, had to live. It was a divinely ordained reality, for the time being, to which one ought to offer as much obedience as one could while hoping for (and indeed requesting) sufficient liberty of worship as to make direct disobedience to it unnecessary. The earliest evidence for this Christian perspective lies in the NT. Here we encounter an important overarching theme: that the kingdom of God has already come, and will one day fully come, displacing the kingdoms of this world whose authority is always contingent on the will of the one true God. In considering these ultimate questions, the apostolic writings—the book of Revelation most obviously—can sometimes portray Rome as illustrating worldly power gone wrong, and consequently bringing suffering upon Christians (as it once did upon Christ). Yet at the same time Paul reminds the Christians in Rome that "[t]he authorities that exist have been established by God" for the sake of the common good and, as such, they should be obeyed (Rom. 13:1–5). The progress of the Gospel itself is described in Acts as "assisted rather than hindered by the timely exploitation of Roman institutions."[36] The Roman Empire is in fact that which holds back "the secret power of lawlessness" that is already at work in the world. It is the force that in the period prior to the final coming of God's kingdom creates space in the world in which "the message of the Lord may spread rapidly and be honored" (2 Thess. 2:6–7; 3:1). The empire is, therefore, something of a contingent good in the world, albeit one that will ultimately pass away.

Precisely because it *will* pass away, however—because it is not an ultimate but a temporary reality—the NT shows little interest in the empire from a missional point of view. There is no expectation that the regime itself can become Christian, and no activism is endorsed that might contribute to that end. What the NT mainly commends, in fact, is in many ways a notable "withdrawal from the political life of the empire,"[37] including its law courts (1 Cor. 6:1–6), even while Christians should adopt a maximally law-abiding and submissive posture in relation to it (1 Pet. 2:13–17; 3:13–17). On the whole, for example, "[t]he predominant impression in the Pauline epistles is of a profound lack of interest in either local or imperial politics. The empire and its institutions are hardly mentioned except as metaphors for the religious life."[38] This is consistent with the picture of Christians in 1 Peter as living as "foreigners and exiles" in a pagan society (2:11)—an image to which we shall return in chapters 16 through 19, when considering our situation in our own contemporary world.

THE EARLY CHURCH FATHERS

We discover these same perspectives widely articulated in the writings of the postapostolic Church Fathers of the second and third centuries. The end of the world is certainly coming—after six thousand years of apostasy since the Fall, according to Irenaeus in Roman Gaul.[39] Until then, the Roman Empire is the context within which the Church lives its life.[40] It is in fact only of interest to Irenaeus *as* "the arena in which the Christian teaching gains ground."[41] For the empire will soon pass away, but the Church will not: "empire is the platform on which the ultimate rebellion against God's purposes must emerge; world history is the story of the growth of empire and of its final collapse before divine judgment."[42] The early third-century writer Sextus Julianus Africanus agrees: Christian history will only endure for five hundred years after Christ, to be followed by his Second Coming.[43]

Tertullian, writing around 197, takes a similar line, while at the same time developing markedly negative commentary concerning the expansion of the empire, which "was accomplished by wanton destruction of cities, assassination of citizens and priests, and sacking of sacred, as well as profane, buildings."[44] Although Christians form their own universal "state," the empire is the God-ordained context in which the Church operates, and Tertullian is keen to assure his Roman readers that "[w]ithout ceasing, for all our emperors we offer prayer. We pray for life prolonged; for security to the empire; for protection to the imperial house; for brave armies, a faithful senate, a virtuous people, the world at rest, whatever, as man or Caesar, an emperor would wish."[45] Christians pray in this way not least because they value "the complete stability of the empire, and . . . Roman interests in general. For we know that a mighty shock impending over the whole earth—in fact, the very end of all things threatening dreadful woes—is only retarded by the continued existence of the Roman empire. We have no desire, then, to be overtaken by these dire events; and in praying that their coming may be delayed, we are lending our aid to Rome's duration."[46] Indeed, "Caesar is more ours than yours, for our God has appointed him. Therefore . . . I do more than you for his welfare."[47]

Origen of Alexandria (c. 185–254) regards "the contemporaneity of Augustus and Christ [as] a providential act," creating a set of circumstances in which Christian doctrine could hold its own until the end of the world and the subjection of all of Christ's enemies.[48] As to how Christians ought to deal with this on-the-ground, in-the-meantime reality of empire, he too maintains (in agreement with his pagan interlocutor Celsus) that Christians ought "to help the king with all our might," while resisting Celsus' idea that this means "to fight for him; and if he requires it, to fight under him, or lead an army along with him."[49] Rather, the kind of help that Origen has in mind is prayer. He also resists Celsus' exhortation that

Christians should "take office in the government of the country, if that is required for the maintenance of the laws and the support of religion," explaining that "it is not for the purpose of escaping public duties that Christians decline public offices, but that they may reserve themselves for a diviner and more necessary service in the Church of God—for the salvation of men."[50]

Separation

There is in all of this a pronounced ideological separation of Church and state, even as Christians clearly inhabit the state, which is envisaged as lasting until Christ returns. There are two clearly defined spheres of existence—and Christians properly and primarily inhabit the first of these, even if they must also necessarily inhabit in some ways the second. It is to enable successful living in the first sphere—and this is the crucial point—that Scripture is then also primarily read by these authors, in line with apostolic teaching that Scripture is inspired by God precisely so as to be "useful one way or another" for Christians (2 Tim. 3:16)—useful for shaping correct Christian doctrine ("showing us truth") and practice ("exposing our rebellion, correcting our mistakes, training us to live God's way"). That is, Scripture is primarily useful for the Church—the people who "dwell in their own countries, but simply as sojourners. As citizens, they share in all things with others, and yet endure all things as if foreigners."[51] It is not primarily useful for the ongoing affairs of the state, about which it has relatively little to say.

THE BIBLE AND THE EMPIRE

With the conversion of Constantine, however, we begin to find a new kind of Bible reading in what will soon become Christendom. It first appears in the writings of Eusebius Pamphili, who became bishop of Caesarea around 313. A favored subject of the emperor, Eusebius outlived him to write a *Life of Constantine* that glorified him as a Christian saint—and he did so with significant reliance on OT, Israelite analogies.

Noble Moses

In the story that Eusebius tells, Constantine is like Moses in opposing "the tyrants of our day [who] have ventured to war against the Supreme God, and have sorely afflicted His Church," in whose midst—"as that other servant of God had done"—Constantine had previously lived, but without sharing "the manner of life of the ungodly."[52] For even in his early life "his noble nature, under the leading of the Divine Spirit, inclined him to piety and a life acceptable to God." Later, Constantine, aware of the malevolent designs of the emperors then in power, "sought safety in flight, in this respect again keeping up his resemblance to the great prophet Moses."[53] Still later, Constantine confronts Maxentius at the Milvian Bridge. According to Eusebius, he is already a Christian by this point, having seen "with his own eyes the trophy of a cross of light in the heavens, above the sun, and bearing the inscription, 'conquer by this,'" as well as having received a subsequent vision of Christ.[54] This is why he marches against Maxentius carrying the *labarum*, having previously committed himself to the reading of the Scriptures and having "made the priests of God his counsellors."[55] Thus prepared, he defeats Maxentius, who goes to his doom in a manner reminiscent of the Egyptian Pharaoh and his chariots in the book of Exodus:

> For as once in the days of Moses and the Hebrew nation, who were worshipers of God, "Pharaoh's chariots and his host hath he cast into the sea and his chosen chariot-captains are drowned in the Red Sea," so at this time Maxentius, and the soldiers and guards with him, "went down into the depths like stone," when, in his flight before the divinely aided forces of Constantine, he essayed to cross the river which lay in his way.[56]

So it is that the victors have every right

> in the same spirit as the people of his great servant Moses, [to] sing and speak as they did concerning the impious tyrant of old: "Let us sing unto the Lord, for he hath been glorified exceedingly: the horse and his rider hath he thrown into the sea. He is become my helper and my shield unto salvation."[57]

This same theme appears in Eusebius' earlier *Ecclesiastical History*. Here Constantine, prior to the battle, invokes "in prayer the God of heaven, and his Word, and Jesus Christ himself, the Saviour of all, as his aid," before advancing to victory "as in the time of Moses himself."[58]

THE IDEAL KING

This is a significant development. Moses is certainly portrayed in earlier Christian literature as being just as great as other ancient philosophers, and indeed as the source of those philosophers' knowledge. Clement of Alexandria, for example, writes as follows:

> It is the wise man . . . alone whom the philosophers proclaim king, legislator, general, just, holy, God-beloved. And if we discover these qualities in Moses, as shown from the Scriptures themselves, we may, with the most assured persuasion, pronounce Moses to be truly wise.[59]

However, Eusebius' use of Moses moves well beyond this closest analogue to it in earlier Christian writing. In Eusebius, the story of Israel in the OT is no longer "useful" only for establishing correct Christian doctrine and practice. It is also useful in terms of forming our understanding of the history of the Roman Empire under Constantine, and of the man himself. Constantine is not merely emperor; he is, rather (as Paul Stephenson puts it), "the leader of the new elect, the new Israelites."[60] His enemies, by the same token, are not merely his own; they are enemies of God, just like those ancient enemies of Moses—or indeed of the righteous Davidic king. Constantine marches against them under the sign of the cross, authorized by the one true God to do so. It is worth noting here that Bishop Cyprian of Carthage (200–258), building on earlier writers, had already referred to the "sign of the cross" by which "Amalek was conquered by Jesus [Joshua] through Moses"—referring to Moses' posture in Exodus 17:8–13. However, this victory is interpreted not in terms of another earthly victory by a political leader but in terms of salvation for all people who are marked on their foreheads with this sign.[61] For Eusebius, though, the state itself is now the inheritor of the mantle of Israel, and the emperor is Israel's king—"God's vice-regent on earth," which is itself "the microcosm of heaven."[62] Monarchy has "come on earth as the image of monarchy in heaven,"[63] and a kind of messianic kingdom has arrived along with it, in the aftermath of the defeat of Licinius:

> The protector of the virtuous . . . went forth with his son Crispus . . . and extended a saving right hand to all that were perishing. Both of them . . . under the protection, as it were, of God, the universal King, with the Son of God, the Saviour of all, as their leader and ally, drew up their forces on all sides against the enemies of the Deity and won an easy victory . . . [and] formed one united Roman empire as of old . . . Everything was filled with light, and those who before were downcast beheld each other with smiling faces and beaming eyes. With dances and hymns, in city and country, they glorified first of all God the universal King, because they had been thus taught, and then the pious emperor with his God-beloved children.[64]

Perhaps Eusebius is already borrowing these ideas from Constantine and his propagandists rather than developing them independently: "Eusebius' use of the comparison probably reuses much material from Constantine's Moses propaganda, but he also seems to have reshaped some parts of it in order to promote his own interests."[65] In due course the propagandists certainly reinforced the same ideas, deploying with enthusiasm biblical images that hitherto "had never been a feature of imperial art and the language of power."[66] If a slightly later source is to be believed, Constantine himself even designed a "Mosaic" tabernacle for his own use in prayer during planned campaigns in the deserts to his east.[67] Here was the ideal monarch, then: "a model of piety and truth [in Eusebius' words] to all the earth."[68] In his empire "the ancient oracles and predictions of the prophets were fulfilled" and the messianic kingdom of the OT arrived.[69]

THE EMPIRE AS BIBLICAL ISRAEL

In this way of reading the Bible, the Roman Empire has become biblical Israel. The Church, for its part, has been absorbed into the state, just as the ancient Israelite priests once functioned under the authority, first, of leaders like Moses, and then the biblical kings. Urban Christian bishops, "empowered to administer property and wealth bequeathed to the church and to preside over an ecclesiastical court," are now set on a path that will bring them into close relationships with Roman administrators, sharing with them "a vested interest in the survival of ancient patterns of social organisation" and frequently collaborating with them "in the enforcement of imperial decrees," functioning as "an additional arm of secular administration."[70] It will not be long, in fact (as we shall see in chapter 5), before a Christian state puts its legislative and administrative weight behind taxes designed in part to support this priestly class financially—just as in OT times the priests were supported by tithes.

Militarily, Constantine did not himself require Christian faith of his soldiers, and he fought no religious wars.[71] However, "his wars did transform how Christians viewed war, and allowed the transformation of the Roman army into a Christian army in the century following Constantine's victory over Licinius [in 324]."[72] In due course there were Crusades—as we shall see in chapter 6. Politically, Constantine did not create a uniformly Christian state. However, the logic of the appropriation of Israel as a model for empire led inexorably (and soon) to the promotion within the state of one, true biblical religion and the penalizing or suppression of all others as not "rightful." This logic was already playing out in the context of the Arian controversy as it rumbled on after Constantine's death during the reign of his son Constantius II (337–361). Failing to support true religion as the Nicene party understood it, Constantius was opposed by those bishops precisely as an idolatrous king like Saul, or Solomon, or Ahab. He was not the righteous, biblical vice-regent of God that he should have been.[73] The later Theodosius, on the other hand, in closing all the pagan temples and establishing Nicene Christianity as the official religion of the empire, did exactly what a good OT king should do. The same biblical frame of reference is then adopted by later emperors like Justinian in the sixth century, with "his determination to be measured by [the] scale of achievement" of Moses and Solomon—whether in the promulgation of law or the construction of great buildings.[74] For centuries afterwards, this kind of biblical "reading" of the state "provided the basis for a political theory accepted ... by eastern Christians in the [eastern Roman] Byzantine Empire."[75] The theory differed somewhat in the West—as we shall see in chapter 5—but that does not mean that we lack examples in Western Church History of the penalizing and suppression of "Jews, pagans, and heretics." To the contrary, we shall encounter numerous striking examples of the same, with respect mainly to heretics, but occasionally to pagans, throughout chapters 5–13. We shall pick up the threads of the story of the Jews within Christendom, from the Middle Ages onwards, in chapter 14.

THE HERMENEUTICS OF EMPIRE

What are we to make of this kind of Bible reading? Granted that the *Church* is supposed to regard itself as "a chosen people, a royal priesthood, a holy nation, [and] God's special possession" (1 Pet. 2:9–10), what justification is there for regarding the Roman Empire under Constantine in such terms? It is true that Christians are supposed to regard OT characters as models in respect of their own faith and life—whether by way of imitation or the lack of it. We are to imitate Elijah in his prayer life (Jas. 5:13–18), for example, but not the disobedient Israelites who failed to enter the Promised Land (Heb. 8:11). But what is it that justifies the correlation of Constantine with Moses, specifically? And supposing for the moment that the correlation is in some sense appropriate, what lessons are best drawn from it? Are they the lessons drawn by Eusebius?

These are important questions—not least because our answers will not only determine how we judge Eusebius' reading of the OT with respect to Church and state but will also inevitably influence (as they no doubt already reflect) our own. They will play their part in shaping our own convictions about how we too, as Christians, should and should not read the OT as pertaining to the "pattern of a Christian polity" with respect to the contemporary state (as S. L. Greenslade puts it in the epigraph to this chapter). Is it really true that, lacking help in the NT with respect to such a "pattern," we should for that reason look for it in "the portrayal of the People of God in the Old Testament"? Why might one do this? Or why not? So: what are we to make of this kind of Bible reading?

The Old Testament and the Christian State

The truth of the matter is that there is very little reason to think that any Christian *should* do as Greenslade suggests. Finding no pattern of a Christian polity in the NT is certainly no justification, in itself, for trying to find it in the OT; we might just as easily take this absence as a strong hint that we should *not*. Is there any *positive* reason that we should do it?

It is not easy to identify one. As we saw in chapter 2, the OT people of God is a special people called to participate in the mission of God in the world in a limited phase of the great biblical Story of redemption. Biblical Israel is organized, socially, economically, and politically, in such a way as to allow it to fulfil this role in particular places and in particular times. The period in which its existence is most analogous to that of the fourth-century Roman Empire is that of the

Israelite monarchy, during which time kings ruled over territories and even (in the case of David and Solomon) over mini-empires. This is indeed the period to which Greenslade's "simple Christian" naturally turns in considering the question of Christian polity—the part of Israel's story in which we find "the anointed king fully engaged in religious affairs and held responsible by God for his people's faith and worship and conduct."[76] The monarchy, however, is not understood in the OT as an ideal form of government even for Israel.

It was generally unimaginable in the ANE that a state could exist without a king. Kingship as an institution was indeed regarded as primordial, gifted to humanity from the beginning of time by the gods. The king himself was at the very least "like a god," if not himself divine—he was the one human being thought capable of "imaging" divinity. The gods, enthroned over the cosmos, exercised their rule on earth through both their temple images and these other human "images," who were responsible for the enactment of law. An image of the king could in fact be placed in a temple beside the image of his god, giving symbolic representation to the idea that the king was the god's right-hand man.[77] Monarchy was an indispensable, non-negotiable datum in the cosmos.

This was not the case in ancient Israel. According to Scripture, the ancient Israelites existed as a people-group for quite some time before the coming of monarchy. When the institution ultimately arose, we are told, it did so because of a sinful desire among the Israelites to be like the other nations around them, rather than remain radically different from them. Their true ruler was God himself—a warrior-king engaged in a long-term conflict with evil in the cosmos, who from time to time summoned his servants, the Israelites, to help him fight some of his battles (Amos 2:9; Ps. 78:53–55). When the Israelites are being faithful in the OT, these are the battles that they fight—God's battles, and not their own. In 1 Samuel 8, however, the Israelites request a human king precisely so that he can "lead us and to go out before us and fight *our* battles" (emphasis added, 8:20). This request is portrayed as wicked in this passage precisely because it represents a rejection of God's kingship and, in particular, the raising of a standing army for the king's own use. It is the kind of unfaithfulness that elsewhere in the OT leads to God fighting *against* the Israelites rather than alongside them. Earlier in 1 Samuel itself the Israelites bring the Ark of the Covenant into the camp in an attempt to manipulate God into fighting for them against the Philistines (1 Sam. 4); God demonstrates his independence of them by seeing to it that they are routed. The reason is that God's justice in the OT is even-handed; his battle is against evil wherever it is to be found.

So the institution of monarchy in Israel has murky beginnings, associated with rebellion against God. It is nevertheless tolerated by God in 1 Samuel 8 and ultimately integrated into his plans for Israel and the world, albeit within the significant constraints placed around the institution in Deuteronomy 17:14–20. These constraints are designed to prevent the worst possible excesses of monarchy, just like stiff-neck law elsewhere in the Pentateuch is designed to limit the negative effects of other kinds of wrongdoing. The story of monarchy in Israel that is then told in the remainder of Samuel-Kings is not a very happy one, not least because most of the kings have little if any interest in obeying the law of Deuteronomy. Hopes are certainly expressed in various OT texts in relation to the king; ideals are articulated, in terms of reigning at the right hand of God in perfect justice (e.g., in Pss. 2 and 110). However, this is not how things actually work out in terms of Israel's *historical* kings. In the end, the monarchy fails, and Israel is led into exile in Babylonia—back to near the beginning of the biblical Story, in Abraham's place of origin. When the idea of monarchy reemerges on the other side of this failure, it is a very different kind of idea. The focus lies then on a messianic king whom the NT identifies as Jesus, rather than on a local, territorial ruler. Here is the one who sits on God's right hand and rules with perfect justice—the kind of shepherd king that is envisaged in Ezekiel 34 but is so markedly absent in much of the lived history of the ANE generally, and of ancient Israel in particular.[78]

Israel's monarchy is not understood in the OT, then, as an ideal form of government even for Israel; and when it is integrated nevertheless into God's plans for Israel and the world, the ideals attached to it are not envisaged as being capable of achievement by any "ordinary" Israelite ruler—not even by David. Why should we imagine, then, that it is right to think of any *Gentile* ruler as "God's vice-regent on earth," and his kingdom as "the microcosm of heaven," in line with these ideals?[79] Why should Eusebius, as a Christian bishop, have imagined that it was appropriate to dress Constantine in such clothing?

The Real Moses

His choice of *Moses* as an analogy to Constantine is in some ways even more bizarre—for in Scripture, Moses is not a king at all, and he rules no territory. He ends his life, in fact, being barred from the Promised Land (Deut. 32:48–52, 34:1–8). In this respect and in most others, Constantine was not the least bit like Moses, and it requires quite a bit of creative writing on Eusebius' part to suggest otherwise. Constantine did not, in his early adult life, "forsake the royal household," as Eusebius tells us Moses did, "openly acknowledging his true brethren and kinsfolk [i.e., the Christians]."[80] His "flight" from Galerius in 305 in order to be at his father's side, if "flight" is what it really was,[81] bears little likeness to Moses' flight in Exodus 2:11–15 to escape execution for murder; Constantine is *not* here "keeping up his resemblance to the great prophet Moses" in any serious manner.[82] His victory over Maxentius at the Milvian Bridge also bears little resemblance to Moses' (or actually God's) victory over Pharaoh in Exodus 14, aside from the unremarkable fact that the death of the protagonist's enemies happened to involve a drowning in water. Constantine does not here, in fact, advance to victory "as in the time of Moses."[83]

It is only by significantly distorting reality that Eusebius can in fact pull off this analogy between Moses and Constantine—engaging not only in the distortion of the *biblical Story* but also the distortion of the *Constantinian* story. Eusebius' Christian readers should be concerned about both. In the first place, we should decry a reading of Moses that is as shallow and episodic, and indeed as misleading, as this one. It is misleading not just in its detail but in its overall tenor: in the language introduced in our chapters 1 and 2, it is a heroic reading rather than a realistic one. Here the biblical protagonist is only ever "the (great) prophet Moses," destined from a young age to participate in avenging "the wrongs of the afflicted people . . . in obedience to the will of a more powerful Lord" than the oppressors.[84] As a young man he "sought safety in flight" from these oppressive powers,[85] before going on to greater things at the site of the Egyptian defeat in the Sea of Reeds.[86] There is nothing here of the murderer Moses in Exodus 2, or of the Moses in Exodus 3–4 who tries so hard to escape the commission that God is trying to give him to deliver the Israelites. There is nothing in Eusebius' account concerning the Moses who sins against God by breaking faith with him "in the presence of the Israelites at the waters of Meribah Kadesh in the Desert of Zin" and failing to "uphold my holiness among the Israelites" (Deut. 32:51). This Moses is squeaky clean.

THE REAL CONSTANTINE

This is only a partially faithful portrait of Moses, then—and it is drawn into the service of an equally heroic and at least partially *unfaithful* portrait of Constantine. For Eusebius, Constantine is a paragon of Christian virtue from the early years of his life—when he "did not share the manner of life of the ungodly: for from that early period his noble nature, under the leading of the Divine Spirit, inclined him to piety and a life acceptable to God"—until its end, when he is said to "resemble his Saviour, who, as the sown corn which is multiplied from a single grain, had yielded abundant increase through the blessing of God, and had overspread the whole world with his fruit."[87] One would never guess from Eusebius' writings that there might be any legitimate reason to doubt when exactly Constantine began to identify as a Christian, or how serious his confession of faith actually was at any point in his life. One would never guess the extent to which his patron god Sol Invictus (and other gods) continued to be honored in both architecture and coinage in the years immediately following his victory at the Milvian Bridge—indeed, the extent to which "[p]agan symbolism *never* [emphasis added] completely disappeared from Constantine's propaganda."[88] One would have no way of knowing by way of Eusebius that shortly after the Council of Nicea Constantine was responsible for the deaths of both his mother Fausta and his son Crispus, in the context of what even the generously minded Peter Leithart allows may have been "a sordid domestic political affair" speaking to the emperor's "decisive brutality."[89] One would certainly have little insight, after reading Eusebius, into the extent to which the emperor's "new Rome" (the city of Constantinople), re-founded after his victory over Licinius in 324, was not conceived as "a new Christian capital for the Roman empire" but was in fact only sparsely populated with Christian architecture and artefacts.[90]

One of the "Christian" buildings in that city in particular—his own mausoleum—illustrates well the ambiguity of the man. It was designed "to ensure that [the emperor's] mortal remains rested beside those of apostles of Christ."[91] In death, Constantine's sarcophagus was placed in the midst of these others—six on each side of him—"in place of Christ. As Christ ruled in heaven and would return to rule on earth, so Constantine, alone of emperors, continued to rule on earth from heaven."[92] There is more than a whiff here of the old "divine king" ideology that so marks the Roman Empire before Constantine—the very ideology that biblical faith rejects (e.g., in Deut. 17). At the very least we find here evidence of a highly exalted self-understanding on Constantine's part. He was in truth always much more Alexander the Great than Moses.[93] He was a man

immersed in Rome's military culture . . . ambitious for territory and glory . . . willing to use brute force to attain his goals, and he covered his violence with propaganda that makes it impossible to know what actually happened . . . One does not have to be a pacifist to notice unpleasant resemblances between Christian Constantine's career and that of any of a dozen pagan emperors.[94]

CONCLUSION

In short, Eusebius is not an entirely trustworthy guide on how to read Constantine. More importantly for our purposes in this book, he is also not a very reliable guide on how to read the Bible well, either on political questions or in our search for what is right. There is no good reason to believe that *any* king or emperor of postbiblical times should be regarded as "the leader of the new elect, the new Israelites,"[95] whether a Moses or a David—even if that king or emperor identifies as a Christian. Such rulers are only ever some of those many governments in the world appointed by "the Most High [God who] is sovereign over all kingdoms on earth and gives them to anyone he wishes and sets over them the lowliest of people" (Dan. 4:17). Each is God-ordained, at least for a time—one of the many "authorities that exist [that] have been established by God" with the purpose of being a "terror . . . for those who do wrong," bringing "punishment on the wrong-doer" (Rom. 13:1–4). We shall explore this important idea further in upcoming chapters, beginning in chapter 5. My point at the moment is simply that none of these Gentile rulers is more God-ordained than any other, indeed, no more justified in claiming for his kingdom the political mantle of God's ancient OT people—for example, by grounding a "divine right" to perpetual dynastic rule in the OT's description of the Davidic covenant.

There is at the same time no good reason (and we shall also return to this matter, in chapter 9) to think it appropriate to draw an analogy between any such ruler's wars and the holy wars fought by the ancient Israelites—as if a Christian emperor's enemies, just by being so, were evidently also enemies of God worthy of violent repression. There is no good reason to think of these imperial enemies as the "Gentiles" of Psalm 113:30, as Emperor Theodosius I later characterizes them.[96] Connected to this point, there is no good reason to believe that victory in such wars inevitably indicates God's approval of the victorious ruler and his realm, further establishing the legitimacy of his rule. As we have seen, success was "the central criterion of [the] . . . ethics" generated by Constantine's religion—the evidence that "[t]he Christian God [was] . . . the most powerful of all deities."[97] This imperial religion was the chosen means of this "wrathful Christian god" in bringing judgment on his enemies, deployed by a ruler whose interest was above all "to appease the god who had [first] granted him victory" as he rose to power, because he feared this same wrath.[98] Yet in the OT itself, no such direct line is drawn between divine approval and military victory—as the case of the righteous Josiah at the end of 2 Kings reminds us (2 Kgs. 22:1–23:30).[99] But even if it were so drawn, the mere fact that something is true of Israel in the great biblical Story does not of itself mean that it is true of any Christian state.

The consequence of these various hermeneutical mistakes was, in this "Constantinian moment" and in others influenced by it throughout history, a significant distortion of the shape of Christian faith—a very mistaken view of what holiness, for the Christian, entails. Imperial Christianity marched out to war under the sign of the cross, uncriticized by any contemporary Christian bishop in doing so, and indeed sometimes accompanied on its campaigns by clergy.[100] It was, by virtue of being a religion of victory, "not a religion of peace and forgiveness."[101] It was at the same time a religion overly focused on the present at the expense of the future[102]—a present time in which a particular earthly empire could be seen by Eusebius "as a fulfilment of prophecy and a renewed golden age that might last until the end of time."[103] To believe such a thing is to lose biblical focus—and dangerously so. It is bad enough when a Christian bishop encourages a supremely powerful Gentile ruler to regard himself as a biblical king who is especially favored by God and destined to do great things on God's behalf. It is worse when he proposes that this particular ruler's realm is little short of the kingdom of God on earth—thereby "baptizing Hellenistic kingship or the absolutism of Diocletian with a Logos doctrine" and fanning the flames of a self-deception that the ruler himself has already embraced.[104] It is worse again, however, when this particular paradigm of godly government goes on to shape the self-understanding of a whole succession of "mini-Constantines" throughout history, from the Frankish Clovis to the Anglo-Saxon Aethelberht and beyond.[105] No doubt considerable good resulted from the Christian conversion of such pagan kings. Historically, however, the fruit of this accompanying utopian way of thinking about political and military power and its earthly territories has often been bitter. It always *is* bitter when the idolatry of the self, or of the state, is only lightly sprinkled by the waters of biblical teaching rather than plunged right into them—to death.

DISCUSSION QUESTIONS

1. Should Christians read the OT in order to arrive at conclusions about how contemporary political states should best be organized? Why or why not?
2. Is monarchy the God-intended means of ruling every state? Why or why not?
3. Have you been prone to the "heroic reading" of biblical narrative as we have considered it in chapters 1, 2, and 4, or have you encountered it in Christian books and sermons? In which ways?
4. Supposing that Constantine was indeed a true Christian: what *ought* he to have learned from the life of Moses?

5

Not Wholly Roman

The Carolingian Empire

The Byzantine and Arab political systems . . . [did not hold] that the task of the state was in large part the salvation of the community of the realm. This marks the originality of the Carolingian project. The Carolingian state was . . . so confident of itself that the task of salvation seemed actually possible.[1]

Chris Wickham

Already in the fourth century AD the Eusebian "reading" of empire was far from uncontested even among the Christian bishops of the East, and notable churchmen continued to assert, in particular, at least the relative independence of the Church vis-à-vis the emperor.[2] Still, Church and empire were closely allied throughout the succeeding centuries in the East, the former having been "moulded into a very close-fitting relationship with the secular government."[3] Emperors, regarding themselves in Eusebian terms as "divinely sent and divinely guided protector[s] of the Church" possessing "a universal cultural and religious mission," all too often attempted to treat the Church as an arm of the state.[4] The Church for its part "supported the Byzantine emperors in their persistent struggle against the barbarians" who threatened its borders, in line with a belief that "the defence of the empire . . . [was] the defence of the Church."[5] "Barbarian," in Roman usage, simply referred to any foreigner who lived outside the borders of the Empire.[6] Christian bishops greatly benefited in material and social capital by lending their support in this way to the notion that to be a Christian was to be a Roman, just as Roman citizens in increasing numbers concluded that in order to flourish in a Christian Roman Empire it might be advisable to become a Christian. And so long as this empire (centered now on Constantinople rather than Rome) continued to prosper, it remained possible to believe that Church and Empire would be united along these lines until the end of time, perpetuating an OT model in which kings and priests in their appropriate "ruling offices" governed one godly realm together.[7]

THE TRANSFORMATION OF THE WEST

Widespread doubt concerning this long-term unity arose far earlier in the West than in the East. Here the "vision of church-world relations" held by important fourth-century Christian leaders like Ambrose of Milan already had "nothing in common with the Eusebian emperor-theology."[8] The doubts accelerated as a result of various imperial reversals in the West in the late fourth and early fifth centuries. Barbarians from the north, many of them Christianized, first settled by treaty in imperial lands, then invaded Italy, and finally (in 410) captured and sacked Rome.[9] Imperial control of the Western Empire was significantly diminished; vast regions were settled and dominated by Goths and others. It is against this background that Augustine writes his famous treatise, *City of God*—precisely as a rebuttal of Eusebian perspectives and a revival of earlier Christian ideas.[10]

THE CITY OF GOD

Responding to those who blamed Christians for the disaster that had befallen Rome—since Christianity asked its adherents to serve God rather than the state and advocated forgiveness toward enemies—Augustine argues to the contrary that Rome has only lasted as long as it has because it was the will of the one true God by whose power and judgment all earthly kingdoms are established. Rome is only one such kingdom, and Constantine only one such king (cf. the conclusion to our chapter 4). He is not "the hinge of the ages," and his conversion does not "mark a new epoch."[11] The fall of Rome itself is insignificant in the whole scheme of things, for it is not the earthly city that is of ultimate importance in history but the heavenly city of God, in which all human society finds its completion. The earthly city is *important*, not least in constraining the behavior of its sinful, fallen inhabitants and thereby providing some peace and order in the present world. However, it is the heavenly city that human beings should fundamentally pursue, and the Church exists in order to lead them there. Currently "pilgrims and foreigners" in the world, and in truth lacking a "state" of their own, the citizens of the city of God patiently await their glorious future. In the meantime, they obey the emperor so far as their duty to God allows, and they pray for Rome's welfare. They do this not because they regard the empire as just or because they are optimistic about its future but simply because it is the right thing to do, both in the interests of the Church itself and of society at large.

Christian Barbarians

In this way of thinking, then, the story of the Church is once again significantly detached from that of the empire, as it was in the beginning. And it is precisely such detachment that allowed the Church in the Roman West to survive and then to flourish in a period in which "barbarian" peoples were settling and intermarrying there and, as they did so, blurring the previously clear lines of distinction between Roman and non-Roman. For it is not necessary, if one takes an Augustinian view, to identify what is Christian with what has previously been Roman; it is possible, rather, to include in what is Christian what is barbarian.

So it is that we find in the West in the fifth century and immediately afterwards an unprecedented fusion of the Roman, the barbarian, and the Christian (admittedly often Arian rather than Nicene) in lands ruled by independent kings who nevertheless sometimes aspired to imperial recognition.[12] They adopted Roman institutions and Latin language, and governed in the name of Rome, pursuing what has been referred to as a "sub-Roman" way of life. Yet in this "Romanness" they "furnished a royal alternative to the divinizing oriental emperor cult: a portrait of kingship that drew [rather] on Ciceronian and senatorial conceptions of Roman rule."[13] The ethos was Roman, but it was not (in the Eastern sense) imperial. And so it is, also, that we come in due course to the Carolingians—albeit by quickly passing over some important intervening history to which we shall return in chapter 6.

THE CAROLINGIAN DYNASTY

The Carolingians were the eighth- and ninth-century successors of the earlier Merovingians who, under Clovis I and his successors, had established a substantial kingdom of the (Germanic) Franks in Gaul as Roman power declined in that region during the fifth century. The unity of this kingdom, known as Francia, was much aided by its wholesale adoption of Nicene Christianity. By the eighth century, however, the Merovingian kings were little more than figureheads in the realm; the real power was wielded by the Frankish statesman Pepin of Herstal, who died in 714, and his son Charles Martel, who died in 741.

Already in this period, Francia had developed strong connections with the papacy, and in 747 a synod of bishops had "sent its declaration of obedience to Rome, promising to maintain orthodoxy and ecclesiastical unity while accepting the ultimate authority of St. Peter and his successors."[14] So when Charles Martel's son Pepin the Short subsequently wished to formalize his family's rule, it is unsurprising that he sought the sanction of the pope in setting aside the Merovingian royal line. Pepin was duly elected king of the new Carolingian dynasty by the Frankish nobility in 751 and subsequently anointed by the bishops of Gaul and enthroned. This anointing was at the time "an extraordinary ideological innovation," drawing its inspiration from the OT rather than from Frankish tradition.[15] Once enthroned, Pepin "encouraged ecclesiastics to organise and direct reforms of the Frankish church" along Roman lines.[16]

Pepin was succeeded initially by two sons, but soon there was only one. His name was Charles (reigned 771–814)—or Charlemagne, as he has commonly come to be known. Charles soon became more than simply king of the Franks. On December 25, 800, Pope Leo III crowned him Augustus of a revived, Western Holy Roman Empire in the region of the world that now begins to be named for the first time in the sources as "Europe." It is Charlemagne's Holy Roman Empire that will be the focus of our interest in what follows below.

A ROMAN EMPIRE?

The first thing to be said about this empire is that, in truth, it was not wholly Roman. For one thing, it was not centered on Rome but on the new Frankish capital of Aachen, self-consciously developed as a second Rome (or *Roma ventura*, "future Rome").[17] And whereas the "new Rome" in Constantinople "resembled the ancient capital of the caesars," Aachen "remained a very small settlement entirely dominated by the Frankish court, which had not adopted the stiff, ceremonial ritual associated with imperial customs."[18] Charles himself "was careful not to imitate the appearance of the Roman emperors whose title he carried"; he was proud of being one of the Franks, who historically considered themselves "manifestly superior to the Romans."[19] His Roman Empire was a distinctive one, then, "inspired by ancient models, both imperial and Christian," but in no way restoring "Roman traditions . . . unchanged."[20]

One of its inspirations, in fact, was an earlier writer who had been notably hostile to the Roman imperium: the early seventh-century Spanish bishop Isidore of Seville (560–636). According to Judith Herrin, Isidore's works represent the first attempt in the ancient Christian world "to distinguish Christian monarchy from [both] previous imperial and republican forms of domination."[21] In succeeding centuries Isidore was enthusiastically received and widely read, and his view of Christian leadership assumed great authority in particular in Charles' domain, permitting the king's ecclesiastical advisors

> to develop an elevated concept of monarchy while insisting on the church's ultimate authority in a Christian society. The foundations could thus be laid for a different integration of church and state in the medieval West and for a rejection

of other forms of authority that also claimed to be Christian. In these developments, Isidore's repeated condemnation of the eastern empire took on additional
significance.[22]

He was not a fan, in short, of a "Eusebian concept of monarchy as a semidivine
state, the ruler acting in imitation of God."[23] He considered the famous emperor
Justinian to be a heretical tyrant who persecuted orthodox bishops, and he was
suspicious even of the earlier Constantine, whom he believed to be an Arian.[24]

A HOLY EMPIRE

If the Carolingian Empire was therefore not a *wholly Roman* empire, it *was* an
intentionally *holy* one, from the moment that Charles began his reign in 771. His
declared aim, in line with Isidorean canons, "was to create a justly governed society which would have the collective wisdom to live in accordance with scriptural
norms and be thus ensured of divine support."[25]

THE CAROLINGIAN RENAISSANCE

Charles had already inherited a self-consciously Christian kingdom from his
father.[26] The consolidation and expansion of this kingdom was now facilitated
by the transfer to Francia of scholars from all over Europe (including the famous
Alcuin of York) to serve as researchers, teachers, and advisors.[27] In due course this
produced a vibrant, high-caliber educational and cultural environment—a "Carolingian Renaissance."[28] At its heart, inevitably, lay theological interests; for the
purpose of its promotion even of basic literacy was "good behaviour and spiritual
understanding." Beyond this, in a context in which "the horizons for biblical study
were expanded beyond the wildest dreams of the two preceding centuries," the
Carolingian elites were expected to acquire "a proper understanding of the Bible
and theology, without which a path in the Carolingian political world could not
properly be walked."[29]

It was with the help of this "self-conscious group of western intellectuals with
the highest standards and standing in the Frankish territories," then, that Charles
set out to strengthen Christian rule in his domain, gathering together "the strands
of [what was already] a common Christian culture . . . in a single enterprise which
was theocratic in intention."[30] He did so deliberately as the effective leader of
Christendom even before his imperial coronation.[31] The OT, for which the culture displayed a general fascination, played an important part in this endeavor, as
Charles set about "the task of salvation" described in the epigraph to this present
chapter. This was a task that others were urging upon him, and he was happy to
comply.[32]

CAROLINGIAN LAW

The king's *Admonitio generalis* (General Admonition, 789), for example, looks to the biblical king Josiah as an example to follow in reviving "the worship of the true God in the kingdom that God had given him," before rearticulating earlier regulations concerning matters like observing Sunday as a day of rest (i.e., as a "Sabbath," in the terms of OT texts like Exod. 20:8–11).[33] The point is to encourage all of Charles' subjects "to live in peace and justice, and to love their neighbors with evangelical goodwill."[34] It is a great illustration of "the Carolingian conception of theocratic monarchy and the king's own view of his responsibility for the spiritual as well as the temporal welfare of his people."[35]

The slightly earlier Capitulary of Herstal (779) decreed among other things that all Christians should contribute one-tenth of their "income" (i.e., the products of their labor) to the Church when they received the sacraments. Such mandatory "tithing," grounded in the OT Torah (in passages like Deut. 12, 14, and 26), was used from the eighth century AD onwards in the Western Church to finance various endeavors, including assisting the poor, and in due course it allowed the construction of the cathedrals of Europe. Its roots lie with Bishop Caesarius of Arles (c. 469–542) in sixth-century Gaul,[36] who first "applied Mosaic law within a Christian framework" to propose that every Christian *must* give away 10 percent of income to the poor by way of the Church, the remainder being subject to freedom of choice (albeit that the virtuous person would make wise choices with eternal implications).[37] Beginning in the late sixth century, this idea of the ecclesiastical tithe slowly came to dominate in Europe,[38] and in the Capitulary of Herstal Emperor Charles placed the power of the Carolingian state behind it, making it legally binding and enforceable by royal administrators.[39] The innovative nature of this move to mandatory, state-imposed tithing in Christendom is well-illustrated by the fact that more than three centuries later, during the time of the Crusades (which we shall discuss in chapter 6), Christians in the East "found Crusader attempts to introduce the tithe baffling."[40]

The governing presupposition of these and other Carolingian capitularies is that Charles' empire is an "ecclesial society":

> Over and over, royal and imperial capitularies prohibit homicide, theft, fraud, usury, perjury, false witness, sorcery, and augury. They not only prohibit crimes, they prohibit vices as if they were crimes and demand virtuous action from both rulers and ruled, always on the explicit basis of Christian law and morality ... In effect, the Carolingian reform tended to collapse the distinction between Church and society.[41]

In these particular examples drawn from Carolingian law, we see illustrated a general truth concerning the law codes that emerged from the "barbarian Christian kingdoms" of the West in the sixth century and afterwards, with their "enduring attachment to biblically centered, patristic political thought and their adaptation of Latin and Greek imperial traditions to the new circumstances."[42] That is, these codes were marked by "a distinctly biblical motif"—that of "Moses, the first civil legislator, establishing Israelite identity as a chosen race by promulgating a particular collection of divinely revealed laws," followed later by other biblical leaders (like King Josiah) who reform in the same direction.[43]

THE VENERATION OF ICONS

The biblical focus of Charles' capitularies is mirrored in the scrutiny given in the closing decade of the eight century to the deliberations of the Seventh Ecumenical Council of 787 in Nicea (known as Nicea II), which took place against the background of conflict in the Church over the use or veneration of religious images (icons). The papacy throughout the eighth century had consistently been in favour of allowing such use and veneration; imperial policy had run the opposite direction. Nicea II affirmed the rightness of icon-veneration, and thereby represented a victory for Rome.[44] The acts of the council (in Greek) were then transmitted to the West, where that language was by this point little known. They arrived in an unfortunately misleading Latin translation that made it appear to the Franks that Nicea II had affirmed image-worship (forbidden by a biblical passage like Exod. 20:2–6). This contributed to the rejection of Nicea II by the Franks in the *Opus Caroli regis contra synodum* (OC) that was read out at the Synod of Frankfurt in 794:

> The Carolingian view on images can be summed up in a few words . . . God chose words and scripture as his sole medium of revelation . . . According to the OC, images play no part in salvation and have no importance in the Christian religion apart from two practical purposes they serve: they ornate [sic] the Church and remind people of things done in the past . . . The emphasis on *Scripture* as God's chosen medium and the importance placed on correct interpretation are characteristic for the OC.[45]

Consonant with this view, the OC "is filled with . . . allusions to . . . Scripture,"[46] which the Carolingians regard the Byzantines (easterners) as using incompetently in defense of "their erroneous ways."[47] In all of this, the OC is not hostile to art; to the contrary, it insists that art should be taken seriously for its own sake, as the product of an artist who is not inspired but may well be excellent at his craft.[48] Frankish churches of the time were certainly not devoid of art. It is simply that "an image can serve no mystic function . . . no sanctity resides in the common clay, wax, or wood out of which an image is made."[49]

KING AND PRIEST

The OC, it should be understood, opposed Rome *along with* Constantinople, defining "an independent Frankish theology." It provides "clear evidence of the Carolingian capacity for self-confident theological reasoning," which not only "marks another stage in the estrangement of West from East" but also indicates Charles' self-understanding in relation to the bishop of Rome.[50] At Frankfurt,

> the churches of Charles' territories realised an autonomy, which separated them from both Rome and Constantinople . . . "Europa" for the first time denied Rome's right to speak on its behalf and aggressively denounced Constantinople's leadership of the entire Christian world.[51]

The one "speaking" on behalf of Europe in this context is of course ultimately Charles who, like his father, "was commonly called David by court intellectuals" and regarded as "'David's royal son' . . . Christ's representative to rule the new Israel."[52] As such he is contrasted with "the eastern rulers as relics of a defunct world order, pagan emperors rather than true Christians."[53] Already in this concept of kingship, as in the architecture of Charles' chapel in Aachen (compared by Alcuin with the Solomonic temple), his imperial pretensions are clear.[54] It did not take long for the rhetoric to become reality, and for a thousand years afterwards (until Francis II relinquished the title of Holy Roman Emperor in 1806)

> the idea of a Holy Roman Empire in the West, a continuation of the one founded by Charles in A.D. 800, proved just as tenacious as the imperial tradition in the East. Western monarchs, generals, and aristocrats competed for a papal coronation in order to reign over an empire variously defined.[55]

THE HERMENEUTICS OF ICONS

The argument of chapter 4 was that we have no good reason as Christians to consider any king or emperor of postbiblical times as a new Moses or David (or Solomon, or Josiah) appointed by God to lead a new, elect nation of "Israelites"— even if that person identifies as a Christian. This applies as much to Charlemagne as to Constantine, and we need not repeat here the arguments in relation to the former's self-understanding. As John Milton would later rightly say, in a context where a royal claim to rule by divine right was being seriously disputed (see our chapter 9), it is a false claim "that all kings are the Lord's anointed."[56]

At the same time, every Christian ruler—like any other Christian—should attend to the OT's moral vision in matters of faith and life and should certainly regard OT characters as models (whether by way of imitation or otherwise) in respect of his or her own faith and life. This is required as much of a Christian ruler as of a Christian builder, teacher, or farmer. Every serious Christian should look for the wisdom that is "useful" for life in OT Scripture, beginning at the beginning of the biblical Story and reading forward from there to see how the Story develops and thereby instructs us concerning our lives before God. Charlemagne was a serious Christian who wanted a truly reformed clergy in his empire who could lead his people to be real Christians too.[57] He appears to have desired to be exactly the kind of king that his assembled bishops at the Synod of Frankfurt hoped for: one who would "assist the oppressed, console widows, bring solace to the unhappy, and be both master and father, king and priest, and a wise sovereign for all Christians."[58] His "greatest religious desire," Heinrich Fichtenau asserts, "was to be treated among the Just."[59] This was a noble aspiration, and his reign reveals a concerted effort to rule in this manner. On the whole he even treated defeated enemies relatively well; the notable exception was his initial treatment of the Saxons, to which we shall return below.[60]

It was in pursuit of a genuinely Christian life and empire, then, that Charlemagne, along with his advisors, read his OT. How well did they read it? We shall take as a case study their understanding of Scripture in relation to the veneration of icons.

IMAGES IN THE BIBLE

The Ten Commandments in Exodus 20:1–17 are set in the context of God's deliverance of Israel from Egypt in the Exodus and his leading of them to Mount Sinai so that they may begin to learn what it means to serve God rather than the ANE "gods." The question of "gods" is addressed right away:

> You shall have no other gods before me. You shall not make for yourself an image in the form of anything in heaven above or on the earth beneath or in the waters below. You shall not bow down to them or worship them; for I, the LORD your God, am a jealous God.

These are commandments given to the Israelites, but they are rooted in God's character, which in Scripture does not change through time: "I, Yahweh your God, am a jealous God." Consistent with this fact, the difference between the living God and all the many other "gods" that people worship—gods that routinely have the form of something in the created world—is one to which all human beings, and not just Israelites, are called to attend in Scripture (e.g., Isa. 43:8–13; 45:20–25). It is one aspect of the fundamental ontological distinction in biblical faith between Creator and Creation, which we noted already in our chapter 3.

It is precisely this distinction, for example, that the Pharaoh of Egypt has just been compelled to acknowledge in the preceding chapters of the book of Exodus, in what can only be described as an almighty, cosmic battle between the god-king of Egypt (along with Egypt's other gods) and the God of the burning bush. There is only one true God in the book of Exodus, who has ultimate power over both Creation and history; all other "gods" are simply creatures. And this is why those who bow down to the latter are urged to turn instead to the living God (e.g., Isa. 44:6–20; Jer. 10:1–10). For the imaged "gods" are merely the work of human hands (e.g., Deut. 4:28; 28:64). To worship them is foolishness beyond reason, not least because in biblical thought idolatry is not only wrong but also devastating. The worship of any aspect of Creation—including Babylonian or Roman emperors (Daniel, Revelation)—is not only an affront to God and a perversion of the true nature of things; by practicing it, we do damage to ourselves, to each other, and to the world in which we live.[61] This is a truth proclaimed throughout the entirety of the biblical Story (e.g., Acts 15:19–20; 17:16–31; Rom. 1:21–25). We have here, then, an example of creational law—as we might well have suspected when we first saw this injunction about images appearing in the Ten Commandments.

THE VENERATION OF ICONS

The Carolingians were warranted on biblical grounds, therefore, in their Christian opposition to the worship of images. Of course, whether the veneration of icons should necessarily be considered as "the worship of images" in a biblical sense is another matter. The fact that to this day many Christians bow down to icons and indeed kiss them does not of itself indicate such worship. Already in Scripture itself all sorts of bowing down and kissing occurs, and the question is, what does the person intend by these actions?[62] An icon is not necessarily an idol; those who use them often explain them simply as "windows into heaven"— reminders, for example, of the way in which the departed saints are still alive as a "cloud of witnesses" gathered in worship around God's throne. Icons of the saints remind us of this reality. They are not themselves, necessarily, objects of worship, although they may become such, especially among those who have not been theologically well-educated concerning the fundamental differences between paganism and Christian faith. Nevertheless, Nicea II itself insisted that the purpose of "venerable and holy images" was that people should be

> lifted up to the memory of their prototypes, and to a longing after them; and to these should be given due salutation and honourable reverence, not indeed that true worship of faith which pertains alone to the divine nature; but to these, as to [other sacred objects] . . . For the honour which is paid to the image passes on to that which the image represents, and he who reveres the image reveres in it the subject represented.[63]

So the Carolingians were correct in reading a passage like Exodus 20 as banning the worship of images in the Church, but they were misguided in seeing that text as necessarily forbidding the use of icons in Christian worship. Then again, at least they did not make the egregious mistake of some later Western Christians of understanding Scripture as encouraging hostility toward all kinds of representational art, especially in church buildings—as if we could rightly lift the injunction "you shall not make for yourself an image" out of its literary content and thereby consider representational art itself as innately profane rather than sacred.

THE HERMENEUTICS OF TITHING

In the case of tithing, on the other hand, the Carolingians took their stand on much less stable hermeneutical ground. It is true that the OT instructs the people of God, among other ways of giving, to tithe on certain agricultural products and to direct these tithes to certain ends: eating the occasional sacrificial meal together, looking after the Levites (who possess no land), and caring for the vulnerable.[64] What reason is there, however, to think that these arrangements made for the people of God in the OT apply also after the coming of Christ?

CHRISTIAN GIVING IN THE NEW TESTAMENT

There are only three references to tithing in the NT, and none of these gets us close to suggesting that Christians ought to tithe.[65] The paucity of the references is particularly striking when one considers that both Jesus and his apostles spoke and wrote a lot about money and possessions and drew on the OT in other respects when doing so. The NT does have a lot to say about generous giving. The early Christian community in Jerusalem, we read in Acts 4, regarded none of their possessions as their own and shared generously with everyone, so that there were no needy among them (Acts 4:32–35, alluding to Deut. 15:4–8). An organizational structure was later created so that no one would be overlooked (Acts 6:1–6). The creation of a central church fund for such purposes is also implied in 1 Timothy 5:3–16, where the Church is able to help widows whom others (including family members) are for some reason unable to help. Special collections could also be made for the benefit of Christian communities other than one's own (1 Cor. 16:1–4). It was expected, moreover, that churches should support church workers properly, for a "worker deserves his wages" (1 Tim. 5:18, referring to Deut. 25:4); "those who preach the gospel should receive their living from the gospel," just as "those who serve in the temple get their food from the temple, and . . . those who serve at the altar share in what is offered on the altar" (1 Cor. 9:13–14). Generosity was expected, then, in respect of all one's possessions—but tithing, whether of agricultural produce or otherwise, is not referred to in this context. Nor is the eating of any sacrificial meal with any Levite (or apostle) in Jerusalem—which is not surprising, since Jerusalem was not a city to which most early Christians were any longer "going up" for festivals.

OTHER EARLY TEXTS

This same generosity is reflected, as well as exhorted, in other early Christian texts. The *Didache* (late first century) stresses the need to look after prophets and teachers in the Church (who are "your high priest") by way of a selection of "first fruits," which are nonetheless assessed in terms of what "you think right."[66] The *Apology of Aristides the Philosopher* in the second century (c. 135) describes the Christian simply in this way: "he that has, gives ungrudgingly for the maintenance of him who has not."[67] Tertullian further reports on monthly offerings for the benefit of the needy, stressing their voluntary nature: "each puts in a small donation, but only if it be his pleasure, and only if he is able: for there is no compulsion; all is voluntary. These gifts are, as it were, piety's deposit fund."[68]

As time passes we do begin to find Christian writers beginning to mention "a tenth" in the context of Christian giving, but generally only in order "to persuade the faithful to greater generosity in almsgiving," as well as in support of what we nowadays call "clergy."[69] This remains the situation until after Constantine's time, when the idea that tithing is a Christian duty begins to take hold in some quarters.[70] In the case of writers like Augustine and Jerome, however, who could sometimes regard the OT "tenth" as suggesting an acceptable minimum for almsgiving, it remains only one possibility among others (e.g., the story of Zacchaeus giving away half his possessions can also be cited): "Christians certainly had an obligation to give something, but then again even a glass of cold water earned its reward (Matt. 10:42)."[71]

AGAINST TITHING

There is no reason to believe on the basis of Scripture, then, that even voluntary tithing of 10 percent of our "income"—whether given to the Church, to other institutions, or to individuals or groups—should form a component of Christian ethics, and there is not much basis for it in early Christian tradition either. Generosity with respect to all that God has given us, in relation to all who need our support, is the central theme, and our decisions on how this generosity is to be expressed are left to our own wise judgment (2 Cor. 8). This being so, there is certainly no justification for the Church's common practice in ancient times of making its receipt of "the tithe" a compulsory aspect of membership, and no justification either for any state adding legislative and administrative force to such mandatory tithing for "religious purposes" (as well as typically taking very large "mandatory tithes," in modern times at least, in its other forms of taxation!).

Whether or not specific OT laws apply directly to us, of course, we should be open to learning from the OT regarding how best to exercise such wise judgment. We should expect Scripture to be "useful" to us in our economic lives—at least suggestive, if not directly relevant. We recall an earlier example from chapter 3, where I proposed that certain rules in Deuteronomy concerning giving the poor and vulnerable access to agricultural produce were useful to us along precisely such lines. We should also mention here a similar passage in Leviticus in this context: "When you reap the harvest of your land, do not reap to the very edges of your field or gather the gleanings of your harvest. Leave them for the poor and for the foreigner residing among you" (Lev. 19:9–10; cf. Exod. 23:10–12). The central idea in such texts, that God's people should not maximize their profits at the expense of the vulnerable, conforms to the general picture painted through-out Scripture concerning righteous conduct when it comes to money and posses-sions. The concrete examples provided in Leviticus and Deuteronomy may well then help us develop our own concrete ideas about how we too might conduct ourselves righteously in such matters.

CHRISTIAN ETHICS AND THE LAW OF THE STATE

In the two large examples studied in this chapter, it may rightly be concluded that the Carolingian elites were at least partially justified in their application of OT injunctions to contemporary Christian life in their own times. Leaving aside these particular examples for the moment, we must now go on to ask: were they warranted in their serious attempt—by all accounts not an entirely successful attempt—to shape a whole society on the basis of such Christian convictions?[72] Should they ever have engaged in this "task of salvation" that they were so confi-dent they could accomplish?

THE BURDEN OF RULE

All governance is conducted on the basis, first of all, of convictions about the correct answers to very large questions of a philosophical or religious nature con-cerning the larger story in which we human beings find ourselves. These include: where did we come from, where are we going, what is our nature, and how ought we to live? Then, secondly, there will also be convictions about the purpose of the governance of the particular community in question in relation to the larger story. What should the aims of the political process be in the light of this story—this particular philosophy of life? How *ought* this community to live, and what are the responsibilities of the ruler in making this happen? These various convictions, philosophical and political, must be sufficiently widely shared in the community to allow governance to occur at all; minimally, the ruler or ruling body must have sufficient persuasive or military/police power at their disposal to prevent the overthrow of their rule. Even if the convictions are widely shared, however, there will always be the need for some coercion if a governed community is to flourish—a need for punishment, for example, when people break the laws the rulers create in pursuit of their goals. One of the key sets of decisions involved in all governance, in fact, relates to which "positive laws" (specific pieces of legislation) to enact on the basis of convictions about what is ultimately right and wrong, and which incentives and sanctions to attach to these laws. Even powerful rulers will have difficulty in enforcing laws that are widely perceived to be unjust or otherwise inappropriate, and such enforcement may well undermine rather than enhance the overall vision for society that the rulers had in mind in the first place.

THE RULE OF ALL

Christian rulers are by definition not only rulers, tasked with governance, but Christians. As such they possess (or ought to possess) strong *Christian* convictions, based on biblical teaching, about the nature of the story in which all of us humans find ourselves—including convictions about the existence and the nature of creational law. These will inevitably form the context in which all Christians, including rulers, ought to understand the purpose and nature of governance. In fact, the biblical Story itself has something important to say about the topic right at its beginning.

As we saw in chapter 3, the biblical Story begins by informing us that every human being is made in God's image—"like God" and ontologically (i.e., "as to our being") equal before God. As such, we are called together to a particular vocation by God, which is in part that we should jointly "rule" in Creation along with him (Gen. 1:28). It is the destiny of all human beings together to rule over the cosmos. This is a particularly striking claim when we read it against the background of ANE thinking more generally about divine and royal "rule" as described in chapter 4. Here the king alone was considered to be the image bearer of the god who ruled through him the part of the cosmos under his royal control. In this way of thinking one person bears the image and everyone else is simply that person's subject, rather than in any real sense a participant in ruling. Totalitarian, hierarchical, static states, like Pharaoh's Egypt, inevitably arose in the ANE on the basis of this ideology. Against this background, the image-bearing language of Genesis 1 clearly represents a deliberate "democratization" of the notion of kingship and implies a very different view of society and its governance. Whatever particular structures of governance, including civil governance, come into existence in human history, they must rightly be created and maintained with these fundamental ontological and vocational human realities in mind. All rulers rule in the midst of all. Particular rule is always exercised in the midst of a community of rulers, each one of whom is just as important as the other, and all of whom are called to be "like God" (Matt. 5:48).

THE RULE OF GOD

What does it mean, though, to be "like God"—specifically as the ruler of a people-group or state? The biblical Story tells us quite a bit about how God rules in the world, and it is important for our current enquiry that we understand it. The most relevant point at present is this: that God allows his image bearers considerable moral freedom in choosing whether to obey his creational law or not. God himself is perfectly and incomparably good and calls his human creatures toward the same goodness that he displays—yet he continually "lives" with a situation in the world where evil prevails, at least for the moment. The human failure or refusal to be good does not bring the world to an end. Instead, God finds ways in our biblical Story of continuing to work for the good in a world now compromised by evil, pursuing the good rather than, by fiat, imposing it (like a tyrannical ruler). He turns the world as much toward the good as he can, while respecting the moral freedom of the human creatures who inhabit it, such that Joseph (for example) can look back on an early life in which his brothers intended him harm and say: "You intended to harm me, but God intended it for good to accomplish what is now being done, the saving of many lives" (Gen. 50:20).[73] This is, our biblical Story proposes, the characteristic way that God works in the world. To a very great extent he allows the cosmic story to unfold as his image bearers choose, reserving salvation and judgment until its end. He does not "pull up" the weeds in the wheat field but lets them "both grow together until the harvest" (Matt. 13:24–30).[74]

We find an enormous degree of pragmatism—and no utopianism—attributed to God in Scripture, then, when it comes to his rule. God does not impose his kingdom on the world but works with what he finds before him in its pursuit. He does not, as it were, drop the New Jerusalem on our heads but rather points out the path that leads to it and encourages us to walk upon it. Christian thinking about politics must also bear this in mind; a Christian *ruler* must attend to it.

CHRISTIAN RULERS

The implication of all this is that Christians in general, and Christian rulers in particular, must think carefully about the way that they frame their answers to questions of political philosophy. What should the aims of the political process be in light of the biblical Story? How *ought* people in a particular state to live, and what are the responsibilities of the ruler in making this happen? The Christian

answer to such questions, I propose, is always rightly going to emphasize substantial freedom on the part of the ruled to govern themselves. It should be no part of
the agenda of the Church, nor that of the Christian ruler, to seek to outdo God in
imposing the kingdom of God on society—as if this kingdom could, in fact, ever
be produced through coercion.

This is centrally true with respect to the very confession of faith itself—as
Alcuin well understood in relation to Charlemagne's aggressive repression of
Saxon paganism during the opening decades of his reign. This repression involved
among other things forced baptism on pain of death, mass executions, and the
imposition of the death penalty on anyone who offended the Christian religion
and its clergy (e.g., by failing to fast on a Friday). Alcuin's intervention is particularly poignant when we recall that one of the key inspirations for the Carolingian
project was Isidore of Seville, with his advocacy of a kingship that persuaded people "by counsel and good example, rather than by force" and with his antipathy to
the tyrant Justinian (who, like Charlemagne, set out to create the wholly Christian state).[75] Alcuin's strongly expressed view was that "faith arises from the will,
not from compulsion. You can persuade a man to believe, but you cannot force
him. You may even been able to force him to be baptized, but this will not help to
instill the faith in him."[76] Charlemagne's methods in Saxony were in fact generally
condemned at an episcopal conference called in 796 to discuss the question of the
conversion of the Avars in the East. These Avars, at least, "were not to be baptized
without first being instructed and persuaded, while the teaching was to be based
more on love than on terror."[77]

The kingdom of God cannot be achieved through coercion. There will always
be a need, of course, for legislation in any society, and for some coercion in relation to it—not least to prevent people from harming their neighbors. That is
certainly one of the tasks of a ruler—(it is given explicit apostolic warrant in
Rom. 13:1–5) and if a Christian is not willing to engage in the task, then he or
she should not seek to rule. Yet all Christians, including a ruler, should be judi-
cious concerning which aspects of life they wish to see governed by legislation
and which enticements and sanctions should be attached to specific laws. One
aspect that must certainly be considered is the effect that a proposed law is likely
to have, not only on the majority but also on minority populations in the realm
(e.g., the Saxons)—since Christians are obliged to attend to *those* image-bearing
neighbors as much as to any others (e.g., in Prov. 31:8–9). All of this the Church
must heed for principled reasons arising out of our biblical Story read as a whole,
and not just out of pragmatism; then pragmatism must inevitably enter the conversation as well. For the Christian *ruler* specifically, like all other rulers, must
inevitably make judgments about how effective even a well-intentioned law will

be in the environment in which it is enacted, or whether in fact more harm than good will be achieved by it.

One aspect of possible harm that must surely be considered in this context is injury to the Gospel itself arising from resentment against Christian governing authorities that impose unwelcome laws on people who do not share Christian convictions of—or at least the *same* Christian convictions as—the ruler. Consider our earlier example of tithing. Suppose for a moment that there *were* good grounds for considering tithing to be an aspect of God's creational law. Would it *then* be something that a Christian ruler like Charlemagne, out of concern for the financial support of the Church, would have been wise to impose on his realm as a matter of legislation? I do not think so, and not just because of my general convictions concerning the nature of a Christian political philosophy: that it will emphasize substantial freedom on the part of the ruled to govern themselves. Specifically, such a legislative move cuts right across the emphasis in both Scripture and much of early Christian tradition on voluntarism when it comes to Christian giving. Freedom lies right at the heart of this *particular* matter in our own biblical Story and early Christian tradition. Such freedoms should not lightly be trampled upon, and history reveals that when they are, negative consequences often follow.

In the case of tithing, the removal of wisely exercised individual or community discretion in terms of whom to give to and how much to give certainly produced some of these negative consequences, both at the time and in subsequent European history. On the one side, many of those collecting the mandatory ecclesiastical tithe quickly came to understand that its guaranteed nature meant that they did not have to worry too much about whether or not the donors approved of them (since the donors could not, in fact, decide to the contrary). We subsequently see in the history of the Church a predictable mutation of the "Caesarius option," whereby the tithe "merged with the church's regular income and served all those who had a claim on ecclesiastical resources"—of whom the poor were only some.[78] The tithe inevitably became bound up, then, with the notable financial abuses that so evidently marked the Church of the High Middle Ages.

On the other side, and in response to such abuses, we encounter some early resentment morphing into considerable later hostility, which eventually contributed mightily to the advent of the Reformation.[79] This hostility continued thereafter. For example, in the midst of discussion concerning rights and freedoms in the course of the English Revolution (1642–1649), the republican and democratic Levellers, who were "opposed to kingship and advocated complete freedom in religion and a wide extension of the suffrage [the vote]," also demanded among other things the abolition of tithes.[80] Already during Charlemagne's own reign, Alcuin drew attention to the same kind of problem with respect to the Saxons.

He was of the opinion that the king had extended his system of tithes too quickly to Saxony

> with the result that Saxons associated the imposition of Christianity with violent extortion: "the tithes, they say, destroyed the faith of the Saxons." He speculated on what would have happened if the apostles had endeavored to exact tithes from their listeners, after Christ had sent them abroad to preach his word." [81]

As a pious, willing royal advisor, Alcuin confessed in fact that he himself found it difficult to pay his full share of the tithe! [82]

THE RULE OF CHARLEMAGNE

All of this said, it is not clear to me that the Carolingians *were* warranted in their attempt to shape a whole society on the basis of their Christian convictions. I see little reason to believe that this is the God-ordained purpose of government, to which idea we shall return in later chapters. With the benefit of so much of Church History now behind us, we are particularly capable of understanding clearly just how dangerously unproductive such a view of government can be. As we shall also see in later chapters, it is not necessarily good news for anyone, Christian or not, when the state takes on the "task of salvation."

CONCLUSION

As we look back on our discussion in this chapter concerning the Carolingian approach to the OT and the Christian life—and especially on the two issues we selected for particular analysis—what are we to say? We are obliged to conclude, first, that the Carolingians were correct in thinking that OT teaching on image worship applied in their present moment to all Christians, who were still in this sense "my people"—but that their interpretation of this teaching as necessarily applying to the veneration of icons is unconvincing. When it comes to tithes, secondly, there is simply no strong reason to think that the OT teaching any longer applies to the (NT) people of God at all; Christians are "not my people" in this matter. The OT may well be "useful" to us in all sorts of ways when we pursue what is right in our economic lives—but not, directly, in *this* way. There is no evident continuity of this kind between the Testaments when it comes to tithing. Thirdly, even where the Church remains "my people," Christians (including those with political power) need to think very carefully about the ways in which Christian convictions about God's creational law should, and should not, form the basis for positive law in any particular territorial state. The Church remains the Church; it is not the same thing as the state, and not all the considerations pertaining to the former pertain in the same way to the latter (and vice versa).

DISCUSSION QUESTIONS

1. Should any government set out to accomplish "the task of Christian salvation" within its borders? Why or why not?
2. Thinking of your own government in particular, do you think it ought to legislate so as to make adultery illegal? If such legislation already exists, should it be repealed?
3. Is it acceptable for Christians to enjoy art—even in church?
4. If "the rule of all" is an important biblical idea in Genesis 1, what does this imply about the best forms of government in both Church and state? Should they be democratic? Need they be?

6

Journey to the Center of the Earth

The First Crusade and Jerusalem

It is perhaps hard for us to appreciate the full importance of the holy places for contemporary chroniclers, exegetes, and theologians. The terrestrial fate of Jerusalem was suffused with transcendental meaning. The Christian Old Testament provided a template for reading providential significance into its military and political fortunes.[1]

Brett Whalen

Charlemagne's empire did not long survive him. His son Louis the Pious (reigned 814–840) struggled to keep control of it and passed it on in fragmented form. In 842 it was formally subdivided into East and West, marking the beginning point of what became France (West Francia) and Germany (East Francia); the Treaty of Verdun in 843 also created a third kingdom between them, which included Italy; its ruler, Lothar, received the imperial title. Conflict continued throughout the succeeding decades, however, and the empire soon fell apart. In due course a different dynasty rose to prominence in East Francia, resulting in the crowning of Otto I as emperor by Pope John XII in 962. So it was that German kings inherited the mantle of empire. It is not long thereafter that we encounter our first German pope—Gregory V (bishop of Rome from 996–999), the cousin of the king who appointed him (Otto III). This Ottonian dynasty was in turn replaced by the Salian dynasty, which produced four German kings all subsequently crowned as emperor: Conrad II (1024–1039); Henry III (1039–1056); Henry IV (1056–1106); and Henry V (1106–1125). It was during the reign of the third of these, Henry IV, that the papacy unleashed the First Crusade on Palestine—the central event that will occupy our attention in this chapter.

If we are to understand this event properly, however—and not least the fact that the pope, and not the emperor, was its crucial initiator—we must first fill in some gaps that remain in view of our approach in chapter 5, which involved passing over much of the history of the Roman Empire between the fall of Rome in the early fifth century and the rise of the Carolingians in the eighth. We must attend, indeed, to the rise to power of the papacy in the West throughout this period and up to the eleventh century, both in conjunction and in tension with the Holy Roman Empire.

ROME, CONSTANTINOPLE, AND FRANCIA

In the middle of the sixth century the emperor Justinian made a serious attempt to reestablish direct control over the western part of what was still (notionally) his empire. He did so with only mixed success, however, and with disastrous consequences for much of Italy in general and for Rome in particular, which became "no longer a centre of great importance or significance to the East."[2] Indeed, his "failure to reestablish Old Rome as a political centre" made it "the weak link in imperial defence in the West," encouraging further incursions into Italy from the north (in the shape of the Lombards).[3]

THE RISE OF THE PAPACY

At the same time this failure contributed greatly to the rise to preeminence in the West of the bishop of Rome, who since the early decades of the fifth century had been the city's natural leader in the absence of effective secular government—"negotiating with hostile forces, maintaining food supplies, and succouring the population in times of plague and floods."[4] Since that time, too, successive popes had pressed Rome's claim (as the foundation of St. Peter) of authority over other bishops. In the absence of adequate help from "new Rome" (Constantinople) in the face of renewed plague and famine and of the Lombard threat, it was Pope Gregory the Great (bishop of Rome from 590–604) who stepped up to deal with the situation, thereby facilitating Old Rome's "successful move from ancient political capital to ecclesiastical centre."[5] It was a center that even in Gregory's time had significant reach, with influence as far away as Gaul and Britain, and his work laid the foundation for the medieval papacy that followed, in the course of whose development Gregory's successors managed to establish a claim not only to the spiritual but also the temporal independence of the papal see (seat of government).[6] It was a mere two hundred years after Gregory, in fact—as we have seen—that Pope Leo III crowned Charles, king of the Franks, as emperor.

TUMULTUOUS CHANGE

This was an astonishing development, which reflected tumultuous change in the world in the intervening seventh and eighth centuries. "The traditional theory of a universal church protected by an empire that also embraced the entire known world [had already become] increasingly unconvincing" by the end of the sixth century as a result mainly of events in the West.[7] As we enter the seventh, however, we find the Eastern Roman Empire itself under pressure, not least from Islamic armies that soon managed to reduce "the empire of East Rome to a tiny fraction of its sixth-century size."[8] Then as we reach the middle of the eighth century (751), the Italian city of Ravenna, the "chief centre of [remaining] Byzantine authority in the West," falls to the Lombards—"a turning point in the history of Europe."[9] Rome was once again at the mercy of the Lombards and without imperial support. Pope Stephen II (bishop of Rome from 752–757) appealed for help to the newly elected king of the Franks, Pepin; it was this relationship between Rome and the Franks that soon produced the new Frankish emperor Charles—the result of an

> uneasy alliance of two different kinds of heirs to Roman power in the West, papal and Carolingian . . . [each striving] to make the inheritance of imperial traditions, however transformed, its own. This interaction of vicars of St. Peter with claimants to the imperial title was to become one of the determinants of western European development thereafter.[10]

ROME AND FRANCIA

The terms of the agreement struck between Stephen and Pepin in this context bound the Carolingian dynasty firmly to the ongoing defense of the papacy at that time and in the future.[11] In the short term this "brought Rome both territorial security and strong military protection."[12] It accorded to Pepin, on the other hand, a papal tribute that was Constantinian in its echoes: he was "a new Moses and David," favored by God, along with his descendants, "as the leaders of the Franks in perpetuity."[13] As such, Stephen urged upon him resistance, along with Rome, to the interests of Constantinople in the region—an idea to which Pepin was only too happy to accede as he sought to extend and consolidate his own political power. Stephen's successor Pope Paul I would go on to quote in relation to the Franks a NT text that we have already noted in chapter 2: "a chosen people, a royal priesthood, a holy nation, God's special possession" (1 Pet. 2:9–10).[14] These new arrangements in the Roman West were in due course provided with further legitimacy by the *Donation of Constantine*. This was a forged document originating in Rome around this time that envisaged Constantine, prior to his departure for his new capital of Constantinople, bestowing upon the bishop of Rome supremacy over the universal Church and full authority over the Western Empire—including the right to appoint its rulers.[15]

EMPERORS AND POPES

It is precisely the ideology of the *Donation* that was being played out, from the Roman side, in the coronation of Charlemagne in Rome in 800: "By putting the crown on the new emperor's head, the pope de facto claimed the supremacy of papal authority over imperial authority."[16] This was not Charlemagne's view, however, and when he moved to crown his son Louis emperor in preparation for the succession (813), he made sure that it happened in Aachen rather than Rome—and thus that Louis was "acclaimed not by the Romans but by the Franks."[17]

THE SUPREME LEADER

In Charlemagne's own mind, and that of many others in the West, "if Christendom had a supreme leader, then that leader was the king of the Franks and certainly not the pope."[18] The pope's duty was to support the emperor in prayer—even as the emperor ruled in Christian humility and service and governed justly under God.[19] In fact, "Charles controlled his kingdom, organized his peoples, and maintained public order almost as much through the Church" as through any other means: "Bishops and abbots were the pillars of public order and answered to the emperor as though they . . . were in every sense officials appointed by him, which after all they usually were."[20] The only appointments requiring papal approval were those of "bishops in Italy who were suffragans [appointed to help diocesan bishops] of the Roman see, and . . . archbishops."[21]

This remained the imperial view and practice in the centuries immediately after Charlemagne; emperors even deposed and appointed popes, who had to swear oaths of loyalty to them. Although they were "barbarians," then, these emperors had ultimately inherited the Eusebian idea that "the [Holy] Roman Empire had a critical role to play in the triumph and spread of the Church."[22] Indeed, as the year 1000 approached, the figure of the emperor became strongly associated in some quarters with the events of the end times before the coming of Christ. In 954, for example, Abbot Adso of Montier-en-Der "predicted the rise of a final emperor . . . who would defeat the infidels, lay down his scepter and crown on the Mount of Olives, and bring about the 'end and consummation of the Roman and Christian Empire.'"[23] As this prophecy implies, the reality of Islamic power (which by this time controlled Jerusalem) was much on people's minds when speculating in this manner, although the basic idea was not new; the fourth or fifth century Tiburtine Sibyl had already spoken of a final Roman ruler who would "summon all of the pagans to baptism" and in whose time "the Jews will convert to the Lord, and His tomb will be glorified by all."[24]

THE PAPAL AGENDA

The papacy's view of its relationship with both Church and empire did not, however, wither and die. It is embodied with respect to the Church most notably in the events of the "Great Schism" of 1054, when the legates of the reforming Pope Leo IX (bishop of Rome from 1049–1054) excommunicated the Patriarch of Constantinople. As Brett Whalen describes it, this was "an important landmark in the papal concept of Christendom, above all the relationship between its Western and Eastern halves." A "reform movement" in Rome thereafter worked diligently to establish substantive papal sovereignty over the empire as well as the Church. The accession of the child-emperor Henry IV in 1056 gave Pope Nicholas I (bishop of Rome from 1059–1061) the opportunity to establish a new, fixed system for appointing popes by way of a vote that was restricted to cardinals (1059); the emperor had no right to intervene except where permitted to do so by papal agreement. This event was closely followed by the election of Pope Gregory VII (bishop of Rome from 1073–1085), who energetically pressed the claims of Rome to rule the world: "anyone who did not recognize the authority of Rome was a heretic," and this included emperors, whom the pope could depose.[25] In pursuit of the interests of Christian orthodoxy, indeed, the pope could legitimately "take a more active hand in directing violence for its own purposes," sanctioning Christian laity to "act as 'soldiers of St. Peter' against the enemies of the papacy."[26]

Internally in the Holy Roman Empire, Gregory's agenda led on directly to the "Investiture Controversy," which concerned the question of who possessed the authority to appoint local bishops and abbots. These were typically members of the ruling nobility who passed on their titles and privileges to their children. Gregory claimed sole rights in these matters (1075); Henry IV strongly asserted his sovereignty in response, rejecting the legitimacy of Gregory's papacy. Gregory then excommunicated Henry and released all Christians from their oath of allegiance to the king (1076). Under pressure from rebels, Henry backed down and apologized (1077). The crisis rumbled on until the Concordat ("agreement") of Worms (1122), a compromise whereby the person chosen by the clergy would first do homage to the emperor in respect of his secular powers, privileges, and lands before receiving his "spiritual" powers and lands from his ecclesiastical superior. In the meantime, externally to the Holy Roman Empire, the Gregorian agenda led on indirectly to the First Crusade, which focused on the city of Jerusalem.

A BRIEF HISTORY OF POSTBIBLICAL JERUSALEM

This city had at one time been the capital of a self-governing state in Palestine, as described in our biblical books of Samuel and Kings. By the time of the Holy Roman Empire, however, those days lay far in the past. The last self-governing Jewish state of any duration had been the Hasmonean kingdom of Judea, which existed from the middle of the second until the middle of the first century BC. Thereafter the Jews of Judea found themselves to be in the first instance, like many Jews elsewhere, inhabitants of the pagan Roman Empire. Their life in this empire was not generally harsh, as we saw in chapter 4, since its emperors were inclined on the whole to tolerate Judaism. One of the things that the Romans did not tolerate, however, was rebellion, which was exactly what the last Roman prefect of Jerusalem provoked in AD 66 by stealing funds from the temple treasury. This resulted in the city's destruction by the Roman general Titus in AD 70. It was rebuilt in the early second century only as a Roman colony (Aelia Capitolina) containing a shrine honoring Jupiter Capitolinus (built on the surviving temple platform), with another dedicated to the goddess Aphrodite (constructed on the present site of the Church of the Holy Sepulcher). As a result of another Jewish revolt in 132–135, Jews were forbidden by imperial decree from living in the city. The consequences of that particular uprising were generally very severe: widespread destruction of Jewish settlements in Judea, great numbers of people sold into slavery, and fierce Roman repression of Judaism in the immediate aftermath. The center of Jewish life in the region thereafter passed to Galilee. The history of the earthly city of Jerusalem appeared to be over. In the main "Jerusalem" remained important now only as a vision among the faithful of the distant future.

CONSTANTINE AND THE SARACENS

All of this changed during the first Christian emperor Constantine's reign. Very much in line with the general idea explored in chapter 4 that his own earthly empire was a fulfilment of prophecy that might last until the end of time, Constantine rebuilt Jerusalem (under its old name) and constructed a new "temple" in the city (the Church of the Holy Sepulcher). It was a physical shrine, constructed in accordance with the prophecy of Ezekiel and standing at the center of an earthly city conceived of as the very center or "navel" of the world.[27] The city of Jerusalem mattered now in the Roman Empire in a way that it never had before. The city was later expanded, in the fifth century, when a church was built by the empress Eudocia (460) as a repository for the relics of the first Christian martyr, Stephen. A couple of decades earlier she had permitted Jews to live once again in Jerusalem. In the sixth century Justinian built another church, dedicated to the

Virgin Mary. However, in 614 a Persian army conquered Jerusalem, destroyed most of the churches, and again expelled the Jews.

A short time later Jerusalem came under Islamic rule (from 638 onwards)—or "Saracen" rule, as Christian writers of the time often referred to it. An impressive Saracen building program was initiated in what was now the third most holy city in Islam after Mecca and Medina. For example, the imposing Dome of the Rock, built on the Temple Mount, was completed in 691. The first Saracen caliphs, ruling from Damascus and later from Baghdad, generally treated their new subjects well, and many Christians held important offices under them. A king like Charlemagne, who often sent financial assistance to Christians in Jerusalem, could intercede successfully with a Saracen ruler like Harun al-Rashid on their behalf.[28] However, the situation began to deteriorate during the later ninth century, as a resurgent Byzantine Empire sought to recapture territories previously lost to the Saracens, including Jerusalem. Christians who supported these moves were regarded as traitors and dealt with accordingly. Toleration began to dissipate, and many churches and synagogues were destroyed wholly or partially—including, in 1009, the Church of the Holy Sepulcher (by Caliph al-Hakim, 996–1021). This was regarded as a powerful provocation throughout the Christian world.

Pilgrimage

Jerusalem, from the first Christian century onwards, was not only a city in which Christians *lived*. It was also a city that Christians *visited* on pilgrimage. They did so in increasing numbers after Constantine; in fact, apart from the early example of Origen, our surviving descriptions of such journeys date only from the fourth century onwards. Pilgrimage was exemplified in that century by people like Constantine's mother Helena and the Church Father Jerome (347–420), and its popularity was only to be expected, if Jerusalem with its new "temple" was indeed now the center of the world. The criticisms of the practice by other notable Church leaders did little to dampen this enthusiasm as the centuries passed.[29]

The Saracen conquests did not initially interfere greatly with this Christian pilgrimage, in line with the early Caliph Umar's promise to Sophronious, the patriarch of Jerusalem, to allow freedom of religion and access to Jerusalem for Christian pilgrims.[30] However, during the early eleventh century migrating Seljuk Turks from the Russian steppes began to cause problems for both the Byzantines and the ruling caliphs in Palestine, and Seljuk conflict with the latter in particular caused great difficulty for pilgrims. The Great Seljuk Sultanate ultimately reached its height under Malik Shah I, whose forces captured Palestine in 1073. This was an unwelcome development in Jerusalem, and in 1077 the city revolted, resulting in a subsequent massacre. The region and the city were retaken by their previous Muslim rulers in 1098.

This, then, is the *broader* background to the First Crusade. Its *immediate* background is a plea to the resurgent papacy in 1090 by the Byzantine emperor Alexius I Comnenus for Western support against the Seljuk Turks, followed by the appearance of his ambassadors before Pope Urban II at the Council of Piacenza in 1095. It was later in that same year, at the Council of Clermont, that this pope called for the Crusade, having laid the groundwork beforehand.[31]

POPE URBAN II

Pope Gregory VII himself had already mooted the idea of a crusade in 1074. Writing to Duke William of Burgundy, he urged him and other nobles—"faithful men of St. Peter"—to take up arms in defense of the beleaguered Eastern Christians. To Henry IV he wrote of warring against "the 'enemies of God', pushing all the way to the 'sepulcher of the Lord' in Jerusalem," and thereby reunifying the Church around Rome.[32] Some contemporaries did in fact believe, in those times of heightened apocalyptic expectation, that Henry "was fated to recover the Holy Sepulcher and defeat the forces of paganism."[33] In the event Gregory's idea foundered on the rocks of his conflict with the same emperor over investiture. However, his "three related goals—internal reform, Christian unity, and opposition to infidels—would inhabit the historical imagination of the Roman Church for centuries to come."[34] Indeed, his promise in the early 1080s that those who took up arms against the emperor on Rome's behalf would receive "remission of all their sins" grounded "the concept of sanctified violence within a penitential framework—an idea that would become part of the essence of crusading."[35]

THE SERMON AT CLERMONT

It was left to his former advisor Pope Urban II (bishop of Rome from 1088–1099), then, to initiate Gregory's war. Saracen control of Palestine, he believed, was a result of past sin on the part of God's people—just as Jerusalem in the OT could be harassed or seized as a result of the sins of the Israelites. Christendom was now in the process of departing from its past sins in a new age of reform; therefore, it could anticipate "a renewal of the churches' ancient glory after bondage under non-believers."[36] It is on this foundation that Urban preached his famous "crusade sermon" in Clermont in 1095—although none of those involved in the events of the time called it a crusade. It was instead a "journey" or a "pilgrimage."[37]

The sermon was received as a summons to the assembled knights to set aside their sinful infighting and fight together in defense of the Eastern Church, and as a call to liberate Jerusalem and its holy places from the wicked and unclean Saracens. Spiritual rewards would accrue for those participating in the crusade for the right reasons; these rewards were attractive to lay Christians who feared God's judgment for their sins and required nonmonastic ways of dealing with them. "The performance of a purgative devotional journey (or pilgrimage)" was one such sanctioned means.[38] According to Guibert of Nogent, apocalyptic themes were important in the sermon: "To fulfil biblical prophecies . . . Christianity must be thriving in Jerusalem and its environs before Antichrist would arrive on the scene and begin his vicious persecution against the faithful before his final defeat at the end of time."[39]

RHETORIC AND TRUTH

The threat of Islam to Christendom and to Christians was greatly exaggerated in this entire exercise. "Europe was by no means engaged in an urgent struggle for survival on the eve of the crusades . . . In fact, after the first forceful surge of Islamic expansion, the interaction between neighbouring Christian and Muslim polities had been relatively unremarkable."[40] Nor were religious minorities in Muslim lands in the Near East subject to ethnic cleansing, or even "widespread and sustained oppression."[41] It is true that the Church of the Holy Sepulcher had been extensively demolished by the Fatimid caliph al-Hakim in 1009—but his son had already agreed in 1027–1028 to allow its rebuilding and redecoration, and substantial work had been completed by 1048. It is also true that substantial numbers of Western Christians had reported new difficulties (to add to all the old ones) and had suffered some notable violence in getting to Jerusalem in the latter part of the eleventh century.[42] On the other hand, a Spanish Muslim pilgrim visiting the city in 1092 describes the city as "a thriving centre of religious devotion for Muslims, Christians, and Jews alike" and gives "no hint that pilgrims . . . were suffering abuse or interference."[43] This helps to remind us that

> when Latin crusading armies arrived in the Near East . . . they were not actually invading the heartlands of Islam . . . [but] fighting for control of a land that, in some respects, was . . . a Muslim frontier, one peopled by an assortment of Christians, Jews, and Muslims who, over the centuries, had become acculturated to the experience of conquest by external force.[44]

It was simply not true (as Pope Urban declared at Clermont) that "Christianity was in dire peril" from Islam at this time, and there is little reason to believe that, in reality, the Muslims in charge of Jerusalem were "bent upon ritual torture and unspeakable desecration"[45] and that Christians under their rule were generally prone to "forced circumcision, protracted disembowelment, or ritualized immolation," their women suffering "appalling violation."[46]

PURIFICATION THEOLOGY

These exaggerations, combined with Urban's other words, helped to produce what we can only describe as the highly toxic "apocalyptic purification theology" that informed the First Crusade—a theology at whose heart lay religiously sanctioned violence. There was the self-inflicted violence of the pilgrimage itself—an arduous journey designed to purge the pilgrim of sin. And then there was the violence inflicted on the "unclean others," who must not be permitted to continue to contaminate Christendom and who deserved to die in any case because of their own sins. And all of this was given a pressing urgency by the imminent approach of the end times. Unsurprisingly, the strong distinction drawn in this theology between "my people" and "not my people" caused trouble not only for Muslims once the Crusade got going; Jewish communities were also attacked along the way. And in subsequent times, as we shall see in chapters 8 and 9, the lines around the "pure" were drawn more and more narrowly within Western Christendom, as a "crusading mentality" took hold of the culture—with disastrous results for those perceived as "not one of us."

THE FIRST CRUSADE

In the immediate historical moment, Urban was successful in sending a very large number of people (tens of thousands) from Europe to Palestine to fight in the First Crusade and thereby to purge their sins. And as things turned out, the Crusade was itself (in the end) remarkably successful from a military point of view.[47]

SHORT-TERM SUCCESS

By June 7, 1099, the Crusaders had glimpsed Jerusalem for the first time, "that longed-for city, for which they had suffered so many hardships, so many dangers, so many kinds of death and famine."[48] The air crackled with apocalyptic expectation. When the city was eventually captured on July 15, 1099, after three days "fasting, praying, and carrying out a ritual procession," Joshua-like, around the city's walls, its "purification" was immensely bloody—as had been the whole campaign, on all sides.[49] Vengeful soldiers indulged in "barbaric and indiscriminate slaughter," killing "men, women, and children, both Muslims and Jews, all the while engaging in rapacious looting," as was the grim custom of the day when a resistant city fell to a siege.[50] It is estimated that at least three thousand people died; six months later a Western visitor reported "that the Holy City still reeked of death and decay."[51] One cleric who witnessed these events was unmoved, however: "It was truly by the just judgment of God that this place should be filled with the blood of those from whose blasphemies it had suffered for so long."[52] Indeed, the first day of slaughter in the city concluded with Christian worship.

The successful outcome of the Crusade, which "stunned Latin Christendom,"[53] was widely understood as confirming its divine mandate—another example of the "success theology" already criticized in chapter 4 above, whereby (in the words of the epigraph to the present chapter) Christians read "providential significance into . . . military and political fortunes." It was also understood as a fulfilment of biblical prophecy.[54] In its aftermath, Jerusalem experienced a century of Crusader rule as the capital of the Latin Kingdom of Jerusalem. Its population was about thirty thousand, the vast majority of these Christian and of French descent; Jews and Muslims were not permitted to live in the city. The Crusaders refurbished the Church of the Holy Sepulcher, completing it in 1149, and engaged in many other building works (e.g. St. Anne's Church, inside St. Stephen's gate). The Dome of the Rock was converted into a Christian church with a cross affixed to its dome. The occupation lasted until 1187, when the Crusaders surrendered Jerusalem to Saladin, founder of the Ayyubid dynasty.

LONG-TERM IMPACT

The long-term impact of the First Crusade was more profound. "From 1099 forward, the fate of [Jerusalem] . . . came to occupy a place of immense priority in the historical memory of the Latin Church."[55] Crusading, reform, and the reunification of the Western and Eastern Church became strongly associated with each other. Insofar as this involved ongoing "holy warfare" against Muslims, specifically, it mirrored the earlier Islamic practice of military *jihad* against infidels and also reciprocally reinforced it.[56] Increasingly in the aftermath of the First Crusade, however, we also encounter a reformist crusading mentality that is more inward looking. As we shall see in chapter 8, a strong distinction between "my people" and "not my people" that was developed originally in terms of enemies *external* to Christendom was now brought to bear upon "enemies" within. In short, the First Crusade

> became a template, a model for subsequent Christian action both at home and abroad when self-proclaimed members of the Western Church confronted heresy and unbelief, saw themselves as threatened, and, in certain circumstances, desired to propagate their faith.[57]

The motivation remained that of purification: "Battle lines were being drawn between faithful Christians, on the one side, and the enemies of God on the other, the latter including heretics, schismatics, pagans, Jews, and other opponents of Christendom." This included, in many Western quarters, a hardening of attitudes toward the Eastern Church.[58] It was to make "crusades" against these internal enemies easier to prosecute, in fact, that the thirteenth-century papacy first established the Inquisition. The intolerance directed within Christendom at

"Jews, pagans, and heretics," first noted in our chapter 4, was thereby considerably ramped up as the thirteenth century gave way to the fourteenth and the fifteenth. Thomas Aquinas (1225–1274) captures the mood of the times well when he writes that heretics "deserve not only to be separated from the Church by excommunication but also to be shut off from the world by death."[59]

THE HERMENEUTICS OF JERUSALEM

We shall return to the violence of it all in chapters 8 and 9—to the questions of whether there is any biblical warrant for Christians either to endorse the execution of heretics (and others) or physically to fight wars in pursuit of the goals of the Church or their state. At present, though, I want to ask another question raised by the First Crusade. Why should any Christian ever have believed that ongoing attention to the earthly city of Jerusalem is an important aspect of Christian faith? Positive convictions on this point have had a highly significant impact throughout Church History on Christian ethical and political reflection. It is important, then, to consider the matter.

DAVID'S CITY

Jerusalem does of course play an important historical role in much of the OT narrative, from the moment that it is captured by David, extended and provided with a palace, and established as his capital (2 Sam. 5:6–12). Here the Ark of the Covenant, the symbolic throne of the invisible God, is installed, "inside the tent that David had pitched for it" (2 Sam. 6:17); Jerusalem is now not only the city of David but also the city of God. Yet it is not a typical ANE "city of a god," possessing a "house" (a temple) at its core for its patron deity. This God does not require a house for himself (2 Sam. 7:5–7). Instead, he promises to build the king a "house" (i.e., a dynasty): "your house and your kingdom will endure forever before me; your throne will be established forever" (2 Sam. 7:16). David's response in prayer correlates this with God establishing "your people Israel as your very own forever" (2 Sam. 7:24). Jerusalem is now associated, then, with a "covenant" made by God with David (2 Sam. 7:28).

This connection is emphasized once again in 1 Kings 8, when Solomon eventually does build a temple in Jerusalem (1 Kgs. 5–7) and David's previous arrangements are superseded (1 Kgs. 8:3–9). In a dedicatory prayer Solomon now asks God to "keep for your servant David my father the promises you made to him when you said, 'You shall never fail to have a successor to sit before me on the throne of Israel'" (v. 25). The promises are bound up with the temple as well as the dynasty; the temple is said to be "a place for you [God] to dwell forever" (v. 13). As such, prayers may be directed toward it—not only by Israelites but also by Gentiles (vv. 41–42). Indeed, to the extent that God is moved by prayer to "uphold the cause of his servant and the cause of his people Israel," it is "so that all the peoples of the earth may know that the LORD is God and that there is no other" (vv. 59–60).

Jerusalem and its temple are evidently important in Scripture. Yet there was a long period before the city's capture when God already had a relationship with his people—when he was "moving from place to place" along with them (2 Sam. 7:6; cf. Acts 7:44–53). All through that time, and still during David's reign, he had "a tent as my dwelling" (same verse). It is well worth noting, moreover, that when we do eventually find both a city and a temple in the OT narrative, the biblical text goes out of its way to relativize the importance of both. God does not in fact "dwell" in Jerusalem in any normal sense of the word; his real "dwelling place" is heaven (1 Kgs. 8:27), and it is from there that he *looks* at the temple and hears prayers offered toward it. It is in fact only his "Name" that is found in Jerusalem. The city is important, at least at this point in Israel's history, as an intermediary in God's relationship with his people (and indeed with others). The centrally important matter, however, is the relationship itself.

JERUSALEM IN THE PSALMS

This is equally clear in the book of Psalms, which routinely speaks about Jerusalem and its temple in extravagant ways. The chosen city is God's "resting place for ever and ever,"[60] Mount Zion where "the LORD bestows his blessing, even life forevermore" (Ps. 133:3). Its temple, therefore, is where the pilgrim wishes to "dwell ... forever" (Ps. 23:6). The city itself is a "holy mountain ... beautiful in its loftiness, the joy of the whole earth"; it is "like the utmost heights of Zaphon" (Ps. 48:1–2). It is the source of life-giving springs of water (Ps. 46:4).[61] It is the location where the living God defeats the waters of chaos that threaten to overwhelm it (Ps. 93:3–4).[62] Indeed, it is a city that God unfailingly protects from enemy attack. Psalm 46 goes on to say that "God is within her, she will not fall; God will help her at break of day" (v. 5).[63] This is the Holy City (with its temple), then, in which God dwells along with his king.

LANGUAGE AND HISTORICAL REALITY

In our present context, the most important thing to notice about this language is how it so evidently outstrips the reality of earthly Jerusalem in the OT narrative. The city of the Psalms is a lofty mountain like Mount Zaphon (Jebel Aqra, 1,717 meters high) and is apparently the focal point of global attention (Ps. 48:1–2); but earthly Jerusalem was always built on quite a small hill (765 meters high), and in ancient times (at least) it was never the focal point of global attention. The

Psalmist's city is the source of life-giving springs of water (Ps. 46:4); but so far as we know, the water systems of earthly Jerusalem have only ever produced mundane waters. Seated in the city of the Psalms, God defeats the seas; but no physical waves have ever smashed into the foundations of earthly Jerusalem, which has always lain well inland from the sea. Nor would any ancient pilgrim to Jerusalem have stayed there very long before leaving again; no one would have expected to "dwell in [that] house of the Lord forever."

The city of the Psalms is, moreover, holy, but the Jerusalem of the biblical narrative is far from it. In 2 Samuel 11:1–17, it is the city in which David lingers in order to commit adultery with Bathsheba and where he plots the death of her husband Uriah. It is a city polluted by sin, and not only David's—a city inhabited by a dysfunctional, wicked royal family (2 Sam. 13–15). It is a city from which both the king and the Ark of the Covenant are for a time exiled (2 Sam. 15–20, noting 15:24–29). Later, it is the city in which Solomon builds shrines for other gods (1 Kgs. 11:7). Later still, in the eighth century BC, Isaiah catalogues the city's sins (e.g., Isa. 3:8–17), selecting King Ahaz of Judah as an archetype of the king who will not trust in God and promising God's judgment (7:1–17; cf. 2 Kgs. 16). Micah speaks of rulers who "build Zion with bloodshed, and Jerusalem with wickedness" (Mic. 3:9–10). Because of them "Jerusalem will become a heap of rubble, the temple hill a mound overgrown with thickets" (v. 12). Little more than a century later, in the aftermath of the dreadful reign of King Manasseh (2 Kgs. 21), we read that a Babylonian army "set fire to the temple of the Lord, the royal palace, and all the houses of Jerusalem. Every important building he burned down . . . [they] broke down the walls around Jerusalem (2 Kgs. 25:9–10). The only surviving Davidic king, Jehoiachin, is imprisoned in Babylon. Jerusalem's sins have caught up with her.

This brings us to the final way in which, in the OT narrative, the language of the Psalms so evidently outstrips the reality of earthly Jerusalem. The Psalmist's city is one that God unfailingly protects from enemy attack—and it is clear that many Judeans prior to the fall of Jerusalem believed that this was indeed true of their capital, no matter how they behaved. Yet already during King Josiah's reign the prophet Jeremiah assails this belief.[64] If the people persist in their misguided theology and practice, he promises, God will do to the temple in Jerusalem what he once did to the sanctuary in Shiloh "where I first made a dwelling for my Name" (i.e., destroy it), and "thrust you from my presence, just as I did all your fellow Israelites" (7:12–15). This is exactly how things turn out. It is not earthly Jerusalem, it turns out, that God unfailingly protects from enemy attack; it is not *that* city and its temple that last "forever."

This truth is already foreshadowed in 1 Kings 9, in the passage that immediately follows the narrative about temple building and temple dedication in

1 Kings 5–8. After reading that God's promise to David about an everlasting *dynasty* is bound up with the question of holiness ("if your descendants watch how they live … you will never fail to have a successor on the throne of Israel," 1 Kgs. 9:4), we learn that the fate of the earthly dwelling place of God is also bound up with this "if." God's name will be there "forever," and his eyes and his heart "will always be there" (v. 3); however, if the kings (and the people) turn away from God and do not observe his "commands and decrees" but "go off to serve other gods and worship them", then Israel will be exiled from the land and the temple "will become a heap of rubble" (vv. 4–9). The holy God can dwell, in the end, only with those who are holy.

GREATER REALITIES

When we read about Jerusalem in the OT, then, we must recognize that it is always a city that points beyond itself to realities greater than itself. It does so in language that would have made immediate sense to readers steeped in ANE culture but which modern readers need to work harder to grasp. Ancient readers knew that generally the gods were envisaged as living on high mountains, in temples that could be pictured as being built on the waters that had produced life on earth in the first place—waters now ordered so that life could flourish but always trying to break out of their bounds and reassert chaos. Genesis 1–2 also reflects these motifs in describing the garden in Eden, which is portrayed as a kind of temple inhabited by images of God (in this case, human beings).[65] "Jerusalem," in this way of thinking, is simply where the one *true* God truly dwells, sovereign over the powers of chaos in such a temple, pouring out blessing (indeed, the river of life) on his "faithful people" who "sing for joy."

When the Psalmist proclaims that he wants to "dwell in the house of the LORD forever," this is the house to which he refers. He experiences something of this reality each time he goes to Jerusalem for a festival, of course—but he does not stay "forever," secure with the living God in his impregnable mountain fortress that cannot be conquered by his enemies. It is indeed with such hopes that the earthly Jerusalem is associated; but that city has never fulfilled them. The situation is in fact analogous to that of the monarchy (see our chapter 4). Jerusalem and its temple, just like the monarchy, are integrated in our biblical Story into God's ultimate plans for his people and for the world at large; ideals are articulated in relation to these institutions. But just as the ideals attached to the monarchy in the OT are not envisaged as being achievable by any ordinary Israelite ruler, so too the hopes bound up with "Zion" far transcend any mundane ANE city or temple.

The Once and Future City

Does Jerusalem have a future in the biblical Story after the city and the temple are destroyed by the Babylonians? It does; but it is important to note which kind of Jerusalem this is. Isaiah, for example, envisages "in the last days [a] mountain of the Lord's temple [that] will be established as the highest of the mountains . . . exalted above the hills," to which "all nations will stream" in an age of universal peace (Isa. 2:2–4). This is an event at the end of time when, as the reference to the height of the mountain suggests, Jerusalem will at last conform to hopes earlier associated with it. Indeed, Isaiah 65:17–25 speaks of God creating Jerusalem in this way in the context of creating "new heavens and a new earth" in which "[t]he former things will not be remembered."

Likewise, Joel 3:17–18 speaks of Jerusalem becoming holy at last, associating this with "mountains [that] drip new wine," hills "[flowing] with milk," and "[a] fountain [that flows] out of the Lord's house and will water the valley of acacias." This is the Jerusalem that provides life-giving, rather than simply mundane waters. In Ezekiel, likewise, when the prophet envisions a New Jerusalem and its temple in the future (Ezek. 40–48), his vision is set "on a very high mountain, on whose south side were some buildings that looked like a city" (Ezek. 40:2). He sees "water coming out from under the threshold of the temple toward the east" sustaining "a great number of trees on each side of the river" as well as "[s]warms of living creatures . . . large numbers of fish . . . [f]ruit trees of all kinds" (47:1–12).

This is the predominant emphasis of our biblical materials when they consider the future of Jerusalem and its temple—two aspects of what biblical theologians typically refer to as biblical "eschatology" (the part of theology concerned with "final things" like death, judgment, and final destiny). Sometimes they do show interest in a more ordinary, earthly Jerusalem (and temple) restored only for the Israelites (e.g., in Ezra-Nehemiah; Haggai). They are much more interested in a Jerusalem that transcends such a reality, however—the Jerusalem that stands at the center of the cosmos and represents (for both Jew and Gentile) communion with God; being forever safe with God in his mighty fortress; being forever nourished and given life by God.

Jerusalem in the New Testament

This interest is even more clearly on display in the NT. Jerusalem plays a key role in the life of Jesus, but although it is referred to as the "Holy City" (Matt. 4:5, 27:53), it is at the same time the place of the OT prophets' martyrdom and of Jesus' temptation, future suffering, and death (Matt. 4:5; Mark 8:31; Luke 13:33–35). Its temple is meant to be a house of prayer for both Jew and Gentile, but it has become (as an economic institution) a den of robbers (Isa. 56:6–7; Luke 19:45–46). Jesus can only weep over this city, envisaging its destruction (Luke 19:41–44).

At the end of his life the temple curtain is torn (Mark 15:38), foreshadowing the building's destruction and suggesting that its importance in the biblical Story is now at an end. All people now have immediate access, in Christ, to the holy of holies, where God "is." The same idea is articulated in Hebrews 6:19–20; 9:8–14; and 10:19–22, where Christ's body is the "curtain." The temple's importance has already been relativized by Jesus himself in John 4:21–24, in his conversation with the Samaritan woman: "a time is coming when you will worship the Father neither on this mountain nor in Jerusalem . . . when the true worshipers will worship the Father in the Spirit and in truth . . . God is spirit, and his worshipers must worship in the Spirit and in truth." It is Jesus, and not the temple, who is the center of the cosmos—the one who "became flesh and made his dwelling among us" (John 1:14), whose very body is equated with the gateway to heaven and the temple (John 1:51, 2:18–21). It is to Jesus, then—and not to the temple—that people from all the nations come in order that God "will teach us his ways, so that we may walk in his paths" (Isa. 2:3). It is in Jesus that they encounter God and find life (John 10:11), and from Jesus that the water of life flows out to a thirsty world (John 4:13–14).

The early Christians, post-Pentecost, still met together in the temple courts (Acts 2:46), while recognizing that "the Most High does not live in houses made by human hands" and that the city's unrighteous inhabitants had a long history of persecuting and killing prophets (including Jesus, Acts 7:48–53). Very soon, however, the Gospel begins to spread outside of Jerusalem (Acts 8:1–8) and into the whole Roman world. One of the earliest recipients of the Gospel in this context is an Ethiopian man who has "had gone to Jerusalem to worship." He does not truly understand the meaning of the OT, though, until he begins his journey back *from* the city to his homeland. On this journey home he meets Philip—at which point, and only then, does he go "on his way rejoicing" (Acts 8:26–40).

Jerusalem remains important in NT times thereafter as the location of the originating, apostolic Church community, but not as a city in itself. In fact, the apostle Paul, in writing to the Galatians about the important difference between the OT and the NT, explicitly (and sharply) contrasts "the present city of Jerusalem" from "the Jerusalem that is above," the latter being "our [Christian] mother" (Gal. 4:25–26). In Hebrews 12:22–24, moreover, it is in Christ that Christians have already "come to Mount Zion, to the city of the living God, the heavenly Jerusalem." The Church is now as the body of Christ "the temple of the living God," and individual Christians are mini-temples within it.[66]

As such, Christians await the joining of heaven with earth, as the New Jerusalem comes down from the former to the latter (Rev. 3:14). This Jerusalem appears only at the end of time, and not before—only when there is "a *new* heaven and a *new* earth" (Rev. 21:1). It is only then that "God's dwelling place" can truly and ultimately be said to be "among the people" (21:2). Predictably, there is no "temple in

[this] city, because the Lord God Almighty and the Lamb are its temple" (21:22). We *do* find "the river of the water of life," however, "flowing from the throne of God and of the Lamb down the middle of the great street of the city" (22:2).

CONCLUSION

In sum, there is no reason why any Christian should ever have believed that ongoing attention to the earthly city of Jerusalem is an important aspect of the Christian search for what is right. There is no reason to think (in the words of the epigraph to this chapter) that "[t]he terrestrial fate of Jerusalem [is] suffused" after Christ "with transcendental meaning." Even in the early stages of our biblical Story, the terrestrial fate of the city and its temple is not the most important thing about either. This is still more clearly the case in the NT. With the coming of Christ, the people of God are no longer one people-group in one land, possessing one capital city with one temple. God's people are now both Jew and Gentile, scattered throughout the world in many cities (and towns and villages), on a pilgrimage together to a "greater" Zion. We walk that path, in pursuit of what is good, in the company of a risen Davidic king who, having offered himself as a sacrifice in that city on our behalf, fulfils in his own person all the hopes surrounding the Jerusalem temple. He is our temple and—as his body—we ourselves are that temple. So it will be until the end of time, and the coming of a new heaven and a new earth. The earthly city of Jerusalem should be of no more importance to the Christian, then, than any other city—nor should it ever have been. Our Christian history was set on a most unfortunate trajectory by Constantine's attention to Jerusalem, illustrated by Urban's decision to fight for it. For there can be no question but that the Christian hermeneutic that ties post-Pentecost Jerusalem to the earth in such a manner, often in the context of utopian and indeed apocalyptic politics, lies at the root of a considerable amount of trouble in the history of the Church.

DISCUSSION QUESTIONS

1. Do you find the argument in this chapter about how Christians should think about "Jerusalem" convincing? Why or why not?
2. Whatever you think about "the end times," are Christians justified in sanctioning the oppression or killing of people in pursuit of their "eschatological" goals?
3. What can we learn from Pope Urban's rhetoric and actions about how we should and should not approach the question of Islam, specifically, in our own day?
4. Is success in war a sure sign that God is with us?

7

The Foulness of Fornication

Sex and Marriage in John Calvin's Geneva

To sum up [in relation to the seventh commandment], then: we should not become defiled with any filth or lustful intemperance of the flesh. To this corresponds the affirmative commandment that we chastely and continently regulate all parts of our life. But he expressly forbids fornication, to which all lust tends, in order through the foulness of fornication . . . to lead us to abominate all lust.[1]

John Calvin

The Investiture Controversy of the eleventh and early twelfth centuries, described in chapter 6, demonstrated the limits of the Holy Roman Emperor's power. Not only did the pope succeed in depriving the latter of the support that he had customarily enjoyed from ecclesiastical officials—forbidding them under pain of excommunication from aiding him—but he emboldened elements of the German nobility who were likewise interested in limiting imperial absolutism. Increasingly powerful local dukes and princes, controlling extensive territory and large military forces, began to emerge. When the Salian dynasty ended with Henry V's death in 1125, the nobles chose to elect not his next of kin but the Duke of Saxony. When he died in 1137, they also avoided his heir and elected a nephew of Henry V.

The accession of Frederick I Barbarossa as German king in 1152 and emperor in 1155 resulted in a period of resurgent imperial power in relation both to the German nobles and the papacy, but he died in 1190 in the course of the Third Crusade. After his death the empire devolved into a multiplicity of independent states ruled by ecclesiastical and secular princes—we shall encounter two ecclesiastical "prince-bishops," for example, in this and the next chapter. Ultimately (in the fourteenth century), election to the imperial throne came to depend on the votes of four secular electors (the King of Bohemia, the Count Palatine of the Rhine, the Duke of Saxony, and the Margrave of Brandenburg) and three spiritual ones (the archbishops of Mainz, Trier, and Cologne). Papal approval was no longer required. From 1438 until 1806 (with only a brief pause in 1742–1745), the emperor was always a king of the Habsburg dynasty of Austria.

THE TRAVAILS OF ROME

The fortunes of the papacy varied over this same period. The later twelfth century was marked first by a schism between different claimants to the bishopric of Rome in the context of Frederick I's struggle with the papacy. This was also the time in which various Italian cities sought to secure independence from imperial or episcopal control (ultimately creating the conditions for the Renaissance), and in which we see the growth of "heretical" movements such as the (proto-Anabaptist) Waldensians and the Albigensians. The reign of Pope Innocent III (1198–1216) represents the beginning of a renewed upswing in papal fortunes. Remembered as "one of the most powerful popes of the Middle Ages," among others things he initiated the Fourth Crusade (1202–1204), which led to the sack of Constantinople; the Fifth Crusade (1217–1221), which ran aground in the sands of Egypt; and the Albigensian Crusade, which was intended to end the Cathar heresy in southern France.[2] In the first and third of these crusades we see nicely illustrated, in its Roman form, the tendency already mentioned in chapter 6 whereby a reformist crusading mentality is brought to bear on enemies *within* Christendom, and not only outside it.

Innocent's immediate successors further extended papal authority in the course of the thirteenth century, bringing "the realities of the papal monarchy and the theories of its universal dominion into their closest proximity."[3] However, in the aftermath of the Second Council of Lyons in 1274—"the last hopeful year in the Middle Ages"[4]—a growing perception emerged that the papacy was faltering in its leadership: "The gap between the imagined Christendom and the circumscribed reality of the Roman Church's position in the world was starting to widen rather than close."[5]

THE AVIGNON PAPACY

Shortly after the Council of Lyons, the overreach of Pope Boniface VIII (bishop of Rome from 1294–1303) led to his downfall at the hands of King Philip IV of France and to the subsequent relocation of the papal court to Avignon (1309). All the popes during the subsequent "Avignon papacy" (1309–1377) were French, and ruled within easy reach of the French king and his troops. Here they deployed their considerable income from tithes and other sources to produce a papal court patterned on the royal court, populated by wealthy cardinals who were often related to the pope. The period of Gregorian reform was well and truly over, and corruption was rife, giving rise to calls for further reform. When the papacy eventually returned to Rome, however, a number of the cardinals found themselves disenchanted by the new Italian pope, Urban VI. They elected one of their own number as Pope Clement VII, who took up residence once again in Avignon.

POPES AND COUNCILS

The papacy was now divided along national lines and lost further respect within Christendom. A growing conciliar movement emerged, arguing that a general council of the Church had greater authority than a pope. A third pope was ultimately elected in 1409 (the Cardinal of Milan, who became Pope Alexander V). He was succeeded shortly afterwards by Pope John XXIII, who in 1414 convened the Council of Constance. This council deposed John, received the resignation of the Roman pope, Gregory XII, and dismissed the claims of the Avignon pope, Benedict XIII—which opened the way for the election of Pope Martin V as sole pope in November 1417.

This was also the council that condemned as a heretic the Bohemian proto-Protestant reformer Jan Hus (1370–1415), resulting in his death; among other things, he had advocated the supremacy of biblical authority over that of the Church. The immediate cause of his trouble, however, was his opposition to the sale of indulgences authorized by Pope John XXIII to help finance his campaign against Pope Gregory XII. Indulgences were designed to distribute to those who received them the excess "merit" accumulated by Christ and the saints, such that the recipients received forgiveness for their sins. Jan Hus publicly denounced their sale in Bohemia, even though they had been approved by his previous ally King Wenceslas IV (who shared in the proceeds). In important ways, then, Hus foreshadowed Martin Luther and the Protestant Reformation that was shortly to destroy the papacy's control over the West forever.

MARTIN LUTHER

Martin Luther was born in 1483 in Eisleben, in what is now northeast Germany. Educated first in Madgeburg (1497–1498) and Eisenach (1498–1501), he went on to study liberal arts as an undergraduate at the University of Erfurt (1501–1505) before joining the Augustinian order of monks in that city out of a concern for the salvation of his soul. In the course of only a few years a spiritual crisis developed, and his life came to be marked by overwhelming terror and despair. He found the strength to endure this crisis through his Bible reading, in the course of which he came to his crucial insight about what "righteousness" means in the Bible and ultimately developed a reformed theology that would transform much of Europe.

In 1511 this still-troubled young monk was transferred from Erfurt to Wittenberg, where became a professor in Bible (1512). Only a few years later, on March 31, 1515, Pope Leo X granted a "plenary [complete] indulgence ... which was intended to finance the building of the new St. Peter's Basilica in Rome."[6] By Luther's time, letters of indulgence had become a major instrument for financing the Church. It was his reflections on the events surrounding their sale in northeast Germany during the spring and summer of 1517 that ultimately spurred him into publishing his famous ninety-five theses, in which he invited public debate about indulgences and other matters.

Almost immediately the theses were being read throughout Germany, and within a few months (by way of the relatively new moveable-print technology invented by Johannes Gutenberg) they had reached the rest of Europe. Soon Luther was in serious trouble with Rome, and the Reformation movement was threatening to tear the Catholic Church apart. Summoned to an Imperial Diet (parliament) in the city of Worms in 1521 to answer for his various writings by the recently elected Holy Roman Emperor, Charles V (1519), Luther left the subsequent proceedings alive—but now officially both a heretic and an outlaw. Nevertheless, for the remainder of his life until his death in Eisleben in 1546, he continued to debate with opponents, to teach, and to write tracts in pursuit of his vision of a reformed Church.

THE REFORMATION AND BIBLICAL INTERPRETATION

At the heart of this part of our story lie questions of authority and—intrinsically connected to these—biblical interpretation. Luther's belief was that Scripture, and not the bishop of Rome, should be the final authority in matters of faith and life—that Christians should consult Scripture alone (*sola Scriptura*) for guidance on doctrine and practice, subordinating all other authorities to the Bible. As literature inspired by God, who speaks through it to the Church and to the world, the Bible is infallible in its guiding work; it does not lead its faithful readers into spiritual error. One of the reasons that this is so is that Scripture is "perspicuous" (clear). No one equipped with a Bible translation that faithfully represents the original Hebrew and Greek texts, and possessing an understanding of some rudimentary rules of reading, should have any great difficulty in understanding its "simple" sense. This is also the literal sense—what someone like Moses said and meant back in his own time, now read in the context of the whole canon of Scripture stretching from Genesis to Revelation. No one should read texts otherwise; all of them should be read in the context of the whole unfolding covenantal story of Scripture (the principle of "the analogy of Scripture"). Nothing should be inferred from a difficult or unclear passage that is not evident from other, clearer passages (whose existence is what provides Scripture overall with "perspicuity"). The point is, though, that all Christians should be reading their Bibles and learning from them what is "useful" for faith and life.[7]

It is evident from this that in Reformation Europe the question of what is "biblical" in terms of the good life, both individually and corporately, was bound to be much discussed by more people than ever before—and that perhaps quite radical consequences would follow, as people decided that what had happened in Christendom beforehand was not quite biblical enough. In this chapter and the next, we shall examine two early examples of how this renewed attention to "being biblical" shaped the life of a European city: in chapter 8, we focus on the German city of Münster; and here in chapter 7, the Swiss city of Geneva. So it is that we move on immediately now from Martin Luther—unusual among the early German and Swiss Reformers in "living in a territorial and princely state"—to a Reformer who operated in a "free" urban location (see further below).[8] His name was John Calvin.

JOHN CALVIN

In 1509, while the young Martin Luther was still wrestling with life as a monk in Erfurt, John Calvin was born in Noyon, north of Paris, about four hundred miles to the west. He would later recall the piety of this childhood environment as typifying the "abominable sacrilege" that was medieval Catholic practice.[9] Educated at the universities of Paris, Orléans, and Bourges, he developed in his early years a commitment to the reforming Renaissance humanist movement in France, with its emphasis on the Bible and biblical languages. As a result of this commitment, in 1535 Calvin left an increasingly intolerant France and found his way to Protestant Basel in Switzerland, where he allied himself clearly with the Reformation. It was here that he completed the first edition of his *Institutes of the Christian Religion*, published in Latin in 1536 and later amended for the first time in 1539. For our immediate purposes the most important section of this work comes at its end, where Calvin addresses the question of civil government.

CIVIL GOVERNMENT

Such government, he writes, "has as its appointed end . . . to adjust our life to the society of men, to form our social behavior to civil righteousness, to reconcile us with one another, and to promote general peace and tranquility," for so long as this imperfect world endures and there are people whose "wickedness [is] so stubborn, that it can scarcely be restrained [even] by extremely severe laws."[10] As such, its task is not only to ensure that people "breathe, eat, drink, and are kept warm" and to keep the public peace but also to prevent "idolatry, sacrilege against God's name, blasphemies against his truth, and other public offenses against religion from arising and spreading among the people."[11] That is, "civil government [has] the duty of rightly establishing [true] religion," for no one should "make laws according to their own decision concerning religion and the worship of God."[12] This is so whether we are thinking about kings or "other rulers."[13] Calvin was well aware that in his time in Europe there existed "self-governing cities, in the German case those known as Reichsstädte—'imperial cities'—or Freistädte— 'free cities'—in effect independent civic republics that were also, from the 1520s onwards, pioneers of urban religious Reformation."[14] Basel was one of these, and Strasbourg another. There was biblical precedent for such governance, Calvin also believed, in the other "lordships" described in the OT (such as those exercised by Joseph and Daniel) and in the "civil rule among a free people" that involved "Moses, Joshua, and the judges."[15]

All such "magistrates" (the general term used by Calvin for rulers) should "remember that they are vicars of God" and should therefore rule justly, even as those who are ruled must recognize that if they "rail against this holy ministry" they "revile God himself" (just like the Israelites who refused Samuel's rule in 1 Sam. 8).[16] This just rule will sometimes require the shedding of blood—as when Moses "by slaying three thousand men in one day . . . took vengeance upon the people's sacrilege" (Exod. 32:27–28), or when David "ordered his son Solomon to kill Joab and Shimei" (1 Kgs. 2:5–6).[17] The wise magistrate must sometimes behave likewise, even while attending also to mercy, "lest by excessive severity he either harm more than heal; or, by superstitious affectation of clemency, fall into the cruelest gentleness."[18]

THE MORAL LAW

What are the laws by which the magistrate should govern? They are the laws of God. Yet here Calvin enjoins upon his readers a consideration that I have also already pressed upon mine in chapter 3: what is there in these laws "that pertains to us," and what is there that does not?[19] The core of what pertains to us, in Calvin's view, is what he calls "the moral law," which "commands us to worship God with pure faith and piety" and "to embrace men with sincere affection"—"the true and eternal rule of righteousness, prescribed for men of all nations and times, who wish to conform their lives to God's will." These are design parameters of Creation that I refer to in this book as creational law. This "moral law" Calvin distinguishes from "the ceremonial law" used by God to train his OT people "as it were, in their childhood, until the fullness of time should come," and from "the judicial law," which imparted "certain formulas of equity and justice, by which they might live together blamelessly and peaceably," but also possessed "something distinct from [the] precept of love" for God and neighbor.[20] These do not have the same universal and eternal validity as the moral law. It is equity itself (and justice) that remain forever; indeed, equity is the goal toward which all right law everywhere presses,

> because it is natural . . . the law of God which we call the moral law is nothing else than a testimony of natural law and of that conscience which God has engraved upon the minds of men . . . this equity alone must be the goal and rule and limit of all laws.[21]

How do we learn of God's moral law, then? As this quotation begins to suggest, and as Calvin has already made clear earlier in the *Institutes*, it is found both in the natural law and then also (and much more clearly) in the Ten Commandments. We note here the correlation of creational or "moral" law with the "natural" law that we discussed at length in chapter 1, albeit with an important (and correct) prioritizing of God's special revelation in Scripture over his revelation in Creation in general. Calvin's moral law is not found in the mere words of the Ten Commandments themselves, however, but in their broader consideration—an idea that is much more fully worked out in the 1539 edition of the *Institutes* than in the original.[22] The fifth commandment, for example, enjoins us not only that we should honor our parents but "that we should look up to those whom God has placed over us, and should treat them with honor, obedience, and gratefulness."[23] The sixth concerns not only killing but "all violence, injury, and any harmful thing at all that may injure our neighbor's body."[24] The seventh enjoins us not only to avoid adultery but (as we see in the epigraph to this present chapter) to avoid becoming "defiled with any filth or lustful intemperance of the flesh."[25] Nor should we "seduce the modesty of another with wanton dress and obscene gestures and foul speech."[26] We shall obey the eighth commandment not only if we refrain from stealing but also "if we do not seek to become wealthy through injustice . . . if we do not madly scrape together from everywhere, by fair means or foul, whatever will feed our avarice or satisfy our prodigality."[27] We shall keep the ninth commandment not only by avoiding bearing false witness but "when our tongue, in declaring the truth, serves both the good repute and the advantage of our neighbors."[28] As to the tenth, "we must banish from our hearts all desire contrary to love."[29] The moral law is not reducible to the words of the Ten Commandments alone, then. Indeed, Calvin often gives great weight to Torah found outside the Ten Commandments in determining how Christians should live, and how the laws of the Christian state should be formed. In other words, other kinds of Torah also have the force of moral law.

GENEVA BEFORE CALVIN

It was this kind of thinking about the nature of the Christian state that John Calvin brought with him to Swiss Geneva, briefly in the late 1530s and then for a longer period from 1541 onwards. This city had for some time been on the road to independence from the dukes of Savoy, who viewed themselves as its overlords but had previously recognized Geneva's General Council (comprising all qualified citizens) as its central legislative body. Beneath the General Council stood the Council of Two Hundred (meeting on special occasions to discuss important matters), the Council of Sixty (drawn from the two hundred and mainly dealing with problems in relation to other governments), and the Small Council—an executive committee of twenty-five, supervising the criminal justice system, from whom four were chosen every year ("syndics") to serve as its presiding officers. In 1535 Geneva managed to escape from external control completely—not only from the dukes but also from the Savoyard prince-bishop, Pierre de La Baume, who was (confusingly) legally answerable to the Holy Roman Emperor rather than to Savoy. In 1536 the newly independent Genevan republic declared itself Protestant, casting off both the Roman Catholic Church and its canon law in favor of biblical teaching. One result over the next few years would be the arrival in Geneva (deeply resented by the natives) of increasing numbers of French religious refugees, attracted by this "New Jerusalem" in the middle of Europe where both the pastors and the magistrates were so evidently intent on being biblical in a Reformation manner.

Throughout all these events, life in Geneva was dominated by factionalism—factions loyal to the rulers of Savoy; opposed to Savoy but loyal to the prince-bishop; and opposed to both (not least because many citizens desired to curtail the power and great wealth of the Church and be rid of "foreign clerics").[30] Substantial numbers of people were exiled as a result of ending up on the losing side; the victorious then almost immediately began to argue among themselves. The consequence of it all—and of ongoing fear of encroachment not only from Savoy but also from Protestant Bern (a notional ally) and Catholic France—was that the Geneva that John Calvin entered in his early years there was a city governed (although he did not yet know it) by "a newly established, but already faction-ridden, ruling elite extremely wary of foreigners and foreign domination, jealous of its liberties, surrounded by implacable foes and allies of dubious quality."[31] It was a Protestant city—but as much for pragmatic political and economic reasons as any other; its residents certainly could not overthrow a prince-bishop and expropriate Church finances and still hope to remain Catholic.

CALVIN IN GENEVA

Calvin's first encounter with Geneva was in 1536, when he made an intended over-night stop on the way (it seems) to Strasbourg. He was persuaded to stay longer by the Reformed pastor Guillaume Farel (1489–1565) in order to help "advance the Gospel" there.[32] It was not a very satisfactory sojourn and ended in 1538 with both men being exiled in the midst of "a lively debate over the role of the ministers and the degree of freedom and authority they were to have in the context of a much wider political dispute."[33] Geneva was not yet quite ready for Calvin's ideas about governance. For the next three years he found employment in Strasbourg. By 1541, however, the church in Geneva was in turmoil, and he was invited back to the city to restore both morale and order.

The Ecclesiastical Ordinances

The *Ecclesiastical Ordinances* agreed upon by Calvin and the city's Small Council (hereafter simply "Council") in the same year created a constitution that would govern both Church and republic in the future. This was one of many earnest moves made in the subsequent years with a view to transforming Geneva from a Catholic city governed by canon law into a Protestant city governed by Scripture. The *Ordinances* outline first the duties of pastors, doctors, elders, and deacons.[34] The tasks of the elders are particularly important in the context of our discussion in this chapter. First, they are "to watch over the life of each person, to admonish in a friendly manner those whom they see to be at fault and leading a disorderly life," before referring unheeding persons to the pastors. Secondly, they are to meet with the pastors once a week in a "Consistory," in order "to see whether there is any disorder in the Church and to consult together concerning remedies when necessary."[35] Attendance by Geneva's citizens when summoned to this Consistory is to be compulsory; if anyone "should refuse to appear," the council is to be informed "so that remedial steps may be taken." An obstinate person "should be admonished for a number of times until it becomes apparent that there is need of greater severity, and then he shall be forbidden the communion of the supper and denounced to the magistrate." Failing to attend church services or despising ecclesiastical order can also lead to admonition, and even (in the case of a recalcitrant person) to permanent excommunication and denunciation to the magistrate.

All this, the city councilors were careful to add to Calvin's draft, "must be done in such a way that the ministers have no civil jurisdiction" and that "there is no derogation by this Consistory from the authority of the Seigneury or the magistracy; but the civil power shall continue in its entirety." Yet it is clear that from the beginning the Consistory was designed by Calvin "to control the behavior of the entire population, to see to it that all Genevans not only accepted the new Reformed teachings set out in sermons and statutes but lived them in their daily lives," and where necessary suffered the consequences of failing to do so.[36]

The Reformation Consolidated

Within a few years Calvin had reshaped the pastorate in Geneva, producing a mainly French company possessing a "high level of learning, expertise, and quality."[37] The Consistory had a stable membership and was gaining traction, especially in holding the citizenry accountable for religious irregularities (magical practices, Roman Catholic practices, failing to attend church services, and errors in catechetical examinations).[38] The idea was by no means new in Geneva that there should be moral and legal accountability for sin, and certainly this idea did not originate with Calvin:

> Legislation against immorality predated the Reformation but specific laws were passed in February 1534 against blasphemy, two years later against blasphemy and card-playing, and by 1537 shops were ordered to be closed during the sermon [church service] hours ... In 1538 strict laws against immorality with heavy fines were passed, connecting, for the first time, morality offences with automatic, secular punishments.[39]

By the middle of the 1540s, nevertheless, "the Consistory was finally prepared to apply itself fully and vigorously to the control of Geneva's domestic life," and it did so with a level of commitment that provoked serious resistance among Genevans for a decade afterwards.[40] We know, for example, that in 1546 it dealt with 170 interpersonal disputes and 40 "public" disputes (rioting, disobedience to authority, and attacks on ministers or French immigrants), and in 1550 with 238 interpersonal and 66 public disputes.[41] "It penetrated life in almost all of its aspects in sixteenth-century Geneva."[42]

In line with the *Ordinances*, relatively insignificant cases would be dealt with by way of rebuke or exhortation; more significant ones by requiring public penitence, or by a ban from the next quarterly communion (a consequential matter in those days). This might be followed later by permanent excommunication (a controversial matter in the early years of Consistory operations).[43] The most serious cases proceeded to the magistrates, who were themselves concerned, independently, with policing both religion and morality in Geneva and could sanction infringements in various ways (e.g., fines, beatings, exile, imprisonment, and execution). For example, the prosecutions of Jérôme Bolsec in 1551 for attacking Calvin's views on predestination did not pass through the Consistory. Nor did that of Michael Servetus in 1553 for rejecting infant baptism and proclaiming that the Christian doctrine of the Trinity is not based on biblical teachings but on Greek philosophy.[44] These were the Council's initiatives, albeit with rather different outcomes—banishment for Bolsec and death for Servetus (the first execution in the city for heresy).[45]

From 1555 onwards, however, this distinction was a fuzzy one: the city by this point was clearly "Calvin's Geneva," inhabited by "a largely Calvinistic population" (including more French refugees), many exposed through education in their younger years "to a lengthy course . . . in Christian doctrine according to John Calvin" and now voting in city elections accordingly.[46] It had taken almost two decades since Calvin's return in 1541, but "[t]he consolidation of the Reformation in Geneva along lines consistent with Calvin's ideas of a godly state" was now complete, and the Consistory was at the height of its power.[47]

SEX AND MARRIAGE IN REFORMED GENEVA

Sex and marriage ranked highly among the concerns addressed by the reforming party in Geneva, both in law and practice. For example, in 1545 and again in 1546 Calvin presented to the magistrates a Marriage Ordinance that informed Consistory and Council deliberations throughout the immediately succeeding period, even though it was not formally adopted until later.[48] "Another long series of statutes governed public and private sexual morality," addressing "adultery, fornication, prostitution," as well as "public bathing, dressing, dancing, parties, dissolute songs, sumptuousness, and much more."[49] The records then reveal that "[w]ell over half of all the hundreds of cases heard by the Consistory each year concerned sexual and family issues," including "[a]dultery and fornication . . . incest, polygamy, rape, [and] sodomy."[50] The Consistory could be remarkably and officiously intrusive in all of this, although at the same time highly attentive to "the innocent, the needy, and the abused."[51] A great deal of its time was spent trying to arrange reconciliation among parties in dispute, and where punishment was handed down by the Consistory (or then by the magistrates) it could be relatively mild. However, sins and crimes considered to be serious—like prostitution, which had previously been tolerated in Geneva—were handled "with startling new severity."[52] Important in both forming statutes and dealing with cases was of course the Bible, to whose rules (especially those in the OT) Calvin and his colleagues "were inclined to give the force of law."[53] To that extent we may rightly say that Calvin's Geneva was not simply a godly republic but a specifically "Hebraic" one. In this chapter we shall take incest as our case study.

CONSANGUINITY AND AFFINITY

The canon law that preceded the Reformation already assumed that "men and women could not marry those who were related to them by blood or by marriage;"[54] there were many specific rules concerning these matters of "consanguinity" and "affinity," ultimately based to a significant degree on OT passages that had also been cited on such matters by the Church Fathers. These rules were embedded in a general philosophy of marriage that viewed it as a

> created, natural institution . . . subject to the law of nature, communicated in reason and conscience, and often confirmed in the Bible. This natural law . . . communicated God's will that fit persons marry when they reach the age of puberty, that they conceive children and nurture and educate them, that they remain naturally bonded to their blood and kin, serving them in times of need, frailty, and old age. It prescribed heterosexual, lifelong unions between a couple, featuring mutual support and faithfulness. It required love for one's spouse and children. It proscribed bigamy, incest, bestiality, buggery, polygamy, sodomy, and other unnatural relations.[55]

To marry in defiance of these rules was to commit incest, and incest was a serious matter (whether or *not* a marriage was involved). Protestant Reformers generally regarded this long list of medieval "incest impediments" as exceeding necessary bounds, and Calvin was no exception. He spent considerable time and energy in grounding a new approach to such questions in biblical and natural law and then translating it into Genevan law and practice. His core text in dealing with incest was Leviticus 18:6–18, where "Moses set out the blood and family ties that rendered sinful any sexual relations between parties."[56]

LEVITICUS 18

These verses form part of a passage that begins by urging the OT people of God not to follow the practices of the people "in Egypt, where you used to live" or "in the land of Canaan, where I am bringing you"; instead, they are exhorted to obey God's laws and "live by them" (Lev. 18:1–5). Before its final verses, which among other things require that those who break the laws "must be cut off from their people," the passage forbids a man from having sexual relations with a woman during her monthly period, with his neighbor's wife, with another man, or with an animal, and also from sacrificing any of his children to the god Molek (vv. 19–30). The rules about consanguinity and affinity are embedded between these bookends. They are headed by a general statement in verse 6, "[n]o one is to approach any close relative to have sexual relations," with the following verses apparently providing examples rather than an exhaustive list (e.g., a sexual relationship between a father and a daughter is not explicitly mentioned). A man may not have a sexual relationship with a woman who is or has been his father's wife, a prohibition that includes his mother (v. 7) but extends beyond that (v. 8)—since the father may have (or have had) more than one wife (cf. Lev. 20:11; Deut. 22:30; 27:20). Also prohibited are sexual relationships between a son and a full- or half-sister (v. 9) as well as "the daughter of your father's wife" (v. 11)—most likely a daughter from a former marriage adopted by the father. A father may not have a sexual relationship with a granddaughter (v. 10) or with a daughter-in-law (v. 15), and a son may not lie with an aunt (vv. 12–14). No one may have a sexual relationship with a sister-in-law (v. 16),[57] or with both a mother and her daughter or granddaughter (v. 17). Finally, a man may not marry his wife's sister while his wife is still living; this law of course explicitly presupposes the practice of polygamy in these ancient times.

THE MARRIAGE ORDINANCE (1546)

The Marriage Ordinance of 1546 is based on these examples but also broadens the definition of incest to include other sexual relations. For example, "[f]athers and mothers were newly prohibited from relationships with their stepdaughters and stepsons"; forbidden also was "marriage between a man and his brother's widow . . . between a woman and her sister's widower . . . . [and] between parties who had earlier committed adultery with each other."[58] First cousins were also prohibited from marrying. In defence of such additions Calvin mainly deployed (as we might expect) the concept of natural law. The impediments in Leviticus represented "the core of God's law . . . and they could not be breached under any circumstances." But at the same time they were "specific illustrations of a more general principle of natural law . . . that direct and collateral relatives and their parents, their spouses, and their children could not marry."[59] This is evident from the fact that "other ancient legal systems, particularly the pre-Christian Roman law, had adopted a similar set of impediments."[60]

INCEST IN GENEVA

Incest was such a serious matter in Calvinist Geneva (as it had been in the High Middle Ages) that when it was committed intentionally people could be executed. Most cases, where the evidence was clear, went directly to the Council. The Consistory only dealt with instances where incest was merely suspected; sometimes it came across the infraction in the course of other inquiries. In a case like that of the widow Antoine Chapuis in 1556, for example, the accused was confronted with evidence that she had had sexual intercourse with her nephew. She admitted that he did often stay at her home but denied wrongdoing. Under strong suspicion, she was sternly admonished about the scandal that their conduct had caused, but no further action was taken. By contrast, in 1557 Andre Duplot was brought before the Consistory for having sex with his widowed aunt, Jeanne Court. She also admitted that he had stayed with her, but both denied wrongdoing. They were not believed, and the Consistory, ordering them to stop spending the night together, sent them to the Council, which fined and imprisoned them. A potentially more serious outcome awaited Jeanne Marcellin in 1556. She confessed to having committed adulterous incest (i.e., while married) with her husband's brother—a capital offence. Indicted before the Council, she was instructed "to kneel in the Council chamber to beg for God's mercy and justice," and she did; "the Council chose to banish her from Geneva and ordered her not to return, on pain of whipping."[61]

THE HERMENEUTICS OF SEX AND MARRIAGE

The reader who has digested the Christian political philosophy briefly outlined at the end of our fifth chapter will have already guessed, no doubt—given my advocacy there of substantial freedom on the part of the ruled to govern themselves and of restraint in coercion—that I am not a great fan of everything that the Reforming party in sixteenth-century Geneva said and did. To be sure, much good was accomplished, as John Calvin's "comprehensive new theology and jurisprudence . . . made marital formation and dissolution, children's nurture and welfare, family cohesion and support, and sexual sin and crime essential concerns for both church and state."[62] It is a tribute to his success that "a good number of these reforms have found their way into our modern civil law and common law traditions."[63] Yet the cost in terms of human freedom was high, and whether the repression of liberty by endless statutes concerning such matters as "public bathing, dressing, dancing, parties, dissolute songs, sumptuousness, and much more" could ever in reality advance the kingdom of God by any great distance is a good question.[64]

In this chapter with its limited space, however, I do not intend to discuss further aspects of public life in Calvin's Geneva; we shall return to a broader discussion of questions of freedom and coercion in chapter 11. I am much more interested in this chapter in the narrower ethical question. Leaving city and state aside, what reason is there to think that a chapter like Leviticus 18 might have something to say to *the NT people of God themselves* (the Church) about sexual and marital relationships? After all, the NT itself is "virtually silent on the subject of impediments" that occupied so much of John Calvin's energy in this area.[65] Does this not indicate that Calvin must have been very wide of the mark in his assessment of the importance of Leviticus 18 for the Christian life?

First, it is true that the NT is "virtually silent on the subject of impediments." The exceptions are significant, however. The first passage of relevance is Matthew 14:3–4: "Now Herod [Antipas] had arrested John and bound him and put him in prison because of Herodias, his brother Philip's wife, for John had been saying to him: 'It is not lawful for you to have her.'" Three of the four Gospel writers (also Mark 6:17–18; Luke 3:19) refer to this marriage in apparent agreement with John the Baptist's assessment. The basis for the criticism is Leviticus 18:16, which instructs: "Do not have sexual relations with your brother's wife" (also Lev. 20:21). This example comes from before Pentecost, of course; but post-Pentecost, secondly, the apostle Paul also alludes to Leviticus in addressing the church in Corinth about a particular relationship in their own midst: "It is actually reported that there is sexual immorality [Gk. *porneia*] among you . . . A man is sleeping with his father's wife" (1 Cor. 5:1). "The body," he will shortly go on to say of a different matter, "is not meant for sexual immorality but for the Lord, and the Lord for the body" (6:13); the Corinthians should "flee" from such immorality (6:18). The term *porneia* is a generic one, covering all kinds of illicit sexual intercourse, but incest is the focus in 1 Corinthians 5, as in Leviticus 18:8, which commands, "do not have sexual relations with your father's wife." This is something, Paul maintains to the Corinthians, "that even pagans do not tolerate."[66] The Christians in Corinth, building their lives on the biblical tradition, should likewise abhor it, and indeed they should "put out of your fellowship the man who has been doing this" (1 Cor. 5:2). This appears to be an interpretation of what is said in Leviticus 18:29—that the lawbreaker should be "cut off from his people." Whether the Christians in Corinth are required by the apostle to do anything more than this to their wayward brother is a question to which we shall return in chapter 8.

From this it appears that there is certainly apostolic warrant for believing that an OT passage like Leviticus 18 has continuing relevance for the NT people of God—that at least a number of its rules are not of the kind represented by the tithing regulations discussed in chapter 5 but represent rather some of the wisdom of the ages that is important for all, and not only some people.

It is important to notice, in relation to this, that when the early apostolic leaders gathered in council in Jerusalem in Acts 15 and were making their initial decisions about how far OT Torah still applied to Gentiles, they summed up their reflections in a letter in this way: "You are to abstain from food sacrificed to idols, from blood, from the meat of strangled animals, and from sexual immorality [*porneia*]" (Acts 15:29). This apostolic concern that all Christians should avoid such sexual immorality is often in evidence in the remainder of the NT. Second Corinthians 12:21, for example, speaks about those who "have not repented of . . . impurity, sexual sin [*porneia*], and debauchery"; Galatians 5:19 lists among the acts of the flesh "sexual immorality [*porneia*], impurity, and debauchery"; and Ephesians 5:3 urges that "among you there must not be even a hint of sexual immorality [*porneia*], or of any kind of impurity, or of greed, because these are improper for God's holy people."[67] Gentiles, and not only Jews, must be holy in such matters. These rules pertain not only to God's specially called people in OT times but to all people—all of God's image bearers, in the language of Genesis 1, through all of time. They are aspects of creational law.

Insofar as Leviticus 18 also reflects this same law, then of course it will be "useful" for Christians in directing us toward a holy life—in this case, specifically in the realm of sex and marriage. Certainly the OT is elsewhere in the NT generally recognized as having important things to say about such matters (e.g., Eph. 5:31, referring back to Gen. 2:24).

ETERNAL IMPEDIMENTS?

This creational law comes to expression in Leviticus 18, of course, in the midst of Mosaic Torah. And this brings up a question that Calvin himself prompts in the *Institutes* but does not sufficiently consider (in my view) in dealing with an OT passage like this one. Granted that there is good reason to think that at least *some* of the rules in Leviticus 18 represent creational law—and even in increasingly pagan post-Christendom it is still probably true that the majority of people would regard sexual intercourse between a son and his mother, or between a human and an animal (Lev. 18:23), as wrong—is it safe simply to assume that *all of them* do? Surely it is clear, to the contrary, that at least to some extent—as the reference to offering children as sacrifices to the god Molek suggests, for example (18:21)—they have more to do with the specifically Israelite context in which this ancient people is to differentiate itself from both the Egyptians and the Canaanites, lest the Promised Land "vomit you out as it vomited out the nations that were before you" (Lev. 18:28). So is it necessarily true that all the "impediments" in Leviticus represent "the core of God's law" and cannot "be breached under any circumstances"?[68] If they are at least partially addressed directly to the circumstances in which ancient Israel found itself (including the environmental reality of polygamy, for example), and those circumstances have changed—what then? After all, by this point in the biblical Story Abraham has already married his half-sister Sarah (Gen. 20:12) in what is the founding marriage of Israel. Moses himself is the product of a marriage between a man and his aunt (Exod. 6:27). There have already been "breaches under . . . circumstances."

Calvin's own thinking about the OT Torah as expressed in the *Institutes* allows for this kind of question about discontinuity in the midst of continuity to be pressed. Aware that there are people in his own time who believe that God's law should simply be obeyed by Christians "as written"—who say that "the law of God given through Moses is dishonored when it is abrogated and new laws preferred to it"—Calvin counters by arguing that there is no such dishonor when a "law is abrogated which was never enacted for us" in the first place.[69] The moral law is eternal, but how it is expressed in judicial (positive) law will always depend on circumstances: for example, "[t]here are countries which, unless they deal cruelly with murderers by way of horrible examples, must immediately perish from slaughters and robberies," and others "inclined to a particular vice, unless it be most sharply repressed."[70] How the moral law is expressed at particular times and in particular places will depend upon such factors, for "the Lord through the hand of Moses did not give that law to be proclaimed among all nations and to be in force everywhere."[71] Each nation is "free to make such laws as it foresees to be profitable for itself," just so long as they are "in conformity to [the] perpetual rule of love [of God and neighbor], so that they indeed vary in form but have the same purpose."[72]

We need to recognize, then, that some of the examples given in Leviticus 18 in terms of not approaching "any close relative to have sexual relations" might have made great sense in an ancient Israelite context in the Promised Land but might not make as much sense outside that context. They represent instances in which God's creational law "touches down" in Israelite society in particular ways that no longer pertain to us (see our chapter 3). We may understand them, perhaps, as contributing greatly to the stability of the extended ancient family by placing certain relationships decisively off-limits—by making them inconceivable, in fact—for family members. Yet we must also ask whether they are needed in circumstances, for example, where extended families are no longer the norm. In other words, we need to consider, in Calvin's own terms, whether some of these rules are of the kind that enable God's OT people to "live together blamelessly and peaceably" in their own historical moment but are not of permanent validity.[73] This frees us, then, in this area of consanguinity and affinity (for instance), not only to set aside the particular rules that no longer appear to make sense to us as we now read the great biblical Story but also to create others that are "profitable" for us in this matter of close relatives and sexual relations. On the one hand, for example, it is not entirely clear why Christians should consider marriage to a dead brother's wife as being intrinsically wrong. On the other hand, Leviticus 18 does not explicitly forbid the marriage of first cousins—but knowing what we now know about the consequences that can sometimes follow from such marriages, we might well agree with Calvin (albeit not for the same reasons) that we should not enter such marriages.[74]

CONCLUSION

These caveats having been entered, however, there is certainly ample Scriptural warrant for believing that the Church ought to attend to the OT in its pursuit of the good life with respect to sexual ethics (including in the area of incest)—not least in how it handles a *lack* of holiness in its midst. For just as it is generally true that "any community of values has a systemic aspect which needs to be maintained by some principle of internal 'order' or 'discipline' if its boundaries are not to disintegrate,"[75] it remains the case in NT as in OT times (as we saw in 1 Cor. 5) that at least in some circumstances God's people must protect the community by removing individuals who persist in rejecting Christian norms of sexual behavior. John Calvin was justified, then, in his view that the OT has something to say to the Church about sex, even if he was not always right in his assessment of *what* the OT teaches about sex.

DISCUSSION QUESTIONS

1. What do you think of John Calvin's view of the purpose of civil government? Is it biblical?
2. Was Calvin wise in his general approach to creating a godly Christian society in which sex was closely monitored? Would you like to see a Consistory established in your hometown? Why or why not?
3. Read Leviticus 18:22. Is this an aspect of God's creational law that still applies to us, or something else? Give reasons, rather than sharing feelings.
4. Read Leviticus 19:19. Are these aspects of God's creational law that still apply to us, or something else? Give reasons, rather than sharing preferences.

8
Apocalypse Now
The New Jerusalem in Münster

It is as if this [sound evangelical] doctrine looked to no other end than to wrest the
scepters from the hands of kings, to cast down all courts and judgments, to subvert all
orders and civil governments, to disrupt the peace and quiet of the people, to abolish
all laws, to scatter all lordships and possessions—in short, to turn everything upside
down![1]

John Calvin

John Calvin's thinking about the nature of the godly society was not formed in a vacuum. In fact, on more than one occasion in his *Institutes* he himself mentions one of the environmental factors impacting upon it: the Anabaptist rebellion in the German city of Münster in 1534–1535. As the excerpt in the epigraph above from his prefatory address to King Francis I already makes clear, it is one of Calvin's explicit purposes in writing his work that his own kind of reformism should not be confused with this other one that turns "everything upside down." As the modern editor of the *Institutes* rightly notes, "Calvin undoubtedly continued to feel the importance of stating a positive conception of politics as a part of his apologetic for the Reformation, and as a practical defense of the doctrines asserted throughout the treatise."[2] It is to this Münster rebellion that we now turn in the present chapter. In order fully to understand it, though, we must again backtrack a little, to the centuries just prior to the Reformation.

APOCALYPTIC EXPECTATION

We noted in chapter 6 the way in which the First Crusade in the late eleventh century was conducted in the midst of apocalyptic expectation in many quarters. This expectation continued to mark reformist thinking in the Western Church in the twelfth century.[3] In Brett Whalen's view, "the latest and greatest reformist apocalyptic thinker of the twelfth century" was Abbot Joachim of Fiore (1105–1202)—a man who claimed "to have privileged insights into the Bible and the meaning of history."[4]

Joachim developed earlier Christian ideas concerning the seven ages of history in a novel manner, dividing the sixth age (in which he believed he lived) into subages marked by the opening of the seven seals of the biblical book of Revelation. The opening of the sixth seal was imminent, and the sixth age would thereafter last only two generations more. It would be a time of tribulation in the Church, marked by a struggle against the Antichrist, but also a time in which the Jewish people would turn to Christ and "the Greeks, who had fallen into heresy through their own rejection of Roman doctrine and authority, would undergo their own form of conversion to the more spiritual faith of Rome, the 'new Jerusalem.'"[5]

This New Jerusalem is much more important to Joachim than the old one. The First Crusade and the capture of the physical Jerusalem are of no significance in his scheme; indeed, he felt "the effort to liberate Jerusalem was misguided."[6] When the OT prophesies about a "land" that is to be reoccupied by God's people, he believes it refers not to the "arid province of Canaan . . . but more so to the universal Church."[7] However, before the coming of the final "Sabbath Age," "the corruption and decadence of Rome" would itself become evident."[8] The Antichrist, who had already been born in Rome, would in fact one day become pope."[9]

All of this would precede the seventh age, which Joachim saw as part of history and prior to the Last Judgment. It is correlated in his thinking to the third "status" in history, in which we move from the time of the Father and then the Son into the time of the Holy Spirit, when people will live in the liberty of the Spirit alone. The precursors to these "spiritual men" are the medieval orders of monks; the regular, more "carnal" clergy belong firmly in the "status" of the Son. The position of the bishop of Rome in this scenario is ambiguous:

> In his *Tract on the Four Gospels*, the abbot seemed to flirt with the idea that the Roman papacy would somehow pass away when the monastic order assumed a place of priority over the clerical order. For the most part, however, Joachim appeared to envision a continued rule for the "spiritualized" papacy in the coming Sabbath age . . . "the universal pontiff of the New Jerusalem."[10]

The first idea, nevertheless—associating "spiritual men" with a New Jerusalem soon to appear and distinguishing them from a largely corrupt Church—was to prove a potent one in the succeeding centuries.

RADICAL POSSIBILITIES

The radical possibilities in Joachim's ideas were not at first much developed. Pope Innocent III, for example, was able to absorb the abbot's insights into his own worldview without great difficulty, "reading" Joachim in a way that allowed for the sack of Constantinople in 1204 by the soldiers of the Fourth Crusade to be a providentially designed event within the ongoing framework of papal authority. This authority was much extended by Innocent's immediate successors.[11]

THE SPIRITUAL AND THE CARNAL

With the Church's recognition of the Franciscan (1209) and Dominican (1216) monastic orders, however, it became natural as the thirteenth century progressed to associate these monks with the "truly 'spiritual men' of Joachite schemes [who] would take the lead in renovating the Roman Church and extending the word of Christ to the peoples of the world under the auspices of a purified papacy."[12] Apocalyptic thinkers grew bolder at the same time in criticizing not only contemporary clergy in general but also the contemporary papacy specifically—even as notable Franciscan and Dominicans tried to rein them in. For example, on the one hand Gerard of Borgo San Donnino taught that the NT would be rendered null and void in the year 1260 and that "the 'carnal' Church of the NT would be superseded with the coming of a more spiritual age," with a "sterile clerical order" giving way to "the monastic order and its more spiritual form of living."[13] On the other hand, the Dominican Thomas Aquinas returned to the older Augustinian view that no one could gain "specific and privileged knowledge of future events" from Scripture. He disputed both the idea that there would be within history a "transformative spiritual age" and the notion that "the apocalypse was imminent." The Gospel must yet reach all the peoples of the world. The Franciscan Bonaventure likewise denied "any future dispensation of the Holy Spirit."[14] By the beginning of the fourteenth century, nevertheless, we encounter "a flood of increasingly subversive prophetic literature, much of which favored the Spiritual position and condemned ... opponents, including the current popes in Rome."[15]

The Avignon papacy and the subsequent papal schism did nothing to improve the situation. Joachim's scheme was serially reworked: new identifications of historical heroes and villains were arrived at, and new dates established for the end of the sixth age. The recent popes of Rome (or Avignon) do not typically come out of these apocalyptic exercises well. Instead, *Jerusalem* begins to emerge as the seat of "the highest pontiff" who arises after the Antichrist. For example, in the work of the Spanish Franciscan John of Rupescissa (writing around the middle of the fourteenth century), "[t]he center of the Christian world, transferred to Rome by Saint Peter, would be transferred once again back to Jerusalem, where it would remain for one thousand years."[16]

In fact, more and more inhabitants of Europe were coming to "imagine the expansion of their faith without the claims of papal monarchy to universal dominion."[17] When at the close of the fifteenth century the Dominican Girolamo Savonarola "predicted a coming age of spiritual renewal, he located the centre of this new world order not in Rome or even in Jerusalem but rather in the city-state of Florence."[18] In this apocalyptic way of thinking, the New Jerusalem could now potentially be any "truly Christian" community. Indeed, in a "transformative spiritual age" governed by a "new law of the Holy Spirit," it could also take any *shape*. For if Calvin's godly city was premised on the conviction that the spiritual life still had to be lived in an enduringly imperfect world of the flesh where "wickedness [is] . . . stubborn"[19]—and therefore that it must be governed by God's age-old law—it was open to apocalyptic "spiritualists," who believed that they were living in a new age, to take a very different view.

FREE SPIRITS

So it is that the radical potentialities in Joachim's ideas were developed in a particular way in northern Europe, for example, by the "Brethren of the Free Spirit"—a collective way of referring to a mysticism that "tended towards a form of speculative pantheism," whose adherents "apparently believed that they could be entirely liberated from conventional moral norms through attaining perfect union with God and were accused in particular of sexual profligacy."[20] Nicholas of Basel, for example, was ultimately burnt at the stake as a heretic in Vienna in the last decade of the fourteenth century for (among other things) demanding "obedience from his followers, whom he could release from their obedience to the Church into a state of primal innocence."[21] The accusations of sexual libertinism directed at such mystics must of course be treated with caution, since "[a]gain and again, over a period of many centuries, heretical sects were accused of holding promiscuous and incestuous orgies in the dark" and indulging in other similar horrors, and it is not likely that this was always, or even often, the case.[22] Nevertheless, it is not unreasonable to suppose that some people who believed themselves "to have attained a state of total oneness with God, in which all things were permitted to them," would have acted on these beliefs with respect to all kinds of societal norms, sexual and otherwise.[23]

The violence that could arise in communities released in this way from ancient moral obligations in a spiritual age is well-illustrated by the fifteenth-century

Taborites—"so called from their fortified stronghold south of Prague to which they gave the OT name of Mount Tabor."[24] A radical arm of the Hussite reform movement in Bohemia, they were proto-Protestant in many of their beliefs, insisting on receiving communion in both kinds (bread and wine) while denying transubstantiation, replacing the Latin with a Czech liturgy, endorsing married clergy, and rejecting all the sacraments with the exception of Baptism and the Eucharist. They were also marked by the crusading mentality that we have already described in chapter 6 and at the beginning of chapter 7—but now set free from its Roman context. With the last days on the horizon, their duty as they saw it was to eradicate sin. Internally, this meant a return to a classless society, with everything held in common (including wives, since there is no marriage in God's kingdom, Matt. 22:30). Externally, this meant fighting battles, sacking churches and monasteries, and destroying libraries (since when the kingdom of God arrives, "no longer will they teach their neighbor, or say to one another, 'Know the LORD,' because they will all know me, from the least of them to the greatest," Jer. 31:34). These violent activities aroused widespread hostility among their neighbors, however, and the Taborite army was defeated decisively in 1452.[25] Allegedly some of their number, the "Adamites," took primal innocence to its logical conclusion and went around naked much of the time, imitating the original state of Adam and Eve. In the new age, when existing ecclesiastical institutions were to be overthrown on the way to a pure, biblical Church, that which had once been wicked was no longer necessarily so.

RADICAL MÜNSTER

This is the broader background against which we must set the events of the Anabaptist rebellion in Münster. The narrower background is the rise of the Anabaptist movement in general. Its name already reveals one of its adherents' most important distinctives: they rejected infant, and practiced adult baptism (which meant, from an outsider's perspective, that they practiced a *second* baptism—thus "*Ana*baptist," from the Greek). Since infant baptism in Europe at this time was also one's point of entry into an established political community, Anabaptists were understood to be repudiating loyalty to any such community—which in terms of primary loyalty, indeed, they were. For they believed that the Church, as a community of believers who had voluntarily and actively confessed their faith, stood apart from the established state. They refused to swear oaths to civil authorities, therefore, and mostly opposed the use of coercive measures (including war) to maintain the social order. For such reasons they were rigorously persecuted by both Protestant and Roman Catholic states—which confirmed to them that they were indeed faithful Christians of the kind first persecuted by the Roman state

for many of the same reasons. They often saw this persecution, in fact, as evidence
that they were living in the end times.

THE MELCHIORITES

The Anabaptist communities that arose out of this ferment were of various
kinds,[26] but crucial to this part of our narrative is the German mystic Melchior
Hofmann (1495–1543). Hofmann established a large following in the Netherlands in the early 1530s for his teaching that the world would soon end (in 1533)
and that the new age would begin in the city of Strasbourg (the New Jerusalem, of course). He ultimately died in prison in that city, rejected by his fellow
Anabaptists and having failed to see his vision materialize. Two of his disciples,
however, are particularly important for what happened next in Münster, three
hundred miles to the north. Here an originally peaceful, nonviolent Anabaptist
community had absorbed into its midst in 1533–1534 thousands of other, persecuted Anabaptists, including many "Melchiorites" from the Netherlands. Among
these were Jan van Leiden and Jan Matthijs. The position of the Anabaptists
in Münster was much strengthened at the beginning of 1534 when Franz von
Waldeck, the prince-bishop of Münster, Osnabrück, and Minden, tried to regain
control of the city by force.[27] He had previously granted religious freedom to the
city and had hitherto regarded the Anabaptists as rather innocent, peaceable people. His intervention had the effect of bringing the city council behind the Anabaptists, whom the prince-bishop had wanted exiled:

> Soon baptism replaced the civic oath as the constitutional basis for Münster's soci-
> ety. Furthermore, the Anabaptists demanded the voluntary surrender of property
> [i.e., a radical community of goods]. From the middle of February, the stream of
> Anabaptist refugees to Münster increased. When the election of the council took
> place on 23 February 1534 according to the old statutes, the radical party won.[28]

As a result, Jan Matthijs became the city's principal leader. To many of its inhabitants, Münster (rather than Strasbourg) was now the New Jerusalem, and they
hoped that within its walls they might "escape the last day of judgment [now]
expected on Easter 1534"—the date prophesied by Matthijs himself.[29]

JAN MATTHIJS

Jan Matthijs did not hesitate to employ violence in pursuit of his goals; he was
indeed, in the words of the Dutch Anabaptist leader Obbe Philips (1500–1568),
a man "so fierce and bloodthirsty that he brought various people to their deaths;
yea he was so violent that even his enemies for their part were terrified of him."[30]
Two days after the election that brought him to power he proclaimed that, in
order to build the kingdom of Christ on earth, it was necessary to purify the city

of all "uncleanness"—that is, of all those who dissented from Anabaptist teachings. This new "crusader" meant indeed to execute all the Lutherans and Roman Catholics who had not yet fled. A compromise was reached, however, as a result of which these latter were either exiled from the city or forced to accept adult baptism.

Von Waldeck responded by laying siege to Münster—an assault that was in turn regarded inside the city as "the final apocalyptic confrontation between the evil powers of the fallen world and God's new creation"—between Christ and Antichrist.[31] Münster's inhabitants prepared for the end by cutting all ties to earthly life—burning all books except the Bible and destroying "all documents representing the former political and spiritual dominion"—and by summoning others from abroad to join them as members of "the 144,000 elect ... [who] should gather to start the conquest of the entire world in preparation for the coming millennium."[32] When Easter 1534 arrived, Jan Matthijs—responding to what he believed to be a divine command—charged out of the city against the besieging army with only a small group of supporters (a veritable biblical Gideon); he was killed. His enemies were in fact "so incensed that they did not just kill him ... but hacked and chopped him into little pieces."[33]

JAN VAN LEIDEN

Undaunted, Jan van Leiden took over the leadership, replacing the city council with twelve "Israelite" elders who published a new code of law, tightening up the rules about community of goods and introducing draconian punishments for sin—the death penalty, for example, for scolding one's parents, adultery, spreading scandal, or complaining.[34] In July of 1534 van Leiden tried to introduce polygamy in Münster (or more precisely, polygyny, permitting the men to take more than one wife but not vice versa). This resulted in significant internal opposition and the execution of numerous dissenters. Polygyny then became mandatory (on the basis of the OT examples of people like Abraham), and all females twelve years and older were forced to marry. "Leading by example, [van Leiden himself] eventually married a total of sixteen women."[35]

At the end of August a monarchy was introduced, on the basis of OT teaching that in the last days God would appoint a king who would have universal dominion. Van Leiden himself called a town meeting to announce the news: "Now God has chosen me to be king over the entire world. What I do, I must do, because God has ordained me."[36] With this, "Münster became a 'Davidic theocracy' in charge of the apocalyptic crusade against the unbelievers."[37] The idea came straight out of Melchior Hoffman's teaching "that the 'godless' would be purged before the final judgment" and that Christ's Second Coming would follow the emergence of "a second Solomon, who would prepare the earth for Christ's arrival." [38] As the Davidic king who would therefore rule the earth until this Second Coming, van Leiden

> set up a grand household with an extraordinary royal suite and a wide array of court officials. His jewelry and stately attire, his royal insignia . . . bespoke his claim to world dominion . . . two swords symbolized the spiritual and secular powers he united . . . [he] had new coins minted with inscriptions that reflected his aspirations to rule the world. [39]

By late fall, "Münster was fighting not only the bishop and the neighboring [Lutheran and Catholic] princes; the Anabaptists' daring enterprise had rallied the entire empire against them." [40] Food began to run out, and increasing numbers deserted. Van Leiden remained optimistic, predicting the liberation of the city on Easter 1535. This date came and went as well, however, and Münster finally fell on June 25 of that year. Many died. The leaders were brutalized and executed on January 22, 1536, and their corpses exhibited in metal baskets that can still be seen to this day hanging from Münster's St. Lambert's Church. [41]

ANABAPTISM AFTER MÜNSTER

Against the background of the Peasants' War in 1524–1525, the Anabaptist "kingdom" of Münster, although short-lived, aroused much anxiety in a Europe already in turmoil as a result of the Reformation more generally. Reform was one thing, and revolution another. Paradoxically, then, "the experience of 'Münster' acted in the end as a profoundly stabilizing factor" in Europe; the reprobates, everyone agreed, "threatened the cohesion of the family, the principles of the economy, and the political hierarchy," and must be stopped. [42] Where there was an unwillingness to distinguish "Münsterites" in particular from Anabaptists in general, this was particularly bad news for the latter. The whole movement could easily be characterized as the common enemy inside the Holy Roman Empire—the mirror image of the Ottoman Turks on the outside—whom many agreed in the midst of their own confessional differences were a threat to peace and good order.

CONTINUING TERROR

The Anabaptist cause was not helped in this respect by the ongoing violence of groups like those led by Jan van Batenburg and his successors in the Netherlands. Van Batenburg was also regarded by his followers as a new David, and he too believed in the illegitimacy of property law, in polygyny, and in the use of coercive force to achieve his ends. In particular, killing "infidels" (non-Anabaptists) was pleasing to God, and so was taking them on as servants of the Anabaptist elite. Indeed, this was regarded as the only way in which non-Anabaptists could survive the coming apocalypse, since after the events at Münster they could never now be baptized; that window of opportunity had closed.[43]

MENNO AND MÜNSTER

In reality, however, mainstream Anabaptism followed a very different course from this crusading "Münsterism" in the years after 1535. This is well-illustrated in the life and work of the Anabaptist leader Menno Simons, from whom the Mennonites take their name.[44] Menno preached openly against the Münster rebellion from its beginning and produced a tract (unpublished in his lifetime) *On the Blasphemy of John Leiden*, apparently in response to the enthronement of van Leiden as messianic king on August 31, 1534.[45] He rejected physical violence as the means by which to realize the kingdom of God; the New Jerusalem cannot be built by human will and force. He was particularly outraged by van Leiden's claim to be the Messiah: "Christ was and is the only Messiah, the fulfillment of the promises of the Old Testament."[46] Further, Scripture teaches that no one knows when Christ will return. Van Leiden was a false prophet, misinterpreting Scripture and leading Menno's brothers and sisters in Münster astray.

This distance between Menno and the Münsterites becomes increasingly visible in his later writings. While never repudiating "the early peaceful phase of the magisterial Anabaptist reformation of Münster," his critique of van Leiden's concept of the New Jerusalem is consistently scathing, and all attempts to associate it with Menno's Anabaptism are resisted.[47] God's kingdom does become a visible reality on earth in the present world, but it is "defined by Christ himself ... His way as the suffering servant became the unsurpassed way of life for all." For Menno, then, "[a]s long as heaven and earth exist, there will be no other." The Münsterite kingdom was "an aberration without any biblical foundation, for only by following Christ's way of suffering love could believers participate in the anticipation of God's kingdom."[48] This ongoing apologetic was entirely necessary, because a full sixteen years after the fall of Münster, in 1551,

[t]he main accusations against Menno and his followers ... were still that they were Münsterites, rebels eager to take over cities and lands, that they practiced sharing their wives as well as their possessions, that they claimed to have reached perfection, and that they taught that salvation can be gained by merit.[49]

Menno rejects these accusations, appealing to his critics to understand that he "and his brothers and sisters [are] not Münsterites but sincere Christians who seek only the Christian way of life and peace."[50] These appeals gained some traction:

Menno's major success in the 1550s seems to have been the recognition of his radical disassociation from Münster by many well-disposed German citizens and magistrates. Finally they recognized the peacefulness and harmlessness of the pious followers of Menno Simons, whose growing quietism in the anticipation of the New Jerusalem no longer posed a threat to worldly kingdoms.[51]

THE HERMENEUTICS OF PUNISHMENT: THE PENTATEUCH

There are all kinds of interesting connections between this chapter and preceding ones. Here again in the case of Münster we see the powerful attraction of King David and his future son to Christian leaders conceiving of their domain as a new Israel—or, as in this case, a New Jerusalem. The OT, as often beforehand, is the basis for the abolition of previous law and the enactment of new law. All of this is bound up with apocalyptic expectation. The "reforms" of the moment are given a particularly important, crusading edge in the light of what is expected imminently to occur. Sin must be expunged and sinners confronted, because the end is nigh—and, in fact, so as to bring that end still closer.

In the remainder of this chapter I want to examine one recurring and important issue in our travels that we have thus far largely passed over but which ought to be a matter of serious interest to the Christian who is committed to the search for what is right—to reading OT Scripture "for life." It is starkly on display in the story of Münster. I proposed in chapter 5 that all governed communities wishing to flourish will have some need of coercive measures (punishment) in order to deal with people who break the laws set in place by governments in pursuit of their goals. If this premise is granted, though, what are we to make of the widespread assumption in Christendom, throughout the period from Constantine to Jan van Leiden and his opponents, that appropriate coercion in pursuit of the common good in Church and society includes the use of execution?

SIN AND DEATH IN GENESIS 1–9

The sixth of the Ten Commandments enjoins us not to kill (Hb. *ratsakh*, Exod. 20:13). As its wider literary context demonstrates, however, it does not thereby forbid all instances of taking a life.[52] Its intent is actually to place a prohibition against premeditated, illegitimate killing (murder) right at the heart of God's creational law, among the other actions that are identified in the Ten Commandments as always and everywhere wrong (adultery, stealing, and so on).

The serious nature of this sin has already been announced early on in the biblical narrative, in Genesis 4:1–16—long before we get to Mosaic Torah. Here Cain murders his brother Abel (Gen. 4:1–16), whose blood "cries out to [God] from the ground" for vengeance (v. 10). It is in the close context of this story that we get our first biblical allusion to death as an appropriate punishment for a crime. It is found in Genesis 9, looking back to Genesis 1: "And from each human being, too, I will demand an accounting for the life of another human being. Whoever sheds human blood, by humans shall their blood be shed; for in the image of God has God made mankind" (9:5–6). We already discussed this idea of image bearing in chapter 3. Each image-bearing life is precious—and the one who destroys it by murder will be in serious trouble with its Creator. God "will demand an accounting for the life" of this other human being, and this accounting will be in terms of a life for a life: "Whoever sheds human blood, by humans shall their blood be shed." This is something that God will do in respect of every life, and not just an Israelite life. It is a universal law.

I have chosen to write "allusion to death" in the previous paragraph quite deliberately, however. Certainly death is envisaged as an appropriate punishment for murder in this passage, in which equity is the central concern (a life for a life). However, the manner in which this punishment is to be enacted is far from clear: "by humans shall their blood be shed" allows for more than one possibility. Are we to think of general providence, whereby the murderer's sins catch up with him and he "gets what he deserves" in terms of how his life works out—a kind of "poetic justice" ("all who draw the sword will die by the sword," Matt. 26:52)? Or are we to see here a reference to officially sanctioned human authority—for instance, the "avenger of blood" within Israelite society, who was a close relative of the deceased tasked with the duty of exacting retribution (e.g., Num. 35:11–28)? We are given no explicit answer to these questions in Genesis 9. When Christians have read this passage as unequivocally justifying the death penalty within human judicial systems, then, they have been guilty of over-reading.

When they have gone on to insist that Genesis 9 demonstrates that only the death penalty is *appropriate* in cases of premeditated murder, they have then been guilty of a further reading mistake: they have failed to read the passage in context. For in Genesis 4, the God who later declares that "whoever sheds human blood, by humans shall their blood be shed" does nothing to bring about this outcome in the case of Cain. God does not put the murderer to death, nor does he urge any human authority to do so; instead, Cain is sent into exile. Moreover, in exile God looks after him, promising that "anyone who kills Cain will suffer vengeance seven times over" (v. 15). He even puts "a mark" on Cain so that no one who finds him will kill him. In other words, God goes out of his way to *prevent* other human beings from exacting blood in revenge for the blood of Abel.

What we should rightly deduce from Genesis 1–9, then, is this: murder is a terrible sin—the destruction of a divine image bearer—for which the perpetrator deserves to die. It is not yet clear who has the authority to kill him, however, and the question has been raised as to whether any human authority constituted by

God, and seeking to be "like God" in an image-bearing capacity, should always (or even often) actually do the killing.

THE DEATH PENALTY IN MOSAIC LAW

When we eventually encounter the Mosaic Torah in the course of the biblical Story, we now find—already within the narrative concerning the initial law giving in Exodus 20–23—that human authorities are explicitly authorized to carry out executions for murder within ancient Israelite society. In Exodus 21:12–14 we read that "[a]nyone who strikes a person with a fatal blow is to be put to death," except if it is done unintentionally. Leviticus 24:17–20 underlines the equity that still lies at the heart of the matter, placing murder within a much broader context:

> Anyone who takes the life of a human being is to be put to death. Anyone who takes the life of someone's animal must make restitution—life for life. Anyone who injures their neighbor is to be injured in the same manner: fracture for fracture, eye for eye, tooth for tooth. The one who has inflicted the injury must suffer the same injury.

Here the pre-Mosaic principle of Genesis 9 is enshrined in a judicial context: societal retribution in respect of death or injury is to be proportionate to the offence. "Poetic justice" (you get exactly what you deserve) is given legislative form and human sanction. As in Genesis 1–9, however, there are reasons to wonder whether we are reading about a principle of retribution that *must* be enacted on every occasion, or whether the concern is more to limit the vengeance that "authorities" might ideally like to take on perpetrators. Certainly in the ongoing biblical narrative after the Pentateuch, as beforehand with Cain (and indeed Moses, who murders an Egyptian overseer in Exod. 2:12), it is not always the case that a murder is met with execution. For example, David is later effectively guilty of the murder of Uriah the Hittite (2 Sam. 11:14–17), but he avoids lethal retribution on his own person for this crime.

If however there is at least evident *equity* in the idea of executing a murderer, the reader of the OT certainly struggles to find it in many of the other instances in Torah where people are said to be deserving of death. These include kidnapping, cursing one's parents (Exod. 21:16–17), having sexual relations with an animal (22:19), breaking the Sabbath (31:14), adultery (Lev. 20:10), some forms of incest (20:11–21), homosexual acts (20:13), and being a medium or a spiritist (20:27). It is not the "life for life" principle that is dictating the choice of penalty in these cases. Rather, it is the seriousness of these sins, relative to other ones, within the ancient Israelite context. Each punishment is disproportionate in relation to the sin itself, but presumably necessary as an option in that particular historical context in order to maintain Israel's viability as a polity.

I say "option" because in these "disproportionate" cases, too, there are questions to be asked about the precise relationship of the rule to actual practice in society. For example, "if a man commits adultery with another man's wife—with the wife of his neighbor—both the adulterer and the adulteress are to be put to death" (Lev. 20:10). However, it seems very likely that "in practice ... the penalty for adultery in Israel was more flexible, and further, that the initiation of proceedings against the offenders was the exclusive right of the husband."[53] Proverbs 6:34–35, for example, envisages the adulterous man arousing "a husband's fury" and showing "no mercy when he takes revenge"—implying thereby that mercy (and perhaps reconciliation) is at least an option (involving, perhaps, financial compensation, which Num. 35:31–32 specifically disallows in the case of murder). Divorce may have been another option (Jer. 3:8; Hos. 2:4), as well as public humiliation (Jer. 13:22–26; Ezek. 16:37, 39). David the adulterer, we note, was permitted to marry the equally adulterous Bathsheba (2 Sam. 11:27). Execution may well have been the most serious punishment possible, but this does not mean that it was always necessarily enacted. The same must surely have been true with respect to cursing one's parents.

We would be wise to set these observations about law and social practice in the OT within the larger context of the ANE in which ancient Israel lived:

> Our modern case law describes precedent that sets limits on what kinds of rulings the lawyers and the judges are allowed to make. Ancient legal wisdom instead tried to instruct the judge on what rightness and wrongness looked like so [that] he ... would be able to produce rightness and eliminate wrongness with his verdicts ... As judges and magistrates absorb[ed] what [the law] communicates, they [would] be better able to recognize wrongness and rightness and make decisions appropriately.[54]

The point is that one cannot predict from a particular legal prescription itself what would necessarily have followed when a particular case, no doubt involving many factors, was being heard.

THE HERMENEUTICS OF PUNISHMENT: CHURCH AND STATE

Our most important question here, however, does not concern what the ancient Israelites were authorized to do, and did do, in respect of murder, adultery, and the like. It is whether there is any good reason to believe that such stipulations about lethal punishment have anything directly to say to the people of God outside of that ancient context. Does the Church, as the new Israel, have the same authority as the old Israel to execute people for such sins?

The Death Penalty and the Church

There is no reason to think that it does—no reason to think that in this area Christians are still "my people" rather than "not my people." Of course it is the case that God's creational law applies as much to Christians as to those in the times before there were Christians—to everyone, in fact. As we have seen throughout chapters one through seven, however, the NT people of God is very differently constituted from the OT people of God, and nothing in the NT suggests that the former has a mandate to bring lethal justice on sinners for their various faults. Like ancient Israel, the Church does need to maintain a strong witness to "overt beliefs, values, and lifestyles,"[55] sometimes disciplining members of the body who refuse to walk in God's ways—but as we saw in chapter 7 (in relation to 1 Cor. 5), this does not involve killing them. It may well be that Leviticus 20:11 says that "if a man has sexual relations with his father's wife . . . both the man and the woman are to be put to death." In recommending to the Christians in Corinth how they should handle such a case, however, the apostle Paul chooses to allude instead to the language of being "cut off from their people" in Leviticus 18:29, and to interpret this in a nonlethal manner: "put out of your fellowship the man who has been doing this" (1 Cor. 5:2).[56] Christians should still obey God's creational law as it is the reflected in OT Scripture—but the Church is not a body that dispenses lethal punishment when one of its members commits, say, incest.

The same is true in the case of murder. When we read that the sixth commandment enjoins us not to murder, the Christian will be anxious to obey it (as indeed the NT proposes; e.g., Matt. 15:19–20; 19:17–19). Each human being remains one who is created in the image of God, and whose life is precious. It is indeed true, in all times and places, that nothing less than a life can compensate for a life. Unlike the "disproportionate" punishments discussed above, then, we can reasonably ground execution for illegitimate killing in the Mosaic Torah in this broader environment that speaks of proportionate retribution in respect to all image bearers. Yet even so, it is not for the post-Pentecost people of God to *enact* such retribution. The Church is not simply "Israel Redux."

"Terror for those . . . who do wrong" (Rom. 13:3)

Does the post-Pentecost *state*, then, have God-given authority to execute? Certainly the NT provides some reason for thinking so. God has appointed rulers to keep order in the world by bringing "terror" upon "those who do wrong," and for that reason they "bear the sword," bringing "punishment on the wrongdoer" (Rom. 13:1–5). The immediate context is provided by the Roman Empire, of course, and, beyond the general permission granted here to the state to use coercive measures to restrain wickedness, the specific allusion appears to be to "the authority (possessed by all higher magistrates) of inflicting sentence of death" in pursuit of social order.[57] Here the right of the state to punish lethally, at least under certain circumstances, appears to be recognized. It is not Paul's pressing concern in Romans 13, of course, to inform his readers about what those circumstances are; he certainly does not refer to the OT in order to clarify the point. This is right and proper, for as we have established already in this book, no post-Pentecost state should be regarded as "Israel" in such a manner, and the punishments prescribed for sins in Israel cannot supply any such state in any simple "one for one" manner with a guide for its own practices in such matters—for its own "positive law." The Church, for its part, should not *expect* the state to punish its citizens for certain sins just because the Israelites did.

An influential argument to the contrary that has often been deployed throughout the ages is based on 2 Corinthians 5:5 where, in regard to the man who has been sleeping with his father's wife, Paul instructs the Christian in Corinth: "hand this man over to Satan for the destruction of the flesh, so that his spirit may be saved on the day of the Lord." This has been interpreted as a secondary stage of the process of discipline, whereby a person is first of all excommunicated by the Church and then also handed over to the secular authorities for punishment. This is, however, a poor interpretation of the text in question. The sinner is being delivered into the custody here, not of the state, but of Satan (which may just be another way of saying that he is being excluded from the community).[58] Moreover, he is not necessarily envisaged as physically dying or even suffering as a result: "the punishment of the offender *may or may not* have included physical suffering in its outworking."[59] Rather, the reference may be to "the 'fleshly' *stance of self-sufficiency* of which Paul accuses *primarily the community* but surely *also the man*," from which Paul hopes that the man can be rescued.[60] After all, "the messenger of Satan" sent to Paul himself in 2 Corinthians 12:7–10 (his "thorn in the flesh") does not cause his death "but through subduing any sense of self-elation 'teaches him lessons of patience and dependence on God.'"[61] More generally, it is entirely unlikely that Paul would advocate handing over recalcitrant Church members to the local magistrates, only to go on immediately to exhort the Corinthians to avoid taking lawsuits "before the ungodly for judgment" (1 Cor. 6:1). We recall again from our chapter 4 the "profound lack of interest" in the NT "in either local or imperial politics"—including systems of law.[62] Certainly Paul recognizes here the need for some coercive measures in pursuit of community flourishing not just in the state but also in the Church—but the latter have nothing here to do with the former.

To pick up again the main thread of the argument: the NT recognizes the right of the state to punish lethally, at least in certain unspecified circumstances. In terms of what is warranted by biblical faith, which are the sins (in the context of the Church) that should also be capital crimes (in the context of the state)? Only one is directly warranted, and it is murder. Here a positive argument can be articulated, on the basis of our biblical Story as a whole rather than simply Exodus through Deuteronomy alone, in respect of the proportionate justice of the matter.

AUTHORITY AND OBLIGATION

The Christian belief that the state has the *authority* to execute a murderer does not of itself imply, of course, any consequent belief that the state *should in fact* ever carry out such a sentence, much less the idea that it has an *obligation* to do so. Here we return in the first instance to Genesis 4, and to God's own decision not to take Cain's life, nor to authorize its taking. All human beings, including magistrates, are image bearers called to be "like God" in how they conduct their lives—and in Genesis 4, God is merciful.

This mercy is often celebrated in the Bible: "The LORD is compassionate and gracious, slow to anger, abounding in love. He will not always accuse, nor will he harbor his anger forever; he does not treat us as our sins deserve, or repay us according to our iniquities" (Ps. 103:8–10). Ezekiel 33 pictures God in this way: "I take no pleasure in the death of the wicked, but rather that they turn from their ways and live. Turn! Turn from your evil ways! Why will you die, people of Israel?" To be like God is to take no pleasure in the death of the wicked but to prefer their repentance—not to treat people as their sins deserve. It is to treat kindly even a very wicked king like Ahab (partly responsible for a judicial murder by his wife Jezebel, 1 Kgs. 21:1–14), responding positively to just this kind of repentance (21:27–29). Following the theological logic here, Christians should regard the execution of a murderer as something that is best avoided—a last resort, rather than a norm.

We see this logic clearly at work in the early postapostolic Church in the thinking of Augustine. The civil magistrate in the "earthly city" (not the city of God) ensures social stability *within* the state, creating the circumstances in which repentance can follow. Because repentance is the goal, severity must always have the end of mercy in mind, and appropriate restraint must be practiced. For this reason, Augustine is ambivalent about the death penalty. Authorized persons who "have put to death wicked men . . . have by no means violated the commandment, 'Thou shalt not kill.'"[63] Yet Christian rulers are righteous

if they are slow to punish, ready to pardon; if they apply that punishment as necessary to government and defence of the republic, and not in order to gratify their own enmity; if they grant pardon, not that iniquity may go unpunished, but with the hope that the transgressor may amend his ways.[64]

Keenly aware of the Christian calling to love, Augustine reminds the proconsul Donatus in 409 that Christians do not seek the death of their enemies, "but their deliverance from error ... by the help of the terror of judges and of laws." He urges Donatus, therefore, "when you are pronouncing judgment in cases affecting the Church ... to forget that you have the power of capital punishment."[65] The dead cannot be reconciled. Indeed, they may not even be justly dead. Augustine was skeptical about the ability of the state to deliver justice: "true justice has no existence save in that republic whose founder and ruler is Christ."[66]

This Christian ambivalence about the death penalty is already evident in the earlier postapostolic centuries prior to Constantine, in the significant reluctance to agree that it was the business of Christ-followers to involve themselves in the violence of the state at all. We saw traces of this already in our chapter 4. This is why early Christian baptismal rules "consistently treat the military as a problematic profession" and why civil magistracy is also a matter of concern—precisely because magistrates had an "official duty to impose capital punishment and to take evidence under torture."[67] The felt incompatibility of the Christian with the Roman life in such respects is well expressed by Tertullian:

> Shall it be held lawful to make an occupation of the sword, when the Lord proclaims that he who uses the sword shall perish by the sword? And shall the son of peace take part in the battle when it does not become him even to sue at law? And shall he apply the chain, and the prison, and the torture, and the punishment, who is not the avenger even of his own wrongs?[68]

Judicial violence may not necessarily be wrong in itself—but a "son of peace" should not involve himself in it. Christ-followers have other business to attend to. Yet this surely raises an uncomfortable question. If, when all has been carefully considered, the death penalty turns out to be the *right* penalty in a particular case—the best action that can be taken in the circumstances—should a Christian refuse to participate in the dreadful deed, preferring that someone else should do what is necessary? Is this in truth to love one's neighbor? It is difficult to see how it can be. On the contrary, it seems rather selfish. To be like God is to be *slow* to punish—not to renounce punishing *altogether*, even when it is called for.

CONCLUSION

Looking back on the whole chapter now, we come to our conclusion. There is very little basis indeed for the widespread assumption in Christendom up to and including Jan van Leiden and his opponents that appropriate coercion in pursuit of the common good in Church and society includes the use of execution. The only sin that should be regarded as deserving of such lethal punishment is murder. By extension, an argument could also be made for a deadly intervention to prevent murder, where no other means are likely to succeed—restraining the violent from violence by way of violence. However, to acknowledge that lethal responses may in principle be just in such a case is not to accept that the *Church* has a right to respond in such ways. The state, on the other hand, does clearly have the authority to do so, but in view of the character of the God who authorizes, it ought not *necessarily* to do so. Nor should Christians encourage the state to act in such ways—particularly if they are in doubt (as Augustine was) concerning the ability of their state to deliver justice (generally, or in capital cases in particular).[69] Murder is a terrible sin, and it ought also to be a crime—and yet, even the murderer might turn from his sins and be saved.

Measured against this biblical standard, a considerable number of the executions that occurred in Christendom within the timespan covered by this book thus far—executions for blasphemy, heresy, witchcraft, incest, adultery, rioting, or other misdeeds—must be judged unequivocally wrong. A number of others, in response to murder, were not for that reason unequivocally right. In the midst of seeking what is right, historically, we must conclude that many people got lost.

DISCUSSION QUESTIONS

1. What were your first reactions, and what are now your thoughts, about what you learned in the first part of this chapter about eschatological ("end-times") expectation in the later Middle Ages?
2. If you had had the chance in 1534–1535 to speak at length in Münster with Jan Matthijs and Jan van Leiden, and if they had been prepared to listen, what would you have said to them about their biblical interpretation (hermeneutics)?
3. Do you find the overall argument advanced about the death penalty in this chapter convincing? Why or why not?
4. In which circumstances should Christians support, or even participate in, the execution of a murderer?

9

Men of Blood

The English Revolution

Where there are magistrates of the people, appointed to restrain the willfulness of
kings . . . [and wielding] such power as the three estates exercise in every realm when
they hold their chief assemblies . . . I certainly do not forbid them to withstand, in
accordance with their duty, the fierce licentiousness of kings. In fact, if they turn a
blind eye to kings who violently fall upon and assault the lowly common folk, I declare
that . . . they dishonestly betray the freedom of the people, of which . . . they have been
appointed protectors by God's law.[1]

John Calvin

The Reformation described in chapters 7 and 8 quickly spread from mainland Europe to the British Isles. In England the Church seceded from Rome
in 1534, during the reign of King Henry VIII, and the Protestant cause in that
country advanced rapidly under his son Edward VI (reigned 1547–1553). After
a reversion to Roman Catholicism under Henry's older daughter Mary Tudor
(1553–1558), during which time many Protestant exiles found their way to Calvin's Geneva, Henry's younger daughter Elizabeth came to the throne (1558–
1603). She sought to deal with the religious differences destabilizing the country
by way of what has become known as the "Elizabethan Settlement." This was an
attempt to chart a middle course in English religious life, involving (centrally)
the imposition of external liturgical conformity in line with an updated *Book*
of Common Prayer while allowing latitude internally to individual conscience.[2]
This settlement was satisfactory neither to the queen's devout Calvinist nor to
her devout Roman Catholic subjects—the former fervently believing (and this

will not surprise the reader of our earlier chapters) that "England ... was an elect nation destined by God to play a great part in destroying Rome" and finding the settlement too Roman.[3] It did not please the pope, either, who in 1580 proclaimed Elizabeth a heretic.

In Scotland, meanwhile, the leading spokesman of the Reformation movement, John Knox, had been carried off as a slave on a French ship (1547) and subsequently installed as a preacher by the English in the garrison town of Berwick-upon-Tweed, exercising thereafter an itinerant preaching ministry in the south. He too fled England during Queen Mary's reign; ending up in Geneva, he became the pastor of the congregation of English exiles there. He returned to Scotland for good in 1559 and was a crucial figure in ensuring the success of the Scottish Reformation. Here the national church was Calvinist in theology and Presbyterian in polity (governed by elders of equal rank) rather than episcopal (governed by bishops with a hierarchy of clergy beneath them). It was this kind of church to which significant numbers of reforming Calvinists in England also aspired—people like Thomas Cartwright (1535–1603), who was forced into exile in Geneva for a while after publicizing his views in 1570.

THE PURITANS

The name by which these English reformers came to be known was "Puritans." Some soon separated themselves from the state church entirely and formed voluntary congregations in line with what they believed to be proper doctrine and practice; they are typically referred to as "Independents" and rejected the rule of both bishops and presbyteries. Such separation was illegal in England at this time, and many of those who followed such a path were persecuted for it (like the Anabaptists in continental Europe) and fled to mainland Europe seeking refuge. The majority of Puritans persevered within the Church of England, essentially setting up a non- or minimally conformist church within a church.[4]

Puritan hopes of further progress toward a "proper" reformation of the English church were raised when in 1603 King James VI of Scotland—a Calvinist— succeeded Elizabeth as King James I of the separate states of England, Scotland, and Ireland (1603–1625). These hopes were quickly disappointed; James turned out to be anything but an enthusiast for either reform or Puritan nonconformity within the Church of England—or for that matter within the Church of Scotland, where he attempted both to establish episcopacy and to introduce Anglican ritual. His son Charles I (1625–1649) was even less to the liking of the Calvinist reformers. This contributed greatly to the problems that Charles had with his Parliament in London (which we shall refer to hitherto simply as "Parliament") right from the beginning of his reign, which were ultimately to lead to his untimely death.[5]

A BRIEF HISTORY OF PARLIAMENT IN ENGLAND

The origins of Parliament (a collective way of referring to what were actually in this period many episodic "parliaments") as it was constituted in Charles I's time lie a few hundred years earlier, in the thirteenth century. At this time, English kings—routinely taking advice from a royal Privy Council—would from time to time also call together a wider range of subjects to discuss judicial and financial matters. They did so especially when they wanted to raise funds by way of taxation in order to fight a war. For example, a highly representative parliament (the so-called "Model Parliament") was summoned in 1295 by King Edward I when he needed financial support for his wars in Scotland and France. It included not only lords of the realm (earls, barons, and bishops), but also "lower clergy" from each cathedral and diocese as well as representatives from each shire, city, and borough.[6] Time-honored custom required, the king said, that matters affecting all should be approved by all. Here we see in action the "three estates" of the epigraph to this present chapter (clergy, nobles, and commons), meeting separately from each other to agree how much funding to grant the king. Eventually all meetings of Parliament comprised these three estates, with the representatives of the commons chosen by election—albeit that the right to vote in the "constituencies" of counties and boroughs that emerged after 1430 and produced these members of Parliament was quite restricted.[7]

Early in the fourteenth century there developed the custom of debating within two "chambers" or "houses"—a House of Lords (both spiritual and temporal) and a House of Commons—with legislative initiatives or "bills" emerging from this process. In due course it became accepted on all sides—Crown, Lords, and Commons—that legislative change should normally involve just such a procedure of debate and agreement, requiring the assent of not only the king but also of both Houses of Parliament. For a king to try to govern by royal prerogative and proclamation alone was, by this point, to risk unpopularity.

KING CHARLES I

This does not mean that kings always cared much about the risk. King James I, for example, held strong, theologically based convictions concerning the nature of kingship. Building on earlier ideas that we have tracked in previous chapters, James asserted that kings inhabited a higher realm than other mortal men, deriving their authority from God, and that within their realm they were not accountable to other earthly authorities, such as Parliament. Kings had preexisted other estates and ranks, and others owned their lands at the king's pleasure. On this absolutist understanding of monarchy, the king could in fact create law simply by royal proclamation. James also made sure that his sons, Henry (d. 1612) and

Charles, imbibed this philosophy and understood that they should not summon Parliament except out of dire necessity. James himself (unsurprisingly) had a fraught relationship with that institution throughout his reign.

DIVINE RIGHT AND PARLIAMENTARY PREROGATIVE

When Charles ascended to the throne in 1625, then, he did so as a king inclined to distrust Parliament, and especially the House of Commons. In his first Parliament in the same year, the Commons turned out to be dominated by Puritans, who in turned distrusted the king, not least because his own religious tendencies did not align with theirs. Determined to have its grievances about surcharges previously imposed by James I addressed, Parliament immediately flexed its muscles by refusing to accord Charles the right, in line with precedent, to collect customs duties for life. Charles simply went on collecting his customs duties anyway. The second Parliament of the reign in 1626 was also dissolved under contentious circumstances.[8] In the third gathering of 1628–1629, members introduced a *Petition of Right* into the proceedings, in which the rights and privileges of Parliament, especially in fiscal matters, were asserted against the king.[9] The king moved once again to dissolve Parliament.[10] Before its members dispersed, however, three resolutions were passed, attacking anyone "promoting popery or Arminianism . . . in the English Church" or collecting or paying the disputed custom duties without being so authorized by Parliament.[11] Charles duly imprisoned the parliamentary leadership. For the next eleven years he managed to get by without that institution. He governed in his own person and on the advice of his Privy Council, living from the proceeds of the customs duties and other taxes and economizing where he could.[12]

THE ARCHBISHOP, THE STOOL, AND THE COVENANT

In the meantime, in 1633, the committed anti-Puritan William Laud was appointed Archbishop of Canterbury, whereupon he launched a relentless campaign against the Puritans throughout the English realm, enforcing strict conformity with the provisions of the Elizabethan Settlement. To the more radical within the Church of England, of course, this was to endorse idolatry and "popery." In the same year he accompanied King Charles to Edinburgh for his Scottish coronation, during which the Anglican rites were employed. By 1637 a royal commission had produced a new prayer book for use in the Church of Scotland, designed to bring the Scottish liturgy more into line with the liturgy in the Church of England.

This prayer book was first used in St Giles' Cathedral in Edinburgh on Sunday, July 23, 1637—and it provoked a riot. Tradition has it that the instigator of this riot was one Jenny Geddes, an Edinburgh market trader, who threw the stool upon which she was sitting at the Dean of Edinburgh when he began to read part of the newly prescribed service. The rioting then spread across Edinburgh and to other Scottish cities. What followed was the Scottish National Covenant, which committed its signatories to the defense of "the true Christian faith and religion" that was likewise "defended by many and sundry notable kirks and realms, but chiefly by the Kirk of Scotland, the King's Majesty, and three estates of this realm, as God's eternal truth and only ground of our salvation." The king, we note, is carefully associated here with the Reformed Christian faith and the "three estates of this realm," even as the text rejects any attempt to force the Scottish church to conform to English liturgical practice and church governance. Its signatories explicitly promise therein that they will "defend his person and authority with our goods, bodies, and lives" *as well as* the "liberties of our country, ministration of justice, and punishment of iniquity, against all enemies within this realm or without."[13]

THE BISHOPS' WAR

Nevertheless, King Charles chose to interpret this move as rebellion and in 1639 initiated the "First Bishops' War" against the Scots, which did not go well. After dissolving the uncooperative "Short Parliament" called to raise taxes to fund the continuing war effort and following the occupation of northern England by a Scottish army, the king was forced to summon Parliament once more. Once again, there was a strong Puritan presence in the House of Commons, but the discontent among its members was much more broadly based than that, and they held a wide variety of views concerning what needed to be done about it.[14] On this occasion Parliament sat for a long and highly consequential period of time (1640–1653), causing it later to be known (unimaginatively) as the "Long Parliament." With the benefit of recent experience, one of its earliest moves was to pass an act forbidding its own dissolution without its consent.

THE ENGLISH REVOLUTION

John McNeill, the modern editor of Calvin's *Institutes*, has referred to the text cited in the epigraph to this chapter as that "brief, startling passage" that subsequently "became a commonplace of political treatises," envisaging as it does the three estates of contemporary nations as "constitutional defenders of the people's liberty against the oppression of kings."[15] Precisely along such lines, Parliament now set about undermining the king's personal rule as much as it could, binding him to Commons and Lords by making it virtually impossible for him to levy taxes without their agreement. The Earl of Strafford, much involved in setting the direction of the kingdom under Charles and in the war on the Scots, was executed for treason in May 1641—precisely as one who had attempted to "introduce an arbitrary and tyrannical government" and had been prepared "to use his Irish [and Catholic] army against the King's others subjects" (namely, the Scots).[16] For the time being it was the king's advisors, and not the king, who were being held explicitly accountable for the current state of affairs.[17] This was soon to begin to change, as the Great Seal, necessary for governance in England, followed the king out of London, and both Charles and Parliament mobilized troops in preparation for war.

THE SOLEMN LEAGUE AND COVENANT (1643)

The detailed course of the first round of the English Civil War that followed from 1642 to 1646 need not detain us here. It began with the inconclusive Battle of Edgehill in October 1642, and it ended in the aftermath of the decisive Parliamentarian victory at Naseby in June 1645. I simply want to highlight under the next few headings a few aspects of and developments in religion and politics in this period that are of importance to our larger theme in this book.

We begin in September 1643. With the Royalist cause in the ascendancy, Parliament concluded an agreement with the Scots known as the "Solemn League and Covenant," which was also ratified by the "Westminster Assembly" that had been meeting since the previous July.[18] By the terms of this Covenant the Scots agreed to provide the Parliamentarians with military support in their struggle with the Royalists, and all agreed to work for a civil and religious union of England, Scotland, and Ireland under a Presbyterian and Parliamentary system. By its ratification, then, the soldiers of the Parliamentary army were (for the moment) bound "to solidarity with the Presbyterian cause."[19] The immediate effect of the agreement was to put a large Scottish army in the field in the north of England, substantially changing the military dynamics. The Battle of Marston Moor near York in July 1644, in which English and Scottish armies fought as one, was a decisive victory for the anti-Royalist forces and contributed greatly to the eventual outcome of the war.

OLIVER CROMWELL

Among the wounded in this battle was a very important player in the events that followed: Oliver Cromwell (1599–1658). A Puritan member of the Parliament of 1628–1629, he was already known as a strong critic of episcopacy and "popish" ritual and as possessing Independent sympathies. In 1640 he was elected again to Parliament; in 1642 he was an early organizer, in Cambridge, of armed detachments preparing to fight in a war against the king. As soon as the war broke out, he raised a troop of cavalry in Huntingdon. He fought at Edgehill and soon distinguished himself as an effective leader.

Some of Cromwell's words in the aftermath of victory at Marston Moor helpfully reveal the mindset of many of the Puritans fighting in the Parliamentary cause: "It had all the evidences of an absolute victory obtained by the Lord's blessing upon the godly party principally."[20] Cromwell is not just fighting for Parliamentary prerogative; he is fighting as one of the "godly party" against the ungodly. For many Puritans, likewise, with their long tradition "of interpreting all political events in an apocalyptic or millenarian sense," the war quickly became not so much about limiting the king's temporal power as about defeating the forces of darkness.[21] *The Souldiers' Catechisme* of 1644 accordingly describes the Royalist enemies not as "countrymen or kinsmen or fellow-Protestants, but rather as enemies of God and our religion and siders with Anti-Christ, and so our eye is not to pity them nor our sword to spare them [cf. Jer. 48:10]."[22] Particularly the Independent Puritans in the army—and there were many of these, swelled in number by returning exiles from abroad—were engaged in a holy war (a crusade) that they were determined to win, thereby significantly changing (they hoped) the nature of English society. This differentiated them from their often less enthusiastic, Presbyterian (and often ennobled) colleagues in the struggle, who were more concerned not to *lose* the war and thereby to lose their heads once Charles was (inevitably, they believed) restored to his throne. By November 1644 the gulf between this "peace party" in both army and Parliament, looking for compromise, and the "war party," looking only for victory, was widening, and serious conflict within the Parliamentary cause was on the immediate horizon.[23]

THE NEW MODEL ARMY

In pursuit of victory, Cromwell argued successfully in a speech in Parliament in December 1644 that the armed forces should be reorganized. The result was the significantly modernized New Model Army. The "Self-Denying Ordinance" of April 3, 1645, further sought "to remodel Parliament's armies for a more vigorous war effort by separating military and political commands," forcing members of Parliament to step down from military office.[24] This disproportionately affected the hereditary lords, typically Presbyterian, who could not relinquish their seats in the Lords, effectively putting the army under Independent command. The terms of the appointment of the new commander-in-chief, the radical Sir Thomas Fairfax, were particularly ominous in this regard. Unlike his predecessor, and all who adhered to the Solemn League and Covenant (including the Scottish Presbyterians), Fairfax was not required "to protect the King's person." This represents "the abandonment of the fiction that [Parliament was] fighting the king's evil counsellors, and the first step towards the conversion of a civil war into a revolution."[25] Nor were Fairfax's soldiers required to take an oath committing to the Covenant, even though the Self-Denying Ordinance had required it.

It was this New Model Army, with Cromwell as its Lieutenant-General (in striking defiance of the Self-Denying Ordinance) that crushed the Royalists at Naseby on June 14, 1645. This outcome left the king without a viable army and without negotiating strength. After some time on the run, Charles surrendered his person to the Scottish army in the north in May 1646.

THE END OF THE KING

As our narrative so far has revealed, King Charles I was not good at compromise, and Parliament was now similarly minded.[26] Captive to the Scots in Newcastle, Charles received Parliament's peace terms, still framed in terms of the Solemn League and Covenant; he rejected them as "destructive to his just regal power."[27] Parliament responded by destroying the Great Seal, which had recently come into its possession. Both parties were entirely convinced that God was on their side and either had vindicated or would vindicate them. Early in 1647 the exasperated Scots handed Charles back into Parliamentary custody and marched home across the border; in June of that year, he was kidnapped by radicals within the New Model Army, who were looking to increase their bargaining power with a Parliament they now distrusted. They had begun to circulate their own Independent rather than Presbyterian proposals about what should happen next, premised on ideas of religious toleration, freedom, and equality. These were ideas familiar to social and political radicals like the Levellers, but they were certainly not acceptable to the Presbyterian-dominated Parliament. They were not entirely acceptable even to Independent-minded army leaders like Fairfax and Cromwell, who pursued a more modest agenda that still envisaged at this stage the restoration of the king. For the radicals, on the other hand, Charles was already by September 1647 the biblical Achan (Josh. 7) who must be removed if the people were once again to flourish. He was soon to become the "man of blood" in the land "who must be purged by execution" (Num. 35:33; cf. 2 Sam. 16:7–8) so that the land would once again become undefiled.[28]

Charles was indeed executed just a couple of years later, on January 30, 1649, after a second, brief phase of civil war—to the dismay, even at this stage, of the majority of the English population. The execution occurred under the supervision of a small "Rump Parliament" that had been purged at the beginning of the previous month by the Independent-dominated army of over one hundred unreliable (Presbyterian) members.[29] Those who engineered the execution did so as the self-evidently godly party to whom God had given victory not once, but twice, thereby legitimating their rule.[30] They also did so in the conviction that "key prophecies from the Bible were about to be fulfilled and that justice upon the King was the only godly course," clearing the way for "the reign of the righteous and Christ's second coming."[31] Charles, according to this apocalyptic view, was one of the ten horns of the beast from Revelation 17 who had yielded his kingdom to Rome, and after whose passing Christ himself would rule. The English army would be the vanguard by which the godly revolution would be carried into all lands.

THE FIFTH MONARCHISTS AND THE FIRST PROTECTOR

The monarchy and the House of Lords were immediately abolished, and a Council of State was elected. England was now a republic. The Scottish parliament immediately moved to proclaim Charles' son as king (Charles II). Like their Presbyterian English neighbors, they were appalled by the regicide, "which seemed to herald not New Jerusalem but a New Münster."[32] Both groups were also hostile to the religious toleration that was important to the Independents who controlled the English government. The Levellers were hostile to the new government for different reasons: that it was "centralist, unrepresentative, nonreformist and despotic."[33] Those most committed to the apocalyptic theology described above were in turn unhappy about "the secular nature of the Council of State and pressed for government by the Church."[34] Some of these "accepted the Münster Anabaptists as their greatest inspiration."[35] Dissatisfaction, in sum, was widespread. The government responded with repression and ultimately (early in 1650) required all males over the age of eighteen to swear an oath of allegiance to the republic.

The Fifth Monarchy

The most radical believers influenced by this apocalyptic theology were the Fifth Monarchists, who in the aftermath of the king's death looked for "a theocratic regime in which the saints would establish a godly discipline over the unregenerate masses and prepare for the Second Coming."[36] By 1653 it was antagonistic to previously held ideas about Parliament (and to the just-dissolved Rump Parliament, in particular), although without an agreed alternative. One idea was that the government of England should lie in the hands of an assembly of godly men "based on the Old Testament Sanhedrin with seventy members," and chosen, perhaps, from the counties, or from the army. Cromwell himself, a second Moses, should choose the representatives—as indeed he ultimately did, along with his officers, in part using a list of names submitted by Independent churches.[37]

The "Barebones Parliament" that ensued, with twelve identifiable Fifth Monarchists among its ranks (out of a "biblical" total of 144; Rev. 14:1) began in great expectation that "the reign of the saints was beginning."[38] The immediate goals of the twelve were radical law reform—in the eyes of many, this meant replacing

"English common law with the biblical Mosaic law" (i.e., with the entirety of the judicial law)—and the abolition of the national church.[39] In pursuit of the latter, there was an early move to abolish tithes.[40] In some respects these goals overlapped with those of the now-marginalized Levellers.[41] The radicals in the assembly were sufficiently successful that their more moderate colleagues quickly became alarmed and by subterfuge engineered the surrender of the assembly's power to Cromwell, who assumed the role of Lord Protector. The Barebones Parliament had lasted all of six months. The Fifth Monarchists now joined the unofficial Opposition in relation to Cromwell's Protectorate, many of them viewing their former hero as a terrible apostate.

The Cromwellian Protectorate

Cromwell had been just as frustrated as the Fifth Monarchists with the Rump Parliament's failure to carry out significant reforms; this is very likely what drove him to use military force to dissolve it on April 20, 1653. Clearly he hoped that a new assembly of "godly men" would do better—although his definition of "godly" was more generous than that of the Fifth Monarchists, such that most members of the Barebones Parliament were "moderate religious Independents, who wanted liberty for individual consciences within a broad national Church."[42] From Cromwell's own point of view, his decision to receive power back from this assembly and become Lord Protector of the realm had nothing to do with "apostasy" but everything to do with his and others' conviction "that if it were allowed to continue not only would the existing social and political order collapse and religious anarchy ensue but the chances of bringing about any reform in the future would all but disappear."[43] Social and political stability after the marked instability of the preceding years were important to Cromwell and to many of those who promoted the Protectorate; so were the rooting out of corruption and the achieving of greater justice, not least by proper reform of the law. Central to it all, however, was a commitment to at least some liberty of conscience in Christian society, which was threatened by the tendency of the radicals in the Barebones Parliament (as one observer put it) to fasten the "name of Antichristianism" upon everything they liked not."[44]

Of course, this liberty of conscience had hard limits. It did not extend to Roman Catholics, for example, to whom the Puritans in general were quite content to attach the "name of Antichristianism." What could follow from this stark antithesis between the holy and the unholy is strikingly illustrated in Cromwell's Irish campaign on behalf of the Commonwealth after the civil war in England had finished. In 1649 he had landed with fifteen thousand troops in Ireland determined to subdue a Royalist rebellion there. He is still remembered in that country for his first siege, of the city of Drogheda, and the subsequent massacre of nearly thirty-five hundred people, including civilians, prisoners, and priests; the pattern was later replicated at Wexford. The crusading, "chosen people" Puritan mentality so evident in the English civil war is also clearly on display in this Irish one. For Cromwell and his associates, the invasion of Ireland was akin to the invasion of Canaan by the Israelites. His troops were informed of this on more than one occasion during the campaign: their destiny was to annihilate the idolatrous Canaanites.[45]

THE HERMENEUTICS OF WAR

A number of important questions arise from this and the previous chapter about governance (among other things). Granted that Christians are encouraged to see the authorities that exist as having been established by God for the sake of the common good, and to obey them as such (Rom. 13:1; 1 Pet. 2:13–17; 3:13–17), how are such legitimate authorities to be recognized? What if there is more than one (as Calvin envisages in the epigraph above), and they get into conflict—a king and a parliament, say, or an elected republican government and a duke or an emperor? How many authorities might there be, and on what grounds might we agree that this is so? We shall defer discussion of such questions, however, until chapter 11. The time has come at this point in our grand narrative concerning the good (biblical) life to give our attention, rather, to the violence of war—violence that has wound its way like a turbulent stream all the way through our reflections in this book so far.

The conversion of Constantine, we recall from chapter 4, brought Church and state into a close relationship with each other, and ultimately Christianity became the official religion of the empire. Christian emperors, thinking of themselves as Moses or David, led the new people of Israel against their enemies, who were also God's enemies, attributing victory to this same God. If it is true that "Constantine [himself] was no holy warrior, still less a crusader," it is also the case that by the time we get to the period of the rise of Islam in the seventh century, the emphasis had shifted in Christendom "from the emperor as divinely inspired, to individual soldiers, whose spiritual purity became essential to the empire's success."[46]

The Holy Roman Emperor Charlemagne certainly regarded himself as a Moses or David in this way, tasked with the governance of an Israel whose whole salvation lay in his hands. This embrace of "a salutary kingship," modeled on the kings of Israel, impacted not only his internal but also his external policy. The Franks had always enjoyed fighting wars, but "now, more than ever in the past, these [Frankish] wars of aggression took on an unequivocal religious legitimacy."[47] On the whole (as we saw in chapter 5) Charles treated his defeated enemies well.[48] However, the violence inflicted on the Saxons during his reign illustrated what could happen even when such a king knew he should "subordinate [his] actions to the demands of Christianity."[49]

The First Crusade underlined what could further happen when the Church, in a time of heightened apocalyptic expectation, "sanctified violence within a penitential framework," promising full remission of sins for those who would inflict violence on others in pursuit of the restoration of Jerusalem.[50] It was natural for the crusading mentality to associate this particular "conquest of Canaan" with the earlier, biblical one. Reflecting on the loss of Crusader Jerusalem to Saladin in 1187, for example, the monk Rostang of the Burgundian monastery of Cluny

> wrote that the sinful mixing of Jerusalem's Christian inhabitants with peoples of "diverse languages and customs" had angered the Lord, much like the Israelites mixing with the Canaanites in the Christian Old Testament, leading God to take back the gift which he had given his people.[51]

The reforming apocalyptists who followed in the twelfth through the sixteenth centuries simply followed the same plotline while introducing local variations with respect to the nature of "Jerusalem"—leading us in the end directly to the horrors of Münster, both inside the city while it was under siege from the imperial forces and after its fall. And now we have seen one aspect of the sequel, in the English Revolution and its aftermath during the Cromwellian Protectorate. The godly party rides out to war against the enemies of God, looking to defeat these Canaanites in war and establish the New Jerusalem in England's green and pleasant land—enemies that end up being in Scotland and Ireland too, as well as (potentially) all over the world.

What are we to make of this widespread assumption in Christendom throughout the period from Constantine to the English Commonwealth that the exhortations to and descriptions of war that we find in the OT warrant post-Pentecost authorities, both Church and state, to fight similar wars—or indeed any war?

The Wars of God

That the OT people of God was birthed and lived out its existence in a violent world is self-evident. Obvious, too, is that the living God whom they come to know in the course of the OT narrative involves himself in the violence of the world—sometime initiates it, in fact, and involves his people in it by way of war. For example, God initiates the violence that leads to the Israelite settlement in the Promised Land as described in the book of Joshua. He does not do so because the Israelites have any right to the land; in biblical thinking it is fundamentally a gift from God, given to them in pursuit of God's long-term (and good) plans for the whole world.[52] In line with this universal perspective, ethnicity also has nothing to do with what happens to the previous inhabitants of the land. They do not lose it because they are Canaanites but because they are wicked, inhabiting a culture that has been corrupt for a very long time.[53] The Israelites themselves eventually lose the land again for the same reason.[54] The point is not, then, that the Israelites are involved in a turf war with the Canaanites and have recruited God to help them win. The point is that God is involved in a long-term conflict with evil, and like an ancient king he has summoned his servants to help him fight some of his battles.[55] In this conflict, in biblical thinking, God can fight just as well *against* Israel as alongside her. In chapter 4 we noted another example of this in 1 Samuel 4 concerning the Ark of the Covenant.[56]

In all of this, the core of God's concern is justice—even-handed justice. When war is described in the OT, this justice is never very far away. We see this in narratives like Judges 11, for example, where a battle is preceded by a long preamble concerning the justice of the case (vv. 12–28). We see it, too, in Deuteronomy, in the very idea that there are *rules* of war concerning such matters as proper regard for the land when a siege is taking place (Deut. 20:19–20) and proper treatment of prisoners of war (21:10–14). Readers of Deuteronomy and Joshua often seem to get distracted in respect of this truth by a number of texts that depart from the normal biblical way of speaking about the demise of the original inhabitants of the land (i.e., that they were "driven out" of the land, just like the Israelites later).[57] These other texts appear to tell us instead of all of the original inhabitants being wiped out—a disproportionate punishment *not* suffered later by the Israelites.[58] Yet there are clearly many Canaanites still living in the land in the *aftermath* of Joshua's victories—people who are not ultimately even *expelled* from the land, much less killed.[59] It is very likely, then, that in the cases where we encounter fierce language that appears to suggest otherwise, we are dealing with examples of the kind of hyperbolic language that is typical of other ANE conquest accounts when they describe comprehensive military victories.[60]

God fights for what is good and right in Scripture, and when the Israelites are being faithful, they always fight God's battles and not their own; sometimes they are not even asked to fight but simply to stand still and to trust, as God, who has his own army, takes care of things (e.g., 2 Kgs. 6:7–23; 19:20–36). Their request for a human king in 1 Samuel 8:7–20 is portrayed as wicked, as we also saw in chapter 4, precisely because it signals a desired departure from this norm. The Israelites here want to be "like all the other nations, with a king to lead us and to go out before us and fight *our* battles" (8:20, emphasis added).

THE PEACE OF GOD

Who is the God who fights in this way, bringing justice on the wicked? It is the same God whom we encountered in chapter 8, who is "compassionate and gracious, slow to anger, abounding in love [and] . . . does not treat us as our sins deserve, or repay us according to our iniquities" (Ps. 103:8–10). It is the God who takes "no pleasure in the death of the wicked" but prefers "that they turn from their ways and live" (Ezek. 33:11).

This is a God, then, who does not take up arms against the Canaanites until many generations have come and gone, and "the sin of the Amorites has . . . reached its full measure" (Gen. 15:16). This is a God who, when the wickedness of Assyria has "come up before" him (Jonah 1:1), sends his prophet Jonah to encourage them to repent, rather than his armies to destroy them, because of his "concern for the great city of Nineveh, in which there are more than a hundred and twenty thousand people who cannot tell their right hand from their left—and also many animals" (4:11). God *does* bring his justice on his Creation, in biblical faith, but his preference is for mercy—even for very wicked cites like Sodom and Gomorrah (Gen. 18:16–33). He is a God who "does not willingly bring affliction or grief to anyone" (Lam. 3:33). His wars against his enemies, then, must always be understood in the context of his love for those same enemies and of his overall salvific plan. This is a plan in which his two most notable enemies, for example— the Egyptians and the Assyrians—will one day worship together (Isa. 19:23–25).[61] It is a plan in which all nations "will beat their swords into plowshares and their spears into pruning hooks. Nation will not take up sword against nation, nor will they train for war anymore" (Isa. 2:4). It is not war that lies deepest in the heart of God, but peace.

It is this same God who, in biblical faith, becomes incarnate in Jesus Christ, and who in Christ's earthly ministry and thereafter remains the God who actively but patiently seeks the salvation of all his human creatures, "not wanting anyone to perish, but everyone to come to repentance" (2 Pet. 3:9). As we have seen in chapters 1 through 8, however, his new mission partner is very differently constituted from her predecessor in the OT. The NT people of God is no longer a nation surrounded by other nations, nor is it one that has been promised a particular land in which to live. This is one obvious aspect of the discontinuity that exists between the OT and the NT—that a specific people, gifted a particular land, centered on one city and its temple, has now become a generalized people found in all lands and living in thousands of cities, journeying together as mini-temples on a pilgrimage toward a new heaven and a new earth. Is this new people of God sometimes called, like the old one, to take up physical arms and fight physical wars? There is nothing in the NT to suggest that this is the case—even though we can be confident that God is still sovereign over all the nations and is still working out his good purposes in the world in terms of justice and salvation in the midst of their wars.

The predominant note struck in the NT literature is, in fact, clearly one of nonviolence. We must pray for those who persecute us (Matt. 5:44), turn the other cheek to those who slap us (Luke 6:29), and strive to live at peace with everyone (Rom. 12:18). We are of course still called, as members of a universal Christian community, to fight alongside God against evil and in pursuit of what is right. The kind of warfare that he now requires of us, however, is described in Ephesians 6. It involves putting on "the full armor of God" and struggling "not against flesh and blood but against the rulers, against the authorities, against the powers of this dark world and against the spiritual forces of evil in the heavenly realms," not least in prayer (vv. 10–20). Only at the end of time will the divine warrior himself ride out on his white horse and "with justice" wage war against the recalcitrant powers of darkness (Rev. 19:11–21), bringing down the New Jerusalem from heaven to earth and creating an eternally peaceable environment: "He will wipe every tear from their eyes. There will be no more death or mourning or crying or pain, for the old order of things has passed away" (Rev. 21:4). In the meantime, we are to pursue peace, not war.

WAR AND STATE

If there is no biblical warrant, then, for the Church to engage in any kind of physical warfare, what about the post-Pentecost state? There is such warrant—but not on the basis that any such state is a new "Israel" led by a new prophet or king like Moses or David (chapter 4). John Milton was right to say, in his iconoclastic tract against Charles I in 1649, that it is a false claim "that all kings are the Lord's anointed."[62] It is also a false claim, however, that any *republic* bears this divine imprimatur (whether based in Geneva, Münster, or London).

However, we do not need to go to Moses or David, specifically, to find the warrant. As in the case of punishment in chapter 8, it is reasonable to ground the state's authority to go to war more generally in its God-ordained nature as articulated in a passage like Romans 13. All governance requires some recourse to coercive measures if a governed community is to flourish, for there are always threats to this flourishing. These threats are not only *internal*—the threats that we considered in chapter 8. They are also *external*. It is reasonable to believe that rulers appointed by God to keep order in the world by bringing "terror" upon "those who do wrong" and authorized by God to use lethal violence where necessary to bring "punishment on the wrongdoer" (Rom. 13:1–5) are thereby also appointed and authorized to fight wars, at least in certain circumstances.

As in the case of punishment more narrowly, Romans 13 does not of itself help us to discern precisely what those circumstances might be. It does, however, predispose us to think about this question within the framework of justice—a framework within which all human (and not merely Israelite) governance is set in the Bible.[63] No war can possibly be justified that is not fought for a just cause, and indeed in a just manner—an expectation that already lies behind Amos' fierce criticisms of Gentile rulers for war crimes in Amos 1. No war can possibly be justified that is about something other than bringing "terror" upon "those who do wrong" or upon those who are clearly *about* to do wrong, and about bringing "punishment on the wrongdoer." This already rules out many different kinds of war. It rules out mere wars of expansion, for example—wars fought to gain territory and control over the peoples and goods of a territory, which is theft (we recall Tertullian's comments about Rome's wars in chapter 4). It rules out wars designed merely to force others into alignment with one's own governing beliefs and values—crusading wars, designed merely to suppress diversity of belief or practice. It also rules out wars in which the lethal violence enacted is disproportionate to the faults of the people being attacked, and it certainly forbids imposing such violence on people who are not directly blameworthy at all or should otherwise be excluded from punishment (including noncombatants). Minimally, these are the kinds of things involved in unjust, impermissible war.

Moreover, the Christian belief that the state has the *authority* to execute lethal violence in war under certain circumstances does not of itself imply any consequent belief that the state *should in fact* do so in particular cases. The situation is analogous to that of lethal punishment generally. Given that it is not war that lies deepest in the heart of God but peace, Christians should regard any resort to war by the state in which they reside as something that is best avoided—a last resort rather than a norm, even in a very wicked world. They should certainly not encourage even just wars or rejoice in them. In the words of one modern author, "violence is [only] justified in the Christian tradition as a lesser evil in a situation of restricted choice among unattractive options."[64] Even when wars are just, they are to be lamented—as Augustine rightly said long ago.[65] Augustine's own view of just war is in my view quite inadequate, not least because he draws precisely the direct connection between Israel's wars and those subsequent to Pentecost that I have warned against above, writing (for example) of "the 'splendid victories over ungodly enemies' with which God has crowned Christian emperors."[66] However, in lamenting even just wars he is surely correct.

THE JUST WAR AND THE CHRISTIAN

Just wars there may sometimes be, in any case—but should Christians involve themselves in them? Augustine's opinion was that it was acceptable to do so, albeit that a Christian should never delight in the shedding of blood.[67] The earliest of the Church Fathers, however—prior to Constantine—took a different view, questioning whether Christians could even be soldiers in the Roman army at all.

The First Apology of Justin Martyr, for example, assures the Roman Emperor Antoninus Pius in the second century that Christians look for a kingdom that is not of this world (the kingdom of peace prophesied in Isa. 2), starkly differentiating "the soldiers enrolled by you, and who have taken the military oath," from "we [Christians] who . . . refrain from making war upon our enemies."[68] He thereby identifies "nonviolence as an essential attribute of discipleship."[69] In the same century the pagan Roman bureaucrat Celsus confirms, as he complains about the fact, that Christians in his time refuse to fight in defense of the Roman Empire. At the turn of the third century Tertullian manifests "categorical opposition to the military profession, notwithstanding that his father was a Roman centurion."[70] For him it is a matter of true worship, on the one hand, and idolatry, on the other.[71] Tertullian acknowledges that God's people fought wars in the OT, but asks: "how will *a Christian man* war, nay, how will he serve even in peace, without a sword, which the Lord has taken away?"[72] What if someone who is already a soldier converts? He may choose to remain a soldier, writes Tertullian, but he must recognize the virtually impossible position in which this places him as a man with now conflicting loyalties.[73]

Writing in the third century, and again referencing Isaiah 2, Origen claims that Christians "no longer take up 'sword against nation,' nor do we 'learn war anymore.'" We have become, he says "children of peace, for the sake of Jesus, who is our leader, instead of those whom our fathers followed, among whom we were 'strangers to the covenant.'"[74] He is keenly aware of the difference in this respect "between the constitution which was given to the Jews of old by Moses, and that which the Christians, under the direction of Christ's teaching, wish now to establish."[75] Ancient Israel, possessing "a land and a form of government of their own," was for good reason given "the right of making war upon their enemies" as well as "putting to death or otherwise punishing adulterers, murderers, or others who were guilty of similar crimes."[76] The situation now, however, is not the same.

In the early Church prior to Constantine, then, we find a principled rejection of any idea of Christians engaging in physical warfare, although some writers stopped short of absolutely requiring converted soldiers to leave the army. It was generally agreed that it was not the business of a Christ-follower to involve himself in the necessarily coercive, violent, political life of the Empire, even though it *was* his duty to pray for the emperor and for the security to the empire. This *spiritual* warfare was not only commended but regarded as more efficacious than the alternative: "none fight better for the king than we do," Origen claimed, referencing the apostolic injunctions about spiritual warfare in Ephesians 6. "We do not indeed fight under him, although he require it; but we fight on his behalf, forming a special army—an army of piety—by offering our prayers to God."[77] These are prayers "on behalf of those who are fighting in a righteous cause, and for the king who reigns righteously, that whatever is opposed to those who act righteously may be destroyed!" These comments remind us of Tertullian's earlier claim, noted in our chapter 4, that Christians pray fervently, among other things, "for brave armies."[78]

Yet here a question arises that has already been considered in a different form in chapter 8. If a cause really is righteous, and it is authentically Christian to *pray for* brave armies that will lead to its triumph—if war is discovered to be the "lesser evil in a situation of restricted choice among unattractive options"—why would it be forbidden to Christians also to *serve in* those brave armies? Is it not rather selfish, in fact, to affirm others' right to prosecute a just war—fighting against evil and in pursuit of what is right—while staying safely at home? It seems that we are on the horns of a Christian dilemma in such a case, and many have sharply felt the point. It is not difficult to conceive of a situation in which love of both our far-neighbors who need defending and our near-neighbors who have agreed to go and defend them would surely require our own, self-sacrificial involvement in a war, even if it meant taking up arms against still other neighbors who are the aggressors. If we believe as Bible readers that there is such a thing as "appropriate coercion" in suppressing evil, it is very difficult to see why we would expect others to do the suppressing without our own involvement. This is why many Christians through the ages, while fully recognizing the calling of the Church to pursue peace with all of its energy and to the maximal degree possible, have not found themselves able to become principled pacifists. Love of one neighbor, they have concluded, sometimes necessitates coercive violence against another.

CONCLUSION

Looking back on the entirety of chapter 9, then: there is very little to be said for the widespread assumption in Christendom throughout the period from Constantine to the English Commonwealth that the exhortations to and descriptions of war that we find in the OT warrant post-Pentecost authorities to fight similar wars. There is in any event certainly no biblical warrant at all for the post-Pentecost fighting of expansionist wars, nor any kind of war involving disproportionate, indiscriminate violence—nor crusading, utopian wars of purification fought in pursuit of any vision of "Jerusalem." No post-Pentecost army is the army of Israel, called by God to do what the latter sometimes did. It may occasionally be necessary for Christians to support their state in fighting a just war—but only as a last resort, and with deep regret. It may also be necessary for Christians not only to support such a war but to fight in it. Much will depend in both cases on how the "evils" of the situation are weighed so as to reveal the least of the ones that confront us. This very difficult calculation will need to take account (among other things) of whether the outcomes of the war are likely to be worth the inevitable suffering involved in fighting it. Outcomes are, of course, almost impossible to predict, and even wars in what many would consider a just cause can produce grim realities in their wake.[79]

Measured by such a standard, the great majority of the wars that we have touched upon so far in the book—like the great majority of the executions—were unequivocally wrong. They were unjust either in principle, or in their conduct, or in both respects. There is something particularly grotesque, indeed, in associating the name of Christ, the Prince of Peace, with the truly dreadful violence carried out by the various "men of blood" involved in so many of these conflicts, albeit that they believed themselves to be faithful servants of God in enacting it.

DISCUSSION QUESTIONS

1. Should Christians celebrate the military forces of the state in which they live?
2. Is it ever right to take up arms against a God-ordained government? Under what circumstances?
3. Name a just war that you know about. What made it just? Was there any injustice about it?
4. Should Christians ever participate in warfare? In which circumstances, and in which roles?

10

A City upon a Hill

The Godly Republic in New England

There was a people, of whom the God of heaven said, This people have I formed for myself, they shall shew forth my praise. And if there be such a people anywhere under the cope of heaven at this day, 'tis the English nation. But of the English nation, certainly there is no colony, or plantation that hath more cause to shew forth the praise of the Almighty, than that which is now and here convened.[1]

Cotton Mather

The reader will recall from chapter 9 that King James I of England, Scotland, and Ireland believed in religious conformity. So did his son Charles I. One consequence of this was that during these two reigns in England many nonconformists decided to go into exile, with some taking the significant step of moving to North America. The most well-known of these settlers in the "New World" are often known today as the "Pilgrim Fathers." Travelling from England to America, by way of a short stay in the Dutch Republic, on their now-famous ship the *Mayflower*, in 1620 they landed at Plymouth, Massachusetts, and founded there the first permanent settlement in New England. However, a much more important and consequential migration began about a decade later, when thousands of Puritans of non-Independent origin decided to leave Charles I's England and founded the colony of Massachusetts Bay to Plymouth's north. Although they had hoped initially to reform the established Church of England, in the Americas they adopted the "congregationalist" form of church government established by the Pilgrims—that is, each congregation was responsible for its own life and did not need to refer to a higher church authority such as a bishop or a presbytery. By

1640, just prior to the outbreak of the English Civil War (when many returned to England to fight), New England was home to around twenty thousand mostly Puritan immigrants (in addition to the many Native American people who were already living in the region). They were fervent in their belief that, like the ancient Israelites, God had called them to their new home out of bondage in an "Egypt" where they were not permitted to worship their God. Having crossed the sea in order to escape—just like their biblical forebears—they were destined now to inhabit this new, American, Promised Land.

JOHN WINTHROP (1588–1649)

The idealistic self-understanding of these Puritan settlers is well-represented in the words of a sermon preached in 1630 by John Winthrop, prior to taking up his position as the first governor of the Massachusetts Bay colony. Who are these immigrants, in his view? They are a new Israel, called to follow the counsel of the OT prophet Micah that God's people should "act justly and . . . love mercy and . . . walk humbly with your God" (Mic. 6:8), also endeavoring to "keep the unity of the Spirit through the bond of peace" (Eph. 4:3). If they succeed in this, Winthrop claims, God will delight to "dwell among them" as he once did in the tabernacle in the wilderness (Exod. 29:46). If they fail, they will become a proverb and a "byword through[out] the world" (1 Kgs. 9:7), and like the Israelites during the later monarchy, they will be driven out of "the good land" whither they are going (1 Kgs. 14:15). Winthrop concludes his remarks by referring to "that exhortation of Moses, that faithful servant of the Lord, in his last farewell to Israel" in Deuteronomy 30:

> Beloved there is now set before us life, and good, death and evil, in that we are commanded this day to love the Lord our God, and to love one another . . . that the Lord our God may bless us in the land whither we go to possess . . . But if our hearts shall turn away so that we will not obey . . . we shall surely perish out of the good Land whither we pass over this vast sea to possess it.[2]

It is in this context that Winthrop refers to the Massachusetts Bay colony, in words that have been much quoted since, as "a city upon a hill." The whole world looks upon this city—this New Jerusalem—waiting to see which path it will follow and what the outcomes will be: "the eyes of all people are upon us." Winthrop spent the remaining years of his own life actively trying to ensure that his fellow settlers walked on the right path. He guided them as they built their new towns (like Boston), with their churches, and as they created a new civil society. He also dealt with the inevitable conflicts that arose in spite of his exhortations about keeping "the unity of the Spirit through the bond of peace."

THE CHARACTER OF THE CITY

The primary motive for the founding of the New England colonies was that the colonists would be free to worship God in line with their beliefs about right and wrong in this matter, without consequent persecution and penalty. As the reader might guess from having read chapters eight and nine, however, this did not mean that individuals among the first settlers had the right to follow their consciences wherever they might lead. They were bound, rather, by their covenant with God and by other later covenants that were built upon it.

A Covenant People

There were, first of all, church covenants setting the rules of each congregation in terms of membership and mutual accountability. Except in Rhode Island, to which we shall return shortly, "church attendance was mandatory in all of the colonies . . . [although] church membership was far from automatic."[3] One had to demonstrate a good knowledge of Calvinist doctrine, as well as a holy life, in order to qualify for church membership, and in most congregations there was then an expectation of "mutual surveillance and admonition for the purpose of keeping church members on the straight and narrow."[4] In addition to these church covenants there were also civil covenants, by which emerging communities agreed how they would govern themselves. In sum, "the Puritans did not envision their polities as mere aggregations of individuals pursuing their private welfare but as sacred corporations dedicated to higher principles."[5]

These ecclesiastical and civil polities, although separate, greatly overlapped—in many ways just as they had earlier done in Calvinist Geneva. The law was shaped to some extent by OT law, and although the pastors could not be magistrates (or vice versa), they did expect to be consulted about new proposals for civil law, so that any conflicts with divine law could be avoided. Again, disciplinary measures within each congregation (including excommunication) were distinguished from civil penalties in each society, and ruling elders were distinguished from magistrates—yet in practice "there was a considerable degree of informal cooperation between ruling elders and magistrates."[6] This seventeenth-century godly (and indeed significantly "Hebraic") republic, in these and other respects, reminds one of the earlier sixteenth-century one—not least in the way that education was a high priority (because literacy was essential if people were to study their Bibles).[7] A new feature of the Massachusetts Bay experiment, however, was the way in which the strong distinction just described, between church members and the remainder of the population (the "inhabitants"), impacted political life. In theory, if not always in practice, the "inhabitants" could not hold office or vote; those privileges were reserved for male church members ("freemen," or citizens).

The Massachusetts Body of Liberties

The importance of OT law to the shaping of this new society can clearly be seen in the *Massachusetts Body of Liberties* (1641), which is often considered to be the first modern bill of rights.[8] For example, in this document "[n]o man shall be put to death without the testimony of two or three witnesses, or that which is equivalent there unto."[9] Servants who flee from "the tyranny and cruelty of their masters" shall be given refuge, and if a servant is maimed or disfigured by a master, he or she is to be released from service; servants who "have served diligently and faithfully to the benefit of their masters seven years shall not be sent away empty."[10] There is to be no

> bond slavery, villeinage [feudal tenancy] or captivity among us, unless it be lawful captives taken in just wars, and such strangers as willingly belie themselves or are sold to us. And these shall have all the liberties and Christian usages which the law of God established in Israel.[11]

Finally, the death penalty shall apply in the following cases (and Scriptural references are provided in the document in each case): worshipping any god but Yahweh; being a witch (male or female); high-handed blasphemy, or cursing God; willful murder; killing another in a moment of anger or passion; killing another through poison or another subterfuge; sexual intercourse with an animal; a male homosexual act; adultery; kidnapping; and bearing false witness in trying to have someone else executed.[12]

To readers who do not know much about Puritan New England but have at least read something about the witch trials that rocked the region in 1692–1693, it is probably the severe sanction pertaining to witchcraft that stands out in this list. In this brief period of time, in the midst of mass hysteria, over two hundred people were accused of practicing witchcraft in the port town of Salem to the northeast of Boston. After the first execution in June 1692 of a woman named Bridget Bishop, Cotton Mather (1663–1728)—a pastor whom we shall meet again shortly—wrote to the magistrates urging caution. In the short term, unfortunately, his advice was ignored, and further executions followed. Ultimately twenty people were executed, and four more died in prison before the trials were declared unlawful in 1702.

TROUBLE IN PARADISE

It is not, however, to the impact of the OT on New England Puritan attitudes to and practices concerning witchcraft that we shall attend in this chapter— nor indeed anything else mentioned in the *Massachusetts Body of Liberties*. The focus of our interest will lie instead on the rules concerning, and the practices discouraged on, the Lord's Day (Sunday). Before we get to that specific topic, however, I want to spend a little more time tracking the New England Puritan story more generally down through both the seventeenth century and the opening decades of the eighteenth.

The Vision Challenged

It was not long before the originating Puritan vision of the kind of society they were called by God to establish in the new Promised Land was challenged even within New England itself. Expulsions and other departures enabled this vision to endure for a time,[13] but especially after the restoration of the monarchy in Britain and Ireland in 1660 it began to lose its strong grip. Church membership restrictions were somewhat relaxed in many congregations (not least to give automatic "half-membership" to members' children), and the importance of orthodoxy to participation in civil life began to decline. As Philip Gorski puts it, in the closing decades of the century "[g]odly republicanism was rapidly evolving into civil republicanism" in public life outside the realm of the Church itself. The change was generated both internally and externally. The royal Massachusetts Charter of 1691, in establishing the Province of Massachusetts Bay under a crown-appointed governor, removed many of the colony's previously exercised rights of self-government, made property ownership rather than church membership the qualification for voting, and granted broader toleration of religious dissent.

The Wars against the Canaanites

Looking to the outside, the earliest contacts with the native populations of the eastern seaboard had not generally been confrontational, and indeed the contemporary American Thanksgiving holiday commemorates each year the early help provided by some natives to the new arrivals.[14] As more and more land became occupied by European settlers, however, tensions also heightened. These led, first, to a brutal conflict with the Pequot people in 1636–1637.[15] Later, just as New England society was changing in the second half of the seventeenth century in the ways described above, the settlers found themselves embroiled in a second, even bloodier conflict known as "King Philip's War" (1675–1776)—"relative to population ... the bloodiest war in American history."[16] It will not surprise the reader of our various preceding chapters to learn that this second war was quickly set within a biblical framework, in which the Native American opponents of the settlers were characterized as Canaanites who could never "join or mix with us to make one Body."[17] This was by no means the only way of thinking about the natives among seventeenth-century New England Puritans but, as the century came to a close, it certainly became a dominant one. One of its more famous exponents was the aforementioned Cotton Mather, who preached a sermon along these lines at the outset of King William's War (1689–1697)—the first of the so-called French and Indian Wars in the succeeding period. This sermon encourages Mathers' contemporary "Israelites" setting out on this particular "just war" to consider the enemy as Canaanites and Ammonites.[18] They are, after all, the colonial representatives of "the English nation" which, just like the Israelites (he will later say—see the epigraph to this chapter), has been formed by God to "shew forth [his] praise."

THE HISTORY OF SUNDAY

It is against this much broader background of Puritan conviction in New England concerning the identity of their community as "Israel," then, that we return now to the particular question of how they handled the matter of the Lord's Day, and what they thought it had to do with Sabbath rest as it is described in the OT.

We must first acknowledge that the practice in Christian society of observing Sunday as a day of rest from ordinary work long predates New England Puritanism. The earliest legislation pertaining to this topic is found just as soon as there exists a state in which Christian faith has been offered protected status. In the year 321, Constantine, in typically ambiguous language, published an edict that mandated that on the "day of the sun . . . the magistrates and people residing in cities" in the Roman Empire should rest.[19] With this edict Constantine created space for all Christians, for the first time, to rest from their ordinary labors on the "Sun Day" of each week—a day on which Christians had been accustomed for a long time to gather for worship and to which they often referred as "the Lord's Day" (the day of the resurrection of Christ). The subsequent Council of Laodicea (364) urges them to continue "honouring the Lord's Day" in this way, "and, if they can, resting then as Christians."[20] Subsequent Christian rulers sought to encourage their subjects along similar lines, often regarding this Christian Sunday as the equivalent of the OT Sabbath. We mentioned in chapter 5, for example, the way in which Charlemagne's *General Admonition* (789) addresses this matter.[21] One explicit purpose of the rest prescribed in that case is that people should gather to worship God. Keeping the Sabbath was also important in Calvin's Geneva, specifically so that people could attend the morning and afternoon worship services (which attendance, we recall, was compulsory).[22] That many of Geneva's citizens did not in fact care much about this connection between rest and worship is evidenced in Calvin's own preaching.[23] So it was, Scott Manetsch tells us, that between 1542 and 1609 the Geneva Consistory not only "frequently interviewed and sometimes reprimanded people for working on Sunday" but also "disciplined people for engaging in recreational activities on Sunday that were deemed inappropriate for spiritual refreshment, such as hunting, dancing, banqueting, playing tennis or billiards, or bowling skittles."[24]

This same concern for the proper use of Sunday was a marked feature of Puritan thinking in England in the seventeenth century. The *Westminster Confession of Faith*, for example, exhorts everyone to "observe an holy rest all the day from their own works, words, and thoughts about their worldly employments and recreations," using the entirety of the day "in the public and private exercises of [divine] worship, and in the duties of necessity and mercy."[25] It is because the Puritans looked at Sunday in such a way that they objected so strongly to the *Declaration of Sports* (or *Book of Sports*) issued by King James I originally in 1617 and republished in 1633 by King Charles I with instructions to all clergy to read it under pain of punishment. This book represents a royal intervention into the ongoing debate between Puritans and their adversaries since the reign of Queen Elizabeth precisely about what should be permissible on a Sunday. It lists "archery, dancing, leaping, vaulting, or any other such harmless recreation as permissible sports" once a person has attended divine worship, and it permits "May-games, Whitsun-ales, Morris dancing and the setting up of Maypoles." At the same time it specifically excludes "the cruel but popular bear- and bull-baiting, and also gambling games such as bowling."[26]

SUNDAY IN NEW ENGLAND

It is to be expected, against this background, that the proper observance of the Lord's Day would be important to the Puritans of New England as they sought to live righteous lives away from the watchful eye of the Stuart kings and their successors. Indeed, in the view of Alice Earle, "Nothing can more plainly show their distinguishing characteristics, nothing is so fully typical of the motive, the spirit of their lives, as their reverent observance of the Lord's Day."[27] The centrality of the day is well-illustrated by the simple fact that, as soon as each successive settlement was established in the New World, the new community would immediately construct a building for public worship.[28] This meetinghouse was central to the settlement, both spiritually and geographically. To these gathering points, then, the worshippers would come, summoned by various instruments (for example, drum, horn, or conch shell) and sometimes by gunfire.[29] They were typically well-armed in case of hostile natives or wild animals, which were in fact the only permissible targets on a Sunday.[30] As in Geneva, there were two Sunday services, in the morning and the afternoon. In the pause between them, congregants who had traveled some distance might move from the often freezing-cold meetinghouse to an adjacent "noon-house," where they could sit by a stone fireplace in front of a blazing wood fire and eat their midday packed lunch.[31]

THE SUNDAY SERVICES

The congregants sat on hard wooden pews that were not of their own choosing.[32] The men and the women entered the meetinghouse through separate doors and sat on different sides; the boys "usually sat on the pulpit and gallery stairs, and constables . . . were appointed to watch over them and control them," employing physical coercion as necessary.[33] In nearly all Puritan towns black people had seats reserved for them separately or sat with Native Americans. The stool of repentance was set aside for particular sinners undergoing discipline. It was not only the young boys who were assigned constables, or "tithingmen." Dozing adults could find themselves assailed by one of these same church officials.[34] The tithingmen had other responsibilities during the week as well, keeping general watch over (usually) ten families (a "tithe") to ensure that they remained on the straight-and-narrow. As fierce as they were, these men did not always deter those from outside the Puritan community from disrupting the Sunday services in order to present their own point of view—"wanton gospellers," as the Puritans called them (meaning Baptists, Quakers, and the like).[35]

The drowsiness just alluded to was no doubt partly attributable to the length and style of the Sunday services: "Sermons which occupied two or three hours were customary enough."[36] Cotton Mather apparently recorded in his diary that "at his own ordination he prayed for an hour and a quarter, and preached for an hour and three quarters." As Nathaniel Ward put it: "We have a strong weakness in New England that when we are speaking, we know not how to conclude."[37] Yet the members of these early Puritan congregations

> did not dislike these long preachings and prophesyings; they would have regarded a short sermon as irreligious, and lacking in reverence . . . [and] when Rev. Samuel Torrey, of Weymouth, Massachusetts, prayed two hours without stopping, upon a public Fast Day in 1696, it is recorded that his audience only wished that the prayer had been much longer.[38]

In addition to these various other activities in the Sunday services, the congregants would sing psalms. The very first book printed in New England, in fact, was "The Bay Psalm-Book," published in 1640 "for the use, edification, and comfort of the saints in public and private."[39]

THE ENFORCEMENT OF REST

The Puritans of New England were determined to enforce a strict observance of the Sabbath in society in general, and not only in respect of Sunday worship. Indeed, their Sabbath often involved the Saturday evening as well as the Sunday:

All the New England clergymen were rigid in the prolonged observance of Sunday. From sunset on Saturday until Sunday night they would not shave, have rooms swept, nor beds made, have food prepared, nor cooking utensils and tableware washed. As soon as their Sabbath began, they gathered their families and servants around them . . . and read the Bible and exhorted and prayed and recited the cat-echism until nine o'clock.[40]

Even visitors and travelers from abroad were expected to heed the strict rules about Saturday evening that were enforced in towns like Boston, where a sea cap-tain like Archibald Henderson was once dragged off to prison for walking for half an hour, in ignorance, after sunset.[41] Whether on Saturday evening or on Sunday,

> [n]o work, no play, no idle strolling was known; no sign of human life or motion was seen except the necessary care of the patient cattle and other dumb beasts, the orderly and quiet going to and from the meeting, and at the nooning, a visit to the churchyard to stand by the side of the silent dead.[42]

So it is that we hear of a fisherman in New London fined for catching eels on a Sunday, and two lovers tried for "sitting together on the Lord's Day under an apple tree." In Plymouth a man was whipped for shooting game and a woman fined for wringing and hanging out clothes; another man was brought before the magistrate for driving some cows a short distance without need. In Wareham a man was fined for picking apples, and in Boston another sea captain was placed in the public stocks for two hours for kissing his wife publicly on the Sabbath Day, on the doorstep of their own home, after he had just returned after a three-year absence. Profaning the Lord's Day was a serious matter. It was particularly so in New Haven, where the law code stated that "profanation of the Lord's Day shall be punished by fine, imprisonment, or corporeal punishment; and if proudly, and with a high hand against the authority of God—with death."[43]

THE HERMENEUTICS OF THE LORD'S DAY

What are we to make of this striking Puritan commitment to a particular kind of Lord's Day observance? Were they warranted in believing that Scripture com-mands such observance? Should we follow their example?

READING BACKWARDS AND FORWARDS

In the opening chapters of this book I wrote about self-identifying "NT Chris-tians" who tend to regard the 25 percent Bible (the NT) as their primary authority for faith and life and to read the OT only through the lens of the NT as (at best) a kind of "secondary Scripture." Essentially, they read the Bible "backwards." His-torically, these Bible readers have typically taken a negative view of any attempt to associate the NT Lord's Day with the OT Sabbath in the way that the Puritans did. They point out that the fourth Commandment is never explicitly cited in the NT as having relevance for the life of the post-Pentecost people of God. We encounter no clear statement indicating that post-Pentecost Christians *ought* to keep a weekly Sabbath. The apostle Paul in Colossians 2:16–17, moreover, exhorts the Christians in Colossae not to "let anyone judge you by what you eat or drink, or with regard to a religious festival, a New Moon celebration, or a Sabbath day. These are a shadow of the things that were to come; the reality, however, is found in Christ." This has often been regarded as something of a "proof text" in relation to Christian observation of the Sabbath; Paul tells Christians not to observe it, and that is the end of the matter.

It has been the argument of this book thus far, on the other hand, that anyone who takes the teaching of Jesus Christ and his apostles seriously is obliged *precisely as* a "NT Christian" to regard the OT, not merely as *secondary* Scripture but rather as fundamental, originating Scripture that is itself "useful for teaching, rebuking, correcting, and training in righteousness, so that the servant of God may be thoroughly equipped for every good work" (2 Tim. 3:16). It is the major part of the literature by which Christians ought to measure what the good life looks like—the 75 percent of the primary source material that we must indeed consult *first of all* when we want to know what to believe and how to live. And *then* we should also take the NT equally seriously as *subsequent* Scripture that everywhere builds on what has gone before but which we shall not properly understand if we limit ourselves to reading only from its pages. That is, we need to read the Bible "forwards," from beginning to end, in just the way that we would read any story, and we need to try to situate each individual text within the sweep of the whole biblical Story read in that manner.

This is the broader context in which the significance of something like the "silence" of the NT concerning Christian Sabbath observance must be assessed. This is also the broader context in which we must read a text like Colossians 2:16–17, which derives from the very same apostle (we must remember) who is responsible for 2 Timothy 3:16. Reading the Bible well is never a matter of "proof texting" with one or two texts found in either Testament. It is always a matter of reading cumulatively and contextually, trying to see how all the different texts together comprise a coherent (if sometimes complex) pattern touching upon a particular doctrinal or ethical matter. Sometimes we may well be unable to *see* how one text fits into the overall pattern suggested by the remainder. That is not a good reason to set aside the majority of texts in favor of the one—if indeed we have rechecked our work on the majority and found it to be well-founded. It *is* a good reason to keep wrestling with the one text in order to ascertain how we might better understand its connection with the many.

The Old Testament Trajectory

The correct place to begin in reflecting on the question of the Christian and the Sabbath, then, is not in the NT but in the Pentateuch. Here the weekly Sabbath day of rest is first mentioned in the Ten Commandments in Exodus 20:8–11, whose content is substantially repeated in Deuteronomy 5:12–15. The two versions of the Commandment vary mainly in connecting Sabbath rest with God resting after creating the world, in the first case, and with the Israelite escape from Egypt, in the second case, which is essentially portrayed in Exodus as a new creation: God's people once again emerge on dry land out of the midst of water and are given a vocation. The idea of one day of rest each week for God's creatures is thereby linked closely with the Creator himself "resting" after creating them. The Sabbath is an uncommon, holy day "(belonging) to the Lord your God" (Exod. 20; Deut. 5:14), and it is be marked as such by such cessation from labor. Deuteronomy especially emphasizes rest for the servants or slaves of the Israelites, who were themselves once slaves in Egypt. Sabbath allows that "your male and female servants may rest, as you do" (Deut. 5:14).

The Sabbath is first of all about God's people imitating God in resting after each week's "creative works," then, and in so doing caring not only for oneself but also for God's other creatures—his other image bearers, both male and female (son and daughter, male and female servant, foreigner), as well as his nonhuman Creation (animals; Deut. 5:14 specifies ox and donkey). It is, secondly, about very deliberately not constructing a society like the one in ancient Egypt. God's people are to remember that they were oppressed by the god-king Pharaoh in Egypt and avoid oppressing others in the just society of Yahweh. That is, the Sabbath is the central symbol of the difference between the good society ordained by Yahweh and the oppressive society ordained by the false gods. For the world created by Yahweh has at its heart a seventh day of rest, in which there is space for all creatures to remember that life is more than work, and that the universe is more than an object to be manipulated in pursuit of gain. The world of Pharaoh, on the other hand, is one in which there is no rest but only feverish productivity (Exod. 1–2). We are presented in the Sabbath with an "alternative to the exploitative ways of the world that begin in self-serving idolatry and end in destructive covetousness."[44] All of this is what this "holy day" represents—a day set apart each week from others, removed from the sphere of the normal and the commonplace. Other OT texts then unpack for us more of what this looks like. God's people should prepare for the Sabbath on the previous day, ensuring that they do not need to cook or bake on the day itself.[45] It is a day of sacred assembly, when offerings are made and psalms are sung.[46] It is a day when normal commercial activity should be suspended.[47]

Taking all of this material together and setting it against the background of our preceding chapters, we are already well on the way to building a strong case for the proposition that the injunctions concerning the Sabbath are not only addressed to God's OT but also to his NT people. In chapter 2 we noted the way in which Christ-followers (or would-be followers) are urged still in the NT to keep the Ten Commandments, with specific allusion or reference made to honoring both father and mother, avoiding the worship of other gods, the making of images, adultery murder, stealing, and coveting. In chapters 5 and 8 we built further on this foundation in discussing the particular Commandments concerning the worship of other gods and murder. Both were shown to represent creational law for all of God's image bearers. There is every reason to think about the Commandment concerning the Sabbath in the same way. Just as it is always right to love God and neighbor by refraining from worshipping creatures as gods and from murder, so it is always right as worshippers of Yahweh to love them by setting aside one day in each week in which all creatures can rest from their labor—thereby being helped to remember that they are creatures and not autonomous gods, and responding to that truth in their own worship. The general thrust of the OT part of the biblical Story points in this direction, as do particular texts like Isaiah 56:1–7, which describe what life will be like in the future (NT) time when God gathers in all his people from exile and his temple becomes "a house of prayer for all nations" (56:8):

> Maintain justice and do what is right, for my salvation is close at hand and my righteousness will soon be revealed. Blessed is the one who does this—the person who holds it fast, who keeps the Sabbath without desecrating it, and keeps their hands from doing any evil . . . foreigners who bind themselves to the LORD to minister to him, to love the name of the LORD, and to be his servants, all who keep the Sabbath without desecrating it and who hold fast to my covenant—these I will bring to my holy mountain and give them joy in my house of prayer. (Isa. 56:1–7)

A reading of Scripture that begins at the beginning, then, and proceeds to the end of the OT, certainly leads us to anticipate that keeping the Sabbath holy will mark the life of the Yahweh-worshipper in NT as well as in OT times.

CONGRUENT NEW TESTAMENT TEXTS

The overwhelming majority of the NT texts that touch on Sabbath are clearly congruent with this same idea. The concern of the Gospels, first of all, which tell us quite a bit about Jesus' own activities on the Sabbath (including his teaching in synagogues on that day), is not *whether* the Sabbath should be kept but *how* it should be kept by the Jesus-follower—since Jesus is "Lord of the Sabbath," and he knows its true intent (Matt. 12:8).[48] For example, the Sabbath commandment should not be read as forbidding hungry people from eating (Matt. 12:1–8). It does not mean that sick people cannot be healed on the Sabbath,[49] any more than it forbids someone from rescuing an animal from a pit or giving it water, or saving a child or an ox that falls into a well, or having one's infant boy circumcised.[50] In the NT, mercy remains more important than sacrifice, or indeed any rituals—as is already the case in the OT (Hos. 6:6; Matt. 12:7). It is always "lawful to do good on the Sabbath" (Matt. 12:7, 12), not least because "the Sabbath was made for man, not man for the Sabbath" (Mark 2:27). Therefore, it is just fine for a man who has been healed by Jesus to carry his mat throughout Jerusalem (John 5:1–15). In none of this material is there any idea that the fourth Commandment concerning observance of the Sabbath has lapsed in the time of the New Covenant.

It is not surprising, then, that we read in Acts about the apostles, post-Pentecost, continuing their previous custom of attending synagogue on the Sabbath. In Acts 13, for example, we read about Paul and his companions entering the synagogue in Pisidian Antioch on the Sabbath and participating in the meeting (vv. 13–41). They stay on afterward to do so again the following week (vv. 42–44). In Acts 16 they look for a place of prayer by a river on the Sabbath, and in Acts 17 Paul spends three Sabbaths reasoning with the congregation from the Scriptures (v. 2). In Corinth, on "every Sabbath he reasoned in the synagogue, trying to persuade Jews and Greeks" (Acts 18:4).

Paul's Concern in Colossians

Nothing thus far leads us to expect that Paul in Colossians, then—the very apostle who directs us to OT Scripture as our foundation for the good life in general, and who specifically emphasizes elsewhere in his writings the importance of the Ten Commandments for the Christian life—will be found opposing the Christian observance of Sabbath. If that was Paul's intention in this letter, we would surely expect a detailed theological and hermeneutical argument as to why the fourth Commandment alone, quite against expectation, no longer applies to the Church. That is certainly not what we find in Colossians 2:16–17. So we need to look again at these verses in order to see whether Paul is, in reality, saying what people have sometimes *maintained* that he is saying.

When we engage in this review it immediately becomes clear that Paul is not in the least concerned with whether the Colossians are or are not observing the Sabbath as commanded by Exodus and Deuteronomy, or whether they should or should not be doing so. He is concerned instead with ensuring that the Colossian Christians are not dissuaded from pursuing orthodox Christian faith by some heretics in their community who are propagating the "hollow and deceptive philosophy" mentioned in 2:8.[51] This heresy is marked by such things as "false humility and the worship of angels" (2:18) and rules about what can be handled, tasted, and touched (2:20)—by ascetic tendencies involving attention to what people "eat or drink" (2:16, 23). They have certainly incorporated Jewish-like ideas into this heresy—ideas about how to observe religious festivals, New Moon celebrations, and Sabbath days, for example—and Paul is certainly adamant that the Colossians should not be led by "judgment" of their own religious practice to accommodate themselves to what the heretics wanted them to believe and to do concerning such matters. They must not "submit" to the heretics' "rules" concerning true religion (2:16, 20). However, this heretical "package," including its Jewish elements, is explicitly described by Paul as being of human and not divine origin. It is a "philosophy" that "depends on human tradition and the elemental spiritual forces of this world rather than on Christ" (2:8), comprising rules that "are based on merely human commands and teachings" (2:22). The Sabbath commandment in the OT, on the other hand, is of divine origin. So it is clear that the contrast Paul is drawing here is not between OT and NT religion, both of which involve God revealing his will to his people, but between a sub-biblical "shadow" religion of human origin and a revealed biblical religion whose core reality "is found in Christ" (2:17). It is analogous to the twisted religion that Isaiah describes in Isaiah 1:10–15—in that case, a religion that is orthodox in outward form but is being practiced by people who are behaving like residents of Sodom and Gomorrah rather than like Israelites (1:10). This being the case, Isaiah's audience may as well give up on observing "New Moons, Sabbaths, and . . . festivals" as well as sacrifices. In that context God is said to find their religious practices "meaningless," "detestable," and "worthless" (1:13)—to "hate [them] with all my being," in fact. But here, too, it is not the validity of such practices in themselves that is problematic—as if God-revealed OT religion were not in fact "revealed" at all. It is their association, rather, with false religiosity. The sacrifices, we note, "were 'false', 'abominations', and 'detestable', terms normally saved for pagan sacrifices like those instituted by Manasseh (2 Kgs 21:2, 11)."[52]

We are not able, therefore, to make any deduction from Colossians 2 about what Paul thought about Christian Sabbath observance in principle even in Colossae, much less in general. To exhort fellow Christians not to allow others to "judge" them with regard to their own rules about observing "a Sabbath day" within their own religious system is not of itself to forbid them from observing the Sabbath in other ways. Indeed, Jesus himself *kept* the Sabbath while being judged by many of his contemporaries in respect to *how* he did so (John 7:24).

A REASON FOR SILENCE?

The more interesting issue concerning the NT and the Sabbath concerns not Paul's allusion to it in the letter to the Colossians but his and the other apostles' general silence about it in their correspondence. If the fourth Commandment remains as one aspect of the Torah that Jesus-followers should embrace, is it not surprising that the apostles never explicitly say this?

It might at first appear so. However, we should remember as we ponder the matter Paul's reading in Ephesians 6:2–3 of the *fifth* Commandment, which I believe offers us a helpful analogy here (see our chapter 3). It is always right to honor one's parents—but the way in which Paul reminds the Ephesians of this fact takes account of the discontinuity *as well as* the continuity between the OT and the NT peoples of God. The latter no longer live in a particular land where they "may live long" (Exod. 20:12); they live instead in *all* lands, traveling onwards to the eschatological Promised Land (as the Letter to the Hebrews itself reminds us). It is precisely this change in circumstances, I believe, that provides us with the best explanation for the silence in the NT concerning the implications of the *fourth* Commandment for Christians. This Commandment as written presupposes that its addressees have free agency in deciding whether to work on a particular day or not and whether to allow or force *others* to work (son or daughter, servants/slaves, the visiting foreigner, or animals). This was certainly true of the ancient Israelite patriarchs and elders in the land of Canaan back in OT times. It was also true, to a qualified extent, of Jewish communities under later Roman domination. Jews were in principle a privileged class when it came to work, because they "could observe the Sabbath according to their religious laws within the Roman empire"—albeit that the edicts relating to these privileges "were reissued or appealed to with some frequency."[53] Their freedom of agency was not complete, but it was substantial.[54] Indeed, it caused much resentment among their pagan neighbors, for "when they stopped working, the rest of the empire did not."[55] It was a common pagan complaint, in fact, "that Jews were lazy and the observance of the Sabbath was merely a way of avoiding work.[56]

If Jews possessed substantial freedom in this area, however—and along with them Jewish Christ-followers, as long as they continued to be recognized as Jews—the same was certainly not true of the majority of the Gentile Christians who, after Pentecost, quickly came to dominate the worldwide Church numerically. Living in various "lands," with no one land of their own that they controlled, and often being people of little or no power in Roman society (women, slaves, and so on), such choices were not open to them. This is why in the Roman Empire before Constantine even Sunday worship-gatherings occurred early in the morning.[57] The remainder of that day, like all the other normal days, was inescapably a working day for many of the participants.[58] It is not in the least surprising that in such circumstances we find eschatological Sabbath rest, rather than "normal" Sabbath rest, elaborated upon in the NT (Heb. 3:7–4:13)—especially when one considers how quickly in the first century various Roman authorities developed an uncomprehending antipathy to the Christian Church because if its "un-Roman" ways. There is a palpable concern in a letter like 1 Peter not to give this wider Roman society any more reason than necessary to respond negatively to the Church—and wives and slaves are specifically addressed in this context (1 Pet. 2:11–3:6). It would have made no sense, in such a context, to press the implications of the fourth Commandment on Gentile Christians.

Arguments from silence are, of course, dangerous entities, in whichever direction we argue them. Nevertheless, when we find in the first century (as indeed later, in the second) that "the Sabbath is never treated with the special regard that its place in the Decalogue would seem to demand," we are entitled to enquire into why that might be so.[59] A plausible answer is simply that, for contextual reasons, the apostles did not *in this case* press upon the early Christians the implications of the moral vision of the OT. It is nor a unique case in this respect. As we shall see in chapters 12 and 13, there are certainly other instances in which we might reasonably understand Scripture as "demanding" a certain outcome in respect of the Christian life, and yet we find nevertheless that the NT writers do not, in their own historical moment, accede to the demand—very likely, once again, for reasons of immediate context.

SABBATH AND SUNDAY

If this hypothesis is correct, then we might expect to find in the early postapostolic period of the Church's life a variety of views arising among Christian people about how to think about Sabbath rest. This is indeed the case: "The early church had no single answer to the question of the relevance of the Sabbath commandment to Christians."[60]

We know of Jewish Christians, first of all, who continued the practice of observing the Jewish (Saturday) Sabbath rest, typically also gathering with other Christ-followers on a Sunday morning—which certainly by at least the beginning of the second century, as Justin Martyr reveals, had become a normative event.[61] He acknowledges that there are true (Jewish) Christians who still "keep the Sabbath."[62] This high regard for the Sabbath could be shared by Gentile as well as Jewish Christians.[63] Especially from the early third century onwards we encounter "rather widespread Gentile regard for the Sabbath, expressed primarily in prohibition of fasting on the Sabbath and in the practice of Christian worship on the Sabbath (in addition to worship on Sunday)."[64]

We also encounter Christian hostility to Sabbath keeping, with attempts being made to distinguish the Sabbath sharply from the Lord's Day. The letter of Ignatius of Antioch to the Magnesians in the early second century is one such example.[65] More generally, "the dominant trend of second-century Christianity was toward a forthright rejection of Sabbath observance along with Jewish practices in general."[66] It is not that the Commandment has nothing to do with Christians; it is, rather (broadly in line with the idea of Hebrews 4) that it is understood as demanding holiness all the time, rather than rest once a week. This "perpetual sabbath" is the holy life which, as Tertullian writes, is to be lived "not only every seventh day but through all time."[67] The merits of this kind of rest are often played off against those of weekly, physical rest of the kind that Jews enjoy—echoing pagan complaints about the "mere idleness" that marks the Jewish Sabbath.[68]

Is there any evidence before we get to the time of Constantine that Christians believed that their "Sabbath rest" possessed ordinary, weekly, physical as well as eschatological dimensions—and that such rest should be taken on their Christian rather than on the Jewish day of worship? Even though for the most part we might not expect this (given what I have said above), there are hints that some Christians were already thinking in this direction. Tertullian acknowledges to some sun-worshipping pagans, for example, that "we [Christians] make Sunday a day of festivity" and in so doing "are not far off from your Saturn and your days of rest."[69] In another place he writes, similarly, that "if we devote Sun-day to rejoicing, from a far different reason than Sun-worship, we have some resemblance to those of you who devote the day of Saturn to ease and luxury, though they too go far away from Jewish ways, of which indeed they are ignorant."[70] In yet another text he speaks of "deferring even our businesses" on the Lord's Day.[71] These statements taken together imply that at least to some extent Sunday was a day of rest in Tertullian's North Africa, and that the OT Sabbath informed the character of this Christian Sunday to some degree.

It is in any event this latter line of thinking that is developed by Eusebius of Caesarea, writing on Psalm 92 in the aftermath (sometime after 330) of Constantine's "Sunday edict." In these reflections Eusebius continues to develop earlier ideas about the entire sabbatical life lived by those who abstain from everything that turns them away from God, and who give themselves over "wholly to the contemplation of divine realities." This continual contemplation is the ideal. Yet as a help in this direction for ordinary people (non-priests), Moses "appointed a particular day for the people so that on this day at least they should leave their ordinary work and have leisure for meditation on the law of God." This leisure was explicitly not "idleness," still less for "feasting and drinking and disorder." It was for worship. So it remains, Eusebius writes, for God's NT people. They have also been given the opportunity on Sundays to live a life like that of the OT priests, devoted to the worship of God. It is, implicitly, Constantine's edict that now allows this.

UNDER THE APPLE TREE

Were the Puritans warranted, then, in believing that Scripture commends the kind of Lord's Day observance that they not only encouraged but actually enforced in New England in the seventeenth century and afterwards?

ON KEEPING SUNDAY SPECIAL

As to the core of the matter, which has to do with whether all of God's creatures should rest from their labors on one day of each week, they were indeed so warranted. There is no generally good reason to believe that, this being right and good for the OT people of God, it would have ceased to be so after the coming of Christ. Nor is there any particular reason to think so from the teaching of the NT. Christians, their neighbors, and their animals still require regular physical rest from their labors in order to flourish physically and spiritually, just as their OT forebears did. They still require to be protected, indeed, from those who think otherwise, or just do not care—those whose vision of life has more in common with the Pharaoh of Egypt than with Yahweh, and whose "unbridled capitalism," making of us "atomized, isolated souls," has already ripped apart "the temporal preserves that used to let us cultivate the seeds of civil society and nurture the sadly fragile roots of affection, affinity, and solidarity."[72]

The Puritans were also justified, in my view, in continuing the earlier Christian practice of taking Sunday rather than Saturday as this day of rest. Sunday is the Lord's Day (the day of resurrection), which from the earliest phases of Church History has been a special day upon which Christians gather together for worship; already in John 20:19 it is the day when Jesus "came and stood among" the gathered disciples "and said, 'Peace be with you!'" (cf. John 20:26–29). It was a logical and theologically coherent step when Christians in Constantine's time and afterwards, given general liberty by way of Roman law to rest on that day but being offered no other alternative, began to interpret the Lord's Day in the light of the Sabbath. Worship and rest were thereby kept together on one day. The consequence was discontinuity as to *day*, for sure—but in the service of a deeper continuity as to *story*. The people of God in both testaments have been those who, for most of history, have set aside a special day each week for both rest and worship. The Christian tradition having thus been established and given legal protection "outside the land" envisaged in the OT, and with no other options available to most people throughout the remainder of history either, it would have made little sense for seventeenth-century Christians to make an issue of which day was "properly" the God-ordained day of rest, even if they had thought of doing so. Even nowadays it is only those who have an unusual degree of liberty and agency who spend much time pondering the question. The majority are glad enough, still, to be given *any* extended time on one day of each week to gather together with other people to exercise freedom both to worship and to rest. For the false gods of the cosmos are always against Sabbath rest, whether they retain their ancient clothing or (like Mammon) are always changing to keep up with the times. It is always the norm, in small ways and in large ones, that we live in Egypt and that we are trying, as best we can, to leave and to discover God's land instead.

If that space were offered to us on a Friday instead (for example), I believe that we would be wise to consider its merits. It just so happens that for most of Christian history it has been offered to us on a Sunday.

Which Kind of Sabbath?

If logical and theological coherence has indeed been evident in past decisions in general about the Lord's Day Sabbath in the Church, the same cannot be said, unfortunately, about a considerable amount of the detail. This is as true of the New England Puritans as of other "sabbatarians" throughout history. At the heart of the problem has often lain a quite unbiblical dichotomy between the spiritual and the physical—the soul and the body. This has in turn led many Christians to emphasize in particular ways what the purpose of Sabbath rest is and is not. It is for corporate worship, for prayer, and for Bible-study ("holy" activities); it is not for anything else ("unholy" activities). The Sabbath is for God, who is Spirit; and is not for his creatures, at least in their physicality.

Yet this is not at all what Scripture teaches about Sabbath rest. The fourth Commandment does not even mention the worship of God specifically, although it undoubtedly occurred (e.g., Ps. 92). The fourth Commandment focuses on what is good for God's creatures. As Jesus himself taught us, "the Sabbath was made for man, not man for the Sabbath" (Mark 2:27). It *also* involves worship—but that is not its main point. And the biblical regulations that fence it around—concerning preparing for the Sabbath on the previous day, so that people do not need to cook or bake on the day itself, or the cessation of normal commercial activity—are not designed to force the worship of God, or even to encourage it; they are pointedly designed for the good of the physical, creaturely participants *in general*.

Unfortunately, many human beings love regulations, and this includes religious human beings, who in pursuit of the good life have often (bizarrely) loved them even more than God does. So it is that the Sabbath, and then later the Lord's Day, has accumulated regulations from ancient times until the present like flies on a cow pie. Jesus was already dealing with such point-missing and counterproductive regulations during his own earthly lifetime—for example, the one deriving from the sectarian Jewish Qumran community that stated that one could not rescue an animal if it fell into a pit on the Sabbath day.[73] It has not been any better since Pentecost, as we have already discovered in this chapter.

So when we see the Puritans of New England insisting that the whole of Sunday should be holy, this is fine and well. But it is very difficult to see any good reason, from the perspective of biblical faith, why this would involve preparing for the day by not shaving, or having rooms swept, or food prepared. It is impossible to affirm the calling to account of two lovers for sitting together on the Lord's Day under an apple tree—as if indeed it were biblically true that physical rest without any "holy" dimension is "idleness" and a bad thing. It is unconscionable that our exuberant sea captain was placed in the public stocks for two hours for kissing his wife publicly on the Sabbath. The biblical idea of Sabbath rest does not in the least forbid such things, any more than it forbids the enjoyment, after a morning service, of archery, dancing, leaping, vaulting, and the like. In this respect, at least, King James I was right, and the Puritans (in England, on this occasion) were mistaken. But in general, quite a bit of what the Puritans believed that Sabbath rest required of them was mistaken, and the mistakes have not been trivial in their consequences. For together they have misrepresented who God is, biblically speaking, and this misrepresentation has entered deeply into the psyche of what are now post-Calvinist societies, not just in New England but all over the world.

CONCLUSION

In continuity with most of the Christians who have gone before us we *ought to* observe a Lord's Day of Sabbath rest if we can—to the extent that we possess the freedom to do so, and recognizing that in practice this freedom may be just as limited as it was for most people in the early Church. We should also encourage others to rest as well, for this is a good thing for them to do, and for society in general (whether they worship with us or not). Where we have power over others (as employers, say), we should certainly create the circumstances for them in which they can make such good decisions (or not). However, we should be careful to observe, and to commend, the Lord's Day in a properly biblical manner— emphasizing the particular freedom that God gives to all his creatures on this day, not only to worship him in resurrection hope but also simply to rest from work and to enjoy all the many wonderful aspects of God's good Creation.

DISCUSSION QUESTIONS

1. Should Christians keep the OT Sabbath on a Saturday? Why or why not?
2. Should the OT Sabbath legislation have any impact on the way that Christians spend their time on a Saturday or a Sunday? Why or why not?
3. If Christians *are* to keep the Sabbath, should they also observe the Passover? Why or why not?
4. A few years ago in the UK there was a broad-spectrum "Keep Sunday Special" campaign aimed at preventing the abolition of age-old Sunday trading restrictions. Numerous Christian organizations and churches participated. Would you have taken part? Why or why not?

11

God's Servant for Your Good

Tyranny, Freedom, and Right Government

When Adam delved and Eve span, who was then the gentleman? From the beginning
all men by nature were created alike, and our bondage or servitude came in by the
unjust oppression of naughty [wicked] men . . . therefore I exhort you to consider that
now the time is come, appointed to us by God, in which you may (if you will) cast off
the yoke of bondage, and recover liberty.[1]

John Ball

The end of the second phase of the English Civil War can be dated to August
27, 1648, with the fall of Colchester to the Parliamentary forces—just a few
months before the execution of the king.[2] It happens that this was also the year
that saw the Peace of Westphalia, which among other things brought to an end
the Thirty Years' War in continental Europe (mainly on German territory)—one
of the longest and most destructive wars in European history, which had resulted
in the death of millions by sword, plague, and famine, and the displacement of
millions more. It was a war that had arisen, ultimately, out of the unstable political conditions created by the tumultuous events of the preceding Reformation
era.[3] England had been itself involved in the early phases of the Thirty Years' War,
both directly and indirectly, until the local events of the Civil War intervened to
take it out of that conflict.

With the end to pervasive war in Europe in the middle of the seventeenth
century we find a palpable desire on all sides to avoid its repetition in the future.[4]
Since religious differences had fueled so much of this warring, it was perhaps
inevitable that, in the second half of the seventeenth and on into the eighteenth

century, the role that religion ought to play in the ongoing life of the emerging European states and their colonies would come under increasing scrutiny.[5] The concern related to both inter- and intrasocietal affairs. In turn, this questioning raised questions about the very nature of the state itself. How best should it be organized? In all of this, biblical interpretation (as always) played a significant role, and in this chapter we shall attend to some dimensions of this historical reality, on the way to asking which kind of political governance is "biblical" and which steps (if any) should Christians take in pursuit of it? As we do so, we shall develop further some ideas about a viable Christian political philosophy that were first outlined in chapters four and five. We begin with a brief, illustrative history of religious toleration.

FROM LACTANTIUS TO THE PURITANS

In chapter 4 we considered the pre-Constantinian Church—born into a Roman Empire that could not comprehend it and often actively persecuted it—and then the Christian writer Lactantius, who argued that the Roman state should protect Christian religious freedom. In due course, the so-called Edict of Milan (313) allowed Christians—along with everyone else—the liberty to follow whichever kind of religion they thought best. It was not long, however, before Theodosius made orthodox Christianity the official religion of the Roman state (380) and the Christianized Empire became increasingly intolerant of "Jews, pagans, and heretics." This general model of "the Christian state" then became in different ways (especially in how precisely the "magistrate" was conceived) the default for later Christian thinking about the *polis* in both East and West during the fourth to the seventeenth centuries—as we have seen throughout chapters five to ten.

ERASMUS OF ROTTERDAM (1466–1536)

This is not to say that the question of how far orthodox Christian rulers should actually use state power to suppress non-Nicene religion was never asked. Since this was an important aspect of the general question raised in chapter 5 concerning the proper bounds of government coercion, it certainly was asked, at least by some. Alcuin asked it of Charlemagne, for example (chapter 5). Several centuries later, just as the Reformation was beginning in the sixteenth century and accusations of heresy were being hurled back and forth on all sides, Erasmus of Rotterdam asked it once again. "[T]he greatest Christian humanist in Europe of the generation that spanned the beginning of the Reformation," we discover in his various writings a markedly tolerant temperament when it comes to questions about Christian dissent and how it should be handled.[6] For Erasmus, piety and virtue are the most important things about the Christian religion; we do not have to agree on all matters of doctrine in order to be saved. Force should not be used, then, to bring "mere" heretics into line (i.e., those whose dissent from the Church's teachings does not touch upon what is essential). Certainly Anabaptists should not be tolerated, since they are not merely heretics but also rebels against God-ordained princely authority. Generally, however, forceful coercion in relation to dissent is both wrong and counterproductive. Here Erasmus explicitly leans on Augustine's views concerning capital punishment (our chapter 8), and the need to retain room for repentance.[7]

LUTHER AND CALVIN

On the other side of the Protestant/Catholic divide, Martin Luther was of a different temperament: "not generally tolerant" after the early years of the Reformation and in particular "highly intolerant of Catholicism" as well as Judaism.[8] He was not even very understanding of his fellow magisterial Reformers, and he was especially hostile to the Anabaptists. As the Lutheran Reformation spread, in fact, the general result was "the rise of confessional states based on a single official church and worship to which subjects were required to conform without regard for individual conscience or personal belief"—although the extent to which conformity was actually enforced varied from place to place and time to time.[9] Religious toleration, anyway, was in limited supply. John Calvin's attitude toward the toleration of heresy is well-illustrated in the case of Michael Servetus (our chapter 7), against whom he appeared before the magistrates as an expert witness. Calvin certainly did not disapprove of the verdict, nor of the death sentence, although he did try to have Servetus spared from burning and executed instead by some other less horrible means. For Calvin, Scripture demanded that heresy should not go unpunished, and it was simply disobedience when a magistrate failed to follow through in such a matter.

SEBASTIAN CASTELLIO (1515–1563) AND THE ANABAPTISTS

It is in this Protestant context that we nevertheless encounter the writings of one of the most significant figures to influence "the struggles over religious toleration in the later sixteenth century and throughout the seventeenth" in Europe.[10] His name was Sebastian Castellio.[11] Castellio agrees with Erasmus: we do not all have to agree on matters of doctrine in order to be saved. Persecution on account of religious belief is both wicked and futile. Specifically attacking Calvin, he maintains that when Servetus fought with reasons and writings, he should have been answered with reasons and writings—and not with violence. For after investigating the meaning of the word "heretic," Castellio asserts, he "can discover no more than this, that we regard those as heretics with whom we disagree"—and disagreement is no reason for killing someone.[12]

Similar ideas were also found during the Reformation period among Anabaptist groups who did not follow the Münster/Melchiorite line but held to voluntarist and to a certain extent noncoercive ideals. They were very different, then, from the leaders of the Münster Anabaptists, who—as we saw in chapter 8—were highly intolerant of both Lutherans and Roman Catholics and (in the end) of anyone except themselves. Melchiorite "exclusions" resulting from doctrinal and other differences tended to be of a drastic, and often lethal kind. The broader Anabaptist movement, to the contrary, although it did not necessarily object to some kind of exclusion from the Christian community on account of heresy or sin, was quite opposed to executions for the same.[13] The strong emphasis of the Radical Reformation generally on the right to dissent has indeed led some to see it as having played a pivotal role in producing the more tolerant Europe that began to emerge in the eighteenth century.[14]

THE PURITANS

The achievement of some toleration of religion in England, as we saw in chapter 9, was already an important agenda item for the early seventeenth-century Independent Puritans who fought in the English Civil War—as opposed to the Presbyterians, who looked for complete, outward conformity to an established (Calvinist) religion.[15] "The so-called Toleration Act of 1650" was a step in this direction, repealing as it did "all acts requiring attendance at [a particular] church on Sundays."[16] The *Instrument of Government* (1653) that established the Protectorate reinforced this freedom, emphasizing persuasion rather than force in respect of true religion—and indeed, "not one person died for religion in Protectoral Britain."[17] Yet the toleration advocated by Puritans like Cromwell did not amount to the granting of "unlimited religious liberty."[18] It certainly did not extend to Roman Catholics, of whom the godly were quite convinced they needed to be *intolerant*, since in no sense did they follow true, biblical religion (the religion of the Hebraic republic).[19] Jews, perhaps, could be tolerated—but not people who were faithful to the bishop of Rome.[20]

Many of the Puritans who emigrated to New England failed to extend a significant degree of toleration even to fellow non-Catholics who differed somewhat from their own precise convictions. For example, Roger Williams was banished from Massachusetts in the mid-1630s for what amounted to an anti-Constantinian advocacy of a strict separation between church and state and support for the right of privacy in religious belief (and nonattendance at church services). He went on to found the town of Providence and the colony of Rhode Island (1636). There the kind of strong link that existed in Massachusetts between the godly (narrowly defined) and the government was broken, and the rights of the individual con-science were given far greater weight.[21] However, banishments were not the only way in which people left Massachusetts in the 1630s and went on to forge fresh visions of Christian society in the colonies. Ongoing voluntary settlement also provided the opportunity for differing polities to flourish. Thomas Hooker, for example, who did not agree with the strict religious conformity insisted upon by other Puritan clergy, led part of his congregation out of Massachusetts to settle in Connecticut in 1636. *The Fundamental Orders of Connecticut* (1639) subsequently gave the right to vote to all freemen, and not just church members.

AFTER WESTPHALIA

So it is that we circle back to the middle of the seventeenth century in Europe, and first of all to the Peace that "restored a Protestant-Catholic balance [in much of Europe] in some respects more favorable to the Protestants than the Peace of Augsburg of 1555."[22] The central ideas of Westphalia were that princes in each of the three main confessions—Roman Catholic, Lutheran, and Calvinist—were allowed to impose general conformity to their chosen confession on their sub-jects, free from outside interference, albeit that Catholics in Protestant realms and Protestants in Catholic ones were allowed to practice their own religion at home, to attend their religious services, and to bring up their children according to their religion.

Minority Reports

This was certainly a significant step in the direction of general toleration, although the agreement itself was restricted to the three confessions mentioned and even the "authorized" minority populations in states that were party to the treaty often faced difficult times thereafter. By the 1670s the French Protestants (Hugue-nots), for example, were under serious state pressure in France, where the Roman Catholic "Sun King" Louis XIV (reigned 1643–1715) eventually revoked (1685) the earlier Edict of Nantes (1598), which had granted them significant rights well before Westphalia. This led immediately to a mass Huguenot migration to more pluralist regions of Europe and her colonies. Life for nonconforming minorities in nonsignatory England had already become harder just a few years earlier, in the wake of the restoration of the monarchy under Charles II (1660–1685) and espe-cially after the passing of the Test Act of 1673. As a result, serious penalties were once again imposed for lack of conformity in respect of the established church.[23]

    Of all the European states of the seventeenth century after Westphalia, the Dutch Republic (comprising seven northern, Calvinist provinces of the Habsburg Netherlands), which had formally established its independence from Spain during the Westphalia process, was the most broadly tolerant. This had something to do with the fact that it was "a commercial republic, and many influential leaders were well aware of the benefits for trade that wide toleration meant."[24] It had something to do, also, with religious and philosophical conviction, including skepticism—the skepticism of someone like Benedict Spinoza (1632–1677), for example, whose family had escaped the Inquisition in an increasingly intolerant Portugal and had emigrated to the Republic. His *Theological-Political Treatise*, published anonymously in 1670, argues centrally that the stability and security of society is not undermined but enhanced by freedom of thought and expression. These ought to be guaranteed to subjects by a sovereign power that possesses authority in respect of the practice of religion but requires adherence only to a minimalist "creed."[25]

TOLERATION AND ENLIGHTENMENT

A similar line was taken a little later, in various publications, by the English philosopher John Locke (1632–1704), upon whom the revocation of the Edict of Nantes and its consequences had "made an indelible impression."[26] From 1667 onwards Locke argued that the state should have no interest in a person's religious views and practices unless that person (or his community) became dangerous to the state. Granting general tolerance (with some exceptions), Locke maintained, would bring an end to religious wars by turning "sectarian" adherents into faithful subjects of the realm.[27] It seems likely that these publications played some part in shaping the English Act of Toleration that was passed by Parliament in 1689 in the aftermath of the "Glorious Revolution" of 1688 (see further below), and which allowed at least freedom of worship under certain circumstances to Trinitarian Protestants who dissented from the Church of England, removing "some of the most burdensome penal laws that had [previously] been passed against them."[28] This act represents the beginnings of a manner of separation between Church and state in England—"the first political recognition and acceptance in England of religious pluralism"—that in the ensuing centuries would contribute much to the internal stability and peaceableness of that country.[29]

The world that followed immediately in the eighteenth century was increasingly shaped by forces that sought to curtail the political power of organized religion in pursuit of greater liberties of various kinds—often failing, but sometimes succeeding. It was the world of the Scottish Enlightenment, for example, which significantly emerged out of a city (Edinburgh) that had seen the last execution in Britain for blasphemy in 1697. It was a world of Enlightenment in general, which trusted reason and argument as much as, or more than, divine revelation and preaching to produce peaceable and flourishing societies.[30] It was a world in which notions of a principled separation between Church and state in pursuit of such dreams gained ever more traction, greatly influencing (for example) the way in which the U.S. constitution was eventually written.[31] It was a world of growing freedom for people to believe and to speak as they desired, even about religion, so long as they did not disturb the peace of society at large. It was a world, in short, in which the state was steadily becoming less and less "Israel" in substantive ways and more and more something else—a community whose citizenship was increasingly defined in terms other than a particular, fairly narrow, religious confession.

THE HERMENEUTICS OF TOLERATION

What are we to make of these significant developments in how the place of religion in society was conceived? We have already considered in the latter stages of chapter 5 some of the broader parameters pertaining to this question. There it became clear (first) that, from the perspective of biblical faith, particular rule is always exercised in the midst of a community of image-bearing rulers, each one of whom is just as important as the other, and (secondly) that it should always be exercised in imitation of God. It is the second of these proposals that is especially important in this section of our current chapter.

What does it mean to be "like God" in one's rule? God himself, we noted, allows his image bearers great liberty in choosing what to believe and how to live their lives. It follows that these image bearers, too, should extend to others of their kind the same liberty, recognizing (as Alcuin did) that "you can persuade a man to believe, but you cannot force him"[32] Ruling, in this biblical Story, cannot be about imposing the kingdom of God wholesale on the world, because God himself does not do so; the kingdom of God cannot be achieved through coercion. Any truly biblical view of society, then, drawn from the entire biblical narrative and locating the Israelites in their correct position within it, must be one in which toleration is given great weight: "the principle of granting and respecting freedom is fundamental to Christian faith."[33]

Religious toleration, specifically, is going to be very important. This is not because it is wrong to believe that others are wrong. It is simply to acknowledge their right to be wrong and to deny that they should suffer penalties merely for being wrong. It is, of course, another matter if someone holding certain beliefs proceeds to act in ways that are harmful to others; in that case, love for the other neighbor required intervention. In general, however, we should allow even quite deluded image-bearing neighbors to remain so, unencumbered, hoping that they will take the same approach when faced with our errors and insanities (as they understand them).

In other words, Christians ought to favor a society that is substantially liberal. This being so, we should celebrate the thinkers, including the ones mentioned in the preceding pages, whose religious and philosophical reflections on religious toleration had already, by the end of the eighteenth century, produced the beginnings of such liberal societies. Measured in terms of biblical faith, their fundamental thinking was often sound, even if not everything they said was good or helpful. And it would be perverse, in the midst of our own often-flawed pursuit of the good life, if we criticized them for what they got wrong while declining to commend them for what they got right.

It is important to emphasize that this Christian favor toward religious toleration ought to be a principled one—rooted as it is deep in the biblical narrative—and not simply a pragmatic and temporary one adopted out of self-interest. All too often in Christian history, unfortunately, when religious toleration has been promoted, it has been so only because the promoters themselves have had something to gain from it. That is, they have wanted their own opinions and ways of life tolerated, but they have had little interest in protecting the rights of others and have indeed been adamant that those rights do not exist. So it is that Lutherans have desired toleration from Roman Catholics but have then failed to extend it to Anabaptists; Presbyterians have sought it from Anglicans but then denied it to Independents; and so on. We ought to be able to do better than this. As conservative as we may be theologically, there are excellent, biblical reasons for believing that we should be liberal politically. And then, in the context of our liberal commitments, we can decide together which laws and punishment are truly necessary in society, touching on religion or anything else—not so that people may be "saved" but simply so that they may be prevented from unduly harming one another.

PRINCES OF THE REALM

The language of "deciding together" about civil matters, however, brings us to the second issue that I want to discuss in this chapter: the issue of governance itself. This too was a question that was actively debated in the late seventeenth and then the eighteenth centuries in Europe and its colonies—not least because the question of one's "rights" to such benefits as freedom of religion inevitably begged the question as to whence the rights might derive and how they might best be protected against those who wished to remove them. Which form of government, then, was after all the best? What was it, indeed, that provided any government with its legitimacy, and under what circumstances might this legitimacy be lost?

The default position on such matters since the beginning of Christendom had of course been that monarchy was the right form of government. Kings had been ordained by God to rule Israel since the time of David (and even of Moses, if truth be told), and maintained their legitimacy in the post-Pentecost period as well as a result of this same ordination. Monarchs ruled, that is, by divine appointment, tasked with the work that God had always given kings to do in ordering the world's chaos in a godly manner. So it would always rightly remain, until the end of time. Toward the beginning of our story we saw that both Constantine and Charlemagne, for example, held such a view of their vocation; in our more recent deliberations we encountered the Stuart kings James I and Charles I, who certainly believed the same. This philosophy of government remained the predominating one in the aftermath of Westphalia, even as the power of the Holy Roman emperor declined and that of the princes of Europe increased. However, precisely how monarchy was understood in relation to other "powers" in each realm varied.

The Divinity of Kingship

It could still be understood, first, in precisely the highly exalted way that James and Charles had understood it. This was how things were in Russia, for example, where in the "third Rome" that was Moscow "the czar was a sacred ruler, imagined as Christlike and merciful and as casting a golden glow over the soil of Russia."[34] In this case, a strong doctrine of the "divine right of kings" predominated, in which, because kings derived their authority directly from God, they could not be held accountable by any earthly body such as a parliament. In this absolutist view of monarchy, indeed, to obey God was quite straightforwardly to obey the king, and one's political duty was thereby only one aspect of one's religious duty. This idea also continued to be propagated in the late seventeenth century by the restored Stuart monarchy in England, Scotland, and Ireland—albeit much more seriously by James II (1685–1688) than by his brother and predecessor Charles II.

As a result, James—the last Stuart and the last Roman Catholic king of these domains—ended his days as an exile in France, where coincidentally the same, exalted view of monarchy predominated. It was defended in that land, for example, by Bishop Jacques-Bénigne Bossuet (1627–1704)—a prominent apologist for the above-mentioned Roman Catholic King Louis XIV—whose *Politique tirée des propres paroles de l'Écriture sainte* ("Statecraft Drawn from the Very Words of Holy Scripture") draws heavily on the Bible in making its case. His ideas on divine right helped to legitimate this "absolute state created by the Bourbons of the seventeenth century," tightening "the ideological links between God and France" that had been forged earlier (in the late thirteenth century) when the idea that the French were God's chosen people first began to be emphasized.[35]

Louis XIV's successor, his great-grandson Louis XV (1715–1774), displayed the same absolutist, individualistic tendencies, but reigned much less competently and died a hated man. His successor, Louis XVI (1774–1792), facing a financial crisis as a result of war, found himself compelled in 1788–1789 to summon the "Estates-General"—a parliament comprising the three estates of clergy, nobility, and commoners—for the first time since 1614. It was a fateful decision, accompanied by an intransigence with respect to his "royal dignity" that is reminiscent of the earlier Charles I of England. Both led to the same outcome, in the midst of a French rather than an English Revolution (1787–1799): Louis was executed. In the end he was just as unable as Charles to accept the constraints on his royal power that would have saved him—and unlike James II (but like Charles) he was not permitted to leave the scene of the crime. In all three cases what the kings conceived of as "divine right" was, to their opponents, "tyranny."

Constitutional Monarchs

Monarchy could be understood secondly, though, as bounded by some constraints—and rightly so, rather than merely as an unfortunate (and hopefully temporary) circumstance. The traditional princely houses that ultimately survived in Europe did so because they came to accept their permanently "constitutional" nature in the context of such constraints, and thus avoided (generally) being regarded as tyrannical. That is, the prince, while remaining the head of state and perhaps still believing himself to have received such a position from God, accepted that political power was rightly shared with others, including the elected representatives of the people, in meaningful ways.

The English Bill of Rights (1689), for example—containing the terms and conditions upon which the English throne was jointly offered by Parliament in 1688 to William of Orange and his wife Mary (James II's daughter)—represents a significant step in such a direction. It states clearly, contractually, and in writing what kings and queens cannot legally do.[36] In this kind of constitutional arrangement, kings and queens are bound by the positive laws of the realm (and not merely by "higher," divine law as they understand it); they are certainly not a law unto themselves. They live in a society, moreover, in which there is a substantial division of powers within the entire body politic and a commitment to transparency and predictability (non-arbitrariness) in how government is exercised. They inhabit a kingdom in which it is agreed that the governed ought to be represented in the government and that the latter ought to be accountable to the former.

THE REPUBLICAN IDEAL

Of course, it was also possible to conceive of a law-governed society that lacked any kind of king or queen at all. Already in medieval Europe certain towns and cities had achieved self-governance on the basis simply of agreements among prominent individuals within them who regarded each other as equals. There were some strong city-republics in northern and central Italy in the Middle Ages, for example. Such republics were often left largely alone by kings and emperors, either because of the economic or other advantages to be gained from them or simply because of the difficulty involved in controlling them. We noted that by John Calvin's time Geneva had also managed to become such an independent city-republic, ridding itself of its prince-bishop and being ruled by its citizens through elected officers (chapter 7). Münster also briefly escaped from the effective control of its own prince-bishop in the years leading up to the rebellion.

A Republic without a King

The idea that an entire territorial state could function without a monarch then became a prominent one in the course of the English Civil War—although for many (including Cromwell himself) it was accepted only with great difficulty (chapter 9).[37] Still, the notion that the right kind of society—indeed, a more biblical society—should not have a king at all was strongly mooted by some of the radicals involved in that struggle. For them, it was not simply that Charles I was personally a tyrant but that the whole hierarchical system of governance (and law) that had a monarch at its pinnacle was innately unjust. It was against nature. It was also against Scripture, whose OT story begins with equality in the Garden of Eden, before any less equal kind of society comes into existence, and whose major NT apostle (Paul) insists that in Christ there is "neither slave nor free" (Gal. 3:28).

For those who know the earlier history of England, the echoes here of John Ball's words in the course of the Peasants' Revolt (1381), cited in the epigraph to the present chapter, are striking. In line with such earlier sentiments, many of Cromwell's New Army radicals were supportive of the argument that all power in the English realm "is originally and essentially in the whole body of the people of this nation . . . and . . . the supreme power of the people's presenters, or Commons assembled in Parliament [ought forthwith be declared]."[38] That power had been stolen from "the people" by both kings and lords, and they wanted it back; it was a matter of natural, inalienable human right. It is on the same foundation of natural justice and equality that they then proposed particular reforms, including a significant extension of voting rights—since "every man that is to live under a government ought first by his own consent to put himself under that government."[39]

The Social Contract

These particular radicals were not able, in the end, to take their ideas very far. In the course of the century that followed, however, many of them were developed by other people, who explored the circumstances under which "every man . . . [gives] consent to put himself under . . . government" and might later also legitimately withdraw it. We shall focus here only on the aforementioned John Locke; a fuller account would also need to discuss, at a minimum, both his predecessor Thomas Hobbes (1588–1679) and his successor Jean-Jacques Rousseau (1712–1778).

Locke's reflections begin, like those of Hobbes before him, with "the state of nature," which for him (but not Hobbes) is already governed by the *law* of nature—the basis for all morality, given to us by God. This law already teaches us that our liberty as individuals to pursue our own interests and agendas should not be exercised at the cost of the well-being of others, who are also created by God.[40] Indeed, in the state of nature we are all already members of voluntary communities (possessing family ties, for example) and not simply isolated individuals. This being so, the state of nature is not one of constant war (as Hobbes believed) but of relative peaceableness. The "relative" is important, however; some people do disobey the law of Nature, infringing on the "property" of others (by stealing land, say, or by taking away a life). The need to restrain and punish them is one of the best reasons possessed by individual men (representing their families) to "contract" together to form a civil government, submitting themselves to its authority. This is how they come to "consent" to put themselves "under . . . government," with the purpose of ensuring "common weal" (in a Commonwealth). They sign up to a "social contract."

This consent is in relation to limited ends only, however. It is quite possible for government to overreach and become tyrannical, acting against rather than in pursuit of the people's interests—in which case the consent of the governed can rightly be withdrawn, the social contract dissolved, and a new contractual process initiated. For Locke, unlike Hobbes, sovereign power is not "untouchable," since it is not absolute. In the end the reasons for this, interestingly, are broadly biblical; Locke's whole account of the state of nature is premised on the Christian story of the Creation and the Fall, which provides the larger context within which he understands the purpose of government (and specifically, the story of monarchy).[41]

THE REVOLUTIONARY RESULTS

The impact of such social-contract theorizing on the thinking of the later eighteenth century in Christendom was substantial. As articulated by Locke and Rousseau, it played a notable role in the overthrow of two monarchies and the eventual establishment of two republics in their stead, in France and the United States of America. We can track its effects quite easily in the major documents of this revolutionary era, such as the American Declaration of Independence and the Declaration of the Rights of Man and the Citizen (first described in our chapter 1). These documents in turn greatly influenced liberal thought more broadly in the nineteenth century, resulting in pressure on the remaining European kings and princes for further constitutional concessions.

What is first of all noticeable even about the earlier of the two documents is that its authors' thinking about legitimate government is no longer rooted directly in the Bible, and certainly not in any idea that the people-groups making these declarations are versions of "Israel" that have been provided with a form of God-ordained rule that lies beyond question. This is not to say that the idea of the "godly, Hebraic republic" that came to New England in the early 1600s (chapter 10) was no longer playing an important role in shaping American self-understanding in the late 1700s and beyond. To the contrary, we shall see in chapter 12 that it was. It is simply to note that this particular notion of the republic has left no trace on the Declaration of Independence itself. As we noted earlier in reflecting on the matter of toleration, in the eighteenth century we find ourselves increasingly inhabiting a political landscape that is less and less shaped by such categories, and more and more by different ones. In fact, to the extent that biblical influence is still directly detectable at all in either the American Declaration or the later Declaration of the Rights of Man, it does not derive from the story of Israel as such but from the biblical accounts of Creation and Fall that precede it. It is as human beings in general that we play our part in these dramas and not as citizens of "Israel" in particular. Our rights, as well as our duties, do not derive in the first instance from Moses but from the fact that we are creatures of God— and the legitimacy of government itself is measured against that truth.

In much of the republican rhetoric of the succeeding decades biblical influence tends to become still more indirect. The French are still conceived of as "a chosen people," but their mission is the avowedly secular one of liberating themselves "from priests and kings," as well as carrying "this message to an enslaved world."[42] The United States of America are still chosen as a redeemer nation for a mission—but after the American Civil War (1861–1865) those affirming American exceptionalism tend less and less to refer directly to the OT to explain it. The OT would in fact "never regain its former stature or exercise the dominance it possessed in the politics of the nation" prior to that watershed moment in American history.[43]

THE HERMENEUTICS OF GOVERNANCE

If it is true that, from the perspective of biblical faith, particular rule is always exercised in the midst of a community of image-bearing rulers, each one of whom is just as important as the other—what judgments must this lead us to concerning the models of governance described above? Who was right and wrong—or more right and less wrong—both in their thinking and their actions?

ABSOLUTIST MONARCHY

We cannot enter a positive judgment concerning absolutist monarchy as an institution, even if we acknowledge that some individual monarchs in the past may have ruled relatively benignly. As we saw in chapter 4, this kind of monarchy was already well-known in the ancient world out of which our OT literature first emerged. When a divine-right theorist like King James I writes of kings inhabiting a higher realm than other mortals and preexisting other estates and ranks; of others holding their lands at the king's pleasure; of royal proclamation as the basis of law—it is in fact this ANE view of kingship that he is unknowingly reflecting. It is not biblical faith, which resolutely sets its face against such exalted views of monarchy. As we saw in chapter 5, this is precisely the point of the image-bearing language of Genesis 1; it represents the deliberate "democratization" of the notion of kingship in that ancient context. The biblical Story begins by simply dismissing ancient divine-right kingship in principle. It proceeds then, throughout its scope, to give example after example where the "god-kings" of the ancient world are cut down to size by the one true living God, and their ordinariness (including their mortality) is emphasized.[44] When tolerable monarchy for Israel is described in Deuteronomy 17, moreover, it is rule under law by one "brother" among many, who must not be a foreigner who is liable to introduce false ideas of rule into the community (Deut. 17:14–20). This king is explicitly not to "consider himself better than his fellow Israelites" (v. 20).

CONSTITUTIONAL MONARCHY

If Scripture is to be read as justifying any kind of monarchical governance, then, it can only be a low-key, "constitutional" monarchy, in which one "brother" or "sister" takes on a particular leadership role for the common good in the midst of the community of image bearers as a whole. It is only when a constitution is agreed upon, and principled constraints are thereby placed around a king or a queen, that monarchical government even begins to reflect to a degree biblical teaching on the topic of "the rule of all." For here the powers of governance begin to be distributed in society as of right, and not merely in accordance with the judgments and desires of an absolute ruler, and at least many *more* people participate in governance than previously.

Can Scripture really be plausibly read as a whole, though, as justifying even *this* kind of monarchy? The biblical Story goes out of its way, after all—as we saw in chapter 4—to emphasize the institution's murky beginnings in Israel, its perennial dangers, its disastrous history, and its ignominious end. Israel's monarchy is not understood in the OT as an ideal form of government even for that people. So even if one believes that post-Pentecost states have any right to think of themselves as a biblical "Israel" in the first place, the biblical narrative represents an exceedingly flimsy foundation upon which to build a case for monarchy of any earthly kind as an ongoing, post-Pentecost institution. As a matter of fact, however (chapter 4), no aspiring post-Pentecost Christian monarch *can* reasonably claim to stand in a line of succession that goes back to the kings of Israel—to be essentially a "David," anointed by God to sit on his right hand. No Gentile ruler can reasonably claim to be God's vice-regent on earth in this way. Our Lord Jesus Christ has already ascended to sit on the Father's right hand, in the only such position that is available (e.g., Acts 2:33–34).

We are compelled, then, to agree with those who in the past—directly or indirectly "reading" the biblical texts that touch upon kingship in the context of the whole biblical Story that begins with Genesis 1—have concluded that we ought not to be governed by monarchs (other than Christ). This includes many of those who have paid lip service to constitutional monarchy but have in reality given support to what is substantively a republic in which, at least for the time being, public, symbolic space of increasingly marginal relevance has been created for the descendants of the real monarchs of old.

The Republican Alternative

This brings us naturally to republicanism. Does the republican vision of society, compared to the monarchical one, align more closely with the grain of the general theology of governance that I have been outlining above? How are we to assess the republic? Much depends here on what we mean by "republic." We might mean to refer to a society in which the ontological equality of all human beings, their right to co-rule in society, and (among other things) their right to dissent from majority religious opinion, are given constitutional recognition and legal force. If so, then from the perspective of biblical faith a republican approach to governance is commendable. This is not least the case because within the bounds of such a republic power is distributed, and it is more difficult than in other governance systems for tyranny to establish itself in a concentrated manner and for people's liberties (including their religious ones) to be suppressed. At best "it manifests positive and crucial Christian values such as justice, the dignity of all people, due process, transparency, honesty, liberty, responsibility, love of one's neighbor, and the humility to recognize the fallibility of both individuals and systems, including the state itself."[45] Historically, however—and this is important—many republicans have not meant by the term "republic" this kind of society. Indeed, republicans have proved just as capable of claiming a divine right to rule as any absolutist king, and just as liable to rule in an absolutist way.[46] So we are required to go into this matter more deeply, which we shall indeed do in chapter 12.

Subjection to Authority

Leaving this particular issue aside for the moment: what are Christians justified in doing in order to ensure that their society is governed in better rather than in worse ways? In chapter 4 we noted that in the NT "[t]he authorities that exist have been established by God" as "God's servant[s] for your good." As such, they should be obeyed; "whoever resists authority resists what God has appointed" (Rom. 13:2, NRSV).[47] The Roman Empire (in this case) is something of a contingent good in the world, albeit that it will ultimately pass away. This passage, along with 1 Peter 2:13–17 and 3:13–17, has sometimes been read as forbidding Christians from doing very much at all—perhaps even anything—to ensure that civil governance is better rather than worse. These Scriptures have certainly been read as forbidding the pursuit of *change* of government or governance structure and as ruling out absolutely any *violence* in pursuit of such goals. It is for the government to govern, and for the subjects to obey; no one should resist authorized power.

However, this interpretation of the relevant passages immediately raises some serious questions for the reader of the entire biblical narrative—and in the search for what is right, remember, it is crucially important to attend to the whole. For one thing, we have the example of the apostles in Acts 5:29 to consider: "We must obey God rather than any human authority." Apparently, there *are* times when Christian disobedience to human authority is justified. Then again, we are called not only to love God but also our neighbor. This must surely mean that, minimally, we must exert such pressure as we can in our various societies in defense of the fundamental rights of our image-bearing neighbors—such as freedom of religion. This may well involve, at some level at least, "resisting" the authorities in terms of how (left to themselves) they would rather behave—even if all we are doing is making humble representations to absolute power. It seems most unlikely on first reflection, then, that passages like Romans 13 intend to teach that no Christian should ever, in any sense, resist authorized power. Indeed, 1 Peter 3:14 envisages that sometimes, at least, we will "suffer for what is right"—which implies that we have gone on living as we *think* is right, even though the state disagrees. That is, we already have resisted authority.

A closer look at the NT passages in question then reveals what they do and do not actually say. It is particularly important to notice first that one of the underlying assumptions of Romans 13:1–5 is that God-ordained authorities hold "no terror for those who do right, but for those who do wrong"—that they are "agents of wrath to bring punishment on the wrongdoer" (vv. 3–4). The possibility that the one who does right will suffer any other fate than being "commended" (v. 3) is not considered here; the state is conceived of only as just. This is also the emphasis of 1 Peter. The authorities generally "punish those who do wrong and to commend those who do right" (2:14), and those who are "eager to do good" in general have nothing to fear from them (3:13–14). Christians are being instructed in these passages, it seems, concerning the correct posture toward government that is generally behaving as it should and, as such, ought to be respected out of concern for the common good: "the one in authority is God's servant for your good" (Rom. 13:4). It is to such government—not perfect but behaving sufficiently justly—that we are to be "subject." These passages do *not* address the question, what if governments *do* in fact routinely hold "terror for those who do right" and regularly "bring punishment" on the one who has done *no* wrong? What if they are intent on harming those who are "eager to do good"? If a government has abandoned its God-ordained responsibilities in respect of justice and is using its power (say) mainly to oppress its population, is it acceptable *then* to resist or oppose it (Rom 13:2)?[48] Love of neighbor surely requires it, in general, even if these passages, in particular, do not help us with the question.

THE RIGHT OF RESISTANCE

How far may we rightly take such resistance? Failing to address the question of resistance to corrupt government at all, these same NT passages certainly do not tell us about the appropriate *boundaries* of such resistance. In general terms we would be justified in thinking that it must be maximally peaceable both in intent and conduct—in line with many biblical imperatives governing Christian conduct, as explored already in chapters eight and nine. Some of the God-ordained systems of governmental authority that exist in the world have typically offered greater opportunities for such peaceful change than others—systems that involve a complex of balancing authorities, for example, not all of which are equally corrupt all at the same time, and most or all of which govern as a result of elections. This is not the kind of system envisaged by Peter, of course; he knows, to the contrary, of a seamless hierarchy in which the emperor "sends" and his governors enact his just will (1 Pet. 2:13–14). Other systems have evolved in the meantime, however, that have essentially involved people entering into "contracts" from the outset and (or) later. This is the kind of situation John Calvin has in mind in the quote offered in the epigraph to our chapter 7. Here God-ordained authority involves both kings and others "appointed to restrain the willfulness of kings … perhaps, as things now are, such power as the three estates exercise in every realm when they hold their chief assemblies." The governance structure itself provides checks on arbitrary power.

What happens, though, if all attempts at necessary but peaceful change in society fail, and our neighbors continue to find themselves oppressed? What happens if tyranny rather than liberty still remains the prevailing reality? Many have taught that there is nothing more to be done except pray; under no circumstances should Christians involve themselves in violent coercion with a view to overthrowing a government and (or) changing a governance structure. It is for God alone to remove a wicked "magistrate" that he has put into power. This is a strange position to adopt, however. Preceding OT Scripture already recognizes (just like the NT) that it is "the Most High [God who] is sovereign over all kingdoms on earth and gives them to anyone he wishes" (Dan. 4:17). Yet it also certainly suggests that individuals and groups are sometimes authorized to participate in the process by which God's wishes are fulfilled. That is, they participate in "legitimate regime change." This is not just true within Israel (as in the example of Jehu, who in 2 Kgs. 9–10 launches a divinely approved military coup to overthrow the existing authorities in his time). It is also true on the wider world stage. In Daniel 5, Belshazzar, for example, having set himself up "against the Lord of heaven" (v. 23), is deemed to have forfeited his legitimacy and is killed by unnamed assailants; "Darius the Mede" takes over the kingdom in his place (vv. 30–31). It seems a little bold, then, to propose that under *no* circumstances should Christians participate in the violent overthrow of a government or a governance structure. What if, as in the case of a war, revolution represents "a lesser evil in a situation of restricted choice among unattractive options"?[49]

CONCLUSION

Our reflections on war in chapter 9 provide in fact precisely our best guidance in resolving the question we have just been discussing in this one. Christ-followers are called to pursue the kingdom of God, which involves a strong commitment to peacemaking and the avoidance of violence, as well as respect for and obedience to government. Yet obeying the total number of the imperatives involved in this calling, all at the same time, is not always a straightforward matter. In our current case, our neighbors may need defending from the government—not least in terms of their religious liberty. The common good may require, moreover, a change to governance structure. Our submission to our government, as Christians, cannot be unqualified, just as our loyalty to our state cannot come at the expense of our loyalty to our King. There is often more than one matter that must also be attended to. As Thomas Aquinas long ago proposed, then, whenever "government is directed not towards the common good but toward the private good of the rule," and the rule has thereby become the "unjust and perverted" governance of "a tyrant," it may become necessary to involve oneself in overt, and perhaps violent resistance to government—but as in the case of just war, only as a last resort, and with deep regret.[50]

Much will depend here, of course, on how the "evils" of the situation are weighed so as to reveal the least of those that confront us. As in the case of war, this will always be a very difficult calculation. We shall need to take account (among other things) of whether the outcomes of overthrowing a government are likely to be worth the inevitable suffering involved in making the attempt—given that we should never expect a perfect government but only an adequate one—and whether those who emerge as leaders on the other side of revolution will rule any more justly than the overthrown (often they do not). As the American Declaration of Independence itself puts it: "Prudence . . . will dictate that governments long established should not be changed for light and transient causes." The mere presence of oppression in society, then, may not justify such radical action. It all depends.[51]

Is the world generally speaking a better place, though, as the result of decline in the course of the last two centuries of absolutist monarchies, and their replacement with other forms of governance? We must surely answer, "certainly, it is"— even though many of our Christian forbears, firmly committed to absolutism in government as "biblical," would be shocked to hear us say so.

DISCUSSION QUESTIONS

1. Benedict Spinoza believed that the stability and security of society is not undermined but enhanced by freedom of thought and expression. Is he correct, and (given that he was not a Christian) should we care?

2. Is it really possible (or even right) for a Christian to be a theological conservative but a political liberal? Why or why not? And if it is right, why are there are not more of these people?

3. In spite of the argument of this chapter, would it still be more in line with God's will if modern countries were ruled by monarchs rather than by some other kind of government? Why or why not?

4. It is self-evident that it is not "self-evident . . . that all men are created equal" (Hindus do not believe this, for example). Does this obvious mistake mean that Christians should not affirm the fundamental equality of all human beings as the foundation of their political philosophy?

12

Conceived in Liberty?

Race, Slavery, and the People Of God

I have always considered Christianity as the strong ground of republicanism . . . It is only necessary for republicanism to ally itself to the Christian religion to overturn all the corrupted political and religious institutions in the world.[1]

Benjamin Rush

In chapter 11 we asked the question: does the republican vision of society, compared to the monarchical one, align more closely with the grain of the general theology of governance that I have been outlining in this book—with the "design parameters" laid down by God for Creation? I proposed that much depends on what we mean by "republic." For the biblical teaching that each and every human being is an image bearer of God implies that the good society will be one in which the ontological equality of all human beings, their right to co-rule in society, and (among other things) their right to dissent from majority religious opinion, are given constitutional recognition and legal force. Yet many republics, historically, have not been so constituted.

THE REPUBLIC OF ATHENS

For example, the ancient republic of Athens was a resolutely hierarchical society, where the only people fully involved in the political life of the city were the adult male citizens who had completed their military training. The majority of the population was excluded from governance—among them the women, and also the huge number of slaves that was essential to the city-state's prosperity. This was not an accident; it followed logically from the Athenian worldview. We shall return to the matter of slaves shortly; for the moment let us simply recognize how this played out in the case of women. Here is Aristotle on female nature: "[t]he male is by nature superior, and the female inferior; and the one rules, and the other is ruled." Again, "[t]he male is by nature fitter for command than the female" and "the inequality is permanent."[2] The Athenian understanding of the state of nature inevitably shaped the politics of the republic, excluding women from public affairs.

If we pass from the real Athens to the ideal world of Plato's *Republic*, the situation does not significantly improve. Plato does assign women a role nearly equal to that of men in this republic, because he reads the state of nature differently. However, most human beings in Plato's ideal society (male *or* female) remains subordinate to the few, wise "Guardians" who make all political decisions without reference to—and are unaccountable to—the population at large. Plato's republic is essentially a totalitarian state. Absolutist monarchy has been displaced, but the monarch's place has been filled by elites who still behave like god-kings without taking the name.

NO MEMORY OF RECORD

As we have already seen in chapter 11, a strong argument, grounded in human equality in the state of nature, was advanced by radical thinkers within the Parliamentary movement during and after the English Civil War who were in favor of a significant extension in voting rights in England. Since the reign of King Henry VI (1421–1471), only freeholders of a property freehold worth at least forty shillings had been entitled to vote in English county elections. In practice this involved mainly men, but as a consequence of custom rather than statute: "Ancient voting rights did not specifically prohibit women's suffrage [their right to vote]," and "[t]here is some evidence that there were women who believed they had the right to vote both in county and borough seats."[3] Still, the property qualification placed a significant restriction on participation in the political life of the state, and in the aftermath of the defeat of Charles I in 1646, the radicals put considerable weight behind a proposal to abolish it. Their conviction was that "[e]very person in England has as clear a right to elect his representative as the greatest person in England."[4]

When such sentiments were expressed in the course of the New Army's Putney Debates in 1647, however, they were greeted with incomprehension by the leadership. Their main spokesman, Cromwell's son-in-law General Henry Ireton, steadfastly resisted the idea of even a reduction (much less the abolition) of a property threshold for the right to vote. As long as Englishmen could remember, he maintained, the country's civil constitution had been as it now was; its current form was "original and fundamental, and beyond [it] I am sure no memory of record goes."[5] It would be a novelty without any justification in ancient custom to grant a universal franchise. Here Ireton depends on "a mediaeval statute" that sought to legitimize the Norman Conquest of England in 1066 by "limiting the making of legal claims and the legality of any 'record' including land title to the period after 3 September 1139 when Richard I acceded to the throne."[6] "Legal memory" did not extend beyond that date. It was impossible, therefore, even to contextualize the present constitution in a larger, more ancient story involving the Anglo-Saxons, and on that basis argue for change. It was certainly absolutely impermissible to appeal beyond that history to an "absolute natural right," placing it above "civil right."[7] That could lead only to anarchy.

The army leadership succeeded, in the end, in their quest to continue to exclude very considerable numbers of Englishmen from governance, not least because Cromwell himself, proud of having been born a gentleman, had no time for the Levellers' insistence on "levelling and parity."[8] He was soon to be found arguing for their suppression. So it was that, under his Protectorate, the property qualification relating to the franchise was not only retained but raised to the extremely high figure of £200. It was not until nearly two hundred years later, under a constitutional monarch rather than a republic, that the Great Reform Act of 1832 extended voting rights in even a small way in England and Wales—albeit specifically limiting the vote for the first time to *male* householders. It was not until 1918 that universal male suffrage based on residence rather than property ownership was established, and not until 1928 that women achieved voting rights equal to those of men.

MORE TO THE STORY

From a Christian perspective, of course, the problem with Henry Ireton's argument against the likes of the Levellers is that any attempt to understand the world must begin "in the beginning" and not in the eleventh century AD in England—or for that matter, in the sixth century BC in Greece. All national and personal history must necessarily be read by Christians within the much larger context of the biblical Story, with its much longer "memory." This was well understood by the radicals at Putney.

UNWORTHY TO PETITION

It was also clearly comprehended by the women who rose up in protest against the brand-new English republican government early in 1649, after a number of male Levellers had been arrested for criticizing it. In response to these arrests, Katherine Chidley, Elizabeth Lilburne, and Mary Overton organized Britain's first ever all-women petition, which was signed, astonishingly, by over ten thousand women. In presenting it to the House of Commons on April 25, 1649, they justified their activism precisely on the ground of "our creation in the image of God, and of an interest in Christ equal unto men." They were dismissed arrogantly and with incredulity by the assembled members of the male Parliament. Elizabeth Lilburne refers to this reaction in her follow-up petition in May of the same year: "we cannot but wonder and grieve," she says, given our assurance that we are created in the image of God, "that we should appear so despicable in your eyes as to be thought unworthy to petition or represent our grievances to this honourable House."[9] Simply replacing a monarchy with a republic, it turns out, does not in itself produce a society in which people's image-bearing nature is taken seriously when it comes to governance—or even to equal treatment under the law more generally. Republics have in fact quite often not taken it seriously, even at the theoretical level. To the extent that this has been the case, they require significant critique from the perspective of biblical faith.

THE APPEAL TO THE PEOPLE

This is also true of republics that *have* embraced the theory but in practice have not *functioned* in ways that are consistent with it. There are cases, for example, where the political rhetoric explicitly and often refers to the rights and liberties of "the people," even while it is evident that many of them in reality either do not possess those rights and liberties at all or do so in a measure very different from those who control the rhetoric. In such cases, the "people," in practice, have little voice in the conduct of the republic's affairs; the "social contract" does not actually include many, or even most of them. In practice, many republics that have theoretically been governed by "the people" have in reality been run by powerful, aristocratic families or oligarchies, defined by wealth, or status, or both. Sometimes they have been governed, at least for a time, by a powerful and manipulative demagogue. "The people" are invoked in such cases not in order to describe reality but so as to disguise it.

But this is not the only kind of disjunction between theory and practice that we must consider—for the fact is that "the people" would not necessarily manage the republic any better than the aristocrats and oligarchs if they *did* have more power than they often do. Even in a genuine democracy, there is such a thing as the tyranny of the majority, which cannot necessarily be trusted to look after, or even to tolerate, minorities. This, too, is a problem from the perspective of biblical faith. The tyrants in this case are not the same people as they were before—but they are still tyrants, failing to attend to the God-given rights and freedoms of their neighbors.

The Pursuit of the Good

It may well be, then, that *in principle* a participatory, democratic, constitutionally grounded republic offers greater potential for a better society that any kingdom (short of the kingdom of God) ever could—not least because within the bounds of such a republic power is distributed, and it is more difficult than in other governance systems for tyranny to establish itself in a concentrated manner. Yet we need to recognize frankly that getting from principle to practice as we pursue right governance is fraught with difficulty. One of the fundamental challenges is that it requires of us something that is not natural to us: a committed, ongoing love for all our image-bearing neighbors, even if they are our enemies. To the extent that we lack this love—this willingness seriously to consider the interests of our fellow image bearers alongside our own—we are likely to fail again and again in trying to bring the just republic actually into existence. We shall do so in diverse ways, often by overreacting to previous failures.

This failure is not in itself a problem, if our recognition of it leads to fresh striving for greater success—to determination to make the needed adjustments in order to ensure that all of our neighbors are "in" the social contract rather than outside it. The real problem arises when we cease to notice or perhaps to care that we are failing—when, for whatever reason, we lose the capacity both for empathy for some of our neighbors (especially those who are different from us) and also for self-criticism. This is almost inevitable, in particular, if we already pride ourselves as inhabiting the "best" form of society (e.g., a democracy) as well as the best version of that form—if we think of ourselves, in our current way of existing, as "chosen." One cannot improve, after all, on perfection. If the perfection is God-sanctioned, indeed, we may well imagine that we risk losing the divine favor in trying to do so.

The Usefulness of Christians

It is precisely at this point that people consciously inhabiting the whole biblical Story rather than simply their national (or even their tribal) story should be capable of great service to the *polis* in which they live. Understanding the multiple ways in which even the best human attempts at good governance inevitably "fall short of the glory of God" (Rom. 3:23), we should be less prone to the nationalistic pride that so often blinds people to the faults in their society. Recognizing that no way of organizing society guarantees that many of the governed will not suffer tyranny, we should be better able to identify it when it appears than those who believe that it simply *cannot* exist in "a free society." Having the capacity to be more clear-sighted than those possessing the blinding, idolatrous commitments that all too often mark the world of politics, we should be able to tell more truth, over a longer period of time, than others can manage, concerning the gaps that exist between the theory and the practice of governance. And above all, of course, having a Gospel that not only commends the love of neighbor without which a just society cannot exist but also generates it, we should be eager to share it with others for the common good.

We *should* be capable of great service in just these ways. Of course, we are often actually not of much help at all, for we do not in fact stand apart from our culture in a manner that enables us to exercise this prophetic calling. Devoted to the society we already know, we are quite unwilling to "read" it within the context of the entire biblical Story in order to discern whether a better one awaits—and then to encourage our fellow citizens to pursue it. In the midst of our worldly enthusiasms and commitments, compromised by vested interests, we end up contributing to our society's problems rather than helping to resolve them.

THE IMPORTATION OF PERSONS

In pursuing these thoughts further, let us now consider—in the earliest stages of its development—a third republic: the United States of America. We begin this part of our story in November 1863, in the midst of the American Civil War. It was in this month that President Abraham Lincoln delivered his famous, brief address at Gettysburg, Pennsylvania, which captured a particular vision of the American republic. Referring to the American Declaration of Independence eighty-seven years earlier, he reminded his listeners that "[f]ourscore and seven years ago our fathers brought forth on this continent, a new nation, conceived in liberty, and dedicated to the proposition that all men are created equal." The Civil War must now be brought to a successful conclusion, he said, so that "this nation, under God, shall have a new birth of freedom, and that government of the people, by the people, for the people, shall not perish from the earth." These are stirring words. Yet between the American Declaration of Independence in 1776 and the Gettysburg Address in 1863 we must reckon with the United States Constitution of 1788.

THE CONSTITUTION OF THE UNITED STATES

This is a document that sits uneasily within the context of the other two. It opens with a general commitment to "promote the general welfare and secure the blessings of liberty to ourselves and our posterity," before proceeding in Article I to describe elections to the House of Representatives "by the people of the several states." Right away we discover an important distinction in the document between "free persons" and "other persons" who, for the purposes of apportioning representatives and direct taxes to the states, are each counted as three-fifths of a free person (section 2). A little further on, in section 9, we read of "the importation of . . . persons," which shall be subject to taxation while it continues (at least until 1808). We begin to realize, in fact, that the American citizens that the Constitution invests with rights and duties do not include very large numbers of people residing within the bounds of the republic. It is only some who are "entitled to all privileges and immunities of citizens in the several states" (Article IV, Section 2)—who benefit directly from the commitment of "[t]he United States . . . [to] guarantee to every State in this union a republican form of government" (Article IV, Section 4). The Declaration of Independence notwithstanding, all are not "equal" in this republic—and certainly this includes slaves.[10]

How are we to explain this mismatch between Lincoln's words and the Declaration of Independence, on the one hand, and the original U.S. Constitution, on the other? How is it possible, indeed, that "[a]lthough by the late eighteenth century Europeans at home and many in the Americas began calling for universal and equal civic and human 'rights', slavery not only survived in the United States into the second half of the nineteenth century but actually boomed"?[11] In pursuit of understanding we must deepen our knowledge of the history of the colonies and then the republic before the Civil War.

SLAVERY IN THE AMERICAN COLONIES

The important fact that must be grasped, first of all, is that African slaves in large measure "underwrote the economic and political elites who emerged" in the New World during this era.[12] The former were crucial to the success of much of the latter's enterprise from the beginning. This was strikingly the case, for example, in Virginia—the first of the North American colonies to be permanently settled. Here an entire slave society quickly emerged—that is, a society "sustained and defined by African slavery."[13] It was not long before there began a steady influx of slaves into the various other southern colonies that had by now come into existence. At the same time more and more legislation came to define the institution itself. In the process the rural south became strikingly black, while the rural north remained predominantly white.[14] Two very different collections of nascent states were now emerging, then, north and south of the "Mason-Dixon Line."[15]

By the time we get to the American War of Independence (1775–1783), it is estimated that there were around six hundred thousand slaves in the British American colonies overall. This was a large number of people facilitating a lively economy, representing (from the owners' perspective) a huge economic investment without which their great prosperity could not continue. The institution of slavery was deeply and legally embedded in the culture of the south in particular; it had "always been there," taken for granted as part of the hallowed tradition of the ancestors. It had been, from time immemorial, a "fact of life in the Americas."[16]

From the Southern slave owners' point of view, then, as we approach the date of the composition of the U.S. Constitution, "ending slavery was as impracticable as it was undesirable."[17]

INALIENABLE RIGHTS

And so, even though the Declaration of Independence at the beginning of the Revolutionary War trumpets in idealistic fashion the inalienable rights of "all men . . . created equal," the Constitution composed soon after its close reflects the reality on much of the ground at that time: "[t]he sheer tenacity of the slaveholding classes, their political weight, and the deeply entrenched legality of slavery for the most part confined the rights issue to whites."[18] This remained the case in the new republic for a considerable period of time afterward as well. While the northern states soon moved to abolish slavery, in the line with the sentiments of the Declaration, the southern ones continued much as before, using the Fifth Amendment of 1791 to great effect in affirming their constitutional rights: that no person should be "deprived of life, liberty, or property [including slaves], without due process of law."[19] Only a few decades later the Northern abolitionist William Garrison (1805–1879) would famously refer to the Constitution as "a covenant with death, and an agreement with hell," before burning it in public.[20]

NATURAL AND NORMAL

However, it was not only that many citizens of the new American republic regarded the abolition of slavery as impracticable and undesirable for economic and social reasons. It was also that they did not believe its abolition *necessary* from a religious or a moral point of view. To the contrary, they believed slavery to be *right*—and they went on believing it all the way through the nineteenth century. This conviction arose from at least two sources, as different historical models of "the republic" shaped people's thinking about its proper current nature.

THE CLASSICAL LEGACY

The first of these models was Athens—a republic that had built its own economy on the foundation of slave labor, and where the slaves in question (included young children who worked in the silver mines of Laurium) were regarded as living tools, much like animals, whom the master could treat as he wished. As Aristotle once wrote: "The use made of slaves and of tame animals is not very different, for both with their bodies minister to the needs of life."[21] The reason that it "is not very different" is that in key respects slaves and animals are *by nature* not very different: "[s]laves and brute animals . . . cannot [form a state], for they have no share in happiness or in a life of free choice."[22] It was in fact the *general* Athenian (and Greek) sentiment that slavery was a good and necessary institution not least because it took serious account of the *nature* of slaves. American republicans who tended to draw their inspiration from classical sources often shared this view:

> In the ancient world, slavery and republicanism were of a piece . . . classical republicans from Plato to Cicero saw slavery as a natural consequence of human inequality. Pro-slavery thinkers in the South built on the classical legacy, arguing that the labor of the slave . . . freed all white men from onerous forms of labor, thereby ensuring a fundamental social equality and civic solidarity between them.[23]

In the words of South Carolinian John C. Calhoun (1782–1850), speaking in the U.S. Senate in 1838, slavery is "the most safe and stable basis for free institutions."[24] People's *experience* of slavery in the South then reinforced such convictions about what was "natural," and specifically about the nature of the "Negro." As white people encountered slaves in this environment, the latter often seemed to them "to be incompetent and utterly dependent . . . docile, testy, or lazy . . . Planters recorded slave torpor and indifference, sometimes as natural traits."[25] It was natural, then, that there should be slaves, and black people were self-evidently suited by nature to be those slaves. Indeed, after the first generation, they were in a very obvious way born to it. So it was, then, that the prominent proslavery advocate Albert Bledsoe, writing in 1856, even while accepting that in some sense all men are created equal, nevertheless maintains that rights are not granted at birth but rather accumulated as people acquire the ability to handle them. This being so, it is evident that "the Negro race [is] already so degraded as to unfit it for a state of freedom"—slavery being designed not for the enlightened but only for the "ignorant and the debased."[26] Alexander Stephens could further celebrate in 1861 that the cornerstone of Southern civilization "rests upon the great truth that the Negro is not equal to the white man, that slavery—subordination to the superior race—is his natural and normal condition."[27] Viewed in this manner, slave owning was "a moral and religious blessing to both owner and slave."[28]

NOT OUR EQUAL

We get some idea of just how deeply this notion of a fundamental, natural difference between black and white people had penetrated into the American republican consciousness by the time of the Civil War by considering the case of Abraham Lincoln himself. In a letter to Albert Hodges in 1864 he wrote that he was "naturally antislavery. If slavery is not wrong, nothing is wrong. I cannot remember when I did not so think, and feel."[29] Yet just a few years earlier, in 1858, he had proclaimed in a speech that "[c]ertainly the negro is not our equal in color—perhaps not in many other respects,"[30] and he had reassured James Brown as follows:

I have expressly disclaimed all intention to bring about social and political equality
between the white and black races . . . I have made it equally plain that I think the
negro is included in the word "men" used in the Declaration of Independence . . .
But it does not follow that social and political equality between whites and blacks
must be incorporated, because slavery must not. The Declaration does not so
require.[31]

Even an ardent abolitionist proposes here that, in deciding how the American
republic should be constituted, weight must be given to what is true about blacks
and whites as to nature. Neither Lincoln nor Jefferson before him "could concede
that blacks, by nature or condition, could be made equal to whites."[32] In fact, both
are on record as believing, in common with a great number of American whites
of this era, that the only solution to the "race-problem" in the United States, ultimately, was "gradual emancipation and the expatriation of the slaves to Africa."[33]

THE HEBRAIC REPUBLIC

The second historical model of the republic to which American republicans
turned in justifying their belief that slavery was right was the Hebraic republic of
Moses. In this context the argument was not that slavery was from the beginning
natural but that it was nevertheless ordained by God.

THE MOSAIC CONSTITUTION

We noted in chapter 10 the way in which the idea of the "godly, Hebraic republic" shaped the self-understanding of the New England settlers from the early
1600s onwards, leading them to think of themselves as a "new Israel." As Eran
Shalev has recently shown, the reach of this same idea "expanded with the onset
of the Revolution throughout the colonies-turned states as Americans repeatedly heard that they were 'at present the People of Israel,' or were establishing 'our
Israel.'"[34] It thereby enabled the revolutionaries "to conciliate a modern republican experiment with the desire for biblical sanction."[35] In many quarters ancient
Israel was in fact consciously preferred over Greece as the model for American
republicanism. By the time of the Civil War, "it was not uncommon to hear that
'the popular idea taught our youth,' namely that 'civil liberty was born and cradled
in the ancient States of Greece and Rome,' was false."[36] In truth it derived from
the Hebrews. Generations of Americans from the Revolution to the Civil War
therefore read the OT

as a civic humanist text to explore and propagate their republicanism . . . [appeal-
ing to] . . . the "Mosaic constitution" as a template for organizing their community
and justifying their distinct republican federalism . . . and that they relied on the

Old Testament's distinct language, narrative forms, and history to formulate a biblical past for America and sanctify their present.[37]

For Samuel Langdon (1723–1797), for example, the Hebrew polity was "a 'perfect republic' endowed with a godly constitution."[38] He was only one of many "articulate late eighteenth- and nineteenth-century Americans [who] saw the origins of their republic as rooted not in the classical political tradition but in biblical Israel."[39]

SLAVERY IN THE BIBLE

As Americans turned to the OT for help, then, in conceiving their own godly republic, they noticed first of all that it was God who created the very first slaves. In Genesis 9:20–27 Noah is apparently treated disrespectfully by his son Ham, and as a result he utters what has become widely known as "the curse of Ham." This brief story became very important in Southern circles, where older ideas associating the name Ham with both "blackness" and "heat" were developed in the cause of demonstrating the inferiority of the "Negro" and the virtue of subjugating him in slavery.[40] Ham was the father (it was said) of the black people who came from hot Africa, and who had been predestined by God for slavery. His grandson Nimrod, traditionally identified in Judaism as the builder of the Tower of Babel, was at the same time identified with those defying the ancient, divinely ordered separation of the races that ought still to be maintained.[41]

Then, secondly, it was noted that later in Genesis Abraham and Sarah and their descendants owned slaves, and that not a breath of criticism attaches to them in the Bible for doing so.[42] In fact, slaves are one aspect of God's blessing upon them (Gen. 24:35). Consistent with this idea, thirdly, the constitution of the Mosaic republic permitted slavery, albeit bringing it under legislative control.[43] Slavery was legal in the OT, in other words, and it was also moral. When the righteous Job proclaims his innocence before God in Job 31, giving numerous examples, he does not claim to have set his slaves free. He claims only that he has not denied them justice when they had a grievance against him (Job 31:13).

In the NT, likewise, slavery is unproblematic. Jesus never criticizes it; in fact, he uses the slave as a model for Christian behavior (Matt. 20:26–27).[44] Slaves are actually instructed by the apostle Paul to "obey your earthly masters with respect and fear."[45] He does advise Philemon to receive his slave Onesimus back "no longer as a slave, but . . . as a dear brother" (v. 16)—but he does in fact *send* him back, as a slave to a master. Nowhere does Paul suggest that slavery as such is a problem and that it ought to be abolished; the same is true of Peter's letters.[46]

In sum, Christian Scripture presents the institution of slavery as one of which God approves, albeit expecting that everyone involved in its practice (including masters) will behave in a virtuous manner. God himself blesses people with slaves. Scripture teaches that the black people of Africa, in particular, have been cursed by God to suffer perpetual enslavement at the hands of other races. Since all of this is true, it is "incumbent upon all devout believers to defend slavery as 'the cause of God and religion. The abolition spirit is undeniably atheistic.'"[47]

THE HERMENEUTICS OF SLAVERY

What are we to make of the biblical hermeneutics at the heart of this attempt to defend the institution of slavery? Do they possess any cogency, such that they might inform our own pursuit of the good life in our present circumstances?

THE CURSE OF HAM

To begin at the weakest point, what has often been called the "curse of Ham" is not in fact a curse on the person so named but actually a curse on his son Canaan (Gen. 9:25–27). There is, further, nothing in Genesis 9 that implies that perpetual slavery is the intended result. For one thing, divine pronouncement like curses in the OT are not like Greek "fates." They do not describe realities that are unavoidable no matter which choices their recipients make in response to them. We shall return to this matter in chapter 13. For another thing, however, there is in fact a good case to be made that this particular curse finds its "fulfillment" already in Genesis 14, where the Canaanite cities (Gen. 14:4) are said to be enslaved to Elam, the eldest son of Shem according to Genesis 10:22. Among Elam's allies are the Goiim, descendants of Japheth (Gen. 10:5; cf. 14:1, 9). If Genesis 14 does not describe the fulfillment of the curse, the most obvious other period in biblical history with which to connect it is that of the occupation of the land of Canaan by the Israelites and the following period of domination of the Canaanites by David and Solomon. There is no good reason to think that it extends any further than that.

Even if we were to think of it as a curse on Ham rather than Canaan, moreover, there is no reference in Genesis 9–10 to Ham or his descendants being black (notice the wide diversity of Hamite peoples in Gen. 10:6–20), and his name "is not related to the Hebrew or to any Semitic word meaning 'dark,' 'black,' or 'heat.'"[48] In short, "[t]o the early Hebrews ... Ham did not represent the father of hot, black Africa and there is no indication from the biblical Story that God intended to condemn black-skinned people to eternal slavery."[49]

ON LAW AND NARRATIVE

It is true, secondly, that the patriarchs in the story prior to Moses owned slaves and that slavery is not forbidden in Mosaic Torah. The question is not "are these things true," but "what are we to make of them?" Specifically, and in the first instance, it is: how are we obliged to understand them as we set them in the context of a Pentateuch that is designed to be read as a whole, beginning with Genesis 1–2?

It is necessary that we ask this latter question precisely because, first of all, we already know from our reflections in previous chapters that a considerable amount of the material in OT Torah is not creational but stiff-neck law. It does not reflect what was true "from the beginning" but arises (e.g., in OT divorce law) "because your hearts were hard" (Matt. 19:8). This being so, the mere fact that some degree of "permission" is granted to some forms of slavery in Mosaic Torah provides insufficient warrant for believing that slavery in ancient Israel was "right," or that people of biblical faith in later times should regard it in their own contexts as "right." Nineteenth-century proslavery writers like Albert Bledsoe appear to have been entirely oblivious to this obvious point. They simply assumed that the presence of material in the OT "sanctioning" slavery proved that the institution was intrinsically compatible with the command to love one's neighbor— that it was "good." The fact is, however, that the presence of material in the OT "sanctioning" divorce evidently does *not* prove that *this* institution is intrinsically good—that divorce should be considered as unproblematic by people genuinely committed living a good life. Seeking what is right evidently and necessarily involves us, rather, in considering all such realities from "the beginning."

Secondly, the mere fact that biblical characters are described as *doing* certain things is no sure sign that they are right to do them, and the mere fact that they make certain statements is no sure sign that what they say is true. This is the case for "heroes" of the faith as much as for anyone else, for they *live* like everyone else in a world where humanity at large (from Gen. 3 onwards) has departed from God's creational law. Even generally faithful people like Abraham fall short of what is right—as in his pretense in Genesis 12:10–20 that his wife Sarah is his sister. So merely noting what Abraham and Sarah *do* in the biblical narrative with respect to slavery is of itself no sure guide as to what we, in our own pursuit of the good life, *ought to do*—nor is what one particular slave on one occasion said about this (Gen. 24:35). Noting further that Abraham is not explicitly criticized for what he is doing in this regard does not settle the matter either—for it is not in the nature of Hebrew narrative to be "explicit." It is more inclined to "show" rather than to "tell"—to invite the reader to draw deductions from what is narrated than to instruct him or her on which deductions to draw.[50] These deductions must necessarily be drawn from the whole narrative in which the individual episode sits, and not only from the episode itself. Otherwise one might well assume that Solomon remains faithful to God all the way through 1 Kings 3–10 (for example), or that Elijah does so all the way through 1 Kings 19, whereas in fact there are good reasons in both cases to believe the opposite.[51]

READING FROM BEGINNING

So: how are we obliged to understand both Pentateuchal narrative and law touching upon slavery when we read the relevant passages in the context of the whole? The "design parameters" of Creation, we recall from chapter 3, lay out for us how we ought as God's image bearers to relate to God, to each other, and to the rest of Creation (Gen. 1–2). With respect to our fellow human beings we are indeed to *regard* all of them as being, like ourselves, image bearers of God, whose vocation is to rule together with us over the cosmos. They are neighbors who are to be "kept" (looked after) rather than harmed by us (Gen. 4:9, 9:6). In none of this material in the opening chapters of Genesis is there any idea that slavery is "natural" for some human beings, either at the beginning or as a result of the Fall. In biblical faith, God does not create "races" in "the state of nature," or classes, or individuals who are meant to be eternally subservient one to the other; he certainly does not create humans who in Aristotelian terms are equivalent to "beasts." It may not in fact be "self-evident" in any general way "that all men are created equal" (chapter 1) but from the perspective of biblical faith it is certainly true nevertheless; it is an important aspect of creational law as it is revealed to us by God. Nor does God, after the Fall, "ordain" that there should be such eternally subservient groups of people. Genesis 10–11 aside, the institution of slavery simply "appears" in the Story as something that fallen people (evidently) desire—including the Patriarchs—and that God (evidently) grants them the moral freedom to choose. It is in this respect exactly like the institution of monarchy later in the Story (1 Sam. 8).

LAWFUL AND WRONG

This being the case, we are clearly obliged to interpret the legislation relating to slavery in the Mosaic Torah precisely along the same lines as the divorce law already mentioned: it is stiff-neck law. When asked about whether divorce was "lawful" (Matt. 19:3), Jesus conceded that in a certain sense it was—but that this did not make it right (cf. Mal. 2:14–16). It was simply that divorce had become a feature of fallen Israelite society by the time of Moses and needed to be regulated so that at least its worst effects might be negated. So it is also with the institution of slavery. It has "arisen"—and God sets out through Moses to regulate it.[52] The point, we note, is not to legislate slavery entirely out of existence; we have noted before, in chapter 5, the pragmatic rather than utopian approach to Creation that is commonly attributed to God in Scripture when it comes to his rule. He does not impose his kingdom on the world but works patiently with what he finds before him in its pursuit. It is in line with this idea that, in dealing with his people Israel as a lawgiver, God is portrayed as accepting an important constraint that necessarily binds any other lawgiver whose citizenry possess genuine agency: in seeking to control evils, the lawgiver must inevitably "offer them concessions" (as Leon Kass puts it in our chapter 3). So slavery itself is "permitted" to continue in Israel—but under regulation. It surely remains the case even today that, to the extent that slavery or practices similar to slavery exist, it is much better to regulate them than to do nothing, even while working toward their eradication.

THE VIRTUE OF JOB

In none of this material is there any foundation upon which to base a positive argument *for* the institution of slavery. There is no reason to believe, on the basis of reading the Pentateuch as a whole, that a person seeking what is good *should* own slaves or *should* defend the rights of others to do so. On the contrary, the important truth that all human beings are my image-bearing neighbors pushes the seeker precisely in the opposite direction.

We see this dynamic at work already in the moral thinking of the slave-owning Job as it is exemplified in Job 31. Here we have an OT passage that in various ways already explicitly reflects what some Christians wrongly believe to be only a "NT truth": that virtue involves more than simply keeping Mosaic Torah.[53] Most importantly for our present purposes, Job tells us that he has not denied justice to his slaves whenever they have brought a "complaint" against him (31:13). This is to move far beyond the terms of the master-slave relationship as they are laid down in Moses' rules. It is, instead, to treat the slave as a neighbor. Indeed, the *basis* for Job's approach is explicitly the common humanity of both the master and the slave (31:15). Both are fashioned by God in the womb; in the language of Genesis 1, both are created in the image of God. It is difficult to see how Job, had he truly followed this thought through to its logical endpoint, could possibly have remained the master of slaves, rather than becoming the friend of neighbors.

SLAVERY IN THE NEW TESTAMENT

This same creational imperative is fundamental to the apostles' teaching in the NT. Here too all human beings hold exalted status as image bearers of God. In Christ, indeed, they have put on a "new self, which is being renewed in knowledge in the image of its Creator. There is no Greek or Jew, circumcised or uncircumcised, barbarian, Scythian, slave or free, but Christ is all, and is in all" (Col. 3:8–11). In the humanity that is now being renewed, we notice, distinctions on the basis of race, class, and religion that separate people from each other and distribute status and power unevenly among them have been abolished. These were not present in the beginning, and they are not present now.[54] Everyone stands on equal terms in Christ, as Paul also informs the Galatians (3:26–28): "There is neither Jew nor Greek, slave nor free, male nor female, for you are all one in Christ Jesus." In the words of Richard Longenecker, those having the image of God restored in them in Christ possess an "equality that has both spiritual and social dimensions."[55] This being so, they are urged throughout the NT to behave toward each other in ways that confirm this truth. James, for example, addresses the question of rich and poor along these lines (Jas. 2:1–4): if a man comes to a Christian meeting "wearing a gold ring and fine clothes" while another comes "in shabby clothes," his readers are not to treat them in accordance with this social difference. They are equals before God. Paul, likewise, expects that what he has to say to the Galatians about there being "neither Jew nor Greek" (Gal. 3:28) will lead to changes in the way that they view the world and conduct themselves. Jews have no privileges over Gentiles, and the latter are not to conform to Jewish law. Nor, on the other hand, are Gentiles to use their freedom from the law for any purpose other than to serve other people. "Brother" and "sister" are now (once again) the fundamental categories that shape all relationships.

These were not generally the favorite NT texts of slave owners in the southern parts of North America between colonization and the American Civil War when it came to slavery. They much preferred other texts that both describe the nature of virtuous behavior in the master-slave relationship and encourage it— for these texts they interpreted as "approving" the institution.[56] Yet the first set of texts, rooted in God's overall plan in Creation and new Creation that spans the entirety of Scripture, must certainly provide the framework within which we understand the second, just as Mosaic Torah must be read against the background of "the beginning." Specifically, the fact that the apostles often urged both slaves and masters to treat each other well in Christ cannot plausibly be taken to imply that they "did not really mean it" when they so often wrote of an equality in Christ, with social and political implications, that includes masters and slaves. We must assume, rather, that they did "mean it," and in fact their own writings suggest that Christian slaves understood what they meant. For example, why would Paul advise Titus (Titus 2:9) to "[t]each slaves to be subject to their masters in everything, to try to please them, not to talk back to them," unless they were tempted to behave otherwise—presumably, as a result of their new, Christian understanding of reality. The situation is likely similar to the one in 1 Timothy 6:2, where "[t]hose who have believing masters" are tempted to "show them disrespect just because they are fellow believers."

AGAINST UTOPIA

If, then, the apostles were undoubtedly serious about Christian equality, why did they not urge in their writing the abolition of slavery? The best answer to this question is that, like the God whom they worshipped, the apostles were not inclined to utopianism in their politics. They were instead considerably pragmatic, content to some extent to play a waiting game. Our earlier reflections in chapter 9 concerning the Sabbath may help us here. In that chapter, I noted that the early Christians had to live in a Roman Empire in which they typically possessed little or no power, and limited choices—an empire whose authorities were quite capable of antipathy to the Church because of its "un-Roman" ways. Consistent with this reality is the NT evidence that the apostles, while being deadly serious about equality in Christ, were also anxious about any Roman perception that Christians represented a threat to the current social order. Noticeable, public changes in the master-slave relationship as a result of an ideology of equality would certainly have been perceived in this way. The memory was still vivid in the empire of the first century BC revolt led by the slave and gladiator Spartacus, whose forces had overrun most of southern Italy before being defeated. The Roman retribution on the defeated slaves was fierce and designed very deliberately to put them back in their place. It is entirely understandable in this context that Peter (for example) would in general urge the readers of his first letter, although they are "free people," to be careful in their use of their freedom, specifically showing "proper respect to everyone" and giving "honor [to] the emperor" (1 Pet. 2:16–17).

None of this implies to the slightest degree, however, that the apostles "approved" of slavery. Paul urges the Christian in Corinth who is a slave, indeed, to gain his freedom if he can (1 Cor. 7:21). And as to masters, in the end we must return to Philemon. He is to regard the returned runaway slave Onesimus as "no longer as a slave, but . . . as a dear brother" (v. 16). Similarly to the case of Job, it is very difficult to see how Philemon could possibly have adopted this perspective wholeheartedly and at the same time have kept Onesimus (in any normal sense of the word) a slave. There were other ways of working toward the abolition of slavery than overtly attacking it.

CONCLUSION

What are we to make, then, of the biblical hermeneutics at the heart of the attempt to defend the institution of slavery in North America in the seventeenth through the nineteenth centuries? To be frank, they were very poor. Genesis 9 was read, first, in an absurd way that is beyond defense. Patriarchal behavior and Mosaic Torah were read, secondly, without attention to their context within the entirety of the Pentateuch, and especially its opening chapters concerning the image-bearing, ontological equality of all human beings. Thirdly, the way in which this same image-bearing equality in Christ provides the framework in which the various cautions about master-slave relations in the NT are set was also disregarded.

The consequence was that large sections of the Christian Church in the United States in the nineteenth century, already greatly benefiting from slavery in all sorts of ways, were entirely unable to see the republic that actually existed in the light of the republic that *should have* existed, and could not provide the prophetic critique that might have helped their contemporaries to change course. Their sloppy reading of the Bible, fueled by vested interests, simply confirmed them in their conviction that their republic was already entirely benign, when in fact it was significantly wicked. Even those who opposed slavery (for whatever reason they did so) were often compromised by (white supremacist) views of race that cannot be reconciled with biblical faith and which, surviving the abolition of slavery, have continued to damage the American republic and its citizens down to the present day. Yet in all this lack of proper attention to Scripture, the Bible was much quoted—as it is to this day.

This is all a great pity, and one of the things that we learn from it is that Christian faith—and we have seen this in earlier chapters as well—is not necessarily very helpful in forming a just society. It all depends on which kind of faith it is, associated with which kind of Bible reading. It is worth mentioning in this connection the disruption introduced into the established norms of much American Christian life by the revivalist Second Great Awakening between 1800 and 1840, as a result of which, in Eran Shalev's view, America was by 1850 "considerably more religious and Christian than the young republic it had been a few decades earlier."[57] At the heart of this kind of Christianity was a pronounced emphasis on individual persons, black or white, in relation to God—their spiritual and moral freedom, as well as their responsibility to seek to change society for the better. This Awakening, then, proved to be fertile ground in which a number of nineteenth-century reform movements found deep roots, and abolitionism was one of these. One cannot take for granted, however, that Christian faith will always be helpful in forming the just republic in such ways.

The comments of Benjamin Rush (1745–1813) in the epigraph to this chapter require nuance in this regard. A fervent evangelical Christian who signed the American Declaration of Independence, and an early opponent of slavery, Rush appears to recognize in this letter to Thomas Jefferson no impediment to the arrival of utopia in the world, if only republicanism can be joined in holy matrimony to "the Christian religion." This marriage, he seems to think, will inevitably "overturn all the corrupted political and religious institutions in the world." It turns out that he seriously underestimated the depths of the challenges involved in bringing an end to such corruption. As Scripture, history, and experience together proclaim, it certainly requires much more of us than simply allying Christian faith to a particular governance philosophy.

Indeed, it is worth noting, specifically with respect to the central subject matter of our present chapter, that the British with their constitutional monarchy, reforming slowly in the mid-to-late 1800s and the early 1900s precisely in order to avoid republican revolution, passed legislation abolishing the institution of slavery in their domains a full three decades before this occurred in the United States. We may further note, along the same lines (and with an eye to our upcoming chapter 13) that in spite of the explicit commitment to human equality that is expressed in the Declaration of the Rights of Man and the Citizen, the British ended up granting women voting rights equal to those of men one and a half decades before the French Third Republic agreed do so (1928 and 1944). It is not necessarily the case that one state will be very different from another simply because its governance system has theoretical advantages over the other. The difficulty involved in predicting the correlation is one of the factors that should make us think very carefully before overthrowing one system in favor of another.

DISCUSSION QUESTIONS

1. Ancient Athens has often been described as "the cradle of Western democracy," and as something of an example for other democracies to follow. What do you think of this?

2. In considering possible solutions to the interracial problems confronting the United States in his time, Abraham Lincoln once said this: "What I would most desire would be the separation of the white and black races" (1858). What do you think about this? Is it consistent with biblical faith?

3. Slavery did not end in the nineteenth century; it simply changed some of its forms. Nowadays it is less about some people owning others and more about people being trapped in exploitative circumstances (e.g., in forced labor, including sexual exploitation). What have we learned in this chapter that might help us in addressing this modern reality—or indeed the reality of racial prejudice and its consequences?

4. Given that Scripture appears to be comfortable with the idea of accommodating the lesser of two evils even while pursuing what is good, can you think of any circumstances in which a Christian might nowadays voluntarily become either a slave or a slave owner?

13

A Monstrous Regiment?
The Vocation and Rights of Women

*There is no form of human excellence before which we bow with profounder deference
than that which appears in a delicate woman, adorned with the inward graces and
devoted to the peculiar duties of her sex: and there is no deformity of human character
from which we turn with deeper loathing than from a woman forgetful of her nature,
and clamorous for the vocation and rights of men.*[1]

Albert Bledsoe

In August 1835, following a proslavery riot in Boston, the abolitionist William
Garrison received a letter of support from a woman named Angelina Grimké
(1805–1879). Writing from Philadelphia, whither she had followed her sister
Sarah from South Carolina in 1829, she urges Garrison not to give up.[2] Thereafter
both Sarah and Angelina became deeply involved in the abolitionist movement.
In 1836 the latter—a devout Christian, for whom "the Bible is my ultimate appeal
in all matters of faith and practice"—wrote a pamphlet, *An Appeal to the Christian Women of the South*, in which she urged her readers by all means possible to
help bring an end to slavery.[3] They should try, for example "to persuade . . . husband, father, brothers, and sons, that slavery is a crime against God and man."[4]
They can set their own slaves at liberty, and if "they wish to remain . . . pay them
wages . . . [and] teach them."[5] The laws of the state "ought to be no barrier in the
way of your duty" in such matters, she suggests.[6] "The women of the South," she
affirms, "can overthrow this horrible system of oppression and cruelty, licentiousness and wrong."[7]

Sarah Grimké followed this bold pamphlet with one of her own in the same year: *An Epistle to the Clergy of the Southern States.* No doubt the reader can easily imagine the impact together of both publications, addressed to Southerners by Southerners; the sisters were reviled in their originating communities. This was not only because of their views on slavery, however. They were despised also because, as women, they were transgressing widely accepted contemporary boundaries marking out the domain of acceptable female conduct. Although the words of the Southerner Albert Bledsoe in the epigraph to this chapter—we last met him in chapter 12—come from a couple of decades later (1856), they reflect this earlier reality. To a Southern man like Bledsoe, the appropriate kind of woman was a "delicate" one, "devoted to the peculiar duties of her sex." These duties absolutely did not include conducting public campaigns about political (or indeed any) matters.

WHO THEN IS A SLAVE?

The interesting thing about this particular perspective, however, is that in 1837 it was every bit as much "Northern" as "Southern." So when in the course of that year the Grimké sisters, under the auspices of the American Anti-Slavery Society, found themselves addressing increasingly large audiences of both women and men about the abolition of slavery, they attracted strong criticism for doing so. Even people who were far from being proslavery, and who were not necessarily anti-abolitionist, responded negatively to the sisters' engagement with "promiscuous" audiences (as some called them) in this way.

FREE STATES (NOMINALLY)

Angelina's *Appeal to the Women of the Nominally Free States* in May 1837 already reflects this reality, alluding as it does in its opening remarks to those who "scoff and gainsay whenever [a woman] goes forth to duties beyond the parlor and the nursery" and who claim that slavery is a "political subject with which women have nothing to do." One is reminded of the reaction of the earlier English Parliament to the petitioning women of 1649 (chapter 12). Angelina's response to such sentiments is to recount example after example of "political women" historically, both inside and outside the Bible, before saying this: "The denial of our duty to act, is a bold denial of our right to act; and if we have no right to act, then may we well be termed 'the white slaves of the North'—for, like our brethren in bonds, we must seal our lips in silence and despair."[8] This is provocative rhetoric, of course: if white women in the North have no right to act as "public persons," then they are just like most black men (mainly) in the South. They are enslaved.

FEMALE CHARACTER

Yet this right to act was soon "officially" questioned by clergy in Massachusetts in a pastoral letter.[9] The involvement of women in matters of public controversy, they asserted, threatened "the female character with widespread and permanent injury." The "power of woman," they proposed, lies "in her dependence, flowing from the consciousness of that weakness which God has given her for her protection." It is best exercised at home. For "when she assumes the place and tone of a man as a public reformer . . . her character becomes unnatural." Therefore, the clergy complain, "[w]e cannot . . . but regret the mistaken conduct of those who encourage females to bear an obtrusive and ostentatious part in measures of reform."

In other words, these Northern clergy may or may not have believed that slavery was "natural," but they certainly thought that a certain way of being a woman was. So did many women themselves. Writing to Angelina in 1837, Catharine Beecher reminds her of woman's divinely ordained subordination to men, which carries with it a "mode of gaining influence and of exercising power . . . altogether different and peculiar."[10] It is indeed important for female well-being that women should stay within their allotted boundaries, for behaving like a man by taking on the role of public advocate and speaker is not only wrong, but dangerous.[11]

THE EQUALITY OF THE SEXES

Sarah Grimké's fifteen *Letters on the Equality of the Sexes and the Condition of Woman*, written later in 1837 and published together in 1838, represent a robust response to this kind of view of women. In this correspondence she takes the opportunity, among other things, to reexamine the Scriptures often used by the sisters' opponents to criticize them.[12]

NOT ONE PARTICLE OF DIFFERENCE

Scripture teaches, she maintains, that God created man and woman equal. In all the "sublime description of the creation of man" in the first chapter of Genesis, "there is not one particle of difference intimated as existing between them."[13] In Genesis 2, likewise, the female is a companion to the male, "in all respects his equal."[14] Here she is immediately at odds with much prevailing opinion which, although granting men and women equal status before God as to their essential being, insisted that our first ancestress Eve finds herself in these opening chapters of Genesis in a secondary and inferior position vis-à-vis Adam. The main features of the argument are, first, that the women is created after and out of the man as his helper—she is a subordinate "part" of him (2:18, 20–22); and, secondly, that the man later gives expression to his authority over the woman by naming her, just as he previously named all the animals (2:19–20, 23). For Sarah Grimké, however, it is only with the entrance of evil into the world in Genesis 3 that we see "subordination" also entering the biblical account, as a "struggle for dominion" develops. God foretells that this struggle will lead to male ascendancy—but both male and female remain image bearers nonetheless. In the view of many of her opponents, on the other hand, the "subordination" of Genesis 3 represents only an intensification of what we already seen in Genesis 2. Even if this is not so, God does not *foretell* male ascendancy in Genesis 3 but rather *ordains* it. It is one aspect of his cursing of the fallen world that, because of her sin, the man will rule over her (Gen. 3:16).

AT ODDS WITH THE WORLD

When Grimké holds that woman is subject to God alone, then, and is accountable only to God for the way in which she uses her God-given gifts, she is entirely at odds with majority opinion. And where she affirms that "I am unable to learn from sacred writ when woman was deprived by God of her equality with man,"[15] her opponents cite many Scriptures that are said to speak precisely to that issue. The same subordinate status announced in Genesis 2–3 is everywhere to be seen in the OT narrative, they claim, and it is also a marked feature of the Mosaic law, where women are by no means equal to men but are instead, like slaves, the property of a male master (e.g., Exod. 20:17; Deut. 22:13–21). The situation in the NT is no different. The apostle Paul tells us that "the head of the woman is man" (1 Cor. 11:3), and that man was not "created for woman, but woman for man" (11:8). Since "the husband is the head of the wife as Christ is the head of the church ... [then] as the church submits to Christ, so also wives should submit to their husbands in everything."[16] First Timothy 2:11–15 clearly forbids a woman to assume authority over a man. This same submission is recommended by Peter (1 Pet. 3:1–6).

THEOLOGY AND PRACTICE

These very different understandings of biblical teaching were of course closely connected with very different understandings of contemporary nineteenth-century society and what had preceded it. For Sarah Grimké, dominion was given to both man and woman "over every other creature, but not over each other."[17] That is how things should have remained. All over the world, however, men have in reality made of women both slaves and "pretty toys or as mere instruments of pleasure."[18] This is also the case in the United States—a country in which, for example, women's education consists "almost exclusively in culinary and other manual operations."[19] It is to be lamented that woman has thus "lived so far below her privileges and her obligations" rather than as "her Creator designed her to move."[20] In responding to this state of affairs, Grimké goes on among other things to attack the legal conditions that prevent American women from operating as full citizens: "the laws which have been enacted to destroy [woman's] independence, and crush her individuality," and that grant her "no political existence."[21] She urges men "to repeal these unjust and unequal laws, and restore to woman those rights which they have wrested from her."[22]

The position that she opposes, on the other hand, holds it to be natural and right, indeed "biblical," that women should be subordinate to men. Whatever it is that image-bearing in Genesis 1 implies, it cannot be that there should be substantial social and political equality between men and women in society. For those who hold this position, this would make nonsense of the remainder of the Bible, which tells us clearly that it is for men, and not women, to rule in family, Church, and society at large. It is entirely right, then, that contemporary society is arranged in the way that it is. Women should not have access to the same education as men, for example, for they do not need it in order to carry out their God-ordained role. They should not have legal rights and protections equivalent to men, because men as their rulers are already their advocates and protectors. Women should certainly not have the same voting rights as men, because this *would* in fact make them co-rulers. This is simply to name but a few of the implications of this position's understanding of "gender," as I shall hitherto refer to it.[23] Such arrangements must be left as they are, for they are the bastions of an orderly, civilized, and peaceable society. To meddle with them is to court disorder and disaster.

ALL ORDER AND VIRTUE

It should be clear by this point in the discussion how the hermeneutical battle lines thus being drawn in relation to gender are closely bound up with those relating to slavery. The advocates for the current societal arrangements, in both cases, advance certain claims about what is natural on the basis of what Scripture teaches about what is "God-ordained." These claims are reciprocally related to societal ideas about what is natural and unnatural (with respect to slaves or women) that arise more from lived experience (e.g., slaves are lazy, and women are dependent). All of this is then deeply connected with a "conservative" view of society that holds that change in either case is both wrong and dangerous. So are the biblical hermeneutics that inexorably bring about such change in *both* cases. Albert Bledsoe pursues exactly this line in warning an audience that already fears that the abolition of slavery will lead to significant social disorder of an even darker future if his opponents' "violent perversions of the sacred text" are accepted.[24] Such Bible reading will inevitably bring an end to all social subordination, to all security for life and property, to all guarantee for public or domestic virtue. If our women are to be emancipated from subjection to the law which God has imposed upon them, if they are to quit the retirement of domestic life, where they preside in stillness over the character and destiny of society; if they are to come forth in the liberty of men, to be our agents, our public lecturers, our committee-men, our rulers . . . we shall soon have a country . . . from which all order and all virtue would speedily be banished.

He concludes thus: "It would not be fair to object to the abolitionists in this way . . . were not these opinions the legitimate consequences of their own principles. Their women do but apply their own method of dealing with Scripture to another case." Emancipate the slaves, he warns, and you will end up having to emancipate women—with disastrous consequences for society at large.

For Sarah Grimké, on the other hand, both emancipations would be a good thing. In pursuit of both she challenges the opposition's *claims* about what is "natural" or otherwise God-ordained, first on the basis of what she believes Scripture actually *teaches* about the created state and its relation to the fallen state. She is not shy, at the same time, about challenging various related claims about what it is "natural" for slaves or women to be and to do. In the latter case, of course, the way in which she is living her life is already presenting such a challenge. The reform programs that she advocates in respect of both slaves and women then flow quite naturally out of the Bible reading that she advocates.

WOMEN'S RIGHTS IN THE UNITED STATES

By the middle of the nineteenth century, in different parts of the Christianized world where the Bible had profoundly shaped the culture, "emancipating women" was becoming an ever- more pressing agenda item for some, even as many men were at the same time fighting for their own further emancipation.[25] It would not be long (relatively) before some gains were made in the cause of gender equality. We may illustrate the point by resuming the thread of our *American* storyline, first of all, in the year 1848. The publication of Sarah Grimké's influential letters in book form stand now ten years behind us, and we find ourselves in Seneca Falls in the State of New York.

Here a convention has been called that is commonly regarded as having publicly launched the women's suffrage movement in the United States. At the opening of this gathering in her hometown, Elizabeth Cady Stanton reads out the Declaration of Sentiments (hereafter "Sentiments") that was already described in our chapter 1. The prospective signatories are pointedly asked to affirm that "we hold these truths to be self-evident: that all men *and women* are created equal" (my emphasis).[26] We recall from chapter 12 that the proper sense of the word "man" in the original Declaration was already a matter of dispute in the decades following its publication. "Sentiments" proceeds then to provide a list of grievances that American women wish male government urgently to address.

Specifically identified as a demand in the resolutions accompanying "Sentiments" is the right to vote: "it is the duty of the women of this country to secure to themselves their sacred right to the elective franchise." At the time, this was almost too radical an idea even for many of those assembled at the convention; it was certainly ridiculed by observers. Yet with the end of the Civil War in 1865 and the passing of the Thirteenth Amendment to the U.S. Constitution abolishing slavery, something fundamental changed in American society, and not just for those who had been slaves. They were of course the most immediate beneficiaries in terms of new rights, emerging from servitude as a new "Hebraic republic" in a landscape where others had by now largely abandoned the old one.[27] The weaknesses in the two further Amendments granting these rights would soon become apparent, but they certainly represented massive change.[28] Their contribution to the cause of women's suffrage lies in the fact that so many men previously disenfranchised were now suddenly allowed to vote—and in such circumstances, it no longer seemed quite so inconceivable as before that women might also be granted suffrage.[29] It was not long before Wyoming became the first U.S. state to grant women the right to vote in all its elections (1890), and a mere thirty years afterwards the Nineteenth Amendment to the Constitution explicitly extended that right throughout the country.

WOMEN'S RIGHTS IN FRANCE

We may also track the progress of the cause of gender equality during this time period by way of the ongoing but rather different storyline in France—the second revolutionary republic considered in chapter 11. In mid-nineteenth-century France, as in the United States, many people were already well aware of the gap between what the founding "declaration" of the republic had apparently promised and what the republic had actually become. They had been so for some time, as we noted in chapter 1 in describing the initiatives taken during the French Revolution to get women's rights onto the revolutionary table.

The cause of gender equality stalled in France for some time afterwards, as the First Republic gave way to the rule of Napoleon (1799–1814, and 1815) and his Civil Code of law (1804), in which even the limited prior gains with regard to female property rights were undermined. This code, which served as a model for law codes throughout nineteenth-century Europe, firmly established women as subordinate to men, particularly in the case of those who were married: "men of all social classes were ... reauthorized ... to wield a quasi-absolute legal authority—as husbands and fathers—over their wives and children."[30]

The 1848 revolution in France—which sparked popular democratic revolts against authoritarian rule all over Europe and led to the creation of the Second French Republic—briefly produced optimism of a kind similar to that in Seneca Falls that progress could once again be made. It soon proved ill-founded. This was a time, after all, when even a man whom history considers to be "an important friend of the women's movement," the liberal Edouard Laboulaye (1811–1883), could voice the opinion that the Civil Code "provided the capstone to French-women's civil equality."[31] It is unsurprising that he also held the view that the kingdom of women does not lie in the public sphere; it is, rather, "in the domestic foyer, in the family sanctuary that they are truly sovereigns."[32] Under the Second Republic, then, France became the first major European nation to institute universal male suffrage without any property qualification; at the same time, the republic failed to advance the suffrage of women at all—much less attend to their other disadvantages under the law.

With the collapse of the authoritarian regime of Emperor Napoleon III (1852–1870) yet another opportunity presented itself. The republican movement in the subsequent Third Republic (1870–1940) was supportive in principle of extending women's rights, and some notable people stood strongly in favor of it.[33] For pragmatic reasons, however, not much could immediately be achieved.[34] Only in the 1880s did some educational and marriage reform become possible. Voting reform never did; even after the First World War "[v]itriolic arguments were used against giving women the vote."[35] In fact, French women did not obtain the right to vote until 1944. More generally, the Napoleonic Code survived essentially unaltered for all of the intervening period—becoming thereby, ironically, the most enduring legacy of the French Revolution.

REFORM AND RESISTANCE

Almost two hundred years later we can now look back and see how the Christianized world as a whole, and not only these two republics, has significantly changed as a result of the women's movement, or what has become widely known since the introduction of the language in France in the 1890s as "féminisme" (feminism). Consider the United Nations Charter (1945), for example, which commits the various member nations of the UN to the ongoing promotion and encouragement of "respect for human rights and for fundamental freedoms for all without distinction as to race, sex, language, or religion." And such "promotion and encouragement" actually continues to occur all around the world at this present time, even in the midst of sometimes violent opposition. The quest to ensure gender equality in both private and public life has never been an easy one, and it remains challenging.

Among those who have made it difficult have been substantial numbers of Christians, both men and women. At every turn they have opposed moves designed—often by other Christians—to promote the equality of men and women and to guarantee it under law. They have often done so out of strong convictions about what is "biblical." In this they have followed notable forebears throughout Church history—the Scottish Reformer John Knox, for example, whose 1558 polemic *The First Blast of the Trumpet against the Monstrous Regiment of Women* provides the title for our present chapter. Knox's particular targets were the monarchs of his own time—the women who ruled in spite of God's Creation ordinance in Scripture that disallows it. It is to this "rule" that the word "regiment" refers in the sixteenth-century English of Knox's title. The word "monstrous" that qualifies it means "unnatural." It is in this case "unnatural" because it is unbiblical—it is not the way that God ordained society to function.

The opponents of substantial change in female participation in society have *also* often taken their stand, however—after the middle of the nineteenth century, just as beforehand—out of strong convictions about what is "natural" for a woman that have *little to do directly* with the Bible. As in the case of slavery, they have appealed here much more to what is said to be "self-evidently" true. In this way of thinking Christians have regarded female "regiment" as "monstrous" not only in the older but also in the more modern sense of the term: "having the qualities or appearance of a monster."[36] In such cases we are not dealing simply with a view about, but also with a visceral reaction to, a woman "behaving like a man." It is the horror of Dr. Frankenstein upon encountering for the first time his own monstrous creation: "How can I describe my emotions at this catastrophe, or how delineate the wretch whom with such infinite pains and care I had endeavoured to form?"[37] Bledsoe's words in the epigraph to this chapter betray similar emotion. He does not merely disagree with the woman who has "come forth in the liberty of men." He *loathes* her as one suffering from a *deformity* of human character. It is disturbing prose, revealing a troubling attitude toward a fellow image bearer.

THE HERMENEUTICS OF GENDER: THE OLD TESTAMENT

Returning as we must to the world of rational and biblical thought, what are we to make of the various important and consequential arguments that we have touched upon above concerning biblical teaching on the matter of male and female? Which are the more compelling, such that even though we have seen them developed in a nineteenth-century context we are required to follow their logic in our own search for what is right now? In approaching these questions we shall of course adopt the same overall approach that we have been developing throughout the entire book.[38]

THE RULE OF WOMEN

This means, once again, that we must begin at the beginning, where in Genesis 1 we are told that humanity comprises "male and female" created "in the image of God" (Gen. 1:27). In *this* "declaration," at least, there is no room for hermeneutical confusion of the later French and American kinds concerning the humans who are said to be "equal." Both men and women are made in God's image, a little lower than God himself (as Ps. 8 will later say). We are ontologically equal, and of extraordinarily high status.

As such we are also called, together, to "rule" in Creation along with God (Gen. 1:28). This is our joint and very high vocation. The rule of God in Creation is thus mediated through the rule of all his human creatures, each one of whom is just as important as the other. We have touched on this important idea a number of times in previous chapters when discussing governance of various kinds. It implies that whichever particular structures of governance arise in the world as communities organize themselves to best effect, they must always express the rule of all the image bearers of God—all blacks and whites (and others), and all men and women. Every other proposal about what is "natural" to this or that class of persons must be assessed within this framework, as must all ways of governing.

Measured in this way, Aristotle's opinions (for example) about male and female—mentioned in chapter 12—are found to be wrong. For Genesis 1 does not in the least imply that "[t]he male is by nature superior, and the female inferior; and the one rules, and the other is ruled." Nor does it permit us to think that "[t]he male is by nature fitter for command than the female."[39] This is simply not true, from the perspective of biblical faith. As Sarah Grimké rightly said back in 1867, in Genesis 1 dominion is given to both men and women over every other creature, but not over each other. Men and women are co-rulers over Creation under God. So it is that—embarrassingly also for John Knox—the biblical Story opens by clearly affirming the "regiment" of women, along with that of men. There is nothing "monstrous" about it.

THE SUITABLE HELPER

Many have insisted that a "proper" reading of Genesis 2 undermines the reading of Genesis 1 that I have just offered. If true, this would be surprising. Typically we would expect a second chapter that follows on from a first in any story to cohere with it, while perhaps developing its themes. Further enquiry reveals that this is in fact the case also here in Genesis. There is no reason to read the second chapter "against the grain" of the first.

The woman is created after and out of the man as his helper, it has been argued—a subordinate "part" of him (2:18, 20–22). However, there is no reason (first) to regard the order in which aspects of Creation come into being in Genesis 2 as telling us anything about their relative importance or authority. We might as well argue that the ground out of which the man was formed is of greater importance and authority than the man. Secondly, the language of "help" is used most often in the OT of God helping mortal human beings (e.g., in Hos. 13:9). Its use in Genesis 2 does not at all imply a subordinate or inferior status or role for the woman. We can and should read the text, rather, as telling us that the man needs her aid so that he (with her) can fulfil the human vocation of ruling that is described in Genesis 1. Without the woman, in fact, humanity is not yet in its fully created state, which is "good" (e.g., Gen. 1:25). It exists still in an unfinished, "not-good" state (Gen. 2:18). As such, it cannot do its job.[40]

It has also been argued that the man in Genesis 2 indicates his authority over the woman by naming her, just as he had previously named all the animals (2:19–20, 23). However, although it is true that elsewhere in the OT it often happens to be authority figures like parents who name others, this is not necessarily so. In Genesis 16:13, for example, Hagar names God. One cannot deduce from the action anything about the nature of the relationship. We are better advised to interpret the "naming" in Genesis 2 in the light of its typical function in creation accounts elsewhere in the ANE world. Here it is bound up with how things come into existence and find their place in the cosmos.[41] When the man in Genesis 2 names the animals, the woman, and *himself* (notice), he is simply describing where all of God's creatures "fit" in the cosmos. As he does so, he draws attention in his word choices not to *difference* between the humans (in status, or in anything else) who are called together to rule in Creation, but precisely to *commonality*. One is "man" (Hb. *'ish*) and the other is "woman" (Hb. *'ishah*)—male and female forms of the same humanity.

There is nothing in the second chapter of Genesis, then, that leads us to adjust or abandon the understanding of woman that we derived from the first. Genesis 2 simply tells us more about how the co-rulers described in Genesis 1 came to exist, and what their nature is. Sarah Grimké was correct on this point also.

A New Plan?

There is in Genesis 1–2, then, no idea of female subordination available for "development" in what follows, as some have thought. We may leave this idea aside, therefore, as we consider Genesis 3, where many have argued that certainly now, if not before, God ordains that men should have dominion over women. God has cursed the fallen world, such that aspects of both the woman's calling to rule (giving birth to and raising children) and the man's (working the land) will now become marked by a new level of struggle (3:16–19). In the midst of a vivid description of this general reality we then read that the woman's "desire will be for your husband, and he will rule over you" (3:16). In the world dominated by "the curse," at least, the female is now to be subordinate to male.

This is a curious reading of Genesis 3. It appears to be premised, first, on the notion that divine pronouncements like those in this passage are somewhat like Greek "fates," describing upcoming reality that is unavoidable no matter which choices the recipients make in response to the pronouncements. The remainder of the OT does not, however, support this view. The ground may be cursed in Genesis 3, for example, but abundant, agricultural fertility is celebrated in many later OT passages (e.g., Deut. 11:13–15). This is consistent with a broader reality: that the remainder of the OT does not view the Fall as having significantly altered the nature of the cosmos as God's good Creation. Consider the great Creation psalms, for example (like Ps. 104), which describe it in exactly the same terms as Genesis 1–2. Even after the entrance of moral evil into it, Creation remains substantially the place that it always was, in which it is possible still to "walk with God" (5:24; 6:9) and to know his blessing. It is not necessary to follow the path of the curse. It is in fact God's constant invitation to his OT people, when they are tempted to walk on such a path of death, to choose life instead (e.g., Deut. 30:15–20). It is seriously to misread Genesis 3, then, to propose that it concerns God's introduction of a new "plan" for Creation in which he "ordains" that things should be very different in the post-Fall world than they were before.[42]

God does not *ordain* that men should have dominion over women in Genesis 3, then. Rather, God *describes* how the male-female relationship will in fact play out in a fallen world where sin is allowed to define it. As he does so he mentions two aspects to the problem. The man will seek mastery over the women as if she were one of the other creatures over which they are jointly designed to rule; that is the significance of the Hebrew verb *mashal* in Genesis 3:16, which reappears in Psalm 8:6 concerning human dominion over the animals ("[y]ou made him *ruler* over the works of your hands"). The woman will reciprocate in kind, for her "desire" for her husband (Hb. *teshuqah*) is analogous to sin's desire to gobble up Cain (Gen. 4:7). She will desire to control, even to consume, her husband. Designed for joint dominion over Creation, male and female will often now find themselves entangled in a struggle for dominion over each other. This, too, is not inevitable; they can choose instead to turn back to God and live in accordance with his design parameters. The Song of Songs, for example, exemplifies this refusal to live out dysfunctional reality. There was no "struggle for dominion" in the beginning, as Sarah Grimké again rightly proposes, and there need not and should not be one now.

NARRATIVE AND LAW

This is the context in which we must then consider the biblical narratives that follow Genesis 3, as well as the Mosaic Torah. It is true, as Sarah Grimké's opponents observed, that the subordinate status of women in relation to men is everywhere to be seen in the OT narrative, and that it is also a marked feature of the Mosaic Torah. As in the case of slavery, however—where men have likewise sought mastery over their co-rulers as if they were instead the creatures over which they were designed legitimately to rule—the question is not "are these things true" but "what are we to make of them?" Grimké's opponents "make of them" that the subordination of women to men is good and right. Viewing them as part of the continuation of the Story that begins in Genesis 1–3, however, we cannot conclude any such thing.

We are obliged instead to read biblical narrative as describing, in this respect, not a right path that people *ought* to have taken but simply a wrong path that often *was* taken. Like slavery, female subordination to men was not "instituted" by God; it simply "appears" in the biblical Story as something that fallen people (evidently) desire and that God (evidently) grants them the moral freedom to choose. It is not thereby "sanctioned." It is indeed often subverted in various ways in the OT. Stories are told, for example, that reveal how brutal the consequences can be for a woman who is legally simply one of a man's possessions and has no rights of her own (e.g., Judg. 11:29–40)—the dangerous double-standards that lie at the heart of such male-dominated societies (Gen. 38). These "biblical tales of terror" are indeed very frank in portraying "the horrible things that happen to women under [such] patriarchy."[43] Biblical stories are also told that go out of their way to remind us that women who in a male-dominated society are considered more as instruments than anything else are in fact fully formed, image-bearing persons for whom God cares. The courageous Hagar is a good example (Gen. 16; 21): doubly disadvantaged as both a slave and a woman, a "victim of use, abuse, and rejection," she is nevertheless "the first person in scripture whom a divine messenger visits and the only person who dares to name the deity," as well as the first woman "to receive a divine promise of descendants."[44] Many other narratives likewise bring to the fore woman's image-bearing qualities, including leadership qualities. Deborah is an obvious example (Judg. 4)—a "non-delicate" woman, of course, who exercised authority over men.

We are also obliged to understand *Mosaic Torah* on women in the same way as we did in the case of slavery. This is not material that speaks of woman's full, image-bearing equality with men. Rather, it addresses a society that has already fallen short of treating women in accordance with this reality. In doing so the goals of Torah are necessarily limited by the circumstances of time and place. It is good law, in the sense that it restrains evil and seeks to mitigate to some extent the damage done to women by the hardness of men's hearts. Yet as in the case of slavery, it involves concessions to the very evils that it seeks to restrain. So it is that the tenth Commandment, for example, does not set out directly to confront a society that has already blurred the ontological distinction between a female human being and an "ox or donkey" (Exod. 20:17)—just as Genesis 3:16 anticipated that men *would*. This Commandment sets out instead—and at least—to forbid the coveting of wives (as well as oxen and donkeys). This does not mean that God "sanctions" the societal view in question, any more than the rules in Leviticus 27:1–7 setting equivalent values for females in respect of dedicatory vows at levels lower than those for males mean that "in fact" they are worth less than men. This is not what Scripture *teaches*.

THE HERMENEUTICS OF GENDER: THE NEW TESTAMENT

I find no basis in fundamental Christian Scripture, then—the earliest Scripture, whose authority for the Church is emphasized by both Jesus and his apostles—for the idea that women are designed by God not to be equal but subordinate to men, being "ruled" by them rather than jointly ruling *with* them. I also find no basis in this fundamental Scripture for the consequentially unequal position in which women have often found themselves with respect to such matters as access to education and employment, legal and political rights, and indeed leadership roles in Church and society. In fact, Scripture to this juncture presses strongly in the opposite direction on all points, insisting as it does that we begin all our ethical reflection "in the beginning" and move forward from there.

BROTHER AND SISTER

As we move forward again now into the NT, what do we find? Here too, as we already saw in chapter 12, all human beings are image bearers of God. In Christ that broken image is being restored, such that distinctions on the basis of race, class, and religion that separate people from each other and distribute status and power unevenly among them have been abolished. These distinctions were not present in the beginning, and they are not present now that Christ has died, has risen, and sits now at the right hand of the Father. Among the passages noted earlier, we need to pay particular attention here to Galatians 3:28: "There is neither Jew nor Greek, slave nor free, male nor female, for you are all one in Christ Jesus." Men and women stand on equal terms in Christ, just as slaves and masters do. "Brother" and "sister" are now the fundamental categories that shape their relationships too (e.g., Rom. 16:1).

It is in line with this that we discover that Jesus himself was hugely affirming of women as he ministered to the needs of everyone during his earthly ministry.

In particular he accepted them as disciples who were, like the men, capable of instruction.[45] We also discover (although Bible translations sometimes make it difficult for us to do so) that women held leadership positions in the early Church. Phoebe is described in Romans 16:1 as a "deacon" (Gk. *diakonos*), which means that she *might* have held a leadership position,[46] and Junia is described as an apostle in Romans 16:7, which means that she *did*. Women also actively participated in church meetings, at least in Corinth, speaking to God on behalf of their brothers and sisters in prayer and "leading in *preaching* a pastorally applied message or discourse *from God*" ("prophesying," 1 Cor. 11:5).[47] These are only some of the gifts that Paul exhorts all the "brothers and sisters" in the Corinthian church to "desire" to possess and to exercise for the common good (12:1, 31)—including those that suit people to be apostles, prophets, teachers (12:28). The point is that it is *Spirit gifting* that suits people to their roles in the life of the Church, and not gender or status (e.g., whether one is slave or free, 12:11).

The equal status of women with men before God, then, that is found "in the beginning" and restored in Christ in this way, strongly associated with joint governance over the rest of Creation, is not merely theoretical but also practical. As we would expect from our discussion of slavery in chapter 12, it has social and political implications. It affects, and ought to affect, how individuals and groups behave.

Cultural Subversion

It is in within this larger context of the whole Story of Scripture as it develops from beginning to end that we must now set some NT texts that may initially appear to stand in tension with the creational imperative pertaining to "co-rule." It will be helpful as we do so to recall the arguments in chapters 9 and 12 concerning Sabbath and slavery. In both chapters I pointed out that the early Christians lived in a Roman Empire whose authorities were quite capable of antipathy toward the Church because of its "un-Roman" ways, and that the apostles had to take account of this reality as they offered advice to their brothers and sisters on how to live "in exile." In considering slavery in chapter 12, I specifically proposed that public changes in the master-slave relationship as a result of a Christian ideology of equality would certainly have been perceived as a threat to the current social order, which outcome the apostles appear to have been anxious to avoid, especially against the recent historical background of the Spartacus revolt. So it is that Peter (for example) urges the readers of his first letter, although they were "free people," to be careful in their use of their freedom, showing "proper respect to everyone" and giving "honor [to] the emperor" (1 Pet. 2:16–17). There is a palpable concern throughout this section of the letter (1 Pet. 2:11–3:6) not to give wider Roman society any more reason than necessary to respond negatively to the Church. And it is in this context that Peter turns from slaves to consider wives, offering his famous advice that the latter should "submit" themselves to their husbands (3:1–6).[48] The historical background that we need to know about here does not concern a particular slave revolt but a more general Roman concern. In the Roman Empire

> legislating and enforcing the "proper" behavior of women was a major concern for authorities because they believed that disorder in the household had seditious ramifications for the welfare of the empire. Therefore, cults and sects were often attacked because of the wild behavior of the women participants.[49]

For the mission of the Church to succeed in such a context, it was important for Christian women "to fit into the culture" as much as possible "while remaining ethically pure."[50] This was a challenging task, given that the fundamental perspectives of biblical faith concerning women's nature and vocation stood starkly at odds with those of the Roman Empire, where the ontological inferiority of the female (in line with Aristotle's opinions) was commonly presupposed. Nevertheless, it had to be attempted. This is the context in which we must understand passages like 1 Peter 3:1–6.

It is important to note at the same time the proposal of Paul in Ephesians 5:21–23 that this submission is to be offered by the Christian woman only in the context of the *mutual* submission of husband and wife (5:21). The codes of the Roman world that described right relationships in a household typically "concentrated solely on the obligations of the subordinate members of the household— wives, children, and slaves—outlining their duties such as obedience, honor, and submission to their authorities."[51] The apostle does not proceed in the same way; there is in fact much more in this passage about the husband's "submission" to his wife than about the reverse. By focusing on the husband's (radically new) responsibilities in this way Paul, while not directly challenging the Roman approach to gender roles, does thereby subvert it. Here the husband essentially performs services for his wife in the domestic realm reserved in that culture for women and slaves: he does "women's work," like the laundry.[52] He does so in imitation of his own "head," who is Christ (5:25–30). The language of "head" here and in 1 Corinthians 11:3–16, incidentally, does not of itself necessitate that we see any idea in either passage of the subordination of women to men. The Greek word can also mean "source"—the originating point of her life, as in Genesis 2—and there is no need to choose a different meaning in these two Pauline cases.[53] To do so would indeed create an unnecessary tension between the apostle and his foundational OT Scripture, which (as we have seen) provides no basis for believing that women are created (or redeemed) to be subordinate to men. Both NT passages in fact clearly reflect the Genesis 1–2 ideal of male-female relationships as we have earlier described it. In 1 Corinthians 11 Paul "makes a careful statement of interdependency and reciprocity between man and woman."[54] In Ephesians 5, "mutual submission is expressed in mutual service."[55] It may well be that woman initially "originated" from man "but then subsequently every man comes from woman so that woman is also the origin of life" (Gen. 3:20); therefore, "through God's design, female and male are not independent of each other."[56]

None of this implies that, in spite of everything else we have read in this chapter so far, the apostles after all "taught" the subordination of women to men, "contradicting, reinterpreting, or qualifying the authority of women in the Creation account in Genesis 1:27–28."[57] Given the revolutionary nature of the Christian message within the Roman context, however, they were certainly committed to employing caution and intelligence in promoting it. As in the case of slavery, there were other (and at the time better) ways of working toward social change than direct confrontation.

Abuse and Control

This brings us in the end to 1 Timothy 2:11–15, which has at times in discussions of "male and female" in biblical faith come to provide "a lens or exegetical grid through which all other Scripture is applied to woman."[58] This is, to begin with, an indefensible way in which to approach the matter. The right thing to do with this passage is to read it in the context of the entire biblical Story, from "the beginning" until the end, which includes all sorts of Scripture that applies to woman. As we do this, our expectation will naturally be that it will prove to be consistent with the conclusions toward which the aggregate of Scripture is already leading us. It would be surprising if it did not. *If* it did not, then we should have to make a decision: whether to be guided on an important ethical issue by a well-developed argument bringing together the great majority of relevant texts into a coherent whole, or by our interpretation of one recalcitrant passage that we cannot seem (yet) to "fit into" this larger picture. In reality, though, that should not be a difficult decision to make.

The text that is of primary interest to us here is found in verse 12, where Paul tells Timothy that "I do not permit a woman to teach or to assume authority over a man." This has often "been used up to the present time to ban women from certain activities and functions with the church [specifically], regardless of a woman's training, skills, or spiritual gifts."[59] It is already difficult to imagine, however—not least because of Paul's own teaching in 1 Corinthians 11–12 (as we have seen) and in Romans 12:3–9—that he means to tell Timothy here that female teaching and leadership in the Church are universally wrong. A better way of understanding 1 Timothy 2:11–12, rather, is to see these verses as Paul's solution to the problem of false teaching that has been introduced into the Christian community in Ephesus by some women who, like Eve, have been "deceived" (2:14; cf. 1:3–7). A plausible reconstruction of one aspect of this deception, inductively derived, would be that they had come to think of "Eve" as better than "Adam," and that they were consequently subjecting their husbands to "abusive or controlling" behavior—a much better way of taking the verb behind the NIV's "assume authority over."[60] That is, what Paul refers to here is not generic "authority" but rather the kind of tyrannical rule attributed to the Gentile rulers in Matthew 20:25 that no Christian, male or female, should exercise.[61] Paul's solution to the problem of these Ephesian females passing on false teaching is that they should "be quiet" while having their error corrected "in quietness and full submission [at home]" by their (evidently competent) husbands whom they have hitherto been treating in a very wrong way.[62] Read in this way, what Paul writes to Timothy is entirely consistent with everything that has gone before. He is addressing a particular situation in the church in Ephesus rather than laying down a general rule about the roles that women can and cannot play in the Church. We saw something rather similar in chapter 10, when we were discussing what Paul had to say to the Christians in Colossae about a certain kind of Sabbath observance (Col. 2:16–17).

In sum: in a situation where a number of women are using their power in an unchristian way and with the purpose of spreading heresy in the Ephesian church, the apostle looks to "quieten" them and thus move them back into a better place with respect to Christian doctrine and practice. One of the objections to this interpretation is of course that Paul appears to ground his teaching here in the Genesis story of Creation, thereby giving the impression that he is laying down creational law for everyone rather than merely resolving a local and temporary difficulty: "For Adam was formed first, then Eve. And Adam was not the one deceived; it was the woman who was deceived and became a sinner" (1 Tim. 2:13–14). Yet we must surely read these words, too, as relating to the situation in Ephesus—as an ad hoc argument capable of persuading the Ephesian women, given their own beliefs about Adam and Eve, that they must rethink their position. If we do not take this view, then we immediately encounter a huge problem: that Paul himself here proposes a reading of Genesis 2–3 that ought to strike non-Ephesian readers of the chapter as deeply unpersuasive. For as we saw earlier in the present chapter, Genesis itself does not draw any conclusions from the order in which aspects of Creation come into being concerning their relative importance or authority. We may now add to this that Genesis itself does not distinguish between the man and the woman in terms of their capacity for being deceived and drawn into sin. Eve is evidently the one who *represents* humanity in its verbal exchanges with the serpent—but Adam is evidently "with her" throughout the encounter (Gen. 3:6), and he is equally culpable, just as Romans 5:15 indicates in teaching that "many died by the trespass of the one man [Adam]." If we were not to regard Paul's comments about Genesis in 1 Timothy 2:13–14 as ad hoc, then, we should be obliged to regard him as a poor exegete in this case of the very Scriptures than he himself advocates that we should carefully read.[63]

CONCLUSION

Having now reached the end of the Story, I still find no basis in Scripture for the idea that women are designed by God not to be equal but subordinate to men. The argument in favor of this view depends on reading both biblical narrative and Mosaic Torah (as in the case of slavery) without proper attention to their context within the whole Story, whose first chapter (Gen. 1) is in the case of women particularly explicit about their equality of being *and* overall role vis-à-vis men. This unconvincing argument next proceeds to subject the second and third chapters of the Story (Gen. 2–3) to entirely implausible interpretation in the context of what comes beforehand as well as afterwards (in the case of Genesis 3 in particular). This has not put Bible readers in a good position to go on to read the various NT texts touching on women very well—that is, coherently as a group, within the whole sweep of Scripture—and they have often in fact failed to *do* it well. In particular, they have failed to give the NT material developing the idea of image-bearing equality between men and women in Christ the proper weight that it requires as the framework within which particular apostolic advice and comment about male-female relations must be understood. At the same time (and connected to this), they have often underestimated the extent to which this advice and comment reflects temporary accommodations to culture rather than providing mandates for the life of the Church in perpetuity all over the world.

The consequences of these hermeneutical mistakes have been serious. Rather than pushing, with as much apostolic caution and intelligence as we can muster in our various cultural contexts, to build a different community that as much as possible genuinely reflects the freedom that we have in Christ, the Church has all too often merely reflected and reinforced cultural norms of understanding (in respect of the "nature" of men and women) and practice (in respect of their proper relationships). So it is that women, irrespective of the God-given gifts they possess, have been denied (for example) the privileges of leading in the Christian community, as well as of preaching and teaching. The Church has then found itself all too often reinforcing rather than challenging such norms in the wider society, even when constructive cultural change in a Gospel direction was possible—which it has not always been, historically, especially where the majority religious and ethical sentiment has not been Christian. Often Christian have forgotten, it seems, that in biblical faith legitimate accommodation to culture is only one momentary step on a journey that ought to result in its holy transformation. Accommodation is an important but temporary means, and not an end.

This forgetfulness has then inevitably led many Christians all too often to take up entirely wrong positions when faced with legitimate demands (often originating from and supported by other Christians) that women should be accorded in society the same rights and privileges as men with respect to matters like equality before the law, access to education and employment, and participation in political processes. That is to say, the Church has often provided, historically, primary ideological support for thoroughgoing gender discrimination in society; it has not proved itself to be a friend to female image bearers. And *that* is to say that it has interacted with the "gender issue" in precisely the same way as the "slavery issue." It is all very well for conservative Christians *nowadays* to claim (as they often do) that they are pressing only for female subordination to males within the Church (and the families of the Church), and not in society at large. We must recognize, however, that our forebears typically made no such distinction—and the reality is that the political commitments of such contemporary Christians quite often reveal that many of them, too, are not particularly strongly committed to maintaining it. If they were able to do it, they would in fact impose on the wider society their understanding of "the will of God" for women in line with "female nature."

This is a shameful legacy, which among other things makes it difficult for the contemporary Church in postmodern Western culture to speak with any credibility about the "gender issue" as it confronts us now. Many people do not expect it to say anything about it that is true or good, or—when they possess substantial power—to act in virtuous ways pertaining to it. And this must be regarded as more than a pity by Christians who remain convinced, in their pursuit of the good life, that the Story of Scripture is precisely where we find infallible guidance for our journey in all its aspects.

DISCUSSION QUESTIONS

1. If you had had the opportunity to address your Christian brother Albert Bledsoe in 1856 concerning his views on women, what would you have said to him?

2. In a 2019 posting on a Christian website concerning the new "Captain Marvel" movie, the (male) author mourns "how far we've come since the days when we sought to protect and cherish our women." He laments that "along with Disney" we have abandoned "the traditional princess vibe and seek to empower little girls everywhere to be strong like men." How would you respond to *this* Christian brother, and why?

3. Read again Galatians 3:28: "There is neither Jew nor Greek, slave nor free, male nor female, for you are all one in Christ Jesus." Is this merely a set of nice ideas about what our lives will be like in heaven, or are we supposed to

act upon these truths in our present circumstances on Earth? What are its implications?

4. Should Christians fight for women's rights in countries where the predominant religious beliefs and ethical norms stand against the extension of such rights? Consider both the potential upsides and downsides of doing so.

14

Staying Alive
Jews, Palestinians, and the Holy Land

> *The Land of Israel was the birthplace of the Jewish people. Here their spiritual,*
> *religious and political identity was shaped. Here they first attained to statehood,*
> *created cultural values of national and universal significance, and gave to the world*
> *the eternal Book of Books.*[1]
>
> *The Israeli Proclamation of Independence*

On May 14, 1948, only a few hours before the official end of the arrangements under which the British had ruled Palestine since 1922, a new "declaration" was presented to the world—not in France or the United States, on this occasion, but in what was now the new state of Israel. It was read out by David Ben Gurion, Israel's first prime minister, to a small number of people gathered at the Tel Aviv Museum and broadcast live on the radio to many more.

RESTORATION

It begins, as we see in the epigraph above, by reminding its readers of the history of the Jewish people in the land of Israel. Forcibly exiled from it, they have "never ceased to pray and hope for their return to it and for the restoration in it of their political freedom," and Jews have attempted "in every successive generation to reestablish themselves" in it. Significant events in recent history are then described. The first is the convening of the First Zionist Congress in 1897, which "proclaimed the right of the Jewish people to national rebirth in its own country." The second and third are a statement of British support for "the establishment in Palestine of a national home for the Jewish people" dating from 1917 (the Balfour Declaration), and "the Mandate of the League of Nations" that "gave international sanction ... to the right of the Jewish people to rebuild its National Home" (1922). The fourth is the immediately preceding massacre of millions of Jews in Europe under Hitler's Nazi regime (the Holocaust), which demonstrated to the world "the urgency of solving the problem of [Jewish] homelessness" by establishing a state that would "open the gates of the homeland wide to every Jew and confer upon the Jewish people the status of a fully privileged member of the community of nations." The Proclamation refers, finally, to the 1947 UN General Assembly resolution that recognizes "the right of the Jewish people to establish their State."

It is on the basis of this "natural right of the Jewish people to be masters of their own fate, like all other nations, in their own sovereign State" that the state of Israel is now established. It will be a state "open for Jewish immigration and for the Ingathering of the Exiles." It will "foster the development of the country for the benefit of all its inhabitants," being "based on freedom, justice, and peace as envisaged by the prophets of Israel." It will further "ensure complete equality of social and political rights to all its inhabitants irrespective of religion, race, or sex," as well as guaranteeing "freedom of religion, conscience, language, education, and culture" and safeguarding "the Holy Places of all religions."

Against the background of everything that we have been thinking about in this book so far, what is striking about this new declaration is not only the ways in which it is similar to the previous two mentioned above (in deploying the concept of "natural right," for example) but also the ways in which it is different. This is not only a matter of improved clarity on particular points (e.g., "complete equality of social and political rights to all its inhabitants irrespective of religion, race, or sex"). It is different also in connecting contemporary political events so explicitly and extensively with the Bible. In this declaration a strong continuity is posited, between the people of God in what Christians call the OT and the people who are now establishing their state in the same region as these forebears. The new state of Israel will facilitate "the ingathering of the exiles" envisaged by the biblical prophets, reconstituting an ancient people in its rightful environment. It will take its lead from the ancient prophets of that people as the new society is built in "freedom, justice, and peace." Particular interpretations of the "eternal Book of Books" (epigraph) that this ancient people first gave to the whole world are clearly playing a significant role here as this new state emerges. The first part of the Bible provides the most fundamental narrative within whose context the authors of this document wish this modern Israel to be understood.

Biblical interpretation was also very much bound up with *Christian* perspectives on the new state both at this time and beforehand, and has been ever since.

Our task in this chapter is to explore the hermeneutics bound up with these Christian perspectives, on the way to answering this question: how are we best to read the OT, in the context of the whole of Scripture, on the matter of Israel/ Palestine? But first we need to become better acquainted with a considerable amount of history. We need to comprehend more deeply the further and nearer background against which the Israeli Declaration of Independence was published and understand in particular exactly what it refers to when cataloging the recent "significant events" that it mentions.

JEWS IN CHRISTENDOM: THE MIDDLE AGES

The "problem of . . . homelessness" identified in the Proclamation goes back, of course, a long way in history, if by "home" we mean a self-governing Jewish state of any duration. Already by the first century AD no such state existed, and the Jews were scattered throughout the Roman Empire and beyond. We have briefly explored in chapters four and six what their lives were like in this pagan empire— and how they changed with the conversion of Constantine and the creation of a Christian Empire in the fourth through the sixth centuries. Protected to some extent by Christian law as they had been previously by pagan law, they were nevertheless a vulnerable minority—second-class citizens who were the targets of constant and foul rhetoric that reinforced the general distaste that many Christians already felt toward Jews and could lead to violence. Jews should be content, we recall the Christian emperor Justinian stating, "with merely 'staying alive.'"[2] Our task here is to pick up the threads of this narrative about the Jews in Christendom in the Middle Ages, focusing mainly on the West.

Conversion and Expulsion

That medieval Jews themselves recognized the protections afforded them, as well as the opportunities that existed for them, in this environment is strongly implied by the important fact that throughout the Middle Ages the "world Jewish population was slowly but steadily shifting from its prior center in the Islamic Near and Middle East to Christian Europe."[3] Whatever the vulnerability involved in living there, then, Jews cannot have been experiencing "[a]n environment unceasingly hostile and harmful."[4] On the other hand, the ongoing vulnerability of Jews within Christian society is also well-illustrated by a mid-tenth-century letter sent by the archbishop of Mainz to Pope Leo VII (reigned 936–939) asking whether it would be better forcibly to convert Jews or to expel them from Christian communities; the options here are stark. The pope replies by telling the archbishop not to coerce Jews to be baptized but certainly to expel them if they refuse voluntary baptism, since "we must not live in society with God's enemies."[5] Pope

Leo at least is apparently aware, as the archbishop and many others in his time are not, of the existing Christian tradition that forbids the forced conversion of Jews (and indeed of pagans; cf. Alcuin in chapter 5).[6] The pope himself is also stepping outside Christian tradition, however, in his advice concerning not living in society with Jews. The point is that, even before the time of the Crusades, Jews could never *depend* on Christian authorities to remember or to enforce either law or tradition. Jewish communities existed very much at the pleasure of the majority—including the majority mob.

SICUT JUDEIS

As the crusading mentality first described in chapter 6 then took a firm hold of Western Christendom, even "staying alive" in this European environment turned out to be far from straightforward for Jews. The reader will recall from that chapter a brief reference to the fact that even as the soldiers of the First Crusade were setting out from Europe to the Holy Land, some of them turned aside along the way to attack Jewish communities. Driven by the ugly rhetoric that characterized Jews as Christ killers, they targeted in particular the wealthy communities of the Rhine Valley in Germany, including those in Mainz, Cologne, and Worms. Even the intervention of the Holy Roman Emperor himself, as well as local bishops, did not dissuade them, and over five thousand Jews were murdered as a result, their property stolen. The Crusaders then moved on to Jerusalem, where they slaughtered many more Jewish men, women, and children along with their Muslim neighbors. The pattern repeated itself in the Second Crusade (1147–1149), in spite of exhortations from Bernard of Clairvaux that the Crusaders should leave the Jews alone. The prevailing mood is reflected more by Peter of Cluny than by Bernard: "Why travel to the end of the world to fight God's enemies when the Jews, much worse than they, live among us?"[7]

Both crusades brought a strong response from the papacy in the form of protective decrees known as "*Sicut Judeis* Bulls" that confirmed previous Church policy on the Jews. They were of limited effectiveness, however. Part of the reason is that, even while seeking to offer protection, they repeated the strong and antagonistic rhetoric of earlier times.[8] When the "purification" of Christendom was the pressing goal, as it had now become (chapter 6), every enemy of God— heretic, Jew, or whoever—was a potential target of holy violence. In the thirteenth century Pope Innocent III held to the same *Sicut Judeis* line, but his rhetoric concerning the Jews was even more inflammatory than his predecessors', and he promoted Jewish servant or slave status very rigorously.[9] He it was who prevailed upon the Fourth Lateran Council of 1215 to dictate that Jews should henceforth at all times wear identifying markers or clothing so that their separate status within

Christendom was immediately obvious. The early thirteenth-century popes who succeeded Innocent followed his example in both attacking and protecting the Jews at the same time, albeit that Innocent IV did go further than others in a non-protective direction: he allowed one expulsion of Jews from Vienne (in Provence) in 1253, where they were allegedly threatening "the souls of Christians."[10] This "threat" would be used more than once in the following centuries to justify a kind of "suspension" of the normal rules of *Sicut Judeis* where there was a desire to do so.

THE BLACK DEATH

Nevertheless, the "normal" *Sicut Judeis* approach is very evident in the fourteenth century in official Church responses to what happened to Jews all over Europe in the course of the outbreak of the Black Death in 1348–1351. These happenings in turn illustrate once again their vulnerability as a vilified, if legally tolerated minority within Christendom. Although this devastating plague affected Jews just as much as Christians, it came to be widely believed (especially in Germany) that it was the result of a Jewish plot to kill Christians by poisoning their wells. Pope Clement VI issued a papal bull declaring this rumor false, but many Christian authorities and those whom they governed continued to believe it. Terrible massacres of Jews followed everywhere in Germany, and many others were forcibly baptized. In the prosperous city of Erfurt in northeast Germany, for example, where there had been a well-integrated Jewish community since the late eleventh century, attempts were made deliberately to entrap the entire group in the city in a surprise attack, and in the ensuing violence around nine hundred people were murdered (1349).[11] From the Black Death onwards the Jews in all German towns understandably lived in perpetual fear of similar attacks, even where enforcement of legal protection was promised by both Church and state. On the other side of the equation, the civil authorities were increasingly attracted to expulsion as a means of solving their "Jewish problem" altogether. Erfurt, again, provides a good example. A second community of Jews settled in the city only a few years after the pogrom, in 1354, and a new synagogue was built at the city's expense. In 1453, however, with anti-Jewish sentiment again on the rise, the authorities revoked their protection of the Jews, obliging them to leave for good.

Although it is true, then, that we encounter "significant and influential philosemitic tendencies" in later as in earlier medieval Europe, this was clearly an environment in which Jews routinely "encountered serious difficulties—popular hostility, recurrent violence, and . . . expulsion."[12] By the close of the Middle Ages, "relatively few professing Jews were allowed in [western] Christian Europe," and the papacy itself had come to share the widespread cultural view that there was no place for Jews in Christian society.[13]

THE PHILOSEMITIC IMPULSE

The rise of Renaissance Humanism in Europe in the fifteenth century brought with it a renewed interest in all matters historical and philological respecting the ancient Jews, and this "Christian Hebraism" in turn had a positive impact on attitudes toward contemporary Judaism at least among the intellectual elites, creating a "framework for cultural dialogue between Jewish and Christian scholars possibly unprecedented in extent and intensity."[14] Even if these Christian Hebraists could be just as convinced as anyone else of the collective guilt of the Jewish people in respect to Christ, and just as committed to missionary efforts directed at the Jews, they tended to be strongly opposed to forced baptism (for example). In addition, many are known to have protected the rights of Jewish colleagues. These developments helped to prepare the way for the more tolerant attitudes that we encounter in the course of the Enlightenment.

MARTIN LUTHER

Perhaps surprisingly in view of my comments on the Reformers and their general intolerance in chapter 11, the early Martin Luther is also found on this philosemitic trajectory, briefly showing empathy toward the Jews both in their suffering and in their alleged stubbornness in refusing to accept Christianity in the preceding centuries. It was perfectly right and reasonable that they should have rejected the Roman Catholic view of the Christian faith, Luther believed, especially given their treatment at these "Christian" hands: "They have dealt with the Jews as if they were dogs rather than human beings."[15] Luther advised his readers to treat the Jews instead with gentleness and respect in the hope of seeing their conversion. Unfortunately this advocacy did not survive his own experience of sharing his Protestant faith with them, and all too soon he was to be found endorsing the worst of what had happened to Jews in Christendom before the Reformation: the burning of synagogues, the destruction of homes, persecution, and mob violence.[16] These sentiments, which enjoyed a long posthistory contributing to ongoing German antisemitism, naturally alarmed the Jews of Europe.

AFTER THE REFORMATION

Out of the Reformation, nevertheless, there also flowed some lasting and significant streams of philosemitism. Already in the seventeenth century we see this among many of the Puritans in England, whence the Jews had been expelled in 1290 by King Edward I and whither they had only slowly (and unofficially) been returning in small numbers over the intervening centuries. These Puritans, with their own commitments to Christian Hebraism, strongly identified with the Jews as fellow "Israelites" and fellow sufferers under the persecution of Rome. With ideas of English "manifest destiny" in the air (chapter 11), they believed that they had a special responsibility to care for them—not least by facilitating their resettlement back in England, where they would be able to hear the true (Calvinist) Gospel and perhaps convert. In line with a long interpretive tradition, they saw the general conversion of the Jews as a precursor to the Second Coming of Christ.[17] By 1656, as a result of this "republican philosemitism," Edward I's edict of 1290 had been informally set aside, and resettlement had begun.[18]

Also in the seventeenth century, in Lutheran Germany, we find Philipp Spener integrating the early Luther's sentiments about Jews into his new Pietist program, which stressed personal, individual faith and serious Christian living. In Spener's way of thinking, too, Christ would not return until the Church took seriously its responsibility to evangelize the Jews, and this necessarily involved approaching them with genuine love and concern. This strong Pietist emphasis on individual devotion and compassion for fellow human beings, including Jews, then influenced and was mirrored in the eighteenth century Enlightenment, in the course of which proposals for reform in respect to the Jews were widely discussed all over Europe in the context of debates about toleration more generally (chapter 11).[19] By this point the legal situation respecting Jews had already somewhat improved here and there, and it further did so in the course of the nineteenth century all over Europe and its (former) colonies, particularly as a result of the French and American revolutions.[20] This process, often referred to as "Jewish emancipation," was substantially complete in much of Europe by the end of the third quarter of the nineteenth century. It provided the legal framework as a result of which "German Jews [for example] began to emerge from the ghettos in which many of them had lived since medieval times and enter mainstream German society."[21] The Enlightenment elites considered it very much to the advantage of Christian society that this should be the case, since it made the Jews "contributing citizens" of each state rather than a noncontributing, impoverished drain on its resources. For their own part, Jews in large numbers enthusiastically embraced this opportunity to assimilate into the dominant culture—especially in Western Europe.

These changes to law, however, had been hard-won in the face of much opposition in Europe, and the new laws were powerless to dissipate the widespread antisemitism that had informed this opposition. Indeed, in the course of the nineteenth century it had evolved in order to take account of the new situation, focusing now on race rather than religion. "The old hatred of Jews had been aimed at the alien, different Jew"; the new version "targeted the Jew who looked like anyone else, who spoke the local language, whose appearance and behavior was middle class, who took part in and even created national culture."[22] "Mainstream society" proved much more difficult to join, in such circumstances, than many Jews had hoped.

ZIONISM AND THE ZIONIST STATE

This is the context in which we must now set the first articulations of Zionism as a political philosophy and examine the events of the early twentieth century that led up to the creation of the state of Israel in 1948. The first key figure in this part of the story is Theodore Herzl (1860–1904).

THEODORE HERZL

Herzl was, first of all, a beneficiary of the changes in the legal status of Jews just described and an example of the integration of Jews into European society by the end of the closing decades of the nineteenth century. His parents were prosperous, middle-class citizens of the Austrian Empire in what is now Hungary, and as a teenager Theodore attended for a while a mainstream secondary school in Budapest before the family moved to Vienna. In both cities, however, Herzl encountered antisemitism firsthand. Moves to Vienna and then to Paris (as a journalist) followed. In France he was dismayed to encounter, in a country that had enacted its first Jewish emancipation laws one hundred years beforehand, exactly the same antisemitism that he had experienced in Budapest and Vienna. This raised questions in his mind about the efficacy of assimilation in overcoming prejudice (and indeed threat). The famous Dreyfus Affair (beginning in 1894), upon which he reported, confirmed his worst fears, and indeed made clear to many observers worldwide that an assimilated Jew was still in reality an outsider when it really mattered—even in republican France.[23] Convinced, then, that European antisemitism was "grounded in a deep-seated mindset that rational thinking could not overcome" and constitutional equality would not dissipate, Herzl began to develop a plan to create a safe haven for Jews somewhere in the world, possibly in their traditional homeland.[24]

He laid out his vision in a pamphlet, *The Jewish State*, in 1896, and it immediately proved a divisive document among Jews, with strong voices on each side of the debate. Aside from religious objections (to which we shall return below) and practical problems, it was by no means obvious to many that forming a Jewish nation-state was a good idea from a strategic point of view, both because of the negative consequences it might have for Jews living in other states and because it would gather so many Jews in one place as an easy target. Jews in the West (including the United States) were largely opposed.[25] In an effort to consolidate support for his ideas, nevertheless, Herzl organized in the following year (1897) the First Zionist Congress in Basel. Significantly, most of the delegates who attended came from central and eastern Europe (and Russia) rather than from the West. The declared goal of Zionism as it emerged from this congress was the creation of a publicly guaranteed homeland for the Jewish people in Palestine, which at this time was part of the Ottoman Empire and home to only a modest number of Jews.[26] At this juncture in the story it appeared to be an impossible dream.

The Balfour Declaration

The crucial political development in the course of the next two decades involved a letter from British Foreign Secretary Arthur Balfour to prominent Jewish peer Lord Rothschild announcing the British government's "sympathy with Jewish Zionist aspirations," their favorable view of "the establishment in Palestine of a national home for the Jewish people," and their commitment "to facilitate the achievement of this object." The caveat was that "nothing shall be done which may prejudice the civil and religious rights of existing non-Jewish communities in Palestine or the rights and political status enjoyed by Jews in any other country."[27] It was not the only view communicated as "the British government's view" on the Middle East to various parties at this time, and it was not everything that the Zionist lobby in Britain had been hoping for. It proved to be a consequential document, however, because with the victory of the British and their allies in the First World War and the subsequent partition of the defeated Ottoman Empire, the promise in the Balfour Declaration was incorporated into the "mandate" to govern Palestine given to Great Britain by the League of Nations in 1922. Recognizing "the historical connection of the Jewish people with Palestine and . . . the grounds for reconstituting their national home in that country," the mandate tasked Britain with "putting into effect" the Balfour Declaration, while reinforcing the caveat concerning the civil and religious rights of non-Jews. It was in line with this caveat and with previous British promises to the Arab leaders in the region that it was agreed soon afterwards that the Jewish national home would be created only on the west, and not on the east side the Jordan River (which ultimately became the kingdom of Jordan).

The State of Israel

As the British subsequently attempted to manage Zionist hopes concerning mass Jewish immigration and settlement while placating indignant Arabs who rejected even the idea of a Jewish homeland in the midst of their majority culture and feared that in reality the whole region might eventually become a Jewish state, the difficulty of actually creating the homeland while taking seriously others people's rights soon became apparent. As early as 1922 the Arabs had been reassured by the British that "immigration cannot be so great in volume as to exceed whatever may be the economic capacity of the country at the time to absorb new arrivals."[28] Yet immigration markedly increased in volume after Hitler's rise to power in Germany in 1933 as German Jews—who, among other contributions, had fought for their country in large numbers during the First World War—now began to learn their own bitter lesson about the "protection" offered by assimilation in the face of virulent antisemitism. Violent confrontations between Arabs and Jews also increased in number and intensity, as their very different outlooks on life and agendas collided.[29] In the aftermath of the full-scale Arab Revolt that rumbled on from 1936–1939, the British government announced its intention of limiting future Jewish immigration and of making much of it conditional on Arab consent, while preparing the way for Palestine eventually to become an independent state with an Arab majority. Zionist opposition to this proclamation was put on hold during the Second World War, but it resumed in 1945 at a time when the entire world was beginning to learn about what antisemitism had on this occasion done to the Jews—unimaginable horrors inflicted on millions of people—and what some of the implications had been, therefore, of limiting Jewish immigration to Palestine. If the majority of Jews in the world before this time had not been Zionists, the shock of this discovery certainly led many to reconsider—including many Americans. It also released a tsunami of humanitarian angst and support for Jews among Gentiles.

Faced with outrage not only in relation to previous policy but also to its ongoing refusal to facilitate the mass immigration of surviving European Jews to Israel—and dealing now also with Zionist violence directed against its rule and policies—the British government soon became weary of the struggle to find a workable solution to the Palestinian problem. It announced its intention of terminating the mandate. The humanitarian sentiment generated by the Holocaust was an important factor in what happened next at the United Nations, which passed a resolution in 1947 in favor of partitioning Palestine and creating both a Jewish homeland and an Arab state. While this plan was acceptable to most Jews living in Palestine at the time, it was entirely unacceptable to most Arabs, as well as to militant Zionists, and civil war immediately broke out. The British, having emphasized repeatedly that their troops would not impose a settlement unless it was acceptable to both sides, began to disengage from Palestine late in 1947 in the midst of this civil war; with the expiration of the mandate in May 1948 they departed the region entirely, leaving the newly formed state of Israel to fight it out (successfully) with its Arab neighbors. Once the dust of war had settled, it was revealed that Israel now controlled all of the area that the UN had designated as the Jewish homeland, as well as over half of the area designated for the Arabs. Hundreds of thousands of Palestinians found themselves as refugees, being replaced in Israel in the immediately succeeding period by an equivalent number of immigrating Jews.

CHRISTIAN ZIONISM

Despite the biblical allusions in the Israeli Declaration of Independence, the Jewish Zionism that ultimately led to these outcomes was, on the whole, not particularly religious in nature. Traditional Jewish belief had held that the return of the Jews to their homeland would only be brought about by the Messiah when he came; in the meantime Jews must accept and endure their fate as a dispersed people in the world. Zionism set itself explicitly in opposition to this point of view, taking power into its own hands. It was clearly understood as doing so by the majority of Jews, who were not prepared at this time to exchange a holy land for a contemporary homeland.

Judaism and Zionism

If the early Zionists therefore understood the land and its possession in ways that were not traditionally religious, the same is true of their view of the people who would inhabit it. Virtually all Zionists in 1897, claims Paul Mendes-Flohr, "shared an insistence that the Jews must be a 'normal' people. In the name of the desired normalization, they consciously sought to jettison the idea of election [chosenness]."[30] When we then consider the key founders of the state of Israel, moreover—people like David Ben Gurion—we discover that they were on the whole committed secularists who desired to establish a secular, and not a religious Jewish state.[31] These founders were excited about welcoming devout, religious Jews to Zion—but mainly so that they could shape them into modern, Enlightenment Jews by way of a good education. It was in part their own poor decision making (relative to their goals) that led to a different outcome—for example, allowing exemption from military service to those who wished to study the Torah; permitting the establishment of religious schools; and delegating to the rabbis the definition of Jewish identity. In part, though, their vision was simply overtaken by the sheer volume of very religious Jewish immigrants (often poor and uneducated) who in successive waves significantly strengthened the religious "party" in Israel. It also did not help the secularist cause that religious Jews turned out to have much higher birth rates than secular ones. The overall result has been an Israel whose level of religiosity many early Zionists did not envision, driven by specifically biblical ideas like the possession of the biblical "promised land" to a degree that the latter did not contemplate.

A Special Calling

The Christian Zionism that necessarily had to exist in order for the Jewish Zionist goals to be achieved, on the other hand, has been highly religious from the start. It began its life during the Reformation (although it was not called "Zionism" until much later) but really came into its own for the first time among the seventeenth-century English Puritans whom we discussed earlier. Christian theologians before this time, while certainly often anticipating the widespread conversion of the Jews in the end times, had generally regarded this conversion as involving the end of a distinct Jewish identity. In this scenario, in which "the Jews had no distinctive eschatological role," there was no space for any return by Jews to a physical land of Israel.[32] The peculiar aspect of Puritan philosemitism, on the other hand, was that this end-time conversion was associated with a Jewish return to their historical homeland in the aftermath of the fall of the Ottoman Empire. It was the special responsibility of Protestant nations, in particular England, not only to seek the conversion of Jews but also to pray for this return. An important early modern influence here was Thomas Brightman (1562–1607), "the first Judeo-centrist to offer a detailed scriptural exposition of the position."[33] His idea was that God had separate earthly plans for Jews and Gentiles that would remain radically different in the future. He anticipated a modest conversion among the Jews in 1650, followed by a pilgrimage to Israel and a more general conversion in 1695–1696. This same restorationist belief then travelled with the Puritans to the American colonies and from there out into the general culture of the emerging United States, such that American self-understanding became in the course of time bound up with the success of Zionism.

As we saw in chapter 12, both the United Kingdom and the United States were later deeply impacted by the kind of revivalist, personal Christianity that was one of the eventual consequences of Pietism spreading outside Germany, and which created the circumstances in the nineteenth century in which activism of various kinds flourished (including reformism vis-à-vis slavery). Since this Pietism was also philosemitic in nature, urging benevolent action toward the Jews in pursuit of their conversion, it was natural that these two streams of Protestantism should coalesce. This created a set of passionately held convictions among many British and American Christians (especially) that it was their duty, as they looked for God's blessing on their own countries, to pursue both Jewish conversion and their recovery of their homeland: "I will bless those who bless you," God had said to Abraham, "and whoever curses you I will curse" (Gen. 12:3).[34] It was the "biblical" position to adopt. This very way of thinking about the matter was itself distinctively Christian and especially Protestant, and not traditionally Jewish. Prior to the nineteenth century, when Jews began to participate fully in Christianized culture, the Bible had been "considered secondary to Jewish oral

law . . . It was the Protestants who discovered the Bible and extolled its importance in educating the younger generation."[35] The Protestants in turn passed on
to nineteenth-century Jews key ideas "from the Bible" about the return to their
ancient homeland that they subsequently embraced as their own.

In Britain this innately religious, Christian Zionism was a major factor in
the creation of an environment in the nineteenth century in which the Balfour
Declaration could be produced in the early twentieth—an environment in which
"Britain came to command unchallenged mastery of the seas after [the Battle
of] Trafalgar, and the Ottoman Empire appeared ever more unstable," making
"the possibility of a national restoration of the Jews to Palestine . . . increasingly
realistic."[36] The British prime minister at the time of the Balfour Declaration
was David Lloyd George, "a Protestant brought up on the Bible . . . [who] was
greatly influenced by the romantic idea of the Jews returning to their ancient
homeland that was prevalent in nineteenth-century Britain and fired up by the
Zionist idea."[37] In the United States, the same Christian Zionism was a major
factor in prompting strong American support for the state of Israel right from
its beginnings, and it remains an extremely important driver of political support
for Israel to this day across a broad spectrum of Protestant evangelicalism, most
notably in its Pentecostal and charismatic (and often dispensationalist) forms.
Since these kinds of evangelicalism are global in nature, Christian Zionism has
also now become a markedly global phenomenon as well, popular in Latin America, Africa, and Asia.

BIBLICAL ROOTS

How do its adherents understand the Bible? They note first of all God's promise
of Canaan to Abraham and his posterity in the book of Genesis (Gen. 12:6–7),
subsequently repeated to Isaac (26:3–4), who prayed that the promise would be
fulfilled in Jacob (28:4; cf. 28:13–15). Joseph later announced to his brothers that
"God will surely . . . take you up out of this land to the land he promised on oath
to Abraham, Isaac, and Jacob" (50:24). This is the land in which the Israelites later
settled under God's guidance and leadership (Joshua and Judges) before losing it
again as a result of repeating the sins of the previous inhabitants (2 Kings). The
most important thing to notice about this promise, however, is that the land is
given "to you and your offspring *forever*" (Gen. 13:15). Consistent with this promise, sealed in Genesis by a solemn covenant, is the fact that even in exile (Lev.
26:44–45 tells us) God will not break his covenant with Abraham's descendants.
It is a one-sided covenant, in the making of which God passes through the midst
of the sacrifices while Abraham is sleeping (Gen. 15:12); it is valid for all time, no
matter what Abraham's descendants do. Israel's sin, then, only causes the temporary loss of parts or all of the land for limited periods; in terms of the overall

picture, "I will not violate my covenant or alter what my lips have uttered" (Ps. 89:34). So it is that in the biblical prophets we read of a return of the Jews to their land from exile—the great "ingathering" alluded to in the Israeli Declaration of Independence itself.[38]

All such promises are to be taken "literally"—this was a notable emphasis of Christian Zionist Bible reading from the beginning, and it continued to be important when premillennial, dispensationalist elements were added to the mix in the succeeding centuries. Cyril Scofield, author of the influential *Scofield Reference Bible*, once put it this way: "Not one instance exists of a 'spiritual' or figurative fulfilment of prophecy . . . Jerusalem is always Jerusalem, Israel is always Israel, Zion is always Zion . . . Prophecies may never be spiritualised, but are always literal."[39] When Scripture is read literally in this way, we immediately understand that God has two distinct purposes in the world, relating to two peoples: an earthly people (the Jews) and a heavenly one (the Christians). He makes different promises to each group, and it is crucial that we should not become confused about which promises pertain to which group. The promises about the land, specifically, pertain only to the Jews, to whom it has been given by God as an eternal inheritance but who have never yet fully occupied it—for it is said in Genesis 15:18 to extend "from the Wadi of Egypt to the great river, the Euphrates" (i.e., it includes at least modern Jordan, Lebanon, and Syria). Christian Zionists look forward to the day that the Jews do fully occupy it. They do so in company (as they see it) with Jesus, who presupposes an Israel restored to the land at his Second Coming (Matt. 19:28; 24:30; Luke 13:34–35),[40] and with the apostles, who anticipate this time when "God [will] restore everything" (Acts 3:21).[41] They typically express profound disappointment, therefore, when Israeli expansion in the region slows down or halts, or when the government of Israel even decides to withdraw from parts of "biblical Israel" it had previously occupied.

Particularly in its premillennial, dispensationalist forms, Scripture has additionally been read as providing a considerable amount of information pertaining to current and future events in the world that have the restored people of Israel at their center. This has typically involved a fairly detailed predictive eschatological timetable involving a rebuilding of the temple in Jerusalem, the reconsecration of a priesthood and the reinstitution of sacrifices there, and various other events leading ultimately to the final battle of Armageddon and the end of world history.

THE HERMENEUTICS OF THE LAND

What are we to make of this Bible reading and of the Christian Zionism that it has produced, and whose program it has in turn legitimated? Is this the correct way for the person in search of what is right to interpret Scripture, and therefore their Christian responsibility toward the Jews? If not, how should Scripture be read better, and what implications follow for the good life?

ISRAEL IN BIBLICAL CONTEXT

First of all, the reader of the book to this point will no doubt have realized in engaging with the immediately preceding description of how Christian Zionists read the Bible that it differs fundamentally, at the "big-picture" level of Story, from the way in which I have been proposing that we *ought* to read Scripture. Already in chapter 3 I argued that the Story itself makes it clear that God's choice of the descendants of Abraham and Sarah as his primary mission partner in the world was a temporary one. It lasted only until the coming of the One who does indeed make a new covenant with all his followers, as described in Jeremiah 31. With the coming of Christ, the primary mission-partner is no longer one particular people-group, defined by physical descent, but a universal Church comprising both Jew and Gentile, defined by faith in Christ. It is the Church, comprising both Jewish and Gentile followers of the Messiah, who together as "fellow citizens" (Eph. 2:19–20) have become "chosen people . . . royal priesthood . . . [and] . . . holy nation" (1 Pet. 2:9–10). It is these people, who "belong to Christ . . . [who are] Abraham's seed, and heirs according to the promise" (Gal. 3:29). The Church is now called both to live authentically in the kingdom of God that has come in Christ and to proclaim it—which (obviously) only believers in the Messiah can do. This NT people of God is deeply continuous with the OT people of God but also significantly discontinuous with it. As such—as we have seen in preceding chapters—it ought not to obey exactly the same Torah, much of which was designed to reinforce the temporary separation between Jew and Gentile that has come to end in Christ (chapter 3 and others). It ought not to look for a Davidic king other than Christ to rule a kingdom other than his own universal one. It ought not to regard the terrestrial fate of either the city of Jerusalem or its temple as being suffused any longer with transcendental meaning—as if it were of any greater importance to the Christian than any other earthly city.

It follows that if this account of the overall shape of the Story is correct—and I believe it is—then the Christian Zionist understanding of Scripture is fundamentally (and not just in its detail) wrong. It creates an ongoing "chosenness" for the OT people of God in the post-Pentecost period of history, independently of Christ, when there is no compelling reason on the basis of Scripture to believe that one exists. It then gathers around that center other ideas (like the ongoing importance of earthly Jerusalem, and ultimately of both its temple and its priesthood) that also lack clear Scriptural warrant. New Testament Scripture, in particular, knows nothing of these notions, although as the Church has long believed it does express the hope "for the Israelites . . . that they may be saved" (Rom. 10:1 and following), *in* Christ and along with everyone else. The core problem of Christian Zionist hermeneutics, then, is a failure to read the story of Israel sufficiently carefully within its literary, canonical context.

LITERAL READING

Ironically enough, this represents a failure to read Scripture "literally"—at least as we defined this reading in chapter 2. When Cyril Scofield tells us that in biblical prophecy "Jerusalem is always Jerusalem, Israel is always Israel, Zion is always Zion" and cautions us against spiritualizing the text, he has already begged an important question that the truly literal reader will always want to ask: which kind of Jerusalem/Zion and Israel is the text talking about? In chapter 6 we noted that the OT presents a multifaceted picture of Jerusalem, in the course of which its rhetoric regularly outstrips the reality of earthly Jerusalem. That is, Jerusalem and its temple routinely point to realities greater than themselves; the hopes bound up with "Zion" far transcend any mundane city or temple. The NT clearly identifies for us what those realities are: Christ has fulfilled in his own person all the hopes surrounding the Jerusalem temple, and the full reality of this will become apparent in the course of time. He is our temple and—as his body—we ourselves are that temple. It is literal reading that leads us to this overall picture—that is, attending carefully to all the individual instances in which "Jerusalem is always Jerusalem . . . Zion is always Zion" within the context of the movement of the entire biblical Story.

THE LAND IN BIBLICAL CONTEXT

This is of course how we should also approach the question of the land in Scripture. It is a land first introduced to us in the biblical Story in Genesis 12, where the God who created the entire earth (Hb. 'erets, Gen. 1:1) now calls out a particular people through whom all peoples will be blessed (Gen. 12:3). To this people is given a particular land (Hb. 'erets, Gen. 12:1) in which they may live, under certain conditions, while God works out his plan through them for the redemption of the whole cosmos. As such—and very much like Jerusalem and its temple—the language used in relation to the land in the OT regularly outstrips historical reality. Before the people of Israel first enter Canaan we read that, if the Israelites obey God in it, "he will bless the fruit of your womb, the crops of your land . . . the calves of your herds and the lambs of your flocks . . . none of your men or women will be childless, nor will any of your livestock be without young. The LORD will keep you free from every disease" (Deut. 7:13–15). We know from the remainder of the OT, however, that many righteous Israelites living in the land did not live such untroubled lives. Then again, when Isaiah describes the return of the sixth-century exiles to this same land, he writes about it in extravagant language; so does Ezekiel. [42] We know from the remainder of the OT, however, that the returning exiles did not inhabit a territory like the one these prophets describe. The extravagant language in both segments of the OT part of the biblical Story, both pre- and postexile, constantly presses upon the reader the question of *reference*: what is it, in the end, to which this language about the wonderful land refers? And this leads us to consider the overall trajectory of the entire biblical literary corpus that ends not with a restoration of anyone to the *land* of Israel but with the provision of a new heaven and a new *earth*, in which these astonishing prophetic words are said indeed to come true. The land of Israel, it turns out—like everything else that has to do with Israel in the OT—must be read within this larger context. Like Torah, it sits within a Story in which certain things have been true "from the beginning" and others will be true in the end. And the question we must ask in pursuit of "literal reading" is, what role does the land play within this larger Story?

Beyond the manner in which the Story ends, the NT confirms in a number of ways what the correct answer is to this question. We think of Hebrews 3:7 to 4:13, for example, where the only Promised Land in the future of God's people is the "land" of ultimate Sabbath rest with God. We also think of Matthew 5:5. When there was a particular people of God in a particular land, the promises of God to the righteous were understandably often focused on the particular: "the meek will inherit the *land* (Hb. *'erets*) and enjoy peace and prosperity" (Ps. 37:11). However, the Creator God was always looking for meekness across the entirety of Creation, not just in one land (Hb. *'erets*, Isa. 11:4). As we are transitioning in Jesus' time, then, from one particular people of God in one land to a universal people of God in all lands, Jesus says this: "Blessed are the meek, for they will inherit the *earth*" (Matt. 5:5). Likewise, in Romans 4:13 Paul writes of "Abraham and his offspring" receiving a promise that they would inherit not the *land* of Israel but "the *world*" (Gk. *kosmos*). That is what the promise to Abraham is really "about"—the people of God inheriting the earth, of which the land is only an initial token. And in Ephesians 6:2–3, as we saw in chapter 3, Paul advises Christians that they should honor their father and mothers *not* so that they "may enjoy long life in the land" but so that they may do so "on the earth" (Exod. 20:16; Eph. 6:2–3).

Time is not cyclical in biblical faith; it is, rather, an arrow. It moves horizontally, from beginning to end, and always on to what is new, leaving the old behind. In the course of this process we move on from a chosen people living in one land to a people living in all lands; from one earthly city to many cities; and from one earthly temple and its priesthood to the temple and its high priest who are Christ, and to the temples and the priests who are all believers in Christ. It is to miss the communicative intent of Scripture to think otherwise. It is to fail to read literally. That God's promises to his people concerning the "territory" in which they are destined to live are indeed "forever" is not in question. However, we saw in chapter 6 that his promise to David that "your house and your kingdom will endure forever" did not mean that "ordinary" Davidic kingship would endure eternally.

We also saw that God's promise that the Jerusalem temple would be "a place for you [God] to dwell forever" did not mean that the ordinary temple in that city would endure forever, or that the pilgrim of Psalm 23 expected that he himself would "dwell in [that] house of the LORD forever." So it is with the land. It always pointed beyond itself to something greater.

CONCLUSION

If there is therefore no good reason to think that the Bible has anything at all directly to say about any return of modern Jews to their historical, God-given homeland and about their founding of a modern state in it after all the centuries of dispersion they have experienced since the time of the Roman Empire—where does this leave us? Does it mean that Christians have no obligation to love the Jews, or to support the modern state of Israel?

Many people appear to fear that this is so—which is one of the reasons why contemporary debate about Zionism is so emotionally charged. In such an environment, even to articulate the above reading of the Bible vis-à-vis the OT and the NT peoples of God runs the risk of being labeled "supersessionist" at best (see chapter 3)—which many people just seem intuitively to know is a "wrong" view held by "bad" people—or antisemitic at worst (a *very* wrong posture adopted by *very* bad people). In the highly polarized world of public discourse that is all too often the norm nowadays, it is apparently the case that one can be a member of only one of two mutually antagonistic tribes: philosemitic and Zionist on the one side and non- or anti-Zionist and antisemitic on the other. Indeed, the members of these tribes themselves often seem determined to prevent any other tribe from ever emerging, shouting down and shaming (as they do) all attempts at discourse in the middle ground. One way or another, only true, dogmatic believers are allowed in this angry (and actually intolerant) world, and the point is not, in the end, to debate at all, but only to win. It is a new holy war.

I want to insist as strongly as I can, on the other hand, that a Christian who has come to the conclusion that the Bible provides no warrant for Christian Zionism is still obligated by Scripture itself to love the Jews and to support the modern state of Israel. The basis for this love and support lies precisely in the reading of the whole biblical Story that I have just set against the deeply flawed Christian Zionist one, and which I have been developing throughout this whole book. This reading is grounded in the biblical imperative that we must love all of our image-bearing neighbors and strive to be their "keepers" (Gen. 4:9)—in this particular case, neighbors whom the Church throughout its history has notoriously and dreadfully, in all kinds of ways, failed to love and keep. Of *course* we should love and support them wherever they live, now as well as in the future, when they are just as likely as in the past to be the targets of despicable rhetoric and egregious violence. In this I do not disagree with Christian Zionists at all. At the same time, this same biblical Story, as I read it, makes it clear that God requires us to love and keep *all* of our image-bearing neighbors, and not just some. Specifically, God requires us to love and keep Arabs as well as Jews. This leads me to a particular view of the right and Christian way in which to approach the matter of Israel/Palestine. It is very much at odds with the approach typically adopted by Christian Zionists, whose faulty biblical hermeneutics lead them to moral and political positions (and actions) with respect to Israel/Palestine that are entirely indefensible on the basis of explicit biblical teaching itself. I shall have more to say about this in chapter 16.

DISCUSSION QUESTIONS

1. Should Christians be committed to fostering "philosemitism" (positive attitudes toward Jews)? Why or why not?
2. Does Christian philosemitism require that Christians support the modern state of Israel? If so, what kind of support should it be?
3. What is our Christian responsibility toward the Palestinian inhabitants of Israel/Palestine, including the large numbers of Palestinian Christians (around two hundred thousand)?
4. In chapter 6 I asked whether Christians are justified in sanctioning the oppression or killing of people in pursuit of their "eschatological" goals. Having read this far in the book, is your answer the same as or different than before you began reading? Why?

15

On Looking After the Garden
The Good Life and Environmental Ethics

It used to be understood that we have a sacred duty to pass on to future generations
a world that is as rich as or richer than the one we came into . . . For most of our
existence, people knew that we were deeply embedded in nature and that our very
survival depended on nature's generosity. We understood that everything in the world
was connected, that what we did had repercussions, and that therefore every act was
laden with responsibility.[1]

David Suzuki

In 1992 the United Nations sponsored what has informally become known as the first "Earth Summit." It met in Rio de Janeiro in Brazil and "was unprecedented for a UN conference, in terms of both its size [172 governments participated] and the scope of its concerns."[2] The UN goal was "to help Governments rethink economic development and find ways to halt the destruction of irreplaceable natural resources and pollution of the planet."[3] It produced the last of the "declarations" that I want mention in this book: the Rio Declaration on Environment and Development.[4]

THE RIO DECLARATION ON ENVIRONMENT AND DEVELOPMENT (1992)

After a brief preamble, in which among other things "the integral and interdependent nature of the Earth, our home," is recognized, this declaration enunciates twenty-seven principles. The first proclaims that "[h]uman beings are at the centre of concerns for sustainable development. They are entitled to a healthy and productive life in harmony with nature." The document proceeds then to affirm that sovereign states possess "the sovereign right to exploit their own resources pursuant to their own environmental and developmental policies," with the caveat that "[t]he right to development must be fulfilled so as to equitably meet developmental and environmental needs of present and future generations" (principles two and three). As we move on, we encounter commitments to "cooperate in the essential task of eradicating poverty as an indispensable requirement for sustainable development" and to give careful consideration to "the least developed and . . . most environmentally vulnerable" countries (principles five and six). Everything should be done "in a spirit of global partnership to conserve, protect, and restore the health and integrity of the Earth's ecosystem" (principle seven). Indeed, all kinds of people worldwide are explicitly mentioned as playing an important role in this mission. "Women have a vital role in environmental management and development," for, example and so do "[i]ndigenous people and their communities, and other local communities" (principles twenty and twenty-two).

Why is it that this declaration was made in 1992 rather than (say) 1792? For that matter, why had the very first global environment conference occurred only twenty years beforehand, in 1972, rather than in 1772—the UN Conference on the Human Environment in Stockholm? A trivial set of answers to these questions would focus on pragmatic matters: obviously, the UN did not exist in the eighteenth century, and no effective means of organizing such a global conference existed back then. A deeper set of answers, however—and it is these in which I am interested—should focus on how the majority of human beings prior to the rise of modernity thought about the world around them and their relationship to it. It is this reality that would above all have prevented humanity, even if it had been able, from organizing a global conference and issuing a declaration concerning "the environment." To understand this important point we must yet again delve into some historical background, on the way to reflecting on what Scripture has to say to Christians seeking what is right with respect to this matter of "environment ethics"—or as we should call it, "Creation care."

DARK GREEN RELIGION

It is regularly claimed nowadays that our contemporary ecological problems are the ultimate result of something that happened long ago: the advent of "civilization." Before the Neolithic agricultural revolution and the domestication of animals, human (Paleolithic) societies were based on "the principle of relatedness [that] is at the heart of indigenous wisdom: traditional intimacy with the world as the immanent basis of spirituality."[5] But then (it is said) this "reverence for the earth-centered was broken," and the human began to take precedence over the natural.[6] In order to save ourselves now, we must somehow retrieve a "religion that considers nature to be sacred, imbued with intrinsic value, and worthy of reverent care."[7] We must abandon modern world religions that "promote and justify violence, bigotry, and anthropocentrism and focus 'exclusively on the superiority and divinity of the human species,'" and we must substitute for these a spirituality in which anthropocentrism is replaced with biocentrism—in which "interspecies equality allows a sense of planetary belonging."[8] Contemporary indigenous peoples can help us greatly on this quest, since "scientists and indigenous peoples have similar insights regarding ecological interdependence, and . . . they often share common ethical and spiritual perceptions about the intrinsic value and sacredness of nature."[9] These indigenous peoples are indeed "the best remaining stewards of . . . critically important spiritual and ecological knowledge."[10]

Those who have adopted such a view of the past, with its significant implications for how we should live in both the present and the future, have been described by contemporary author Bron Taylor as having embraced "dark green religion." This religion, he suggests, is at the present time "as widespread as most religions, more significant than some, and growing more rapidly than others."[11] Its practitioners have certainly made a huge impact on UN deliberations concerning the environment. Reporting on the Earth Summit in Johannesburg in 2002, for example, Taylor writes of the dominant conviction among the participants

> that most people used to live sustainably but that a fall from an earthly paradise occurred, resulting (variously, depending on the speaker) from agriculture, hierarchy, patriarchy, monotheism, technology, and capitalism, all of which disconnect us from nature and produce greed, indifference, and injustice.[12]

The important point that must be emphasized is that, in this way of thinking, "most people used to live sustainably" in a highly conscious, knowledgeable manner. They did not do so accidentally. It was their ecological wisdom that enabled them to live more ecologically sensitive lives than we modern people do—and that is why they are important for us now.

A CONVENIENT MYTH

Whether it is a dominant conviction of Earth Summiteers or not, we are obliged to insist that there is in fact no good reason, empirically speaking, to believe in such a "dark green golden age" in the Paleolithic era of human history. We certainly lack *direct* evidence that this is how the world was back then, and the indirect evidence that has allegedly been drawn from the observation and analysis of modern hunter-gatherer societies is not at all compelling.[13] I have offered an extensive summary of the modern research that bears on this question in another

book, and I do not intend to repeat much of that detail here.[14] It is worth reproducing a little of it in the present context, however, so that the reader can get a
sense of where it leads us.

THE AMAZON

The native peoples of Amazonia have often been depicted in popular writing
as possessing an innate "conservation ethic," preserved from ancient times, from
which we might learn something important in our modern mission "to conserve,
protect, and restore the health and integrity of the Earth's ecosystem" (Rio Declaration, principle seven). However, the evidence clearly suggests that what looks
like "conservation" among these peoples arises in reality simply as an accidental
by-product of the main business at hand: surviving as best one can in challenging
circumstances. It is resource constraints that drive their practices, not an environmental philosophy. As one researcher, Michael Alvard, has put it, "The appearance of balance between traditional native groups and their environment has
more to do with low human population densities, lack of markets, and limited
technology than it does with any natural harmonious relationship with nature."[15]
Such claims are of course, as Allyn Stearman notes, "certain to disturb those who
romanticize indigenous peoples according to their own ethnocentric perceptions
of how native societies relate to nature."[16] Since they are based on solid empirical
evidence, however, they need to be taken seriously.

NORTH AMERICA

Other studies have tracked just how destructive of their environments premodern people have often been when resource constraints have not been in play—
typically "using the richest resources with pitiless energetic efficiency" and thereby
radically changing the world around them.[17] Contrary to the assumption of many
people, for example, that "native North Americans had little impact on the flora
and fauna of the continent," the truth is that these early native peoples "created
the very ecosystem that we now consider 'natural'" in that part of the world.[18]
Very likely they are to be implicated, first, in the eradication of some thirty-five
genera of mostly large animals around 10,000 BC—the "Pleistocene extinctions."
Even if they were not directly or entirely responsible for these extinctions, they
certainly "drove populations of highly desirable 'target species' or 'preferred prey'
to low levels, or even to local extinction,"[19] just as one would expect of a people
pursuing an optimal foraging strategy with no effective conservation practices."[20]
When Europeans first encountered North America, they generally found abundant wildlife only where the native inhabitants were absent or greatly diminished
in number.[21] None of this speaks to "conservation practices" on the part of Native

American peoples historically. It was, again, a matter of staying alive in the immediate circumstances; ecological wisdom did not come into it.

Mind and Matter

These examples are aspects of a larger pattern, which has been described by Bobbi
Low in her study of 186 traditional societies worldwide. People in such societies "do not, at least to their ethnographers, express a widely held conservation
ethic," and "their low ecological impact ... results not from conscious conservation efforts but from various combinations of low population density, inefficient
extraction technology, and lack of profitable markets for extracted resources."[22]
Consequently (as Thomas Neumann says), it is "important to surrender the
image of the aboriginal peoples living in idyllic harmony with host ecological systems."[23] They have not done so recently, and there is no reason to think that they
ever did so in previous eras.

The most important point to grasp here is not only that premodern people
have not typically practiced "conservation" but that the very concept has not arisen
in their minds—and for good reason. Conservation (W. T. Vickers reminds us)
"is not a state of being. It is a response to people's perceptions about the state of
their environment and its resources, and a willingness to modify their behaviors
to adjust to new realities."[24] In order for a "conservation ethic" to arise, then, two
things are minimally necessary. First, there must be "stress on the resource base,
made tangible through scarcity and/or increases in work effort, with significant
repercussions for the user group."[25] Secondly, there must be a belief that human
hunting or farming behavior (or whatever) is responsible in some way for the
problem and that changes to human habits will improve the situation. This is
manifestly not how premodern people have typically looked at the world, however. On the one hand, they have often lived in the midst of plenty rather than
scarcity (not least because of low population pressure on their environments).
On the other, their belief systems have generally not led them to believe that
there is any correlation between scarcity and their behavior (retrospectively or
prospectively).

Ironically, that is to say, it is precisely the premodern "nature-spirituality" so
appreciated by the dark green religionists that has prevented the acquisition of
"ecological wisdom" by the people who have practiced this spirituality. Consider
those Plains Indians in North America, for example, who believed that buffalo
were created in countless numbers underground, or in a certain lake, emerging
each year onto the prairie to supply their needs. If the buffalo could not be seen,
it was not because of population decline or some such modern concept. It was
because they had not (yet) left their point of origin. It is not easy to see how anything approaching a conservation ethic could ever have arisen out of such a belief

system, and no evidence that it ever did—since "scarcity" here has no connection, conceptually, with human behavior. The comments concerning the past by David Suzuki that are noted in the epigraph to this chapter, then, are quite misleading. Many people in the past did understand that they were "deeply embedded in nature and that [their] very survival depended on nature's generosity"—that, indeed, "everything in the world was connected." This did not, however, lead them to believe that they had a role to play, much less a "sacred duty" to perform, in passing on "to future generations a world that is as rich as or richer than the one we came into." Their "responsibility" with respect to "repercussions" simply was not understood in such a manner.

THE RISE OF MODERNITY

To put this in a different way: in order even to conceive of an Earth Summit that will "help Governments rethink economic development and find ways to halt the destruction of irreplaceable natural resources and pollution of the planet," one already needs to have registered that scarcity is a present or an imminent problem (along with pollution), that human beings have to some degree created the problem, and that we are also capable of doing something to solve it. One needs to have already embraced a "modern" view of the world and our role in it, and to have abandoned premodern ones—at least the ones I have just described.

THE ROOTS OF THE MODERN

I put the matter in precisely this way because of my convictions about where what we call "modernity" came from, and what its roots in premodernity were. Again, I have explained these convictions at great length in a different book, and I have insufficient space here to do more than simply outlining them.[26] The core of the argument is this: that what we now call modernity arose out of a particular version of the Christian worldview that was deeply rooted in OT Scripture, which in the centuries BC had already set its face against the "nature spirituality" that was ubiquitous in the ANE. Modernity arose as this biblically based worldview began fully to gain its own voice by freeing itself from the undue influence of certain streams of Greek philosophy (especially that of Aristotle) that had been dominant in the centuries AD stretching from the first to the fifteenth.

Aristotle held that every object in the cosmos possesses two elements: form and matter. Neither is created; both are simply "there." The *form* of an object is its essential reality; the *matter* is merely the imperfect vessel in which the form is realized. The point of natural philosophy (what modern people call "science") is to penetrate to the essence (the form), which one accomplishes by way of reason (rational contemplation). Our senses cannot get us there—they only tell us about the matter, not the form, and if we depend upon them they will mislead us as to essential reality. It follows, then, that Aristotelian natural philosophy—which permitted observation to play some initial role in the process of gaining knowledge—did not ultimately value empirical enquiry. The main point was to clarify what nature *must* be like, a priori, by way of logical and dialectical argument. All that remained beyond that was the observation of mere examples reflecting (however dimly) the rational, necessary truth of the matter.

It was this Aristotelian philosophy of nature that was self-consciously rejected by early modern science as it began to emerge in the late sixteenth and then the seventeenth centuries, leading us thereby into the modern world. This modern science depended on the idea that God had created both the heavens and the Earth, which possessed an order imprinted upon it by God (and therefore obeyed "laws"). Creation is nevertheless distinct from God and represents a legitimate object of enquiry *in itself*. This enquiry must be empirically based, since God (being God) stands outside the cosmos, and his actions in creating it cannot be predicted rationally. There is therefore no necessity about Creation. We cannot know what God *must* have done. Rather, one has to look and see what God has *actually* done. It was in setting aside Greek ideas about nature, then, and substituting others in their place, that modern science became possible.

Where did these "un-Greek" ideas originate? They originated in the biblical, Christian doctrine of Creation, so long prevented from radically changing the world by its unfortunate marriage to a Greek philosophy of nature of which too many Christian theologians were overly enamored.[27] "The modern investigators of nature," Michael Foster tells us, "were the first to take seriously *in their science* the Christian doctrine that nature is created."[28] The Reformation played a crucial role in this cultural shift, since it insisted on the authority of "the Bible alone," read according to its literal sense. Indeed, the new science was promoted most enthusiastically in those parts of Europe where the older, medieval ideas had become the most marginalized—that is, in Protestant rather than in Roman Catholic areas.

REASON EXPLORING NATURE

For many of the early modern scientists, science was fundamentally about telling the truth about how the world works, first to the glory of the God who created it, and secondly so that we can live more holy lives within it. The famous Johannes Kepler (1571–1630), for example—who had wanted to be a theologian—became quite content in the end with being an astronomer instead, since (he wrote) "through my [scientific] effort God is being celebrated in astronomy."[29] It did not take very long, however, for modern science to begin to shake itself free of the constraints (as many saw it) of traditional Christian confession and to view

"Nature" (as it had once again come to be known) as a self-standing entity that could be studied using scientific method alone. Indeed, the potential of such study for producing fundamental *change* in the world was quickly appreciated.

This was true not only at the scientific and technological but also at the social and political levels, as fresh convictions about what is "natural" became the basis for various proposals as to how the modern state should organize itself. This is the context, for example, in which we must understand the various "declarations" that we have pondered in the course of this book (beginning in chapter 1) concerning natural and self-evident rights that we must absolutely recognize in how we live our lives.[30] It was also true, however, at a technological level. Already in the writings of the English philosopher Francis Bacon (1561–1626) in the early seventeenth century, we find that "reason exploring nature," unencumbered by any previous form of tradition, philosophy, or religion, is the path to true knowledge.[31] This knowledge is to be acquired, moreover, not so that humanity may live in greater *agreement* with it—as in a typical "natural law" argument—but so that we may *master* it. Such an approach to "nature" was still inevitably (in the seventeenth century) influenced by some biblical ideas. They were now relocated, however, within a thoroughly this-worldly, utopian story about reality that justified (as biblical faith does not) the bending of everything in nature to human ends and was optimistic about the ability of human power to reach these ends.

In Francis Bacon, then, we already see foreshadowed the development of modern science as a totalizing worldview in principle independent of the doctrinal and ethical constraints of Christian religion—or of any religion, for that matter. We are still dealing today with the consequences of the birth of this creature. It is indeed just at this point in history, and not before, that the seedbed is truly constructed from which the flower of our current ecological crisis eventually emerged. A reductionistic science sets off, now, on its quest for total knowledge of certain kinds concerning the totality of "Nature," with a view to total mastery of it, convinced that such "progress" must always, in all respects, be a good thing. It does so without any apparent sense of obligation to account for itself in terms of larger, holistic ideas concerning what "the good" looks like, and with little reflection on whether some "goods" are in fact much more important than others. This journey was bound from the beginning to end badly. It simply took a few hundred years for us to realize just how bad the ending might be.

TOWARD ENVIRONMENTALISM

Strenuous objections to this new and modern way of looking at the world already began to emerge in Europe and its colonies in the eighteenth and nineteenth centuries, associated with the movement typically referred to as "Romanticism." It was just before and during this period that the myth that we discussed earlier concerning the idyllic "state of nature" among premodern peoples first arose and was widely disseminated. This happened as influential people expressed their own dissatisfaction with the way in which early modern civilization was turning out and contrasted it with native society, especially in the Americas. The Baron de Lahontan's popular travelogue, *New Voyages to North America* (1703), provides a good example, in which "science and the arts are the parents of corruption. The savage obeys the will of Nature, his kindly mother, therefore he is happy. It is the civilized folk who are the real barbarians."[32]

ROMANTICISM

The celebration of the spontaneous, the visceral, and the natural, along such lines, lay at the core of Romanticism. Feeling was a more reliable instructor than intellect, nature a better and a purer teacher than civilization. William Wordsworth put it in this way: "One impulse from a vernal wood / May teach you more of man / Of moral evil and of good / Than all the sages can."[33] Romanticism was thus a reaction against the scientific rationalism of modernity as such, but also against the massive changes happening in society as a result, as modern science harnessed "natural forces" such as water and wind, and "natural products" such as coal, to produce the Industrial Revolution and its attendant pollution, poverty, and ugliness (symbolized by Blake's "dark Satanic mills").

Romanticism not only contributed in general ways to what became environmentalism, but also in very specific ones—for out of this context emerged some important writings that have had a long-lasting influence on modern culture. One of these is Henry David Thoreau's *Walden* (1854).[34] The writings of John Muir about the Sierra Nevada (1872–1913) also deserve special mention.[35] Important Romantics in Great Britain during this era include John Ruskin, Octavia Hill, and Edward Carpenter. The passionate interest in nature that is evident in such authors is also reflected in the creation of various early modern organizations designed to protect aspects of it from the further encroachment of modern industrialist capitalism. Among these were (in Great Britain) the Society for the Protection of Birds (1889) and the National Trust for Places of Historic Interest or Natural Beauty (1894); and (in the United States) the National Audubon Society, which set out to save "plume birds" from the ladies' hat trade, and the Sierra Club, established by John Muir and others to defend Yosemite National Park.

MAN AND NATURE

What all these initiatives have in common is a keen awareness that humanity in the modern period has been drastically changing the environment far more significantly than ever before, and that it must now—for the benefit of all creatures—constrain its activity and alter its habits. The need for *remedial* action had indeed already been urged back in 1864 by George Marsh in his *Man and Nature*. In this volume he attacked a residual, premodern conviction among his contemporaries concerning the necessarily perpetual bounty that the Earth will bestow upon its creatures. His main concern was the forests, which had been dangerously reduced in size. Human beings have caused this problem, he wrote, and only they can fix it; nature does not heal itself but must be taken under human care. It was, one reader later proclaimed, "the rudest kick in the face that American initiative, optimism, and carelessness had yet received."[36]

The scale of the problems (plural) that "the modern project" has bequeathed to us has only become clearer from the middle of the twentieth century onwards. A significant moment in this process was the publication in 1962 of *Silent Spring* by Rachel Carson, which warned of the severe harm that pesticides, particularly DDT, were causing to birds and other creatures. She was criticized by the chemical industry for saying so, but the book was a bestseller and had a huge impact worldwide, leading to the founding in 1967 of the Environmental Defense Fund by scientists committed to banning DDT. *The Population Bomb*, published in 1968, also became a bestseller; it predicted famine in the wake of global overpopulation. Stunning visual evidence of the modern human capacity to do harm was provided in the following year when an oil rig in California blew out and the oil slick killed ten thousand birds and sea creatures. With "environmental issues" firmly on the table in the United States as a result, the first Earth Day in 1970 brought twenty million Americans out of their homes to demonstrate in favor of a healthy, sustainable environment. By the end of the year President Nixon had created the Environmental Protection Agency.

These are some of the events that lie in the immediate background of the UN Conference on the Human Environment in Stockholm 1972—and I trust that it is now evident why it did indeed take place in 1972 and not two hundred years earlier. By the time we get to the Rio Declaration in 1992, the world had additionally witnessed various other alarming events, including the opening of a hole in the ozone layer over Antarctica. It is not surprising, then, that one of the major international agreements concluded at Rio concerned global climate change.[37]

IT'S ALL GOING TO BURN

It will no doubt already be clear from some of the comments from dark green religionists reported near the beginning of this chapter what they believe the Christian "contribution" to have been with respect to sustaining any kind of care for "the environment." Put simply, they do not believe that Christian faith has made *any* kind of positive contribution, but only a markedly negative one.

The Human Good

This is a view that is widely shared within the environmental "movement," with its overall "critique of Abrahamic anthropocentrism, which is believed to separate humans from nature."[38] It is famously represented by Lynn White's influential 1967 essay characterizing Western Christian tradition as mainly teaching this:

> By gradual stages a loving and all-powerful God had created [nonhuman Creation] . . . Finally, God had created Adam and, as an afterthought, Eve to keep man from being lonely. Man named all the animals, thus establishing his dominance over them. God planned all of this explicitly for man's benefit and rule: no item in the physical creation had any purpose save to serve man's purposes. And, although man's body is made of clay, he is not simply part of nature: he is made in God's image.[39]

The judgment at which White arrives on the basis of this analysis is that "[e]specially in its Western form, Christianity is the most anthropocentric religion the world has seen."[40]

This perspective on Christian faith has continually resurfaced in "green" publications ever since. An early example is James Lovelock, who is well known for his "Gaia theory" about the biosphere as a self-regulating organism (Gaia being the Greek goddess of the Earth). Lovelock's opinion was that "our religions have not yet given us the rules and guidance for our relationship with Gaia."[41] He believed that neither "the humanist concept of sustainable development" nor "the Christian concept of stewardship" were fit for this purpose, because both "are flawed by unconscious hubris."[42] Human beings, in both worldviews, are conceptually simply too far up the chain of being, a major problem for the planet. People who think that God has given us "dominion" over the earth are the last people who are going to take the radical steps necessary to save it.

Just Passing Through

This critique hits the mark to some degree. It is not at all difficult to find marked anthropocentrism in the Christian tradition attached to biblical ideas concerning human "dominion" over nature (Gen. 1:26–28). Consider the theology of Thomas Aquinas, for example, of which one modern author says this (in relation to environmental ethics specifically):

> any Thomistic environmental ethic must be consistently anthropocentric, where this means that nonhuman creatures are finally instruments to the human good. Any duties toward (or restrictions on our activities toward) such creatures must find their moral grounding in the human good.[43]

On this view, "the entire changeable universe is finally for the sake of the human good and species."[44] We find statements trending in the same direction among the writings of John Calvin, for whom "it was chiefly for the sake of mankind that the world was made ... this [is] the end which God has in view in the government of it."[45] The "end for which all things were created ... [was] that none of the conveniences and necessaries of life might be wanting to men."[46]

This kind of view of Creation has then often been wedded to a view of redemption that focuses on human salvation and says little or nothing about the cosmos as a whole. In fact, wherever the Gnosticism first introduced in chapter 2 has deeply penetrated into Christian theology, we find little interest shown in *materiality* at all—since in Gnosticism, salvation is all about human souls escaping their imprisonment in evil matter. The *Gospel*, influenced by this idea, comes to concern the redemption of human souls rather than their bodies. The material world as such, then, becomes of little importance. In the words of the old song, it is a place that "I'm just a-passing through" and in which it is quite wrong to "feel at home," since our "treasures are laid up somewhere beyond the blue."[47] In the words of a newer song, we are souls "stranded in some skin and bones" and waiting only for our rescue at "the dawn."[48]

The present world exists, then, to provide for us the "necessaries of life" while we wait for a future in which "the heavens will disappear with a roar; the elements will be destroyed by fire, and the earth and everything done in it will be laid bare ... everything will be destroyed" (2 Pet. 3:10–11)—and human souls will enter a much better, spiritual eternity. There is indeed *not* much in this way of looking at things that provides much of an incentive to look after the environment. "It's all going to burn anyway," as people have quite often said in certain Christian circles—"so why worry too much about it?" Why monitor global warming except as another sign of the end times (as a number of so-called "prophecy websites" are now actually doing)? Why bother legislating environmental protections?

This kind of perspective is often found nowadays in Protestant dispensationalist circles, where the earth is regarded as "merely a temporary way station on the road to eternal life ... unimportant except as a place of testing to get into heaven," created for the faithful to "use for profitable purposes on their way to the hereafter."[49] We do not need to plunge into the depths of Protestant dispensationalism, however, in order to come across marked Christian anthropocentrism. Consider *Caritas in veritate* (2009) for example—the last encyclical of Pope Benedict XVI. It is a wonderful, modern restatement of the long tradition of Christian humanism, laying out for us in a very helpful way our human duties and responsibilities toward other human beings. However, its love and justice are indeed predominantly, perhaps entirely, for men and women. Creation as a whole serves mainly only as the backdrop against which the human drama is played out.

The pragmatic, instrumentalist view of nonhuman Creation that tends to emerge from such theology is well illustrated by a large glass case containing a stuffed brown bear that I encountered a number of years ago in the airport waiting area in Anchorage, Alaska. Inscribed on the accompanying plaque was some helpful information telling the reader when this bear had been "harvested." When you can talk about "harvesting" a bear, it is no longer a living creature with its own dignified existence apart from your own but simply an object serving your own ends.

THE HERMENEUTICS OF CREATION CARE

What are we to make of this kind of biblical hermeneutic, as developed by some Christians and critiqued by many environmentalists? Leaving aside some of the issues we have already addressed in earlier chapters—Eve as "afterthought," for example, and "naming" as establishing dominance (White)—is this the right way in which to read the biblical Story as it touches upon "nature"?

From the Ground

We begin at the beginning—as we have sought to do throughout this book. "In the beginning God created"—a God whom we soon discover has a tremendous interest in *what* he has created and what is for its good. It is true that human beings are designed to play an important role in this Creation. However, this does not mean that we are intrinsically more important than the other creatures, and certainly not that (in Lynn White's words) "no item in the physical creation had any purpose save to serve man's purposes." For all that these chapters do set humans apart from other creatures, they also go out of their way to make it clear that we are, like them, *part of* Creation—a Creation that in Genesis 1 is already "good" in consisting of many of them, before we come along. We do not have a day of Creation to ourselves, for example, but share the sixth day with the other land creatures—emphasizing the commonality that exists between the humans and the rest of the animal Creation. Genesis 2 underlines this commonality by telling us that humans are "produced" from the earth in the same way as the other animals (Genesis 2:7; 2:19). Humans are humus, made out of soil ("from the dust of the ground") and animated by God, who breathes into us the breath of life that makes a person "a living being" (2:7). In these respects we are no different from the other animals: Genesis 1:20 uses the same phrase ("living being") of the sea creatures, and Genesis 2:19 uses it of the land animals and birds. We are important creatures, then—but we *are* creatures, just like all the others formed "according to their kinds."

So the OT provides no warrant for White's "Christian axiom that nature has no reason for existence save to serve man." The conclusion to the Creation week in Genesis 1:1–2:4 occurs, indeed, not on the sixth day with the creation of human beings, but on the seventh when God "rested." It is this Sabbath rest, not the creation of humanity, that completes Creation and brings its days to the perfect biblical number of seven. And this Sabbath rest was of course later observed weekly in Israel, on which day (as we saw in chapter 10) it was again the *commonality* of all creatures that was emphasized, not the usefulness of some in respect to others (Exod. 20:8–11). On the Sabbath "you shall not do any work, neither you, nor your son or daughter, nor your manservant or maidservant, nor your animals." Other creatures have their own importance; we are not the only show in town. Job 38 and 39 later make exactly this same point, at considerable length.

Just Dominion

It is important next to be precise in the matter of how and for what reason human beings are "set apart" from Creation in Genesis 1–2. We touched on this already in chapter 3. Here I noted that, just as Creation as a whole is conceived of in the OT as God's temple, so human beings are considered to be the images of God that ancient people used to place in *their* temples. Ancient kings also used to set up images of themselves in territories which they claimed as their own. It is not as autonomous beings, then, that humans are "made in God's image and likeness" in Genesis 1. We are instead God's representatives; we govern on behalf of the God who is the only true King, remembering all the while that "[t]he earth is the Lord's, and everything in it" (Ps. 24:1). It does not belong to us.

What does being a king involve? It involves what ancient kings were expected to do on behalf of the gods generally: "ruling and subduing." This implies that there is work to be done in the world, right from the beginning—that human beings are designed to go on working with God in his creative acts, bringing order out of chaos. But the language of kingship also implies *care* for the rest of Creation. For the vocation of kings in the ancient world not only involved ruling and subduing but also looking after the welfare of their subjects and ensuring justice for all. The mandate to rule and subdue, then, is not a mandate to exploit and ravage the earth in one's own self-interest. Genesis does not have in view here absolute and unfettered power that can be used as human beings will, with no moral restraint. Human rule is always to be exercised *on behalf of* the God in whose world we live. It is to be a just, peaceable dominion of the kind described in Psalm 72, governed by people who are able to "judge [their] people in righteousness, [their] afflicted ones with justice" (72:2).

SERVING AND KEEPING

Genesis 2 makes it especially clear, as it exegetes "dominion" in terms of earth keeping, what this looks like in relation to nonhuman Creation. The world is portrayed in this chapter as a garden—an enclosed parkland in which human beings live in harmony with their kin (the animals) and with God. Here the language of monarchy gives way to the language of priesthood, and we find human beings placed in God's parkland "to work it and take care of it"—to "serve it and keep/ guard it" (Hb. *'abad* and *shamar*). This is religious language, which underlines the importance and sacred nature of the task: it is worship and conservation. It is precisely the language used in Numbers 3:7–8, when the work of the priests in the Tabernacle is described.[50] The world is a sacred place, like a temple, and human beings are its priests. We can also turn this around, in line with our reflections in previous chapters concerning what land, city, and temple in the OT ultimately "speak of," and how the OT conceives of governance. Kings and priests in ancient Israel were called to live out in the *land* something of the vocation that all human beings are given with respect to the *Earth*.

The dominion given to human beings in Genesis 1, then, is evidently not a *lording it over* the rest of a Creation that is designed "explicitly for man's benefit" (White). This dominion is instead a sacrificial *looking after* Creation. Our creation in God's image has occurred with the purpose that we should imitate him in his creativity and in his providential care for creatures. In the Genesis story itself we get an extended picture of what this looks like in chapters 6–9, where Noah is "portrayed as uniquely righteous . . . [and] also the arch-conservationist who built an ark to preserve all kinds of life from being destroyed in the flood."[51]

ALL CREATURES GREAT AND SMALL

It must be granted, then, that human beings are indeed conceived of in Genesis "not simply [as] part of nature" but as image bearers of God. It is also true that much of the Story that follows concerns not only how these image bearers treat each other but also how they *should or should not* do so, and that their redemption is clearly regarded as centrally important to God's plans in Creation. "People keeping" (in the language of Gen. 4:9) is therefore a major concern of OT Scripture. Yet "earth keeping" is also, "from the beginning," very important. In the OT literature both inside and outside Genesis, in fact, these two—people keeping and earth keeping—go hand in hand. For Creation can only function properly to the extent that the image bearers delegated to look after it are able to do their job. Conversely, human dysfunction—whether individual or communal— inevitably impacts the rest of Creation grievously. This is precisely *because* the whole of Creation is conceived of in biblical faith as a single "circle of being," in which what happens to one part inevitably affects the remainder. Hosea 4:1–3 starkly describes this reality in the context of the Israel of the eighth century BC:

> There is no faithfulness, no love, no acknowledgment of God in the land. There is only cursing, lying and murder, stealing and adultery; they break all bounds, and bloodshed follows bloodshed. Because of this the land mourns, and all who live in it waste away; the beasts of the field and the birds of the air and the fish of the sea are dying.

Here communal dysfunction involving people-keepers failing to keep each other properly—and, in failing, breaking various of the Ten Commandments— disables the earth-keepers from keeping the earth properly, and grief and death to all follow.

Sometimes there is damage because human violence directly impacts the Earth—a possibility envisaged in Deuteronomy 20:19, for example. Here the text recognizes that war (even in ancient times) could be disastrous for the rest of Creation, and it urges combatants, when they fight, to try to limit the damage: "When you lay siege to a city for a long time, fighting against it to capture it, do not destroy its trees by putting an ax to them, because you can eat their fruit. Do not cut them down. Are the trees of the field people, that you should besiege them?" This is a good example of OT Torah responding to the brokenness of things (stiff-neck law), rather than seeking to inculcate an ideal (creational law): *if* there must be war, then at least leave the trees alone. This is partly for pragmatic reasons (they provide fruit), but partly just because the trees do not deserve to be caught up in the conflict. Trees have rights.

Another reason that communal dysfunction can impact the rest of Creation is that it distorts the relationship between the earth-keepers and what they are called to keep. That is, it places the Earth disproportionately in the hands of those who do not care for God's laws, and who certainly do not accept that "the land is mine and you are only tenants" (Lev. 25:23). The prophets also have a lot to say about this dimension of the problem. In Isaiah 5:8–10, for example, we find "woe" laid upon those "who add house to house and join field to field till no space is left and you live alone in the land."

Just as a whole of Creation thus suffers along with humanity in its fallen state, so the whole of Creation is envisaged in the OT as being redeemed along with its flawed "keepers." Among the OT passages that address this reality is Isaiah 11:6–9, for example, with its vision of a future in which "the wolf will live with the lamb, the leopard will lie down with the goat . . . They will neither harm nor destroy on all my holy mountain, for the earth will be full of the knowledge of the L<small>ORD</small> as the waters cover the sea." Hosea 2:18 goes on to envisage a day when God "will make a covenant for them with the beasts of the field and the birds of the air and the creatures that move along the ground. Bow and sword and battle I will abolish from the land, so that all may lie down in safety."

The Earth and Everything in It

As we come to the NT, we find (unsurprisingly) that the whole world remains God's world: "From him and through him and to him are all things," writes Paul, "the earth . . . and everything in it" (Rom. 11:36; 1 Cor. 10:26; cf. Rev. 4:11). Into this world comes the one in whom human image bearing reaches its high point—"the image of the invisible God," of whom Paul says that "all things were created by him and for him . . . in him all things hold together" (Col. 1:15–20). He it is who "fulfills God's design for all creation and displays what had always been intended for all humankind."[52] The redemption that Christ initiates is naturally cosmic in its scope—as broad as the original Creation: "God was pleased . . . through him to reconcile to himself *all things* [my emphasis], whether things on earth or things in heaven" (Col. 1:19).

For this cosmic redemption the entirety of nonhuman Creation waits, looking "in eager expectation for the sons of God to be revealed"; it is currently "groaning as in the pains of childbirth," waiting for the new heavens and the new earth to be born as a result (Rom. 8:19, 22). Currently "subjected to frustration" (8:20)—it does not function properly, because of human dysfunction (sin)—it looks to be released from this frustrated condition. It *will* be released, once human beings themselves are fully redeemed: "Just as the resurrection hope is hope of a resurrection body, so resurrection life is to be part of a complete creation."[53]

This last quote underlines the need for our thinking about Creation in relation to New Creation to stress continuity as well as discontinuity—just as we have been learning to balance these realities well in general in our Bible reading. A text like 2 Peter 3:10 might well at first appear to tell us about a complete disjunction between present and future reality—"it's all going to burn." This would place it well outside the mainstream of biblical thinking about the future, however, in which what is new represents an "evolution," as it were, of what lies beforehand, rather than a complete break from it. "The wolf will live with the lamb" (Isa. 11:6), "the meek . . . will inherit the earth" (Matt. 5:5), the present will give birth to the future, and our resurrection bodies will be similar to as well as different from our present ones. The present reality may be passing away, and it may indeed be destined for "fire" (Heb. 1:10–12; 12:26–29)—but it seems that it must pass through fire only to become a more purified version of itself. The new heaven and the new earth are, after all, just *that*—and not something entirely different (2 Pet. 3:13). It is moreover the case that our human destiny is to live with God in the New Jerusalem that in Revelation 21:1–3 comes down out of heaven to Earth. We do not fly away (without our bodies) to another destination.

There is nothing in any of this NT material that suggests that God has ceased to care for all of Creation, or that we human beings are no longer called to look after it on God's behalf. Earth-keeping remains one aspect of our human calling, just as destroying the Earth represents a grievous departure from it. And in the New Creation we shall in fact still be "kings and priests," just as we are now (Rev. 5:10).

BACON AND CALVIN

While it is true, then, that versions of Christian theology have existed of the kind that are attacked by environmentalists as overly anthropocentric and insufficiently focused on Creation-in-general, these theologies are not well-grounded in Christian Scripture. They owe a lot more to Francis Bacon, in fact, "who hijacked the Genesis text to authorize the project of scientific knowledge and technological exploitation whose excesses have [indeed] given us the ecological crisis."[54] There is much in the genuinely (as opposed to ex-) Christian tradition that is, to the contrary, well-rooted in Scripture. This includes the writings of John Calvin, whose comments quoted above might not lead us to expect much of him in this respect. Yet while Calvin did believe that it was "chiefly for the sake of mankind that the world was made," he certainly understood that humanity "rules" under God's command and that "dominion" is not an excuse for plundering the Earth.[55] Every human being, rather, should "regard himself as the steward of God in all things which he possesses. Then he will neither conduct himself dissolutely, nor corrupt by abuse those things which God requires to be preserved."[56] Calvin also taught that the whole of Creation, and not only humanity, has a future hope: "God will restore to a perfect state the world, now fallen, together with mankind."[57]

This biblical view of our relationship with and responsibilities toward non-human Creation provides Christians with every reason to continue to be involved in the "environmental movement," as they *have been* in fact, in large numbers, for decades now. One of the first Christian responses to White dates from only three years after his essay, in the form of *Pollution and the Death of Man*, by Francis Schaeffer.[58] Schaeffer argued, rightly, that what was needed in response to the ecological crisis was not a return to nature-spirituality but rather a better form of Christianity, in which Christians actually acted on the basis of the Scripture that they claimed to honor. Other important books followed, such as *Earthkeeping: Christian Stewardship of Natural Resources*, edited by Loren Wilkinson.[59] Many responded in the following years precisely along such lines. The good life in Scripture, Christians began to affirm in large numbers, is a life marked by love, not only for our image-bearing neighbors but also for the remainder of God's Creation; "[t]he righteous care for the needs of their animals" (Prov. 12:10; cf. Deut. 22:1–6). The well-being of the remainder of Creation is in fact intrinsically bound up with our own and our neighbors' flourishing, as both Scripture and our own contemporary experience teaches us: it is especially the poorest people in the world who suffer the most from negative ecological developments.[60]

We are likewise called not only to care for the whole of Creation as we find it now but also to seek to correct the mistakes that we have made in the past, in the belief that God has delegated to us enormous responsibility in "ruling" and "keeping" the planet, and that our decisions will necessarily be very important in determining how things play out. Whether this is a welcome truth or not, it is a matter of Scriptural and empirical fact that human beings do possess "dominion" over Creation. This is why, at all the Earth Summits ever held, the delegates were drawn from only one species (as my friend Loren Wilkinson once said to me). It was not because their organizers were "overly anthropocentric," but because among all of God's creatures it is only human beings who possess the kind of agency that is capable of drastically changing the world for good or for ill, and might even be concerned or worried about doing so.

CONCLUSION

The question is not whether humanity has dominion, then, but how we shall use it. The biblical Story tells us how we should use it, and indeed provides us with the hope that we need to persevere in the task even when it seems difficult and even impossible. For it calls us to live in anticipation of a time when not only human society will be ordered perfectly justly but the entire cosmos will be redeemed—a new Creation. And we have every reason to believe that God himself will gather up everything that is good in this present Creation, including our smallest and most futile-seeming actions, and will carry it forward into this new one, where the righteous who cared for the first version will also get to care for the second. It does not seem likely on the basis of biblical teaching that the unrepentant who failed to look after the first will also get a chance to mess up the latter—which is precisely why "all [will] lie down in safety" (Hos. 2:18). So contrary to the sentiments of authors like James Lovelock, people who truly believe that God has given humanity "dominion" over the earth are in fact likely to be the *first* people who will take the radical steps necessary to save it. It is simply that many people do not truly believe it.

DISCUSSION QUESTIONS

1. Which aspects of the vision of the world held by "dark green religionists" do you find compelling, and why?
2. Are you a Romantic? And is this a good thing or a bad thing?
3. What does "just dominion" of the Earth by humanity look like, so far as you are concerned? Give examples.
4. Should Christians be concerned by climate change, whether or not it is entirely or partially caused by human actions?

III
CONCLUSIONS

Photographer unknown, arastiralim.net via Wikimedia Commons,
https://commons.wikimedia.org/w/index.php?curid=20103197

16

The Sword of the Spirit
The Cutting Edge of Biblical Ethics

What we live through, in any age, is the effect on us of mass emotions and of social conditions from which it is almost impossible to detach ourselves. Often the mass emotions are those which seem the noblest, best and most beautiful. And yet, inside a year, five years, a decade, five decades, people will be asking, "How could they have believed that?" because events will have taken place that will have banished the said mass emotions to the dustbin of history.[1]

Doris Lessing

With the close of chapter 15 we have come also to the end of our various "explorations" in biblical ethics that followed on from our presentation of their "foundations" (chapters 1–3). Throughout the entire exercise we have begun at the beginning of the Christian Bible (Genesis, not Matthew) and we have sought to read what follows in the Story against that background, attempting to develop a consistent approach to the various individual ethical issues that we have addressed. My primary purpose in engaging in these explorations has not been to encourage the formation of sound judgments about Christian interpretations of Scripture in the past—although that has been part of it. It is all too easy with the benefit of hindsight to see the mistakes that others have made—to see how *others* have been caught up in "mass emotions and . . . social conditions" from which they could not detach themselves (our epigraph above). How *could* those English sixteenth-century Puritans have identified Roman Catholics and Native Americans as Canaanites and acted violently against them in the way that they did? How *could* those nineteenth-century

Southerners in the United States have come to believe that plantation slavery was biblical? Or to take a more recent example not previously discussed in the book: how *could* so many twentieth-century German Christians have concluded that support for Adolf Hitler and his policies was consistent with a biblically grounded faith? It is not difficult, looking in our rearview mirrors, to identify such errors, especially if we live in a time and a place in which mostly everyone agrees with our point of view in assessing them.

The real challenge is to avoid making *new* mistakes *in the present* concerning "what's bad and what's good" (Pierre Bezukhov's words in chapter 1)—precisely when we do *not* yet possess the benefit of hindsight and may find ourselves under considerable pressure from society to conform to its current norms. As we take up "the sword of the Spirit, which is the word of God" (Eph. 6:17; cf. Heb. 4:12), does our chosen way of reading it allow it truly to possess the "cutting edge" in contemporary ethical debate of the sort that Paul himself has in mind in using the image:

> The sharp short sword . . . was the crucial offensive weapon in close combat . . . As believers take hold of and proclaim the gospel, they are enabled to overcome in the battle . . . As the Church continues to be the reconciled and reconciling community, the Gospel conquers the alienating hostile powers and brings about God's saving purposes.[2]

Does our way of reading Scripture allow it to deliver truth that people do not currently wish to hear—and that we ourselves may not initially desire to hear? Does it create the possibility that, even under strong familial or cultural pressure, we shall still be able to hear the divine imperative to stand up for what is right? Is it likely that we shall even be able to do this, if necessary, entirely alone—as in the powerful photograph at the beginning of this chapter, taken in 1936 in a shipyard in Hamburg, Germany, following an address to the crowd by Adolf Hitler himself?[3] It is not easy to take such a stand. It requires a strong conviction concerning the right path that derives from somewhere other than majority sentiment—from a way of reading the world, including our authoritative texts, which the vast majority of our neighbors may not share.

My primary purpose throughout our explorations in chapters 4–15 has been precisely to develop a consistent paradigm for interpreting Scripture ethically that will enable us to live the good life *now*—and indeed in the future, when facing moral challenges that we cannot yet envisage. The most important thing about our discussion to this point, then, is not that we have been able to arrive at well-grounded conclusions concerning the individual ethical issues that we have examined—although that is certainly important. The most important thing is that we have been developing along the way (I trust) an interpretive paradigm that will enable us to read Scripture accurately in countercultural as well as in culture-endorsing ways across a whole range of issues that we have not yet discussed—even when the surrounding culture cannot hear this call, and even when the Church itself has significantly accommodated to the culture. In pursuing this purpose, I have been keenly aware of the famous advice that goes as follows: "Give a person a fish, and you feed him for a day. Teach a person to fish, and you feed her for a lifetime." Books filled only with answers to particular ethical questions are always limited in their usefulness in the real world of complicated and changing circumstances, and they can quickly become dated. I have aimed in this book for something better.

What then are the key elements of this paradigm that we have derived from the preceding chapters? Let us review them.

THE BEGINNING

We have learned, first, that the beginning of the Story in Genesis 1–2 represents an important baseline against which to read everything that follows in Scripture, since it communicates some fundamental truths about the Creator God and his Creation. These chapters provide in particular a moral vision pertaining to how all the human persons in Creation are to relate to God and to other creatures. This is where we first learn what it means to love God and our neighbors, both human and otherwise—how God intended the world to be when he created it, rather than how it has in fact become. If we are rightly to understand the biblical Story as a whole, and to know what it means for what we should believe and how we should live, then it is to this beginning that we must constantly return.

For example, in the world as we know it now—the world after Genesis 3—there is such a reality as marital breakdown and a consequent need to legislate about it. However, "it was not this way from the beginning" (Matt. 19:8)—and it is what was true "at the beginning" (19:4) that matters first of all when it comes to our ethical reflections on marriage, since it reveals to us the nature of God's "creational law." The beginning of the biblical Story is the magnetic north toward which our ethical compass must always return in our search for what is right, if we are not to misinterpret the terrain of our journey and get lost.

BIBLICAL NARRATIVE

We have also learned that we must first read the biblical narrative that occupies so much of the space in our Bibles, beginning in Genesis, in the light of "the beginning." Here it is important to register that we are dealing with Scripture that is for the most part overtly *descriptive* rather than *prescriptive*. It describes what people in ancient times *actually did*, rather than directly instructing us about what we *should do*. It *is* provided for our instruction—but in a manner that forces us to think carefully about what we are supposed to learn from it. As we have seen, it is particularly important to recognize that the characters who inhabit this biblical narrative (with the exception of Jesus) are not simply "heroes" of the faith, provided for our imitation. Even the best of them possesses a "dark side," and in a fallen world each one makes moral mistakes—sometimes egregious ones.

For example, Abraham's trust in God is exemplary for much of his story (Gen. 15:6; Heb. 11:8–12), and yet on two separate occasions he pretends that his wife Sarah is actually his sister and gets her involved with another man. Trouble consequently arises (Gen. 12:10–20; 20:1–18). This is not intended as behavior that we should imitate in the course of our next foreign vacation. Moving beyond Genesis, Elijah is a great exemplar of biblical faith in many respects, and he is certainly to be imitated in his prayer life (Jas. 5:13–18). Yet Elijah was a human being just like us (5:17), and in 1 Kings 19 we find him running as far as he can away from both Queen Jezebel and God, who questions him twice about his behavior (19:9, 13). We are not told this part of the Story so that *we* know how to behave. We are told this part of the Story so that we can learn something about *God's* compassion for his broken people (19:5–8).

If we are not to end up learning the wrong lessons from biblical narrative, then, we need discernment. The world after Genesis 3 is a "mixed" world in which there is both good and evil, even within the hearts of God's people. And it is this mixed world that is so truthfully and powerfully revealed to us in biblical narrative, in all its beauty and its horror, in the love and warmth that make it wonderful, and in the hatred and the coldness that make it intolerable. The Holy Bible, it turns out, frequently describes a stunning lack of human holiness, often providing us with examples *not* to follow rather than with role models.

MOSAIC TORAH

It is the particular narrative of the Pentateuch that provides, thirdly, the context for the Mosaic Torah that we encounter in Exodus through Deuteronomy. As we have seen, this Torah is a challenging combination of different kinds of material. We certainly discover there creational law that persists in holding the OT people of God accountable to the moral vision that Genesis 1–2 introduce to us. This instruction is also directly relevant to God's NT people. The Ten Commandments represent the most obvious examples of this eternal law that tells all human beings how we *ought* and *ought not* to live.

THE QUESTION OF RELEVANCE

However, we also encounter other kinds of instruction that we have good reason to believe possesses less relevance for the Church, or perhaps no direct relevance at all. The need for it arises only because of the entry of moral evil into the world as described in Genesis 3. This instruction is designed to enable the OT people of God to survive and flourish in their particular, ancient, fallen context until the point in God's redemptive plan when Israel's calling as God's primary mission partner is taken over by a global people comprising both Jew and Gentile. This kind of Torah seeks to achieve its goal in various ways. Some of it is designed to maintain strict boundaries between Jew and Gentile so that Israel maintains its identity *as* God's people. The requirement that male children should be circumcised is a good example. Some of it is stiff-neck law, designed to legislate in respect of moral failure so as to minimize damage and provide some kind of recompense to its victims. A good example here is the divorce law mentioned earlier.

THE TATTOO AND YOU

It matters greatly that we understand which kind of Torah we are reading in any particular case. This requires not only that we read all of it in the context of the entire biblical Story but also that we try to understand it all against its historical and cultural background. In this way we shall be able to arrive at well-grounded conclusions about what to do with a particular Mosaic law, especially in cases where the right answer is initially not clear. For example, Leviticus 19:28 in the NIV instructs the reader as follows: "Do not cut your bodies for the dead or put tattoo marks on yourselves." This verse is sometimes cited nowadays in relation to the modern practice of tattooing. The immediate context within the verse itself, however, suggests that the prohibition relates to incisions made on the human body in connection with pagan funeral rites: "Do not cut your bodies for the dead." We read about such practices in ancient Ugaritic myth concerning the death of the god Baal, whereupon the chief god El reacts as follows: "With a stone he scratches incisions on his skin, with a razor he cuts cheeks and chin."[4] Both verse 28 and the preceding verse 27, then ("do not cut the hair at the sides of your head or clip off the edges of your beard"), concern the need for God's OT people not to get involved in the pagan rites of their neighbors. They thereby speak indirectly to the ongoing need of God's NT people to keep themselves appropriately separate from their surrounding (often very idolatrous) cultures, so that their lives testify to what is true rather than what is false (2 Cor. 6:14 to 7:1). They have nothing directly to say, however, concerning contemporary trends in fashion. This is not to say, of course, that such trends are necessarily beyond Christian critique, in so far as they are bound up with and symbolically communicate problematic beliefs—for example, the belief that my body belongs exclusively to me and that I may do with it as I wish.

FROM THE PROPHETS TO THE NEW TESTAMENT

Fourth, the remaining OT literature, which we may summarily describe as the Prophets (e.g., Isaiah) and Wisdom (e.g., Job), provides us with still further guidance about how to read the whole Story from the beginning to the end, including the Mosaic Torah that is embedded within it.

PROPHETS AND WISDOM

The prophetic literature does this by interpreting the past in the context of each prophet's present moment and then looking into the future where the NT sits. We saw in chapter 10, for example, how the vision of Isaiah 56:1–7 helps us to interpret correctly the Sabbath commandment in Exodus and Deuteronomy. In the context of the eighth-century BC religion of "Sodom" and "Gomorrah" that is the book's concern in Isaiah 1 (1:10), the prophet dismisses Israelite observation of the Sabbath as futile (1:13). Yet when the book looks to the future in chapter 56, it envisages a time when "justice" and "right" will still include observing the Sabbath. Among the righteous who will in this way "keep the Sabbath without desecrating it and . . . hold fast to my covenant" will be "foreigners," whom God will "bring to my holy mountain and give them joy in my house of prayer" along with the Israelites (56:1–7).

Likewise, a chapter like Job 31—in making the case for Job's righteousness—helps us to differentiate between creational and other law in the Pentateuch by appealing throughout to the former rather than the latter. For example, right at the beginning of the chapter (as we have seen), when Job mentions loving his female neighbor properly, he does not refer to the Commandment in Exodus 20 concerning adultery; what he says is that "I made a covenant with my eyes not to look lustfully at a girl" (31:1). For the person seeking what is right, it not only adultery that is a problem—it is also lust. The entirety of Job 31 continues in the same vein. It is not just that Job has left the edges of his fields so that the poor can glean there; he has in fact been extraordinarily generous (31:16–20). It is not just that Job has avoided idolatrous acts or coveting what belongs to his neighbor; he has avoided apostasy in his heart and also trusting in wealth (31:24–28). He has been generous to enemies and strangers alike (31:29–40), and he has always treated his slaves as image-bearing neighbors (31:13–15). Refusing to confuse the different types of Torah with each other, Job has fully embraced the relational moral vision of the kingdom of God.

THE NEW TESTAMENT

The next move, into the NT, clarifies the moral vision of the Bible still further, just as the meaning of the NT is itself clarified. As we read from the beginning of the Story *forwards*, in the direction of this NT ending, we are better able to identify discontinuity between the Testaments where it really does exist. At the same time, we are better equipped to refrain from calling "new" in the NT what is not in fact new. We are also better able to identify with accuracy—in the NT as in the OT—the biblical teaching that is of ongoing, general relevance for the Church and to distinguish it from the teaching that is likely more particular and occasional. All of this is important, although it seems clear that for contemporary Christians the most pressing danger lies on the side of underemphasizing the *continuity* rather than the reverse.

I have often heard it claimed, for example, that Jesus' Sermon on the Mount introduces a new kingdom ethic into the world, in which "internal" matters of the heart are more important than "external" matters of obedience to rules. Only someone who has never spent much time with the OT, and in particular with the OT "Sermon on the Mount" in Job 31, could possibly say such a thing. The contrast that Jesus draws in Matthew 5–7 is not between revealed OT and revealed NT ethics; it is between what the OT Scriptures really teach about the good life and what people have *heard* about this from their teachers. To be precise, throughout this discourse Jesus challenges inadequate contemporary understandings of certain aspects of Scripture by drawing attention to other parts of Scripture with which he expects them to be consistent.

For example, Scripture teaches that we should not murder, but it also teaches that "anger resides in the lap of fools" and that "a wise man keeps himself under control" (Eccl. 7:9, Prov. 29:11). It exhorts the reader to "refrain from anger and turn from wrath," since "it leads only to evil" (Ps. 37:8). Anger can indeed lead to murder (Gen. 4:5–8). This is the larger context in which we must read Matthew 5:21–26. Likewise, if people are going to make oaths, they should certainly keep them (Lev. 19:12), but people of integrity should not need to make oaths in the first place (Matt. 5:33–37; Jas. 5:12). And in remembering that appropriate justice is specified in various circumstances in Torah along the lines of "eye for eye, and tooth for tooth" (i.e., when vengeance occurs it should be appropriate, not excessive), we should not forget the general scriptural imperatives to treat other people compassionately and mercifully, just as God does. He himself offers such compassion and mercy even to those who are his enemies, and whom he is said to "hate" because of their evil deeds (Matt. 5:38–48; cf., e.g., Ps. 5:5; Mic. 7:18).[5] It is evident at this point, incidentally, that we do not represent Scripture entirely correctly when we say that it describes God "loving the sinner but hating the sin," as if the actor were somehow not quite responsible for the action. Rather, God is very angry with *sinners* (the actors) but at the same time loves them and seeks their repentance, being unwilling that "any . . . should perish" (Matt. 18:14).

THE CHURCH AND ITS SOCIETAL CONTEXTS

In this careful reading of Scripture, finally, we should remember that the Bible is first and foremost designed to be "useful" to the Church in respect of "teaching, rebuking, correcting, and training in righteousness, so that the servant of God may be thoroughly equipped for every good work" (2 Tim. 3:16–17). It is not first and foremost addressed to the broader societies within which Christians live. Its primary purpose is to shape the "reconciled and reconciling community" mentioned in the quote earlier in this chapter—the Church that is called to deploy the "sharp short sword" of "the Spirit that is the word of God" in its "close combat" with the dark powers of the cosmos and thereby bring about "God's saving purposes." Certainly Christians are called to live and work in the culture at large, mediating God's truth to the world for the common good. Before they can do this effectively, however, the sharp, cutting edge of the sword of the Spirit must be felt in the Christian community itself.

As we have seen throughout this book, the Christian enterprise from Constantine onwards has often been marked by a failure to make a sufficiently clear distinction of this kind between the Church and the world. This failure has had evidently negative consequences of varying degrees of severity. Yet because one of the things that history teaches us is that history teaches us nothing, we still encounter in the present day large numbers of Christians in different countries throughout the world whose instinct is to collapse the spheres of Church and broader society into one, rather than keep them appropriately separate. What is ethically right for the Christian and for the Christian community becomes at the same time, and without further reflection, the basis for a political program and eventually for a legislative agenda pursued by the state. The unspoken assumption appears to be that, ideally, everything that is moral ought to be legal, and that everything that is immoral ought to be illegal. That is: the law of God ought also to be the law of the land.

UNLIKELY BEDFELLOWS

In this respect Christians often share a perspective on the nature of "good" public life with unlikely bedfellows—contemporary people with whom they have little otherwise in common, and whose ideologies they would otherwise firmly reject. Among these bedfellows are radical Islamists, for whom "it is the task of the Islamic state to enforce obedience to the revealed law of Islam"—the Shari'a—which is the timeless manifestation of the will of Allah that applies to all of life and should therefore be imposed on people everywhere when Muslims have the power to do so.[6] Also among this number are the leftist secularists who in many ways dominate the contemporary educational and political scenes in large swathes of the post-Christian Western state. They too are seemingly very comfortable with the idea of leveraging the power of the state to coerce others into right thinking and action in line with their secular "religion." Their belief system is perhaps more difficult to spot than that of the Islamists, in part because they are typically so oblivious to possessing one, and they do not speak as if they do. Their rhetoric is in fact routinely filled with misleading self-identifiers like "liberal," "tolerant," and "pluralist," suggesting a kind of ideological neutrality. The reality is, however, that they are none of these things, except within very tight ideological lines. Their "tolerance," in particular, is neither philosophical nor ethical in nature—that is, they are not in the least tolerant of philosophical or ethical perspectives different from their own. We shall return to this particular matter in chapter 19.

THE END OF DEMOCRACY

It is of course impossible for a genuinely liberal, democratic, and pluralist society long to endure in the face of this kind of fusion of the private, the familial, and the communal with the public sphere and those who control it. Everyone who currently lives in countries where freedom of thought and action—and indeed reputation and employment—are under threat from such illiberal forces (whether from the left or the right) ought therefore to be concerned about it and should be active in resisting it for the good of all. People of biblical faith, as I have sought to demonstrate in this book, possess particularly good reasons to be in the forefront of expressing such concern and resistance. For a genuinely Christian political philosophy is always rightly going to emphasize substantial freedom on the part of all the members of a given society to believe what they wish and to live in accordance with those beliefs. Consistent with this, it should be *no* part of the agenda of the Church to seek to outdo God in imposing the kingdom of God on society at large, any more than we wish to see similar "impositions" by Islamists or secularists. To the contrary, the biblical imperative to seek the good of all our neighbors even if they are also our cultural, religious, or political opponents or even enemies requires that we think very carefully about how Christian ethics should shape public space. We should reflect even more carefully on how to present our conclusions about this to others who do not share our fundamental convictions about reality. The first task of the Church is always to be the Church, not simply a band of religious cheerleaders for particular political programs or legislative agendas, whether of the left or the right, promoted by external organizations that are focused on strictly temporal matters.

ON SEARCHING THE SCRIPTURES

In all of this we have seen that reading the Bible for life is not a simple matter. By giving us the kind of Scripture that we now possess—not a straightforward set of rules but a literature that requires *engagement* with it in order to make progress in understanding it—God himself has ordained in his wisdom that our search for what is right should not *be* simple. This is the same God, after all, who when Incarnate in first-century Judea and Samaria so frequently spoke in parables rather than plainly, forcing his listeners to think hard about his words, wrestle with them, and ask questions about them. The search for what is right is indeed a *search*.

On the other hand, we are also promised in general that if we seek we shall find (Matt. 7:7), and we have every reason to believe in particular that if we put the required effort into searching the Scriptures in pursuit of the truth, we shall be successful in finding it. The Bible cannot be useful to us, after all, if we are not able in the end to make sense of it. Jesus himself always teaches in the Gospels in the expectation that open-hearted people will be able to recognize that his interpretation of Scripture is true, even though the truth *can* initially be obscured from them. It is significant in this regard that, in speaking to the two disciples on the Emmaus Road in Luke 24, Jesus assumes that Scripture is clear in the way that it prophesies of "the Christ"; the OT is not to blame for their lack of comprehension of it. The problem lies rather in the fact that these disciples are "foolish" and "slow of heart to believe" with respect to "all that the prophets have spoken." The Scriptures in themselves are what Peter later describes as "a light shining in a dark place" (2 Pet. 1:19). They are "perspicuous."[7]

Our own explorations in the preceding chapters bear this out. It has not been difficult, by way of what I hope has been a biblically grounded, patient, and consistent approach to Scripture, to work out what we should think about the shape of the good life according to Scripture across a whole range of important matters. It has not been difficult, either, to make progress in our consideration of how this might affect our public as well as our private lives. None of this has been *simple*—but it has also not been difficult. The core qualities that we require in the pursuit of the good life along such lines are simply a desire to know God's will (first) and a perseverance in discovering it (secondly), more than anything else. It is not rocket science.

ON PUSHING HOT BUTTONS

I am equally confident that it will not prove difficult, employing this same interpretive paradigm, for my readers to work out what they should think about the shape of the good life according to Scripture when it comes to other matters that we have not discussed in this book. To a very great extent I shall need to leave these readers to discover for themselves whether this is true, since we are now coming toward the end of an already long book.

However, I explicitly promised in chapter 14 to return to one specific issue before we get there; I committed to outlining my own view, against Christian

Zionism, of the right and Christian way in which to approach the matter of Israel/ Palestine. Beyond that, I would be remiss if I did not offer at least some reflection on other, "hot-button" issues that contemporary Christians are (or ought to be) concerned about. In chapter 17, therefore (along with Israel/Palestine), we shall discuss global warming, abortion, and euthanasia/assisted suicide; and in chapter 18, transgenderism and same-sex sexual relationships. Our discussion of these important, contemporary issues—although they will mainly be brief, relative to all the literature than has been written about them—will hopefully be helpful to readers when they later turn to reflect on still other matters that I have been forced to neglect. In an Appendix that follows chapter 20 I shall also provide a list of resources for further study on the topics covered in both chapters seventeen and eighteen.

As we proceed, I shall be making significant use of the biblical metaphor of "exile," along the lines of 1 Peter 1:13–17 and 2:11:

> Therefore, with minds that are alert and fully sober, set your hope on the grace to be brought to you when Jesus Christ is revealed at his coming. As obedient children, do not conform to the evil desires you had when you lived in ignorance. But just as he who called you is holy, so be holy in all you do; for it is written: "Be holy, because I am holy." Since you call on a Father who judges each person's work impartially, live out your time as foreigners here in reverent fear . . . Dear friends, I urge you, as foreigners and exiles, to abstain from sinful desires, which wage war against your soul.

We always live in exile, as Christ-followers, and as we seek to live our good and holy lives there, it is important that we try to understand how the "mass emotions" of our time have shaped and continue to shape the *landscape* of that exile in our particular case. All times are not the same. What do our current neighbors believe, then—perhaps the majority of people—about the nature of "the good," both generally and specifically? This will help us to form a realistic appreciation of the challenges that we shall face on our journey through this landscape, and what we need to do in order to rise to them.

In my estimation, this is particularly important at the present time when it comes to the issues of sexual orientation and gender identity. Chapter 19 turns our attention, therefore, to these particular aspects of the contemporary "landscape" for many Christians worldwide, focusing in particular (as an example) on my home country of Canada. This will lead us in chapter 20 to reflect more broadly on the disciplines that we all need to cultivate in order to maintain our Christian integrity "as foreigners here," so that we may persist as a shining light even in very dark cultures, enabling our neighbors (hopefully) to see the darkness *as* darkness, and to turn instead toward the Light.

CONCLUSION: THE JOURNEY AHEAD

At this point in the book, however, I am disinclined to proceed (as it were) on my own. I would prefer it if my readers, having read thus far, were to begin to take up their own responsibility to think carefully about these important matters from a biblical perspective. Therefore, before I offer my own analyses of each topic covered in the following pages, I would like my readers in each case to "test out the paradigm." To facilitate this exercise, the discussion questions at the end of chapters sixteen and seventeen will focus not on topics *previously* covered in the book but on those *about to be* covered on the following pages. My proposal is that, before you have seen my own argument, you should in each case do two things. First, consider *how* you are going to approach the matter in order to arrive at the best answer. This will involve the question not only of how to read Scripture but also of how to access and process other information that you may need. If you are reading this book in a group, you may wish to assign group members different research tasks in advance of the discussion. Secondly, develop what you believe to be the best answer, bearing in mind that we need to distinguish between what Scripture has to say to the *Church* and what the implications of this might be for our engagement with our *culture*. I shall see you on the other side of your first set of questions—that is, at the beginning of the next chapter.

DISCUSSION QUESTIONS RELATING TO CHAPTER 17

1. "[Most] climate scientists agree that climate-warming trends over the past century are extremely likely due to human activities, and most of the leading scientific organizations worldwide have issued public statements endorsing this position" (https://climate.nasa.gov/evidence/). The implications for life on earth if these warming trends continue are serious. How should Christians respond?

2. Since the end of the Six-Day War in 1967, Israelis have been divided over two competing ideas of what to do with the territories captured in the war. The "Land for Peace" advocates argue that Israel should evacuate most of the area in exchange for a peace agreement that provides Israelis with peace and security. By contrast, the proponents of "Greater Israel" insist that the land is part of the biblical homeland of the Jews and should become a permanent part of Israel (https://www.jewishvirtuallibrary.org/facts-about-jewish-settlements-in-the-west-bank). How should Christians respond?

3. Many people at present hold a moral position concerning abortion that is similar to the Stoic position encountered by the early Christians in the Roman Empire: just as fruit belongs to a fruit tree, so an unborn child belongs

to its mother, who may therefore do what she pleases with it up to the point of birth (and perhaps even immediately after birth). How should Christians respond?

4. The view that many contemporary people take of suicide is also similar to the prevailing view in ancient Rome where, in the general absence of sociological, religious, or ethical barriers to the practice, suicide was common. How should Christians respond?

17

The Moral Maze of the Moment
A Brief Guide for the Perplexed

maze noun . . . 1a: a confusing intricate network of passages; b: something confusingly elaborate or complicated . . . 2: chiefly dialectical: a state of bewilderment.[1]

Merriam-Webster Dictionary

The Moral Maze is a well-established, live radio discussion show on the BBC Radio network in the UK; its website describes it as "combative, provocative, and engaging live debate examining the moral issues behind one of the week's news stories."[2] *Wikipedia* tells us that on the show "a series of 'witnesses'—experts or other relevant people—are questioned" by four regular panelists "who then discuss what each witness said." It also tells us that "the discussions . . . often revolve around whether newer liberal values are eroding more traditional values," although "this binary split is often complicated by differing philosophical views the panel hold which do not conveniently sit in a simple left-right political divide."[3]

We are engaged in a similar exercise in this book. We too have been questioning witnesses in search of answers to moral questions—in search of what is right. The witnesses in whom we have been primarily interested, however, have not been modern experts but ancient ones: the authors of Christian Scripture. Moreover, our "maze" has not in fact turned out to be "confusingly elaborate or complicated," leaving us bewildered (see the epigraph above). This is because *our* witnesses have provided us with a reliable map that we are well able, with some reasonable effort, to read. The search for the good has not been in vain, then, although it has perhaps sometimes surprised the reader, since its outcomes, like the philosophical views of the *Moral Maze* panel, "do not conveniently sit in a simple left-right political divide." At times the search has endorsed what have often been considered "newer liberal values"; at others, it has led to the affirmation of "more traditional values." This is as it should be, since nothing in Scripture suggests that when the Word of God is properly heard, it will be found simply to endorse the settled lists of beliefs and values of any human community within God's good but fallen world. If it had turned out, then, after our careful deliberations concerning how best to read Scripture ethically, that all of our conclusions corresponded neatly to the slates of politically correct prejudices to which our modern "tribes" of both the left and the right subscribe, then we should all have had reason to doubt the objectivity of the exercise, as well as its purpose.[4]

Our task in chapters 17 and 18 is to bring this same biblical "map" of the "maze" to bear on some further, contemporary moral questions—the kinds of questions that do indeed frequently turn up at present in "the week's news stories." Because in the case of the first two topics in the present chapter I am developing arguments from earlier ones, I can afford to be quite brief. I shall need to give more space, however, to the third and fourth topics.

ALL WHO LIVE IN IT WASTE AWAY

In chapter 15 we established from Scripture that God possesses a great interest in everything that he has created and in what is for its good. This interest is evident not least in some aspects of the vocation he has bestowed upon the human creatures who are made in his image and whom he has called to exercise just dominion over the earth. We are not only to "keep" our human neighbors (Hb. *shamar*, 4:9) but also to "keep" the rest of Creation (Hb. *shamar*, 2:15; NIV's "take care of it"). When we are unable or unwilling to do so because of our dysfunctional relationships with God and each other, "the land mourns, and all who live in it waste away; the beasts of the field and the birds of the air and the fish of the sea are dying" (Hos. 4:3). That is, God has chosen to create a world whose well-being depends to a significant extent on how his image bearers behave.

GLOBAL WARMING

All this being so, the contemporary idea that human behavior might have contributed to significant global warming should not be in the least surprising to the person who confesses a biblical faith. The associated idea of consequent, severe impact on the flourishing of both human beings and other creatures in different parts of God's world also makes biblical and theological sense. These are absolutely *not* ideas that only make sense in connection with (for example) "the rising political clout of modern feminism."[5] *Whether* such global warming is in fact an empirical reality has of course been much debated in recent decades, and many people remain skeptical about it. Among conservative Republicans in the United States, for example, 2019 figures suggest that only 42 percent agree that it is a reality, and indeed analysis of Gallup poll data from 1990 through 2015 suggests that in particular among American Christians during those years "the likelihood that a . . . respondent expressed a great deal of concern about climate change dropped by about a third "[6] It is always important, of course, to interrogate properly the empirical evidence upon which scientific claims are based, in order to check that they are well-founded. Yet the evidence in this case appears to overwhelmingly supportive of the thesis, such that "most of the leading scientific organizations worldwide have issued public statements endorsing" the view "that climate-warming trends over the past century are extremely likely due to human activities."[7]

FAITH, SCIENCE, AND COMMITMENT

It is open to us then to adopt a skeptical posture, of course, in relation to the scientific community that "agrees" on this matter. However, we must recognize the risk in doing so without very good reason—that as people who identify as truth seekers we shall in fact end up by deliberately cutting ourselves off from important aspects of the truth. Christians have found themselves in this kind of position before. We remember the large numbers of believers in seventeenth- and eighteenth-century Europe, for example, who simply refused to swap their medieval cosmology for the new Copernican one, even as the empirical evidence in support of the latter became overwhelming.[8] This kind of commitment to ignorance has only ever had devastating consequences for the credibility of the Christian faith in the public square. Even more seriously in the present case, however: how are we to fulfil our vocation to look after God's garden if we simply refuse to look at the evidence pertaining to what might be ailing it?

Even if there *were* any doubt about the extent of global warming and its main causes, we should still be obliged by Scripture to respond as creatively and constructively as we could to its negative effects, so far as we could ascertain them— the erosion of human and animal habitats, for example, and consequent species loss. As Christians in search of biblical righteousness we should not need to agree on every fine point of the debate about the significance and causes of climate change in order to agree on our duty of care for a planet that is currently clearly suffering from its effects. Global warming ought to matter to us, as biblical Christians, and we ought to be fully engaged with others in responding to its challenges as well as we can. Whether we ourselves initially warm to this idea or not, we must hear the divine imperative in Scripture to do what is right in this area of our lives, even if others choose to ignore it—including our Christian neighbors or our political allies. So it comes down to this: created as earth-keepers, we should be striving to live in ecologically committed ways in our personal lives and in our Christian communities. In the realm of public discourse, we should be urging our politicians to consider in all of their decision-making the common good not only of all *people* but of all *creatures*. People are important, and their interests should certainly not be ignored in pursuing the common good of all—but nor should human interests lead us to neglect the interests of our nonhuman neighbors.[9]

THE GOD OF JEWS—AND GENTILES

This question of the common good of all *people*, specifically, necessitates that we next pick up the threads of the discussion in chapter 14, where I argued that the Christian Zionist understanding of Scripture is fundamentally wrong. There is no good reason to think that the Bible has anything at all directly to say about the return of modern Jews to their historical homeland, and their founding of a modern state in it. This does not mean that Christians have no obligation to love Jews, however, or to support the modern state of Israel.

INDISCRIMINATE LOVE

All human beings, whether Jew or Gentile, are created as image bearers of God who should rightly expect to be "kept" by their neighbors. We are to love all of these neighbors in imitation of God, who "causes his sun to rise on the evil and the good and sends rain on the righteous and the unrighteous" (Matt. 5:43–48). God himself "does not show favoritism" in respect of Jews and Gentiles (Rom. 2:9–11). Among other things, this indiscriminate love to which we are called means looking out for our neighbors wherever they are vulnerable to enemies seeking to do them harm—whenever they find themselves oppressed by the wicked, and like "the foreigners, the fatherless, and the widows" of biblical Torah they need our special protection (e.g., Deut. 14:29). Ezekiel 37 lays particular emphasis on the just treatment of the foreigner in the Promised Land when the Israelites return there from exile.[10] God himself is an advocate for and defender of the vulnerable and oppressed in these ways—a "father to the fatherless, a defender of widows" (Ps. 68:5)—and we are called to be the same. At the same time we are called to be peacemakers (Matt. 5:9), just as God himself is "the God of peace" (Rom. 16:20; 1 Cor. 14:33) who was "reconciling the world to himself in Christ, not counting people's sins against them" (2 Cor. 5:19). Christ "himself is our peace," who has "destroyed the barrier, the dividing wall of hostility" between Jew and Gentile, reconciling "both of them to God through the cross, by which he put to death their hostility" (Eph. 2:14–16). Christ-followers are therefore to "make every effort to do what leads to peace and to mutual edification" (Rom. 14:19), exercising "the ministry of reconciliation" that God has committed to us (2 Cor. 5:18–19). Like God, we must be committed to seeing enemies reconciled.

THE LOVE OF JEWS

It is true that God's choice of the people descended from Abraham and Sarah—ancient Israel—as his primary mission-partner in the world was a temporary one, and that with the coming of Christ this role no longer belongs to one particular people-group but to a universal Church. This does not mean, however, that God no longer loves the Jews (as if "not chosen" meant "hated"), or that Jews have ceased to be image bearers—with all that this status entails. God remains "the God of Jews" just as he remains "the God of Gentiles" (Rom. 3:29); "there is no difference between Jew and Gentile—the same Lord is Lord of all and richly blesses all who call on him" (Rom. 10:12). It remains our Christian duty, then, to love our Jewish neighbors, which includes protecting them when their enemies seek to do them harm. It is a duty that comes into particularly sharp focus in the light of the many Christian failures in the past to provide such protection (see our chapters, six, and fourteen). In fact, people identifying as Christians, entirely misunderstanding what Scripture required of them, have themselves often persecuted Jews. It is obscene, for example, and not only absurd, that some of our forebears inflicted violence on Jews as "Christ-killers," when Christ himself urges us to forgive our (and his) enemies. It is impossible (I propose) for any morally sensitive person who knows the full history of antisemitic sentiment and action in the world, down through the Holocaust and beyond, to disagree with the conclusion drawn from it by many modern Jews: that the Gentile nations cannot be trusted to "keep" Jews within their domains and therefore that Jews once again need their own national state. In accepting this conclusion it is not in the slightest degree necessary to agree, however, that the eventual creation of the contemporary state of Israel represents the fulfilment of biblical prophecy. The Christian duty of love toward vulnerable neighbors is a sufficient ground for supporting the existence of a modern state of Israel, and it is this same duty that requires us to be committed to its ongoing security in the face of intent to damage or destroy it. Similarly, Christians are obliged to work for and engage in the protection of Jews in other countries from an antisemitism that is ever attempting to reestablish itself as mainstream ideology in Gentile contexts.

THE LOVE OF PALESTINIANS

At the same time, God also continues to love his *Gentile* image bearers—just as much as his Jewish ones—and it is our Christian duty to love them, too, as our neighbors. This includes protecting *them* when their enemies, including their Jewish ones, do not treat them with the respect and solicitude that they are due and indeed seek to do them harm. God "does not show favoritism" in respect of Jews and Gentiles, and nor should we. Christians ought to be as concerned for Arabs in Israel/Palestine, then—whether they are Christian, Muslim, or otherwise—as they are for Jews. They ought to be concerned both about the injustices that non-Jews in the region have suffered in the past and about those they continue to suffer daily in the present. They ought to put serious effort into at least preventing the latter, even if it is challenging realistically to do much to recompense people in respect to the former.[11] Christians ought to be concerned also about the overt racism that often lies at the heart of this unjust treatment by Israeli Jews of their neighbors.[12]

It is entirely unacceptable from the perspective of biblical faith, then, that so many self-identifying Christians in the world are opposed in principle to criticizing the state of Israel when it engages in moral wrongdoing, on the specious ground that God is against those who "curse" Israel (Gen. 12:3) and is for those who support Israel.[13] To confront a neighbor about wrongdoing is not to "curse" that neighbor, and if criticizing Israel is also to "curse" it, then God must have been "against" all the biblical prophets who did so. Modern Israelis do not get a "free pass" on their moral obligations to their neighbors just because they are Jews—and if it is antisemitic to hold them accountable for their actions, then many Jews themselves (who are also determined to hold them accountable) are also antisemitic.[14] In Scripture, it is the false prophets who offer partisan support, no matter what, to the Israelite state. True prophets are marked by their willingness, where necessary, to condemn it.[15] Christians, likewise, cannot play "favorites" in Israel/Palestine.

THE CALL TO PEACEMAKING

To the extent that we do so, in fact, we destroy our own capacity to be the peacemakers in the region that we are called to be. Reconciliation there will be difficult enough to achieve without Christians unthinkingly continuing to pour money without conditions into Israel at the expense of very much support at all for the Palestinian Arabs. Persisting in supporting settlement expansion by Israelis into the West Bank, East Jerusalem, and the Golan Heights that is overwhelmingly regarded in the global community as standing in violation of international law will also not help.[16] It is extraordinary to find Christ-followers anywhere who are in these ways so uncritically "for" a contemporary foreign state—more supportive of it even than many of its own citizens—when we are forbidden so clearly in Scripture from offering unqualified endorsement even of our *own* state (chapter 11). But of course the fact is that many of the Christians who are "pro-Israel" in this particular manner have already stepped away from biblical faith in embracing uncritically nationalistic sentiments *concerning* their own countries. Each of us needs to return to true faith, responding to the divine imperative in Scripture to do what is right in this area of our lives, even if many others in our "tribe" (again) choose to ignore it.

In summation: in our personal lives and in our Christian communities we should commit to loving Jews and Palestinians equally well, and our lives in general and our giving in particular should reflect this. In the realm of public discourse we should urge our politicians, first, to deal with the situation in Israel/Palestine as even-handedly as they can and, secondly, always to consider what will contribute to a lasting peace in the region that is also as just a possible under the circumstances.

IN THE WOMB

If all human beings, whether Jew or Gentile, are created as image bearers of God who should rightly expect to be "kept" by their neighbors, does this include those who are still in the womb? Are these, too, among the vulnerable persons—like "the foreigners, the fatherless, and the widows" of biblical Torah—whom we must protect from harm? If so, what does this mean for how I approach the question of abortion (the deliberate termination of a human pregnancy), both in my personal and family life and in my advocacy in the realm of public discourse?

THE CONTEMPORARY CONTEXT: KATE GREASLEY

It will be helpful to set these questions first in the context of contemporary debate about abortion among those who are not arguing the matter on explicitly Christian or even religious grounds. The philosopher Kate Greasley, for example, has recently set out her views on abortion as follows. She begins by conceding that "if the fetus is a person, equivalent in value to a born human being, then abortion is almost always morally wrong and legal abortion permissions almost entirely unjustified."[17] She immediately then launches into a discussion of definitions. She notes that by the word "person" philosophers "generally mean to capture a category of beings with strong moral rights, in particular, the almost inviolable right to life." "Person" is to be distinguished from the term "human being," which is used "to denote individual members of the human species." All embryos and foetuses "are certainly human beings, in that they are all individual human organisms. But this does not mean that they are all necessarily persons."[18] If they are not persons, she argues, then "not only is abortion morally permissible but denying women the abortion right is a serious injustice."[19] After elucidating why this is so, she concludes thus: "To prevent women from exercising reproductive control through abortion can force on them serious and unequal costs to their well-being (as well as forcing on them a new parental identity), such that it cannot be justified if abortion is not seriously immoral."[20]

Pausing only to dismiss the argument that abortion does not actually deliver the benefits to women that they seek—"the women-protective claims have to be exaggerated beyond reasonable belief to speak against abortion rights"—she moves on to the question of prenatal personhood as such. Noting the complexity of the issue,[21] she expresses her preference for the idea that "the core constitutive features of a person are developmentally acquired capacities" rather than features like mere "human genetic coding."[22] This is why, given the choice between saving numerous embryos or one fully formed baby, people would typically choose the latter. It is not, then, "humanity per se [that] is the basis for moral status." Rather, "moral status and the fundamental right to life supervene on capacities that embryos and fetuses do not possess . . . such as reasoning ability, language, and self-consciousness."[23]

She then turns to deal with the objection that this account of personhood excludes many "people" from the category of "persons": young infants, for example, or adults in comas or suffering from severe cognitive disabilities. She acknowledges the problems but sticks to her view. She notes that the opposing "theory that ties moral status to human species membership [and] has no trouble including infants, the comatose, or the radically cognitively defective within the remit of full rights-holding individuals" at the same time "extends equal moral protection to zygotes [fertilized ova] and embryos as well"—and this, too, is problematic. On what basis can it be argued that "all human beings as of conception are full rights-holding persons"?[24] In the end, then, acknowledging that "birth does not amount to a transformative moment in which the moral status of the early human being is radically altered," Greasley nevertheless opts for birth as the "abortion threshold."[25] Termination of human life "will be justifiable before birth but not afterward"—even though prenatal human beings are very little different from new-born babies.[26]

THE CONTEMPORARY CONTEXT: CHRISTOPHER KACZOR

In responding to Kate Greasley and making considerable use of the difficulties she has faced in trying to draw defensible distinctions among different human beings as to their "personhood," Christopher Kaczor works backwards, as it were. Given that we now possess a right to life such that someone else is not simply permitted to kill us, he asks, when did we gain that right? And when did we not possess it? In exploring this question, he first draws on an academic paper from 2013, whose authors (Giubilini and Minerva) argue that "there are no morally significant differences between a newborn and a fetal human being in utero."[27]

Neither one is a "person"—therefore, "if abortion is ethically permissible, then post-birth abortion is also ethically permissible."²⁸ The authors do not explicitly say at what moment killing a child becomes ethically wrong, but Kaczor deduces from their argument that the answer is around two years of age, when children typically become aware of their own existence and can take an interest in, and indeed *desire*, its continuance. If this conclusion is unacceptable, Kaczor points out, "then something is wrong with Giubilini and Minerva's argument."²⁹ He believes that what is mainly wrong with it is precisely the idea that the right to life has to do with (in Greasley's words) "developmentally acquired capacities," at least of the postnatal kind. Suicidal human people, for example, "do not desire their continued existence, but it would still be wrong to kill them."³⁰ In fact,

> we desire things (like continued living) because we (rightly or wrongly) think that such things are good. So, what is relevant in determining whether someone has been wronged is not simply whether they were deprived of something they desired but also whether they were deprived of something good . . . What we desire can be insane, tyrannical, unjust, uninformed, sexist, or racist. What is relevant ethically is not undermining someone's desires but undermining someone's good.³¹

There is indeed in Giubilini and Minerva's thinking a pronounced body-self dualism, Kaczor maintains, whereby my body is not really my "self." Instead, my "self" comprises my aims, desires, and awareness—which means, of course (as Kaczor wittily, but very pertinently, points out), that one human being with dissociative identity disorder may actually be sixteen persons, and that every one of them has a right to live. This seems (to most people) implausible; among other things, it turns the successful psychiatrist into a mass murderer.

Having demolished Giubilini and Minerva's thesis, Kaczor turns next to the idea that the right to life begins at birth. He denies, however, that birth is the "magic moment" giving rise to this right.³² Next comes the question: does the right to live begin at some point during gestation? One popular version of the affirmative response in this case places "viability" at the heart of the matter (as promoted in the famous *Roe v. Wade* case in 1973 in the United States): the point at which "the fetus . . . presumably has the capability of meaningful life outside the mother's womb."³³ The "conscious desires account," secondly, holds that the right to life begins at twenty-five to thirty-two weeks after conception, while the "sentience account" (thirdly) connects it to the capacity to experience physical pain. Still others (fourthly) connect the right to life with fetal movement, or fetal brain waves. Then there are those who hold (fifthly) that the right to life "gradually strengthens as the prenatal human being develops physically and psychologically."³⁴ Kaczor methodically analyses each of these positions and finds them wanting.³⁵ In the course of his argument he explicitly rejects for a number of reasons Greasley's argument concerning the saving of a fully formed baby in preference to numerous embryos. Among these reasons is that "[t]he right to life is the duty of agents not to intentionally kill anyone with this right"; it is not the same thing as a right to be rescued in a situation where lesser-of-two-evils considerations apply.[36]

Kaczor's position in the end is that one's right to life begins when one begins to exist. When is that? It is when one is an embryo, sharing as a member of the human species in the "self-directed activities" of all living organisms, including "assimilating nutrition, growing proportionately, and reproducing new cells," and possessing the ability to die. Every human being has the right to life from that point onwards Indeed, he contends,

> [i]f we learn anything from history about ethical judgment, it is that our past errors of exclusion were seriously wrong. We now face another moment in history in which we must choose between the ethics of inclusion and the ethics of exclusion. We can affirm that all human beings are created equal and endowed with inalienable rights. Or we can affirm that only those human beings who are like me have rights but those human beings who are not like me do not.... Although human beings in utero are not like us, not powerful, unable to protect themselves, and as vulnerable as a human can be, these characteristics do not change in the least the fact that they are just as human as any of us.[37]

He thereby endorses an "endowment account of personhood," in which human beings have intrinsic value, over against a "functional" view, in which they have a value based on how they function on a sliding scale (e.g., in relation to sensitivity to pain, or rationality).[38] This guarantees human beings their rights for the whole of their lives, no matters what happens to their "functions," and it removes the need for any calculations about degrees of personhood in relation to "thresholds"—whether inside or outside the womb. Only such a view of rights, including the right to life, protects us from what Steven Pinker has referred to as a "nasty feature of human social psychology: the tendency to divide people into in-groups and out-groups, and to treat the out-groups as less than human."[39]

ABORTION IN THE BIBLE

How does biblical faith inform our participation in this debate about the rights and wrongs of abortion? It has been suggested by some that certain biblical texts specifically address the issue. Genesis 38 has been drawn into the discussion, for example, and also Numbers 5—implausibly, in both cases.[40] The most commonly mentioned passage has been Exodus 21:22–25, where we read about a situation in which people fighting with each other "hit a pregnant woman and she gives birth prematurely [or has a miscarriage] but there is no serious injury." In such a case, "the offender must be fined whatever the woman's husband demands and the court allows." However, "if there is serious injury," the principle of lex talionis applies: "you are to take life for life, eye for eye, tooth for tooth, hand for hand, foot for foot, burn for burn, wound for wound, bruise for bruise." This is not a text that concerns abortion, of course, but it has been considered relevant because of what it is alleged to say about the relative value of the mother and the child.

The fact is, however, that it allows us to say nothing for certain about this matter. Is the point of the law that lex talionis only applies in a case where either the child or the mother come out of the fight with serious injury? In this case, mother and child are being treated equally under the law. Or is the point that, whatever happens to the child, the result is only a fine and that lex talionis applies only in the case of serious injury to the mother? The passage, in itself, is not at all clear. If the latter interpretation were to be considered the correct reading, then we need to recognize that this, in itself, would not mean that "the Bible teaches" that unborn children are less valuable than postnatal humans. We should still need to consider the character of the law in the context of the whole biblical Story, as we have been doing throughout this book. The need for such reflection is already pressed upon us by the immediately surrounding verses, which concern slaves (vv. 20–21 and 26–27). The premise of these laws is that slaves are "property" (v. 21) and that violence against them is not to be assessed in the same way as for freemen. In particular, lex talionis does not apply in their case, which is why special provisions are made in the case of lost eyes and teeth (there is no "eye for eye, tooth for tooth" possibility). It would be quite wrong to deduce from all of this that "the Bible teaches" that slaves are any less the image bearers of God than anyone else—as we saw in our chapter 12.

Therefore, if Scripture is to be "useful" to us in reflecting on this question of abortion, it will not be on the basis of specific texts that directly address the question.[41] It will be on the basis of what Scripture teaches us more generally about relevant matters, as we seek as Christ-followers to "live out of" our biblical Story.

LIFE AND DEATH IN THE BIBLE

Most importantly, what does Scripture have to say about life and death in general? We inhabit a Story that begins with the important, large idea that human beings are *creatures* of a *Creator* (Gen. 1:1)—some of the many creatures into whose nostrils God has breathed the breath of life, making us "living beings" (Gen. 2:7; cf. 6:17; 7:15, 22). Life comes to us as a gift; we are not our own creators. As Psalm 100:3 puts it: "Know that the LORD is God. It is he who made us, and we are his." We are the clay in relation to the potter; "we are all the work of your hand" (Isa. 64:8). It is God who gives life, and it is God who sustains it; without his ongoing involvement as life-giver, his creatures would die. Psalm 104:29–30 speaks to this truth: "when you take away their breath, they die and return to the dust. When you send your Spirit, they are created, and you renew the face of the ground."[42] God gives life, and God takes it away, after a lifespan that is determined by the Creator himself (Job 14:5; Dan. 5:26), such that worrying about the matter is futile (Matt. 6:27). As the giver of life—as we have seen already in this book— God is passionate about preserving it and angry with all those who illegitimately take it away. This is why his creational law forbids murder (Exod. 20:13), and why those who act in such life-destroying ways in our biblical narrative find themselves subject to his justice—Cain in Genesis 4, or Ahab in 1 Kings 21, for example. Anyone who "sheds human blood" in such ways, as we saw in Genesis 9:6, stands outside the will of God, "for in the image of God has God made mankind."

We shall get to end-of-life issues shortly, before this chapter itself ends. But when does the individual life *begin*, in biblical faith? It begins in the womb. Job 10:10–11 speak obliquely about this reality: "Did you not pour me out like milk and curdle me like cheese, clothe me with skin and flesh, and knit me together with bones and sinews?" Psalm 139:13–16 is clearer:

> For you created my inmost being; you knit me together in my mother's womb. I praise you because I am fearfully and wonderfully made; your works are wonderful, I know that full well . . . all the days ordained for me were written in your book before one of them came to be.

It is this same perspective that is reflected in Jeremiah 1:5, where God tells the prophet: "Before I formed you in the womb I knew you, before you were born I set you apart"; and in Galatians 1:15, where Paul speaks of God setting him apart for his apostolic role "before I was born." The mystery of the creative process is the subject of Ecclesiastes 11:5: "As you do not know the path of the wind, or how the body is formed in a mother's womb, so you cannot understand the work of God [in general], the Maker of all things." The mystery of our *fallen* as well as our *created* condition from before our births is the subject of Psalm 51:5–6: "Surely I was sinful at birth, sinful from the time my mother conceived me. Yet you desired faithfulness even in the womb; you taught me wisdom in that secret place." God is deeply involved already with the prenatal human being. Yet in this fallen world it is precisely the fact that all human beings, no matter what their current state, are created by the same God in the womb that is the ground for their equal status before God and their rights: "Did not he who made me in the womb make them [Job's slaves]? Did not the same one form us both within our mothers?" (Job 31:15).

CHRISTIANS AND ABORTION

All of this taken together clearly implies that people of biblical faith are bound to regard God-given, human life in the womb as being just as sacrosanct as human life outside the womb and to regard the illegitimate destruction of this prenatal human life as wrong—as a violation of God-ordained human rights, in fact. Human beings *in utero* do not possess the right to life because they have managed to accumulate certain "developmentally acquired capacities" such as "reasoning ability, language, and self-consciousness" (Greasley). They possess the right to life because their life belongs to God, and it can only rightly be taken away by (or with the sanction of) God. From the perspective of biblical faith, all the contemporary arguments about when *we humans* might wish to consider an *in utero* life worthy of the attribution of personhood, and therefore worthy of our protection from deliberate harm by others, are irrelevant. They are just as irrelevant as arguments about "proper" personhood from birth onwards, whether these arguments pertain to healthy infants, challenged minors, or impaired adults. The value of a human being, in biblical faith, lies not in "developmentally acquired capacities," or indeed in anything that we might think makes him or her "more like us," or more useful to society, or whatever. The value of a human being lies in the mere (but glorious) fact that he or she is an image bearer of God—someone in the care of God, from the moment that God starts creating him or her until the end of life. Kaczor is right, then, in his endorsement of an "endowment account" over against a "functional account" of personhood. Human beings have intrinsic value from the beginning. It does not matter how they "function" on a sliding scale of human devising.

The only question that remains is whether there is ever any situation in which the destruction of life in the womb can rightly be considered "God-sanctioned." This question relates to Greasley's "almost" language above: "if the fetus is a person, equivalent in value to a born human being, then abortion is *almost always* [my emphasis] morally wrong and legal abortion permissions almost entirely unjustified."[43] What might the exceptions be, for a Christian? One of the most often discussed of these is the case where the continuation of a pregnancy risks the life of the mother. Is abortion ethically permissible in such a case? Here we must be clear about our terms. It is not properly "the deliberate termination of a human pregnancy" if a mother elects to have necessary surgery (for example) that will lead, as a consequence, to the death of her unborn child; the death of the child is obviously not her goal. As Kaczor puts it: "It is permissible to do one action with two effects, one good and one bad, so long as the action itself is ethically acceptable, the evil effect is not chosen as a means or as an end, and there is a proportionately serious reason for allowing the evil side effect."[44]

Another, more difficult case that is commonly discussed is that of a pregnancy resulting from a rape. Rape is, of course, a devastating, wicked sin, and it is
a heroic person who continues a pregnancy resulting from such a terrible assault.
If it is heroic to continue the pregnancy, however, is it also morally permissible
to end it? If one genuinely believes that the child in the womb is a person, it is
difficult to see how the answer to this question could be "yes." Although it is a
painful truth to articulate in this context, it remains a truth: it does not follow
that because one has been terribly harmed by the wicked, it is morally acceptable
to inflict terrible harm on the innocent.[45] This second act can in fact prove to be
much more difficult to come to terms with than the first one, precisely because
it was done to another rather than to oneself. Conversely, many female rape victims who have kept their babies have been grateful in the end to have made this
decision, and their children have also been thankful in later years that this was
the decision taken.[46]

It is because the early Christians so wholeheartedly embraced biblical teaching on the sacrosanctity of life along such lines that they themselves took such a
different view from their own contemporaries, the Stoics, of both abortion and
infanticide. The Stoics, decidedly anthropocentric in their thinking, were happy
to endorse both practices as "reasonable." In the first case, they held that what
nature teaches us about ethics is taught by the tree and its fruit. A baby is part of
the mother's body, just as the fruit belongs to the fruit tree, until both (fruit and
baby) "fall." Therefore, up to the point of birth, the mother could do anything she
pleased to the baby.[47] In the second case, babies with mental or physical abnor-
malities were judged "useless" as opposed to "sound," and like all useless things
they were to be discarded by reasonable people.[48] They lacked the appropriate
"developmentally acquired capacities." The early Christians took a very different
view. The *Didache*, for example (late first or early second century), explicitly states
that "thou shalt not procure abortion, nor commit infanticide."[49] The *Epistle of
Barnabas* (from the same period) says something very similar, and prefaces its
prohibition with another, positive command: "Thou shalt love thy neighbor more
than thine own soul. Thou shalt not slay the child by procuring abortion; nor
again, shalt thou destroy it after it is born."[50] The prenatal human being is not part
of its mother, but a "neighbor." It was such commitments that among other things
led the early Christians frequently to visit the rubbish dumps of Rome to rescue
children left there by their families to die. The contemporary Church, likewise, is
called to be a place of refuge, safety, and support for young and yet-unborn children, as well as their parents, who are also our neighbors and are often in need of
very significant support in walking the right path in this area of life.

ABORTION AND THE LAW

Throughout this book we have been reflecting not only on what Scripture has
to say to the Church concerning the good life but also on what the Church
might advocate for in the culture at large that relates to each theme that we have
explored. The two are always going to be related to each other, but the one will
not necessarily entirely predict the other, not least because not everything that is
immoral should necessarily be made illegal, even if we had to power to make it so.
What I have proposed in earlier chapters, in fact, is that in thinking about such
matters, Christians ought to be principled political liberals, advocating and working for a society marked by freedom—one in which we Christians ourselves are,
of course, at liberty among other things to preach the Gospel and call our non-
Christian neighbors to (freely chosen) repentance. What does all of this mean
when it comes to abortion?

It has sometimes been proposed that freedom in this case means that abortion, although it is wrong, should not be illegal: individuals should be allowed to
make their own conscientious choices about this matter. The problem is that at
least *two* parties are involved in the case of abortion, and not only one, and the
rights and freedoms of both must be considered. At least in countries historically
shaped by Christian faith, we have not typically allowed our neighbors the freedom to behave immorally if it involves the intentional harm of another. In fact, we
already have many laws in the statute books that are designed to protect the innocent from serious harm precisely along such lines. If we truly believe that children
in the womb are persons, then it follows that we are obliged to advocate for legal
protections with respect to their right to life, wherever and whenever we can do
so—for entirely new protections, where necessary, or for the further expansion
of current ones. We are called at the same time to resist proposals concerning the
further deployment of abortion—for instance, as a way of maintaining population control in a period of global warming.[51] This is one obvious way in which it
really does matter that we hold a properly Christian view of our calling as earth
keepers, rather than simply a lightly baptized non-Christian one. For a Christian
view of earth keeping does not allow for the neglect at the same time of people
keeping, including the keeping of persons in the womb.

In seeking such legal protections for the unborn, however, we need to be
careful, first, to consider the consequences of any particular legislation for the
mothers of those unborn, in particular, and we need to take serious (and indeed
self-sacrificial) steps to minimize the negative impact of those consequences.[52]
We live in a messy world, in which even noble aspirations can lead to unjust outcomes for some, often according to the rule of "unintended consequences."[53] Secondly, we should also (as always) avoid utopianism in our politics. We may well
believe—I am convinced that we *should*—that any form of abortion is absolutely

wrong in itself. We may further believe that its legalization in any form is bound to contribute (and has already) to the further erosion of our societal commitments concerning right-to-life issues more broadly. This is precisely because such legalization means that the right to life is no longer being assigned automatically to a human being. The onus now falls on the human individual to demonstrate that (s)he is worthy of the right to life in line with other people's judgments about whether his or her "developmentally acquired capacities" are sufficient to gain status in the "in-group." The *legalizing* of the taking of a human life for such "failure to demonstrate" *normalizes* such killing, and reduces resistance to further analogous killing, as we have seen in the case of those arguing in favor of infanticide. All this being said, however, seeking legislative change is not an all-or-nothing affair. As we have learned from OT Torah at various points in this book, some legal protections for the vulnerable are better than none. They form part of what is "good." So if we cannot win a political argument on abortion in terms of what we believe would be *best*, we should remain willing for the moment to compromise and accept what is less than best, rather than help to deliver the *worst*—which is no abortion law at all, and indeed no legal prohibition of infanticide either.[54]

In the meantime, Christian health professionals are obliged, like every other kind of Christian, not to involve themselves in abortion. In many parts of the world, then, the immediate focus of our engagement with the public domain will be to create, or to maintain, a legal right of conscience in respect of facilitating abortions that will protect Christian health professionals and enable them to do their jobs while keeping as far away as possible from this grievous moral error.[55]

ONE FOOT IN THE GRAVE

The best way into our final topic in this chapter is by way of a comment by Christopher Kaczor already recorded above. Suicidal people, he states, "do not desire their continued existence, but it would still be wrong to kill them."[56] Many people at the present time appear to disagree with him, at least to some degree. They hold that it is morally acceptable actively to cause another's death (e.g., by administering a lethal substance) if that person requests it. This is typically referred to as "voluntary *euthanasia*" (from the Gk. meaning "a gentle and easy death"). If someone believes this, then they will also likely believe that "assisted suicide" is morally unproblematic: the provision of *help* for the person requesting to die, in the form of (e.g.) putting drugs within their reach when they are unable to fetch them for themselves. All of this is to be distinguished in principle from *nonvoluntary* euthanasia, such as would occur in the cases of infanticide described above, or in cases where third parties decide that an adult's life is not worth (or no longer worth) living and proceed to deprive them of life without their consent. Although this is also an important moral issue, it will not be the main focus of this section of our chapter (although we shall inevitably touch upon it, for reasons that will become clear). We shall mainly consider in what follows only interventions to deprive (or help to deprive) people of life *with* their consent. How does biblical faith lead us to think about such interventions?

THE BIBLE AND SUICIDE

The most fundamental question to be considered here is the morality of suicide as such. We do not need to do much new work in reflecting on this question, since we have already explored earlier in this chapter the character of the Bible's "big picture" concerning life and death in general. Human life is a gift from God; it is not something that we ourselves "own." It is God who gives it, and it is only God (or those who are sanctioned by God) who can take it away, at which point "the spirit returns to God who gave it" (Eccl. 12:7). These are already sufficient grounds for believing that to end one's own life is morally wrong. The Catechism of the Roman Catholic Church rightly interprets the biblical tradition when it says this:

> Everyone is responsible for his life before God who has given it to him. It is God who remains the sovereign Master of life. We are obliged to accept life gratefully and preserve it for his honor and the salvation of our souls. We are stewards, not owners, of the life God has entrusted to us. It is not ours to dispose of.[57]

That is, we are stewards of our own life just as we are stewards of God's good Creation in general. This is the larger context in which we must then read the individual Scripture passages that describe suicide, which in the eyes of some lead us to the view that "the biblical attitude toward suicide ranges from ambivalence to praise."[58] This is a rather extraordinary statement, however, especially when we consider who the people *are* who commit suicide in the biblical Story.[59] These are not "heroes" set before us for our imitation; in none of these cases are the actions of these biblical characters praised by anyone.[60] This includes Judas Iscariot, of whom Darrel Amundsen wryly says that "it is reasonable to assume that he would hardly have been regarded as a model of Christian probity."[61]

As we read on in the NT, indeed, we find at least one suicide prevented (Acts 16:25–34), but more importantly, we encounter Christian teaching that very much presses in a direction contrary to the practice. In Romans 14:7–8, for example, Paul tells the Roman Christians that "none of us lives for ourselves alone, and none of us dies for ourselves alone. If we live, we live for the Lord; and if we die, we die for the Lord. So, whether we live or die, we belong to the Lord." "Do you not know," Paul asks the Christian in Corinth, "that your bodies are temples of the Holy Spirit, who is in you, whom you have received from God? You are not your own; you were bought at a price. Therefore honor God with your bodies" (1

Cor. 6:19–20). This is the very point: our lives belong to Christ, and they are not our own, to do with as we please. To this we must then add—since suffering is a common reason for suicide—all the NT material that touches on the need for, and virtue of, Christian endurance even under the most trying of circumstances. In Romans 5:3–4, for example, Paul writes that we Christians "glory in our sufferings, because we know that suffering produces perseverance; perseverance, character; and character, hope." This is just one example of the way in which "the New Testament encourages patience, stresses hope, commands perseverance, and so strongly emphasizes the sovereignty of God in the life of Christians and the trust that they should exercise, knowing that God will ultimately cause all things to work out for their good."[62] This does not mean, of course, that we should *look* for suffering, nor that we should fail to relieve it where we can legitimately do so. It does nevertheless remind us that life with God itself involves some suffering and that good things can follow from it.

SUICIDE IN THE POSTAPOSTOLIC CHURCH

There is no ground in any of this material for believing that Scripture countenances the notion of noble or morally right suicide of the kind that we find in Graeco-Roman thinking, exemplified most famously by Socrates (469–399 BC), who "chose to drink hemlock rather than endure exile, a choice enthusiastically endorsed by most of the philosophical schools at the time."[63] It is true that the NT authors never explicitly forbid the practice, but in the light of what they *do* teach about life, endurance (explicitly *in* "exile"), and death, it is most unlikely that this is because they had no strong feelings about it. It is much more likely because suicide "was so inherently contrary to Christian values and priorities as not to be considered a viable option for Christians"—even though Christian lives in the Roman Empire could be quite grim, and they could *end*, in particular, very badly.[64]

Certainly as we move into the early postapostolic period we do begin to find explicit negativity toward the practice. The author of the *Shepherd of Hermas* (early second century), for example, regards "the suicide of one who resorted to it owing to distress as so serious that anyone who could have helped him but failed to do so not only had committed a serious sin but was also guilty of his blood."[65] Later in the same century Tertullian, reflecting on the biblical idea that a Christian should give to the one who asks, cautions his readers to be thoughtful about this command, pointing out that it does not mean giving "wine to him who has a fever ... [or] poison or a sword to him who longs for death."[66] This strongly implies that both suicide and assisting suicide are morally wrong. Finally, by way of example (and this is not an exhaustive account), we should mention the fourth-century scholar Lactantius, first encountered in our chapter 4, who bluntly asserts that "they are accursed and impious . . . who even taught what are the befitting reasons for voluntary death; so that it was not enough of guilt that they were self-murderers, unless they instructed others also to this wickedness."[67]

The only exception that some Christian leaders allowed throughout this period from the second to the fourth centuries was suicide by women in order to preserve their chastity, and especially their virginity.[68] It is this "anomaly in early Christian thought" that then "precipitates Augustine's digression on suicide in Book One of the *City of God*"—an author in whose writing "[a]ll the implicit and explicit [prior] condemnations of suicide in Christian literature . . . are encapsulated and elaborated."[69] Augustine adds only an "unequivocal condemnation of suicide to preserve chastity."[70]

CHRISTIANS AND EUTHANASIA/ASSISTED SUICIDE

If Scripture leads us, in company with Christians before us, to consider suicide to be morally wrong, then it follows that assisting others in achieving it, or acting as their agent in doing so, is also morally wrong—as Tertullian already implies, and as the Roman Catholic Catechism explicitly states: "Voluntary cooperation in suicide is contrary to the moral law."[71] It is morally wrong even where it is legally permitted. In particular—since this is the real core of the issue at present—it is morally wrong, from the perspective of biblical faith, for a Christian healthcare professional to involve himself or herself in what is often called physician-assisted suicide (PAS), even where the intention is to alleviate suffering. It is equally wrong for that professional to engage in any kind of voluntary euthanasia.

The pressure on physicians to do so is great, especially in cultural environments that greatly value patient autonomy—one of "the two commonest reasons advanced in favor of physician-assisted suicide and euthanasia" among physicians in general.[72] Yet there are significant problems with this notion of patient autonomy even if, for the moment, we leave Christian faith aside. Suppose that we allow that "a competent adult ought to have a right to physician-assisted suicide for the relief of suffering. But why must the person be suffering? . . . Why are not the person's desires or motives, whatever they be, sufficient?"[73] Why should physicians deny "any competent person the right to be killed, sick or not"?[74] Is that person's mere claim to self-determination a sufficient reason for a physician to comply with his or her request? But

> doctors quite rightly have never been willing to do what patients want solely because they want it. To do so would reduce doctors to automatons, subordinating their integrity to patient wishes or demands . . . our culture has, traditionally, defined a physician as someone whose duty is to promote and restore health . . . That is why a mere claim of self-determination, which requires no reference to

health at all, is not enough. A doctor will not cut off my healthy arm simply because I decide my autonomy and well-being would thereby be enhanced.[75]

This "historical resistance" has its origins not only in Christian but also in pagan Greek thinking, where the question of assisted suicide is explicitly addressed in the Hippocratic Oath: "I will neither give a deadly drug to anybody if asked for it, nor will I make a suggestion to this effect." As Leon Kass notes, "the Hippocratic physician rejects the view that the patients' choice for death can make killing the patient—or assisting the patient in suicide—right."[76] Later he says this: "Medicine has never, under anyone's interpretation, been charged with *producing or achieving death itself.* Physicians cannot be serving their art or helping their patients ... by making them disappear."[77] Daniel Callahan adds this: "Physical pain and psychological suffering among those who are critically ill and dying are great evils. The attempt to relieve them by the introduction of euthanasia and assisted suicide is an even greater evil."[78] We cannot cure one evil with another.

This brings us to compassion, the second of "the two commonest reasons" given in favor of physician-assisted suicide and euthanasia. In Christian faith (unlike Stoicism), compassion is in itself good. But like all our passions, "compassion can be distorted, self-defeating, and even harmful ... [it is] not, of itself, a sufficient moral justification for ending a human life."[79] When it is treated as such—"absolutized ... as a social value"—it is inevitable that an obligation will be created "on the part of physicians to be the preferred instruments of hastening death," but this must be resisted.[80] Compassion can and does express itself in other ways, such as ensuring excellent palliative healthcare for the already dying, where the goal of medical intervention is not to kill or to facilitate self-killing, but rather "the alleviation of suffering, the optimization of quality of life until death ensues, and the provision of comfort in death."[81] These two expressions of "compassion" are entirely different, and we must resist the cynical inclusion of both under a category heading like "medically assisted dying," which aims to obfuscate the difference.[82] It is in fact precisely the existence of high-quality palliative care that is threatened by the rising acceptance of suicide as a kind of "end-of-life care," since the latter is cheaper, and therefore very attractive to modern states facing burgeoning healthcare costs because of the existence of

> a reservoir of relatively defenceless persons, perceived, through bigoted "ageism," as unproductive and pejoratively dependent. In them, modernization has created a population stratum that, in a state of nature or conditions of scarcity economics, "ought" to be dead.[83]

In such a situation the pressing societal question can quickly become (in Margaret Somerville's words), not "should the baby live?" (as in our previous section) but "should the grandparents die?"—or indeed persons with disabilities, or anyone else considered by majority society to be in the "out-group."[84] Christians must seek in every possible way to work against such a trend in societal thinking, putting effort and money into life-affirming initiatives that enhance the life of our elders and other vulnerable people, protect them from harm, and afford them at the last a "death with dignity" that does not involve medical intervention intended to speed its arrival. For we must agree that "an ethical indictment of PAS . . . entails moral duties on the part of [a person's] surrounding community . . . to provide effective means of ameliorating [that person's] physical and existential suffering."[85]

SUICIDE AND THE LAW

If Christians should not commit suicide, and should not assist others in doing so, for what should we advocate in our wider societies? The case is similar to abortion. We must at the very least strive for the creation or maintenance of a legal right of conscience in refraining from facilitating suicide that will allow Christian health professionals to continue to live their professional lives in a Christian manner. However, we are required to do much more, even as we advocate and work for a free society.

For although it might at first seem that the "liberal" approach to the issue of suicide must simply concede that adult citizens should have the legal right to kill themselves if they choose, with help if necessary—as long as it is not Christian help—it is not in fact as simple as that. We are obliged to consider not only the freedom of the individual, but also the good of the community as a whole. Respect for individual autonomy is important, but not at the expense of "the needs, safety, and protection of the community, especially its vulnerable members, such as persons with disabilities or those who are old, fragile, or mentally ill."[86] And the fact of the matter is that "[e]xperience in countries which have legalized euthanasia, in particular the Netherlands and Belgium, shows that legalized euthanasia threatens such people with abuse that could place even their continued existence at risk."[87] It may begin with a concern to alleviate the physical suffering of consenting, terminally ill patients, but euthanasia has the evident potential then for extension (as in the Netherlands) to "people with mental, but not, [sic] physical illness, as well as to babies and children."[88] The pressure then grows simply to have a legal right to die, with medical assistance, whenever one wishes, and especially (as in Belgium) when one is "tired of life."[89] Once the "do no harm" boundary has been crossed, it is not difficult for this kind of progression to take place, including the practice of involuntary euthanasia out of "compassion."[90] For *legalizing* euthanasia *normalizes* euthanasia, and

[t]his makes it perhaps all too easy for people to request euthanasia, and to be granted such a death as a "way out" of painfully difficult situations and circumstances, rather than addressing underlying issues of inequality and a lack of adequate support for people with very complex needs.[91]

This particular comment pertains to the "consenting" person with disabilities in particular, who is often said to have the right to make an "informed choice." But the whole business of "choice" in this area is much more complex than is often admitted, for such choices are never made in a social vacuum. Prejudice regarding disability, along with failure of proper care can, for example, deprive "patients who might otherwise want to live of the feeling that they have a [genuine] choice."[92] *Elderly* people who think, and have indeed been led to believe, that they are a burden to their family or to society as a whole can likewise easily be led into making the "right" choice. This is especially likely to happen in hedonistic cultures where there is a strong will to remove constraints, economic or otherwise, on younger people's ability to pursue (right now) their desires and dreams—the kind of younger people who already believe that "life after 50 must be awful and that it's 'downhill all the way.'"[93] Rusty Reno perceptively characterizes the mood of this "empire of desire" as follows: "As long as we cannot imagine anything lasting and true other than primitive instincts, we might as well concentrate our minds on the economic, medical, psychological factors that promise to maximize our satisfaction."[94]

It is particularly dangerous that euthanasia and assisted suicide should be legal in such an empire. For it is not only babies in the womb who must now demonstrate that they are worthy of the right to life on account of their "capacities" but also young infants, persons with disabilities, the elderly, and indeed, in principle, *everyone*. And "capacities" aside, they must also demonstrate that they do not represent an inconvenience standing in the way of the majority's "satisfaction." It is not in the least surprising that in this steadily encroaching "culture of death" we should be hearing calls, for example, for assisted suicide to be available to (expensive-to-maintain-and-therefore-inconvenient) prison populations.[95] In the culture of death, anyone can find himself or herself in the "out-group" rather than the "in-group," as a result of a failure to demonstrate both sufficient value and noninterference with the desires of others.

Christians must advocate strenuously in the opposite direction, appealing not so much to the Bible, directly, as to values that people might already hold beyond a commitment to "personal autonomy." One of these values will often be "equality": "Those who claim to uphold equality and relieve the plight of victims should naturally see the disabled, the debilitated, and the dying in the same light: as vulnerable groups in danger of being thought unequal to the rest of us."[96] Protection of the vulnerable, indeed, will often be another value. We should know ourselves well enough by now as human beings "to recognize that people . . . cannot be trusted with the right to kill other people, especially people who are socially devalued."[97]

CONCLUSION

To sum up this entire chapter in a brief span: we should love Creation, both Jews and Palestinians, the unborn and their parents, and those who are suicidal (or vulnerable to persuasion in that direction). This does not and cannot mean that we agree with all that our neighbors say or do. It also does not and cannot mean that we take no steps to prevent them from harming themselves or each other; nor does it absolve us from urging society at large to do the same.

DISCUSSION QUESTIONS RELATING TO CHAPTER 18

1. Campaigns are currently under way in various parts of the world to guarantee a child's legal right to choose its own gender on the basis of its intuitions about what its gender identity "really is," and to opt for drug treatment and surgery to make this a reality. How should Christians respond?
2. It has become widely accepted all over the world in recent decades that same-sex relationships are natural for many people, or at least that people who wish to engage in them as a matter of choice have a right to do so. How should Christians respond?

18

Who Am I?

Questions of Identity

*This question . . . suggests that there is actually a plausible answer. Almost as if
our being were a fixed thing . . . The irony is that the more you seek to identify who
you are, the more fragile you are likely to feel about yourself . . . Our identity should be
seen as an ongoing process.*[1]

Mel Schwartz

Identity is a complex phenomenon. Many people appear to believe that it is
fundamentally an "internal" reality—a fixed, stable, entity within the body that
individuals are capable of discovering and naming by empirical means or have
already "found." However, the truth is that "to the degree that identity is not biological (and much, but not all of it is), then it's a drama enacted in the world of
other people."[2] It is in various ways a social product, substantially shaped (if not
determined) by environment, such that we live in a world that is about "I am (in
community), therefore I think," as much as "I think (individually), therefore I
am."[3] Identity is "a set of complex compromises between the individual and society as to how the former and the latter might mutually support one another in
a sustainable, long-term manner."[4] It is a *goal* as much as anything else, involving
"efforts [that] can produce results."[5] Identity *can* be focused "on the past—what
used to be true of one, [and] the present—what is true of one now." However, it
can also be focused on "the future—the person one expects or wishes to become,
the person one feels obligated to try to become, or the person one fears one may
become."[6] Identity shapes behavior, but behavior in turn also shapes identity,

whether in establishing the status quo or opening up the possibility of a different future.

Identity is not, therefore, an individually determined, fixed reality, but a "plastic" reality that is socially constructed in very significant ways. This is especially true among the young, and it is directly related to the great plasticity of their brains themselves, which get wired and rewired through experience, including group experience, as they develop: "brains change over time depending what they do, and what they are made to do."[7] Yet it also remains possible for *adults* to make choices about behavior that impact their identity. Therapists depend on this very reality, for example, in dealing with people who identify as addicts, whether we are speaking of alcohol, drug, or sex addiction. It may be true for such a person that "I am an addict," but it is possible through daily choices, in the midst of strong community support, to progress to "I am a clean addict," and sometimes to a situation in which the power of the addiction over one's life is significantly reduced or even removed.

All of this is widely known among professionals in the relevant fields of study, and it has seeped out in various ways into the world at large. This is why we so routinely find comments on the Internet of the kind that appears in our epigraph above (from a psychotherapist). Here is another, from a clinical psychologist: "we have to realize that identity is the furthest thing from being fixed."[8] Another blogger complains that in current debates about immigration "we end up making identity seem like something that is set in stone."[9] Still another refers disparagingly to the high profile given to "individual identity . . . in western psychology," much of which "is about the individualised self with a supposedly fixed identity."[10]

This provides us with important background as we consider our last two "hot-button" issues in this section of the book: transgenderism and same-sex sexual relationships.

ON SEX AND GENDER

Transgenderism is perhaps the most volatile issue facing Christians in many countries at the present time. In addressing it, we must first of all be clear about what increasing numbers of people now mean by the English word "gender." They no longer use it, in accordance with historical practice from the early fifteenth century until relatively recently, as a synonym for "sex." It is often the case, instead, that "sex" refers to biological reality, while "gender" refers to social or cultural distinctions *rather than* biological ones.[11] It is in line with this distinction that *Merriam-Webster* defines a transgender person as one "whose gender identity differs from the sex the person had or was identified as having at birth."[12] "Gender identity" (as defined in the same dictionary) is in turn "a person's internal sense of being male, female, some combination of male and female, or neither male nor female."[13] From both definitions taken together we deduce that the term "transgender" applies to those who have an "internal sense" that their true identity differs from their birth identity as indicated by their sex.

BODY MATTERS

In the interests of further clarity we must also consider some facts of biology, not least so that we understand the phrasing "or was identified as having" in the above definition, which may well strike the reader as curious. Is it not true, as Scripture already teaches us, that human offspring are either male or female: "God created mankind in his own image, in the image of God he created them; male and female he created them. God blessed them and said to them, 'Be fruitful and increase in number; fill the earth and subdue it'" (Gen. 1:27–28)? If so, what does it mean that in some cases babies have had their sex "identified" by someone?

The reason is not that "the attending obstetrician recorded whichever sex first came to mind."[14] It is instead that in a very small number of cases newborn babies possess a reproductive or sexual anatomy that in relation to the great majority of people is unusual. For example, some individuals are born with "congenital adrenal hyperplasia," a rare condition in which the baby "can have an enlarged clitoris at birth (sometimes very penis-like), due to high levels of androgen hormones in the womb."[15] Such persons used to be regarded as suffering from "disorders of sex development" (DSDs); more recently, and not least because of controversy surrounding whether or when surgical interventions should occur to "correct" a perceived biological "problem," the term "intersex" has increasingly been adopted.

The statistics relating to intersex persons vary depending on where exactly one sets the boundaries of "unusual" in respect of the reproductive or sexual anatomy, but even including "not very unusual at all," it appears that they make up no more than 0.37 percent of the population.[16] It is important to understand this, since the intersex phenomenon is the basis for the commonly repeated claim nowadays that "sex is not binary." In a 2018 op-ed in the *New York Times*, for example, Anne Fausto-Sterling, the Nancy Duke Lewis Professor of Biology and Gender Studies at Brown University in the USA, argued that "[t]wo sexes have never been enough to describe human variety ... It has long been known that there is no single biological measure that unassailably places each and every human into one of two categories—male or female."[17] At most, however, this would only demonstrate that sex is not *entirely* binary, but only mainly so. In actuality, however, as Alex Byrne (Head of the Department of Linguistics and Philosophy at the Massachusetts Institute of Technology) has noted in a response to Fausto-Sterling's essay, even in the most unusual cases, where persons are born with both female and male "elements" to their biology (0.015 percent of the population), "they usually fall within the female/male binary, and ... no one clearly falls beyond it"; "there are no clear and uncontroversial examples of humans who are neither female nor male."[18] That is to say, whatever the atypical nature of their biology in some respects, such persons are designed to produce entirely different "gametes"—large female and small male reproductive cells capable of uniting with those of the opposite sex in sexual reproduction.[19] As evolutionary biologist Colin Wright confirms:

> [W]hile there is evidence for the fluidity of sex in many organisms, this is simply not the case in humans. We can acknowledge the existence of very rare cases in humans where sex is ambiguous, but this does not negate the reality that sex in humans is functionally binary . . . the final result of sex development in humans are unambiguously male or female over 99.98 percent of the time.[20]

Writing of the popular contemporary idea "that the very notion of *biological sex* . . . is a social construct," he says this: "As a biologist, it is hard to understand how anyone could believe something so outlandish. It's a belief on a par with the belief in a flat Earth."

In sum, sex *is* fundamentally binary, from a biological point of view. This corresponds to what Scripture also teaches us. Like the human dominion over Creation that is also described in Genesis 1:28 (see our chapter 15), it is a matter not only of Scriptural teaching but also of empirical evidence. As people who ought to be committed to facts in general (see the comments on global warming in chapter 17), Christians should also be committed to this fact in particular, even while being equally committed to ensuring the well-being of all those who are unusual in terms of their biology. The world can be a very cruel place for people who are "different" in terms of accepted norms of any kind, whether biological or cultural, and no Christian should contribute to the cruelty. We have a duty of care to all of God's image bearers—that is, all human beings. This is itself an excellent reason, however, for holding on to evidence concerning what is true rather than turning aside from it. Falsehood has never helped anyone in the end.[21]

IN THE WRONG BODY

Most intersex people self-identify in accordance with their given biology, and they are not, therefore, "transgender." If they choose at some point to have surgery—since surgery on intersex persons who are too young to consent is now increasingly frowned upon—they do so in order to conform their bodies more closely to its typical male or female form. What is distinctive about a *transgender* person, on the other hand, is the feeling that he or she has been born into the wrong body.

GENDER DYSPHORIA

The currently approved technical term for this is "gender dysphoria," where "dysphoria" refers to significant unhappiness (just as "euphoria" refers to its opposite).

"Gender dysphoria" involves, then, "significant distress and/or problems functioning associated with [a] conflict between the way [people] feel and think of . . . their physical or assigned gender."[22] This condition, too—just like the intersex condition—was widely described by medical professionals until very recently as a disorder: "gender identity disorder," according to the fourth version of the *Diagnostic and Statistical Manual of Mental Disorders (DSM-4-TR)*.[23] This language, although not the associated thought, was altered in *DSM-5* (2013) out of a desire to avoid stigmatizing people by attributing to them a "disorder," while still ensuring that they did not lose access to health care. It is important to emphasize the language in *DSM-5* of "significant distress" or "impairment in major areas of functioning, such as social relationships, school, or home life," without which the manual will not allow a diagnosis of gender dysphoria to be made. The mere fact, for example, that a preschool child sometimes dresses up in clothes typically worn by the opposite sex as part of his or her play does not count; this is a common aspect of child development.

THE TRANSGENDER COMMUNITY

Some of the persons who experience this "significant distress" seek to hide it, and they go on living outwardly in accordance not only with their biological sex, but also with the expectations of their culture concerning the behavior appropriate to males and female (for example, in terms of clothing choices). Others deal with it by strongly defining the essential self, at least for a time, over against biology; this includes some children, who may (for example) express a strong dislike of their sexual anatomy. It is important to emphasize "at least for a time," however, since given appropriate care (and we shall come back to this point) "only a small number of children with gender dysphoria will continue to have symptoms in later adolescence or adulthood,"[24] and some people testify to the disappearance of dysphoria even after it has been part of life for decades.[25] In others in the transgender community, gender dysphoria persists for a considerable time, and in some of these cases the decision is taken to "transition" biologically, as far as possible, to the preferred sex.

In the case of prepubescent children this can involve the administration of puberty-blocking drugs, typically between ten and twelve years of age at the present time. At an older age it will involve hormone therapy, and then surgery in order to make the body more like a man's (a female to male transition, or "FtM") or more like a woman's ("MtF")—"drastic treatments" that in the past have been delayed until the late teens at the earliest, precisely because by that point "doctors can be much more confident in making a diagnosis of gender dysphoria."[26] The treatments are drastic because, while many of the effects of hormone therapy may be reversible if people stop taking the hormones, it all depends how long they have been engaging in the treatment. Some aspects (e.g., breast growth and possible sterility in MtFs) are not reversible at all.[27] Surgeries like double mastectomies in FtMs are also irreversible.[28] And although some professionals claim that after such treatments "most trans women and men are happy with their new sex and feel comfortable with their gender identity," others concede that "feelings of distress may continue" afterwards.[29] The variable reports no doubt have something to do with how long after the surgery the reporting occurs, since the fact is that after the initial "relief afforded by transition, hormones, and surgery," many transitioned transgender people find themselves with serious, ongoing physical, social, and psychological problems (as discussed at length by Dr. Stephen Levine).[30] Among the many personal testimonies that confirm this reality is that of Walt Heyer, a biological male who lived as "Laura Jensen" for eight years. He describes the way in which his own MtF transition initially made him "giddy with excitement" but soon led to renewed gender dysphoria, deeply suicidal thoughts, and ultimately to de-transitioning.[31] We should also mention here the heart-rending FtM testimony toward the end of the 2017 BBC documentary *Transgender Kids: Who Knows Best?*[32]

EXCLUSION AND SUPPRESSION

It is important to emphasize that *all* those who suffer from gender dysphoria are part of the "transgender community." There is a very unfortunate tendency among the "transitioned" in that community, and among those who are keen to support them, to claim the term only for themselves. Surprisingly for people who may themselves not have been listened to and may even have been abused, they quite deliberately exclude both those who have chosen not to transition, as well as those who have de-transitioned. They seek to ridicule their testimony and suppress their voices; the abuse suffered by the de-transitioned can be particularly severe.[33] One excellent example of the impulse toward suppression is the successful pressure brought to bear in Canada on the Canadian Broadcasting Corporation not to air the BBC documentary mentioned above. The purpose of all this behavior appears to be to create a climate of opinion in which it becomes self-evident to the majority in the surrounding culture that there is only one way—their own way—of rightly interpreting and properly "handling" gender dysphoria. They are well on their way to succeeding in this goal in Canada, even though their convictions on this point rest on what our preceding discussion in this chapter suggests is a weak foundational idea: that people attesting to the condition, including very young children, are necessarily testifying thereby to a fixed internal "identity," to which the external body *must*, rightly, conform. The testimony of the de-transitioned leads of course in a very different direction, cautioning that treating persons "suffering from gender identity issues as if they really were persons of the opposite sex only serves to lead those that are suffering with such issues away from finding the serenity and wholeness of being at peace with their bodies and identities."[34]

A CHRISTIAN RESPONSE TO TRANSGENDERISM

In framing a response to transgenderism that is consistent with biblical faith, we need to recognize that this is not an issue where we shall be able to quote particular biblical texts that go directly to its heart. The Bible simply does not speak explicitly about transgenderism as such.[35] If Scripture is to be "useful" to us in this case (as in the case of, say, abortion), it will need to be on the basis of what it teaches us more generally about relevant matters, as we seek as Christ-followers to "live out of" our Story.

SOME FUNDAMENTALS

Here we must return to some fundamentals of biblical faith that were first introduced in chapter 1—and these same fundamentals will inform our upcoming discussion of same-sex sexual relationships later in the present chapter. How do we know what is good? The answer is that God reveals himself to us so that we begin to understand who he is and what goodness looks like. The Bible itself plays a central role in this divine revelation. Goodness should not be defined in the end by family, tribe, culture, or state. Most importantly for this present chapter, goodness should not be defined by what is said to be instinctually and behaviorally "natural" to human beings—whether this is a claim about human beings in general or about the individual in particular. Biblical faith teaches us, in fact, that each one of us individually, as well as communities of people collectively, possesses a variety of instincts or desires that need to be *ignored* in pursuit of what is right. To quote again Christopher Kaczor (last encountered in our chapter 17), as he criticizes the view that *personhood itself* is defined by "desire" for existence: "What we desire can be insane, tyrannical, unjust, uninformed, sexist, or racist."[36] To identify what is "natural" to us, then, is not thereby to ascertain what is right, since to discover an "is" is not yet to establish an "ought"—even if in fact we could "discover," in a reasonably objective manner, what the "is" might be. Modern people tend to be very optimistic about their capacities in this latter regard, but Scripture is not, because it holds that in our fallen condition "the heart [our inner person, including the mind] is deceitful above all things and beyond cure. Who can understand it?" (Jer. 17:9).

In biblical faith, then, we do not possess twenty-twenty vision when it comes to understanding reality, including our own internal reality. We need help from God, by way of his revelation, if we are to see things clearly, both in terms of who we really are and how we ought to live. It follows from this, before we even get to matters of sex and gender, that Christ-followers are bound by the terms of their discipleship, in determining what is good and right, to reject *any* argument presented by their culture that prioritizes what is said to be "natural" to us over what God has revealed to us. Indeed, at the point at which a Christian accepts that his or her internal sense of the self (for example) is the decisive factor in defining how he or she is to live, that person has actually given up on being a Christ-follower, subject to Jesus' lordship, and has become someone else. This is not so much a criticism as simply a statement of fact. Biblical faith teaches us that our feelings are not a reliable guide in the pursuit of a good life and will certainly often lead us astray. To reject this teaching is to reject the canon of Scripture that Christ himself has provided for us in order that we can "measure" our lives and discover if they are good. Followers of Christ are obliged to prioritize the divine imperatives in Scripture over everything else—even if others choose to ignore them. This is, incidentally, one of the reasons why it is entirely wrong-headed to suggest that matters of sex and gender are "secondary" matters in the Church that should not be permitted to fracture Christian unity—a fairly common aspect of contemporary Christian discourse, unfortunately. It is absolutely *not* a secondary matter to substitute a non-Christian for a Christian way of thinking about how we discover the nature of the good in any area of our lives.

GOD, SEX, AND GENDER

What, then, has God revealed in Scripture about sex and gender? Beginning at the beginning of the Story in Genesis 1–2, we read that God created human beings "male and female"—two clearly differentiated sexes designed neverthe- less to complement each other (Gen. 1:27–28). The difference and the comple- mentarity somehow reflect a difference and yet complementarity within God himself: we are created in two distinct sexes that together "image" God. This is our first "identity marker" from a biblical point of view, and one that will never change over time: we are image bearers. As such, we are created in order to procreate, as "a man leaves his father and mother and is united to his wife, and they become one flesh" (2:24). Sex is in fact intrinsically bound up with the formation of *family* by the said male and female—their response to the divine command to humanity in general that it should "be fruitful and increase in number" (1:28). In the biblical Story that follows, however, sex is not viewed in a purely functional way. The intrinsic beauty and joy of sexual intimacy is celebrated, for example, in a book like the Song of Songs.[37] Sexual intercourse is certainly *bound up* with procreation, but that is not all that must be said about it. Companionship is also an important emphasis in Genesis 2, for "it is not good for the man to be alone" (2:18).

The NT picks up this Genesis material directly when it speaks of our lives as sexual beings—as we would expect it to do when dealing with God's creational law. The union of a man and a woman in marriage is compared to Christ's relationship with the Church (Eph. 5:21–33, quoting Gen. 2:24)—an inviolate and permanent bond "as long as they both shall live." The NT strictly prohibits violation of this bond, whether through divorce (Matt. 19:1–8), adultery (Matt. 5:27–28), or prostitution (1 Cor. 6:12–20), or even through what we spend our time *thinking* about (Matt. 5:27–28). In all of this, it is the vision of Genesis 1–2 that is fundamental to the articulation of NT teaching.

In none of this biblical material is there a basis for the idea that any "gender" exists that is not connected intrinsically to a person's God-created biological sex. There are men and there are women, created as such by God. It is, of course, true that in Scripture, as in life, persons of each sex express their masculinity and femininity in a diversity of ways (e.g., in culturally specific ways). This is an important thing to say, especially in light of the pronounced tendency in a considerable amount of Church culture, historically, to insist that "proper" expressions of masculinity and femininity occur only within very narrowly drawn lines; we saw this illustrated, for example, in chapter 13. Concerning the question of what it means, biblically, to be a "real" woman and a "real" man, we must certainly think more critically than has often been the case in the past.[38] Scripture gives us no reason at all, however, to interpret such diversity of expression as evidence of the existence of multiple genders that can be dissociated from biological sex. Biblical faith holds that there are two genders (and not, for example, eighty-one).[39] We may well feel otherwise, in our "empire of desire"; a considerable number of people nowadays, especially younger people, say that they do. Scripture gives us no reason to believe that such feelings are a reliable guide, however, as to what is actually true.

In the particular case that we are currently discussing, Scripture also gives us no reason to believe that the "true" identity of any human born with a male body is in reality female, or vice versa. Again, some people feel otherwise—as we have seen, they possess (at least for a time) an internal sense that their true identity differs from their given biological sex. Neither the OT nor the NT, however, offers any support for the notion that *these* feelings are a reliable guide to what is actually true. Nor does Scripture provide us with any foundation for the engineering of our given bodies so as to make them more like those of the opposite sex. As we already saw in chapter 17, our bodies are not our own to do with just as we like: "you are not your own; you were bought at a price" (1 Cor. 6:19–20).

Until very recently the vast majority of people living in countries within what was formerly Christendom, whether or not they read their Bibles very much, would themselves have given very little credence to any claim about an individual's "true identity" that did not match up with his or her physical, biological form.

Christopher Kaczor depends on this fact in developing his argument against Giubilini and Minerva's thesis concerning personhood (chapter 17). He criticizes their "body-self dualism," whereby my body is not really my "self," but instead "I" am the sum of my aims, desires, and awareness. We recall his argument that, on this view, one human being with dissociative identity disorder is actually sixteen persons, and every person has a right to live. This seems to most people, he suggests, implausible, since among other things it makes the successful psychiatrist into a mass murderer—the killer of fifteen "persons." What is "plausible" to people depends, however, on context. To many people nowadays, the idea that a person's true identity is "internal" to them and may have little to do with that person's bodily form, is actually self-evidently correct. Our current situation is already predicted by a letter that I read in the *Vancouver Sun* in 2000, in which a sixteen-year-old girl opined that "on the Internet you don't have to have a name, you don't have to have a body or a gender, you can be truly yourself." It is our modern version of the ancient Gnosticism that was first described in our chapter 2 and mentioned again in chapter 15.

THE DISORDERED (CHRISTIAN) LIFE

Rejecting the heresy of Gnosticism (as he or she must), the orthodox Christian is obliged also to reject the idea that his or her "gender identity" is determined by an "internal sense of being male, female, some combination of male and female, or neither male nor female."[40] In line with this, transgender "transitioning" must also be rejected as a legitimate Christian life-choice. So how *are* we to deal with the very real and distressing condition of gender dysphoria?

There is no reason to think that we ought to depart from the general biblical answer pertaining to *any* aspect of our lives where we find our experience currently in tension with, or even at odds with, God's calling to holiness. Biblical faith teaches us that we live in a good but disordered world—that in all sorts of ways the divine order of Creation has been negatively impacted by the poor moral choices of human beings in the past and at the present time. Each of us inherits this disorder, and also adds to it. This is our second identity marker: we are not only image bearers but *fallen* image bearers. This, too, will not change through time, until we arrive at its end. One set of resulting disorders, in the midst of many, relates to sex and gender. In fact, in the first chapter of his letter to the Romans, Paul identifies these particular disorders as high-ranking ones—implicitly, this is precisely because they concern core "identity" issues. These disorders follow on immediately from idolatry, and they lead on subsequently to other serious deviations from God's creational law (Rom. 1:18–32). That being said, "there is no one righteous, not even one" (3:10); we are all disordered in multiple ways. Gender dysphoria is just one example of such disordering, and as such it is equally accurate to name it "gender identity disorder." Perhaps this description might not even have become so widely regarded as problematic if it had not been contrasted with "normal" but instead described as "one example of the universally disordered human condition." If there is indeed "stigma" to be attached to "disorders," then it must be attached to us all—but in fact, there should *be* no stigma attached to aspects of our lives over which we have no direct control, whether these be physical, mental, or emotional in nature.

So how are we *generally* to deal with aspects of our Christian lives where we find our experience currently in tension with God's calling to holiness? Recognizing that as Christ-followers we are still "in process" on our journey through life and that, like Paul in Philippians 3:12–14, we have not

> already arrived at [our] goal, [but we] press on to take hold of that for which Christ Jesus took hold of [us] . . . Forgetting what is behind and straining toward what is ahead, [we] press on toward the goal to win the prize for which God has called [us] heavenward in Christ Jesus.

Here is our third identity marker: we are not only fallen image bearers, but we are "in Christ Jesus" and on our way toward a "goal." This is the biblical version of the general idea mentioned in the introduction to this chapter, that identity can be focused on "the future—the person one expects or wishes to become." That journey requires "others who endorse and reinforce one's selfhood, who scaffold a sense that one's self matters and that one's efforts can produce results."[41] The Christian journey requires precisely this as well: we should not try to undertake it alone. We need a community of like-minded and like-committed friends around us (a church) to whom we can speak honestly about our struggles in the sure knowledge that they will listen to us, cry with us, encourage us, and support us in remaining on the right path, even when it is very difficult to walk. Depending on what the issue is, and how severe it is, we may well need specialist counselling that is both competent and at least consistent with a Christian way of looking at the world. This will require some careful research, since some counselling (Christian or not) is of a poor quality and can be very damaging, some non-Christian counselling is greatly in tension with fundamental Christian beliefs, and not even all "Christian" counselling is truly grounded in the Christian Story or has Christian goals firmly in mind.

As we move along in our journey with our friends in Christ and others who can genuinely help us, we can expect that over the course of time—this is the testimony of the Church throughout the ages—we shall find some of our many "disorders" becoming easier to manage and even ceasing to cause us much difficulty at all. We can also expect, however, that some of them will remain a challenge to us until the end of our earthly lives. Biblical faith is not a "quick fix" faith, as Paul himself reminds us (mercifully) in referencing his famous thorn in his flesh in 2 Corinthians 12:7–8: "a messenger of Satan, to torment me." Some Christians are only ever one drink away from falling back into alcohol addiction, one Netflix movie away from turning back to pornography, and one marital argument away from deep depression. Some are like the main character (analogously, not literally) in the movie *A Beautiful Mind* who, suffering from paranoid schizophrenia, must learn to ignore continually other people in the room whom he "sees" as real, and yet whom he knows, in his right mind, are not really there. We need to learn to ignore what seems intuitively obvious in favor of what we trust to be true.

CHRISTIANS AND GENDER DYSPHORIA

In the case of gender dysphoria in particular, then, Christians should certainly not hide from others the unhappiness and even the "significant distress" that we experience as a result of our condition. We really must share this unhappiness and distress with other trusted people in our community, looking for their friendship and support in the midst of it, and we would be wise also to seek good Christian counselling that will help us to make progress in understanding and managing our condition. Perhaps we may even be able ultimately to move beyond our gender dysphoria; certainly some have testified to that reality.[42] This will not necessarily be the case, however, and then our hope must lie, as with so much in the Christian life, not in healing in this life but in the resurrection of the body and the life of the world to come.

If this is indeed the right pathway through life for Christian *adults* suffering from gender dysphoria, then of course this will have a very great influence on how we respond to our *children* if they display symptoms that are consistent with the condition. They, too, must be encouraged to talk openly to us about their feelings, and also to other trusted adults, including (again) trusted health professionals. The question of "trust" is particularly crucial here, however, precisely because identity is forged in community. Parents must therefore do their research and be absolutely confident that the adults recruited to help (teachers, perhaps, and doctors) will not be overly compromised by an ideology that is not consistent with Christian values. Unfortunately, it may become increasingly challenging in the near future to find such adults, for reasons we shall discuss in chapter 19. One way of getting some perspective on what professionals are advising us is to find a networking group for parents whose experiences have led them to see the *dangers* involved in certain kinds of professional advice that they now regret having followed.[43]

In any case our children must certainly be listened to, taken seriously, and within reason accommodated, in the hope that in the course of time through love, good communication, and effective counselling they will prove to be among the majority of children whose symptoms of gender dysphoria disappear by the onset of puberty. I say "within reason," because of course Christian parents ought still to believe what most parents have believed until very recently: that just because children, in their assertion that their gender is opposite to their biological sex, are "persistent, consistent, and insistent" about it—the kind of language that appears in much contemporary advice concerning the diagnosis of gender dysphoria— this does not mean that these claims should simply be conceded to.[44] When our children reach adulthood, of course, they will need to make their own decisions about how to handle their lives, and we can only hope and pray that by that point they will be well-prepared to make decisions in line with Christian faith rather than otherwise, continuing to honor God with their bodies because their identity is *first* in Christ before it is anywhere else.

SAME-SEX ATTRACTION

The strong predisposition of many people in contemporary culture to privilege the "internal sense" of the self above everything else in deciding how to live one's life is evident in matters not only of gender identity but also of sexual relation- ships. Here the "internal sense" relates not to whether one is "really" male or female but rather to the question of desired sexual partners *as* a male or a female. An important aspect of this question concerns a person's perception of his or her "sexual orientation": "a person's sexual identity or self-identification as bisexual, heterosexual, homosexual, pansexual, etc."[45] In this section of chapter 18 we are concerned only with the question of a desire for a sexual relationship with some- one of the same sex (same-sex attraction) and its implications for the actions that might follow on from this desire.

THE GAY COMMUNITY

People who find themselves with same-sex attraction often refer to themselves as "gay," and this is also the terminology that I shall use in this chapter, while recognizing the fraught complexity of our contemporary linguistic environment in such matters. The gay community, like the transgender community, is a broad one. It includes people who have experienced same-sex attraction for as long as they can remember, going back into early childhood, as well as others who had no such feelings until they were well into adulthood.[46] Some of these peo- ple have sought to hide their feelings and have gone on living outwardly as if they do not experience them, sometimes for the whole of their lives. Some have dealt with their feelings by "coming out" as gay, and this has increasingly been the case, at increasingly younger ages, as many of the societies comprising the "empire of desire" (Reno's words from earlier) have become more accepting of same-sex attraction and also of same-sex sexual relationships and have legalized gay sex, and more recently same-sex marriage. "Coming out" as gay does not necessarily mean, however, that people enter into gay sexual relationships. Some have chosen to remain celibate, and some have married a person of the *opposite* sex and had a family with that person, even though they are predominantly attracted to persons of the *same* sex.

Nor does entry into a gay sexual relationship necessarily mean that a person will always, ever after, experience sexual attraction for people of the same rather than the opposite sex. The evidence suggests, to the contrary, that this aspect of people's perceived and confessed "identity" is not necessarily any more stable over time than others. A 2002 study already suggested, for example, that "women's sexuality and sexual orientation are potentially fluid, changeable over time, and variable across social contexts."[47] A 2011 article confirms such findings and adds that "there is evidence that male sexual attractions and behaviors can also be fluid."[48] A 2016 study categorically states that "arguments based on the immutability of sexual orientation are unscientific, given what we now know from longitudinal, population-based studies of naturally occurring changes in the same-sex attractions of some individuals over time."[49] A still more recent academic study suggests that, "far from being a fixed preference . . . sexual identity and attraction undergo extensive and often subtle changes throughout a person's life, continuing long past adolescence and into adulthood, with women showing slightly more fluidity than men.[50] Since this is true even of those who have entered into gay sexual relationships and have thereby through experience participated in "wiring" their brains in that direction, it is not surprising that some people who at one time experienced same-sex attraction but *never* entered into a gay sexual relationship have reported that they no longer experience such attraction. That is, they report that their "sexual identity" has undergone "extensive . . . changes" in the course of their lives.[51] Among other things, "the formation of [new] emotional attachments may facilitate unexpected changes in sexual desire."[52]

SEXUAL ORIENTATION

This does all raise a question, of course, about what we might properly mean by referring to a gay "sexual orientation" (or for that matter *any* sexual orientation). Clearly this terminology does *not* refer necessarily to a stable, unchangeable feature of a person's life. A particular instance of it may in fact be a passing phase in one's life, whether it is experienced by a younger or an older person. And this leaves to one side the important additional question as to whether in a highly sexualized culture people might not in any case entirely misunderstand their feelings of "attraction" for another person, perhaps confusing admiration or a desire for intimate friendship (for example) with sex. This is one respect in

which Hollywood in general, and the pornography industry in particular, have
been wildly successful. They have managed to create a language for our feelings
whose purpose is (in George Orwell's words in 1984) "to narrow the range of
thought"—a general reality and not one pertaining specifically to the gay community. Being human, in that dysfunctional world, is "all about sex." We shall return
to 1984 in chapter 19.

For the moment, we simply need to register this important point: that in
spite of what is commonly stated in public discourse at the present time, and
reinforced by recent movies like *The Miseducation of Cameron Post* (2018) and
Boy Erased (2018)—that sexual orientation is fixed and immutable—the evidence
suggests otherwise.[53] Nor are proactive attempts to change it, once routinely
described by the acronym SOCE (sexual orientation change efforts), necessarily
"misguided, cruel, and psychologically disastrous"—another common belief of
our time.[54] Even the 2009 American Psychological Association (APA) report on
appropriate therapeutic responses to sexual orientation, which was produced by a
highly unrepresentative group of psychologists (and one psychiatrist)[55] who were
certainly not advocates of "psychological interventions to change sexual orientation," was only prepared to state in opposition to them that "there is insufficient
evidence to support [their] use."[56] Noting that "[r]ecent research reports indicate
that there are individuals who perceive they have been harmed and others who
perceive they have benefited from nonaversive SOCE," the report says this:

> Early and recent research studies provide no clear indication of the prevalence
> of harmful outcomes among people who have undergone efforts to change their
> sexual orientation or the frequency of occurrence of harm . . . we cannot conclude
> how likely it is that harm will occur from SOCE. However, studies from both
> periods indicate that attempts to change sexual orientation may cause or exacer-
> bate distress and poor mental health in *some individuals* [my emphasis], including
> depression and suicidal thoughts.[57]

The term "nonaversive" is important. It intends to distance activities like counselling, prayer, visualization, social skills training, and psychoanalytic therapy, from
"aversive" treatments that most people nowadays would find unacceptable. These
include electric shock treatment and the administration of nausea-inducing
drugs accompanied by the presentation of homoerotic stimuli. As to nonaversive
SOCE, the report tells us, there is testimony to both positive and negative outcomes. It is unfortunate that it is the testimony only of the harmed individuals
that appears to be influencing contemporary discussion about SOCE, and with
great effect. The positive testimony of many others as to the benefit they derived
from these efforts *at least to some extent*, if it is known at all, is simply not taken
seriously.[58] Even the public statements of distinguished medical professionals are

ignored.[59] It is not that all or even most people with same-sex attraction can be "converted" (which is an unfortunate word to which we shall return in chapter 19). It is simply that, *evidently*, some change is possible at least for some people. Moreover, it is *evidently* the case (as the academic studies on this topic reveal) that exploring this possibility by way of nonaversive SOCE, whatever the outcome may be, is not necessarily, or even normally harmful.[60]

Suppression and Exclusion

This brings me naturally to my final point in this section of the chapter. As in the case of the transgender community, it is important to emphasize that *all* those described above who testify to experiencing same-sex attraction are rightly described as members of the "gay community." There is a tendency among particular sections of this community and those who are keen to support them—as with the transgender community—to claim the language only for themselves and to disparage or even abuse those who have made decisions about their way of life that are different from their own, including decisions to participate (happily) in SOCE. These moves are apparently motivated by a desire that these other gay narratives should not in any way undermine their own, specifically in relation to their strong belief that because same-sex attraction is natural to them, their gay sexual relationships are self-evidently right (and indeed inevitable). This attempt at exclusion should not be regarded as acceptable.

THE BIBLICAL PERSPECTIVE

We already covered, in reflecting on transgenderism, some of what needs to be said from a Christian point of view about same-sex attraction and relationships, specifically as it relates to how we discover what goodness looks like. We need to depend on what God has revealed to us through Scripture, and not on what is natural to us. What does the biblical Story tell us? Right at its beginning, in describing God's creation of human beings as "male and female" (Gen. 1:27–28), it describes also the context in which human sexual intercourse is designed by God to occur. It describes a particular kind of relationship—a marital relationship—*between* a male and a female, as "a man leaves his father and mother and is united to his wife, and they become one flesh" (2:24). Reproduction stands at the center of God's purposes here—sex is intrinsically bound up with the formation of *family*—although companionship is also an important emphasis (2:18). We already noted earlier how the NT picks up these same themes when it speaks of our lives as sexual beings, viewing the union of a man and a woman in marriage as reflecting Christ's relationship with the Church. Our male-female relationships are (or ought to be) about a lot more than sexual intercourse, of course, and in the future of God's kingdom this particular kind of intercourse will apparently play no part in these relationships at all.[61] When telling the great story of our humanity, orthodox Christian theology knows of only a limited role, in space and in time, for specifically *sexual* intercourse. That being said, *if* the question concerns the proper place for such intercourse in the here-and-now, Scripture is clear in its answer.

The Negative Implications

It is this positive Scriptural vision of sexual expression—what God is *for* rather than *against* in this area of our lives in our present world—that makes sense of what Scripture then has to say negatively about activities that fall outside of God's purposes in Creation. This is precisely why Scripture takes such a dim view of adultery, for example, which represents a fracturing of the covenant that a man and his wife make with each other. It is because of this positive vision that we also find texts forbidding people from committing sexual acts with animals (e.g., Lev. 18:23). Sexual intercourse is designed *for* a certain kind of relationship, and not for any others. Scripture reinforces this message again and again, both implicitly and explicitly, by providing us with many narrative examples where, for human beings who are alienated from God and fractured in their relationships with each other, sex has become a focal point of those realities. This part of the biblical Story begins with the violent Lamech, the first polygamist (Gen. 4:19–24), and moves onwards from there.

Much of the deviation from God's plan for sex that is reflected in the OT relates to male-female relationships, from which we may perhaps safely deduce that this was the most common kind of deviation that occurred in the world inhabited by the ancient Israelites—as is still the case nowadays. Old Testament Scripture is not silent, however, concerning the matter of people committing sexual acts with others of the same gender—acts that also depart, in their own way, from God's creational law. Consider Leviticus 18:22 and 20:13:

> Do not have sexual relations with a man as one does with a woman; that is detestable.

> If a man has sexual relations with a man as one does with a woman, both of them have done what is detestable.

Of course, since these texts are taken from Mosaic Torah, we must pause to ask the question we already asked of other aspects of Leviticus 18 in chapter 7: are these instructions reflective of God's creational law, representing certain aspects of the wisdom of the ages concerning sex, or are they more like the tithing regulations discussed in chapter 5, which were designed only for the Israelites in their

ancient context? As we saw in chapter 7, in the case of the "incest" elements of
Leviticus 18 a strong case can be made for the ongoing relevance of the passage in
the life of the Church, since the apostle Paul and others regard it precisely in this
way and base Christian ethical instruction upon it. The same is true in the case
of the "same-sex" element in this passage (and in Lev. 20). The Greek translation
of the OT that the NT apostles typically quoted in their letters uses a particular
vocabulary to represent the Hebrew text of Leviticus 18:22 and 20:13:

> Do not lie with a man [Gk. *meta arsenos*] as one lies [Gk. *koitēn*] with a woman.

> If a man lies with a man [Gk. *meta arsenos*] as one lies [Gk. *koitēn*] with a woman ...

This same language is reflected in both 1 Corinthians 6:9–10 and 1 Timothy 1:10.
In the former the wicked who "will not inherit the kingdom of God" include
"adulterers ... male prostitutes [and] *arsenokoitai*." In the latter, "the ungodly and
sinful" include "murderers ... adulterers and *arsenokoitai*." The Greek word *arse-
nokoitēs* here has been invented, possibly by Paul himself, precisely to refer to the
kind of activity referred to in Leviticus 18:22 and 20:13. It is clearly still a huge
problem, in the Church as in ancient Israel, when "a man lies with a man as one
lies with a woman." To persist in behaving in this way is to inhabit the part of the
human community that "will not inherit the kingdom of God."

THE FIRST CHAPTER OF ROMANS

What Paul has to say in these passages about sex is unsurprisingly consistent with
what he has to say in Romans 1:26–27. He notes here, in the context of describing
the rebellion of human beings against God and the consequences of that rebellion in idolatry and sexual perversion, that some women have "exchanged natural
sexual relations for unnatural ones" and that some men have likewise "abandoned
natural relations with women," becoming "inflamed with lust for one another."
That is, people have made up their own sexual rules rather than conforming
themselves to the will of the Creator, whose purpose for sex is that it should
be practiced within a permanent union of a man and a woman. Some modern
readers have tried to evade the force of this argument by maintaining that Paul
is not really writing about moral wrongdoing but only about ritual uncleanness,
which is not something with which Christians need any longer concern themselves. Yet Romans 1 begins by saying that "the wrath of God is being revealed
from heaven against all the godlessness and wickedness of people, who suppress
the truth by their wickedness" (1:18). When Paul later summarizes his foregoing
argument (3:9–11), he likewise writes about already having "made the charge that
Jews and Gentiles alike are all under the power of sin." The very terminology
found throughout Romans 1 clearly leads us in the same direction.[62] Humanity

has first generally, and then specifically and sexually, replaced truth with false-hood. Same-sex relations are contrary to the Creation order, and as such they are morally wrong, whether or not many people engage in them and (indeed) "also approve of those who practice them" (1:32).

There is, then, no uncertainty concerning what biblical faith has to say about sex in general, or about same-sex sexual relationships in particular. Scripture never affirms any form of sexual expression apart from that which occurs within the confines of a marital relationship between a man and woman. It often explic-itly condemns other forms of expression, whether heterosexual or homosexual. It is precisely the clarity of Scripture on such matters that has led the Church to an equal clarity in its traditional teaching pertaining to them, so that Scripture and tradition speak with one voice. If Christians are now departing from this teach-ing, it is not because Scripture has somehow become less clear but only because the general culture in various parts of the world—in the "empire of desire"—is currently speaking strongly in favor of different beliefs and practices based on another authority. Luke Timothy Johnson is candid on this point:

> I think it important to state clearly that we do, in fact, reject the straightforward commands of Scripture and appeal instead to another authority when we declare that same-sex unions can be holy and good. And what exactly is that authority? We appeal explicitly to the weight of our own experience and the experience thou-sands of others have witnessed to . . .[63]

CHRISTIANS AND SAME-SEX ATTRACTION

What are Christians to do, then, when they experience same-sex attraction? As in the case of gender dysphoria, there is no reason to think that we ought to depart from the general biblical answer pertaining to *any* aspect of our lives where we find our experience currently in tension with, or even at odds with, God's calling to holiness. Again, we have dealt with "the general biblical answer" already, so we may pass on. In the specific case of same-sex attraction, as with gender dysphoria, we really must share the reality of our lives, in the course of our repentant walk with Christ, with other trusted people in our Christian community so that we are not journeying alone. We would be wise also to seek good Christian counselling that will help us to make progress in understanding and managing our attraction. Perhaps we may even ultimately find that we no longer experience it. This will not necessarily be the case, however.[64] If this is true for us, then as with any other aspect of our "disordered lives," our hope must lie not in healing in this life but in the resurrection of the body and the life of the world to come. Our children, too, must be encouraged to talk openly to us about their same-sex attraction, as well as to other trusted adults, in the hope that in the course of time, when they reach adulthood, they will be able to make good decisions about how to handle their own lives in line with Christian faith rather than otherwise.

ON LOVE AND BOUNDARIES

Looking back on the whole chapter, then: Christians are called to deal with gender dysphoria and same-sex attraction in more or less the same way, in the context of the biblical Story that tells us who we are and where we are going. It is this Story that provides us with the fundamental, unchanging truths about our identity that we need for our life's journey in community. Our intuitions and feelings, even if they are persistent, provide us with no reliable guidance concerning the nature of the good life.

The Protection of the Flock

Many Christians who either are or have previously been gender dysphoric or same-sex attracted have walked, or are now walking, on the countercultural path that is mapped out by Scripture in this way, although their own testimony about their lives, including their feelings, is often ignored in a climate that is generally hostile to it and to them. They love God and his commandments, and they live accordingly.[65] We need to affirm them strongly and offer them as much support and friendship as we can in our Christian communities, not least because they are often very vulnerable people. It may be that they have never acted on the feelings relating to sex and gender with which they have struggled. It may be that they have acted on them, perhaps with tragic consequences for soul and body. Either way, we need to love them, as an absolute Christian duty.[66]

We are of course called to love all of our neighbors; but we are not called to *affirm* all that they say and do. To the contrary, love often involves disagreeing with what others say, or disapproving of what they do. It may involve actively resisting what they say (including how they interpret their feelings) and what they do (because of how they feel). We cannot with integrity accept the dangerous and illiberal idea that has come to dominate so much Western culture in this and other matters, virtually as core dogma: "it's morally wrong (and unloving) to say or do anything that hurts my feelings."[67] Nor does love require that we *support and befriend* all of our neighbors equally. The primary duty of the Church is to offer support to Christ-followers, including those suffering from gender dysphoria and same-sex attraction, as they faithfully seek to follow their Lord in body as well as soul. Our primary duty is to ensure that these disciples are part of a deep-friendship community that will offer them not only help but also accountability structures. Contrary to much current opinion, it is *not* a primary duty of the

Church to provide a hospitable, welcoming community for those who have made a committed decision to head off in a different direction (note, e.g., 2 John 10–11).

We must certainly love these other neighbors as God loves them (which includes hoping and working for their repentance). But we cannot love them at the expense of the neighbors who are following the right and often painfully difficult path (perhaps in the aftermath of having lived quite differently), and certainly not at the expense of our own children who are being shaped by the Christian community of which they are members. The first duty of the shepherds of the Church is to look after and protect the flock, especially the lambs (John 10:1–18; 21:15–19; Acts 20:28–31; 1 Pet. 5:1–4). And this necessitates that our Christian communities possess firm boundaries, with the sheep on the inside and everyone else on the outside.

The Plural Society

What does our broader love for neighbor entail, outside these boundaries? If my readers still agree with me that Christians should be principled political liberals, advocating and working for a free society, then they ought also to agree (I propose) that our adult fellow citizens ought to have the freedom both to believe that their internal sense of gender identity or sexual orientation is an infallible guide to who they really are and to act on this belief in their decision-making about how they live, within the bounds of respect also for their neighbors' freedoms. We may hold their belief to be false, on both biblical and empirical grounds, and we may consider their consequent actions to be unwise—but that is another matter. Insofar as their adult freedoms do not impinge significantly on the freedoms of others, a free society must seek to protect them. This is part of what it means to love our neighbors, even if they consider themselves to be our enemies. We hope, in return, for a reciprocal recognition of our Christian freedom to believe what we hold to be true about both sex and gender, and to live in consistency with these beliefs.

What does this mean in terms of the kinds of law that Christians might support or oppose, when advocating in the public square? It certainly means that we ought to support the introduction or maintenance of legal protections for gay and transgendered people of the kinds that other citizens enjoy. This further implies, I propose, the acceptance of the legal recognition of a committed one-to-one same-sex relationship of a kind analogous to a Christian marriage. This is not because Christians can rightly recognize it as a marriage, for the very definition of marriage in biblical faith forbids it. The orthodox position on this matter is often caricatured at present as representing opposition to "equal marriage"—but this claim simply begs the obvious question, "but which of God's creatures *may* rightly marry each other?" Equality, from the Christian standpoint, does not come into it. If Christians support the legal recognition of "gay marriage," then, it will not be on the ground of "equality." It will instead be on the ground that committed, one-to-one same-sex relationships are much better for the people involved, and for society as a whole, than the alternatives. As we have already seen in previous chapters, most recently in discussing abortion and euthanasia/assisted suicide in chapter 17, legislation (from a biblical perspective) is often more about the regulation of brokenness than anything else—the best in the circumstances, rather than the highest good.

What are the limits to these freedoms for which we should advocate? As we also saw already in chapter 17, in discussing abortion and euthanasia/assisted suicide, respect for individual autonomy is important, but not at the expense of "the needs, safety, and protection of the community, especially its vulnerable members."[68] Among these vulnerable neighbors are children, of whom Jesus said this: "If anyone causes one of these little ones . . . to stumble, it would be better for them to have a large millstone hung around their neck and to be drowned in the depths of the sea" (Matt. 18:6). So we are especially obliged to pay attention to what is good for them. This clearly implies among other things that we must strongly oppose much of what is currently being allowed to happen to children and older (often highly vulnerable) minors in many countries of the world as a result of the rapid rise to prominence of transgenderism. It should also make us think hard about other questions too, however, such as whether people in long-term gay relationships ought to be raising children. There have been some significant contributions to this debate in recent years from adults—not necessarily religious people—who have grown up in gay homes either without a father or without a mother, and who now view *this* fact as an abrogation of *their* right and freedoms.[69] Here are marginal voices who claim that some of the new adult freedoms being claimed in our various societies have come at their expense. The plural society, if it is to be a good society, must be one in which such voices are taken just as seriously as others—especially given what one expert has described as "the vast and incontrovertible body of evidence" that fatherlessness in particular is "associated with heightened risk for criminality, substance abuse, and poorly regulated sexual behaviour among children, adolescents, and the adults that they eventually become."[70]

CONCLUSION

Who am I? I am an image bearer of the living God, body and soul together. I am a male or a female image bearer, as defined by my biology, created by God to exercise dominion along with my neighbors over the earth that belongs to him. I am a fallen image bearer, but also one who in Christ is saved and destined for a glorious, embodied future. I am wired for relationship, both with God and with other creatures. One of those relationships may well be a lifelong marriage to someone of the opposite gender, involving sexual intimacy and children. That is who I am. And I live my life in exile now, waiting to go up to Zion when God calls me home.

It is now evident, as we come to the end of our reflections in the last two chapters, what consistent Christian belief looks like concerning some of the hot button issues of our day. It is not yet entirely clear what the landscape of exile is like, in which we seek to live out our faith. It is inhabited, for sure, by neighbors whose beliefs in these matters are in many cases very different from our own, and whose ideas of the good life are correspondingly quite different as well. But it is not simply difference of opinion that marks this landscape. There is more to it than that, as we shall see in the next chapter.

DISCUSSION QUESTION
RELATING TO CHAPTERS 17 AND 18

Looking back on both previous chapters, what are the areas in which you experience the most tension with the surrounding culture, and why? How have you sought to negotiate these tensions?

19

The Landscape of Exile
On Living in Dangerous Times

O'Brien held up his left hand, its back towards Winston, with the thumb hidden and the four fingers extended. "How many fingers am I holding up, Winston?" "Four." "And if the party says that it is not four but five—then how many?" "Four." . . . "You are a slow learner, Winston," said O'Brien gently. "How can I help it?" he blubbered. "How can I help seeing what is in front of my eyes? Two and two are four." "Sometimes, Winston. Sometimes they are five. Sometimes they are three. Sometimes they are all of them at once. You must try harder. It is not easy to become sane." [1]

George Orwell

Orwell's dystopian novel 1984 is set in London, England, in the totalitarian state of Oceania, which is ruled by the Party and its leader Big Brother. Using various methods, the Party exercises almost complete control over people's lives in the city. For example, there is excellent surveillance: widespread video and audio monitoring allows the Party to keep track of all its members almost all of the time. The flow of information is strictly controlled and, in line with the idea that the one who "controls the past controls the future," historical records are systematically altered (in the Ministry of Truth) to align them to the Party's desired version. [2] This is one aspect of the propaganda that is constantly communicated by way of the giant telescreen that is found in every citizen's room and is insinuated into the family more subtly by way of children recruited into the "Junior Spies" organization, which in turn encourages its members to spy on their parents and to report any instance of disloyalty to the Party. Additionally, the Party has invented a new language called "Newspeak," whose purpose is "to narrow the range of thought" such that even "thought crime" will ultimately be impossible, "because there will be no words in which to express it."[3] This is important, because the Party is not content for people only to conform outwardly to "the truth" but instead insists upon correct *thinking*; thought-crime is indeed the worst of crimes. This is why everyone who wishes to flourish (and even survive) in Oceania in the meantime must become well-practiced in the art of "doublethink": the ability to hold as true two completely contradictory beliefs at the same time. This is a necessary skill if one does not wish to rebel in the mind against the Party, even when the Party states the exact opposite *either* of what it has previously stated *or* the opposite of what one already knows to be true on other grounds. Newspeak itself requires doublethink of its users, even in dealing with the names of government ministries like the Ministry of Truth, whose mandate is to lie. Consider the Newspeak term "blackwhite," for example, which has

> two mutually contradictory meanings. Applied to an opponent, it means the habit of impudently claiming that black is white, in contradiction of the plain facts. Applied to a Party member, it means a loyal willingness to say that black is white when Party discipline demands this. But it means also the ability to believe that black is white, and more, to know that black is white, and to forget that one has ever believed the contrary. This demands a continuous alteration of the past, made possible by the system of thought which really embraces all the rest, and which is known in Newspeak as doublethink.[4]

It will come as no surprise to learn, then, that in this novel people are typically eager to learn both Newspeak and doublethink in order to "fit in" with their peers, make progress within Party circles, and avoid trouble.

It is against this totalitarian regime that the central character of the novel, Winston Smith, quietly rebels—a low-ranking member of the Outer Party who purchases a diary in which to record his illegal thoughts. Tricked by an Inner Party member named O'Brien into taking home some literature produced by the opposition "Brotherhood," Winston is subsequently tortured and brainwashed by the same man. The dialogue recorded in the epigraph above occurs during this section of the novel, as O'Brien tries to get Winston to perceive reality "correctly." Winston must give up on the idea that two plus two equals four and accept instead that it equals whatever the Party says. Essentially, he must learn to call black white.

WHICH YEAR IS IT?

If my readers greet this dystopian picture of the world with even a glimmering of recognition, it will not only be because of their knowledge or experience of the history of both fascist and Marxist regimes of the twentieth century, or of the obviously totalitarian regimes of our present time. It will also be because they live in the post-Christian, *formally liberal and democratic states* of our present time. For instance, even these societies are already in many respects "surveillance societies." This is not just about video and audio monitoring in order to prevent crime and terrorism—although it is true that citizens have proved remarkably eager in the last couple of decades to give up privacy and freedom in exchange for (perceived) security. More than that, most of us "pass our days under the nonstop surveillance of a telescreen [mobile phone] that we bought at the Apple Store, carry with us everywhere, and tell everything to, without any coercion by the state."[5] Most of us also have a giant telescreen in our home, and if we are not aware of the multiple ways in which we thereby open ourselves up to "propaganda," both political and otherwise, then we have simply not been paying sufficient attention (even while allegedly "watching"). Television and the Internet profoundly shape our view of the world, and if they did not, advertisers would not pay large sums of money for advertising space with a view to selling us their products. Through these means and others, we must constantly contend with the "Newspeak" of our own time, in which words do not mean what they used to mean, or what (at first sight) one might think they *still* mean. Doublethink has thereby become part of our contemporary reality. As Dorian Lynskey has sagely pointed out concerning one of Orwell's own blind spots in this regard, Orwell did not foresee "that the common man and woman would embrace doublethink as enthusiastically as the intellectuals and, without the need for terror or torture, would choose to believe that two plus two was whatever they wanted it to be."[6]

All of this does not yet add up to an Orwellian, totalitarian society. It does, however, create an environment in which conditions exist that are friendly to the steady advance of totalitarian thought and action of various kinds, and perhaps ultimately to the creation of such a state, whether notionally of the right or the left. In a perceptive essay on this theme in 2019, George Packer drew attention, for example, to "the daily load of doublethink pouring from [U.S. President Donald] Trump, his enablers in the Inner Party, his mouthpieces in the Ministry of Truth, and his fanatical supporters among the proles [proletariat]," and to the threat that this poses to a pluralist, liberal democracy.[7] He goes on to note in this essay, however, that there is also such a thing as "progressive doublethink" on the left, among people whose "key word is *justice*—a word no one should want to live without."[8] Yet precisely because "they want to be counted on the side of justice," these progressives generally "assent without difficulty to the stifling consensus of the moment and the intolerance it breeds," and some of their "commissars with large followings patrol the precincts of social media and punish thought criminals" precisely to ensure that nonconformity does not easily arise.[9] "This pressure,"

Packer argues, "can be more powerful than a party or state, because it speaks in the name of the people and in the language of moral outrage, against which there is, in a way, no defense."[10] In such an environment, "intelligent people do the work of eliminating their own unorthodoxy without the Thought Police."[11] The Progressive Party becomes a substantive reality, even though it does not possess a central office.

We need to add to this something that Packer himself does not mention: that this Party often does take on a physical, nonvirtual form in "the letters of mass denunciation which are now commonplace in our universities," as well as the intimidating demonstrations on university campuses and in other locations that are designed to prevent the free expression of ideas that are considered ideologically impure from the Party's point of view.[12] Many younger people appear to think that this is virtuous rather than (truly) appalling, and even if the university and local authorities disagree with their judgment, they have all too often in the recent past shamefully capitulated to the Party's view. This dogmatic opposition to free speech is itself facilitated by Newspeak, because the purveyor of every idea with which these Party members disagree is immediately denounced using one of the vocabulary items defining thought crimes (e.g., racism, sexism, homophobia, transphobia, Islamophobia)—all too often chosen more for their emotional impact than for their descriptive accuracy. The summative vocabulary item that embraces all the other terms is "right wing," whether the person really is right wing or not: it is simply a slur against anyone who does not in any matter "assent . . . to the stifling consensus of the moment" that the Party supports.[13]

In this propensity to slander, "the left" is of course simply the mirror image of what is (genuinely) "the right," which employs the same tactic: everything even slightly to the left of their position is said to be "left-wing." There is no center. It suits ideologues to speak in such ways, and it always has, for their real interest is in power exercised in the interest of their own "tribe" and not in the common good; there is not a true liberal to be found among them. "'Nothing is gained by teaching a parrot a new word,' [George] Orwell wrote in 1946. What is needed is the right to print [and speak] what one believes to be true, without having to fear bullying or blackmail from any side."[14] But this right is actively under threat at the present time, even in societies where the rhetoric of freedom is strong, and we ought all be concerned about it—for without genuine freedom of speech, we cannot defend our other freedoms.

This is the kind of exilic landscape in which many contemporary Christian people in the largely post-Christian West must conduct their ethical reflection and live their good and holy lives, and I want to take the remainder of this chapter further to illuminate its character. I shall do so by way of an extended description and analysis of the situation that currently faces many Christians worldwide when it comes to the questions of gender identity and sexual orientation/practice discussed in chapter 18. My focus will be on my home country of Canada, but I shall include exemplary material from other countries as well. This will lead us in chapter 20 to a broader consideration of the "disciplines of exile" that all Christians require in order to live out the good life more broadly that we have been describing in this book.

CHANGE AND CONVERSION

In 2015 the distinguished psychologist Dr. Kenneth Zucker was fired by the Centre for Addiction and Mental Health (CAMH) in Toronto, Ontario—the largest mental health teaching hospital in the country. This event was connected to the passing of the *Affirming Sexual Orientation and Gender Identity Act* by the Ontario provincial legislature in the same year, which among other things forbade those providing healthcare services from offering "any treatment that seeks to change the sexual orientation or gender identity of a person under 18 years of age."[15] Exceptions were permitted for "services that provide acceptance, support or understanding of a person or the facilitation of a person's coping, social support, or identity exploration or development," and for "sex-reassignment surgery or any services related to sex-reassignment surgery." Another significant exception related to consent to "treatment that seeks to change." It may proceed *if* the minor "is capable with respect to [it] and consents to [its] provision."

ON THE FACE OF IT

On the face of it, all of this together appears to *allow* medical professionals to explore with all minors over the course of time whether or not their feelings about themselves amount to a sexual orientation or a gender identity that is unchangeable. It further *allows* minors with same-sex attraction (for example) to engage consensually in sexual orientation change efforts (SOCE; see our chapter 18). What the legislators are out to *ban* is coercion by health professionals in these matters. Perhaps they had in mind the kind of coercive, boot-camp environments designed by some Christians historically to "cure" their children of the wrong kinds of sexual attractions. This same association of SOCE with coercion is certainly evident in the public statements of other politicians in Canada, and indeed of the federal government, which in July 2019 pointed out that "existing Criminal Code offences—such as kidnapping, forcible confinement and assault—may apply in cases where a person is forced to undergo conversion therapy."[16] This association is also reflected in the Canadian media, as in one journalist's reference to "aversion therapy that attempts to condition a person's behaviour by causing them discomfort through things like electric shocks when they're exposed to specific stimuli."[17]

THE END OF THE RAINBOW

Whatever the legislative intent in Ontario may have been, however, Rainbow Health Ontario—an organization committed to promoting the health of Ontario's LGBTQ communities—argued in the light of the new law that what Zucker was doing in his Child, Youth, and Family Gender Identity Clinic was illegal, and they succeeded in getting him fired and the clinic closed. For reasons that will become clear shortly, it is important to note what these activists accused Zucker of practicing. It was "conversion therapy"—a term that does not appear in the Ontario Act but had previously been used in various other contexts (along with "reparation therapy") to describe SOCE. It is already a misleading term in relation to SOCE as a whole, since the great majority of health professionals involved in SOCE have not believed or advertised that these "change efforts" produce guaranteed results in "gay conversion," but only that they help some people who experience unwanted same-sex attraction. As applied to Zucker's work with young gender dysphoric persons at CAMH, however, the use of the term "conversion therapy" represents nothing other than blatant Newspeak, where (we recall) "words do not mean what they used to mean." For Zucker was certainly not engaged in any kind of "converting" activity. He was simply pursuing the well-established, professional, and patient approach to children with gender dysphoria already described in chapter 18—waiting to see if children grew out of the symptoms. The truth did not save Zucker, however. The label stuck, and he was summarily punished for his "crime" which, as his former colleague Debra Soh notes, was simply that

> he did not blindly follow the current popular dogma of affirming young children who say they want to transition to the opposite sex . . . [it] was not about . . . conducting "reparative" or "conversion therapy" . . . [but] about recognizing that it simply doesn't make sense for a child to undergo the challenges of a social or physical transition if they are likely to grow comfortable in the body they already have, on their own.[18]

Specifically, from the activists' perspective Zucker was unwilling to move quickly enough to affirm a child's "internal sense" of his or her gender identity by recommending to parents early "social" transitioning. This refers to a process in which children adopt the name, hairstyle, or clothing associated with their affirmed gender. It is the precursor to the puberty-blocking, hormonal, and surgical interventions described in our previous chapter.

IDEOLOGY AND SCIENCE

Debra Soh's words come from a post with the subheading "ideology is now tak-ing precedence over science," and in her concluding sentence she returns to this theme: "The issue is no longer about what's in the best interest of these children but about winning, at any cost, the ideological war." In this war, she claims, there is ongoing, extreme pressure on clinicians "to endorse the early transitioning model for their young patients, even when it may not be the best way forward for them."

The Cost of Dissent

This is not only true in Canada. On July 18, 2019, Kirsty Entwistle, formerly a clinical psychologist at the Gender Identity Development Services (GIDS) in Leeds (UK), sent an open letter to her former employer expressing concern that "GIDS clinicians are making decisions that will have a major impact on children and young people's bodies and on their lives, potentially for the rest of their lives, without a robust evidence base."[19] The whole letter is worth reading, but partic-ularly striking is Entwistle's claim that she "went to work at GIDS expecting to do complex assessments and differential diagnosis" but discovered in reality that if she did not arrive at the "correct" diagnosis after assessment, she ran "the risk of being called transphobic."[20]

The pressure is extreme not least because those who do not take the "correct" view on gender and sex are in danger of losing their jobs—just like Zucker did—as the (Progressive) Party purges the public square of thought-criminals. This is also the case in other countries. Consider, for example, the recent firing of the psychiatrist Allan Josephson (already mentioned in chapter 18) by the University of Louisville (United States) for sharing at a conference "his professional opinion on the medicalization of gender-confused youth."[21] In a later interview about this firing, Josephson suggested that many practitioners shared his views but were afraid to speak out, and the interviewer responded that she had "had emails and calls from AAP [American Academy of Pediatrics] members and pediatricians saying pretty much what you said and asking to remain anonymous."[22]

Patients Know Best

Such firings and the fear that they generate will only accelerate a tendency that is already present even in many clinicians who are not members of the Party but who simply want a quiet life: the tendency just to give the customer what he or she demands. They are already under pressure to do this by such organizations as the World Professional Association for Transgender Health, whose view is "that patients know best what they need to be happy," which means that "patient autonomy is the singular ethical consideration" for the doctor in considering a particular case of gender dysphoria.[23] The *clinician's* ethics do not, in the end, matter. We can hardly be surprised, then, when Josephson tells us that he has personally witnessed merely "cursory" evaluations of gender dysphoric children by medical professionals following which "the patient gets hormones" without further ado. More generally, concerning the over fifty gender clinics that have suddenly sprung up in the United States in response to a demand for their services, Josephson says this:

> They're set up almost like . . . a restaurant where a person comes in and orders a treatment. Doctors have always said—you give me the symptoms, and I'll help you with what I think is going on for the diagnosis. But that basic process is being short-circuited by a "this is my diagnosis; this is what I have" approach. And literally they're asking for hormones. And amazingly, doctors are going along with it in many cases. I think it's a travesty of our profession.

This leaves both parents and children without the depth of information and balanced advice that they need in order to make properly informed decisions about how they might best handle gender dysphoria—including full information about the significant risks of the "drugs and surgery" pathway.[24] When medical professionals become in this way merely

> cheerleaders for transition, their behavior indicates to the patient that this is the best solution that only requires a bit of courage. They may lead patients and parents to believe that there is scientific certainty about the wisdom of transition. This is not what the ethical principle of honesty means. The professional's responsibility is to expand the patient's views of the risks of what they are undertaking.[25]

It is particularly shocking that this "listen to the consumer" position should have developed in gender clinics where so many of the consumers are extremely vulnerable people by any definition of the word "vulnerable." A "large percentage of gender nonconforming patients" in some gender clinics at least in the United States are

> runaways, disowned persons, or those who have aged out of foster care. They may be living hand to mouth on the streets and may be periodically homeless. Some of this group turns to criminality and/or sex work. They have a high prevalence of drug abuse and are at high risk for sexually transmitted diseases.[26]

If there is good reason in general to believe, as Stephen Levine writes, "that the patient does not [in fact] always know best," this is certainly true of these "emancipated youth" in particular.[27]

THE SUPPRESSION OF COMPLEXITY

Zucker's transgression, and for that matter Josephson's, was essentially the same as that of the producers of the suppressed BBC documentary also mentioned in chapter 18: to insist that the whole business of gender dysphoria in children is much more complicated than the activists wish anyone to understand. The suppression of such truth is country cousin to the Ministry of Truth's rewriting of history, since among other things it seeks to obliterate from public view what has been normal practice, historically, in dealing with the condition. One aspect of the complexity is that (in Debra Soh's words) "underlying conditions can be mistaken for gender dysphoria, including autism and borderline personality disorder."[28] Another, which Soh does not herself mention, is that no child is an island. Environmental factors, as we saw in chapter 18, play a huge part in the ways in which children perceive themselves and their world, as their identity is being shaped in community—for example, in a family.[29] Beyond the family, however, there is the peer group, which is now global in nature as a result of the Internet. This creates previously unparalleled opportunities for "social contagion" to develop: "the spread of affect or behaviour from one crowd participant to another; one person serves as the stimulus for the imitative actions of another."[30] This is a well-recognized phenomenon among psychologists, and many historical examples can be cited—for example, the "wave of suicides" that swept across Europe in the late eighteenth century in the wake of Goethe's novel *Young Werther*, "as if the very act of suicide was somehow infectious."[31]

Only such "contagion" can possibly explain the dramatic increase worldwide in cases of what used to be the relatively rare condition of gender dysphoria, such that "the Gender Identity Development Service in the United Kingdom alone has seen a 2,000 percent increase in referrals since 2009."[32] The "social contagion" explanation is particularly plausible with respect to the relatively new phenomenon of "rapid onset gender dysphoria," where teenagers (usually girls) with no previous history of the condition suddenly announce their desire to transition to the opposite sex. In a 2018 American study by Lisa Littman, which the Ministry of Truth also sought to suppress, the author notes that 87 percent of her subjects were reported by their parents as identifying as transgender only after spending more time online than was customary, and after friends of theirs had already "come out."[33] This is not particularly surprising in a broadly post-Christian Western context in which a) enormous societal pressures are routinely placed on girls to have a certain kind of body type and personality, which often leads on to self-hatred and self-harm; b) they have been told from a young age (not entirely consistently with [a]) that they can be whoever they want to be; and c) they are aware of countless famous and not-so-famous adults and teenagers who have had surgery precisely so that *they* can be who they want to be.

THE IMPOSITION OF FALSEHOOD

Gender dysphoria has many causes, it turns out, and it requires careful handling to get to the bottom of the causes and to help children and teenagers resolve the problems that it raises for them. So does "sexual orientation," according to many people who have had the opportunity to reflect on the roots of their attractions, and specifically their same-sex attraction—people who have come to the conclusion that in their cases it was the result of factors like "emotional and/ or sexual abuse; unmet emotional needs; depression, OCD, or other unfulfilled needs. In short these issues were childhood wounds to their psychosexual and/or psychosocial development."[34]

THE NOVA SCOTIA ACT

In spite of all this, however, and in spite of widespread, negative reaction to the Zucker firing among his fellow professionals at the time, the imposition of ideology has continued apace in Canada, seeping out from the world of health professionals and into the world in general. This is already clear in the Nova Scotia *Sexual Orientation and Gender Identity Protection Act* of 2018, which first of all specifically places counselling among its prohibited "services or tactics" in pursuit of "change" in sexual orientation or gender identity.[35] The ban is complete, secondly, for children under the age of sixteen, *whether or not they consent.* Much younger minors are apparently old enough to consent to "services related to gender-confirming surgery," such as the administration of puberty-blockers around the age of ten, and of cross-sex hormones between the ages of thirteen and sixteen depending on circumstances.[36] However, even if minors under sixteen feel confused about their gender, or if their same-sex attraction is unwanted, and even if they would welcome counselling to get to the roots of the matter with a view to getting some relief, they are not old enough in Nova Scotia to consent to this. Thirdly, it is not only health professionals who are banned from "change efforts" in Nova Scotia but any "person in a position of trust or authority toward a minor." We must assume that this includes at a minimum parents, pastors, and teachers. No such persons may use "tactics" designed to lead to "change," not even with respect to their own children. The "tactics" explicitly include counselling; do they also include (for example) prayer? It seems that even parents, faced with their child's current perception of his or her sexual orientation or gender identity, are now only permitted to respond to the child with affirmation. They are not permitted to talk to the child, for example, about the possibility that his or her "gender identity or expression" is not an immutable aspect of his or her nature.

This is evidently no longer about preventing coercion. This is about imposing a certain kind of interpretation of reality on the population at large and in so doing requiring that this population accepts as true something that is actually false: that in the young, gender identity and sexual orientation are already "fixed and immutable" and that any moves to "change" them are bound to cause harm.[37] And in pursuing this agenda, the Party is quite willing to intrude not only upon the right of health professionals to treat their patients in the ways that they think best, and upon the rights of parents and others to raise and counsel children as *they* think best, but also upon the rights of minors themselves to make "incorrect" decisions.

SOGI 123

This brings us to the year 2019, and to the situation in my home province of British Columbia (BC). Here the imposition of ideology has an educational as well as a (potential) legal aspect. Together they represent a serious challenge to Christians intent on living good lives and raising their children to do the same.

The educational aspect of the challenge is represented by the "Sexual Orientation and Gender Identity" program (SOGI 123) that has been introduced into BC schools, beginning in kindergarten.[38] This program has been characterized by the BC Ministry of Education as being about freedom from "discrimination, bullying, harassment, intimidation, and violence," and of course all Christians ought to agree that our schools should not allow such behaviour within their premises. However, "harm" is unfortunately the Trojan horse inside of which something else is being smuggled into our British Columbian Troy. For SOGI 123 is not only about preventing "discrimination, bullying, harassment, intimidation, and violence" but also about children being "safe and comfortable enough to live their authentic lives" at school. In pursuit of this goal, the SOGI program simply teaches as a fact—with no acknowledgment of the complexity of, or differing beliefs concerning this matter—that "everyone has a sexual orientation and gender identity."[39] Children themselves, of course, determine what these are.[40] The "SOGI-inclusive school" will simply embrace all their "experiences and identities," so that children can be themselves. Correspondingly, a parent's task is to "open up the conversation and keep it open, by allowing [children] to question, express, and explore their individuality as they wish."[41]

SOGI 123 is not just about treating others with respect even if one disagrees with the weight that they place on their feelings in deciding how to live their lives. It is about compelling one to agree with others that their feelings are in fact an infallible guide to "who they really are" and about placing their subsequent actions beyond any questioning, even of a gentle, listening, and respectful kind. As one website advises us on the "right" way to approach such questions: "if you want to know whether someone is male or female, it may be best just to ask."[42] In the "empire of desire," it is apparently now treasonous to ask questions about what desire *signifies*, and whether others have understood these significations correctly.

This is extraordinary. In BC one cannot drive a vehicle until the age of sixteen, and this is also the age of consent to sexual activity. The voting age is eighteen, and the legal drinking age is nineteen, as is the legal smoking age. One cannot enter a casino until the age of nineteen, nor enter into a binding contract. There are good reasons for all these laws, and they all have to do with the limited capacity of young people to handle important matters optimally. Yet adults in BC are now apparently obliged to affirm even a very young child's interpretation of what his or her childlike feelings mean, right now, in terms of very import-ant questions about his or her personhood. In the course of doing so, we must in particular assent (always, without exception) to the proposition that a boy is really a girl, and a girl is really a boy; to do otherwise is to engage (in Newspeak) in "misgendering," which in BC can get one into serious trouble. To illustrate: under Canadian law, "when someone uses abusive behaviour to control and/or harm a member of their family," that person has committed the offence of "family violence."[43] And as a result of a 2019 BC Supreme Court case involving a father who opposed his fourteen-year-old daughter's decision to begin hormone ther-apy with a view to transitioning to a male-like body, it seemed for a time that "family violence" must include trying to persuade one's child to abandon hormone treatment, addressing her by her birth name, or referring to her as a girl or with female pronouns—"misgendering."[44] Mercifully, the judicial propriety of apply-ing family-violence legislation to such actions was subsequently rejected by the courts. The attempt to do so should not surprise us, however, when we consider the words of the former Canadian politician Cheri DiNovo, who was primar-ily responsible for the legislative changes in Ontario concerning sex and gender: "Being lesbian, gay, bisexual, trans, or queer is who one is; to tell a child that who they are is wrong we consider to be abusive."[45]

"But two and two are four." "Sometimes, Winston. Sometimes they are five. Sometimes they are three. Sometimes they are all of them at once. You must try harder. It is not easy to become sane." Indeed it is not.

CONVERSION THERAPY

Additionally, there is a bill currently before the British Columbia (BC) Legis-lature (2019–2020), the *Sexual Orientation and Gender Identity Protection Bill* (2019), whose wording could be taken to suggest that its sponsors wish, even more than the Nova Scotia legislators, to suppress dissent in such matters.[46] This bill explicitly employs the terminology of "conversion therapy." Mimicking the Nova Scotia Act in prohibiting any "person in a position of trust or authority in relation to a minor" from providing such therapy to a minor, it has however now removed *any consent clause at all*. No person under nineteen years of age may consent to "conversion therapy." Given the history of this language in Ontario, one's first impression is that the BC bill is therefore designed among other things to ban "psychiatrists and other psychotherapists . . . from even exploring with a patient the [likely] underlying psychological basis for [gender] dysphoria," or any similar possibility in the case of same-sex attraction.[47] It is also reasonable to read it as intending to ban parents and other adults from responding to minors in ways that are not entirely affirming of their current perceptions concerning their sexual orientation or gender identity. If so, then gender identity and sexual orientation, as perceived by even quite young individuals, are now to be considered fixed realities like skin or eye color, and no other perspective on such matters is allowed. There is indeed no *room* for "perspective"; the "facts" speak for themselves. The Party, it seems, has pronounced it to be so, and everyone must agree, even if there are many good reasons not to do so.

DISSENT AND CRIME

If all of this were not serious enough, the federal government of Canada has at time of this writing said that they are looking at Criminal Code reforms aimed at deterring the "shameful" practice of conversion therapy.[48] There is in fact a bill before the Canadian Senate that has already been drafted with this aim in mind. Even though many people have testified that "change efforts" have to some degree helped them, this bill aims to criminalize the advertising of "any practice, treatment, or service designed to change an individual's sexual orientation or gender identity *or to eliminate or reduce sexual attraction or sexual behaviour between persons of the same sex* [my emphasis]."[49] It seems clear that this new element in the wording has been explicitly introduced to ensure that "conversion therapy" includes services that only claim to *help* people with unwanted same-sex attraction ("reduce"), rather than to eliminate it. Astonishingly, it is not only minors who are to be deprived of access to such services; the intended ban relates to *all* advertising to *anyone*, consenting adult or otherwise. An additional clause then also criminalizes receiving "a financial or other material benefit" for providing conversion therapy to minors. If this bill were to pass, then among other things its effect would probably be to make health professionals even more likely than at present to avoid "the Zucker mistake" in treating children with gender dysphoria and instead simply to "go with the ideological flow." For anyone in "business" who were to have the "conversion therapy" label successfully hung around his or her neck, however unjust it might be, would now risk not only social shaming and loss of employment but also criminal prosecution.

THE NATURE OF THE HUMAN

We may now sum up the "landscape of exile" in Canada at the present time, as it pertains to sexual orientation and gender identity. The challenge at present is not limited to pursuing authentic Christian lives in exile while respecting the right of our neighbors to hold beliefs about sex and identity and the good life that are very different from our own. The challenge is increasingly (it seems) that significant numbers of these neighbors are intent on imposing their beliefs and derivative moral positions on the rest of us, suffocating dissent and limiting freedom of action.

Many of the people who are so immediately in favor of the campaign against conversion therapy when they hear about it appear to imagine that it is only about outlawing blatantly coercive practices akin to torture in respect of minors who currently think of themselves as members of minority communities. It turns out that this is precisely the case with respect to the main sponsors of the BC conversion therapy bill described above, which of course creates space within which constructive dialogue can occur (and is currently occurring) with a view to amending the language of the bill so as remove its most immediate dangers. Outside BC, however, it does *not* appear that those promoting such legislation in 2019 are *only* trying to outlaw coercive practices. Such legislation is also designed to create a climate of opinion in which it becomes self-evident to the majority of people that there is only one way—the Party's way—of rightly interpreting and properly "handling" matters of sexual orientation and identity. The emotional impact of the term "conversion therapy" is precisely what makes it so useful in this respect, and that is indeed why it is being *used* in proposed legislation, even though (or actually *because*) it is entirely misleading with respect to how "ideologically impure" health professionals and others have been, and still are, dealing with distressed children. It is Newspeak, designed to facilitate the suppression of all kinds of freedoms that we should each of us hold dear, including freedom of speech, freedom of choice (not least in how we parent, practice medicine, and access medical care), and freedom of religion.

"Freedom is the freedom to say that two plus two make four. If that is granted, all else follows."[50] In BC in particular, however, we have our schoolteachers teaching our children and grandchildren (by way of SOGI 123) what the province has proclaimed to be the "right" way of thinking about matters of sex and identity, and it is possible that we are about to be bound by a new provincial law that, if passed in its present form, will certainly discourage all other adults from trying to persuade our young people otherwise.

A GLOBAL AGENDA

At its deepest root, what is this assault on our freedoms really *about*? Our early forebears in the faith had to contend mightily in defence of Christian truth as it pertains to theology: who is God? Their victory established in the public domain of Christendom the truth that God is One and Three, a Trinity comprising the Father, along with the fully divine/human Christ, and the Holy Spirit. The presenting question in the early twenty-first century is different. It is the question of anthropology. What is a human being (Ps. 8:4)? And it is a question with which Christians all over the world, and not just in Canada, will be wrestling for the foreseeable future. We can be confident of this because the landscape of our exile is being intentionally shaped at the behest not only of activists in individual countries but of global forces.

UNITED IN MISSION

We see this, for example, in the appointment by the United Nations in 2016 of an "independent expert on protection against violence and discrimination based on sexual orientation and gender identity," Vitit Muntarbhorn.[51] The word "independent" is an interesting piece of Newspeak in itself, since Mr. Muntarbhorn "was the Co-Chairperson of the drafting committee of the Yogyakarta Principles on the Application of International Human Rights Law in relation to sexual orientation and gender identity in 2006."[52] These Yogyakarta Principles, updated in 2017, would if adopted require all states (among other things) first to "[i]ntegrate within State policy and decision-making a pluralistic approach that recognises and affirms the interrelatedness and indivisibility of all aspects of human identity including sexual orientation and gender identity" (Principle 1).[53] The word "indivisibility" implies, of course, that something like "gender identity" is just as fixed as skin color. Principle 2 urges countries, secondly, to take "all appropriate action, including programmes of education and training, with a view to achieving the elimination of prejudicial or discriminatory attitudes or behaviours which are related to the idea of the inferiority or the superiority of any sexual orientation or gender identity or gender expression." We are no longer permitted to believe in God's creational law concerning sex and gender. Thirdly, states ought to ensure "that education methods, curricula, and resources serve to enhance understanding of and respect for, inter alia, diverse sexual orientations and gender identities" (Principle 16). And so we arrive at SOGI 123. It is a very short step from here to banning the Bible, or parts of it, as hate speech.

WOKE CAPITALISM

The play of global forces is also evident in the way that large corporations are currently falling over themselves both to sell the new ideology along with their products and actively to suppress dissent from it.[54] As a striking example of this selling we may take the multinational Coca Cola, which caused a stir in Hungary by advertising their product during the Sziget music festival using photographs of gay couples, under the headline "zero sugar, zero prejudice." When asked about this, the company said that the festival echoes the company's core principles: "We believe both hetero- and homosexuals have the right to love the person they want, the way they want."[55] That is a principle with considerable latitude in it. A carbonated soft drink manufacturer, it seems, has joined the Party's recruitment wing.

As examples of suppression, we may take both Twitter and Amazon. Writing in late 2018, biologist Colin Wright—last encountered in chapter 18 arguing for the completely "outrageous" (but factually correct) idea that sex is binary— had this to say about Twitter:

> Despite the unquestionable reality of biological sex in humans, social justice and trans activists continue to push this belief, and respond with outrage when challenged. Pointing out any of the above facts [in his essay] is now considered synonymous with transphobia. The massive social media website Twitter—*the* central hub for cultural discourse and debate—is now actively banning users for stating true facts about basic human biology. And biologists like myself often sit quietly, afraid to defend our own field out of fear that our decade of education followed by continued research, job searches, and the quest for tenure might be made obsolete overnight if the mob decides to target one of us for speaking up. Because of this, our objections take place almost entirely between one another in private whisper networks, despite the fact that a majority of biologists are extremely troubled by these attacks to our field by social justice activists. This is an untenable situation.[56]

Twitter has apparently joined the Party's censorship department. So too has Amazon. In early July 2019, activists were successful in persuading Amazon to ban books that they regarded as promoting "conversion therapy"—principally, the books of Joseph Nicolosi. As Ron Dreher has pointed out, this means that one can buy through Amazon Hitler's *Mein Kampf*, Alfred Kotz's *The SS Leadership Guide* (translated from the original German), and the works of Stalin apologist Grover Furr, but not the works of a therapist hated by certain pressure groups of the moment.[57] This is, Dreher claims, "woke capitalism at its finest," and we ought to be troubled by it, because "[n]ine out of ten e-books sold come from Amazon. Forty-two percent of hardcover books sold come through Amazon." The company's power to control information flow, and thereby shape opinion, is immense.

WHAT COMES NEXT?

One can only wonder what may come next, if the current trends continue. In particular, what will come next if our children—now endowed with the absolute right to act authentically on the basis of their "internal sense" of their true identity—continue to have their imaginations shaped by that great carrier of social contagion, the Internet? Are we very far away from lowering, or even abolishing, the age of consent to sexual activity in Canada, which is currently sixteen, on the basis of an "internal sense" in children that it infringes their liberties?

What about a child's "internal sense" that he or she is an alien, and the subsequent request for surgery to make it so?[58] What about minors who claim to have been born in the wrong species—shall we accord them special rights in our human rights codes?[59] Perhaps some members of the Party would be shocked by these ideas. But given their ideology, on what basis would they say "no"?

What about a child's "internal sense" that he or she is "transabled"—that is, suffers from "body integrity identity disorder (BIID, also known, of course, as body integrity *dysphoria*, in order to avoid the word "disorder")? People with this condition experience "an intense desire to amputate a major limb or sever the spinal cord in order to become paralyzed."[60] Like gender dysphoria, BIID also has "an onset in early childhood," and the main rationale given by subjects for body modification "is to feel complete or to feel satisfied inside." Surgery has in this case also been "found helpful in all subjects who underwent amputation." Is this what comes next: the amputation, on demand, of young limbs? Daniel Callahan, defending traditional Hippocratic medicine in our chapter 17, is emphatic that doctors "have never been willing to do what patients want solely because they want it. To do so would reduce doctors to automatons, subordinating their integrity to patient wishes or demands."[61] To illustrate his point, he says this: "A doctor will not cut off my healthy arm simply because I decide my autonomy and well-being would thereby be enhanced." But in a consumer culture dominated by my "right" to live in accordance with my "internal sense" of my identity, this is *precisely* what doctors find themselves doing. It is already happening.[62]

CONCLUSION

In sum, we already live in a world marked by what C. S. Lewis once called *The Abolition of Man*,[63] and it may well be the world in which many of us must live for some time to come:

> a realm of cultural darkness, in which rational argument and respect for the opponent are disappearing from public discourse, and in which increasingly, on every issue that matters, there is only one permitted view, and a licence to persecute all the heretics that do not subscribe to it. This signifies, to my way of thinking, the death of our political culture and the rise of a kind of godless religion in its stead.[64]

The question is: are we equipped for the journey? Do we have what it takes to complete it? Are we ready for the battle?

DISCUSSION QUESTION

Think about (and even reread) the OT narratives that most obviously describe people living in exile: the Joseph story (Gen. 37–50) and the books of Daniel and Esther. Also read the great psalm of exile, Psalm 137. How do these Scriptures inform our Christian understanding of living in exile now?

20

The Disciplines of Exile
On Hearts and Minds

We all want progress . . . [But] if you are on the wrong road, progress means doing an
about-turn and walking back to the right road; in that case the man who turns back
soonest is the most progressive man.[1]

C. S. Lewis

We do not know for sure how things will turn out in the immediate future for Christians in Canada in particular, or in the world in general, with respect to these matters of sexual orientation and gender identity. Perhaps the various representations being made to governments about these matters will make a positive difference; perhaps they will not. Nor do we know what the more distant future will bring our way regarding these same questions, five or ten years further down the road, or other questions than we cannot even yet foresee. Will the political context in which they arise be more to the left or to the right? Will more and more people belatedly realize where the current trends are leading us and hesitate to go there—perhaps even turn back to God in large numbers? We cannot tell. But whatever happens, we shall each of us need to find an authentically Christian way forward in those circumstances, as we live in this world as "foreigners and exiles," looking forward to our new home in God's "new heaven and . . . new earth, where righteousness dwells" (1 Pet. 2:11; 2 Pet. 3:13). Which disciplines shall we need to cultivate in order to do this successfully?

A PSALM FOR EXILES

Psalm 137 is a particularly helpful Scripture when it comes answering this question. It forms part of an entire section of the book of Psalms (107–150) that has been structured so as to address the theme of God's *ingathering* of his people from their general exile in this world at the end of time. This is expressed in particular through the metaphor of pilgrimage to Zion, with a focus on the individual figure of the coming Davidic king. Psalm 137 looks back specifically on the exile of the people of Judah to Babylon in the aftermath of the fall of Jerusalem to the Babylonians in 587 BC (cf. 2 Kgs. 24–25): "By the rivers of Babylon we sat and wept" (v. 1). These "rivers" or "waters" included the Tigris and Euphrates rivers, but also a vast irrigation system distributed across the huge plain of Babylon. This made the region wonderfully fertile—a good place to live, from the point of view of material well-being. Babylon registered highly on the quality-of-life scale in the ancient Near East. This is precisely why, when the Judean exiles later had the chance to return to their homeland, relatively few choose to do so. They assimilated, instead, into the dominant culture.

This would not have surprised the Babylonians in the slightest, because they (of course) regarded their culture as wonderful, and they considered "exile" within it to be a privilege as much as a punishment. So did the Assyrians before them. The Assyrian King Sennacherib's delegate, at the gates of Jerusalem in 701 BC, had this to say to the city's inhabitants: "Make peace with me and come out to me; then every one of you will eat from his own vine and fig tree and drink from his own cistern, until I come and take you to a land like your own, a land of grain and new wine, a land of bread and vineyards, a land of olive trees and honey" (2 Kgs. 18:31). Sennacherib intended to take *these* Judeans into exile in a new promised land (Deut. 8:7–9). It has generally been this way with imperial power throughout the ages: oppression is dressed up as liberation by leaders who present themselves as the fathers of their people, the true guarantors of their ultimate good.

So it is in Psalm 137. "Sing us songs of joy," the Babylonians captors demand of their Judean prisoners; "sing us one of the songs of Zion" (v. 3). You are on the way to the Promised Land—to Utopia. You should be happy. It is a seductive invitation, and the people of God have often encountered it throughout their history. The early Church certainly did so in the Roman Empire, which the NT portrays as the contemporary incarnation of Babylon (1 Pet. 5:13; Rev 14:8; 16:19; 17:5; 18:2, 10, 21): "conform to our Roman norms and all will be well," the first Christians were told. We still hear this invitation now: "forget that you are in exile here and be at home."

Psalm 137 describes three disciplines that will help us resist this invitation. We may summarize them as remembering, resistance, and trust.

THE IMPORTANCE OF REMEMBERING

What was it that led the psalmist and his friends in Psalm 137 to keep clearly in mind that Babylon was *not* "home"? When so many were bedazzled and bewitched by the glories of this *destination*, how did these people retain their understanding of life as a *journey*? The most fundamental answer to these questions is that they *remembered*—and memory, rather than sight or touch, shaped their thinking. They remembered who they were; they remembered where they had come from and where they were heading; and they remembered what Babylon and her allies truly stood for, beneath the veneer of sophistication and civilization presented to their senses. They remembered Zion (Jerusalem, verse 1): what it stood for, and what had been done there. And they committed themselves never to forget it (verses 5–6)—never to forget that their *highest joy* (verse 6) would not be found in their present situation.

REMEMBERING AND SPIRITUALITY

Remembering is a huge and foundational part of biblical spirituality, and much of the Israelite religious system was set up in such a way that it *facilitated* this remembering. The very fact that the Levites were not allotted tribal territory in Israel, "because the LORD, the God of Israel, is their inheritance" (Jos. 13:33), was a constant reminder of the central biblical truth that we are now considering: that true faith is "pilgrim" faith. In NT terms, it is about remembering where our treasure is (Matt. 6:19–21)—for where our treasure lies, there will our heart lie also. The Sabbath was a weekly reminder that God is our Creator and that work is not life, or life work. It was also a reminder that "you were slaves in Egypt and that the LORD your God brought you out of there with a mighty hand and an outstretched arm" (Exod. 20:8–11; Deut. 5:12–15). This kind of remembering of the past is the basis for much of the ethical instruction in the OT (e.g., Deut. 15:15; 16:12). Remember who you are, and act accordingly! And induct your children into these memories, so that *they* know who *they* are:

> Fix these words of mine in your hearts and minds; tie them as symbols on your hands and bind them on your foreheads. Teach them to your children, talking about them when you sit at home and when you walk along the road, when you lie down and when you get up. Write them on the doorframes of your houses and on your gates, so that your days and the days of your children may be many in the land the LORD swore to give your ancestors, as many as the days that the heavens are above the earth. (Deut. 11:18–21)

Notice the all-encompassing nature of this task. Hearts, minds, hands, and foreheads are recruited, standing for our entire being. We are to remember, and to encourage remembrance, when sitting, walking, lying down, and getting up—throughout the entire day. Our physical environment is to be constructed so as to help us in the task: the doorframes of our homes and the gates of our towns, representing our entire space. This task of remembering requires fierce commitment, since biblical faith teaches us (and we know this from experience) that the danger of forgetting is very real. And so we notice that the psalmist in Psalm 137 pronounces curses on his own *hand* and *tongue* if he should forget (verses 5–6). He invites inability of action and speech if his actions and speech are not consistent with his faith and do not reflect where his treasure and his joy ultimately lie. We remember Jesus' own fierce words about what it takes to be a disciple: we must be ready to sacrifice eye, foot, or hand—whatever is important to us—if by keeping these body parts we are led into sin (Matt. 5:29–30; 18:7–9). Discipleship is a serious business and remembering is fundamental to it. But it does not come easily to us. We need to be intentional about it.

REMEMBERING AND BIBLE READING

We realize from all of this that to survive and indeed flourish in exile involves more than simply reading our Bibles well. Much of this book has been about that important matter: reading Scripture well in pursuit of the good life. This is the literature that tells us fundamentally *what* is to be remembered in exile, and it is absolutely necessary that we understand clearly what it teaches us in this respect. But this understanding is not of itself sufficient for our journey. The remembering must still be done. If indeed we find ourselves presently involved in a kind of war, requiring that we "put on the full armor of God, so that [we] can take [our] stand against the devil's schemes" (Eph. 6:11), then of course we must fight with "the sword of the Spirit, which is the word of God" (6:17). But the first battle is actually the battle for our own hearts and minds, which is as crucial to our victory in this conflict as in any other.

THE WATERS OF LETHE

In developing this point, it is appropriate to recall that in Greek mythology there is a river that runs through Hades that causes all who drink from it to lose all memory of their past existence; it is known as the Lethe. My question, then, is this: what are our contemporary waters of Lethe, which interfere with our remembrance of Zion? What are the rivers from which we drink that cause forgetfulness in exile?

SCREEN TIME

Here we must inevitably contrast the picture of daily life presented in Deuteronomy 11 with another, very different picture, comprising several elements. Leaving aside for the moment our life at home and in our Christian community, most of us spend much of each day in work or educational environments shaped by a *Zeitgeist* (a defining spirit or mood of the time) that already offers us little support for our Christian journey. In fact, "the way of the modern world," to quote a colleague of mine, makes it easy "to live as if God doesn't exist."[2] After work or school, we go home. At least in Canada (chosen again simply as an example), over 93 percent of adults are currently joined in these homes by television, primarily through digital cable. They watch, on average, just over twenty-five hours per week (or just under four hours per day).[3] Seventy-five percent of Canadians also admit to logging onto the Internet while watching television. Seventy-three percent spend at least three to four hours each day online (no doubt both at work and in the home). Sixty-six percent spend at least one hour each day online watching TV or movies. The leading online content provider, by some distance, is Netflix (58 percent of the total market).[4]

The shaping power of TV and Internet, as their content is so widely disseminated, is enormous. It is a primary way in which the general cultural environment "seeps into" our lives in our "private" space, shaping our understanding of reality, our imaginations, and our desires and leading us to particular viewpoints concerning what is "normal." This shaping does not need to be a matter of conscious intent in order to be significant, although much of it is intentional: there are well-thought-out agendas at play. Politicians wish us to see the world in a way that suits them; businesses are intent on creating in us the desire to buy their products; and social activists of all kinds are committed, through the transformation of our hearts and minds, to the task of changing the world in general. They no longer need to knock on our doors and talk to us in order to further these agendas, or to persuade us to go out to mass meetings. We are their captive audiences in our own homes, happily absorbing from their rhetoric ideas that range from the true and the good, through to the false and the wicked, by way of the false and the merely stupid.[5] It was the intent of companies like Facebook from the beginning to make us captive in this way, as Facebook's founding president, Sean Parker, admitted in 2017. The question that the founders asked was, "How do we consume as much of your time and conscious attention as possible?" "It's a social-validation feedback loop," he said, "exactly the kind of thing that a hacker like myself would come up with, because you're exploiting a vulnerability in human psychology."[6]

THE POLICY OF NORMALIZATION

So for example, it is not in the least bit accidental that we have recently seen an upsurge in movies and TV shows that include gay and transgendered characters and their relationships, just at the moment when there is an evident general societal push to "normalize" same-sex sexual relationships and the transgendered condition. It is a matter of policy. Responding to ongoing complaints of LGBTQ under-representation in visual media,[7] many more program and filmmakers than before are now striving to redress the balance, to mixed reviews among viewers.[8] The committed among them know that, in terms of changing public opinion, this policy "works." Already in 2015, "[r]espondents who saw a storyline featuring a transgender adolescent on the show *Royal Pains* had more positive attitudes toward transgender people and policies, compared to *Royal Pains* viewers who did not see this particular storyline." Significantly, "neither exposure to news stories about transgender issues, nor the highly visible Caitlyn Jenner [true] story, were associated with (more tolerant) attitudes towards transgender people or policy issues." As the journalist reporting this story comments, "Jenner's story may have been interesting, but it didn't soften hearts; the plight of a fictional character did." Such is the power of our "telescreens" (as Orwell describes them in *1984*) to shape our thinking and feeling.[9]

TIME IN THE STORY

The question, in short, is not only whether we are reading our Bibles well. The question is, how much *time* are we spending in that biblical Story each day, allowing it to shape our thinking, our imaginations, and our desires, relative to the time we spend in the "other world" presented to us each day at work, and in school, and then reinforced at home by TV, the Internet, and social media? How much time are our *children* spending under the instruction of the Lord Jesus Christ, and how much under the tutelage of (say) Dr. Cable, Professor Netflix, or Gauleiter Twitter? If any one of us is spending, say, eight hours per day either online or watching TV, and (say) thirty minutes a day individually in worship, prayer, and Bible study and four hours per week (perhaps) gathering with other Christians to do the same—what is likely to be the outcome of this set of "disciplines" pertaining to our exile? Who is likely to have effective control over our imaginations and desires, and whose view of the world is likely to be the one that we find the more plausible? Adult Christians in post-Christian countries sometimes express surprise at the rapidity of their culture's turn away from Christian faith, and indeed the rapid decline in the number of younger members in their churches. But is it really so surprising, after eighteen years of life in which the Internet (in particular) has been the real catechizer of our young, if at nineteen they no longer find a Christian way of looking at the world convincing?

BETA THROUGH OMEGA

This question underlines our need to recommit in our churches (among other things) to robust Christian education, which on the whole we have been failing to provide for a long time now. Without such a commitment, we cannot possibly expect to survive the cultural tsunami that now threatens to overwhelm us. One thirty-minute sermon each week is not going to be effective.

At the heart of this robust education must lie training in critical thinking. In *1984*, Orwell graphically describes the Party's intent in assailing the general population by way of the telescreen in every citizen's room, with a constant stream of propaganda. It intends thereby to overwhelm the mind's capacity for independent thought. In exhorting the people to "reject the evidence of your eyes and ears" and to believe only what Big Brother says, the Party seeks to control how they interpret truth and reality.[10] The situation is not so different in our own time, even if the goals of the propagandists are not always those of which Orwell's Party would have approved—and we must respond to the challenge. We are immersed in half-truths and lies, but if we cannot *see* them as such, then we cannot combat them. And so we must train ourselves and our children to become better critical thinkers, able to recognize the character of the messaging that is coming our way through advertising, film, and the like, and be capable of rejecting it. We must protect our mind's capacity for independent thought. *Critical Thinking 101* should be regarded as a basic discipleship course—the first course we take after Alpha.[11] Alpha is good, but we also need the further levels: Beta, and then Gamma, through Omega.

THE COURAGE TO RESIST

In this great tale of two cities in which we find ourselves caught up, then, we need first to *remember* by every means possible that Zion is Zion, and that Babylon is Babylon. This remembering requires determination, leading on to the creation of, and adherence to, structures and disciplines of exile that will help keep us and our families faithful to God, rather than slipping, drowsily, away from him. It will enable us then, like the exiles in Psalm 137, to *resist*. Their heads were clear, and their hearts were pure. In NT terms, they had followed the advice of Paul to Colossians: "Set your hearts on things above, where Christ is, seated at the right hand of God. Set your minds on things above, not on earthly things" (Col. 3:1–2). This put them in a position to stand fast against the negative cultural norms and trends of their day.

Their captors wanted the exiles to forget who they were, and to leave behind their pain. They wanted these Judeans to entertain them with "songs of joy" (Ps. 137:3). Remembering reality, however, and in the midst of many tears, the exiles found the nearest trees and suspended from them their musical instruments (v. 2). They retired them for the foreseeable future—a gesture, certainly, of defiance and disobedience. For they realized that weeping was a more appropriate response to their situation than partying—that "blessed are those who mourn" (Matt. 5:4).

Perhaps they also realized the importance, even for their *captors*, of their refusal to capitulate to the false Babylonian worldview. Perhaps they were intent on telling the truth about this civilized Babylonian culture, whose foundations were so stained with blood, precisely so that their captors might one day understand the darkness of what they perceived as paradise. In the fourth chapter of the book of Daniel, King Nebuchadnezzar himself is said to have come to his senses in just this way, raising his eyes toward heaven and having his sanity restored (v. 34).

And so the exiles hung their harps on the trees and refused to play along. They refused to "walk in step with the wicked, or stand in the way that sinners take, or sit in the company of mockers" (Ps. 1:1). They resisted, just like Daniel— that great narrative example of what "respectful resistance to the empire" means for the believing person and of all the good that it can achieve. Daniel and his friends suffered for their resistance, of course; but their suffering changed empires. So did the suffering of the early Christians. We who live in exile now, in this "empire of desire," must resist as well. We must resist false ideas, and we must resist false moralities, and we must refuse to participate in our culture's attempts at normalizing them. We must proclaim the truth, and we must live holy lives, even if it brings suffering—as it sooner or later will.

At the most *general* level, this resistance will involve the continual rejection, mentally, emotionally, and verbally, of the lie that God's law represents a set of chains and shackles that we must cast off in order to be our authentic selves (Ps. 2:3). It will involve the constant affirmation instead that it is the person "whose delight is in the law of the LORD, and who meditates on his law day and night" who is blessed in the end, being like "a tree planted by streams of water . . . whose leaf does not wither" (Ps. 1:1–3). To cast off God's law, we must proclaim, is a path that can only lead to "destruction" (Ps. 1:6). The Progressive Party, including its members who identify as Christians, will of course always present their own path as the path of progress, as will its mirror-image party on the right. For those who have embraced prophetic and apostolic, biblical faith, however, the only progress worth pursuing (as our epigraph above suggests) is by way of a movement backwards to "the right road" delineated by the truth and reality in God's law, and forward again from that point.

CHURCH, WORK, AND SCHOOL

The *particular* form that our resistance takes will depend very much on when and where we live, and what the pressing issues are that confront us in that context. For some of us it will necessarily involve resistance within our *church*. From the beginning, the Church has faced the problem that even within its own ranks are to be found highly acculturated members (like the Gnostics) who do not actually affirm key aspects of the faith and the moral vision articulated in Scripture and may well actively be teaching error. They have substituted a non-Christian for a Christian way of thinking about how we discover what the good life is, and they hold views on important questions of the day that are not easily distinguishable in key respects from those of their non-Christian neighbors. Other kinds of resistance will be futile if we fail to deal with our internally compromised condition. As Paul advises the church in Rome: "I urge you, brothers and sisters, to watch out for those who cause divisions and put obstacles in your way that are contrary to the teaching you have learned. Keep away from them. For such people are not serving our Lord Christ, but their own appetites" (Rom. 16:17–18).

For many of us, our Christian calling will necessarily involve resistance in our *workplace*, since this is the primary location each day in which we engage with Babylon. It will always involve the unspoken resistance of heart and mind, even as we seek respectfully to negotiate a pathway through the challenges involved in the engagement. One is reminded here of Daniel and his friends, living "in exile" in *ancient* Babylon and considering how to be faithful to God in a world that did not know him. Their first move, in Daniel 1, was to discover whether reasonable accommodations could be reached that did not comprise their own identity and integrity (cf. "If it is possible, as far as it depends on you, live at peace with everyone," Rom. 12:18). However, our resistance may sometimes need to be spoken and costly, as we refuse to act in ways that Babylon holds to be virtuous but Zion does not. That is the picture painted for us in Daniel 3. Here there is no flexibility on the side of the idolatrous empire; only complete, worshipful allegiance is acceptable. Resistance must in such circumstances become overt.

SCHOOLING AND PROPAGANDA

Even more importantly, I believe, many of us will be called to resistance in our *school*—another primary location in which (young) exiles engage with Babylon, on most days of the week. This will be especially true if we face the kind of situation described in chapter 19, where the school system itself has become in part the propaganda arm of the imperial government. All parents need to be as sure as they can be that their children are safe at school, and in particular that they are *morally* safe. But is it safe when children are going to be hearing from their teachers, from a young age, that an important part of their business is to discover their sexual orientation and gender identity and (of course) live these out as "authentic selves"? Is it safe when they are spending time every day in environments where a sustained attempt is being made to present this as the normal and right way of looking at the world—for example, by way of reading books from the "Top SOGI Book Choices for Students and Teachers" list?[12] Is this not likely to create confusion, and indeed distress, that was not there to begin with? Clinical psychologist Jordan Peterson certainly believes so:

> The continually expanded plethora of "identities" recently constructed and pro-
> vided with legal status . . . risks generating psychological chaos among the vast
> majority of individuals exposed to the doctrines that insist that identity is essen-
> tially fluid and self-generating (and here I'm primarily concerned about children
> and adolescents whose standard or normative identity has now merely become
> one personal choice among a near-infinite array of ideologically and legally defined
> modes of being).[13]

Might not this confusion then subsequently lead children down a path that they
would not otherwise have chosen? Of course, those who think that one's sexual
orientation and gender identity are individually and reliably "discovered" within
oneself will respond that there is no danger in any of this, because no one can
discover something within that is not already "there." The Campbell River School
District in BC very confidently asserts, for example, that "information and discussion will not make anyone a certain sexual orientation or gender identity."[14] In
chapter 18, however, we saw that in reality who we are, and who we become, have
a considerable amount to do with the environment in which we live, as well as the
interpretations of reality offered within it by both authority figures and peers.

HIGH STAKES

This is why the stakes are so high in the schooling question, and why parents
dealing with an ideologically committed school system cannot afford to be relaxed
about it. It is not only about whether our children continue in their Christian
faith under the influence of contrary but widely accepted ideas permeating our
educational system. It is also about their earthly well-being should they even partially embrace these ideas. For example, we should not want our children's heads
filled with ideas that make it plausible to them to begin "socially transitioning"
to the opposite sex in elementary school. This is typically presented nowadays,
from the adult point of view, as if it were a "neutral" way of treating a child, but
in fact it is itself "a form of social psychological treatment, one that could lessen the
likelihood that the child will psychologically realign with their body by the end of
adolescence."[15] We should not want to prepare the ground in this way for the later
consumption of puberty blockers whose full risks are unknown[16] but which will
almost certainly guarantee (it seems) that the child will progress later to cross-sex
hormones,[17] which possess significant health risks.[18] The next step is irreversible
surgeries that will by no means guarantee the disappearance of the gender dysphoria first diagnosed, or improve the child's happiness in general.[19] We assuredly
do not want (I imagine) to have to answer our child's question later in life—after
irreversible decisions have already been taken and now, perhaps, they would like
to have back the fertility that as a younger person they never imagined they would
miss—"But why did you allow me to start on this path? I was only ten."

We are not alone in this entirely rational concern about where early "affirmation" of gender identity, in particular, can lead. Even "psychologists, social workers, doctors, medical ethicists, and academics" who "tend to be left-leaning, open-minded, and pro-gay rights" are expressing their concern "about the current trend to quickly diagnose and affirm young people as transgender, often setting them down a path toward medical transition."[20] The question that is being raised is a simple one: are we in our public school system *recognizing* a transgender community that already exists from a young age, or are we in fact participating in the *creation* of one?

TERMS OF ENGAGEMENT

In all such situations, we need to resist attempts by others to indoctrinate our children. In the first instance, then, especially with respect to kindergarten and elementary schoolchildren, we need to find out who our teachers are, what they believe, and how they intend to teach. We need to make it clear to them what is acceptable to us in these respects, and what is not, and we need to gain assurances from them that they will keep us fully informed about developments in the relevant areas throughout the school year. We need to be "on top" of our children's education in exile, taking full responsibility for it.

This means educating in the home *even if* we are also using the public-school system—making sure that our young exiles can handle themselves in that system, especially as they get older, and more independent of us. This is where a robust, church-based education would greatly help us. We may even have to opt in the end, unfortunately, for taking over our children's education entirely by way of home-schooling. I say "unfortunately" as a professional educator myself, who believes in the concept of the public school and whose own children went through the BC school system in earlier and quite different times. I believe in Christian participation in the public square. However, if it turns out that this square has been taken over by ideologues who will not listen to us, then we may have no choice but to withdraw from it in order to protect our children.

I also say "unfortunately" because of the evident weaknesses in many home-schooling programs. A genuinely Christian school, staffed by teachers all of whom hold to orthodox Christian beliefs about identity and sex (among other things), would be a much better alternative. This option is simply not affordable for many families, however, even if space in a genuinely Christian school were available within travel distance of their homes. The problem here is compounded by the fact that not all "Christian" schools are especially Christian, especially when it comes to their stance on the pressing issues of the moment. Perhaps one implication of the way in which Babylon is currently trending in many parts of the world is that Christians will need to find ways of funding entirely new networks of

Christian schools that *are* affordable by all families and could indeed be open also
to other neighbors who would welcome some protection for their own children
from unwelcome influences. Protecting our own children is important, but we do
not want to find ourselves standing before God at the end of our lives and unable
to answer this further question: "What did you do to protect children in general?"

THE CONFIDENCE TO TRUST

In exile, then, we need to remember, and we must resist. Along with these two
disciplines belongs a third: the discipline of trust. The final verses of Psalm 137
exemplify it (vv. 7–9). For at least two reasons it is likely that we shall initially
find these verses shocking. First, we may not have lived in similar times, or at
least recognized them as such. Secondly, we are not accustomed to talking to
God about all of the reality in which we live, but only some of it. In particular, we
are accustomed to disguising our true selves both from others (in public prayer)
and from God (in private prayer). In many Church traditions we have in fact
institutionalized the first kind of disguise by simply omitting the gut-wrenching
and raw final verses of Psalm 137 from our prayer books and lectionaries. They are
insufficiently respectable, along with many parts of the other psalms known as
"laments." That is why these numerous alternatives in Scripture to "songs of joy"
inform so little of our sung worship in church services today.

THE NEED FOR LAMENT

The truth is, however, that we need these lament psalms. As reminders of the
suffering of others, and of our need to stand in solidarity with them in prayer,
we need these psalms first to challenge our lack of attention to the darkness of
the world when it does not impinge directly upon *us*. The lament psalms keep us
focused on that darkness when perhaps we would rather forget about it and proceed with the party. Knowing that if we stop addressing God directly about the
lack of justice in the world then we shall soon cease from dealing honestly with
God or caring about justice at all, the lament psalmists force the issue upon us.
They prevent us thereby from falling prey to illusion and delusion with respect
to the nature of the world around us, and from practicing a religion that has
become escapist and cozy, and all too easily adjustable to the favorite ideology of
the moment. If we are truly remembering and resisting in exile, then lament will
naturally follow. It is as fundamental to a properly biblical spirituality as these
other two practices. Conversely, if in our individual prayer and corporate worship
we do not lament as well as praise, then these religious activities will not help us
to remember and resist. Our religion will become Marx's "opium of the people,"
fostering forgetfulness and apathy.

We need the lament psalms, secondly, when we ourselves walk in darkness, and our songs of joy do not help us to talk to God about it. As Eugene Peterson puts it with respect to Psalm 137 specifically:

> Dishonesty in prayer is already rampant enough without assist from bleeding heart editors. The Hebrew editors who selected the psalm for our praying were a tougher breed; they included the third stanza of Psalm 137 deliberately and with good reason: the life of prayer carries us into difficult country, a country in which we become aware that evil is far more extensive than anything we ever guessed, where malignity has worked its way perversely and deeply into the world's ways.

For it is indeed this personally experienced "malignity" in the world, and the hope that God will act to deal with it, that the final verses of Psalm 137 concern. The "children" of the daughter of Babylon—that is, the Babylonians as an entire people-group, just as the "children" of Zion are the inhabitants of Jerusalem and Judah (cf. Lam. 1)—have ravaged the land of Palestine. They have massacred people of all ages. In other words, the exiles have not only left a *land* behind them but also their *dead*—and the psalmist expresses the hope that these horrendous crimes will not be forgotten.

THE COMING OF JUSTICE

He *trusts* that this is so. In the same way that faithful worshippers of God strive always to remember Zion, so the psalmist prays that God will also remember Edom's treachery as well as Babylon's victims, and that justice will be done. He trusts that God, in accordance with the principle of *lex talionis* already encountered in our chapter 17, will ensure that there will be some kind of fitting and appropriate punishment for their crimes. It is this legal realm that the word "repays" (Hb. *shalem*) in Psalm 137:8 recalls.[21] We exiles are not permitted to take personal vengeance on Babylonians, even if they treat us brutally (e.g., Prov. 24:28–29; Matt. 5:38–42; Rom. 12:17–21). We are to love our oppressors, somehow, even as we cannot allow their crimes to pass unnoticed, nor allow the voices of their victims to go unheard. So where is justice to come from? It must come from God. It *will* come from God. *He* will not forget the true character of Babylon, even if her children make every effort to spin it. As invincible as this great city might sometimes appear, Babylon will certainly fall, as the Most High God, who "is sovereign over all kingdoms on earth and gives them to anyone he wishes," weighs her on his justice scales and finds her wanting (Dan. 4:34; 5:27).

IN THE MEANTIME

In the meantime we pursue, with discipline, the good life. We remember, we resist, and we trust. Perhaps such faithful lives will change the landscape of exile itself. Perhaps, like Daniel and his friends, we shall become the means by which the empire repents (Dan. 4). If not, then perhaps we shall at least be able to persuade it to allow us ongoing space to live our own lives in peace and quiet (Dan. 1), looking favorably upon us even in the presence of our enemies (Dan. 6). We should certainly pray and work for such outcomes, along with other brave souls who are in their own way standing up for what is true and good even in the midst of fear about what might happen to them as a result. Our love for even our enemies requires that we do so.

But perhaps none of this will happen. It is entirely possible that our post-Christian Western cultures will only become still more post-Christian. It is possible that the avowedly tolerant (but actually in key respects totalitarian) elites who now hold political and legal power in this postmodern "empire of desire" will offer no space in which the true Church can safely exist—that we shall soon find ourselves back in the Roman Empire prior to Constantine, requesting tolerance and typically failing to obtain it. It is possible that it will soon no longer be acceptable, or indeed legal, to hold to traditionally Christian views on a whole range of matters, including gender and sexuality, and to live out our lives in accordance with those views.

Perhaps we shall change empires, but perhaps not. Perhaps our immediate future in many parts of the world is only as that incomprehensible minority who refuse to define their identity in terms of their work, their gender, or their sexual preferences." Perhaps—as Stanley Hauerwas once said—it is as "those peculiar people who don't abort their babies or kill their elderly," or for that matter their disabled (or otherwise "faulty") infants.[22] Perhaps our future is as traitors to our tribe or class, because we refuse to take the correct (or indeed any) ideological line politically, or to our countries, because we refuse to endorse their nationalistic rhetoric.

We do not know what will happen, and in a very fundamental way it does not *matter* what happens. We must in any case continue in our pursuit of the good life. Living in Babylon, the city of our present exile, we must remain devoted to Jerusalem, the city prepared for us in the future (Heb. 11:10, 16; Rev. 21:2, 10). Our goal is to get there with our heart and minds, and indeed our bodies, intact.

THE GOOD AND THE PERFECT LIFE

With any book concerning Christian ethics, there is always a particular danger to be faced—and I want to end this book by facing it. The danger is that in perceiving in a new and deeper way God's calling upon our lives, and at the same time the challenges involved in responding to it, we feel crushed rather than energized. We recognize in a new way how much we have been conformed to our culture rather to Christ. We are weighed down by our sins, which perhaps we now realize are more numerous and more serious than we ever thought before. Aware of our weakness, and convicted about our lack of courage, we shrink in the face of the difficult path ahead. We are not sure how we shall ever be able to cope without the waters of Lethe to soothe us in our daily troubles.

The good news is that Scripture has anticipated us in these respects and provides us with the reassurance that we need in order to go on. It does so by showing us Isaiah, for example, oblivious to what true holiness looks like until the day that he receives a vision of God in the Jerusalem temple (Isa. 6:1–8). Now he understands for the first time just how unholy he is, and his reaction is appropriate: "Woe to me! . . . I am ruined! For I am a man of unclean lips, and I live among a people of unclean lips, and my eyes have seen the King, the LORD Almighty" (v. 5). The significant moment is the very next one, however. No sooner has Isaiah acknowledged the truth than "one of the seraphim flew to me with a live coal in his hand, which he had taken with tongs from the altar. With it he touched my mouth and said, 'See, this has touched your lips; your guilt is taken away and your sin atoned for'" (vv. 6–7). The problem is immediately dealt with—by God. And this frees Isaiah up to respond eagerly and positively to God's calling: "Here am I. Send me!" (v. 8).

Scripture reassures us also by letting us inside the Apostle Paul's mind to see his turmoil as a person who has also realized, in the aftermath of his conversion to Christ, what God's law really demands—what it truly means that "the law is holy, and the commandment is holy, righteous, and good" (Rom. 7:12). At one level Paul delights in this law (v. 22), but he also sees "another law at work in me, waging war against the law of my mind and making me a prisoner of the law of sin at work within me" (v. 23). He is, therefore, "wretched" and in need of "rescue" (v. 24). The remedy is immediately at hand, however: "there is now no condemnation for those who are in Christ Jesus, because through Christ Jesus the law of the Spirit who gives life has set you free from the law of sin and death" (8:2–3). That is, we are by no means perfect, but we do not need to be, since God has made us in Christ his own children (v. 14). It is in this confidence that we can look ahead on our path with hope, convinced that "our present sufferings are not worth comparing with the glory that will be revealed in us" (v. 18), knowing that "in all things God works for the good of those who love him" (v. 28).

The point is this: that the *good* life in Scripture is not a life devoid of weakness and sin. It is instead the *faithful* life, one aspect of which is resting every moment in the grace of the God who is slow to anger and quick to forgive, and who is indeed able "to empathize with our weaknesses" (Heb. 4:15). It is on this basis, and not on the ground of our moral perfection, that we "approach God's throne of grace with confidence," precisely "so that we may receive mercy and find grace to help us in our time of need" (v. 16). Our *search* for the good is premised on the fact that we have already been *found* by the Good. And it is for this reason that we are able every day (if we choose), with a clear conscience and a joyful heart, to forget "what is behind" (including all our many sins) and strain "toward what is ahead," pressing on "toward the goal to win the prize for which God has called [us] heavenward in Christ Jesus" (Phil. 3:13–14).

The good life, in other words, is not the perfect life. It is only the committed life, in pursuit of "the pioneer of [our] salvation" who was made "perfect through what he suffered" and now makes his pursuers holy (Heb. 2:10–11). It is "a long obedience in the same direction," in company with the Person through whose obedience we have already been made righteous.[23] And this committed obedience, we are promised, will reap great rewards. The journey will be well worth it, in view of what we shall discover at its end.

FINAL DISCUSSION QUESTION

In your own particular context, which challenges do you face in pursuing the good life as described in Scripture and summarized in this book? What are you doing, or what will you do, to prepare to meet these challenges?

Appendix

Resources for Further Study and Engagement with the
Issues Discussed in Chapters 17 and 18

WEBSITES

These websites provide ongoing and up-to-date information about one or more
of the issues discussed in chapters 18 and 19, including about social and political
developments:

- A Rocha, https://arocha.ca/: an international Christian organization
  engaged in scientific research, environmental education, community-based
  conservation projects, and sustainable agriculture.
- ARPA Canada, https://arpacanada.ca/: designed to "educate, equip, and
  encourage Reformed Christians to political action and to bring a biblical
  perspective to our civil authorities."
- BioEdge, https://www.bioedge.org/: "bioethics news from around the
  world."
- Cardus, https://www.cardus.ca/: "a nonpartisan, faith-based think tank
  and registered charity dedicated to promoting a flourishing society through

independent research, robust public dialogue, and thought-provoking commentary."

+ Focus on the Family, https://www.focusonthefamily.ca/ and https://www.focusonthefamily.com/: "helping families thrive."
+ Journey Canada, https://www.journeycanada.org/: "a community-based, Christ-centred discipleship ministry that exists to help people find hope and live life through experiencing Jesus in their relationships, sexuality, and identity."
+ PATH (Positive Approaches to Healthy Sexuality), https://www.pathinfo.org/: "a nonprofit ecumenical coalition of organizations . . . whose main goal is to promote healthy sexuality and traditional family values."
+ REAL Women of Canada, http://www.realwomenofcanada.ca/: "speaks for women who support the values of traditional family and marriage."
+ Telos Group, http://www.telosgroup.org/resources/: an American organization seeking a "time beyond the Israeli-Palestinian conflict, when diverse communities of American peacemakers will stand with both Palestinians and Israelis to sustain security, dignity and freedom for all." They have a compendium of various resources on their webpage.

BIG-PICTURE BIBLICAL INTERPRETATION AND THEOLOGY

+ Iain Provan, *The Reformation and the Right Reading of Scripture* (Waco: Baylor University Press, 2017).
+ Iain Provan, *Seriously Dangerous Religion* (Waco: Baylor University Press, 2014).

ISRAEL/PALESTINE

+ Dale Hanson Bourke, *The Israeli-Palestinian Conflict: Tough Questions, Direct Answers*, The Skeptic's Guide Series (Downers Grove, Ill.: IVP, 2013).
+ Walter Brueggemann, *Chosen?: Reading the Bible amid the Israeli-Palestinian Conflict* (Louisville: Westminster John Knox, 2015).
+ Donald Lewis, *A Short History of Christian Zionism* (Downers Grove, Ill.: IVP Academic, forthcoming).
+ Rosemary Radford Ruether and Herman J. Ruether, *The Wrath of Jonah: The Crisis of Religious Nationalism in the Israeli-Palestinian Conflict*, 2nd ed. (Minneapolis: Fortress, 2002).

CREATION CARE

+ Richard Bauckham, *Living with Other Creatures: Green Exegesis and Theology* (Waco: Baylor University Press, 2011).

- David Bookless, *Planetwise: Dare to Care for God's World* (Nottingham: IVP, 2008).
- Steven Bouma-Prediger, *For the Beauty of the Earth: A Christian Vision for Creation Care*, Engaging Culture, 2nd ed. (Grand Rapids: Baker Academic, 2010).
- Leah Kostamo, *Planted: A Story of Creation, Calling, and Community* (Eugene, Ore.: Wipf & Stock, 2013).
- Douglas J. Moo and Jonathan A. Moo, *Creation Care: A Biblical Theology of the Natural World*, Biblical Theology for Life (Grand Rapids: Zondervan, 2018).

ABORTION

- Robert P. George and Christopher Tollefsen, *Embryo: A Defense of Human Life* (New York: Doubleday, 2008).
- Bernard N. Nathanson, *The Hand of God: A Journey from Death to Life by the Abortion Doctor Who Changed His Mind* (repr., Washington, D.C.: Regnery, 2013).
- Pope John Paul II, *Evangelium Vitae*, http://www.vatican.va/content/john-paul-ii/en/encyclicals/documents/hf_jp-ii_enc_25031995_evangelium-vitae.html.
- Sarah C. Williams, *Perfectly Human: Nine Months with Cerian* (Walden, N.Y.: Plough, 2018).

EUTHANASIA AND ASSISTED SUICIDE

- Ryan T. Anderson, "Always Care, Never Kill: How Physician-Assisted Suicide Endangers the Weak, Corrupts Medicine, Compromises the Family, and Violates Human Dignity and Equality," https://www.heritage.org/health-care-reform/report/always-care-never-kill-how-physician-assisted-suicide-endangers-the-weak.
- Canadian Society of Palliative Care Physicians, http://www.cspcp.ca/cspcp-key-messages-re-hastened-death/: "Key Messages: Physician-Hastened Death."
- *The Christian Medical and Dental Society of Canada*, www.cmdscanada.org: many resources, including a video (*The Gift*).
- Alex Schadenberg, *Exposing Vulnerable People to Euthanasia and Assisted Suicide* (Brisbane: Connor Court, 2014).
- *The Vulnerable Persons Standard*, http://www.vps-npv.ca/: proposed Canadian safeguards designed to protect "vulnerable persons who may be subject to coercion, inducement to suicide and abuse" in the context of legalized euthanasia and PAS."

GENDER DYSPHORIA

+ Evangelical Alliance, *Trans Formed* (London: Evangelical Alliance, 2018).
+ Minnesota Family Council, "Parent Resource Guide: Responding to the Transgender Issue" (2019), available free at genderresourceguide.com.
+ Vaughan Roberts, *Transgender* (Good Book Company, 2016), Kindle edition.
+ Mark A. Yarhouse, *Understanding Gender Dysphoria: Navigating Transgender Issues in a Changing Culture* (Downers Grove, Ill.: IVP Academic, 2015).

SAME-SEX ATTRACTION AND RELATIONSHIPS

+ Denny Burk and Heath Lambert, *Transforming Homosexuality: What the Bible Says about Sexual Orientation and Change* (Phillipsburg, N.J.: P&R, 2015)
+ Wesley Hill, *Washed and Waiting: Reflections on Christian Faithfulness and Homosexuality* (Grand Rapids: Zondervan, 2010).
+ Mark Yarhouse and Olya Zaporozhets, *Costly Obedience: What We Can Learn from the Celibate Gay Christian Community* (Grand Rapids: Zondervan, 2019).

Notes

1   THE GOOD LIFE AND HOW TO RECOGNIZE IT

1   Leo Tolstoy, *War and Peace*, trans. Anthony Briggs (London: Penguin, 2005), 375.

2   The book in question is Ruth W. Grant, ed., *In Search of Goodness* (Chicago: University of Chicago Press, 2011). The advertisement may be found at https://www.press.uchicago.edu/ucp/books/book/chicago/I/bo10998156.html.

3   Alia E. Dastagir, "Are You a Good Person? Morality Experts Say This Is How to Find Out," *USA Today*, December 21, 2018, https://www.usatoday.com/story/news/2017/12/26/you-good-person/967459001/.

4   Matthew 19:17 emphasizes a different aspect of the question, but with the same intent to declare that God alone is the arbiter of the good: "Why do you ask me about what is good?" Jesus replied. "There is only One who is good."

5   Mark Murphy, "The Natural Law Tradition in Ethics," in *Stanford Encyclopedia of Philosophy*, Winter 2011 online ed., ed. Edward N. Zalta, https://plato.stanford.edu/archives/win2011/entries/natural-law-ethics/.

6   *Merriam-Webster*, s.v. "natural," https://www.merriam-webster.com/dictionary/natural.

7   *Merriam-Webster*, s.v. "supernatural," https://www.merriam-webster.com/dictionary/supernatural.

8   *Journals of the Continental Congress, 1774–1789*, vol. 5, ed. Worthington C. Ford et al. (Washington, D.C.: Washington Government Printing Office, 1904–1937), 510–14.

9   U. S. Congress, *French Declaration of the Rights of Man and of the Citizen and the American Bill of Rights: A Bicentennial Commemoration Issued Pursuant to S.J. Res. 317, 100th Congress* (Washington, D.C.: U.S. Congress, Senate, 1989), 1.

10   Lynn Hunt, ed., *The French Revolution and Human Rights: A Brief Documentary History* (Boston: Bedford; New York: St. Martin's, 1996), 119.

11   Olympe de Gouges, "Declaration of the Rights of Woman and the Female Citizen," in *Feminist Writings from Ancient Times to the Modern World*, vol. 1, ed. Tiffany K. Wayne (Santa Barbara, Calif.: Greenwood, 2011), 155–57. Another significant contribution to the question of women's rights from this same era was Mary Wollstonecraft's *A Vindication of the Rights of Woman: With Strictures on Political and Moral Subjects* (Dublin: Stockdale, 1792).

12   Radical as she was in her demands for women's rights, de Gouges was closely allied with the Girondin political faction. They were considerably more moderate than the Montagnards who gained control of the revolution in 1793. She suffered accordingly, executed for treason during the Reign of Terror that followed the coup.

13   Sophie Mousset, *Women's Rights and the French Revolution* (New York: Routledge, 2007), 97.

14   See further Elizabeth Racz, "The Women's Rights Movement in the French Revolution," *SSoc* 16 (1952): 151–74 (166–72).

15   Elizabeth Cady Stanton et al., *History of Woman Suffrage*, vol. 1 (Rochester, N.Y.: S. B. Anthony, 1887), 70.

16   "Such has been the patient sufferance of the women under this government, and such is now the necessity which constrains them to demand the equal station to which they are entitled. The history of mankind is a history of repeated injuries and usurpations on the part of man toward woman, having in direct object the establishment of an absolute tyranny over her." Stanton et al., *Suffrage*, 70.

17   Cited in Ter Ellingson, *The Myth of the Noble Savage* (Berkeley: University of California Press, 2001), 81.

18   David Hume, *Treatise of Human Nature: Reprinted from the Original Edition in Three Volumes*, 3.1.1.27, ed. L. A. Selby-Bigge (repr., Oxford: Clarendon, 1960), 469. I have often taken the liberty in this volume of amending slightly the premodern English of some older texts for the benefit of the reader without (I hope) altering the sense. The original in this case, e.g., refers to "the usual copulations of propositions," which to most modern readers is opaque. The originals can in each case be checked by following the endnotes.

2   THE TWENTY-FIVE PERCENT BIBLE

1   The Apocrypha are books such as the Wisdom of Solomon and Ecclesiasticus that occupied an important place in the life of the early postapostolic Church but whose canonicity had always been a disputed matter. Following the lead of Jerome (c. AD 347–420), the Protestant Reformers excluded them from the canon; the Roman Catholic Church has retained them as "deuterocanonical" texts. See further my book *The Reformation and the Right Reading of Scripture* (Waco: Baylor University Press, 2017), chapters 2 and 3.

2   Andy Stanley, "Aftermath, Part 3: Not Difficult," YouTube video, April 30, 2018, https://www.youtube.com/watch?v=pShxFTNRCWI&feature=youtu.be.

3   The substance of the argument that follows is taken from Provan, *Right Reading*, chapter 2, which readers should consult for further detailed footnote references in respect to the points made here.

4   Romans 1:23; 2:21–22; 7:7–12.

5   Christopher R. Seitz, *The Character of Christian Scripture: The Significance of a Two-Testament Bible*, STI (Grand Rapids: Baker Academic, 2011), 17.

6   Henning G. Reventlow, *History of Biblical Interpretation*, vol. 1: *From the Old Testament to Origen*, trans. Leo Perdue, RBS 50 (Atlanta: Society of Biblical Literature, 2009), 140, 146.

7   For an extensive discussion, see Provan, *Right Reading*, chapters 7 to 9.

8   On Marcion see further Provan, *Right Reading*, 2–43, 158–60, and 166–69.

9   Reventlow, *Biblical Interpretation*, 1:151.

10   Reventlow, *Biblical Interpretation*, 1:155. For some further information about Platonism and Gnosticism in relation to biblical faith see Iain Provan, *Seriously Dangerous Religion: What the Old Testament Really Says and Why It Matters* (Waco: Baylor University Press, 2014), 125–26, 153–55, and 242–44.

11   Irenaeus, *Adversus haereses* (*Against Heresies*) 3.13.1 (*ANF* 1:436). Ancient and medieval sources like this one, from the Church Fathers and other writers, are often cited only in an abbreviated Greek or Latin form. To make life easier for the reader of this book, however,

they will be cited herein on their first endnote appearance using their full Greek or Latin title, accompanied by its English translation. On subsequent appearances, only the abbreviated form of the English will be used.

12   Stephen G. Dempster, "Canon and Old Testament Interpretation," in *Hearing the Old Testament: Listening for God's Address*, ed. Craig G. Bartholomew and David J. H. Beldman (Grand Rapids: Eerdmans, 2012), 154–79 (159).

13   For a detailed description see Provan, *Right Reading*, 160–65.

14   John J. O'Keefe and Russell R. Reno, *Sanctified Vision: An Introduction to Early Christian Interpretation of the Bible* (Baltimore: Johns Hopkins University Press, 2005), 34, 37.

15   Irenaeus, *Against Heresies* 2.28.3 (*ANF* 1:400).

16   Irenaeus, *Against Heresies* 3.12.12 (*ANF* 1:434).

17   Reventlow, *Biblical Interpretation*, 1:163.

18   Irenaeus, *Against Heresies* 1.9.4 (*ANF* 1:330).

19   Irenaeus, *Against Heresies* 1.8.1; 1.9.4 (*ANF* 1:326, 330).

20   For a thorough discussion of what literal reading does and does not involve, see Provan, *Right Reading*, chapter 4.

21   Augustine, *De doctrina christiana* (*Christian Doctrine*) 1.36 (*NPNF¹* 2:533).

22   On the origins of allegorical reading in Greece, see Provan, *Right Reading*, 138–41. The Homeric literature possessed great cultural authority in Greece, but by the fifth century BC many intellectuals could no longer take seriously its perspective (e.g.) on the gods, whose behavior was considered oftentimes to be reprehensible.

23   O'Keefe and Reno, *Sanctified Vision*, 103.

24   Shaye J. D. Cohen, *The Beginnings of Jewishness: Boundaries, Varieties, Uncertainties* (Berkeley: University of California Press, 1999), 190.

25   Cited in Cohen, *Beginnings*, 190.

26   Cited in Cohen, *Beginnings*, 190.

27   Council of Laodicea, Canon 29 (*NPNF²* 14:148).

28   Norman P. Tanner, S.J., ed., *Decrees of the Ecumenical Councils*, 2 vols. (London: Sheed & Ward, 1990), 1:109, 113. For a full description of Theodore's life and work, see Provan, *Right Reading*, 184–90.

29   Cohen, *Beginnings*, 196.

30   Ambrose, *De Jacob et vita beata* (*Jacob and the Happy Life*), in *St. Ambrose: Seven Exegetical Works*, ed. Bernard M. Peebles et al., trans. Michael P. McHugh, FC 65 (Washington, D.C.: Catholic University of America, 1985), 137.

31   Irenaeus, *Against Heresies* 4.31 (*ANF* 1:504–5).

3   IN THE BEGINNING

1   See "Revive 2019," Hebraic Roots, https://hebraicroots.ticketleap.com/revive19/details.

2   For an in-depth description of the earlier Revive 2013 event and its participants, see Menachem Kaiser, "For Some Believers Trying to Connect With Jesus, the Answer Is to Live Like a Jew," Tablet, February 4, 2014, https://www.tabletmag.com/jewish-life-and-religion/161086/observing-torah-like-jesus.

3   For more on this, see Provan, *Seriously Dangerous Religion*, 31–46. Expansions of everything else in this present brief description of the Bible's great Story may also be found in this book.

4   Leon R. Kass, *The Beginning of Wisdom: Reading Genesis* (New York: Free Press, 2003), 168.

5   D. E. Kennedy, *The English Revolution 1642–1649*, BHP (Basingstoke: Macmillan, 2000), 125–28.

4   THE EMPEROR'S NEW CLOTHES

1   S. L. Greenslade, *Church & State from Constantine to Theodosius*, 1953 F. D. Maurice Lectures (London: SCM Press, 1954), 12.
2   For the background, see Paul Stephenson, *Constantine: Unconquered Emperor, Christian Victor* (London: Quercus, 2011), 87–116. Two men held the title of "Augustus" at this time.
3   Stephenson, *Constantine*, 62–86.
4   Peter Leithart, *Defending Constantine: The Twilight of an Empire and the Dawn of Christendom* (Downers Grove, Ill.: IVP, 2010), 40.
5   Stephenson, *Constantine*, 127–31.
6   Stephenson, *Constantine*, 84–86.
7   Stephenson, *Constantine*, 170. For a brief introduction to Lactantius and some excerpts from his *Divine Institutes*, see *From Irenaeus to Grotius: A Sourcebook in Christian Political Thought 100–1625*, ed. Oliver O'Donovan and Joan Lockwood O'Donovan (Grand Rapids: Eerdmans, 1999), 46–55.
8   Stephenson, *Constantine*, 174.
9   Stephenson, *Constantine*, 174.
10   Stephenson, *Constantine*, 134–40. It is in this context that we encounter the famous but problematic story of Constantine's vision of a cross prior to the battle (182–89).
11   Stephenson, *Constantine*, 138; 151–58.
12   Stephenson, *Constantine*, 173.
13   Stephenson, *Constantine*, 182–87.
14   Stephenson, *Constantine*, 216–17.
15   Stephenson, *Constantine*, 256–78.
16   Stephenson, *Constantine*, 256.
17   Leithart, *Defending Constantine*, 126–46.
18   Amnon Linder, "The Legal Status of the Jews in the Roman Empire," in *The Cambridge History of Judaism*, vol. 4: *Late Roman-Rabbinic Period*, ed. Steven T. Katz (Cambridge: Cambridge University Press, 2006), 128–73 (150).
19   Linder, "Legal Status," 152.
20   Judith Herrin, *The Formation of Christendom* (Princeton: Princeton University Press, 1987), 40.
21   Linder, "Legal Status," 140.
22   Linder, "Legal Status," 129.
23   See further on Constantine and the Jews, Peter Schafer, *The History of the Jews in the Greco-Roman World: The Jews of Palestine from Alexander the Great to the Arab Conquest* (London: Routledge, 2003), 180–84.
24   Shlomo Simonsohn, *The Apostolic See and the Jews: History* (Rome: Pontifical Institute of Mediaeval Studies, 1991), 4; Schafer, *History of the Jews*, 5.
25   Schafer, *History of the Jews*, 189–92 (191).
26   Simonsohn, *Apostolic See*, 4.
27   Schafer, *History of the Jews*, 191.
28   Schafer, *History of the Jews*, 192.
29   Schafer, *History of the Jews*, 191.
30   Linder, "Legal Status," 168–69.
31   Linder, "Legal Status," 152.
32   Schafer, *History of the Jews*, 194–95.
33   It was under Justinian's rule, e.g., that Jews were for the first time denied "the right to appear before a court as witnesses against an (orthodox) Christian." They were also "removed from all important offices in the municipal administration [and only] . . . permitted to hold lower

positions 'where the burden of office was greater than the honour'" (Schafer, *History of the Jews*, 194).

34   Schafer, *History of the Jews*, 194–95.
35   Simonsohn, *Apostolic See*, 8. In painting a general picture, of course, one must be careful to offer nuance. The empire of Charlemagne, for example, provided an environment for Jews in which they apparently flourished.
36   Loveday C. A. Alexander, "Rome, Early Christian Attitudes to," in *ABD* 5:836–39 (839), citing Acts 16:37–39; 18:12–17; 21:31–22:29; 23:11–24:12.
37   Alexander, "Rome," 839.
38   Alexander, "Rome," 837.
39   Irenaeus, *Against Heresies* 5.28–29 (*ANF* 1:556–58).
40   Irenaeus, *Against Heresies* 5.26 (*ANF* 1:496–98).
41   Adolf M. Ritter, "Church and State up to *c*. 300 CE," in *Origins to Constantine*, ed. M. M. Mitchell, F. M. Young, and K. S. Bowie, Cambridge History of Christianity, vol. 1 (Cambridge: Cambridge University Press, 2006), 524–37 (530).
42   O'Donovan and O'Donovan, *From Irenaeus to Grotius*, 16.
43   Herrin, *Formation*, 3–4.
44   Ritter, "Church and State," 532. He thereby chooses an emphasis that differs from that of Melito of Sardis (d. c. 180), who proposes that the glory of the empire is a consequence of the favor shown to Christians by the Roman authorities under most of the preceding emperors and urges the incumbent Marcus Aurelius to continue to "protect that philosophy which began with Augustus and was reared along with the empire" (529).
45   Tertullian, *Apologeticus* (*Apology*) 30 (*ANF* 3:42).
46   Tertullian, *Apology* 32 (*ANF* 3:42–43).
47   Tertullian, *Apology* 33 (*ANF* 3:43).
48   Ritter, "Church and State," 533.
49   Origen, *Contra Celsum* (*Against Celsus*) 8.73 (*ANF* 4:667).
50   Origen, *Against Celsus* 8.75 (*ANF* 4:668).
51   Mathetes, *Pros Diognēton 'epistolē* (*Epistle to Diognetus*) 5 (*ANF* 1:25).
52   Eusebius, *Vita Constantini* (*Life of Constantine*) 1.12 (*NPNF*² 1:485).
53   Eusebius, *Life of Constantine* 1.20 (*NPNF*² 1:488).
54   Eusebius, *Life of Constantine* 1.28–29 (*NPNF*² 1:490).
55   Eusebius, *Life of Constantine* 1.30–32 (*NPNF*² 1:490–91).
56   Eusebius, *Life of Constantine* 1.38 (*NPNF*² 1:493).
57   Eusebius, *Life of Constantine* 1.38 (*NPNF*² 1:493).
58   Eusebius, *Historia ecclesiastica* (*Church History*) 9.9.2 and 9.9.5 (*NPNF*² 1:364).
59   Clement of Alexandria, *Stromata* (*Miscellanies*) 1.26 (*ANF* 2:338). Important connections exist between Eusebius and the earlier Jewish author Philo of Alexandria, in his *Life of Moses*. Fin Damgaard, "Propaganda against Propaganda: Revisiting Eusebius' Use of the Figure of Moses in the *Life of Constantine*," in *Eusebius of Caesarea: Tradition and Innovations*, ed. Aaron Johnson and Jeremy Schott, HS (Cambridge, Mass.: Harvard University Press, 2013), 115–32 (123–28).
60   Stephenson, *Constantine*, 209; and see further the entire discussion on pp. 209–11.
61   Cyprian, *Ad Quirinum testimonia adversus Judaeos* (*To Quirinius: Testimonies against the Jews*) 2.21–22 (*ANF* 5:524–25).
62   Averil Cameron, "Constantine and the 'Peace of the Church,'" in Mitchell, Young, and Bowie, *Origins to Constantine*, 538–51 (551).
63   Greenslade, *Church & State*, 10.
64   Eusebius, *Church History*, 10.9.7 (*NPNF*² 1:387–88).
65   Damgaard, "Propaganda," 117.

66 Stephenson, *Constantine*, 219.

67 Stephenson, *Constantine*, 250.

68 Stephenson, *Constantine*, 251, quoting the *Tricennial Oration* in praise of the emperor (AD 336). See further O'Donovan and O'Donovan, *From Irenaeus to Grotius*, 60–65.

69 These are words taken from Eusebius' address upon the occasion of the dedication of the Church of the Holy Sepulcher in Jerusalem in 335 (O'Donovan and O'Donovan, *From Irenaeus to Grotius*, 59). Eusebius cites here Ps. 72:7–8 and Isa. 2:4.

70 Herrin, *Formation*, 58–59.

71 Stephenson, *Constantine*, 189, 228–34.

72 Stephenson, *Constantine*, 189. See the immediate context of this quote for striking examples of what he means.

73 Greenslade, *Church & State*, 46, 48. For a precursor in using OT characters as analogues for those who persecute true Christians, see again Cyprian, who refers to Saul, Ahab, and Nebuchadnezzar (Cyprian, *Ad Fortunatum* [*To Fortunatus: Exhortation to Martyrdom*] 11 [*ANF* 5:502–5]).

74 Herrin, *Formation*, 39.

75 Cameron, "Constantine," 551.

76 Greenslade, *Church & State*, 12.

77 John H. Walton, *Ancient Near Eastern Thought and the Old Testament: Introducing the Conceptual World of the Hebrew Bible* (Grand Rapids: Baker Academic, 2006), 278–86.

78 On the ideal of the shepherd king in the ANE, see Wilfred G. Lambert, "Kingship in Ancient Mesopotamia," in *King and Messiah in Israel and the Ancient Near East: Proceedings of the Oxford Old Testament Seminar*, ed. John Day (London: T&T Clark, 2013), 54–71. In 1–2 Kings the absence of such a shepherd king is explicitly noted by the prophet Micaiah (1 Kgs. 22:17).

79 Cameron, "Constantine," 551.

80 Eusebius, *Life of Constantine* 1.12 (*NPNF*² 1:485).

81 See Stephenson, *Constantine*, 116.

82 Eusebius, *Life of Constantine* 1.20 (*NPNF*² 1:488).

83 Eusebius, *Church History* 9.9.5 (*NPNF*² 1:363).

84 Eusebius, *Life of Constantine* 1.12 (*NPNF*² 1:485).

85 Eusebius, *Life of Constantine* 1.20. (*NPNF*² 1:488).

86 Eusebius, *Life of Constantine* 1.38–39 (*NPNF*² 1:492–93).

87 Eusebius, *Life of Constantine* 1.12; 4.72 (*NPNF*² 1:485; 559).

88 Leithart, *Defending Constantine*, 76 (with a significant medallion example on p. 244). Consider, e.g., the "Great Cameo" of c. 324–326, of which Paul Stephenson says, "Looking at the Great Cameo, one might wonder at the nature of Constantine's Christianity" (Stephenson, *Constantine*, 218).

89 Leithart, *Defending Constantine*, 230.

90 Stephenson, *Constantine*, 201–3.

91 Stephenson, *Constantine*, 203.

92 Stephenson, *Constantine*, 288. See further Leithart, *Defending Constantine*, 93–94, who appears to me to underplay the significance of the evidence.

93 Eusebius, *Life of Constantine* 1.7 (*NPNF*² 1:483).

94 Leithart, *Defending Constantine*, 236–67.

95 Stephenson, *Constantine*, 209; and see further the entire discussion on pp. 209–11.

96 Stephenson, *Constantine*, 300–302, on how the notion of a "Christian army" developed after Constantine.

97 Stephenson, *Constantine*, 278; Leithart, *Defending Constantine*, 86, citing John H. Yoder, and also p. 124.

98   Stephenson, *Constantine*, 248, 256, 262; Leithart, *Defending Constantine*, 82–83.
99   "Neither before nor after Josiah was there a king like him who turned to the Lord as he did—with all his heart and with all his soul and with all his strength, in accordance with all the Law of Moses"—and yet he died an untimely death, reigning for a much shorter time than his wicked grandfather Manasseh (2 Kgs. 23:25, 29).
100 Leithart, *Defending Constantine*, 237, 245.
101 Stephenson, *Constantine*, 230.
102 This is so even after all allowances are made for the truth that a Christian ruler must necessarily attend to the present *as well as* to the future; we shall return to this truth in chapter 5.
103 Leithart, *Defending Constantine*, 287.
104 Greenslade, *Church & State*, 11.
105 Geoffrey Koziol, "Christianizing Political Discourses," in *The Oxford Handbook of Medieval Christianity*, ed. John H. Arnold (Oxford: Oxford University Press, 2014), 473–89 (473).

5   NOT WHOLLY ROMAN

1   Chris Wickham, *The Inheritance of Rome: Illuminating the Dark Ages, 400–1000*, PHE 2 (New York: Penguin, 2010), 424.
2   The great Athanasius of Alexandria (296–373), for example, sharply confronted Constantine over the question of Nicene orthodoxy, and in his *Life of Anthony* recorded Anthony's pointed opinion "that Constantine was no more than a man and that 'Christ is the only true and eternal Emperor'" (Leithart, *Defending Constantine*, 185). The life of John Chrysostom (349–407) further testifies to the truth "that the Latin-speaking West had no monopoly on conflict between ecclesiastical and secular government in the new Christian empire" (O'Donovan and O'Donovan, *From Irenaeus to Grotius*, 89).
3   Herrin, *Formation*, 116.
4   Greenslade, *Church & State*, 79; Leithart, *Defending Constantine*, 292.
5   Leithart, *Defending Constantine*, 292, partially quoting Arnaldo Momigliano.
6   The word itself originated in ancient Greece as a way of referring to people who were from "out of town" and did not speak Greek. It had no necessarily negative connotation beyond that, e.g., "uncivilized." Herodotus used it in referring to the Persians.
7   O'Donovan and O'Donovan, *From Irenaeus to Grotius*, 90, noting Chrysostom's own view of the appropriate relationship between secular and sacred authority.
8   O'Donovan and O'Donovan, *From Irenaeus to Grotius*, 67.
9   Herrin, *Formation*, 25–26.
10   Leithart, *Defending Constantine*, 284.
11   Leithart, *Defending Constantine*, 284n12, 286.
12   Herrin, *Formation*, 28–37. She notes, e.g., the manner in which "Clovis, king of the Franks, celebrated his nomination by Emperor Anastasios to the position of honorary consul in 508" (35–36).
13   O'Donovan and O'Donovan, *From Irenaeus to Grotius*, 170.
14   Herrin, *Formation*, 359.
15   Herrin, *Formation*, 379; Alessandro Barbero, *Charlemagne: Father of a Continent*, trans. Allan Cameron (Berkeley: University of California Press, 2004), 20.
16   Herrin, *Formation*, 391.
17   Herrin, *Formation*, 446–48; Barbero, *Charlemagne*, 87–89.
18   Herrin, *Formation*, 451.
19   Barbero, *Charlemagne*, 16, 104.
20   Herrin, *Formation*, 305.
21   Herrin, *Formation*, 237. For easy access to a couple of selections from Isidore's work, see O'Donovan and O'Donovan, *From Irenaeus to Grotius*, 204–11.

22   Herrin, *Formation*, 248. In Charles' case this break from the imperial Roman past was exemplified in an interesting departure from it in how chronological questions were handled. Herrin, *Formation*, 5–6, 403–4.

23   Herrin, *Formation*, 237.

24   Herrin, *Formation*, 240–41.

25   Paul Fouracre, "Frankish Gaul to 814," in *New Cambridge Medieval History*, vol. 2: C. 700–C. 900, ed. Rosamond McKitterick (Cambridge: Cambridge University Press, 1995), 85–109 (107–8).

26   The Franks considered themselves (in the words of their Salic Law) to be a Christian people "brave in war, faithful in peace, wise in their counsels, of noble body, of immaculate purity … converted to the Catholic faith, free of heresy" (Heinrich Fichtenau, *The Carolingian Empire*, MART 1 [Toronto: University of Toronto Press, 1978], 1).

27   "By 804 the lands ruled by Charlemagne were half again as large as in 768." Wickham, *Inheritance*, 380. It was a huge empire, "larger than any subsequent state in Europe has ever been except for brief years at the height of the power of Napoleon and Hitler" (387).

28   For a brief account of its character, see Wickham, *Inheritance*, chapter 17, and Barbero, *Charlemagne*, chapter 10; further, G. W. Trompf, "The Concept of the Carolingian Renaissance," *JHI* 34 (1973): 3–26.

29   Trompf, "Concept," 14; Wickham, *Inheritance*, 383. This was not an entirely male preserve: "A dense literary education was available to a lay woman by 810 or so, only twenty-five years after Carolingian schooling started" (Wickham, *Inheritance*, 414). It *was* a largely elite preserve, however: "The Carolingians did sometimes contemplate general schooling, but they did not seriously develop it" (idem).

30   Herrin, *Formation*, 426–27; Fouracre, "Frankish Gaul," 108.

31   Barbero, *Charlemagne*, 97–99.

32   In 775, for example, the Irish Christian Cathwulf advised the king in a letter that "ignoring divine instructions would lead to the downfall of the king himself as well as his people. To underline his message, he frequently referred to biblical examples"—particularly OT ones. Charles must always remember that he "was responsible for his people's salvation" (Miriam Czock, "Creating Futures through the Lens of Revelation in the Rhetoric of the Carolingian Reform ca. 750 to ca. 900," in *Apocalypse and Reform from Late Antiquity to the Middle Ages*, ed. Matthew Gabriele and James T. Palmer [London: Routledge, 2019], 101–19 [106]).

33   Herrin, *Formation*, 433; Barbero, *Charlemagne*, 224–25. For some translated excerpts from the text, including what it says about Sabbath rest, see Barbara H. Rosenwein, ed., *Reading the Middle Ages: Sources from Europe, Byzantium, and the Islamic World* (Toronto: University of Toronto Press, 2013), 148–50; and further, our chapter 8 below.

34   Barbero, *Charlemagne*, 225.

35   Marshall W. Baldwin, ed., *Christianity through the Thirteenth Century*, DHWC (New York: Walker, 1970), 114 (with selections from the *Admonition* following on 114–19).

36   Before Caesarius, Christian leaders had typically "used the language of tithing only to discuss almsgiving, which by its nature resisted being made a fixed due." Caesarius, however, wishing "to transform Arles and the surrounding countryside into a Christian city," needed an income stream that was more stable than this, and his new conception of Christian tithing was developed with such stability in mind: "alms and tithing were to be two separate categories, with the former linked with freedom and love, and the latter with obligation and justice" (Eric Shuler, "Caesarius of Arles and the Development of the Ecclesiastical Tithe: From a Theology of Almsgiving to Practical Obligations," *Traditio* 67 [2012]: 43–69 [44, 56–57]).

37   Shuler, "Caesarius," 59.

38   It was given official approval first at the Second Council of Tours in 567 and later at the Council of Mâcon in 585, which observed that few at that time practiced it.

39   Herrin, *Formation*, 432.

40   Shuler, "Caesarius," 44–45.

41   Koziol, "Discourses," 482–83.

42   O'Donovan and O'Donovan, *From Irenaeus to Grotius*, 170.

43   O'Donovan and O'Donovan, *From Irenaeus to Grotius*, 171. By way of contrast in the east, "Justinian's own [earlier] legislative contributions to [his own code of law] conveyed the tradition Hellenic cast of his imperial self-understanding, his devotion . . . to restoring Roman splendor in its political, cultural, and above all, religious aspects . . . as the Socratic philosopher king who, in imitating divine rule, is an image of God to his subjects" (171–72).

44   Herrin, *Formation*, 426–27.

45   Åslaug Ommundsen, "The Liberal Arts and the Polemic Strategy of the *Opus Caroli Regis Contra Synodum* (*Libri Carolini*)," SO 77 (2002): 175–200 (177).

46   Ommundsen, "Liberal Arts," 181. It contains "well over one thousand quotations from the Bible," with a "preference for the Old Testament as an authority over the New" (Ann Freeman, "Theodulf of Orleans and the *Libri Carolini*," *Spec* 32 [1957]: 663–705 [692]).

47   Ommundsen, "Liberal Arts," 192.

48   Freeman, "Theodulf," 695–703.

49   Freeman, "Theodulf," 697.

50   Herrin, *Formation*, 427–28.

51   Herrin, *Formation*, 435.

52   Wickham, *Inheritance*, 381; Barbero, *Charlemagne*, 86; Trompf, "Concept," 23–24.

53   Herrin, *Formation*, 435, 439.

54   Barbero, *Charlemagne*, 87–89.

55   Herrin, *Formation*, 476.

56   John Milton in *Eikonoklastes* (1649), quoted in Kennedy, *English Revolution*, 124.

57   Barbero, *Charlemagne*, 119–20, 142, 245, who tells us that the king's everyday life was shaped by "the liturgical services that he felt himself obliged to take part in with an almost monk-like zeal" (119–20). Fouracre adds that "[t]he reform of the church was directed at the moral welfare of the subject, with the effect of widening the brief for the state's intervention in the subject's life" ("Frankish Gaul," 108). On the seriousness of Charles' promotion of "ethical religion" among his subjects, see further Janet L. Nelson, "Religion in the Age of Charlemagne," in *Oxford Handbook*, 490–514 (505–6).

58   Barbero, *Charlemagne*, 142.

59   Fichtenau, *Carolingian Empire*, 35.

60   He avoided the mutilations that were customary in Byzantium, for example (Barbero, *Charlemagne*, 142). As to the Saxons, all that should be noted in the present context is that when confronted by Alcuin (see below), Charles backed down and changed his Saxon policy. This is significant: "Aristocrats are always violent, corrupt and greedy, but they were at least aware of the ideology of public responsibility in this period" (Wickham, *Inheritance*, 391). To put this in a more positive way, Charlemagne was serious enough about his Christian faith to recognize when he got things wrong and to work to put them right.

61   See further Iain Provan, "To Highlight All our Idols: Worshipping God in Nietzsche's World," *ExAud* 15 (2000): 19–38.

62   Is the intent in bowing down to engage in worship of created things as if they shared in divinity—as in the inappropriate worship offered by Cornelius to Peter in Acts 10:25, or by John to the angel in Revelation 19:10 (also Rev. 22:8–9)? Or does it imply only respect (e.g., Gen. 33:3–7) and/or affection (e.g., 1 Sam. 20:41)? Is the kissing associated with worshiping a "god" (Hos. 13:2)—or with greeting someone (Gen. 29:13), romantic intent (Song 1:2), or expressing respect and affection (Luke 7:44–45)?

63   *The Decree of the Holy, Great, Ecumenical Synod, the Second of Nice* (NPNF² 14:550).

64   Leviticus 27; Num. 18; Deut. 12; 14; and 26. Some reluctance to tithe in the ways described is reflected in Mal. 3:6–11, where the people are promised God's blessing if they amend their ways.

65   In Matt. 23:23 (and Luke 11:42), Jesus rebukes the Pharisees for their careful tithing of herbs while at the same time neglecting the weightier matters of the law. This reflects a generalizing tendency in Judaism in this period, whereby over the course of time all agricultural products, and eventually all forms of income, become subject to the tithe of 10 percent. In the parable of Luke 18:9–14, secondly, the Pharisee thanks God for his own moral virtue, revealed in part by the fact that he gives tithes of all that he gets. In Heb. 7:4–10, thirdly, we are reminded that Abraham gave a tithe to Melchizedek and that the Levites were authorized to take tithes from the people.

66   *Didachē Kiriou dia tōn dōdeka apostolōn* (*The Teaching of the Twelve Apostles, Commonly Called the Didache*), 13, in *Early Christian Fathers*, ed. Cyril Charles Richardson, LCC 1 (New York: Macmillan, 1970), 177–78.

67   Aristides, *Apologia* (*The Apology of Aristides the Philosopher*) 15 (*ANF* 9:277).

68   Tertullian, *Apology* 39 (*ANF* 3:46). See also Justin Martyr, who describes those "who are well to do, and willing," giving at each worship service "what each thinks fit." The offering is then used to look after "orphans and widows and those who, through sickness or any other cause, are in want, and those who are in bonds and the strangers sojourning among us, and in a word takes care of all who are in need" (Justin, *Apologia I* [*First Apology*] 67 [*ANF* 1:186]).

69   Shuler, "Caesarius," 51. At the end of the second century, Irenaeus, for example, mentions the Jewish tithe only to contrast it with Christians who "set aside all their possessions for the Lord's purposes, bestowing joyfully and freely . . . as that poor widow acted who cast all her living into the treasury of God" (Irenaeus, *Against Heresies* 4:18 [*ANF* 1:485]).

70   The late fourth-century *Apostolic Constitutions*, e.g., assign agricultural first fruits (amounts unspecified) to the priests but do instruct the Christian to "give the tenth of thy increase to the orphan, and to the widow, and to the poor, and to the stranger" (*Constitutiones apostolicae* [*Apostolic Constitutions*] 7.2.29 [*ANF* 7:471]).

71   Shuler, "Caesarius," 47–48.

72   "[T]he basically conservative nature of [the culture], and the unmoving social order it represented, meant that on balance custom outweighed innovation when it came to putting into practice any intention to reform the kingdom" (Fouracre, "Frankish Gaul," 108).

73   For a much fuller exploration of this topic, see Provan, *Seriously Dangerous Religion*, chapter 10.

74   For an extended reflection on this parable in relation to the "field" of reality in which we pursue the Christian moral vision, see John. G. Stackhouse Jr., *Making the Best of It: Following Christ in the Real World* (Oxford: Oxford University Press, 2008), 261–66.

75   Herrin, *Formation*, 237.

76   Barbero, *Charlemagne*, 243.

77   Barbero, *Charlemagne*, 244.

78   Shuler, "Caesarius," 69.

79   For a careful assessment of the evidence in the earlier Middle Ages, see Giles Constable, "Resistance to Tithes in the Middle Ages," *JEH* 13 (1962): 172–85.

80   "Levellers," in *ODCC*, 980. Like many such names historically, "Levellers" was not chosen by these people themselves, and they objected to it.

81   Barbero, *Charlemagne*, 243.

82   Barbero, *Charlemagne*, 244.

6 JOURNEY TO THE CENTER OF THE EARTH

1   Brett E. Whalen, *Dominion of God: Christendom and Apocalypse in the Middle Ages* (Cambridge, Mass.: Harvard University Press, 2009), 47.
2   Herrin, *Formation*, 157.
3   Herrin, *Formation*, 141.
4   Herrin, *Formation*, 103.
5   Herrin, *Formation*, 142, and all of chapter 4.
6   Gregory himself had already emphasized in his influential *Liber regulae pastoralis* (*Book of Pastoral Care*) "that bishops should advise the Christian rulers of the West on all topics, not only church matters" (Herrin, *Formation*, 175).
7   Herrin, *Formation*, 186.
8   Herrin, *Formation*, 213.
9   Herrin, *Formation*, 370.
10 Herrin, *Formation*, 446.
11 Herrin, *Formation*, 374.
12 Herrin, *Formation*, 379.
13 Herrin, *Formation*, 379, citing a letter from Stephen to Pepin in 757.
14 Barbero, *Charlemagne*, 16.
15 For easy access to the gist of the document, see O'Donovan and O'Donovan, *From Irenaeus to Grotius*, 228–30. The serious schism that had by this point arisen between east and west is also evidenced in the calling and deliberation of the Lateran Synod in Rome in 769, just one year after Pepin's death. In this synod, attended by twelve Frankish bishops, "the West closed its ranks against the eastern heresy [of iconoclasm]. And with this theological decision, both the papacy and the Frankish monarchy for a while abandoned official contacts with Constantinople," whose emperor was now concentrating on the imperial defense of the east (Herrin, *Formation*, 395). Iconoclasm is a theological position that holds icons (art that depicts God or humans) to be idolatrous and demands their destruction.
16 Barbero, *Charlemagne*, 93.
17 Barbero, *Charlemagne*, 93.
18 Barbero, *Charlemagne*, 97.
19 Barbero, *Charlemagne*, 98; O'Donovan and O'Donovan, *From Irenaeus to Grotius*, 174.
20 Barbero, *Charlemagne*, 168.
21 Barbero, *Charlemagne*, 173.
22 Whalen, *Dominion*, 15.
23 Whalen, *Dominion*, 14.
24 Whalen, *Dominion*, 40.
25 Whalen, *Dominion*, 32.
26 Whalen, *Dominion*, 32. See further, for a helpful introduction to the papacy/empire conflict throughout the eleventh to fourteenth centuries and selections from primary sources, O'Donovan and O'Donovan, *From Irenaeus to Grotius*, 231–387.
27 Eusebius, *Life of Constantine* 3.33 (*NPNF*[2] 1:529); Leithart, *Defending Constantine*, 93–94, 136–39.
28 As a result, "[t]he patriarch of Jerusalem acknowledged [Charles] as the protector of the holy places and sent him the keys to the Holy Sepulchre" (Barbero, *Charlemagne*, 101). The Church in Palestine had declined in size and wealth in this period relative to previous centuries, perhaps prompting an appeal for funds from the west and leading to a careful survey by Frankish envoys to determine firsthand the real needs (Michael McCormick, *Charlemagne's Survey of the Holy Land: Wealth, Personnel, and Buildings of a Mediterranean Church between Antiquity and the Middle Ages: With a Critical Edition and Translation of the Original Text* [Washington, D.C.: Dumbarton Oaks Research Library and Collection, 2011]).

29   "Saint Augustine ... denounced pilgrimages, Saint John Chrysostom ... mocked them, and
      Saint Gregory of Nyssa ... pointed out that pilgrimages were nowhere suggested in the Bible
      and that Jerusalem was a rather unattractive and sinful city" (Rodney Stark, *God's Battalions:
      The Case for the Crusades* [New York: HarperOne, 2009], 81–82).

30   The monastic chronicler Rodulfus Glaber (985–1047) notes in his time an "increase of pil-
      grimages to the holy places of Jerusalem," which he is tempted to see as a sign of the end
      times during which "the faithful would rush to Jerusalem to oppose [the Antichrist] or serve
      him" (Whalen, *Dominion*, 21–22). One such pilgrim was the Anjou warlord Fulk Nerra
      (987–1040), who travelled three times to the city in the hope of purifying his soul (Thomas
      S. Asbridge, *The Crusades: The Authoritative History of the War for the Holy Land* [New York:
      Ecco, 2010], 4–5).

31   Stark, *Battalions*, 100–101.

32   Whalen, *Dominion*, 36–37.

33   Whalen, *Dominion*, 37.

34   Whalen, *Dominion*, 37.

35   Asbridge, *Crusades*, 16–17.

36   Whalen, *Dominion*, 50.

37   Asbridge, *Crusades*, 40.

38   Asbridge, *Crusades*, 12.

39   Whalen, *Dominion*, 55.

40   Asbridge, *Crusades*, 26.

41   Asbridge, *Crusades*, 29.

42   Stark, *Battalions*, 97–98.

43   Asbridge, *Crusades*, 28.

44   Asbridge, *Crusades*, 23.

45   Asbridge, *Crusades*, 33.

46   Asbridge, *Crusades*, 37.

47   For good descriptions see Asbridge, *Crusades*, 41–114, and Stark, *Battalions*, 120–61.

48   Asbridge, *Crusades*, 90.

49   Whalen, *Dominion*, 42.

50   Asbridge, *Crusades*, 101.

51   Asbridge, *Crusades*, 102.

52   Whalen, *Dominion*, 42. For a grim description of what happened when Antioch fell for the
      first time to the Crusaders, e.g., see Asbridge, *Crusades*, 73.

53   Asbridge, *Crusades*, 108.

54   Asbridge, *Crusades*, 108.

55   Whalen, *Dominion*, 71. Interestingly, this is not the case in Islam, in spite of what is some-
      times claimed nowadays about Muslims "harboring bitter resentments about the Crusades
      for a millennium." This resentment is of much more recent vintage (Stark, *Battalions*, 8–9).

56   See Asbridge, *Crusades*, 26, who claims that this notion of "devotional warfare" had lain "dor-
      mant within the body of Islam" in the eleventh century but was now revived.

57   Whalen, *Dominion*, 70–71.

58   Whalen, *Dominion*, 75, 84–86.

59   Thomas Aquinas, *Summa Theologica* 2–2.11.3, trans. Fathers of the English Dominican
      Province, rev. Daniel J. Sullivan, GBWW 20 (Chicago: Encyclopedia Britannica, 1952), 440.

60   God "will bless her with abundant provisions; her poor I will satisfy with food," such that
      "her faithful people will ever sing for joy" (Ps. 132:14–16).

61   "There is a river whose streams make glad the city of God, the holy place where the Most
      High dwells."

62   "The seas have lifted up, O LORD, the seas have lifted up their voice; the seas have lifted up their pounding waves. Mightier than the thunder of the great waters, mightier than the breakers of the sea—the LORD on high is mighty."

63   Psalm 76:1–3 tells us, moreover, that "in Judah God is known . . . His tent is in Salem, his dwelling place in Zion. There he broke the flashing arrows, the shields and the swords, the weapons of war."

64   "Reform your ways and your actions, and I will let you live in this place. Do not trust in deceptive words and say, 'This is the temple of the LORD, the temple of the LORD, the temple of the LORD!'" (Jer. 7:3–4).

65   Provan, Seriously Dangerous Religion, 81–83.

66   1 Corinthians 3:16–17; 6:19; 2 Cor. 6:16; Eph. 2:21.

7   THE FOULNESS OF FORNICATION

1   John Calvin, Institutes of the Christian Religion, ed. John T. McNeill, trans. Ford L. Battles (Louisville: Westminster John Knox, 2011). This work will normally be cited according to the position of the 1539 text within the final four-volume expansion of 1559.

2   Whalen, Dominion, 126.

3   Whalen, Dominion, 151.

4   Whalen, Dominion, 200, quoting Richard Southern.

5   Whalen, Dominion, 179–80; and further, 193–200.

6   For more on the background to, and also the development of, the indulgences "crisis," see Martin Brecht, Martin Luther: His Road to Reformation 1483–1521, vol. 1 of Martin Luther, trans. James L. Schaaf (Philadelphia: Fortress, 1985), 176–92 (178).

7   This paragraph summarizes what may be read at greater length in Provan, Right Reading, 281–312.

8   Michael A. Mullett, John Calvin (London: Routledge, 2011), 40.

9   Carlos M. N. Eire, Reformations: The Early Modern World, 1450–1650 (New Haven: Yale University Press, 2016), 42.

10   Calvin, Institutes 4.20.2.

11   Calvin, Institutes 4.20.3.

12   Calvin, Institutes 4.20.3.

13   Calvin, Institutes 4.20.4.

14   Mullett, Calvin, 41.

15   Calvin, Institutes 4.20.4; further, 4.20.8.

16   Calvin, Institutes 4.20.6–7.

17   Calvin, Institutes 4.20.10.

18   Calvin, Institutes 4.20.10. Likewise, "kings and people must sometimes take up arms to execute such public vengeance," fighting just wars when necessary (4.20.11; also, 4.20.12).

19   Calvin, Institutes 4.20.14.

20   Calvin, Institutes 4.20.15.

21   Calvin, Institutes 4.20.16.

22   Calvin, Institutes 2.8.

23   Calvin, Institutes 2.8.35.

24   Calvin, Institutes 2.8.39.

25   Calvin, Institutes 2.8.41.

26   Calvin, Institutes 2.8.44.

27   Calvin, Institutes 2.8.46.

28   Calvin, Institutes 2.8.47.

29   Calvin, Institutes 2.8.49. As see Witte and Kingdon note, "Sometimes Calvin read volumes of insight into a single verse" (John Witte Jr. and Robert M. Kingdon, Sex, Marriage, and

Family in John Calvin's Geneva, vol. 1: *Courtship, Engagement, and Marriage* (Grand Rapids: Eerdmans, 2005), 7.

30   William G. Naphy, *Calvin and the Consolidation of the Genevan Reformation* (Manchester: Manchester University Press, 1994), 18.

31   Naphy, *Calvin*, 21.

32   Mullett, *John Calvin*, 39.

33   Naphy, *Calvin*, 27–43 (41).

34   For the text from which the citations in this paragraph are drawn, see Philip E. Hughes, trans. and ed., *The Register of the Company of Pastors of Geneva in the Time of Calvin* (Grand Rapids: Eerdmans, 1966), 41–49.

35   For a description of how the Consistory operated, see Witte and Kingdon, *Sex, Marriage, and Family*, 66–71.

36   Witte and Kingdon, *Sex, Marriage, and Family*, 14.

37   Naphy, *Calvin*, 72.

38   See Naphy, *Calvin*, 76–78, for its composition, and p. 109 for a table (14) listing consistory cases for 1542.

39   Naphy, *Calvin*, 30–31, with a chart detailing prosecutions for moral/religious offences.

40   Naphy, *Calvin*, 102.

41   Naphy, *Calvin*, 109.

42   Witte and Kingdon, *Sex, Marriage, and Family*, 14.

43   Witte and Kingdon, *Sex, Marriage, and Family*, 66–67.

44   Michael Servetus, *De trinitatis erroribus* (*On the Errors of the Trinity*, 1531) and *Dialogorum de Trinitate* (*Dialogues on the Trinity*, 1532), in *The Two Treatises of Servetus on the Trinity*, trans. Earl Morse Wilbur, HTS 16 (Cambridge, Mass.: Harvard University Press, 1932).

45   Naphy, *Calvin*, 171–72, 182–83.

46   Mullett, *John Calvin*, 44–45; further, Naphy, *Calvin*, 190–232.

47   Naphy, *Calvin*, 222.

48   Witte and Kingdon, *Sex, Marriage, and Family*, 12–13.

49   Witte and Kingdon, *Sex, Marriage, and Family*, 13.

50   Witte and Kingdon, *Sex, Marriage, and Family*, 15.

51   Witte and Kingdon, *Sex, Marriage, and Family*, 14.

52   Witte and Kingdon, *Sex, Marriage, and Family*, 1.

53   Witte and Kingdon, *Sex, Marriage, and Family*, 18.

54   Witte and Kingdon, *Sex, Marriage, and Family*, 310.

55   Witte and Kingdon, *Sex, Marriage, and Family*, 29.

56   Witte and Kingdon, *Sex, Marriage, and Family*, 312 (and for other relevant biblical passages, pp. 313–14).

57   The exception in OT Torah is the case of the childless widow, where such a "levirate" marriage was expected, albeit not enforced (Deut. 25:5, reflected in Matt. 22:24).

58   Witte and Kingdon, *Sex, Marriage, and Family*, 316.

59   Witte and Kingdon, *Sex, Marriage, and Family*, 316.

60   Witte and Kingdon, *Sex, Marriage, and Family*, 317.

61   Witte and Kingdon, *Sex, Marriage, and Family*, 328 (and for more on all three cases, pp. 324–28, 344–45, 352–53).

62   Witte and Kingdon, *Sex, Marriage, and Family*, 1.

63   Witte and Kingdon, *Sex, Marriage, and Family*, 2.

64   Witte and Kingdon, *Sex, Marriage, and Family*, 13.

65   Witte and Kingdon, *Sex, Marriage, and Family*, 317.

66   Anthony C. Thiselton, *The First Epistle to the Corinthians*, NIGTC (Grand Rapids: Eerdmans, 2000), 385–86, for a brief account.

67   See also Col. 3:5; 1 Thess. 4:3.

68   Witte and Kingdon, *Sex, Marriage, and Family*, 316.

69   Calvin, *Institutes* 4.20.16.

70   Calvin, *Institutes* 4.20.16.

71   Calvin, *Institutes* 4.20.16.

72   Calvin, *Institutes* 4.20.15.

73   Calvin, *Institutes* 4.20.15.

74   Genetics Education Canada tells us that "studies have shown that, when there is no known genetic diagnosis in the family, first cousin unions are at a 1.7–2.8 percent additional risk above the general population risk of 2–3 percent to have offspring with a congenital anomaly. The risk for a more closely related union is higher and for a more distantly related union is lower" ("Consanguinity," Genetics Education Canada Knowledge Organization, https://geneticseducation.ca/educational-resources/gec-ko-on-the-run/consanguinity/). By coincidence, on the same day *The Guardian* newspaper in England reported that in certain populations there "[m]arriage between cousins leading to fatal genetic conditions remain [*sic*] a factor in a significant proportion of child deaths" (Nazia Parveen, "Fatal Genetic Conditions More Common in Children of South Asian Heritage in West Yorkshire City, Study Says," *The Guardian*, February 15, 2019, https://www.theguardian.com/society/2019/feb/15/cousin-marriages-cited-as-significant-factor-bradford-child-deaths).

75   Thiselton, *First Corinthians*, 402.

8   APOCALYPSE NOW

1   Calvin, *Institutes* prefatory address to King Francis I.

2   Calvin, *Institutes* editor's introduction (lxvi).

3   Whalen, *Dominion*, 42–99.

4   Whalen, *Dominion*, 75–76, 101.

5   Whalen, *Dominion*, 102.

6   Whalen, *Dominion*, 116.

7   Whalen, *Dominion*, 122.

8   Whalen, *Dominion*, 103.

9   Whalen, *Dominion*, 123.

10   Whalen, *Dominion*, 119.

11   Whalen, *Dominion*, 135–37.

12   Whalen, *Dominion*, 176.

13   Whalen, *Dominion*, 177–83 (181–82).

14   Whalen, *Dominion*, 186–89.

15   Whalen, *Dominion*, 205.

16   Whalen, *Dominion*, 225.

17   Whalen, *Dominion*, 227.

18   Whalen, *Dominion*, 227.

19   Calvin, *Institutes* 4.20.2.

20   "Brethren of the Free Spirit," in ODCC, 237.

21   "Nicholas of Basle," in ODCC, 1156.

22   Norman Cohn, *Europe's Inner Demons: The Demonization of Christians in Medieval Christendom*, rev. ed. (London: Pimlico, 1993), 73; see further Robert E. Lerner, *The Heresy of the Free Spirit in the Later Middle Ages* (Berkeley: University of California Press, 1972), 10–34.

23   Cohn, *Demons*, 73.

24   "Taborites," in ODCC, 1585.

25   Ernst Werner, "Popular Ideologies in Late Mediaeval Europe: Taborite Chiliasm and Its Antecedents," *CSSH* 2 (1960): 344–63.

26   Hans-Jürgen Goertz, *The Anabaptists*, 2nd ed., trans. Trevor Johnson (London: Routledge, 1996).

27   Helmut Isaak, *Menno Simons and the New Jerusalem* (Kitchener, Ont.: Pandora, 2006), 37n29.

28   Sigrun Haude, *In the Shadow of "Savage Wolves": Anabaptist Münster and the German Reformation during the 1530s*, SCEH 20 (Boston: Humanities, 2000), 12.

29   Isaak, *Menno Simons*, 37.

30   George H. Williams, *The Radical Reformation*, 3rd ed., SCES 15 (Kirksville, Mo.: Truman State University Press, 1995), 371.

31   Isaak, *Menno Simons*, 37.

32   Haude, *Shadow*, 12.

33   Williams, *Radical Reformation*, 371, again quoting Obbe Philips.

34   Richard van Dülmen, *Das Täuferreich Zu Münster, 1534–1535: Berichte U. Dokumente*, Wissenschaftliche Reihe 4150 (München: Deutscher Taschenbuch, 1974), 141; Williams, *Radical Reformation*, 372.

35   Haude, *Shadow*, 14.

36   Norman Cohn, *The Pursuit of the Millennium: Revolutionary Millenarians and Mystical Anarchists of the Middle Ages* (Oxford: Oxford University Press, 1970), 296.

37   Isaak, *Menno Simons*, 62.

38   Isaak, *Menno Simons*, 62n41; further, Eire, *Reformations*, 269–71.

39   Haude, *Shadow*, 15.

40   Haude, *Shadow*, 15.

41   Eire, *Reformations*, 271–76.

42   Haude, *Shadow*, 147–48.

43   On these groups, see James M. Stayer, *Anabaptists and the Sword*, rev. ed. (Eugene, Ore.: Wipf & Stock, 1976), chapter 13.

44   Born in 1496 in the Netherlands, Menno became a Roman Catholic priest in 1524. He quickly came to question his church's teaching about the Eucharist and began to read both the Bible and the writings of Martin Luther. In due course he came to question infant baptism as well.

45   On the authenticity of this work, see Isaak, *Menno Simons*, 34–37.

46   Isaak, *Menno Simons*, 39.

47   Isaak, *Menno Simons*, 105.

48   Isaak, *Menno Simons*, 66.

49   Isaak, *Menno Simons*, 99.

50   Isaak, *Menno Simons*, 100.

51   Isaak, *Menno Simons*, 112.

52   The verb itself can actually be used in the OT of *legitimate* killing (i.e., not murder; Num. 35:26–27).

53   E. A. Goodfriend, "Adultery," in *ABD* 1:82–86 (83).

54   John H. Walton and J. Harvey Walton, *The Lost World of the Torah: Laws as Covenant and Wisdom in Ancient Context* (Downers Grove, Ill.: IVP Academic, 2019), 31, 35.

55   Thiselton, *First Corinthians*, 409, on 1 Cor. 5:9–10.

56   The Hb. allows for such a reading because although "cut off" (*karat*) does often mean "kill," it need not; the verb is used both for the death penalty and simply for exclusion from the covenant people.

57   C. K. Barrett, *The Epistle to the Romans*, rev. ed. (London: Continuum, 1991), 227.

58   So, interestingly, Calvin—see Witte and Kingdon, *Sex, Marriage, and Family*, 323.

59   Thiselton, *First Corinthians*, 396.

60   Thiselton, *First Corinthians*, 396.

61   Thiselton, *First Corinthians*, 399, quoting South.

62   Alexander, "Rome," 837.

63   Augustine, *De civitate Dei contra paganos (City of God)* 1.21 (*NPNF*¹ 2:15).

64   Augustine, *City of God* 5.24 (*NPNF*¹ 2:105).

65   Augustine, *Letter 100* (*NPNF*¹ 1:411–12).

66   Augustine, *City of God* 2.21 (*NPNF*¹ 2:36).

67   O'Donovan and O'Donovan, *From Irenaeus to Grotius*, 2–3.

68   Tertullian, *De corona (The Chaplet)* 11 (*ANF* 3:99).

69   E.g., is the judicial system systemically corrupt? Is it operating in a less-than-even-handed way and failing to provide the same justice to everyone? Is it racked by prejudice or incompetence, such that the outcomes of trials involving murder are sometimes or often dubious?

9   MEN OF BLOOD

1   Calvin, *Institutes* 4.20.31, slightly amended for great clarity, given current English usage.

2   At the heart of the matter were two "acts" of 1559. The Act of Supremacy, first, proclaimed Elizabeth to be the supreme governor of the realm in all spiritual, ecclesiastical, and temporal matters—a denial of papal supremacy—and required of all clergy an oath of obedience to the Crown. It was the Act of Uniformity that imposed liturgical conformity. The updated *Book of Common Prayer* (originally dating to 1549) was similar to the 1552 revision but retained some "high church" or Catholic elements. It affirmed the use of traditional vestments and church furnishings (reversing the 1552 position) and deleted an earlier statement that no adoration of the "real presence" of Christ in the elements was intended by kneeling during the Eucharist. It also deleted a prayer asking for deliverance from the tyranny of the bishop of Rome.

3   Bernard S. Capp, *The Fifth Monarchy Men: A Study in Seventeenth-Century English Millenarianism* (London: Faber and Faber, 1972), 34. The Reformer Martin Bucer in Strasbourg had earlier held a similar view: "His description of a Christian utopia, *De Regno Christi*, was an account of what England might become under Edward VI" (34).

4   John Craig, "The Growth of English Puritanism," in *The Cambridge Companion to Puritanism*, ed. John Coffey and Paul C. H. Lim (Cambridge: Cambridge University Press, 2008), 34–47.

5   The legal and administrative systems of England had been extended to Wales in 1535 and 1542, with the Welsh thereafter electing their own members to the Parliament in London. The union of the English with the Scottish and Irish parliaments still lies in the future of our narrative. "Parliament" in this chapter, therefore, is "the Parliament of England and Wales."

6   I.e., from each county governed by a sheriff, and from each larger and smaller autonomous urban center (not under the control of a sheriff).

7   All who owned freehold property worth at least forty shillings could in principle participate in county elections—but not less-wealthy people, or tenants. One also needed to have a significant income in order to sit as a member of the Commons.

8   This Parliament was even more critical of the king's government, especially of the role played within it by the Duke of Buckingham, who was effectively in charge of foreign policy. Charles dissolved it when it tried to impeach the duke for treason.

9   England was in the midst of a war with both France and Spain, in the course of which the king had resorted to a tactic used by his father to raise money without summoning Parliament: he had imposed "forced loans" on local gentry, which many had refused to pay at risk to their freedom. The *Petition of Right* was Parliament's response.

10   He did so early in 1629 after Buckingham was assassinated, and in the midst of ongoing dissent in Parliament.

11   Kennedy, *English Revolution*, 2. Arminianism was a recently developed anti-Calvinist theo-
       logical position emphasizing the freedom of the human will in response to the love of God.
       It was named after Jacobus Arminius, a theologian in the University of Leiden in Holland
       (1603–1609), who became involved in a high-profile argument on the topic with a Calvinist
       colleague, Franciscus Gomarus.

12   Norah Carlin, *The Causes of the English Civil War*, HASt (Oxford: Blackwell, 1999), 12–24.

13   James Aikman, *An Historical Account of Covenanting in Scotland: From the First Band in
       Mearns, 1556, to the Signature of the Grand National Covenant, 1638* (Edinburgh: Thomas
       Constable, 1851), 80–83.

14   John Morrill, "The Puritan Revolution," in Coffey and Lim, *Cambridge Companion to Puri-
       tanism*, 67–88 (68–72).

15   Editor's preface, lxvii, referring to *Institutes* 4.20.31. Calvin continues in 4.20.32 as follows:
       "In that obedience which we have shown to be due the authority of rulers, we are always to
       make this exception, indeed, to observe it as primary, that such obedience is never to lead
       us away from obedience to him, to whose will the desires of all kings ought to be subject, to
       whose decrees all their commands ought to yield, to whose majesty their scepters ought to
       be submitted."

16   Kennedy, *English Revolution*, 11–12 (11).

17   This is also evident in Parliament's "Grand Remonstrance" to Charles in December 1641.
       This document blames "malignant parties" for what has gone wrong, urging the king now to
       set a new direction in which (among other things) the Church of England will be reformed
       in a moderately Puritan direction, with the power and influence of the bishops much re-
       duced (Kennedy, *English Revolution*, 3). At the same time the Remonstrance does not shrink
       from cataloguing in detail the royal misgovernance arising under the influence of these "ma-
       lignant parties."

18   This assembly, entirely Calvinist by persuasion, had been tasked by Parliament to reform the
       Church of England and would go on to produce the Larger and Shorter Westminster Cat-
       echisms, the Westminster Confession, and the Directory of Public Worship. It comprised
       twenty lay members of the House of Commons and ten from the House of Lords, along
       with over one hundred English clergymen and a number of Scottish Presbyterians.

19   Kennedy, *English Revolution*, 5.

20   Kennedy, *English Revolution*, 28.

21   Capp, *Fifth Monarchy*, 35.

22   Kennedy, *English Revolution*, 5.

23   Kennedy, *English Revolution*, 29–30.

24   Kennedy, *English Revolution*, 30.

25   Kennedy, *English Revolution*, 32, partially quoting Gentles.

26   Since creating its own Great Seal in 1643, in fact, and declaring "those who made use of the
       Royal Seal enemies of the state," it had functioned explicitly as a rival authority to the king
       (Kennedy, *English Revolution*, 37). It was also on record—in peace proposals sent to Charles
       in November 1644—not only as requiring the king to "take the Covenant" and accept the
       reform of the Church of England along Presbyterian lines but also as being determined to
       prosecute a large number of Royalists without mercy. While waiting for a royal response to
       these proposals, it had already (on January 10, 1645) executed Archbishop Laud for treason,
       in defiance of a pardon issued under the Royal Seal in 1642.

27   Kennedy, *English Revolution*, 41.

28   Kennedy, *English Revolution*, 59, 81.

29   The background to this coup can be summarized in the following way. In the aftermath
       of the first phase of war both the army and Parliament negotiated with the king while the
       army leaders sought to contain and manage rank-and-file radicalism: see Kennedy, *English*

Revolution, 64–89, for the fascinating debate within the army. All these negotiations failed. Charles then struck a deal with the Scots, who guaranteed him military assistance to regain his kingship in exchange for promises in line with the Covenant. After the Parliamentary forces had won the ensuing second phase of civil war (1647–1648), and while they were still in the field, the Presbyterian-dominated Parliament "passed a comprehensive Ordinance establishing a Presbyterian system in England without the toleration looked for by the Independents"; at the same time this opened up the way for fresh negotiations with the king (Kennedy, *English Revolution,* 111). The patience of many in the army, which had just fought another war with the same king and were not in sympathy with the Presbyterian agenda, was now at an end, and the purge, and then the regicide, were the result.

30   On war and providence in Puritan thinking more generally, see Stephen Baskerville, *Not by Peace but a Sword: The Political Theology of the English Revolution* (London: Routledge, 1993), 32–33.

31   Kennedy, *English Revolution,* 122.

32   Capp, *Fifth Monarchy,* 45.

33   Kennedy, *English Revolution,* 138.

34   Kennedy, *English Revolution,* 138.

35   Capp, *Fifth Monarchy,* 146.

36   Capp, *Fifth Monarchy,* 14. Their agenda in this regard was unique even in a period marked by apocalyptic fervor, and even though in itself the concept of a "fifth monarchy" following the four earlier ones described in Daniel 2 had a long history behind it and was well-known. Earlier Christians had claimed that the Holy Roman Empire, or the papacy, or the Jesuits, e.g., represented this fifth monarchy, destined to last forever (Capp, *Fifth Monarchy,* 20–21). For a detailed exposition of the agenda itself, see Capp, *Fifth Monarchy,* 131–71.

37   Capp, *Fifth Monarchy,* 63–64.

38   Capp, *Fifth Monarchy,* 67.

39   Barry Coward, *The Cromwellian Protectorate,* New Frontiers in History (Manchester: Manchester University Press, 2002), 19; Capp, *Fifth Monarchy,* 162–71, 177–78.

40   Capp, *Fifth Monarchy,* 70, 74–75.

41   Capp, *Fifth Monarchy,* 89–92, who also rightly emphasizes the great differences.

42   Coward, *Protectorate,* 11.

43   Coward, *Protectorate,* 13. In the succeeding months, in explicitly refuting claims that he had become a worse tyrant than Charles I, Cromwell attacked "the 'mistaken notion' of Fifth Monarchism . . . claiming it threatened law, liberty, and property" (Capp, *Fifth Monarchy,* 106).

44   Coward, *Protectorate,* 20.

45   Denis Murphy, S.J., *Cromwell in Ireland: A History of Cromwell's Irish Campaign* (Dublin: Gill and Son, 1883), 72, 78–79n2.

46   Stephenson, *Constantine,* 306–7.

47   Barbero, *Charlemagne,* 43.

48   Barbero, *Charlemagne,* 142.

49   Barbero, *Charlemagne,* 44–57, 142.

50   Asbridge, *Crusades,* 17.

51   Whalen, *Dominion,* 142.

52   E.g., Gen. 12:1–3; 15:1–16; Deut. 8:7–10; 9:4–5; Amos 2:9–10.

53   E.g., Gen. 15:16; Lev. 18:24–26; Deut. 9:4–5.

54   Texts like Deut. 4:25–28; 1 Kgs. 14:15–16; and 2 Kgs. 21:11 look ahead to this reality, and various other texts describe it retrospectively (e.g., 2 Kgs. 17:7–23).

55   Amos 2:9; Ps. 78:53–55.

56   We find the same idea in passages like Isa. 10:5–6, where the Assyrians are described as the rod of God's anger against Israel, and Jer. 25:9–11, where Nebuchadnezzar is the vehicle of God's anger against Israel.

57   E.g., Lev. 18:24–28; Num. 33:51–56; 2 Kgs. 16:3; 17:7–23.

58   E.g., Josh. 10:40–42; cf. Deut. 7:1–6 and 20:16–18.

59   E.g., Judg. 1:1–3:6; 2 Sam. 24:7; 1 Kgs. 9:15–23.

60   See further K. Lawson Younger Jr., *Ancient Conquest Accounts: A Study in Ancient Near Eastern and Biblical History Writing*, JSOTS 98 (Sheffield: JSOT, 1990). After all, combatants and noncombatants are typically distinguished in warfare elsewhere in the OT, and children, in particular, are not held morally accountable for wrongdoing and are not to be caught up in their parents' wrongdoing (e.g., Exod. 22:24; Num. 14:3; Deut. 1:39; 24:16). The language of total destruction is from multiple points of view, then, very puzzling language if it is not to be understood as hyperbolic in the way that Younger suggests.

61   "In that day Israel will be the third, along with Egypt and Assyria, a blessing on the earth. The LORD Almighty will bless them, saying, 'Blessed be Egypt my people, Assyria my handiwork, and Israel my inheritance.'"

62   Milton, *Eikonoklastes*, quoted in Kennedy, *English Revolution*, 124.

63   The most convincing reading of Ps. 82, for example, interprets this text precisely in terms of God's general expectations of all the self-styled "god-kings" in the world that they will rule justly on behalf of God who himself renders judgment upon them.

64   John Langan, "The Elements of St. Augustine's Just War Theory," *JRE* 12 (1984): 19–38 (26).

65   "It is the wrongdoing of the opposing party which compels the wise man to wage just wars; and this wrongdoing, even though it gave rise to no war, would still be matter of grief to man because it is man's wrongdoing. Let everyone, then, who thinks with pain on all these great evils, so horrible, so ruthless, acknowledge that this is misery. And if any one either endures or thinks of them without mental pain, this is a more miserable plight still, for he thinks himself happy because he has lost human feeling" (Augustine, *City of God* 19.7 [NPNF¹ 2:405]).

66   O'Donovan and O'Donovan, *From Irenaeus to Grotius*, 106.

67   Leithart, *Defending Constantine*, 276.

68   Justin, *First Apology* 39 (ANF 1:175–76).

69   Kirk R. MacGregor, "Nonviolence in the Ancient Church and Christian Obedience," *Them* 33 (2008): 16–28 (18).

70   MacGregor, "Nonviolence," 19.

71   "But now inquiry is made about this point, whether a believer may turn himself unto military service, and whether the military may be admitted unto the faith, even the rank and file, or each inferior grade, to whom there is no necessity for taking part in sacrifices or capital punishments. There is no agreement between the divine and the human sacrament [vow], the standard of Christ and the standard of the devil, the camp of light and the camp of darkness. One soul cannot be due to two masters—God and Caesar" (Tertullian, *De Idolatria* [*Concerning Idolatry*] 19 [ANF 3:73]).

72   Tertullian, *Concerning Idolatry* 19 (ANF 3:73).

73   "All sorts of quibbling will have to be resorted to in order to avoid offending God . . . [for n]owhere does the Christian change his character . . . A state of faith admits no plea of necessity; they are under no necessity to sin, whose one necessity is, that they do not sin" (Tertullian, *The Chaplet* 11 [ANF 3:100]).

74   Origen, *Against Celsus* 5:33 (ANF 4:558).

75   Origen, *Against Celsus* 7:26 (ANF 4:621).

76   Origen, *Against Celsus* 7:26 (ANF 4:621).

77   Origen, *Against Celsus* 8:73 (*ANF* 4:668).

78   Tertullian, *Apology* 30 (*ANF* 3:42).

79   Many have regarded the American Civil War, e.g., as fought for just cause on the part of the North because at the core of what the South was defending lay the institution of slavery. Whatever one thinks of this judgment, it remains the case that the first cost of abolishing slavery was the loss of over six hundred thousand men on both sides of the conflict. We must then add that nearly four million freed slaves were subsequently left to themselves to figure out what to do next, largely becoming "the South's coloured rural underclass, free and oppressed at the same time, and marked in freedom the way colour had defined them in bondage" (Eric Nellis, *Shaping the New World: African Slavery in the Americas, 1500–1888*, ITI [Toronto: University of Toronto Press, 2013], 141). None of this represents a stellar outcome.

10   A CITY UPON A HILL

1   Sermon (1700), cited in Mason I. Lowance Jr., *The Language of Canaan: Metaphor and Symbol in New England from the Puritans to the Transcendentalists* (Cambridge, Mass.: Harvard University Press, 1980), 161.

2   Cited in Michael Parker, *John Winthrop: Founding the City upon a Hill* (New York: Routledge, 2014), 192–93.

3   Philip S. Gorski, *American Covenant: A History of Civil Religion from the Puritans to the Present* (Princeton: Princeton University Press, 2017), 42.

4   Gorski, *Covenant*, 42.

5   Gorski, *Covenant*, 44.

6   Gorski, *Covenant*, 45.

7   This commitment to education can be seen both in the laws that were enacted to create lower schools to teach both reading and writing and in the foundation of Harvard College in 1636 to educate the clergy.

8   Donald S. Lutz, ed., *Colonial Origins of the American Constitution: A Documentary History* (Indianapolis: Liberty Fund, 1998), 70–87.

9   *Body of Liberties*, §47 (Deut. 19:15).

10   *Body of Liberties*, §85–88 (Exod. 21:1–4; 26–27; Deut. 23:15).

11   *Body of Liberties*, §91 (Lev. 25:39–43; Deut. 20:10–15).

12   *Body of Liberties*, §94.

13   Already in the 1620s, e.g., the Plymouth colony expelled for libertinism ("including sexual liaisons with native women") a businessman with Anglican and aristocratic sympathies named Thomas Morton, who went on later to write his *New English Canaan* (1637)—a denunciation of Puritan governance in New England (Gorski, *Covenant*, 49).

14   Ann M. Little, *Abraham in Arms: War and Gender in Colonial New England* (Philadelphia: University of Pennsylvania Press, 2011), 16–18.

15   The Pequot people at that time dominated the entirety of modern-day Connecticut and eastern Long Island and controlled the fur and wampum (bead) trade there. Various tribes that were subservient to these Pequot saw the English settlers as a means to the end of escaping their overlords and forged alliances with the colonists. After the death of some English traders in 1636, the Bay colony sent a small force against the Pequot and their allies to exact revenge, and war followed. It involved casualties among men, women, and children on both sides. Many natives were also taken into slavery by the Puritan victors (including by John Winthrop himself), and from there they were often deported to the West Indies, where they were exchanged for enslaved Africans.

16   Gorski, *Covenant*, 55. It was named for a Wampanoag chief in the region and was fought between the settlers and their Indian allies (such as the Mohawks), on the one hand, and

various opposing tribes, on the other—most centrally, the Narragansetts. The deeper background lies in the simmering, ongoing tensions in the region during the decades intervening since the 1630s; the immediate flashpoint was the execution for murder in 1675, by the colonial authorities, of three of Philip's warriors. By the war's end the colonists and their allies had managed to destroy much of their native opposition in New England, killing thousands and selling many more into slavery.

17   Gorski, *Covenant*, 56, quoting a sermon by Samuel Nowell from 1678.

18   Cotton Mather, *Soldiers Counseled and Comforted: A Discourse Delivered unto Some Part of the Forces Engaged in the Just War of New England against the Northern and Eastern Indians* (Boston: Samuel Green, 1689). He exhorts them thus: "You are fighting for the defence and succour of the blessed thrones which our David, our Jesus has here erected for himself . . . 'tis for Christ, and with Christ, that you are concerned . . . You are fighting, that the churches of God may not be extinguished . . . [The enemy] shall all shortly perish by the arms of his *New English Israel* . . . you may look to be instruments of executing what God has denounced on them" (32, 35).

19   It was later incorporated into the Code of Justinian (3.12.3): "Let all judges, the people of the cities, and those employed in all trades, remain quiet on the Holy Day of Sunday. Persons residing in the country, however, can freely and lawfully proceed with the cultivation of the fields; as it frequently happens that the sowing of grain or the planting of vines cannot be deferred to a more suitable day, and by making concessions to Heaven the advantage of the time may be lost" (S. P. Scott, ed., *The Civil Law: Including the Twelve Tables, the Institutes of Gaius, the Rules of Ulpian, the Opinions of Paulus, the Enactments of Justinian, and the Constitutions of Leo*, vol. 12 [Cincinnati: Central Trust, 1932], 275).

20   Council of Laodicea, Canon 29 (*NPNF*² 14:148).

21   "And we also decree, according to what the Lord ordained in the law, that there be no servile work on Sundays, as my father, of good memory, ordered in the edicts of his synods, that is: that men do no farm work, either in plowing fields or in tending vineyards, in sowing grain or planting hedges, in clearing in the woods or in cutting trees, in working with stone or in building houses, or in working in the garden; nor are they to gather for games or go hunting. Three tasks with wagons may be performed on Sunday, the arms' cart or the food wagon, or if it is necessary to bear someone's body to the grave. Likewise, women are not to work with cloth nor cut out clothes, nor sew or embroider; nor is it permissible to comb wool or crush flax or wash clothes in public, or shear sheep, to the end that the honor and quiet of the Lord's day be kept. But let people come together from all places to the church for the solemnities of the mass and praise God on that day for all the good things He has done for us" (Baldwin, *Christianity*, 118–19).

22   All shops had to remain closed during these hours. Beyond this, "all Genevan workers, with the exception of those who provided essential daily services such as bakers and city guards, were required to refrain from their daily labors on Sunday so that they might participate in sacred services and experience physical and spiritual refreshment" (Scott M. Manetsch, *Calvin's Company of Pastors: Pastoral Care and the Emerging Reformed Church, 1536–1609*, OSHT [Oxford: Oxford University Press, 2013], 130).

23   "If there be one day in the week reserved for religious instruction when they have spent six days in their own business, they are apt to spend the day which is set apart for worship, in play and pastime; some rove about the fields, others go to taverns to quaff; and there are undoubtedly at this time as many at the last mentioned place, as we here assembled in the name of God" (Sermon on 1 Tim. 3:16, quoted in Manetsch, *Company*, 131).

24   Manetsch, *Company*, 131, with examples.

25   *Westminster Confession* 21.7–8, in Westminster Assembly, *The Confession of Faith, Agreed upon by the Assembly of Divines at Westminster, with the Assistance of Commissioners from the Church of Scotland* (Haverhill, N.H.: Goss, 1821), 93–94.

26   Trevor James, "King James' Book of Sports, 1617," *Hist* 134 (2017): 42.
27   Alice M. Earle, *The Sabbath in Puritan New England* (New York: Scribner's Sons, 1891), 327.
28   The first of these meetinghouses "were often built in the valleys, in the meadow lands; for the dwelling-houses must be clustered around them, since the colonists were ordered by law to build their new homes within half a mile of the meetinghouse" (Earle, *Sabbath*, 4).
29   Earle, *Sabbath*, 26.
30   The men "always rose when the services were ended and left the house before the women and children, thus making sure the safe exit of the latter" (Earle, *Sabbath*, 24).
31   Earle, *Sabbath*, 102.
32   The Puritans, "though bitterly denouncing all forms and ceremonies, were great respecters of persons; and in nothing was the regard for wealth and position more fully shown than in designating the seat in which each person should sit during public worship. A committee of dignified and influential men was appointed to assign irrevocably to each person his or her place, according to rank and importance" (Earle, *Sabbath*, 45).
33   Sometimes bad behavior could result in an appearance before the magistrate, as in the case of one youth who allegedly "sported and played and by indecent gestures and wry faces caused laughter and misbehavior in the beholders" (Earle, *Sabbath*, 56–57).
34   The tithingman was "equipped with a long staff, heavily knobbed at one end, with which he severely and pitilessly rapped the heads of the too sleepy men," as well as "the too wide-awake boys." The other end of his stick sported a foxtail, with which he more gently awakened the women (Earle, *Sabbath*, 66–67).
35   Earle, *Sabbath*, 230.
36   Earle, *Sabbath*, 78.
37   Earle, *Sabbath*, 79.
38   Earle, *Sabbath*, 81.
39   Earle, *Sabbath*, 144.
40   Earle, *Sabbath*, 254.
41   Earle, *Sabbath*, 255.
42   Earle, *Sabbath*, 258.
43   Earle, *Sabbath*, 248.
44   Walter Brueggemann, *Theology of the Old Testament: Testimony, Dispute, Advocacy* (Minneapolis: Fortress, 1997), 185. The Sabbath command looks to "a human community . . . peaceably engaged in neighbor-respecting life that is not madly engaged in production and consumption, but one that knows a limit to such activity and so has at the center of its life an enactment of peaceableness that bespeaks the settled rule of Yahweh."
45   Exodus 16:21–23.
46   Leviticus 23:3; Num. 28:9–10; 1 Chr. 9:32; 2 Chr. 2:4; the heading to Ps. 92.
47   Nehemiah 10:31; 13:15–22; Jer. 17:19–27; Amos 8:5–6.
48   See further, e.g., Mark 1:21–28; Luke 4:14–29.
49   E.g., Matt. 12:9–13; Mark 3:1–6; Luke 4:31–37; John 9:13–16.
50   E.g., Matt. 12:11; Luke 13:10–17; Luke 14:1–6; John 7:21–24.
51   For a full discussion of the nature of this heresy see Peter T. O'Brien, *Colossians, Philemon,* WBC 44 (Dallas: Word, 1982), xxx–xli.
52   Gary V. Smith, *Isaiah 1–39,* NAC 15A (Nashville: B&H, 2007), 108.
53   Herold Weiss, "The Sabbath in the Writings of Josephus," *JSJ* 29 (1998): 363–90 (363).
54   For example, a recent case study of a small Jewish community in first- and early second-century Roman Egypt "shows that it was not always possible to observe the Sabbath strictly when confronted with the governmental power of the Roman Empire, despite the indications of tolerance found in Philo or Josephus. The Jews from Edfu did pay taxes on the Sabbath. When they could collect the taxes themselves, however, namely in case of the Jewish

tax, they took care to observe their religious practices" (Willy Clarysse, Sofie Remijsen, and Mark Depauw, "Observing the Sabbath in the Roman Empire: A Case Study," *SCI* 29 [2010]: 51–57 [57]).

55 Clarysse, Remijsen, and Depauw, "Sabbath," 52.

56 Christopher Rowland, "A Summary of Sabbath Observance in Judaism at the Beginning of the Christian Era," in *From Sabbath to Lord's Day: A Biblical, Historical, and Theological Investigation*, ed. Donald A. Carson (Grand Rapids: Zondervan, 1982), 44–55 (52), referencing Philo, *Special Laws* 2.60, in *The Works of Philo*, trans. C. D. Yonge (Peabody, Mass.: Hendrickson, 1993), 574. In general, Rowland tells us, "[t]he observance of the Sabbath . . . was open to abuse from pagan writers" (51). See further *TDNT* 7:17–18.

57 In the earliest times they may well have taken place on the Saturday evening, if Acts 20:7–12 may be taken as describing a more general practice. Here the Christians appear to be meeting just after the weekly Sabbath is over—after sunset on Saturday, in the Jewish way of reckoning time. From that point of view, they are even at this time, therefore, meeting on the first day of the week. This would have permitted Jewish Christ-followers to observe the Sabbath before moving on to the evening Christian gathering.

58 Paul A. Hartog, "Constantine, Sabbath-Keeping, and Sunday Observance," in *Rethinking Constantine: History, Theology, and Legacy*, ed. Edward L. Smither (Eugene, Ore.: Wipf & Stock, 2014), 105–29 (125–28).

59 Richard J. Bauckham, "Sabbath and Sunday in the Post-Apostolic Church," in Carson, *Sabbath*, 251–98 (268).

60 Bauckham, "Sabbath," 255.

61 Christians gather "on the day called Sunday . . . because it is the first day on which God . . . made the world; and Jesus Christ our Saviour on the same day rose from the dead" (Justin, *First Apology* 67 [*ANF* 1:185–86]). Note also the letter written by Pliny the Younger to the emperor Trajan in the year 107, in which the former reports that Christians are accustomed to meet "regularly before dawn on a fixed day" (Pliny the Younger, *Letters and Panegyrics* 10.96, trans. Betty Radice, vol. 2, LCL 59 [London: Heinemann, 1969]), 289.

62 Justin Martyr, *Dialogus cum Tryphone* (*Dialogue with Trypho*) 47 (*ANF* 1:218).

63 Tertullian mentions that some Christians known to him abstain from kneeling on the Sabbath, thereby treating it in the same way as a Sunday. He further claims that the matter is "on its trial before the churches," suggesting that it involves more than merely a handful of people (Tertullian, *De oratione* [*On Prayer*] 23 [*ANF* 3:689]). "Kneeling . . . was considered a posture of solicitude and humility unfit for days of divine joy (and therefore to be shunned on 'the day of the Lord's Resurrection' . . .)" (Kenneth A. Strand, "Tertullian and the Sabbath," *AUSS* 9 [1971]: 129–46 [133–34]).

64 Bauckham, "Sabbath," 261.

65 Christians are those "no longer observing the Sabbath but living in the observance of the Lord's Day" (Ignatius, *Epistola ad Magnesianos* [*Letter to the Magnesians*] 9.1 [*ANF* 1:62]).

66 Bauckham, "Sabbath," 259. This is also starkly reflected later in the above-mentioned Council of Laodicea (364): "Christians must not judaize by resting on the Sabbath but must work on that day, rather honouring the Lord's Day . . . if any shall be found to be judaizers, let them be anathema from Christ."

67 Tertullian, *Adversus Judaeos* (*Against the Jews*) 4 (*ANF* 3:155); see earlier Irenaeus *Against Heresies* 4.16 (*ANF* 1:481).

68 Irenaeus writes, for example, that "he will not be commanded to leave idle one day of rest, who is constantly keeping sabbath, that is, giving homage to God in the temple of God, which is man's body, and at all times doing the works of justice" (Irenaeus, *Epideixis tou apostolikou kērygmatos* [*Proof of the Apostolic Preaching*], trans. Joseph P. Smith, ACW 16 [New York: Newman, 1952], 106).

69   Tertullian, *Ad Nationes* (*To the Nations*) 1.13 (*ANF* 3:123).
70   Tertullian, *Apology* 16 (*ANF* 3:31).
71   Tertullian, *On Prayer* 23 (*ANF* 3:689).
72   Judith Shulevitz, "Why You Never See Your Friends Anymore," *The Atlantic*, November 2019, https://www.theatlantic.com/magazine/archive/2019/11/why-dont-i-see-you-anymore/598336/. Shulevitz is the author of *The Sabbath World: Glimpses of a Different Order of Time* (New York: Random House, 2011).
73   Geza Vermes, *The Dead Sea Scrolls in English*, 3rd ed. (Sheffield: JSOT, 1987), 95, referencing CD 11:13–14.

11   GOD'S SERVANT FOR YOUR GOOD

1   John Ball, "Address to the Rebels at Blackheath (1381)," in *British Historical and Political Orations from the 12th to the 20th Century*, ed. Ernest Rhys (London: J. M. Dent, 1915), 3–4.
2   Kennedy, *English Revolution*, 110.
3   The Peace of Augsburg in 1555 had attempted to contain this instability by dividing Europe into Roman Catholic and Lutheran "zones," each regional or more local ruler being permitted to choose the confession of his own domain within the overarching reality of the Holy Roman Empire. In the end, however, the omission of Calvinist rulers from the settlement—as well as the territorial ambitions of some of the others—caused this uneasy truce to unravel.
4   For the sake of brevity in what follows, I shall hitherto simply refer to this watershed moment as "Westphalia."
5   As a result of the Peace of Westphalia these states were now "emerging" in a new way, as the effective power of the Holy Roman Emperor and the imperial Diet declined, and the princes of Europe often became absolute sovereigns over their own territories. Indeed, new powers emerged, not least in Austria, Bavaria, and Brandenburg, and others grew in influence and reach, like Sweden and France.
6   Perez Zagorin, *How the Idea of Religious Toleration Came to the West* (Princeton: Princeton University Press, 2003), 50.
7   Erasmus, who remained a Roman Catholic even while holding some rather Protestant-sounding ideas, apparently believed in such limited toleration until the end of his life. If his English friend Thomas More ever truly shared his view, as his own book *Utopia* (1516) might suggest, then he certainly eventually abandoned it. In *Utopia* he envisaged a land in which "for the sake of peace . . . all should be free to follow their own religious faith and to try to convert others, provided they relied solely on persuasion and refrained from abuse." Faced with the Reformation in England, however, he became a "persecutor and scourge of heretics" in that country (Zagorin, *Toleration*, 57–58).
8   Zagorin, *Toleration*, 76.
9   Zagorin, *Toleration*, 82.
10   Zagorin, *Toleration*, 143.
11   Castellio had once been the rector of the College of Geneva, but by 1553 he was working as a professor of Greek at the University of Basel.
12   Zagorin, *Toleration*, 93–144 (107). Castellio was by no means the only "tolerationist" respondent to the Servetus affair; another notable one was the Italian humanist Celio Secondo Curione. For a brief account see Mario Biagoni, *The Radical Reformation and the Making of Modern Europe: A Lasting Heritage*, SMRT 207 (Leiden: Brill, 2017), 139–40.
13   Zagorin, *Toleration*, 83–86.
14   Biagoni, *Radical Reformation*, passim, and the conclusions in chapter 6, specifically pp. 139–42.
15   Morrill, "Puritan Revolution," 74–75.
16   Morrill, "Puritan Revolution," 80.

17   Morrill, "Puritan Revolution," 81, with further discussion of how dissent was handled by Cromwell on pp. 82–84.

18   Coward, *Protectorate*, 59.

19   The *Instrument* itself explicitly does not offer liberty "to popery, prelacy, [or those who] practice licentiousness" (Morrill, "Puritan Revolution," 81). In 1655, as Lord Protector, Cromwell issued a new proclamation "demanding full conformity to the laws against priests, 'who resort to say masses and seduce people to the church of Rome,' and the 'speedy conviction' of popish recusants 'for there had been great neglect'" (Albert J. Loomie, "Oliver Cromwell's Policy toward the English Catholics: The Appraisal by Diplomats, 1654–1658," *CHR* 90 [2004]: 29–44 [33]). Significant persecution of Catholics followed. There is some evidence that Cromwell's own heart was not entirely in some aspects of this intolerance—but on the other hand, he "never abandoned his determined effort to remove Catholic clergy [in particular] from England" (Loomie, "Cromwell's Policy," 43).

20   Coward, *Protectorate*, 58–61. So it was that "for the persecuted majority of the English Catholic community in Ireland and England, Cromwell's [eventual] demise was a welcome liberation" (Loomie, "Cromwell's Policy," 44). Nevertheless, toleration for Roman Catholics *had* been advocated by *some* English Puritans as early as the 1640s (Norah Carlin, "Toleration for Catholics in the Puritan Revolution," in *Tolerance and Intolerance in the European Reformation*, ed. Ole Peter Grell and Bob Scribner [Cambridge: Cambridge University Press, 1996], 216–30). On the Jews and the Puritans, see further our chapter 14.

21   Rhode Island proved an attractive destination, therefore, for religious people who could find no satisfactory home in the Bay colony. For many striking examples, see Earle, *Sabbath*, 292–310. These included Anne Hutchinson, who established a settlement on the island after greatly disturbing the Boston community with her teaching concerning salvation: that one's assurance of salvation was the result not of increasing personal sanctification but rather of the inner witness of the Holy Spirit.

22   John C. Laursen, "Introduction: Contexts and Paths to Toleration in the Seventeenth Century," in *Beyond the Persecuting Society: Religious Toleration before the Enlightenment*, ed. John Laursen and Cary Nederman (Philadelphia: University of Pennsylvania Press, 1998), 169–77 (170).

23   The Test Act made a person's eligibility for public office in England dependent upon receiving the sacraments according to the rite of the reestablished, prerepublican Church of England.

24   Laursen, "Contexts," 174.

25   Benedict de Spinoza, *Theological-Political Treatise*, ed. Jonathan Israel, trans. Michael Silverthorne and Jonathan Israel, CTHP (Cambridge: Cambridge University Press, 2007).

26   Zagorin, *Toleration*, 267.

27   Roman Catholics could not be tolerated, for example, in the main because they owed allegiance to a foreign ruler (the pope), nor could atheists, since human society is impossible once God is removed as the guarantor of oaths.

28   Zagorin, *Toleration*, 245. This was also true of the Frenchman Pierre Bayle (1647–1706), who was himself a Huguenot and would go on to make his own contributions to the cause of toleration (Zagorin, *Toleration*, 267–83).

29   Zagorin, *Toleration*, 267. Substantial civil equality followed in the nineteenth century, with Protestant dissenters being admitted to Parliament in 1828 and Roman Catholics being fully emancipated in 1829; Jews were permitted to join them in Parliament after 1858, and atheists after 1886.

30   Arthur Herman, *How the Scots Invented the Modern World: The True Story of How Western Europe's Poorest Nation Created Our World and Everything in It* (New York: Three Rivers, 2002), 2–10.

31 Consider Article VI, for example, which declares that "no religious Test shall ever be required as a Qualification to any Office or public Trust under the United States."

32 Barbero, *Charlemagne*, 243.

33 Stackhouse, *Making the Best of It*, 300.

34 W. R. Ward, "Response," in *Many Are Chosen: Divine Election and Western Nationalism*, ed. William R. Hutchison and Hartmut Lehmann, HTS 38 (Minneapolis: Fortress, 1994), 51–56 (51).

35 Thomas Kselman, "Religion and French Identity: The Origins of the *Union Sacrée*," in Hutchison and Lehmann, *Many Are Chosen*, 57–79 (57–58).

36 E.g., a monarch cannot suspend laws without the consent of Parliament, maintain an army in peacetime without Parliament's authorization, or interfere with freedom of speech or free elections. This idea that a monarch is "king by contract" was already in the air during the English Revolution (Kennedy, *English Revolution*, 80).

37 Even once King Charles was dead, in fact, the Lord Protector continued to function very much as "a king in all but name," even though he refused point-blank to be crowned as one (Coward, *Protectorate*, 24–25).

38 Kennedy, *English Revolution*, 71, quoting from *The Case of the Army Truly Stated* (1647).

39 Kennedy, *English Revolution*, 74, quoting the Leveller William Rainborowe.

40 Hobbes had agreed with the radicals of the Civil War period that individuals in this state are equal to one another, and that no single individual has an innate "right" to rule over the rest. However, because life in the state of nature is nasty, brutish, and short—a state of perpetual war—we have wisely built civil society on top of it in order to make our existences more tolerable. In order to achieve this, each of us has granted a sovereign (as we must do) absolute power over society. This is the "social contract" into which we have entered, and to which all must remain committed—out of measured self-interest. The alternative is that unrestrained self-interest will destroy civil society and plunge us back into the brutal state of nature. No matter how bad things become under the terms of the social contract, that alternative is always going to be worse. Absolutist monarchy survives in this scenario, then, but not because of divine right, nor indeed for "biblical" reasons at all. It does so because it is necessary for our own survival and because, for that reason, it is chosen by reasonable people.

41 Rousseau also locates his idea of the state of nature within a Creation and Fall narrative, but of a different kind. Human society is at first peaceful and uncomplicated, but this begins to change with the invention of private property, which produces inequality. The property owners then create government by way of an initial, problematic social contract, allegedly to guarantee the rights of all but in reality to entrench the inequality. It is this that explains the nature of the modern society that Rousseau sees all around him; although "[m]an was born free . . . he is everywhere in chains" (Jean-Jacques Rousseau, *The Social Contract*, trans. Maurice Cranston [London: Penguin Books, 1968], 49). How may we now recover our natural liberty while continuing to live in civil society? We may do so by way of agreements freely entered into with other free and equal persons, transferring our individual rights and freedoms to a collective sovereign "body" that will seek the common good. This is the new social contract, according to which the individual will must find its place within the general will. The sovereign here, then, is not a king but a democracy of a particularly direct (i.e., not "representative") kind. The collective body, comprising every citizen, gathers together and makes decisions that represent the general will. Here, too, there are traces of the biblical Story still to be seen in the articulation of the social contract, albeit that generally Rousseau held a negative view of the usefulness of Christian faith for creating a flourishing, modern state; he preferred a version of deism.

42   Kselman, "Religion," 71, referring to Jules Michelet (1798–1874). Similarly, Victor Hugo (1802–1885): "France would not perish because it had a unique mission in the world, a mission to challenge kings and priests and bring liberty to all peoples" (72).

43   Eran Shalev, *American Zion: The Old Testament as a Political Text from the Revolution to the Civil War* (New Haven: Yale University Press, 2013), 187.

44   We think of, e.g., Pharaoh in Exod. 1–15; Sennacherib in 2 Kgs. 18–19; and Nebuchadnezzar in Dan. 3–4.

45   Stackhouse, *Making the Best of It*, 303.

46   It is interesting to note here, e.g., the way in which the English Puritans could claim to be the legitimate rulers of England precisely because Providence had twice given them victory in war over the king. The only difference between Commonwealth and king in this respect, then, was that the victories in war that had in due course placed the latter on the throne as God's vice-regent had happened a longer time ago (Kennedy, *English Revolution*, 67, 83).

47   I depart here from the NIV, which says: "whoever rebels against the authority is rebelling against what God has instituted." This risks giving the Greek a specific sense—that of armed revolution—that is unhelpful. The language is more generally that of "opposes, resisting, standing against."

48   This was how Rom. 13 was read, e.g., by the American revolutionary Jonathan Mayhew. The passage teaches "a natural right to resist unjust rule . . . Paul argues 'not in favor of submission to all who bear the *title* of rulers, in common; but only, to those who *actually* perform the duty of rulers, by exercising a reasonable and just authority, for the good of human society'" (Gorski, *Covenant*, 68).

49   Langan, "Elements," 26.

50   Thomas Aquinas, *On the Government of Rulers* 1:2, in *Aquinas: Political Writings*, ed. R. W. Dyson, CTHPT (Cambridge: Cambridge University Press, 2002), 8.

51   In Aquinas' view, "resistance and even regicide may be legitimate, provided that the tyranny is severe and prolonged, and that the judgment is carried out by public persons" (Gorski, *Covenant*, 252n58).

12   CONCEIVED IN LIBERTY?

1   "Letter to Thomas Jefferson, August 22, 1800," in *Letters of Benjamin Rush*, ed. Lyman H. Butterfield, MAPS 30 (Princeton: Princeton University Press, 1951), 2:820–1.

2   Aristotle, *Politics* I.5.1254b 13 and I.12.1259a 40, trans. Benjamin Jowett (New York: Random House, 1943), 59, 75.

3   Neil Johnston, "The History of the Parliamentary Franchise," CBP:RP 13–14, 7, https://researchbriefings.parliament.uk/ResearchBriefing/Summary/RP13-14.

4   Kennedy, *English Revolution*, 75, quoting the Leveller John Wildman. It was intolerable that under the present rules "many a soldier 'whose zeal and affection to God and this kingdom has carried him forth in this cause'" would find himself "without an estate after years in the Army and therefore without an interest in the future of the kingdom or a voice in elections" (Kennedy, *English Revolution*, 76, partially quoting Rainborowe).

5   Kennedy, *English Revolution*, 76.

6   Kennedy, *English Revolution*, 76.

7   Kennedy, *English Revolution*, 74.

8   Kennedy, *English Revolution*, 89.

9   Julia O'Faolain and Lauro Martines, *Not in God's Image: Women in History from the Greeks to the Victorians* (New York: Harper & Row, 1973), 266.

10   For a brief account of the later debate about the real *intent* of the Constitution, its wording notwithstanding, see C. Bradley Thompson, ed., *Anti-Slavery Political Writings, 1833–1860: A Reader* (Armonk, N.Y.: M. E. Sharpe, 2004), xxii–xxiv, and, at greater length, pp. 133–56.

11   Nellis, *New World*, 4.

12   Nellis, *New World*, 2.

13   Nellis, *New World*, 2. By 1664 the Maryland Assembly had in turn passed a law equating "Negro" with "slave" and mandating lifelong servitude for all such persons and their children (as well as for any children from unions between "freeborn English women" and "Negro slaves"). A 1705 Virginia statute refers to all such slaves as "real estate" (Nellis, *New World*, 90–91).

14   This was not because people in the North necessarily objected to slavery but because of the different economics of the regions: it was predominantly the South that had the large plantations whose economy required extensive forced labor.

15   "By the first half of the eighteenth century, about 2.5 per cent of New England's population [for example] was black . . . Maryland's population was 31.5 per cent black and Virginia's 42 per cent with only a tiny percentage of them free" (Nellis, *New World*, 97.)

16   Nellis, *New World*, 130.

17   Nellis, *New World*, 100.

18   Nellis, *New World*, 129.

19   By 1860 almost half of the states in the union (fifteen out of thirty-three) "had state constitutions protecting the rights of whites to hold slaves as permanent property" (Nellis, *New World*, 133).

20   Dwight T. Pitcaithley, ed., *The U.S. Constitution and Secession: A Documentary Anthology of Slavery and White Supremacy* (Lawrence: University Press of Kansas, 2018), xi.

21   Aristotle, *Politics* I.5.1254b 24–25.

22   Aristotle, *Politics* III.9.1280a 32–34.

23   Gorski, *Covenant*, 87.

24   Thompson, *Political Writings*, xiii.

25   Nellis, *New World*, 98.

26   Albert T. Bledsoe, *An Essay on Liberty and Slavery* (Philadelphia: J. B. Lippincott, 1856), 54.

27   Henry Louis Gates Jr., ed., *Lincoln on Race and Slavery* (Princeton: Princeton University Press, 2009), xxii.

28   Pitcaithley, *Constitution*, 22.

29   Gates, *Lincoln*, xvii.

30   Gates, *Lincoln*, xvii.

31   Gates, *Lincoln*, xvii.

32   Nellis, *New World*, 137. Lincoln's antipathy to interracial marriage follows quite naturally from this. Referring in 1857 to Stephen Douglas' horror "at the thought of the mixing of blood by the white and black races," Lincoln says that he is "agreed for once—a thousand times agreed" (Gates, *Lincoln*, xxxi).

33   Thompson, *Political Writings*, xv.

34   Shalev, *American Zion*, 1–2.

35   Shalev, *American Zion*, 1–2. Even Jefferson—not exactly an orthodox Christian— "envisioned as early as 1776 a Great Seal for the young United States that represented on one of its sides the people of Israel led by the pillar of fire in the desert" (Shalev, *American Zion*, 5). One can readily understand how an Exodus narrative concerning a people who flee tyranny would have been useful for this purpose.

36   Shalev, *American Zion*, 11.

37   Shalev, *American Zion*, 13.

38   Shalev, *American Zion*, 24.

39   Shalev, *American Zion*, 82.

40   David M. Goldenberg, *The Curse of Ham: Race and Slavery in Early Judaism, Christianity, and Islam* (Princeton: Princeton University Press, 2009), 142–44.

41 Stephen R. Haynes, *Noah's Curse: The Biblical Justification of American Slavery* (Oxford: Oxford University, 2002).

42 E.g., Gen. 12:16; 16:1; 24:2; 26:14.

43 Some of this was in principle temporary, debt slavery—a debtor worked voluntarily for a creditor in order to pay off a loan (e.g., Exod. 21:2–3; Deut. 15:12)—but such slavery could become permanent if the slave chose to stay on (e.g., Deut. 15:16–17). People also had the right to sell their children into slavery or use them as security. Prisoners of war could become slaves (e.g., Deut. 20:11–14), and slaves could also be purchased from neighboring nations (e.g., Lev. 25:44–46).

44 The apostle Paul similarly describes Christians as those who "have become slaves of God" (Rom. 6:22). The deepest slavery in life, about which Christians should be most concerned, is slavery to sin (Gal. 4:8–9; 5:1).

45 Ephesians 6:5, 9; Col. 3:22–25; 4:1.

46 In 1 Pet. 2:18 he writes: "Slaves, in reverent fear of God submit yourselves to your masters, not only to those who are good and considerate, but also to those who are harsh."

47 Pitcaithley, *Constitution*, 24, quoting an 1860 sermon by the Presbyterian minister Benjamin Palmer.

48 Goldenberg, *Curse*, 149.

49 Goldenberg, *Curse*, 149.

50 Iain Provan, V. Philips Long, and Tremper Longman III, *A Biblical History of Israel*, 2nd ed. (Louisville: Westminster John Knox, 2015), 128.

51 Iain Provan, *1 and 2 Kings*, UBCS (Grand Rapids: Baker Books, 2012), 84–96 and 146–47.

52 Thus, if a slave is blinded, or his tooth is broken, he is to be freed in compensation (Exod. 21:26–27). If an owner beats his slave to death, he is to be punished (Exod. 21:20). As we saw in chapter 10, slaves are to share in the Sabbath rest (Exod. 20:10), as well as taking part in sacrificial meals (Deut. 12:12). Exod. 21:7–11 protects rights of female slaves who become concubines; Deut. 23:15–16 forbids the person from whom a refugee slave has sought protection from handing the slave back.

53 The speaker does not rest his claim to virtue, e.g., on having avoided adultery (Exod. 20:14) but on having refrained from looking lustfully at a girl (Job 31:1). He is not a righteous person because he has refrained from stealing (Exod. 20:15), but because he has not "denied the desires of the poor or let the eyes of the widow grow weary" (Job 31:16) and he has shared his food with orphans (31:17).

54 Along similar lines Paul, in 1 Cor. 12:13, reminds the Christians in Corinth that they "were all baptized by one Spirit into one body—whether Jews or Greeks, slave or free—and we were all given the one Spirit to drink."

55 Richard N. Longenecker, *New Testament Social Ethics for Today* (Grand Rapids: Eerdmans, 1984), 75.

56 E.g., Eph. 6:5–9 and Col. 3:22–4:1.

57 Shalev, *American Zion*, 163.

13   A MONSTROUS REGIMENT?

1 Willard. M. Swartley, *Slavery, Sabbath, War, and Women: Case Issues in Biblical Interpretation* (Scottdale, Pa.: Herald, 1983), 49–50.

2 "The ground upon which you stand is holy ground: never—never surrender it. If you surrender it, the hope of the slave is extinguished, and the chains of his servitude will be strengthened a hundredfold . . . You must obey our great Master's injunction: Fear *not* them that kill the body, and after that, have nothing more that they can do" (Angelina E. Grimké, "Slavery and the Boston Riot" [1835], https://www.loc.gov/resource/rbpe.05601500/). For a general account of the Grimkés' life see Alison M. Parker, *Articulating Rights: Nineteenth-Century*

American Women on Race, Reform, and the State (Dekalb: Northern Illinois University Press, 2010), 63–96.

3 "I know you do not make the laws, but I also know that you are the wives and mothers, the sisters and daughters of those who do . . . You can do much in every way . . . You can read on this subject . . . You can pray over this subject . . . You can speak on this subject . . . You can act on this subject" (Angelina E. Grimké, *An Appeal to the Christian Women of the South* [New York: American Anti-Slavery Society, 1836], 16–17, http://utc.iath.virginia.edu/abolitn/abesaegat.html).

4 A. Grimké, *Women of the South*, 18.

5 A. Grimké, *Women of the South*, 18.

6 A. Grimké, *Women of the South*, 18. The case of Daniel's friends in Dan. 3 is one example.

7 A. Grimké, *Women of the South*, 26.

8 Angelina E. Grimké, *Appeal to the Women of the Nominally Free States Issued by an Anti-Slavery Convention of American Women* (Boston: Isaac Knapp, 1837), 13–14; cf. the closing argument on pp. 68–70.

9 General Association of Massachusetts, *Minutes of the General Association of Massachusetts. At Their Meeting at North Brookfield, June 26, 1837. With the Narrative of the State of Religion, and the Pastoral Letter* (Boston: Crocker & Brewster, 1987), 20–21.

10 Catharine E. Beecher, *Essay on Slavery and Abolitionism* (Philadelphia: Henry Perkins, 1837), 97, 100.

11 "All the sacred protection of religion, all the generous promptings of chivalry, all the poetry of romantic gallantry, depend upon woman's retaining her place as dependent and defenceless, and making no claims, and maintaining no right but what are the gifts of honour, rectitude, and love" (Beecher, *Essay*, 101–2).

12 Sarah M. Grimké, *Letters on the Equality of the Sexes and the Condition of Woman* (Boston: Knapp, 1838).

13 S. Grimké, *Letters*, 4–5.

14 S. Grimké, *Letters*, 5.

15 S. Grimké, *Letters*, 10.

16 Ephesians 5:23–24; cf. Col. 3:18.

17 S. Grimké, *Letters*, 4–5.

18 S. Grimké, *Letters*, 47.

19 S. Grimké, *Letters*, 49.

20 S. Grimké, *Letters*, 66.

21 S. Grimké, *Letters*, 74.

22 S. Grimké, *Letters*, 82.

23 I shall do so for no other reason than to distinguish the kind of "sexual ethics" discussed in chapter 7 from "the ethics of the sexes" now being discussed in the present chapter. In many ways I would like to avoid the word "gender" in making this distinction, because although it was once commonly used simply as a synonym for "sex," it has now become customary to set the one over against the other—which I certainly do not intend to do here. Yet I cannot think of a good, concise, alternative term. See further on gender and sex our chapter 17.

24 "The history of interpretation furnishes no examples of more willful and violent perversions of the sacred text than are to be found in the writings of the abolitionists. They seem to consider themselves above the scriptures: and when they put themselves above the law of God, it is not wonderful that they should disregard the laws of men. Significant manifestations of the result of this disposition to consider their own light a surer guide than the word of God, are visible in the anarchical opinions about human governments, civil and ecclesiastical, and on the rights of women, which have found appropriate advocates in the abolition publications" (cited in Swartley, *Slavery*, 49).

25 The conflict that arose for pragmatic reasons between these two sets of aspirations, as priorities were necessarily ordered in specific political agendas, would prove to be an important factor in inhibiting the achievement of the first. For example, many of the reforming Chartists who flourished in England between 1838 and 1848 believed in female suffrage, but they omitted a demand for it from their Charter for fear that it might damage their program of achieving universal suffrage for men.

26 Stanton, *Suffrage*, 70.

27 The notion that the United States as a whole is an "American Zion" largely disappears among whites after the Civil War, giving way to the idea of "first and foremost a black Zion," in which it is now the African Americans who are the escaped slaves and white America has become Pharaoh (Shalev, *American Zion*, 184).

28 The Fourteenth Amendment (1868) granted citizenship to "all persons born or naturalized in the United States, and subject to the jurisdiction thereof," guaranteed to those persons equal protection under the law, and authorized the government to punish states that abridged citizens' right to vote. The Fifteenth Amendment (1870) explicitly stated that the "right of citizens of the United States to vote shall not be denied or abridged by the United States or by any State on account of race, color, or previous condition of servitude."

29 The connection between the emancipation of slaves and women in this respect had already been made in Kansas, where linked suffrage referenda had been presented to the electorate in 1867.

30 Karen Offen, *The Woman Question in France, 1400–1870*, NSEH (Cambridge: Cambridge University Press, 2017), 6.

31 Offen, *Woman Question*, 166–71 (167, 170).

32 Offen, *Woman Question*, 171.

33 One of these was Victor Hugo (1802–1885), who in a letter wrote: "This minor before the law, this slave in reality, is woman. Man has inequitably weighted the two balance pans of the Code, whose equilibrium is important to the human conscience; man has put all the rights on his side and all the obligations on woman's side. Because of this, there is a profound problem. Because of this, woman is in servitude. Under our present legislation, she cannot vote, she does not count, she does not exist" (Karen Offen, *Debating the Woman Question in the French Third Republic, 1870–1920*, NSEH [Cambridge: Cambridge University Press, 2018], 17).

34 The problem early on was that "the political climate . . . was still less than auspicious for making drastic reforms in women's status . . . republicans felt that their own objectives were seriously threatened," and that they must prioritize those (Offen, *Debating the Woman Question*, 16).

35 Offen, *Debating the Woman Question*, 618.

36 *Merriam-Webster*, s.v. "monstrous," https://www.merriam-webster.com/dictionary/monstrous.

37 Mary Wollstoncraft Shelley, *Frankenstein: or, The Modern Prometheus* (London: Printed for Lackington, Hughes, Harding, Mavor, & Jones, 1818), 98.

38 The reader will not be surprised, having read chapter 1, that I ask these questions in this way, thereby underlining my intention of refusing to join any ongoing (but futile) debate about what is "natural" to a woman (or a man) that proceeds independently or quasi-independently of Scripture (by way, perhaps, of Mary Shelley). I am interested, rather, in discerning biblical teaching on woman (and man).

39 Aristotle, *Politics* I.5.1254b 13 and I.12.1259a 40.

40 Whether we can in fact properly even call it a "man" is an interesting question (Provan, *Seriously Dangerous Religion*, 80–81).

41 Walton, *Ancient Near Eastern Thought*, 156–69.

42 Provan, *Seriously Dangerous Religion*, 133–37.

43   Tikva Frymer-Kensky, *Studies in Bible and Feminist Criticism*, JPSSDS (Philadelphia: Jewish Publication Society, 2006), 174.

44   Phyllis Trible, *Texts of Terror: Literary-Feminist Readings of Biblical Narratives* (Philadelphia: Fortress, 1984), 28.

45   See, e.g., Matt. 9:23–26; Mark 5:25–34; Luke 10:38–42; John 4:1–26; and, for women as paradigmatic disciples, Matt. 28:9–10. For a more general study of women in the New Testament, see Richard Bauckham, *Gospel Women: Studies of the Named Women in the Gospels* (Grand Rapids: Eerdmans, 2002).

46   The term "could be understood simply in terms of a regular pattern of service undertaken by Phoebe on behalf of her local church," but more likely refers to "a recognized ministry . . . or position of responsibility within the congregation" (cf. 1 Tim. 3:8–13) (James D. G. Dunn, *Romans 9–16*, WBC 38B [Dallas: Word, 1988], 86).

47   Thiselton, *First Corinthians*, 828. The term "prophesying," he informs us, "allows for short utterances or, in accordance with Paul's own wishes, for longer stretches of speech to which the nearest modern parallel is probably that of an informed pastoral sermon which proclaims grace and judgment, or requires change of life, but which also remains open to question and correction by others" (1094).

48   Against the background of 1 Pet. 2:12 ("Live such good lives among the pagans that, though they accuse you of doing wrong, they may see your good deeds and glorify God on the day he visits us") this passage combines exhortation to Christian husbands and wives to love one another as co-heirs of eternal life with attention to cultural norms concerning "immodest or ostentatious clothing" and presuppositions concerning women as the weaker sex and the virtue of her "submission" to her husband.

49   Cynthia Long Westfall, *Paul and Gender: Reclaiming the Apostle's Vision for Men and Women* (Grand Rapids: Baker Academic, 2016), 13.

50   Westfall, *Gender*, 13.

51   Westfall, *Gender*, 93.

52   Westfall, *Gender*, 56–58.

53   Westfall, *Gender*, 61–105. As Tom Schreiner himself notes in disagreeing with Westfall on this particular point, the Greek word does probably mean "source" in some Pauline texts (Eph. 4:15; Col. 2:19) (Thomas R. Schreiner, "Paul and Gender: A Review Article," *Them* 43 [2018]: 178–92 [186]). I do not find persuasive his reasons for failing to understand the word in the same way in the texts currently under scrutiny.

54   Westfall, *Gender*, 99.

55   Westfall, *Gender*, 102.

56   Westfall, *Gender*, 104.

57   Westfall, *Gender*, 104–5.

58   Westfall, *Gender*, 279.

59   Westfall, *Gender*, 279.

60   Westfall, *Gender*, 290–94.

61   Westfall, *Gender*, 293.

62   Westfall, *Gender*, 279–312.

63   I leave aside entirely in the present context the equally puzzling comment that "women will be saved through childbearing" (NIV) and refer the reader on this point to the commentaries.

14   STAYING ALIVE

1   See "Proclamation of Independence," The Knesset, 1948, https://www.knesset.gov.il/docs/eng/megilat_eng.htm.

2   Linder, "Legal Status," 152.

3   Robert Chazan, "Philosemitic Tendencies in Medieval Western Christendom," in *Philosemitism in History*, ed. Jonathan Karp and Adam Sutcliffe (Cambridge: Cambridge University Press, 2011), 29–48 (30).

4   Chazan, "Philosemitic Tendencies," 30.

5   Simonsohn, *Apostolic See*, 11.

6   Consider, e.g., Gregory the Great's letter to the bishops of Arles and Marseille, in which the pope declares that "whoever comes to the baptismal font not by the sweetness of preaching but by necessity, returning to the original superstition dies worse than before," and tries to persuade the bishops to adopt preaching and discourse instead of force (Jessie Sherwood, "Interpretation, Negotiation, and Adaptation: Converting the Jews in Gerhard of Mainz's *Collectio*," in John Tolan et al., *Jews in Early Christian Law: Byzantium and the Latin West, 6th–11th Centuries*, RLMCMS 2 [Turnhout: Brepols, 2014], 119–29 [124]).

7   Simonsohn, *Apostolic See*, 15.

8   Simonsohn, *Apostolic See*, 16–17.

9   Simonsohn, *Apostolic See*, 18–21.

10   Simonsohn, *Apostolic See*, 23.

11   Paradoxically, one end result of this tragedy was that the synagogue became a warehouse, its original function forgotten, and thus survived later anti-Jewish depredations in Germany to become the oldest remaining Central European synagogue still standing from ground to roof. It can still be visited and now houses some treasure abandoned by Jews attempting to flee the 1349 pogrom. See "Jewish Past and Present in Erfurt," https://juedisches-leben.erfurt.de/jl/en/index.html.

12   Chazan, "Philosemitic Tendencies," 48.

13   Simonsohn, *Apostolic See*, 37.

14   Abraham Melamed, "The Revival of Christian Hebraism in Early Modern Europe," in Karp and Sutcliffe, *Philosemitism*, 49–66 (65).

15   Martin Luther, *That Jesus Christ Was Born a Jew* (1523), in *Luther's Works 45: The Christian in Society II*, ed. Walther I. Brandt (Philadelphia: Fortress, 1962), 200. See further the early Luther texts cited in Brooks Schramm and Kirsi I. Stjerna, eds., *Martin Luther, the Bible, and the Jewish People* (Minneapolis: Fortress, 2012), 67–75.

16   It is often said that this bitter Luther was the "later" Luther. In reality, however, documents exist from 1525–1526 whose "extreme negativity . . . toward the Jews . . . is remarkable" (Schramm and Stjerna, *Martin Luther*, 99 [also 104–16]). See further Christoph Bultmann, "Das Wittenberger christlich-jüdische Kontroversgespräch 1526 und Luthers Betrachtung der Juden. Bemerkungen im Anchluss an die Orientierung zum Reformationsjubiläum 'Die Reformation und die Juden' (2014)," in *Religionen in Bewegung: Interreligiöse Beziehungen im Wandel der Zeit*, ed. Michael Gabel et al., VIFRUF (Münster: Aschendorff, 2016), 143–95.

17   We recall from chapter 6, for example, the fourth or fifth century Tiburtine Sibyl's prediction of a final Roman ruler in the world in whose time the Jews would "convert to the Lord." Whalen, *Dominion*, 40.

18   Adam Sutcliffe, "The Philosemitic Moment?" in Karp and Sutcliffe, *Philosemitism*, 67–90 (85).

19   Isaac Eisenstein Barzilay, "The Jew in the Literature of the Enlightenment," *Jewish Social Studies* 18 (1956): 243–61 (246–51). An important figure here was Christian Wilhelm von Dohm (1751–1820), who in 1781–1783 published a large and influential book arguing that Jews should be granted equal rights, freedom in choice of occupation, freedom of worship, and admission to schools.

20   The United States was the first country effectively to emancipate Jews, since the Constitution of 1787 states that "no religious test shall ever be required as a qualification for any office

or public trust under the United States"—although some law in the individual states took a while to conform itself to this imperative. The French Revolution resulted in citizenship rights for all Jews in France, and Jewish equality was also proclaimed in the territories subsequently conquered by Napoleon.

21   Barbara Fischer and Thomas C. Fox, "Lessing's Life and Work," in *A Companion to the Works of Gotthold Ephraim Lessing*, ed. Barbara Fischer and Thomas C. Fox (Rochester, N.Y.: Camden House, 2005), 13–40 (16). Gotthold Ephraim Lessing (1729–1781) had staged in 1749 "one of the first works of German literature to portray a Jew in a positive light" (*Die Juden*), following it up in 1779 with his famous plea for religious tolerance, *Nathan the Wise* (whose central character is a Jewish merchant) (Fischer and Fox, "Lessing's Life," 20). Lessing was an acquaintance of the important Jewish Enlightenment figure Moses Mendelssohn (1729–1786), who encouraged von Dohm to write the important book mentioned in note 19 above.

22   Anita Shapira, *Israel: A History* (Waltham, Mass.: Brandeis University Press, 2012), 22.

23   Alfred Dreyfus, an assimilated, rich Jewish army officer, was arrested and then convicted on exceedingly flimsy evidence of spying and sentenced to life imprisonment on Devil's Island. Irrefutable evidence then appeared in 1896 that cleared him of the crime, but it was suppressed by the army. A public outcry ensued, in the course of which the novelist Émile Zola was convicted of libel for accusing the government and the army of playing to the French public's antisemitism in an attempt to divert attention away from their own failures. Dreyfus' retrial was then marked by violent antisemitic rhetoric in France, and in spite of the clear evidence that he was innocent, he was convicted for a second time—whereupon the liberal president of France pardoned him.

24   Shapira, *Israel*, 25. A similar conclusion concerning antisemitism had already been reached by Jews in Russia as a result of continual anti-Jewish violence there in the last quarter of the nineteenth century (Shapira, *Israel*, 20–22).

25   For a description of the early Jewish opposition to Zionist ideas, see Shapira, *Israel*, 13–15.

26   Shapira, *Israel*, 33–47.

27   Leonard Stein, *The Balfour Declaration* (New York: Simon and Schuster, 1961), i.

28   Shapira, *Israel*, 74, quoting a British government White Paper.

29   "Throughout the entire period [of British rule] there was no significant discourse between Jews and Arabs. The Arabs saw no reason to relinquish their exclusive ownership of Palestine, while the Jews had as yet nothing to relinquish" (Shapira, *Israel*, 93).

30   Paul Mendes-Flohr, "In Pursuit of Normalcy: Zionism's Ambivalence toward Israel's Election," in Hutchison and Lehmann, *Many Are Chosen*, 203–24 (206).

31   "Ben-Gurion was not a religious man. His approach was always rigorously secular: the people had chosen and shaped its gods, and not God his people" (Anita Shapira, "Ben-Gurion and the Bible: The Forging of an Historical Narrative," *Middle Eastern Studies* 33 [1997]: 645–74 [668]).

32   Andrew Crome, *Christian Zionism and English National Identity, 1600–1850*, CTAW (Cham: Palgrave Macmillan, 2018), 37.

33   Crome, *Christian Zionism*, 51–57 (54).

34   On Christian Zionism in England in the nineteenth century, see Donald M. Lewis, *The Origins of Christian Zionism: Lord Shaftesbury and the Evangelical Support for a Jewish Homeland* (Cambridge: Cambridge University Press, 2010). On its entire history in the United States, see Robert O. Smith, *More Desired than Our Owne Salvation: The Roots of Christian Zionism* (New York: Oxford University Press, 2013).

35   Shapira, *Israel*, 23.

36   Crome, *Christian Zionism*, 211.

37   Shapira, *Israel*, 70.

38   For example, Isa. 11:12 tells us that God will "raise a banner for the nations and gather the exiles of Israel." Jeremiah 31:10–12 promises that "he who scattered Israel will gather them and will watch over his flock like a shepherd . . . They will come and shout for joy on the heights of Zion," in a context where the new covenant that God makes with his people in Christ is described (31:31–34; cf. Heb. 8:8–12). Ezekiel 36:24–28 likewise promises that "I will take you out of the nations; I will gather you from all the countries and bring you back into your own land," going on to describe a broader reality that has typically been taken to refer to the period after Pentecost: "I will give you a new heart and put a new spirit in you; I will remove from you your heart of stone and give you a heart of flesh. And I will put my Spirit in you and move you to follow my decrees and be careful to keep my laws" (cf. John 3:5–7).

39   Cyrus I. Scofield, *Scofield Bible Correspondence Course* (Chicago: Moody Bible Institute, n.d.), 45–46, quoted in Stephen Sizer, "The Bible and Christian Zionism: Roadmap to Armageddon?" *Transf* 27 (2010): 122–32 (131n1).

40   One day Jerusalem will bless him as one "who comes in the name of the Lord" (Luke 13:34–35). At his Second Coming all the tribes of the land will mourn (Matt. 24:30, drawing on the statement in Zech. 12:10 that "the inhabitants of Jerusalem . . . will look on me, the one they have pierced, and they will mourn"). Matthew 19:28 further states that "at the renewal of all things, when the Son of Man sits on his glorious throne, you who have followed me will also sit on twelve thrones, judging the twelve tribes of Israel."

41   In Acts 1:6–7 the restoration of "the kingdom to Israel" is mentioned as an event still in the future. In Acts 3:21 Peter uses the same Greek word that the Greek OT employs for the return of Jews from all over the world to the land. In Revelation Jesus stands on Mount Zion, where the new earth with its gates named after "the 12 tribes of the sons of Israel" is also centered (Rev. 14:1; 21:2, 12).

42   "I will make rivers flow on barren heights, and springs within the valleys. I will turn the desert into pools of water, and the parched ground into springs. I will put in the desert the cedar and the acacia, the myrtle and the olive. I will set junipers in the wasteland, the fir and the cypress together" (Isa. 41:18–19). "I will make a covenant of peace with them and rid the land of savage beasts so that they may live in the wilderness and sleep in the forests in safety . . . They will no longer be plundered by the nations, nor will wild animals devour them. They will live in safety, and no one will make them afraid" (Ezek. 34:25–28).

15   ON LOOKING AFTER THE GARDEN

1   David Suzuki, *The Legacy: An Elder's Vision for Our Sustainable Future* (Vancouver: Greystone Books, 2010), 55.

2   These words are taken from the UN Conference on Environment and Development (1992), May 23, 1997, https://www.un.org/geninfo/bp/enviro.html, the UN's own webpage concerning the conference.

3   UN Conference on Environment and Development (1992).

4   The text may be found at http://www.unesco.org/education/pdf/RIO_E.PDF.

5   John Zerzan, *Twilight of the Machines* (Port Townsend, Wash.: Feral House, 2008), 124. I discuss at more length this author and others who advocate for similar ideas in my *Convenient Myths: The Axial Age, Dark Green Religion, and the World That Never Was* Waco: Baylor University Press, 2013), chapter 4.

6   Zerzan, *Twilight*, 28.

7   Bron Taylor, *Dark Green Religion: Nature Spirituality and the Planetary Future* (Berkeley: University of California, 2010), ix.

8   Taylor, *Religion*, 99–101, quoting Paul Watson, the cofounder of Greenpeace.

9   Taylor, *Religion*, 147, referencing David Suzuki and Peter Knudtson, *Wisdom of the Elders: Honoring Sacred Native Visions of Nature* (Vancouver: Greystone Books, 1992).

10   Taylor, *Religion*, 154, referencing Suzuki and other ecologists.

11   Taylor, *Religion*, 147, 217.

12   Taylor, *Religion*, 183–84.

13   For a full discussion of the problems involved even in the *idea* that we might be able learn about the distant past by way of studying modern "primitive peoples," see Provan, *Convenient Myths*, chapter 5.

14   See Provan, *Convenient Myths*, chapter 6.

15   Michael S. Alvard, "Testing the 'Ecologically Noble Savage' Hypothesis: Interspecific Prey Choice by Piro Hunters in Amazonian Peru," *HE* 21 (1993): 355–87 (384).

16   Allyn MacLean Stearman, "Only Slaves Climb Trees: Revisiting the Myth of the Ecologically Noble Savage in Amazonia," *HN* 5 (1994): 339–57 (351).

17   Atholl Anderson, "A Fragile Plenty: Pre-European Māori and the New Zealand Environment," in *Environmental Histories of New Zealand*, ed. Eric Pawson and Tom Brooking (Melbourne: Oxford University Press, 2002), 19–34 (32).

18   Michael S. Alvard, "Evolutionary Theory, Conservation, and Human Environmental Impact," in *Wilderness and Political Ecology: Aboriginal Influences and the Original State of Nature*, ed. Charles E. Kay and Randy T. Simmons (Salt Lake City: University of Utah Press, 2002), 28–43 (29–30); Charles E. Kay, "Are Ecosystems Structured from the Top-Down or Bottom-Up?" in Kay and Simmons, *Wilderness and Political Ecology*, 215–37 (215).

19   Paul S. Martin and Christine R. Szuter, "Revising the 'Wild West': Big Game Meets the Ultimate Keystone Species," in *Archaeology of Global Change: The Impact of Humans on their Environment*, ed. Charles L. Redman et al. (Washington, D.C.: Smithsonian Books, 2004), 63–88 (64).

20   Kay, "Ecosystems," 225.

21   Provan, *Convenient Myths*, 74–79.

22   Bobbi S. Low, "Behavioral Ecology of Conservation in Traditional Societies," *HN* 7 (1996): 353–79 (353, 368).

23   Thomas W. Neumann, "The Role of Prehistoric Peoples in Shaping Ecosystems in the Eastern United States: Implications for Restoration Ecology and Wilderness Management," in Kay and Simmons, *Wilderness and Political Ecology*, 141–78 (143).

24   Cited in Flora Lu Holt, "The Catch-22 of Conservation: Indigenous Peoples, Biologists, and Cultural Change," *HE* 33 (2005): 199–215 (209).

25   Holt, "Catch-22," 205–6.

26   Provan, *Right Reading*, 383–413.

27   "The medieval philosopher had of course believed the Christian doctrine that nature is created. But the belief had been efficacious only in his theology. In his science of nature . . . he had continued to employ the methods of Aristotelian science, entirely oblivious of the fact that Aristotle's science was based upon the presupposition that nature is not created." Michael B. Foster, "The Christian Doctrine of Creation and the Rise of Modern Natural Science," *Mind* 43 (1934): 446–68 (453).

28   Foster, "Creation," 453.

29   From a letter dated to 1595, cited in Gerald Holton, "Johannes Kepler's Universe: Its Physics and Metaphysics," *AJP* 24 (1956): 340–51 (351), who goes on to say that "more than a few times in his later writings [Kepler] referred to astronomers as priests of the Deity in the book of nature."

30   For a focused discussion of how the new science was perceived as holding great promise for building a better world in the aftermath of the carnage of war in the seventeenth century, see Provan, *Right Reading*, 369–82.

31   John C. Briggs, "Bacon's Science and Religion," in *The Cambridge Companion to Bacon*, ed. Markku Peltonen (Cambridge: Cambridge University Press, 1996), 172–99.

32   Paul Hazard, *The European Mind (1680–1715)* (London: Hollis and Carter: 1953), 14. More generally, see Ellingson, *Myth*, 11–41.

33   William Wordsworth, "The Tables Turned," in *Selected Poetry*, ed. Mark Van Doren (New York: Modern Library, 1950), 82–83.

34   Thoreau describes the twenty-six months during which he lived a simple and solitary life in a cabin beside Walden Pond in Concord, Massachusetts, deliberately away from society. Here he was able to contemplate with great attention the natural world around him, which he describes engagingly. Many have found inspiration in his story.

35   Muir emphasized to his readership the importance of experiencing and protecting nature. He was instrumental in the creation of various important national parks in the United States—initiatives that would eventually be consummated in the Wilderness Act of 1964, which set aside just over nine million acres of land to be preserved in perpetuity as wilderness, and subsequent additions in the form of national forests and parks.

36   David Lowenthal, *George Perkins Marsh: Prophet of Conservation* (Seattle: University of Washington Press, 2000), 303.

37   Some of the other "alarming events" are these: the partial meltdown of the Three Mile Island nuclear power plant near Harrisburg, Pennsylvania, and the explosion of the Chernobyl nuclear power plant in the Ukraine; the accidental release of methyl isocyanate at a Union Carbide pesticide factory in Bhopal, India, ultimately causing over twenty thousand deaths; the grounding of the Exxon Valdez Alaska's Prince William Sound, spilling eleven million gallons of oil into the water and killing hundreds of thousands of marine animals, and the marked increase in threatened or endangered species, largely because of habitat loss, throughout the world.

38   Taylor, *Religion*, 75.

39   Lynn White, "The Historical Roots of Our Ecologic Crisis," *Science* 155 (1967): 1203–7. This essay was reproduced in I. G. Barbour, ed., *Western Man and Environmental Ethics* (Reading: Addison-Wesley, 1973), 18–30, and the quote in that version is to be found on p. 25.

40   White, "Crisis," 25.

41   Cited in Taylor, *Religion*, 36.

42   Cited in Taylor, *Religion*, 36.

43   Francisco Benzoni, "Thomas Aquinas and Environmental Ethics: A Reconsideration of Providence and Salvation, *JR* 85 (2005): 446–76 (446).

44   Benzoni, "Aquinas," 446.

45   Calvin, *Institutes* 1.16.6.

46   John Calvin, *Commentaries on the First Book of Moses Called Genesis*, CalC 1, ed. and trans. John King (London: Calvin Translation Society, 1847; repr., Grand Rapids: Baker, 1981), 64–65, 96.

47   The full text can be found at https://genius.com/Jim-reeves-this-world-is-not-my-home -annotated.

48   The full text can be found at https://genius.com/U2-yahweh-lyrics.

49   Ron Wolf, "God, James Watt, and the Public Land," *Audubon* 83 (1981): 58–65 (65). James Watt became Secretary of the Interior in the first Reagan administration in 1981—a controversial figure who put enormous effort into ensuring greater resource development in the USA at the expense of environmental protection. "By turning to Watt ... [President] Reagan was abandoning a moderate Republican policy agenda and a campaign that had stressed coalition building for a far more aggressive, narrow, and ideological strategy. That decision had major implications for the direction of environmental policy initiatives in the first three years

of his administration and for their legitimacy" (Michael E. Kraft and Norman Vig, "Environmental Policy in the Reagan Presidency," *PSQ* 99 [1984]: 415–39 [423]). The religious underpinnings of Watt's politics were made clear on various occasions throughout his brief tenure (until 1983).

50   "They are to perform [*shamar*] duties for him and for the whole community at the Tent of Meeting by doing the work [*'abad*] of the tabernacle. They are to take care of [*shamar*] all the furnishings of the Tent of Meeting, fulfilling the obligations of the Israelites by doing the work [*'abad*] of the tabernacle."

51   Gordon J. Wenham, *Genesis 1–15*, WBC 1 (Waco: Word, 1987), 33.

52   William L. Lane, *Hebrews 1–8*, WBC 47A (Dallas: Word, 1991), 48.

53   James D. G. Dunn, *Romans 1–8*, WBC 38A (Dallas: Word, 1988), 471.

54   Richard Bauckham, *Bible and Ecology: Rediscovering the Community of Creation* (London: Darton, Longman and Todd, 2010), 6.

55   E.g., Calvin, *Genesis* 57, 125; and *Institutes* 3.10.1, where he notes in reference to 1 Cor. 7:31 that "Paul . . . admonishes us to use this world without abusing it."

56   Calvin, *Genesis* 125–26.

57   John Calvin, *Epistle of Paul the Apostle to the Romans and to the Thessalonians*, CalC 8, ed. David W. Torrance and Thomas F. Torrance, trans. Ross Mackenzie (Edinburgh: Oliver and Boyd, 1961), 305.

58   Francis A. Schaeffer, *Pollution and the Death of Man: The Christian View of Ecology* (Wheaton, Ill.: Tyndale House, 1970).

59   Loren Wilkinson, ed., *Earthkeeping: Christian Stewardship of Natural Resources* (Grand Rapids: Eerdmans, 1980).

60   So, e.g., Pushpam Kumar and Makiko Yashiro, "The Marginal Poor and Their Dependence on Ecosystem Services: Evidence from South Asia and Sub-Saharan Africa," in *Marginality: Addressing the Nexus of Poverty, Exclusion, and Ecology*, ed. Joachim von Braun and Franz W. Gatzweiler (Dordrecht: Springer, 2014), 169–80.

16   THE SWORD OF THE SPIRIT

1   Doris Lessing, *Prisons We Choose to Live Inside* (Toronto: CBC Enterprises, 1986; repr. Toronto, Anansi, 2006), 13.

2   Andrew T. Lincoln, *Ephesians*, WBC 42 (Dallas: Word, 1990), 451.

3   The man in this photograph who does *not* have his arm raised in the Nazi salute is probably ex-Nazi party member August Landmesser. The photograph can be seen also at https:// en.wikipedia.org/wiki/August_Landmesser#/media/File:August-Landmesser-Almanya-1936 .jpg.

4   Roy E. Gane, "Leviticus," in *ZIBBC* 1:284–337 (315).

5   See further Provan, *Right Reading*, 115–22.

6   Malise Ruthven, *Islam: A Very Short Introduction* (New York: Oxford University Press, 1997), 4; see further Provan, *Seriously Dangerous Religion*, 251–78.

7   See further on the perspicuity (sufficient clarity) of Scripture, Provan, *Right Reading*, 283–312.

17   THE MORAL MAZE OF THE MOMENT

1   *Merriam-Webster*, s.v. "maze," https://www.merriam-webster.com/dictionary/maze.

2   *The Moral Maze*, BBC, https://www.bbc.co.uk/programmes/b006qk11.

3   "The Moral Maze," Wikipedia, https://en.wikipedia.org/wiki/The_Moral_Maze.

4   Consider as an example of this genre John J. Collins, *What Are Biblical Values?: What the Bible Says on Key Ethical Issues* (New Haven: Yale University Press, 2019), the modus ope-

randi of which, chapter by chapter, is this: "Summarize the Bible. Reveal complications and supposed contradictions. Neutralize the Bible by repeating the axiom that the Bible isn't decisive. Nod knowingly toward today's cultural consensus. Reload"—except with respect to "social justice," where "all his hesitations and hedges go out the window" (Peter J. Leithart, "What Are Biblical Values?" *First Things*, July 19, 2019, https://www.firstthings.com/web-exclusives/2019/07/what-are-biblical-values).

5   James Wanliss, *Resisting the Green Dragon: Dominion not Death* (Burke, Va.: Cornwall Alliance for the Stewardship of Creation, 2010), Kindle edition, chapter 2.

6   Ari Natter, "Republicans Who Couldn't Beat Climate Debate Now Seek to Join It," *Bloomberg*, March 5, 2019, https://www.bloomberg.com/news/articles/2019-03-05/republicans-who-couldn-t-beat-climate-debate-now-seek-to-join-it. See further Jim Hanchett, "Polls Suggest Less Environmentalism among U.S. Christians," Futurity, February 1, 2018, https://www.futurity.org/christians-environment-opinion-1670122.1/.

7   See "Climate Change: How Do We Know?" NASA, https://climate.nasa.gov/evidence/, with references to the academic literature.

8   Provan, *Right Reading*, 368–69.

9   It is important to strike exactly the right balance here, since there are people on each side of the contemporary debate who are not balanced at all. To put it extreme terms, biblical faith encourages neither the anthropocentric, free-wheeling capitalist nor the antihuman, radical, ecoterrorist to think that (s)he is right. We are obliged to look after nonhuman Creation but also to look after our human neighbors, including the poorest and most vulnerable among them who stand to suffer very badly if some of the "great plans" for saving the planet currently under discussion are actually enacted. Many of our youngest people are already suffering unnecessarily from great anxiety because of the horror stories told them about their futures by those who wish to recruit them to the cause.

10   "You are to consider them as native-born Israelites; along with you they are to be allotted an inheritance among the tribes of Israel. In whatever tribe a foreigner resides, there you are to give them their inheritance" (Ezek. 37:22–23).

11   Some of these injustices are very large, but many are of the mundane, local variety that over time, nevertheless, wear people down. Consider, e.g., the public transport situation in the West Bank. Reporting in 2013 his experience of trying to ride on buses along with Jewish settlers, a Palestinian blacksmith stated that "settlers often complain when Palestinians enter their buses. Palestinians can be blocked from boarding, kicked off or subject to verbal abuse once on board . . . Riding with settlers is humiliating and involves a lot of suffering." See Joseph Federman, "Palestinian-Only Buses Set Off Uproar in Israel," Associated Press, March 4, 2013, https://www.apnews.com/f3c61de8ff7f4299a1c983f26263ae96.

12   "In Israel at 70 [years of age], Zionism means a government of the racist, by the racist, for the racist. As a public servant, as an Orthodox rabbi, as a settler, you're free to say anything you want, as long as it's anti-Arab, anti-black, anti-Muslim, anti-Palestinian, anti-immigrant, and, for good measure, anti-Ashkenazi, anti-North American Jew, anti-New Israel Fund and, in general, anti-leftist of all stripes" (Jewish Israeli journalist Bradley Burston, "This Is Zionism as Racism. This Is Israel at 70," *Haaretz*, April 4, 2018, https://www.haaretz.com/opinion/.premium-this-is-zionism-as-racism-this-is-israel-at-70-1.5975641).

13   See, e.g., Christians United for Israel, https://www.cufi.org/; cf. Eric Robert Crouse, *American Christian Support for Israel: Standing with the Chosen People, 1948–1975* (Lanham, Md.: Lexington Books, 2015).

14   See, e.g., Yakov M. Rabkin, *What Is Modern Israel?* English ed. (London: Pluto Press, 2016); cf. https://jewishvoiceforpeace.org.

15   Note, e.g., 1 Kgs. 22:1–28; Mic. 3:5–12.

16   See, e.g., Uri Blau, "Haaretz Investigation: U.S. Donors Gave Settlements More than $220 Million in Tax-Exempt Funds over Five Years," *Haaretz*, December 7, 2015, https://www .haaretz.com/haaretz-investigates-u-s-donors-to-israeli-settlements-1.5429739; and Judy Maltz, "Inside the Evangelical Money Flowing into the West Bank," *Haaretz*, December 9, 2018, https://www.haaretz.com/israel-news/.premium.MAGAZINE-inside-the -evangelical-money-flowing-into-the-west-bank-1.672344.3.

17   Kate Greasley and Christopher Kaczor, *Abortion Rights: For and Against* (Cambridge: Cambridge University Press, 2017), 5.

18   Greasley and Kaczor, *Abortion Rights*, 6.

19   "This is because of what is at stake for pregnant women in securing abortion access. The potential interests that women have in obtaining abortion are threefold: the interest in procreative control, the interest in being free from the bodily burdens of pregnancy, and the interest in sex equality. The strength of these interests is undoubtedly enough to justify abortion morally if the human embryo or fetus lacks the status of a person" (Greasley and Kaczor, *Abortion Rights*, 10–11).

20   Greasley and Kaczor, *Abortion Rights*, 17.

21   "What is it that makes us morally considerable beings, in possession of the fundamental right to life? In virtue of what do we hold such a status? Is personhood a matter of attaining certain capacities, such as rationality, or agency, or self-conscious thought? Or is it a question of being endowed with a certain kind of nature or essence, expressed in genetic programming or human biology? And is it possible that the same creature might be a morally considerable person at one stage of its existence but not at another?" (Greasley and Kaczor, *Abortion Rights*, 24).

22   Greasley and Kaczor, *Abortion Rights*, 27.

23   Greasley and Kaczor, *Abortion Rights*, 40–41.

24   Greasley and Kaczor, *Abortion Rights*, 50.

25   Greasley and Kaczor, *Abortion Rights*, 80.

26   Greasley and Kaczor, *Abortion Rights*, 81–82.

27   Greasley and Kaczor, *Abortion Rights*, 92. The paper is Alberto Giubilini and Francesca Minerva, "After-Birth Abortion: Why Should the Baby Live?" *Journal of Medical Ethics* 39 (2013): 261–63.

28   "The interests of actual people (parents, family, society) override the nonexistent interests of potential people (newborns, prenatal human beings). The financial expense and personal burden of infants can detrimentally affect the interests of actual people. So, killing a newborn is morally permissible" (Greasley and Kaczor, *Abortion Rights*, 93).

29   Greasley and Kaczor, *Abortion Rights*, 94.

30   Greasley and Kaczor, *Abortion Rights*, 94.

31   Greasley and Kaczor, *Abortion Rights*, 95.

32   "The conventional view defending prenatal abortion and condemning postnatal abortion is inherently unstable. The arguments in favor of prenatal abortion often also apply to infanticide. The arguments against infanticide often apply to abortion. It is more consistent to be opposed to killing both before and after birth or to be in favor of killing both before and after birth. Birth, in other words, is not a magic moment that transforms an individual who can be killed at will into someone like us who has a right to live" (Greasley and Kaczor, *Abortion Rights*, 104).

33   Greasley and Kaczor, *Abortion Rights*, 108.

34   Greasley and Kaczor, *Abortion Rights*, 126.

35   E.g., in some cases of conjoined twins, one twin will depend on the other for continued life, but this "makes no difference for their basic rights. So, viability—the ability to live independently from other people with or without technological help—is not necessary for

personhood." As to sentience, "Why should suffering alone count in our moral judgment of what is right and what is wrong?" Also, "there are some human beings who even after birth are incapable of experiencing pain"; does this mean that they have no right to life? (Greasley and Kaczor, *Abortion Rights*, 110–11, 113).

36 Greasley and Kaczor, *Abortion Rights*, 148.

37 Greasley and Kaczor, *Abortion Rights*, 132.

38 Greasley and Kaczor, *Abortion Rights*, 132. See further Edwin C. Hui, "Personhood and Bio-ethics," in *Questions of Right and Wrong: Proceedings of the 1993 Clinical Bioethics Conference*, ed. Edwin C. Hui (Vancouver: Regent College, 1994), 1–15, who states that "the zygote, as a unique life created by God, is already a person with a potential to develop, not merely a potential human person" (14).

39 Greasley and Kaczor, *Abortion Rights*, 141, quoting Pinker.

40 In commanding that his daughter-in-law Tamar should be burned to death (by implication, along with her unborn child), Judah simply commits one more disreputable act in a whole series described in the preceding narrative in Gen. 38. He is not a "hero" to be imitated (Robert Alter, *The Art of Biblical Narrative* [London: Allen & Unwin, 1981], 1–46). Numbers 5, moreover, is not best read as involving "a drink that will cause an abortion if [the wife] slept with another man (regardless of whose child it is)," as proposed (e.g.) by Nynia Chance, "Biblical Abortion: A Christian's View," Rewire.News, June 3, 2012, https://rewire.news/article/2012/06/03/biblical-abortion-christians-view-1/. It is most unlikely that the husband would be so disinterested concerning the possibility of losing his own child, and the water and dust mentioned do not in any case make up an effective abortive agent. In any case, the positive outcome contemplated in verse 28 is not that the woman will be able to birth a child that she is already carrying but that she will be able to *conceive* children (and later birth them). Notice the same vocabulary (Hb. *zara'/zera'*), e.g., in Lev. 12:2: "A woman who *becomes pregnant* and gives birth to a son." The ritual in Num. 5 relates to future barrenness in the guilty party, not to a present pregnancy.

41 The absence of specific texts has been taken by some as evidence that the Bible does not much care about the topic of abortion. So Katha Pollitt, "6 Myths about Abortion," *Time*, November 13, 2014, https://time.com/3582434/6-abortion-myths/. Of course, arguments from silence have to be handled very carefully, and another explanation of this particular silence is simply that there was no need explicitly to legislate about abortion in either ancient Israel or the earliest Church because the practice was already widely regarded as unquestionably wrong. It was certainly regarded in this way in at least one other part of the ancient Near East, where it *was* legislated against: Middle Assyrian law treated the willful destruction of a prenatal human being as a capital offence (Russell T. Fuller, "Exodus 21:22–23: The Miscarriage Interpretation and the Personhood of the Fetus," *JETS* 37 [1994]: 169–84 [177–78]).

42 Ecclesiastes 12:6–7 point to same truth in this poignant exhortation: "Remember him—before the silver cord is severed, and the golden bowl is broken; before the pitcher is shattered at the spring, and the wheel broken at the well, and the dust returns to the ground it came from, and the spirit returns to God who gave it."

43 Greasley and Kaczor, *Abortion Rights*, 5.

44 See further Greasley and Kaczor, *Abortion Rights*, 155–57.

45 See further Greasley and Kaczor, *Abortion Rights*, 154–55.

46 Stephanie Gray, "What Do Rape Victims Say About Their Pregnancies?" Love Unleashes Life, November 6, 2017, https://loveunleasheslife.com/blog/2017/11/6/what-do-rape-victims-say-about-their-pregnancies-by-stephanie-gray. See further the documentary *Allowed to Live: A Look at the Hard Cases*, YouTube video, https://www.youtube.com/watch?v=FfKkWfDEQjc.

47   Edward Westermarck, *The Origin and Development of the Moral Ideas*, 2nd ed., 2 vols. (London: Macmillan, 1924), 1:415.

48   Seneca, *De Ira* 1.15, in *Seneca: Moral Essays*, trans. John W. Basor (Cambridge, Mass.: Harvard University Press, 1923), 145, which translates the Latin in this way: "We drown even children who at birth are weakly and abnormal. Yet it is not anger, but reason that separates the harmful from the sound."

49   *Didache* 2.2, in Richardson, *Early Christian Fathers*, LCC 1, 172.

50   *Barnabas* 19.5 (*ANF* 1:148).

51   Leonard Kahn, "Is There an Obligation to Abort? Act Utilitarianism and the Ethics of Procreation," *Essays in Philosophy* 20, no. 1 (2019).

52   This is not only a matter of ensuring extensive support for parents of the unborn, who are often very vulnerable neighbors themselves, but also a matter of how legislation concerning abortion is framed. For some reflections on this latter point, see Greasley and Kaczor, *Abortion Rights*, 157–60. Earlier in the book Kaczor is at pains to emphasize that "[w]e must distinguish between the objective morality of an action and the subjective culpability of the agent. Conscientious, good people can do things which—objectively speaking—are seriously wrong, and yet they do so without full knowledge and consent to their action . . . Even if every fetal human being has a right to life, it could turn out that those who get abortions or support abortion are honestly and inculpably mistaken in their view that abortion is ethically permissible" (Greasley and Kaczor, *Abortion Rights*, 89). These are the kinds of considerations that all legislation about abortion must account for.

53   As Greasley points out, there is a compelling argument to be made that "[a]bortion practice does not disappear because it is banned . . . prohibiting or restricting abortion in law only drives women intent on procuring abortion to unregulated and unsafe practitioners—the "backstreet" abortionist—resulting in worse overall outcomes." In her own judgment, this consideration cannot "justify toleration of abortion if it amounts to homicide," since it would never be accepted as an argument "against the prohibition of infanticide." Still, it is a matter to be taken seriously (Greasley and Kaczor, *Abortion Rights*, 9–10).

54   I write this in my present context in Canada, where we do in fact have no abortion law at all mainly because our politicians would not compromise on a less than perfect one (from their point of view). Infanticide is not yet legal, thankfully, but one wonders how long this will remain true in in face of strong arguments about the "arbitrary" nature of birth as a "dividing line" in respect of personhood.

55   The threat to such rights of conscience is also a marked feature of the public discourse of our time: "A doctor's conscience has little place in the delivery of modern medical care . . . If people are not prepared to offer legally permitted, efficient, and beneficial care to a patient because it conflicts with their values, they should not be doctors" (Julian Savulescu, "Conscientious Objection in Medicine," *BMJ* [*Clinical Research Ed.*] 332, no. 7536 [2006]: 294–97 [abstract]).

56   Greasley and Kaczor, *Abortion Rights*, 94.

57   Catholic Church, "Suicide," in the *Catechism of the Catholic Church*, 2nd ed. (Vatican: Libreria Editrice Vaticana, 2012), §2280.

58   Paul Middleton, "Suicide in the Bible," Bible Odyssey, https://www.bibleodyssey.org:443/en/people/related-articles/suicide-in-the-bible.

59   In Judg. 9:52–54 the murderous king Abimelek takes his own life with the help of his servant after a woman drops a millstone on his head and cracks his skull. He chooses death so that no one can say that a woman killed him. In 1 Sam. 31:4–5 Saul, the rejected king of Israel holding on desperately to power in spite of God's choice of David, kills himself in order to avoid the justice of God that is shortly to fall upon him at the hands of the Philistine. In 2 Sam. 17:23 the traitorous royal counsellor Ahithophel, intent on David's death, kills

himself because his advice is not followed by Absalom. In 1 Kgs. 16:18–19 Zimri, a king who was famous for "doing evil in the eyes of the Lord and following the ways of Jeroboam and committing the same sin Jeroboam had caused Israel to commit," kills himself to avoid being captured by a besieging army. And in Matt. 27:3–5 Judas, smitten with remorse for betraying Jesus, hangs himself. The case of Samson, the last and most extraordinary of the judges in the book of Judges, is not a true suicide. Rather, he happens to die (knowing that he probably will) in the course of taking revenge on numerous Philistines—that is his main intent (Judg. 16:23–30). In any case, there is no hint in the chapter that the narrator *approves* of Samson's actions here. He has in fact presented this leader in Israel throughout his story as a thoroughly ambiguous character. Of relevance our judgment here is that fact that taking personal revenge on one's enemies is certainly not regarded in Scripture, generally, as virtuous (e.g., Prov. 25:21–22).

60   Later Judaism, drawing on this same literary tradition, generally regarded suicide as a sin, as expressed eloquently in Josephus, *Jewish War*, in *The Works of Flavius Josephus*, trans. William Whiston (Philadelphia: Jas. B. Smith & Co., 1854), 271: "It may also be said that it is a manly act for one to kill himself. No, certainly, but a most unmanly one; as I should esteem that pilot to be an arrant coward, who, out of fear of a storm, should sink his ship of his own accord. Now self-murder is a crime most remote from the common nature of all animals, and an instance of impiety against God our Creator; nor indeed is there any animal that dies by its own contrivance, or by its own means, for the desire of life is a law engraven in them all; on which account we deem those that openly take it away from us to be our enemies, and those that do it by treachery are punished for so doing. And do not you think that God is very angry when a man does injury to what he hath bestowed on him? For from him it is that we have received our being, and we ought to leave it to his disposal to take that being away from us."

61   Darrel W. Amundsen, "Suicide and Early Christian Values," in *Suicide and Euthanasia*, ed. Baruch A. Brody, Philosophy and Medicine 35 (Dordrecht: Springer, 1989), 77–153 (81).

62   Amundsen, "Suicide," 95–96.

63   Middleton, "Suicide."

64   Amundsen, "Suicide," 80.

65   Amundsen, "Suicide," 98. Around the same time Justin Martyr "maintains that it is wrong for Christians to kill themselves because God wants them in the world and the human race needs them, for without Christians there would be no one to instruct humanity in the truth" (Amundsen, "Suicide," 116).

66   Tertullian, *De Fuga in Persecutione* (*Flight in Time of Persecution*) 13.2 (*ANF* 4:124).

67   Quoted in Amundsen, "Suicide," 118. He discusses other postapostolic sources prior to Augustine throughout pp. 116–23.

68   Amundsen, "Suicide," 120–23.

69   Amundsen, "Suicide," 123, 139.

70   Amundsen, "Suicide," 140.

71   Catholic Church, "Suicide," §2282.

72   Edmund D. Pellegrino, "Compassion Is Not Enough," in *The Case against Assisted Suicide: For the Right to End-Of-Life Care*, ed. Kathleen M. Foley and Herbert Hendin (Baltimore: Johns Hopkins University Press, 2002), 41–51 (41).

73   Daniel Callahan, "Reason, Self-Determination, and Physician-Assisted Suicide," in Foley and Hendin, *Assisted Suicide*, 52–68 (62).

74   Callahan, "Reason," 63.

75   Callahan, "Reason," 63–64.

76   Leon R. Kass, "I Will Give No Deadly Drug: Why Doctors Must Not Kill," in Foley and Hendin, *Assisted Suicide*, 17–40 (32).

77   Kass, "Deadly Drug," 35. He means "right medicine," of course, for he himself references Nazi Germany, where doctors did in fact participate in the deaths of millions of people whose lives were regarded as "not worth living."

78   Callahan, "Reason," 68.

79   Pellegrino, "Compassion," 41–42.

80   Pellegrino, "Compassion," 46–47.

81   Kathleen M. Foley, "Compassionate Care, Not Assisted Suicide," in Foley and Hendin, *Assisted Suicide*, 293–309 (297).

82   Margaret A. Somerville, *Death Talk: The Case against Euthanasia and Physician-Assisted Suicide*, 2nd ed. (Montreal and Kingston: McGill-Queen's University Press, 2014), xxiv–xxv.

83   Somerville, *Death Talk*, 13, quoting Gerald Gruman.

84   Somerville, *Death Talk*, 23. She notes earlier in the book the recent increase in "discussion of the healthcare, and sometimes other, costs of caring for aged people, which used to be a forbidden topic in the context of the euthanasia debate … The same is true in relation to discussion of euthanasia for people with dementia … incorporating into the euthanasia debate the discussion of healthcare and other costs of caring for people, or euthanasia for people with dementia, is a frightening development, because it means the former could be accepted as a justification for euthanasia or the latter implemented" (xxiv).

85   Jason T. Eberl, "I Am My Brother's Keeper: Communitarian Obligations to the Dying Person," *Christian Bioethics* 24 (2018): 38–58 (39).

86   Somerville, *Death Talk*, xxiii.

87   Somerville, *Death Talk*, xxiii.

88   Somerville, *Death Talk*, xxx. In Belgium euthanasia is already available for "patients going blind or intractably depressed, but not dying" (David Elliott, "Institutionalizing Inequality: The Physical Criterion of Assisted Suicide," *Christian Bioethics* 24 [2018]: 17–37 [24]). One assumes that both of these come under the heading of "euthanasia practiced upon an incurable and not yet terminally ill … [person] who experiences unbearable physical or mental suffering" that is one of the four "scenarios" envisaged in the Belgian legislation (Herman Nys, "A Discussion of the Legal Rules on Euthanasia in Belgium Briefly Compared with the Rules in Luxembourg and the Netherlands," in *Euthanasia and Assisted Suicide: Lessons from Belgium*, ed. David A. Jones et al., Cambridge Bioethics and Law [Cambridge: Cambridge University Press, 2017], 7–25 [7]). This "suffering" includes that of a person with a psychiatric illness (Joris Vandenberghe, "Euthanasia in Patients with Intolerable Suffering Due to an Irremediable Psychiatric Illness," in Jones et al., *Euthanasia and Assisted Suicide*, 150–72).

89   Raphael Cohen-Almagor, "Euthanizing People Who Are 'Tired of Life,'" in Jones et al., *Euthanasia and Assisted Suicide*, 188–201.

90   Herbert Hendin, "The Dutch Experience," in Foley and Hendin, *Assisted Suicide*, 97–121 (104–6); Rene Leiva et al., "Euthanasia in Canada: A Cautionary Tale," *World Medical Journal* 64 (2018): 17–23. A 2019 legal case in the Netherlands graphically illustrates the problem. Here a doctor was acquitted of unlawful euthanasia even though, *at the point when he practiced it*, his demented patient did not consent; "[i]n fact, the doctor secretly slipped a sedative in the patient's coffee" before administering the lethal injection forcibly, because "the patient suddenly began resisting so strongly that the doctor needed the help of her relatives to hold her down" (Michael Cook, "Dutch Doctor Acquitted of Unlawful Euthanasia," BioEdge, September 15, 2019, https://www.bioedge.org/bioethics/dutch-doctor-acquitted-of -unlawful-euthanasia/13218).

91   Irene Tuffrey-Wijne et al., "'Because of His Intellectual Disability, He Couldn't Cope': Is Euthanasia the Answer?" *Journal of Policy and Practice in Intellectual Disabilities* 16, no. 2 (2019): 113–16 (116).

92 Diane Coleman, "Not Dead Yet," in Foley and Hendin, *Assisted Suicide*, 213–37 (216). Kevin Fitzpatrick and David A. Jones. "A Life Worth Living? Disabled People and Euthanasia in Belgium," in Jones et al., *Euthanasia and Assisted Suicide*, 133–49 (Michael Cook, "US Study Says Assisted Suicide Laws Rife with Dangers to People with Disabilities," BioEdge, October 13, 2019, https://www.bioedge.org/bioethics/us-study-saysassisted-suicide-laws-rife-with-dangers-to-people-with-disabil/13245). For a troubling personal testimony, consider the case of Canadian Roger Foley, as described on his GoFundMe page, "Roger Foley's Assisted Life Fund," GoFundMe, https://www.gofundme.com/f/assistedlife?viewupdates=1&utm_medium=email&utm_source=customer&utm_campaign=p_email%2B1137-update-supporters-v5b.

93 Amelia Hill, "Over-a-Third-of-Britons-Admit-Ageist-Behaviour-in-New-Study," *The Guardian*, August 19, 2019, https://www.theguardian.com/society/2019/aug/19/over-a-third-of-britons-admit-ageist-behaviour-in-new-study.

94 R. R. Reno, "Empire of Desire: Outlining the Postmodern Metaphysical Dream," *First Things*, June 2014, https://www.firstthings.com/article/2014/06/empire-of-desire.

95 Kathleen Messinger, "Death with Dignity for the Seemingly Undignified: Denial of Aid in Dying in Prison," *Journal of Criminal Law and Criminology* 109 (2019): 633–73.

96 Elliott, "Inequality," 31.

97 Coleman, "Not Dead Yet," 237.

18 WHO AM I?

1 Mel Schwartz, "Who Am I?" *Psychology Today*, June 20, 2010, https://www.psychologytoday.com/ca/blog/shift-mind/201006/who-am-i.

2 Jordan Peterson, "Gender Politics Has No Place in the Classroom," *National Post*, June 21, 2019, https://nationalpost.com/opinion/jordan-peterson-gender-politics-has-no-place-in-the-classroom.

3 "First, people do not create themselves from air; rather, what is possible, what is important, what needs to be explained all come from social context . . . Second, being a self requires others who endorse and reinforce one's selfhood, who scaffold a sense that one's self matters and that one's efforts can produce results . . . Third, the aspects of one's self and identity that matter in the moment are determined by what is relevant in the moment" (Daphna Oyserman, Kristen Elmore, and George Smith, "Self, Self-Concept, and Identity," in *Handbook of Self and Identity*, ed. Mark R. Leary and June Price Tangney, 2nd ed. [New York: Guilford, 2012], 69–104 [76]). All human thinking "is influenced by the context in which it occurs, including physical and social features of the external context" (88).

4 Peterson, "Gender Politics."

5 Oyserman et al., "Self," 76.

6 Oyserman et al., "Self," 69.

7 Joseph Brean, "Shattering the Scientific World's History of Gendered Brain Assumptions," *National Post*, July 15, 2019, https://nationalpost.com/news/shattering-the-scientific-worlds-history-of-gendered-brain-assumptions. Brean is offering a summary of the view of neuroscientist, Gina Rippon, *The Gendered Brain: The New Neuroscience that Shatters the Myth of the Female Brain* (London: Bodley Head, 2019). For a briefer introduction to the topic of brain plasticity in general, see Kendra Cherry, "How Experience Changes Brain Plasticity," Verywell Mind, updated June 26, 2019, https://www.verywellmind.com/what-is-brain-plasticity-2794886.

8 Lisa Firestone, "Changing Your Sense of Identity: Five Powerful Actions We Can Take to Challenge Our Negative Self-Perception," *Psychology Today*, December 4, 2017, https://www.psychologytoday.com/us/blog/compassion-matters/201712/changing-your-sense-identity.

9 Jonathan Morgan, "Is Identity Fixed?" *Change Writer*, http://changewriter.net/is-identity-fixed/.

10   Suman Fernando, "Connections," *Openmind* 153 (2008): 16–17 (16).

11   For a brief but helpful history of how we travelled from then to now, see Tomas Bogardus, "Gender's Journey from Sex to Psychology: A Brief History," Quillette, March 13, 2019, https://quillette.com/2019/03/13/genders-journey-from-sex-to-psychology-a-brief-history/.

12   *Merriam-Webster*, s.v. "transgender," https://www.merriam-webster.com/dictionary/transgender.

13   *Merriam-Webster*, s.v. "gender identity," https://www.merriam-webster.com/dictionary/gender%20identity.

14   Jane Robbins, "The Cracks in the Edifice of Transgender Totalitarianism," *Public Discourse*, July 13, 2019, https://www.thepublicdiscourse.com/2019/07/54272/.

15   Alex Byrne, "Is Sex Binary?" ARC Digital, November 1, 2018, https://arcdigital.media/is-sex-binary-16bec97d161e.

16   Byrne, "Is Sex Binary?" citing corrections offered by Carrie Hall to earlier work that arrived at the higher figure of 1.7 percent.

17   Ann Fausto-Sterling, "Why Sex Is Not Binary," *New York Times*, October 25, 2018, https://www.nytimes.com/2018/10/25/opinion/sex-biology-binary.html.

18   Byrne, "Is Sex Binary?"

19   Byrne, "Is Sex Binary?" Here he quotes Simone de Beauvoir in *The Second Sex*: the sexes "are basically defined by the gametes they produce." See also John Skalko, "Why There Are Only Two Sexes," *Public Discourse*, June 5, 2017, https://www.thepublicdiscourse.com/2017/06/19389/: "Our sex—male or female—is determined by our basic capacity to engage in sexually reproductive acts . . . Given that human beings reproduce sexually, they are biologically either only male or female. Men are men, and women are women."

20   Colin Wright, "The New Evolution Deniers," Quillette, November 30, 2018, https://quillette.com/2018/11/30/the-new-evolution-deniers/.

21   As Byrne himself puts it in the case not only of intersex, but also transgender people: "To those struggling with gender identity issues, it might seem liberating and uplifting to be told that biological sex in humans is a glorious rainbow, rather than a square conservatively divided into pink and blue halves. But this feel-good approach is little better than deceiving intersex patients: respect for autonomy demands honesty. And finally, if those advocating for transgender people (or anyone else) rest their case on shaky interpretations of biology, this will ultimately only give succor to their enemies." Byrne, "Is Sex Binary?"

22   American Psychiatric Association, "What Is Gender Dysphoria?" https://www.psychiatry.org/patients-families/gender-dysphoria/what-is-gender-dysphoria.

23   American Psychiatric Association, *Diagnostic and Statistical Manual of Mental Disorders*, 4th ed., text rev. (Washington, D.C.: APA, 2000).

24   "Gender Dysphoria," https://www.psychologytoday.com/ca/conditions/gender-dysphoria; "the majority of children with suspected gender dysphoria don't have the condition once they reach puberty" (NHS, "Treatment," https://www.nhs.uk/conditions/gender-dysphoria/treatment/). See further T. D. Steensma et al., "Factors Associated with Desistence and Persistence of Childhood Gender Dysphoria: A Quantitative Follow-Up Study," *Journal of the American Academy of Child and Adolescent Psychiatry* 52 (2013): 582–90; Kenneth J. Zucker, "The Myth of Persistence," *International Journal of Transgenderism* 19 (2018): 231–245.

25   Note, e.g., the testimony of Linda Seiler, "Becoming the Woman God Made Me to Be," Focus on the Family, December 6, 2019, https://www.focusonthefamily.com/media/daily-broadcast/becoming-the-woman-god-made-me-to-be.

26   The wording is that of UK National Health Service website concerning treatment of gender dysphoria (NHS, "Treatment"). There is evidence, however, that these restrictions are now being challenged by doctors (Robbins, "Cracks").

27 "Information on Estrogen Hormone Therapy," University of California San Francisco, Transgender Care, https://transcare.ucsf.edu/article/information-estrogen-hormone-therapy.

28 They are also expensive. In 2016, "top surgery" (as it is called) cost between U.S. $6,000 and $9,000, and "bottom surgery" (i.e., constructing genitalia) ranged from U.S. $75,000 to $100,000. See Peter Rowe, "How a Girl Born at 2 Pounds Became a Happy Boy," *San Diego Union Tribune*, April 7, 2016, https://www.sandiegouniontribune.com/lifestyle/people/sdut-transgender-teens-new-life-2016apr07-story.html.

29 NHS, "Treatment"; Psychology Today, "Gender Dysphoria."

30 Stephen B. Levine, "Informed Consent for Transgendered Patients," *Journal of Sex and Marital Therapy* 45 (2019): 218–29 (226).

31 Walt Heyer, "Hormones, Surgery, Regret," *USA Today*, February 11, 2019, https://www.usatoday.com/story/opinion/voices/2019/02/11/transgender-debate-transitioning-sex-gender-column/1894076002/. His website is sexchangeregret.com. See further Nicole Russell, "Here's What People Who Used to Be Transgender Are Telling the Supreme Court," *The Federalist*, August 30, 2019, https://thefederalist.com/2019/08/30/heres-people-used-transgender-telling-supreme-court/.

32 As of July 16, 2019 this documentary, which transgender activists have gone out of their way to criticize and suppress, was still viewable at https://vimeo.com/217950594, https://www.dailymotion.com/video/x58s24i, and https://www.thetalentmanager.com/talent/25458/alex-gower-jackson.

33 On this topic see, e.g., some of the comments embedded in Sally Lockwood, "'Hundreds' of Young Trans People Seeking Help to Return to Original Sex," Sky News, October 5, 2019, https://news.sky.com/story/hundreds-of-young-trans-people-seeking-help-to-return-to-original-sex-11827740.

34 Russell, "Supreme Court."

35 The closest it comes is in Deut. 22:5, which certainly reveals a concern at least about the blurring of God-given sex and gender boundaries by way of inappropriate clothing: "a woman must not wear men's clothing, nor a man wear women's clothing, for the Lord your God detests anyone who does this." For a brief discussion of the ANE background, see Eugene E. Carpenter, "Deuteronomy," in *ZIBBC* 1:418–547 (493). The various biblical texts concerning "eunuchs" (castrated males; e.g., 2 Kgs. 9:32) are entirely irrelevant to our discussion, since the medical procedure in this case has nothing to do with individual's pursuit of his perceived gender identity and everything to with ensuring the loyalty of these men to ancient kings and emperors. See further Iain Provan, "2 Kings," in *ZIBBC* 3:151–53.

36 Greasley and Kaczor, *Abortion Rights*, 95.

37 Iain Provan, *Ecclesiastes and Song of Songs*, NIVAC (Grand Rapids: Zondervan, 2001).

38 As one of my daughters pointed out to me, precisely in the context of a discussion of gender dysphoria: "When we ascribe layers of meaning to gender that the Bible does not (e.g., 'real' men are strong, do not cry, are good at sports, do not submit to women, whereas 'real' women are feminine, docile, and sexually desirable), we exclude men and women from their respective genders in a way that God never intended. For example, I do not think there is any evidence that God would give a hoot if a woman wore unfeminine clothing, played sports everyday with male friends, and did not know how to apply makeup. I think there is an important call to the Church to stop mirroring secular culture in ascribing such narrow meaning to gender that many people *do* end up feeling uncomfortable as men or women in a way that they would not if the Church stuck to biblical, noncultural notions of male and female. I think we inadvertently encourage gender dysphoria when we do so."

39 See "63 Genders . . . Now 81 Genders," aPath, March 20, 2000, https://apath.org/63-genders/.

40 *Merriam-Webster*, s.v. "gender identity," https://www.merriam-webster.com/dictionary/gender%20identity.

41 Oyserman et al., "Self," 76.

42 Note again the Linda Seiler interview, "Becoming the Woman." However: "For someone who struggles with gender dysphoria and becomes a Christian, there is no promise that those feelings will go away. But they have been promised the presence of the Holy Spirit, who assures them of their new identity as God's children and gives them a new longing to please him. That will involve recognising that what ultimately matters is not what my feelings may say about myself but who God made me to be, which is who I will be in the resurrection. My origin and destiny in Christ should therefore affect how I live now. And that origin and destiny includes my body, with its sex" (Vaughan Roberts, *Transgender* [Good Book Company, 2016], Kindle edition, 61). Roberts writes as someone who himself struggles as a Christian with same-sex attraction.

43 Ideally this should be a local group, but there are also web-based organizations that parent can check out, like 4th Wave, https://4thwavenow.com/tag/hacsi-horvath/, and Transgender Trend, https://www.transgendertrend.com.

44 As the distinguished American psychiatrist Allan Josephson has said of this advice: "When I saw that, my knee-jerk response was, 'Do these people have children?' Because in the process of raising children, they insistently, persistently, consistently demand lots of things that are not good for them, whether it's turning off the computer, eating your own food, staying up too late, and it's the parents' job then to guide them to say, This is what you need to do to be healthy" (Madeleine Kearns, "Gender Dissenter Gets Fired," *National Review*, July 12, 2019, https://www.nationalreview.com/2019/07/allen-josephson-gender-dissenter-gets-fired/).

45 *Merriam-Webster*, s.v. "sexual orientation," https://www.merriam-webster.com/dictionary/sexual%20orientation.

46 Because of frequent misunderstanding on the point, it is necessary to mention here that the fact that people have a long memory of same-sex attraction cannot be taken to demonstrate that they were "born gay": "The current scientific revolution in our understanding of the human epigenome challenges the very notion of being 'born gay,' along with the notion of being 'born' with any complex trait. Rather, our genetic legacy is dynamic, developmental, and environmentally embedded" (Lisa M. Diamond and Clifford J. Rosky, "Scrutinizing Immutability: Research on Sexual Orientation and US Legal Advocacy for Sexual Minorities," *Journal of Sex Research* 53, nos. 4–5 [2016]: 363–91 [366]).

47 L. A. Peplau and L. D. Garnets, "A New Paradigm for Understanding Women's Sexuality and Sexual Orientation," *Journal of Social Issues* 56 (2000): 330–50 (329).

48 Michael C. LaSala, "Sexual Orientation: Is It Unchangeable?" *Psychology Today*, May 17, 2011, https://www.psychologytoday.com/ca/blog/gay-and-lesbian-well-being/201105/sexual-orientation-is-it-unchangeable.

49 Diamond and Rosky, "Immutability," 370.

50 Carley Cassella, "Here's More Evidence Sexual Orientation Is Fluid Right into Our Adult Years," Science Alert, May 5, 2019, https://www.sciencealert.com/sexual-orientation-continues-to-change-right-through-our-teens-and-into-adulthood.

51 Cassella, "Adult Years."

52 Diamond and Rosky, "Immutability," 363.

53 In many people's minds this conviction appears to be connected with the idea that same-sex attraction is genetically determined. This is not the case. In one recent study, for example, "researchers could not find any way to meaningfully predict or identify a person's sexual behaviour on the basis of their genes" (Michael Cook, "Farewell to the 'Gay Gene' Theory," BioEdge, September 1, 2019, https://www.bioedge.org/bioethics/farewell-to-the-gay-gene-theory/13200); see further Ian Paul, "Are We Born Straight or Gay?"

      Psephizo, October 2, 2019, https://www.psephizo.com/sexuality-2/are-we-born-straight-or-gay/?fbclid=IwAR1fNlQgadsUywLFKGIXFhqYEm45GPAl9jKO5tU_lBvNjeJgk-jGwo2YcuQE.

54   Michael Cook, "Can Sexual Orientation Change? Yes, according to a New Study," MercatorNet, August 21, 2018, https://www.mercatornet.com/conjugality/view/can-sexual-orientation-change-yes-according-to-a-new-study/21629.

55   Joseph Nicolosi, "APA Task Force Report—A Mockery of Science," https://www.josephnicolosi.com/apa-task-force/.

56   APA, *Report of the American Psychological Association Task Force on Appropriate Therapeutic Responses to Sexual Orientation* (Washington, D.C.: APA, 2009), 120.

57   APA, *Sexual Orientation*, 42–43.

58   Such testimonies, along with those of others who have left a gay lifestyle without necessarily engaging in SOCE, are everywhere in evidence, not least in personal form on the Internet; as a starting point, see (e.g.) the Voices of Change website (www.voicesofchange.net), and Focus on the Family, "Do People Change from Homosexuality? Hundreds of Stories of Hope and Transformation (Part I)," https://www.focusonthefamily.com/socialissues/sexuality/freedom-from-homosexuality/do-people-change-from-homosexuality-hundreds-of-stories-of-hope-and-transformation-part-1. For some academic studies on SOCE specifically, see the following: In 2000 a large study found that after receiving therapy and making other efforts to change, only 35.1 percent of the participants who had previously viewed themselves as "more homosexual than heterosexual," "almost exclusively homosexual," or "exclusively homosexual" in their orientation "continued to view their orientation in this manner" (Joseph Nicolosi, A. Dean Byrd, and Richard W. Potts, "Retrospective Self-Reports of Changes in Homosexual Orientation: A Consumer Survey of Conversion Therapy Clients," *Psychological Reports* 86 [2000]: 1071–88). A 2010 study reported among men "dissatisfied with their same-sex attraction" increases in heterosexual self-identity and in reported heterosexual feelings and behavior, along with a decrease in reported homosexual feelings and behavior after SOCE, with "the two most helpful techniques [being] understanding better the causes [of] one's homosexuality and one's emotional needs and issues and developing nonsexual relationships with same-sex peers, mentors, family members, and friends" (Elan Y. Karten and Jay C. Wade, "Sexual Orientation Change Efforts in Men: A Client Perspective," *The Journal of Men's Studies* 18 [2010]: 84–102). A 2011 longitudinal study concluded that "change of homosexual orientation appears possible for some and that psychological distress did not increase on average as a result of the involvement in the change process" (Stanton L. Jones and Mark A. Yarhouse, "A Longitudinal Study of Attempted Religiously Mediated Sexual Orientation Change," *Journal of Sex and Marital Therapy* 37, no. 5 [2011]: 404–27). Finally, a 2018 study surveyed 125 men who had undergone SOCE, 68 percent of whom reported reduction in their same-sex attraction and behavior (ranging from "some" to "much"), as well as an increase in attraction to women. About 14 percent claimed that their orientation had changed from exclusively homosexual to exclusively heterosexual. On the whole, the participants found their therapy helpful; only one reported extreme negative effects (Paul L. Santero, Neil E. Whitehead, and Dolores Ballesteros, "Effects of Therapy on Religious Men Who Have Unwanted Same-Sex Attraction," *Linacre Quarterly*, July 23, 2018, DOI: 10.1177/0024363918788559). This last paper has now been retracted by the journal due to the lack of a prior statistical review of the paper, which does not of course affect its usefulness for those addressing the question of whether SOCE, as such, are perceived by some people as beneficial.

59   Consider, e.g., these words (from 2013) of former APA president Nicholas Cummings: "Gays and lesbians have the right to be affirmed in their homosexuality. That's why, as a member of the APA Council of Representatives in 1975, I sponsored the resolution by which the APA stated that homosexuality is not a mental disorder and, in 1976, the resolution, which

passed the council unanimously, that gays and lesbians should not be discriminated against in the workplace. But contending that all same-sex attraction is immutable is a distortion of reality. Attempting to characterize all sexual reorientation therapy as 'unethical' violates patient choice and gives an outside party a veto over patients' goals for their own treatment. A political agenda shouldn't prevent gays and lesbians who desire to change from making their own decisions." He further reports that in addition to the thousands of gay and lesbian patients whom he and his staff treated over twenty-five years and who attained "a happier and more stable homosexual lifestyle" as a result, he also oversaw many who were seeking to change their sexual orientation, and of these, "hundreds were successful" (Nicholas A. Cummings, "Sexual Reorientation Therapy Not Unethical," *USA Today*, July 30, 2013, https://www.usatoday.com/story/opinion/2013/07/30/sexual-reorientation-therapy-not-unethical-column/2601159/). See also, in the Australian context, David van Gend, "Banning Therapy, Banning Liberty," MercatorNet, March 7, 2019, https://www.mercatornet.com/conjugality/view/banning-therapy-banning-liberty/22255.

60   It is important to note that these concerns about the potential harm of attempting change are hardly ever set alongside the potential harm of entering into or continuing an actively gay lifestyle so that some kind of balanced risk assessment could be attempted. For one example of the latter: "In the general population, anal cancer is a rare disease ... Each year anal cancer is diagnosed in about 2 people out of every 100,000 people in the general population. Current estimates are that HIV-negative MSMs [men who have sex with men] are 20 times more likely to be diagnosed with anal cancer. Their rate is about 40 cases per 100,000. HIV-positive MSMs are up to 40 times more likely to diagnosed with the disease, resulting in a rate of 80 anal cancer cases per 100,000 people" (National LGBT Cancer Network, https://cancer-network.org/cancer-information/gay-men-and-cancer/anal-cancer-hiv-and-gaybisexual-men/).

61   This at least appears to be the implication of Jesus' teaching that "[a]t the resurrection people will neither marry nor be given in marriage; they will be like the angels in heaven" (Matt. 22:30). Whether the language of "angels" then presses us further to envision a post-resurrection state where gender does not exist, or where it has been transcended in some way, is another matter. Early Christian theologians like Gregory of Nyssa had something to say about such matters: "Whatever Gregory has in mind for the resurrection life, it will certainly not conform to anything we can catch and hold in gender stereotypes *in this world*" (Sarah Coakley, *God, Sexuality, and the Self: An Essay "On the Trinity"* [Cambridge: Cambridge University Press, 2013], 283).

62   "Close scrutiny of vocabulary ... reveals ... eight terms that connote sin, together with additional features of the context that contribute to the sense that homosexuality is sinful. True, Paul does not use the word *sin* ... The word *sin* does not occur *anywhere* in the first two chapters of Romans, but the description of sin is clearly their primary subject" (Thomas E. Schmidt, *Straight and Narrow? Compassion & Clarity in the Homosexuality Debate* [Downers Grove, Ill.: IVP, 1995], 84).

63   Cited in Denny Burk and Heath Lambert, *Transforming Homosexuality: What the Bible Says about Sexual Orientation and Change* (Phillipsburg, N.J.: P&R, 2015), 22.

64   It is not true to say that "Christians who experience same-sex attraction will necessarily be freed from those desires completely in this life. Many such Christians report partial or complete changes in their attractions after conversion—sometimes all at once, but more often over a period of months and years. But those cases are not the norm. There are a great many who also report ongoing struggles with same-sex attraction" (Burk and Lambert, *Transforming Homosexuality*, 58).

65   For just one example, see Sean Doherty, "'Love Does Not Delight in Evil, but Rejoices with the Truth': A Theological and Pastoral Reflection on My Journey away from a Homosexual Identity," *Anvil* 30 (2014): 5–16.

66   Readers who wish to think further about what this looks like would do well to read the brief story of "Sara" and then all of chapter 7 in Mark A. Yarhouse, *Understanding Gender Dysphoria: Navigating Transgender Issues in a Changing Culture* (Downers Grove, Ill.: IVP Academic, 2015), 143–61, where he discusses the tensions involved in being both "inwardly" and "outwardly" missional.

67   Peterson, "Gender Politics."

68   Somerville, *Death Talk*, xxiii.

69   See, e.g., "Child of Lesbian Parents Opposes Gay Marriage," ABC News (Australia) YouTube video, https://www.youtube.com/watch?v=V73Y1HsDKWs; "The Other Side of the Rainbow—Millie Fontana's Story," Australian Christian Lobby, YouTube video, https://www.youtube.com/watch?v=tgE3juldK-4&feature=youtu.be.

70   Peterson, "Gender Politics."

19   THE LANDSCAPE OF EXILE

1   George Orwell, *Nineteen Eighty-Four* (New York: Penguin, 2013), 284–86
2   Orwell, *Nineteen Eighty-Four*, 40.
3   Orwell, *Nineteen Eighty-Four*, 60.
4   Orwell, *Nineteen Eighty-Four*, 242.
5   George Packer, "Doublethink Is Stronger than Orwell Imagined: What *1984* Means Today," *The Atlantic*, July 2019, https://www.theatlantic.com/magazine/archive/2019/07/1984-george-orwell/590638/.
6   Quoted in Packer, "Doublethink."
7   Packer, "Doublethink."
8   Packer, "Doublethink."
9   Packer, "Doublethink."
10   Packer, "Doublethink."
11   Packer, "Doublethink."
12   The quote is from Roger Scruton, "The Failure to Stand Up for Conservative Thinking Is Leading Us into a New Cultural Dark Age," *The Telegraph*, July 20, 2019, https://www.rogerscruton.com/articles/20-latest/619-the-telegraph-20th-july-19.
13   I wrote this line before reading this excellent essay (and the comments in response): Toby Young, "Why I Want to Start a Free Speech Trade Union," Quillette, August 1, 2019, https://quillette.com/2019/08/01/why-i-want-to-start-a-free-speech-trade-union/.
14   Packer, "Doublethink."
15   See Government of Ontario, "Affirming Sexual Orientation and Gender Identity Act," 2015, https://www.ontario.ca/laws/statute/S15018.
16   Hannah Thibedeau, "Ottawa Looking at Criminal Code Reforms to Deter 'Shameful' Conversion Therapy," CBC News, July 9, 2019, https://www.cbc.ca/news/politics/conversion-therapy-criminal-code-1.5204919.
17   Alvin Yu, "Conversion Therapy: What You Need to Know," CBC News, July 13, 2019, https://www.cbc.ca/news/canada/conversion-therapy-what-you-need-to-know-1.5209598. The same association is apparent in a recent U.S. Senator's reference to "psychological torture." Michael Cook, "Sexual Orientation," quoting U.S. Senator Scott Wiener.
18   Debra W. Soh, "CBC's Decision against Airing Transgender Kids Doc Should Leave Everyone Unsettled," CBC News, December 18, 2017, https://www.cbc.ca/news/opinion/transgender-kids-documentary-1.4453667.

19 Kirsty Entwistle, "An Open Letter to Dr. Polly Carmichael from a Former GIDS Clinician," Medium, https://medium.com/@kirstyentwistle/an-open-letter-to-dr-polly-carmichael-from-a-former-gids-clinician-53c541276b8d.

20 Entwistle, "Letter." Consider further the interview recorded in the aftermath of the firing of the psychiatrist Allan Josephson by the University of Louisville for sharing at a conference "his professional opinion on the medicalization of gender-confused youth" (Kearns, "Gender Dissenter Gets Fired").

21 Kearns, "Gender Dissenter."

22 Kearns, "Gender Dissenter."

23 Levine, "Informed Consent," 220.

24 Again, for a very full discussion of the risks, see Levine, "Informed Consent," 222–26. As the title suggests, this essay is fundamentally about what truly "informed consent" looks like.

25 Levine, "Informed Consent," 227.

26 Levine, "Informed Consent," 221

27 Levine, "Informed Consent," 227.

28 Soh, "Decision."

29 Walt Heyer reports, e.g., that as a four-year-old boy his grandmother repeatedly, over several years, dressed him in a full-length purple dress and told him how pretty he was as a girl. This led on to later sexual abuse by another family member (Heyer, "Hormones"). In May 2019, secondly, the High Court in the UK affirmed the right of a four-year-old boy to live as a girl after it transpired that his foster parents were sending him to school in a girl's uniform. Two other children assigned to the couple also had gender identity issues (Michael Cook, "4-Year-Old Can Begin Transgender Transition, says UK Court," BioEdge, May 19, 2019, https://www.bioedge.org/bioethics/4-year-old-can-begin-transgender-transition-says-uk-court/13063). A friend in Vancouver informed me, thirdly, that his neighbors were dressing their child alternately as a boy and as a girl, day by day, so that he could eventually choose his gender for himself.

30 Paul Marsden, "Memetics and Social Contagion: Two Sides of the Same Coin?" *Journal of Memetics: Evolutionary Models of Information Transmission* 2 (1998): 171–85. The definition is quoted from *The Handbook of Social Psychology*.

31 Marsden, "Social Contagion."

32 See Michelle Cretella, "I'm a Pediatrician. How Transgender Ideology Has Infiltrated My Field and Produced Large-Scale Child Abuse," Intellectual Takeout, July 5, 2017, https://www.intellectualtakeout.org/article/im-pediatrician-how-transgender-ideology-has-infiltrated-my-field-and-produced-large-scale.

33 Lisa Littman, "Rapid Onset Gender Dysphoria in Adolescents and Young Adults: A Study of Parental Reports," *PLoS ONE* 13, no. 8 (2018): e0202330, https://doi.org/10.1371/journal.pone.0202330. The original study was published on August 16, 2018, and a corrected version, with the conclusions unchanged, was issued on March 19, 2019 after an outcry from some activists working in transgender clinics led to an investigation of the original. See also the comments by Susan Bradley in Douglas Todd, "If Your Child Talks about Being a Different Gender, Take It Slowly," *Vancouver Sun*, https://vancouversun.com/opinion/columnists/douglas-todd-if-your-child-talks-about-being-a-different-gender-take-it-slowly.

34 Voices of Change, www.voicesofchange.net.

35 Nova Scotia Legislature, *Sexual Orientation and Gender Identity Protection Act of 2018*, 2nd session, 63rd General Assembly, Ch. 28 of the Acts of 2018. The act is available online: https://nslegislature.ca/legc/bills/63rd_2nd/3rd_read/b016.htm.

36 Sharon Kirkey, "Puberty Blockers, Cross-Sex Hormones: Canada's Family Doctors Get Guidance on Treating Youth with 'Gender Dysphoria,'" *National Post*, January 31, 2019, https://nationalpost.com/news/puberty-blockers-cross-sex-hormones-canadas-family-doctors

-get-guidance-on-treating-youth-with-gender-dysphoria. Some surgeons in other jurisdictions have actually operated on children under sixteen: in San Diego in 2016, e.g., a fourteen-year-old minor underwent an irreversible double mastectomy on the basis of her perception concerning her true gender (Peter Rowe, "Happy Boy").

37   "Research" is unsurprisingly being produced to prove that this is true, but it is all too often of very poor quality. Consider, e.g., the much-publicized *JAMA Psychiatry* study by Jack L. Turban and others, "Association Between Recalled Exposure to Gender Identity Conversion Efforts and Psychological Distress and Suicide Attempts among Transgender Adults," *JAMA Psychiatry*, September 11, 2019, https://jamanetwork.com/journals/jamapsychiatry/article-abstract/2749479?resultClick=1. Mark Regnerus characterizes this study as follows: "Weak data are being used to make empirical—and then clinical and legal—truth claims while subsidized by nascent political will" (Mark Regnerus, "Does 'Conversion Therapy' Hurt People Who Identify as Transgender? The New *JAMA Psychiatry* Study Cannot Tell Us," *Public Discourse*, September 18, 2019, https://www.thepublicdiscourse.com/2019/09/57145/?fbclid=IwAR0BI7nbxroWWPwwDmIc-EIC1UwlOLLH06yl7GlgGAQrMtpYyRF8KMBCG9g).

38   See "More Students Supported by SOGI-Inclusive Education," Government of British Columbia, May 17, 2019, https://archive.news.gov.bc.ca/releases/news_releases_2017-2021/2019EDUC0040-000975.htm.

39   *Sogi 123*, https://www.sogieducation.org/.

40   "Every student understands and expresses their gender differently, with interests and choices that are common or less common for their biological sex. Some students may be unsure of their sexual orientation. Others may identify specifically as lesbian, gay, straight, bisexual, transgender, queer, two-spirit, cisgender, or other" (*Sogi 123*, "Parents," https://www.sogieducation.org/parents).

41   *Sogi 123*, "Parents."

42   Claire Ainsworth, "Sex Redefined: The Idea of 2 Sexes Is Overly Simplistic," *Scientific American*, October 22, 2018, https://www.scientificamerican.com/article/sex-redefined-the-idea-of-2-sexes-is-overly-simplistic1/.

43   Government of Canada, "About Family Violence," Department of Justice, https://www.justice.gc.ca/eng/cj-jp/fv-vf/about-apropos.html.

44   Douglas Quan, "Legal Dispute between Trans Child and Father Takes New Turn over Freedom of Expression," *National Post*, April 30, 2019, https://nationalpost.com/news/canada/legal-dispute-between-trans-child-and-father-takes-new-turn-over-freedom-of-expression. "Misgendering" was also a core component of a 2019 BC Human Rights Tribunal decision in favor of a transgendered politician judged to have suffered "injury to dignity feelings, and self-respect" as a result of the (certainly inflammatory) speech of a BC Christian, such that it comprised an aspect of "hate speech." The tribunal ordered the accused to pay the complainant $35,000 for his behavior prior to the hearing, and a further $20,000 "as 'costs for improper conduct' for, among other things, referring to the complainant as a male during the hearing" (Geoffrey Trotter, "Legal Worldview and the New Coercion," *Christian Legal Journal* 28, no. 2 [2019]: 22–27 [23]). For the dangers involved in "misgendering" in 2019 in other countries, see (e.g.) Luke Gittos, "Misgendering Is Not a Crime," Spiked, March 25, 2019, https://www.spiked-online.com/2019/03/25/misgendering-is-not-a-crime/.

45   *Transgender Kids: Who Knows Best?* around the eleven-minute mark.

46   See the press release at https://www.andrewweavermla.ca/2019/05/27/introducing-bill-practice-conversion-therapy-british-columbia/, and the text of the bill at http://www.bclaws.ca/civix/document/id/lc/billscurrent/4th41st:m218-1.

47   Robbins, "Cracks," writing of the general state of affairs, not about BC in particular. See further Levine, "Informed Consent," 224, who acknowledges that what used to be widely

considered as an aspect of ordinary, ethical medical care with respect to gender dysphoria—specifically, that "pediatricians and mental health professionals may intervene to help both the parents and the child discuss the issue well before puberty" is regarded by "some activists . . . [as] 'reparative therapy.'" He notes that this view, held by "strangers to the families," is tantamount to the view that "parents have no right to seek help for their concerns about their gender-nonconforming children."

48   Thibedeau, "Conversion Therapy."

49   Parliament of Canada, *An Act to Amend the Criminal Code* (Conversion Therapy), 1st session, 42nd Parliament, 1st reading (April 9, 2019): S-260. Available at https://www.parl.ca/DocumentViewer/en/42-1/bill/S-260/first-reading.

50   Orwell, *Nineteen Eighty-Four*, 81.

51   UN General Assembly, "Resolution Adopted by the Human Rights Council on 30 June, 2016," July 15, 2016, https://www.un.org/en/ga/search/view_doc.asp?symbol=A/HRC/RES/32/2.

52   UN Human Rights, Office of the High Commissioner, "Vitit Muntarbhorn," https://www.ohchr.org/EN/Issues/SexualOrientationGender/Pages/VititMuntarbhorn.aspx.

53   Yogyakarta Principles, "About the Yogyakarta Principles," http://yogyakartaprinciples.org/principles-en/about-the-yogyakarta-principles/

54   This is not even to mention the allegations leveled by Jennifer Bilek concerning the *funding* of the institutionalization of transgender ideology specifically, which she tracks to "exceedingly rich, white men with enormous cultural influence . . . [who] fund the transgender lobby and organizations through their own organizations, including corporations." Her view is that much of this funding is driven as much by a desire to make money as by anything else (Jennifer Bilek, "Who Are the Rich, White Men Institutionalizing Transgender Ideology?" *The Federalist*, February 20, 2018, https://thefederalist.com/2018/02/20/rich-white-men-institutionalizing-transgender-ideology/).

55   "Pro-LGBT Coca-Cola Adverts Spark Boycott Calls in Hungary," *The Guardian*, August 5, 2019, https://www.theguardian.com/world/2019/aug/05/pro-lgbt-coca-cola-ads-spark-boycott-calls-in-hungary.

56   Wright, "Deniers." See also Matt Naham, "Feminist Writer Sues Twitter after She Tweets 'Men Aren't Women' and Gets Banned," Law and Crime, February 12, 2019, https://lawandcrime.com/lawsuit/feminist-writer-sues-twitter-after-she-tweets-men-arent-woman-and-gets-banned/.

57   Ron Dreher, "Amazon.com Surrenders to the Homintern," *The American Conservative*, July 3, 2019, https://www.theamericanconservative.com/dreher/amazon-com-homintern-joseph-goebbels-joseph-nicolosi-reparative-therapy/, who refers in turn to Denny Burk, "Amazon Bans Books on 'Conversion Therapy,'" http://www.dennyburk.com/amazon-bans-books-on-conversion-therapy/. The questions in this case are whether it is acceptable to believe (in Burk's words) that "the Gospel helps us to change, even in our wayward sexual desires," and whether it should be illegal to share this belief with others and work with them toward that end.

58   See "Woman Undergoes Surgery to Become Genderless Alien," InformOverload, YouTube video, March 3, 2019, https://www.youtube.com/watch?v=-X0-L46t4Ig; "Remove my Genitals to Make me a Genderless 'Alien': Hooked on the Look," Barcroft TV, YouTube video May 25, 2017, https://www.youtube.com/watch?v=2lkybOCvLTA. See also Maroosha Muzaffar, "Alien Beauty Invades World of Fashion," Ozy, July 18, 2019, https://www.ozy.com/fast-forward/alien-beauty-invades-world-of-fashion/95394.

59   See, e.g., "20-Year-Old Woman Claims She Is a Cat Born in the Wrong Body," Inside Edition, YouTube video, January 28, 2016, https://www.youtube.com/watch?v=rLmwLcLikXQ. One's initial reaction is to think that this must be a clever satirical commentary on all the other things that are currently going on along analogous lines. In reality, there is no "must"

about it; all things are possible in this new world in which we live. "Modern authenticity encourages us to create our own beliefs and morality, the only rule being that they must resonate with who we feel we really are" (Jonathan Grant, quoted in Roberts, *Transgender*, 27).

60   Rianne M. Blom, Raoul C. Hennekam, and Damiaan Denys, "Body Integrity Identity Disorder," *PLoS One* 7, no. 4 (2012), https://journals.plos.org/plosone/article?id=10.1371/journal.pone.0034702. See also Naveed Saleh, "Body Integrity Identity Disorder," Verywell Mind, July 26, 2019, https://www.verywellmind.com/amputating-a-healthy-limb-1123848.

61   Callahan, "Reason," 63–64.

62   Blom, Hennekam, and Denys, "Body Integrity Identity Disorder," looks *back* on patients after amputation.

63   C. S. Lewis, *The Abolition of Man: Or, Reflections on Education with Special Reference to the Teaching of English in the Upper Forms of Schools* (London: Oxford University Press, H. Milford, 1943).

64   Scruton, "Failure."

20   THE DISCIPLINES OF EXILE

1   C. S. Lewis, *Mere Christianity* (New York: Harper Collins, 1952), 28.

2   Craig M. Gay, *The Way of the (Modern) World: Or, Why It's Tempting to Live as if God Doesn't Exist* (Grand Rapids: Eerdmans, 1998).

3   Amy Watson, "Television in Canada—Statistics & Facts," Statista, May 17, 2019, https://www.statista.com/topics/2730/television-in-canada/.

4   CIRA, "2019 Canada's Internet Factbook," https://cira.ca/resources/corporate/factbook/canadas-internet-factbook-2019.

5   One can hear the weary resignation in the voice of Roger Launius, a former chief historian of NASA, even in the printed word: "The reality is, the Internet has made it possible for people to say whatever the hell they like to a broader number of people than ever before." He is referring to the widely believed falsehood that the moon landings were faked (Richard Godwin, "One Giant . . . Lie? Why So Many People Still Think the Moon Landings Were Faked," *The Guardian*, July 10, 2019, https://www.theguardian.com/science/2019/jul/10/one-giant-lie-why-so-many-people-still-think-the-moon-landings-were-faked).

6   Olivia Solon, "Ex-Facebook President Sean Parker: Site Made to Exploit Human 'Vulnerability,'" *The Guardian*, November 9, 2017, https://www.theguardian.com/technology/2017/nov/09/facebook-sean-parker-vulnerability-brain-psychology.

7   E.g., Kaitlyn Tiffany, "GLAAD on LGBTQ Representation in Film: 'It Is Not Getting Better,'" *The Verge*, May 25, 2017, https://www.theverge.com/2017/5/25/15690404/glaad-lgbtq-representation-film-not-getting-better.

8   Note the robust discussion, e.g., in Quora, "Why Do We See Gay and Lesbian Characters in Almost All US Movies or TV Series?" Quora, https://www.quora.com/Why-do-we-see-gay-and-lesbian-characters-in-almost-all-US-movies-or-TV-series.

9   Tom Jacobs, "TV Dramas Spur Support for Transgender Rights," *Pacific Standard*, August 15, 2017, https://psmag.com/social-justice/tv-dramas-spur-support-for-transgender-rights.

10   Orwell, *Nineteen Eighty-Four*, 92.

11   Readers unfamiliar with this excellent program should consult https://www.alphacanada.org/.

12   "Top SOGI Book Choices for Students and Teachers," http://teach-educ.sites.olt.ubc.ca/files/2018/01/SOGI-Top-Books-List-2018.pdf.

13   Peterson, "Gender Politics." He is responding in part to one striking example of what can happen to children who are exposed to this ideology. See Barbara Kay, "Ontario Family Files

Human Rights Complaint after Six-Year-Old Girl Upset by Gender Theory in School," Barbara Kay, June 17, 2019, http://www.barbarakay.ca/articles/view/1414.

14 Campbell River School District, "SOGI 123," https://www.sd72.bc.ca/studentsparents/SOGI-123/Pages/default.aspx.

15 Kearns, "Gender Dissenter."

16 Paul W. Hruz, Lawrence S. Mayer, and Paul R. McHugh, "Growing Pains: Problems with Puberty Suppression in Treating Gender Dysphoria," *The New Atlantis* 52 (Spring 2017): 3–36.

17 Annelou L. C. de Vries et al., "Puberty Suppression in Adolescents with Gender Identity Disorder: A Prospective Follow-Up Study," *Journal of Sexual Medicine* 8, no. 8 (August 2011): 2276–83. This study found that of seventy young adolescents treated with puberty suppression drugs ("gonadotropin-releasing hormone analogues [GnRHa]"), allegedly "to provide time to make a balanced decision regarding actual gender reassignment," none "withdrew from puberty suppression, and all started cross-sex hormone treatment, the first step of actual gender reassignment."

18 Eva Moore, Amy Wisniewski, and Adrian Dobs, "Endocrine Treatment of Transsexual People: A Review of Treatment Regimens, Outcomes, and Adverse Effects," *Journal of Clinical Endocrinology and Metabolism* 88 (2003): 3467–73.

19 It is sometimes suggested that "transitioning" is a cure for suicidal tendencies in people with gender dysphoria, but there is little reason to think that this is the case. One 2011 study from liberal Sweden actually found that "[p]ersons with transsexualism, after sex reassignment, have considerably higher risks for mortality, suicidal behaviour, and psychiatric morbidity than the general population," concluding that "sex reassignment, although alleviating gender dysphoria, may not suffice as treatment for transsexualism, and should inspire improved psychiatric and somatic care after sex reassignment for this patient group" (Dhejne C. Lichtenstein et al., "Long-Term Follow-Up of Transsexual Persons Undergoing Sex Reassignment Surgery: Cohort Study in Sweden," *PLoS ONE* 6, no. 2 (2011): e16885, https://doi.org/10.1371/journal.pone.0016885). In other words, the community as a whole has an ongoing need, after the hormonal and surgical adjustments, for mental and other health care. This in turn begs the question as to how far the condition would better have been dealt with *from the beginning* as a mental health issue. Generally, "over 90 percent of people who commit suicide have a diagnosed mental disorder." Cretella, "Pediatrician."

20 Robbins, "Cracks," quoting from the private website of the group "Youth Trans Critical Professionals."

21 We find it again in Jer. 51:56, which also contains the Heb. words behind "destruction" and "done" from Ps. 137 (Hb. *shadad* and *gemulah*), although the NIV renders these in the Jeremiah passage as "destroyer" and "retribution."

22 Quoted in Elliott, "Inequality," 31.

23 Romans 5:19; cf. Heb. 5:8; Eugene H. Peterson, *A Long Obedience in the Same Direction: Discipleship in an Instant Society*, 2nd ed. (Downers Grove, Ill.: IVP, 2000).

Bibliography

Aikman, James. *An Historical Account of Covenanting in Scotland: From the First Band in Mearns, 1556, to the Signature of the Grand National Covenant, 1638*. Edinburgh: Thomas Constable, 1851.

Ainsworth, Claire. "Sex Redefined: The Idea of 2 Sexes Is Overly Simplistic." *Scientific American*, October 22, 2018. https://www.scientificamerican.com/article/sex-redefined-the-idea-of-2-sexes-is-overly-simplistic1/.

Alexander, Loveday C. A. "Rome, Early Christian Attitudes to." Pages 836–39 in *ABD* 5.

Alter, Robert. *The Art of Biblical Narrative*. London: Allen & Unwin, 1981.

Alvard, Michael S. "Evolutionary Theory, Conservation, and Human Environmental Impact." Pages 28–43 in Kay and Simmons, *Wilderness and Political Ecology*.

———. "Testing the 'Ecologically Noble Savage' Hypothesis: Interspecific Prey Choice by Piro Hunters in Amazonian Peru." *HE* 21 (1993): 355–87.

Ambrose. *Jacob and the Happy Life*. In *St. Ambrose: Seven Exegetical Works*. Edited by Bernard M. Peebles et al. Translated by Michael P. McHugh. FC 65. Washington, D.C.: Catholic University of America, 1985.

American Psychiatric Association. *Diagnostic and Statistical Manual of Mental Disorders*. 4th edition. Washington, D.C.: APA, 2000.

———. "What Is Gender Dysphoria?" https://www.psychiatry.org/patients-families/gender-dysphoria/what-is-gender-dysphoria.

American Psychological Association. *Report of the American Psychological Association Task Force on Appropriate Therapeutic Responses to Sexual Orientation*. Washington, D.C.: APA, 2009.

Amundsen, Darrel W. "Suicide and Early Christian Values." Pages 77–153 in *Suicide and Euthanasia*. Edited by Baruch A. Brody. Philosophy and Medicine 35. Dordrecht: Springer, 1989.

Anderson, Atholl. "A Fragile Plenty: Pre-European Māori and the New Zealand Environment." Pages 19–34 in *Environmental Histories of New Zealand*. Edited by Eric Pawson and Tom Brooking. Melbourne: Oxford University Press, 2002.

Anderson, Ryan T. "Always Care, Never Kill: How Physician-Assisted Suicide Endangers the Weak, Corrupts Medicine, Compromises the Family, and Violates Human Dignity and Equality." https:// www .heritage .org/ health -care -reform/ report/always-care-never-kill-how-physician-assisted-suicide-endangers-the-weak.

The Ante-Nicene Fathers. Edited by Alexander Roberts and James Donaldson. 1885–1887. 10 vols. Repr., Peabody, Mass.: Hendrickson, 1994.

Aquinas, Thomas. *On the Government of Rulers*. In *Aquinas: Political Writings*. Edited by R. W. Dyson. CTHP. Cambridge: Cambridge University Press, 2002.

———. *Summa Theologica*. Translated by Fathers of the English Dominican Province. Revised by Daniel J. Sullivan. GBWW 20. Chicago: Encyclopedia Britannica, 1952.

Aristotle. *Politics*. Translated by Benjamin Jowett. New York: Random House, 1943.

Arnold, John H., ed. *The Oxford Handbook of Medieval Christianity*. Oxford: Oxford University Press, 2014.

Asbridge, Thomas S. *The Crusades: The Authoritative History of the War for the Holy Land*. New York: Ecco, 2010.

Baldwin, Marshall W., ed. *Christianity through the Thirteenth Century*. DHWC. New York: Walker, 1970.

Ball, John. "Address to the Rebels at Blackheath," 1381. Pages 3–4 in *British Historical and Political Orations from the 12th to the 20th Century*. Edited by Ernest Rhys. London: J. M. Dent, 1915.

Barbero, Alessandro. *Charlemagne: Father of a Continent*. Translated by Allan Cameron. Berkeley: University of California Press, 2004.

Barrett, C. K. *The Epistle to the Romans*. Rev. ed. London: Continuum, 1991.

Barzilay, Isaac Eisenstein. "The Jew in the Literature of the Enlightenment." *Jewish Social Studies* 18 (1956): 243–61.

Baskerville, Stephen. *Not by Peace but a Sword: The Political Theology of the English Revolution*. London: Routledge, 1993.

Bauckham, Richard J. *Bible and Ecology: Rediscovering the Community of Creation*. London: Darton, Longman, and Todd, 2010.

———. *Gospel Women: Studies of the Named Women in the Gospels*. Grand Rapids: Eerdmans, 2002.

———. *Living with Other Creatures: Green Exegesis and Theology*. Waco: Baylor University Press, 2011.

———. "Sabbath and Sunday in the Postapostolic Church." Pages 251–98 in Carson, *Sabbath*.

Beecher, Catharine E. *Essay on Slavery and Abolitionism*. Philadelphia: Henry Perkins, 1837.

Benzoni, Francisco. "Thomas Aquinas and Environmental Ethics: A Reconsideration of Providence and Salvation." *JR* 85 (2005): 446–76.

Biagoni, Mario. *The Radical Reformation and the Making of Modern Europe: A Lasting Heritage.* SMRT 207. Leiden: Brill, 2017.

Bilek, Jennifer. "Who Are the Rich, White Men Institutionalizing Transgender Ideology?" *The Federalist*, February 20, 2018. https://thefederalist.com/2018/02/20/rich-white-men-institutionalizing-transgender-ideology/.

Blau, Uri. "Haaretz Investigation: U.S. Donors Gave Settlements More than $220 Million in Tax-Exempt Funds over Five Years." *Haaretz*, December 7, 2015. https://www.haaretz.com/haaretz-investigates-u-s-donors-to-israeli-settlements-1.5429739.

Bledsoe, Albert T. *An Essay on Liberty and Slavery.* Philadelphia: J. B. Lippincott, 1856.

Blom, Riann M., Raoul C. Hennekam, and Damiaan Denys. "Body Integrity Identity Disorder." *PLoS One* 7, no. 4 (2012). https://journals.plos.org/plosone/article?id=10.1371/journal.pone.0034702.

Bogardus, Tomas. "Gender's Journey from Sex to Psychology: A Brief History." Quillette, March 13, 2019. https://quillette.com/2019/03/13/genders-journey-from-sex-to-psychology-a-brief-history/.

Bookless, David. *Planetwise: Dare to Care for God's World.* Nottingham: IVP, 2008.

Bouma-Prediger, Steven. *For the Beauty of the Earth: A Christian Vision for Creation Care.* Engaging Culture. 2nd ed. Grand Rapids: Baker Academic, 2010.

Bourke, Dale Hanson. *The Israeli-Palestinian Conflict: Tough Questions, Direct Answers.* The Skeptic's Guide Series. Downers Grove, Ill.: IVP, 2013.

Brean, Joseph. "Shattering the Scientific World's History of Gendered Brain Assumptions." *National Post*, July 15, 2019. https://nationalpost.com/news/shattering-the-scientific-worlds-history-of-gendered-brain-assumptions.

Brecht, Martin. *Martin Luther: His Road to Reformation 1483–1521.* Vol. 1 of *Martin Luther.* Translated by James L. Schaaf. Philadelphia: Fortress, 1985.

Briggs, John C. "Bacon's Science and Religion." Pages 172–99 in *The Cambridge Companion to Bacon.* Edited by Markku Peltonen. Cambridge: Cambridge University Press, 1996.

Brueggemann, Walter. *Chosen?: Reading the Bible amid the Israeli-Palestinian Conflict.* Louisville: Westminster John Knox, 2015.

———. *Theology of the Old Testament: Testimony, Dispute, Advocacy.* Minneapolis: Fortress, 1997.

Bultmann, Christoph. "Das Wittenberger christlich-jüdische Kontrovergespräch 1526 und Luthers Betrachtung der Juden. Bemerkungen im Anschluss an die Orientierung zum Reformationsjubiläum 'Die Reformation und die Juden.' 2014." Pages 143–95 in *Religionen in Bewegung: Interreligiöse Beziehungen im Wandel der Zeit.* Edited by Michael Gabel et al. VIFRUF. Münster: Aschendorff, 2016.

Burk, Denny, and Heath Lambert. *Transforming Homosexuality: What the Bible Says about Sexual Orientation and Change.* Phillipsburg, N.J.: P&R, 2015.

Burston, Bradley. "This Is Zionism as Racism. This Is Israel at 70." *Haaretz*, April 4, 2018. https://www.haaretz.com/opinion/.premium-this-is-zionism-as-racism-this-is-israel-at-70–1.5975641.

Byrne, Alex. "Is Sex Binary?" ARC Digital, November 1, 2018. https://arcdigital.media/is-sex-binary-16bec97d161e.

Callahan, Daniel. "Reason, Self-Determination, and Physician-Assisted Suicide." Pages 52–68 in *The Case against Assisted Suicide: For the Right to End-Of-Life Care.* Edited by Kathleen M. Foley and Herbert Hendin. Baltimore: Johns Hopkins University Press, 2002.

Calvin, John. *Commentaries on the First Book of Moses Called Genesis.* CalC 1. Edited and translated by John King. London: Calvin Translation Society, 1847. Repr., Grand Rapids: Baker, 1981.

———. *Epistle of Paul the Apostle to the Romans and to the Thessalonians.* CalC 8. Edited by David W. Torrance and Thomas F. Torrance. Translated by Ross Mackenzie. Edinburgh: Oliver and Boyd, 1961.

———. *Institutes of the Christian Religion.* Edited by John T. McNeill. Translated by Ford L. Battles. Louisville: Westminster John Knox, 2011.

Cameron, Averil. "Constantine and the 'Peace of the Church.'" Pages 538–51 in Mitchell, Young, and Bowie, *Origins to Constantine.*

Campbell River School District. "SOGI 123." https://www.sd72.bc.ca/studentsparents/SOGI-123/Pages/default.aspx.

Cantor, James. "Do Trans-Kids Stay Trans- When They Grow Up?" Sexology Today, January 11, 2016. http://www.sexologytoday.org/2016/01/do-trans-kids-stay-trans-when-they-grow_99.html.

Capp, Bernard S. *The Fifth Monarchy Men: A Study in Seventeenth-Century English Millenarianism.* London: Faber and Faber, 1972.

Carlin, Norah. *The Causes of the English Civil War.* HASt. Oxford: Blackwell, 1999.

———. "Toleration for Catholics in the Puritan Revolution." Pages 216–30 in *Tolerance and Intolerance in the European Reformation.* Edited by Ole Peter Grell and Bob Scribner. Cambridge: Cambridge University Press, 1996.

Carpenter, Eugene E. "Deuteronomy." Pages 418–547 in *ZIBBC* 1.

Carson, Donald A., ed. *From Sabbath to Lord's Day: A Biblical, Historical and Theological Investigation.* Grand Rapids: Zondervan, 1982.

Cassella, Carley. "Here's More Evidence Sexual Orientation Is Fluid Right into Our Adult Years." Science Alert, May 5, 2019, https://www.sciencealert.com/sexual-orientation-continues-to-change-right-through-our-teens-and-into-adulthood.

Catholic Church. "Suicide." In the *Catechism of the Catholic Church.* 2nd ed. Vatican: Libreria Editrice Vaticana, 2012. §2280.

Chance, Nynia. "Biblical Abortion: A Christian's View." Rewire.News, June 3, 2012. https://rewire.news/article/2012/06/03/biblical-abortion-christians-view-1.

Chazan, Robert. "Philosemitic Tendencies in Medieval Western Christendom." Pages 29–48 in Karp and Sutcliffe, *Philosemitism in History*.

Cherry, Kendra. "How Experience Changes Brain Plasticity." Verywell Mind, updated June 26, 2019. https://www.verywellmind.com/what-is-brain-plasticity-2794886.

CIRA. "2019 Canada's Internet Factbook." https://cira.ca/resources/corporate/factbook/canadas-internet-factbook-2019.

Clarysse, Willy, Sofie Remijsen, and Mark Depauw. "Observing the Sabbath in the Roman Empire: A Case Study." *SCI* 29 (2010): 51–57.

Coakley, Sarah. *God, Sexuality, and the Self: An Essay "On the Trinity."* Cambridge: Cambridge University Press, 2013.

Coffey, John, and Paul C. H. Lim, eds. *The Cambridge Companion to Puritanism*. Cambridge: Cambridge University Press, 2008.

Cohen, Shaye J. D. *The Beginnings of Jewishness: Boundaries, Varieties, Uncertainties*. Berkeley: University of California Press, 1999.

Cohen-Almagor, Raphael. "Euthanizing People Who Are 'Tired of Life.'" Pages 188–201 in *Euthanasia and Assisted Suicide: Lessons from Belgium*. Edited by David A. Jones et al. Cambridge Bioethics and Law. Cambridge: Cambridge University Press, 2017.

Cohn, Norman. *Europe's Inner Demons: The Demonization of Christians in Medieval Christendom*. Rev. ed. London: Pimlico, 1993.

———. *The Pursuit of the Millennium: Revolutionary Millenarians and Mystical Anarchists of the Middle Ages*. Oxford: Oxford University Press, 1970.

Coleman, Diane, "Not Dead Yet." Pages 213–37 in *The Case against Assisted Suicide: For the Right to End-Of-Life Care*. Edited by Kathleen M. Foley and Herbert Hendin. Baltimore: Johns Hopkins University Press, 2002.

Collins, John J. *What Are Biblical Values?: What the Bible Says on Key Ethical Issues*. New Haven: Yale University Press, 2019.

Constable, Giles. "Resistance to Tithes in the Middle Ages." *JEH* 13 (1962): 172–85.

"Consanguinity." Genetics Education Canada Knowledge Organization. https://geneticseducation.ca/educational-resources/gec-ko-on-the-run/consanguinity/.

Cook, Michael. "Can Sexual Orientation Change? Yes, according to a New Study." MercatorNet, August 21, 2018. https://www.mercatornet.com/conjugality/view/can-sexual-orientation-change-yes-according-to-a-new-study/21629.

———. "Dutch Doctor Acquitted of Unlawful Euthanasia." BioEdge, September 15, 2019. https://www.bioedge.org/bioethics/dutch-doctor-acquitted-of-unlawful-euthanasia/13218.

———. "Farewell to the 'Gay Gene' Theory." BioEdge, September 1, 2019, https://www.bioedge.org/bioethics/farewell-to-the-gay-gene-theory/13200

———. "4-Year-Old Can Begin Transgender Transition, Says UK Court." BioEdge, May 19, 2019. https://www.bioedge.org/bioethics/4-year-old-can-begin-transgender-transition-says-uk-court/13063.

———. "US Study Says Assisted Suicide Laws Rife with Dangers to People with Disabilities." BioEdge, October 13, 2019. https://www.bioedge.org/bioethics/us -study-saysassisted-suicide-laws-rife-with-dangers-to-people-with-disabil/13245.

Coward, Barry. *The Cromwellian Protectorate.* New Frontiers in History. Manchester: Manchester University Press, 2002.

Craig, John. "The Growth of English Puritanism." Pages 34–47 in Coffey and Lim, *Cambridge Companion to Puritanism.*

Cretella, Michelle. "I'm a Pediatrician. How Transgender Ideology Has Infiltrated My Field and Produced Large-Scale Child Abuse." Intellectual Takeout, July 5, 2017, https://www.intellectualtakeout.org/article/im-pediatrician-how-transgender -ideology-has-infiltrated-my-field-and-produced-large-scale.

Crome, Andrew. *Christian Zionism and English National Identity, 1600–1850.* CTAW. Cham: Palgrave Macmillan, 2018.

Cross, F. L., and E. A. Livingstone, eds. *The Oxford Dictionary of the Christian Church.* 3rd ed. Oxford: Oxford University Press, 2005.

Crouse, Eric Robert. *American Christian Support for Israel: Standing with the Chosen People, 1948–1975.* Lanham: Lexington Books, 2015.

Cummings, Nicholas A. "Sexual Reorientation Therapy Not Unethical." *USA Today,* July 30, 2013. https://www.usatoday.com/story/opinion/2013/07/30/sexual -reorientation-therapy-not-unethicalcolumn/2601159.

Czock, Miriam. "Creating Futures through the Lens of Revelation in the Rhetoric of the Carolingian Reform ca. 750 to ca. 900." Pages 101–19 in *Apocalypse and Reform from Late Antiquity to the Middle Ages.* Edited by Matthew Gabriele and James T. Palmer. London: Routledge, 2019.

Damgaard, Fin. "Propaganda against Propaganda: Revisiting Eusebius' Use of the Figure of Moses in the *Life of Constantine.*" Pages 115–32 in *Eusebius of Caesarea: Tradition and Innovations.* Edited by Aaron Johnson and Jeremy Schott. HS. Cambridge, Mass.: Harvard University Press, 2013.

Dastagir, Alia E. "Are You a Good Person? Morality Experts Say This Is How to Find Out." *USA Today,* December 21, 2018. https://www.usatoday.com/story/news/ 2017/12/26/you-good-person/967459001/.

De Vries, Annelou L. C., et al. "Puberty Suppression in Adolescents with Gender Identity Disorder: A Prospective Follow-Up Study." *Journal of Sexual Medicine* 8, no. 8 (2011): 2276–83.

Dempster, Stephen G. "Canon and Old Testament Interpretation." Pages 154–79 in *Hearing the Old Testament: Listening for God's Address.* Edited by Craig G. Bartholomew and David J. H. Beldman. Grand Rapids: Eerdmans, 2012.

Diamond, Lisa M., and Clifford J. Rosky. "Scrutinizing Immutability: Research on Sexual Orientation and U.S. Legal Advocacy for Sexual Minorities." *Journal of Sex Research* 53, nos. 4–5 (2016): 363–91.

Doherty, Sean. "'Love Does Not Delight in Evil but Rejoices with the Truth': A Theological and Pastoral Reflection on My Journey away from a Homosexual Identity." *Anvil* 30 (2014): 5–16.

Dreher, Ron. "Amazon.com Surrenders to the Homintern." *The American Conservative*, July 3, 2019, https://www.theamericanconservative.com/dreher/amazon-com-homintern-joseph-goebbels-joseph-nicolosi-reparative-therapy/.

Dülmen, Richard van. *Das Täuferreich Zu Münster, 1534–1535: Berichte U. Dokumente.* Wissenschaftliche Reihe, 4150. München: Deutscher Taschenbuch Verlag, 1974.

Dunn, James D. G. *Romans 1–8.* WBC 38A. Dallas: Word, 1988.

———. *Romans 9–16.* WBC 38B. Dallas: Word, 1988.

Earle, Alice M. *The Sabbath in Puritan New England.* New York: Scribner's Sons, 1891.

Eberl, Jason T. "I Am My Brother's Keeper: Communitarian Obligations to the Dying Person." *Christian Bioethics* 24 (2018): 38–58.

Eire, Carlos M. N. *Reformations: The Early Modern World, 1450–1650.* New Haven: Yale University Press, 2016.

Ellingson, Ter. *The Myth of the Noble Savage.* Berkeley: University of California Press, 2001.

Elliott, David. "Institutionalizing Inequality: The Physical Criterion of Assisted Suicide." *Christian Bioethics* 24 (2018): 17–37.

Entwistle, Kirsty. "An Open Letter to Dr. Polly Carmichael from a Former GIDS Clinician." Medium. https://medium.com/@kirstyentwistle/an-open-letter-to-dr-polly-carmichael-from-a-former-gids-clinician-53c541276b8d.

Fausto-Sterling, Ann. "Why Sex Is Not Binary." *New York Times*, October 25, 2018. https://www.nytimes.com/2018/10/25/opinion/sex-biology-binary.html.

Federman, Joseph. "Palestinian-Only Buses Set Off Uproar in Israel." Associated Press, March 4, 2013. https://www.apnews.com/f3c61de8ff7f4299a1c983f26263ae96.

Fernando, Suman. "Connections." *Openmind* 153 (2008): 16–17.

Fichtenau, Heinrich. *The Carolingian Empire.* MART 1. Toronto: University of Toronto Press, 1978.

Firestone, Lisa. "Changing Your Sense of Identity: Five Powerful Actions We Can Take to Challenge Our Negative Self-Perception." *Psychology Today*, December 4, 2017. https://www.psychologytoday.com/us/blog/compassion-matters/201712/changing-your-sense-identity.

Fischer, Barbara, and Thomas C. Fox. "Lessing's Life and Work." Pages 13–40 in *A Companion to the Works of Gotthold Ephraim Lessing.* Edited by Barbara Fischer and Thomas C. Fox. Rochester, N.Y.: Camden House, 2005.

Fitzpatrick, Kevin, and David A. Jones. "A Life Worth Living? Disabled People and Euthanasia in Belgium." Pages 133–49 in *Euthanasia and Assisted Suicide: Lessons from Belgium.* Edited by David A. Jones et al. Cambridge Bioethics and Law. Cambridge: Cambridge University Press, 2017.

Focus on the Family. "Do People Change from Homosexuality? Hundreds of Stories of Hope and Transformation (Part I)." https://www.focusonthefamily.com/ socialissues/sexuality/freedom-from-homosexuality/do-people-change-from -homosexuality-hundreds-of-stories-of-hope-and-transformation-part-1.

Foley, Kathleen M. "Compassionate Care, Not Assisted Suicide." Pages 293–309 in *The Case against Assisted Suicide: For the Right to End-Of-Life Care.* Edited by Kathleen M. Foley and Herbert Hendin. Baltimore: Johns Hopkins University Press, 2002.

Foley, Kathleen M., and Herbert Hendin, eds. *The Case against Assisted Suicide: For the Right to End-Of-Life Care.* Baltimore: Johns Hopkins University Press, 2002.

Foster, Michael B. "The Christian Doctrine of Creation and the Rise of Modern Natural Science." *Mind* 43 (1934): 446–68.

Fouracre, Paul. "Frankish Gaul to 814." Pages 85–109 in *New Cambridge Medieval History.* Vol. 2: *C. 700–C. 900.* Edited by Rosamond McKitterick. Cambridge: Cambridge University Press, 1995.

Freedman, David Noel, ed. *Anchor Bible Dictionary.* New York: Doubleday, 1992.

Freeman, Ann. "Theodulf of Orleans and the *Libri Carolini.*" *Spec* 32 (1957): 663–705.

Frymer-Kensky, Tikva. *Studies in Bible and Feminist Criticism.* JPSSDS. Philadelphia: Jewish Publication Society, 2006.

Fuller, Russell T. "Exodus 21:22–23: The Miscarriage Interpretation and the Personhood of the Fetus." *JETS* 37 (1994): 169–84.

Gane, Roy E. "Leviticus." Pages 284–337 in *ZIBBC* 1.

Gates, Henry Louis, Jr., ed. *Lincoln on Race and Slavery.* Princeton: Princeton University Press, 2009.

Gay, Craig M. *The Way of the (Modern) World: Or, Why It's Tempting to Live as if God Doesn't Exist.* Grand Rapids: Eerdmans, 1998.

General Association of Massachusetts. *Minutes of the General Association of Massachusetts. At Their Meeting at North Brookfield, June 26, 1837. With the Narrative of the State of Religion, and the Pastoral Letter.* Boston: Crocker & Brewster, 1987.

George, Robert P., and Christopher Tollefsen. *Embryo: A Defense of Human Life.* New York: Doubleday, 2008.

Gittos, Luke. "Misgendering Is Not a Crime." Spiked, March 25, 2019, https://www .spiked-online.com/2019/03/25/misgendering-is-not-a-crime/.

Godwin, Richard. "One Giant ... Lie? Why So Many People Still Think the Moon Landings Were Faked." *The Guardian,* July 10, 2019. https://www.theguardian .com/science/2019/jul/10/one-giant-lie-why-so-many-people-still-think-the-moon -landings-were-faked.

Goertz, Hans-Jürgen. *The Anabaptists.* 2nd ed. Translated by Trevor Johnson. London: Routledge, 1996.

Goldenberg, David M. *The Curse of Ham: Race and Slavery in Early Judaism, Christianity, and Islam.* Princeton: Princeton University Press, 2009.

Goodfriend, E. A. "Adultery." Pages 82–85 in *ABD* 1.

Gorski, Philip S. *American Covenant: A History of Civil Religion from the Puritans to the Present*. Princeton: Princeton University Press, 2017.

Gouges, Olympe de. "Declaration of the Rights of Woman and the Female Citizen." Pages 155–57 in *Feminist Writings from Ancient Times to the Modern World*. Vol. 1. Edited by Tiffany K. Wayne. Santa Barbara, Calif.: Greenwood, 2011.

Government of Canada. "About Family Violence." Department of Justice. https://www.justice.gc.ca/eng/cj-jp/fv-vf/about-apropos.html.

Government of Ontario. "Affirming Sexual Orientation and Gender Identity Act," Government of Ontario, 2015, https://www.ontario.ca/laws/statute/S15018.

Grant, Ruth W., ed. *In Search of Goodness*. Chicago: University of Chicago Press, 2011.

Gray, Stephanie. "What Do Rape Victims Say about Their Pregnancies?" Love Unleashes Life, November 6, 2017. https://loveunleasheslife.com/blog/2017/11/6/what-do-rape-victims-say-about-their-pregnancies-by-stephanie-gray.

Greasley, Kate, and Christopher Kaczor. *Abortion Rights: For and Against*. Cambridge: Cambridge University Press, 2017.

Greenslade, S. L. *Church & State from Constantine to Theodosius*. 1953 F. D. Maurice Lectures. London: SCM Press, 1954.

Grimké, Angelina E. *An Appeal to the Christian Women of the South*. New York: American Anti-Slavery Society, 1836. http://utc.iath.virginia.edu/abolitn/abesaegat.html.

———. *Appeal to the Women of the Nominally Free States Issued by an Anti-Slavery Convention of American Women*. Boston: Isaac Knapp, 1837.

———. "Slavery and the Boston Riot." 1835. https://www.loc.gov/resource/rbpe.05601500/.

Grimké, Sarah M. *Letters on the Equality of the Sexes and the Condition of Woman*. Boston: Knapp, 1838.

Giubilini, Alberto, and Francesca Minerva. "After-Birth Abortion: Why Should the Baby Live?" *Journal of Medical Ethics* 39 (2013): 261–63.

Hanchett, Jim. "Polls Suggest Less Environmentalism among U.S. Christians." Futurity, February 1, 2018. https://www.futurity.org/christians-environment-opinion-1670122./.

Hartog, Paul A. "Constantine, Sabbath-Keeping, and Sunday Observance." Pages 105–29 in *Rethinking Constantine: History, Theology, and Legacy*. Edited by Edward L. Smither. Eugene, Ore: Wipf & Stock, 2014.

Haude, Sigrun. *In the Shadow of "Savage Wolves": Anabaptist Münster and the German Reformation during the 1530s*. SCEH 20. Boston: Humanities, 2000.

Haynes, Stephen R. *Noah's Curse: The Biblical Justification of American Slavery*. Oxford: Oxford University, 2002.

Hazard, Paul. *The European Mind (1680–1715)*. London: Hollis and Carter: 1953.

Hendin, Herbert. "The Dutch Experience." Pages 97–121 in Foley and Hendin, *The Case against Assisted Suicide*.

Herman, Arthur. *How the Scots Invented the Modern World: The True Story of How Western Europe's Poorest Nation Created Our World and Everything in It.* New York: Three Rivers, 2002.

Herrin, Judith. *The Formation of Christendom.* Princeton: Princeton University Press, 1987.

Heyer, Walt. "Hormones, Surgery, Regret." *USA Today,* February 11, 2019. https://www.usatoday.com/story/opinion/voices/2019/02/11/transgender-debate-transitioning-sex-gender-column/1894076002/.

Hill, Amelia. "Over a Third of Britons Admit Ageist Behaviour in New Study." *The Guardian,* August 19, 2019. https://www.theguardian.com/society/2019/aug/19/over-a-third-of-britons-admit-ageist-behaviour-in-new-study.

Hill, Wesley. *Washed and Waiting: Reflections on Christian Faithfulness and Homosexuality.* Grand Rapids: Zondervan, 2010.

Holt, Flora Lu. "The Catch-22 of Conservation: Indigenous Peoples, Biologists, and Cultural Change." *HE* 33 (2005): 199–215.

Holton, Gerald. "Johannes Kepler's Universe: Its Physics and Metaphysics." *AJP* 24 (1956): 340–51.

Hruz, W., Lawrence S. Mayer, and Paul R. McHugh. "Growing Pains: Problems with Puberty Suppression in Treating Gender Dysphoria." *The New Atlantis* 52 (2017): 3–36.

Hughes, Philip E., trans. and ed. *The Register of the Company of Pastors of Geneva in the Time of Calvin.* Grand Rapids: Eerdmans, 1966.

Hui, Edwin C. "Personhood and Bioethics." Pages 1–15 in *Questions of Right and Wrong: Proceedings of the 1993 Clinical Bioethics Conference.* Edited by Edwin C. Hui. Vancouver: Regent College, 1994.

Hume, David. *Treatise of Human Nature: Reprinted from the Original Edition in Three Volumes.* Edited by L. A. Selby-Bigge. Repr., Oxford: Clarendon, 1960.

Hunt, Lynn, ed. *The French Revolution and Human Rights: A Brief Documentary History.* Boston: Bedford; New York: St. Martin's, 1996.

Hutchison, William R., and Hartmut Lehmann, eds. *Many Are Chosen: Divine Election and Western Nationalism.* HTS 38. Minneapolis: Fortress, 1994.

Irenaeus. *Proof of the Apostolic Preaching.* Translated by Joseph P. Smith. ACW 16. New York: Newman, 1952.

Isaak, Helmut. *Menno Simons and the New Jerusalem.* Kitchener, Ont.: Pandora, 2006.

Jacobs, Tom. "TV Dramas Spur Support for Transgender Rights." *Pacific Standard,* August 15, 2017. https://psmag.com/social-justice/tv-dramas-spur-support-for-transgender-rights.

James, Trevor. "King James' Book of Sports, 1617." *Hist* 134 (2017): 42.

Journals of the Continental Congress, 1774–1789. Vol. 5. Edited by Worthington C. Ford et al. Washington, D.C.: Washington Government Printing Office, 1904–1937.

John Paul II, Pope. *Evangelium Vitae*. http://www.vatican.va/content/john-paul-ii/en/encyclicals/documents/hf_jp-ii_enc_25031995_evangelium-vitae.html.

Johnston, Neil. "The History of the Parliamentary Franchise." CBP:RP 13–14. https://researchbriefings.parliament.uk/ResearchBriefing/Summary/RP13–14.

Jones, David A., et al., eds. *Euthanasia and Assisted Suicide: Lessons from Belgium*. Cambridge Bioethics and Law. Cambridge: Cambridge University Press, 2017.

Jones, Stanton L., and Mark A. Yarhouse. "A Longitudinal Study of Attempted Religiously Mediated Sexual Orientation Change." *Journal of Sex and Marital Therapy* 37, no. 5 (2011): 404–27.

Josephus. *The Works of Flavius Josephus*. Translated by William Whiston. Philadelphia: Jas. B. Smith & Co., 1854.

Kahn, Leonard. "Is There an Obligation to Abort? Act Utilitarianism and the Ethics of Procreation." *Essays in Philosophy* 20, no.1 (2019).

Kaiser, Menachem. "For Some Believers Trying to Connect with Jesus, the Answer Is to Live Like a Jew." Tablet, February 4, 2014. https://www.tabletmag.com/jewish-life-and-religion/161086/observing-torah-like-jesus.

Karp, Jonathan, and Adam Sutcliffe, eds. *Philosemitism in History*. Cambridge: Cambridge University Press, 2011.

Karten, Elan Y., and Jay C. Wade. "Sexual Orientation Change Efforts in Men: A Client Perspective." *The Journal of Men's Studies* 18 (2010): 84–102.

Kass, Leon R. *The Beginning of Wisdom: Reading Genesis*. New York: Free Press, 2003.

———. "I Will Give No Deadly Drug: Why Doctors Must Not Kill." Pages 17–40 in Foley and Hendin, *The Case against Assisted Suicide*.

Kay, Barbara. "Ontario Family Files Human Rights Complaint after Six-Year-Old Girl Upset by Gender Theory in School." Barbara Kay, June 17, 2019. http://www.barbarakay.ca/articles/view/1414.

Kay, Charles E. "Are Ecosystems Structured from the Top-Down or Bottom-Up?" Pages 215–37 in Kay and Simmons, *Wilderness and Political Ecology*.

Kay, Charles E., and Randy T. Simmons, eds. *Wilderness and Political Ecology: Aboriginal Influences and the Original State of Nature*. Salt Lake City: University of Utah Press, 2002.

Kearns, Madeleine. "Gender Dissenter Gets Fired." *National Review*, July 12, 2019. https://www.nationalreview.com/2019/07/allen-josephson-gender-dissenter-gets-fired/.

Kennedy, D. E. *The English Revolution 1642–1649*. BHP. Basingstoke: Macmillan, 2000.

Kirkey, Sharon. "Puberty Blockers, Cross-Sex Hormones: Canada's Family Doctors Get Guidance on Treating Youth with 'Gender Dysphoria.'" *National Post*, January 31, 2019. https://nationalpost.com/news/puberty-blockers-cross-sex-hormones-canadas-family-doctors-get-guidance-on-treating-youth-with-gender-dysphoria.

Kostamo, Leah. *Planted: A Story of Creation, Calling, and Community*. Eugene, Ore.: Wipf & Stock, 2013.

Koziol, Geoffrey. "Christianizing Political Discourses." Pages 473–89 in *Oxford Handbook*.

Kraft, Michael E., and Norman Vig. "Environmental Policy in the Reagan Presidency." *PSQ* 99 (1984): 415–39.

Kselman, Thomas. "Religion and French Identity: The Origins of the *Union Sacreé*." Pages 57–79 in Hutchison and Lehmann, *Many Are Chosen*.

Kumar, Pushpam, and Makiko Yashiro. "The Marginal Poor and Their Dependence on Ecosystem Services: Evidence from South Asia and Sub-Saharan Africa." Pages 169–80 in *Marginality: Addressing the Nexus of Poverty, Exclusion, and Ecology*. Edited by Joachim von Braun and Franz W. Gatzweiler. Dordrecht: Springer, 2014.

Lambert, Wilfred G. "Kingship in Ancient Mesopotamia." Pages 54–71 in *King and Messiah in Israel and the Ancient Near East: Proceedings of the Oxford Old Testament Seminar*. Edited by John Day. London: T&T Clark, 2013.

Lane, William L. *Hebrews 1–8*. WBC 47A. Dallas: Word, 1991.

Langan, John. "The Elements of St. Augustine's Just War Theory." *JRE* 12 (1984): 19–38.

LaSala, Michael C. "Sexual Orientation: Is It Unchangeable?" *Psychology Today*, May 17, 2011. https://www.psychologytoday.com/ca/blog/gay-and-lesbian-well-being/201105/sexual-orientation-is-it-unchangeable.

Laursen, John C. "Introduction: Contexts and Paths to Toleration in the Seventeenth Century." Pages 169–77 in *Beyond the Persecuting Society: Religious Toleration before the Enlightenment*. Edited by John Laursen and Cary Nederman. Philadelphia: University of Pennsylvania Press, 1998.

Leithart, Peter. *Defending Constantine: The Twilight of an Empire and the Dawn of Christendom*. Downers Grove, Ill.: IVP, 2010.

———. "What Are Biblical Values?" *First Things*, July 19, 2019. https://www.firstthings.com/web-exclusives/2019/07/what-are-biblical-values.

Leiva, Rene, et al. "Euthanasia in Canada: A Cautionary Tale." *World Medical Journal* 64 (2018): 17–23.

Lerner, Robert E. *The Heresy of the Free Spirit in the Later Middle Ages*. Berkeley: University of California Press, 1972.

Lessing, Doris. *Prisons We Choose to Live Inside*. Toronto: CBC Enterprises, 1986. Repr., Toronto, Anansi, 2006.

Levine, Stephen B. "Informed Consent for Transgendered Patients." *Journal of Sex and Marital Therapy* 45 (2019): 218–29.

Lewis, C. S. *The Abolition of Man: Or, Reflections on Education with Special Reference to the Teaching of English in the Upper Forms of Schools*. London: Oxford University Press, H. Milford, 1943.

———. *Mere Christianity*. New York: Harper Collins, 1952.

Lewis, Donald M. *The Origins of Christian Zionism: Lord Shaftesbury and the Evangelical Support for a Jewish Homeland*. Cambridge: Cambridge University Press, 2010.

Lichtenstein, Dhejne C., et al. "Long-Term Follow-Up of Transsexual Persons Undergoing Sex Reassignment Surgery: Cohort Study in Sweden." *PLoS ONE* 6, no. 2 (2011): e16885, https://doi.org/10.1371/journal.pone.0016885.

Lincoln, Andrew T. *Ephesians*. WBC 42. Dallas: Word, 1990.

Linder, Amnon. "The Legal Status of the Jews in the Roman Empire." Pages 128–73 in *The Cambridge History of Judaism*. Vol. 4: *Late Roman-Rabbinic Period*. Edited by Steven T. Katz. Cambridge: Cambridge University Press, 2006.

Little, Ann M. *Abraham in Arms: War and Gender in Colonial New England*. Philadelphia: University of Pennsylvania Press, 2011.

Littman, Lisa. "Rapid Onset Gender Dysphoria in Adolescents and Young Adults: A Study of Parental Reports." *PLoS ONE* 13, no. 8 (2018): e0202330. https://doi.org/10.1371/journal.pone.0202330.

Lockwood, Sally. "'Hundreds' of Young Trans People Seeking Help to Return to Original Sex." Sky News, October 5, 2019. https://news.sky.com/story/hundreds-of-young-trans-people-seeking-help-to-return-to-original-sex-11827740.

Longenecker, Richard N. *New Testament Social Ethics for Today*. Grand Rapids: Eerdmans, 1984.

Loomie, Albert J. "Oliver Cromwell's Policy toward the English Catholics: The Appraisal by Diplomats, 1654–1658." *CHR* 90 (2004): 29–44.

Low, Bobbi S. "Behavioral Ecology of Conservation in Traditional Societies." *HN* 7 (1996): 353–79.

Lowance, Mason I., Jr. *The Language of Canaan: Metaphor and Symbol in New England from the Puritans to the Transcendentalists*. Cambridge, Mass.: Harvard University Press, 1980.

Lowenthal, David. *George Perkins Marsh: Prophet of Conservation*. Seattle: University of Washington Press, 2000.

Luther, Martin. *That Jesus Christ Was Born a Jew*. 1523. In *Luther's Works 45: The Christian in Society II*. Edited by Walther I. Brandt. Philadelphia: Fortress, 1962.

Lutz, Donald S., ed. *Colonial Origins of the American Constitution: A Documentary History*. Indianapolis: Liberty Fund, 1998.

MacGregor, Kirk R. "Nonviolence in the Ancient Church and Christian Obedience." *Them* 33 (2008): 16–28.

Maltz, Judy. "Inside the Evangelical Money Flowing into the West Bank." *Haaretz*, December 9, 2018. https://www.haaretz.com/israel-news/.premium.MAGAZINE-inside-the-evangelical-money-flowing-into-the-west-bank-1.6723443.

Manetsch, Scott M. *Calvin's Company of Pastors: Pastoral Care and the Emerging Reformed Church, 1536–1609*. OSHT. Oxford: Oxford University Press, 2013.

Marsden, Paul. "Memetics and Social Contagion: Two Sides of the Same Coin?" *Journal of Memetics: Evolutionary Models of Information Transmission* 2 (1998): 171–85.

Martin, Paul S., and Christine R. Szuter. "Revising the 'Wild West': Big Game Meets the Ultimate Keystone Species." Pages 63–88 in *Archaeology of Global Change: The Impact of Humans on their Environment*. Edited by Charles L. Redman et al. Washington, D.C.: Smithsonian Books, 2004.

Mather, Cotton. *Soldiers Counseled and Comforted: A Discourse Delivered unto Some Part of the Forces Engaged in the Just War of New England against the Northern and Eastern Indians*. Boston: Samuel Green, 1689.

McCormick, Michael. *Charlemagne's Survey of the Holy Land: Wealth, Personnel, and Buildings of a Mediterranean Church between Antiquity and the Middle Ages: With a Critical Edition and Translation of the Original Text*. Washington, D.C.: Dumbarton Oaks Research Library and Collection, 2011.

Melamed, Abraham. "The Revival of Christian Hebraism in Early Modern Europe." Pages 49–66 in Karp and Sutcliffe, *Philosemitism in History*.

Mendes-Flohr, Paul. "In Pursuit of Normalcy: Zionism's Ambivalence toward Israel's Election." Pages 203–24 in Hutchison and Lehmann, *Many Are Chosen*.

Messinger, Kathleen. "Death with Dignity for the Seemingly Undignified: Denial of Aid in Dying in Prison." *Journal of Criminal Law and Criminology* 109 (2019): 633–73.

Middleton, Paul. "Suicide in the Bible." Bible Odyssey. https://www.bibleodyssey.org:443/en/people/related-articles/suicide-in-the-bible.

Mitchell, M. M., F. M. Young, and K. S. Bowie, eds. *Origins to Constantine*. Cambridge History of Christianity. Vol. 1. Cambridge: Cambridge University Press, 2006.

Moo, Douglas J., and Jonathan A. Moo. *Creation Care: A Biblical Theology of the Natural World*. Biblical Theology for Life. Grand Rapids: Zondervan, 2018.

Moore, Eva, Amy Wisniewski, and Adrian Dobs. "Endocrine Treatment of Transsexual People: A Review of Treatment Regimens, Outcomes, and Adverse Effects." *Journal of Clinical Endocrinology and Metabolism* 88 (2003): 3467–73.

The Moral Maze. BBC. https://www.bbc.co.uk/programmes/b006qk11.

"The Moral Maze." Wikipedia. https://en.wikipedia.org/wiki/The_Moral_Maze.

Morgan, Jonathan. "Is Identity Fixed?" *Change Writer*. http://changewriter.net/is-identity-fixed/.

Morrill, John. "The Puritan Revolution." Pages 67–88 in Coffey and Lim, *Cambridge Companion to Puritanism*.

Mousset, Sophie. *Women's Rights and the French Revolution*. New York: Routledge, 2007.

Mullett, Michael A. *John Calvin*. London: Routledge, 2011.

Murphy, Denis S.J. *Cromwell in Ireland: A History of Cromwell's Irish Campaign*. Dublin: Gill and Son, 1883.

Murphy, Mark. "The Natural Law Tradition in Ethics." In *Stanford Encyclopedia of Philosophy*. Winter 2011 online ed. Edited by Edward N. Zalta. https://plato .stanford.edu/archives/win2011/entries/natural-law-ethics.

Muzaffar, Moroosha. "Alien Beauty Invades World of Fashion." Ozy, July 18, 2019. https://www.ozy.com/fast-forward/alien-beauty-invades-world-of-fashion/95394.

Naham, Matt. "Feminist Writer Sues Twitter after She Tweets 'Men Aren't Women' and Gets Banned." Law and Crime, February 12, 2019, https://lawandcrime.com/ lawsuit/feminist-writer-sues-twitter-after-she-tweets-men-arent-woman-and-gets -banned/.

Naphy, William G. *Calvin and the Consolidation of the Genevan Reformation*. Manchester: Manchester University Press, 1994.

NASA. "Climate Change: How Do We Know?" Updated July 12, 2019. https://climate .nasa.gov/evidence/.

Nathanson, Bernard N. *The Hand of God: A Journey from Death to Life by the Abortion Doctor Who Changed His Mind*. Repr., Washington, D.C.: Regnery, 2013.

Natter, Ari. "Republicans Who Couldn't Beat Climate Debate Now Seek to Join It." *Bloomberg*, March 5, 2019. https://www.bloomberg.com/news/articles/2019-03 -05/republicans-who-couldn-t-beat-climate-debate-now-seek-to-join-it.

Nellis, Eric. *Shaping the New World: African Slavery in the Americas, 1500–1888*. ITI. Toronto: University of Toronto Press, 2013.

Nelson, Janet L. "Religion in the Age of Charlemagne." Pages 490–514 in *Oxford Handbook*.

Neumann, Thomas W. "The Role of Prehistoric Peoples in Shaping Ecosystems in the Eastern United States: Implications for Restoration Ecology and Wilderness Management." Pages 142–78 in Kay and Simmons, *Wilderness and Political Ecology*.

The Nicene and Post-Nicene Fathers, Series 1 and 2. Edited by Philip Schaff. 1886–1889. 28 vols. Repr., Peabody. Mass.: Hendrickson, 1994.

Nicolosi, Joseph. "APA Task Force Report—A Mockery of Science." https://www .josephnicolosi.com/apa-task-force/.

Nicolosi, Joseph, A. Dean Byrd, and Richard W. Potts. "Retrospective Self-Reports of Changes in Homosexual Orientation: A Consumer Survey of Conversion Therapy Clients." *Psychological Reports* 86 (2000): 1071–88.

Nova Scotia Legislature. Sexual Orientation and Gender Identity Protection Act of 2018. 2nd session, 63rd General Assembly. Ch. 28 of the Acts of 2018.

Nys, Herman. "A Discussion of the Legal Rules on Euthanasia in Belgium Briefly Compared with the Rules in Luxembourg and the Netherlands." Pages 7–25 in Jones et al., *Euthanasia and Assisted Suicide*.

O'Brien, Peter T. *Colossians, Philemon*. WBC 44. Dallas: Word, 1982.

O'Donovan, Oliver, and Joan Lockwood O'Donovan, eds. *From Irenaeus to Grotius: A Sourcebook in Christian Political Thought 100–1625*. Grand Rapids: Eerdmans, 1999.

O'Faolain, Julia, and Lauro Martines. *Not in God's Image: Women in History from the Greeks to the Victorians*. New York: Harper & Row, 1973.

Offen, Karen. *Debating the Woman Question in the French Third Republic, 1870–1920*. NSEH. Cambridge: Cambridge University Press, 2018.

———. *The Woman Question in France, 1400–1870*. NSEH. Cambridge: Cambridge University Press, 2017.

O'Keefe, John J., and Russell R. Reno. *Sanctified Vision: An Introduction to Early Christian Interpretation of the Bible*. Baltimore: Johns Hopkins University Press, 2005.

Ommundsen, Åslaug. "The Liberal Arts and the Polemic Strategy of the *Opus Caroli Regis Contra Synodum (Libri Carolini)*." *SO* 77 (2002): 175–200.

Orwell, George. *Nineteen Eighty-Four*. New York: Penguin, 2013.

Oyserman, Daphna, Kristen Elmore, and George Smith. "Self, Self-Concept, and Identity." Pages 69–104 in *Handbook of Self and Identity*. Edited by Mark R. Leary and June Price Tangney, 2nd ed. New York: Guilford, 2012.

Packer, George. "Doublethink Is Stronger than Orwell Imagined: What *1984* Means Today." *The Atlantic*, July 2019. https://www.theatlantic.com/magazine/archive/2019/07/1984-george-orwell/590638/.

Parker, Alison M. *Articulating Rights: Nineteenth-Century American Women on Race, Reform, and the State*. Dekalb: Northern Illinois University Press, 2010.

Parker, Michael. *John Winthrop: Founding the City upon a Hill*. New York: Routledge, 2014.

Parliament of Canada. An Act to Amend the Criminal Code (Conversion Therapy). 1st session, 42nd Parliament, 1st reading (April 9, 2019): S-260.

Parveen, Nazia. "Fatal Genetic Conditions More Common in Children of South Asian Heritage in West Yorkshire City, Study Says." *The Guardian*, February 15, 2019. https://www.theguardian.com/society/2019/feb/15/cousin-marriages-cited-as-significant-factor-bradford-child-deaths.

Paul, Ian. "Are We Born Straight or Gay?" *Psephizo*, October 2, 2019. https://www.psephizo.com/sexuality-2/are-we-born-straight-or-gay/?fbclid=IwAR1fNlQgadsUywLFKGIXFhqYEm45GPAl9jKO5tU_lBvNjeJgkjGwo2YcuQE.

Pellegrino, Edmund D. "Compassion Is Not Enough." Pages 41–51 in Foley and Hendin, *The Case against Assisted Suicide*.

Peplau, L. A., and L. D. Garnets. "A New Paradigm for Understanding Women's Sexuality and Sexual Orientation." *Journal of Social Issues* 56 (2000): 330–50.

Peterson, Eugene H. *A Long Obedience in the Same Direction: Discipleship in an Instant Society*. 2nd ed. Downers Grove, Ill.: IVP, 2000.

Peterson, Jordan. "Gender Politics Has No Place in the Classroom." *National Post*, June 21, 2019. https://nationalpost.com/opinion/jordan-peterson-gender-politics-has-no-place-in-the-classroom.

Philo. *Special Laws*. In *The Works of Philo*. Translated by C. D. Yonge. Peabody, Mass.: Hendrickson, 1993.

Pitcaithley, Dwight T., ed. *The U.S. Constitution and Secession: A Documentary Anthology of Slavery and White Supremacy*. Lawrence: University Press of Kansas, 2018.

Pliny the Younger. *Letters and Panegyrics*. Translated by Betty Radice. Vol. 2. LCL 59. London: Heinemann, 1969.

Pollitt, Katha. "6 Myths about Abortion." *Time*, November 13, 2014. https://time .com/3582434/6-abortion-myths.

"Pro-LGBT Coca-Cola Adverts Spark Boycott Calls in Hungary." *The Guardian*, August 5, 2019. https://www.theguardian.com/world/2019/aug/05/pro-lgbt-coca -cola-ads-spark-boycott-calls-in-hungary.

"Proclamation of Independence." The Knesset, 1948. https://www.knesset.gov.il/ docs/eng/megilat_eng.htm.

Provan, Iain. *1 and 2 Kings*. UBCS. Grand Rapids: Baker Books, 2012.

———. "2 Kings." Pages 151–53 in *ZIBBC* 3.

———. *Convenient Myths: The Axial Age, Dark Green Religion, and the World That Never Was*. Waco: Baylor University Press, 2013.

———. *Ecclesiastes and Song of Songs*. NIVAC. Grand Rapids: Zondervan, 2001.

———. "To Highlight All Our Idols: Worshipping God in Nietzsche's World." *ExAud* 15 (2000): 19–38.

———. *The Reformation and the Right Reading of Scripture*. Waco: Baylor University Press, 2017.

———. *Seriously Dangerous Religion: What the Old Testament Really Says and Why It Matters*. Waco: Baylor University Press, 2014.

Provan, Iain, V. Philips Long, and Tremper Longman III. *A Biblical History of Israel*. 2nd ed. Louisville: Westminster John Knox, 2015.

Quan, Douglas. "Legal Dispute between Trans Child and Father Takes New Turn over Freedom of Expression." *National Post*, April 30, 2019. https://nationalpost .com/news/canada/legal-dispute-between-trans-child-and-father-takes-new-turn -over-freedom-of-expression.

Quora. "Why Do We See Gay and Lesbian Characters in Almost All US Movies or TV Series?" https://www.quora.com/Why-do-we-see-gay-and-lesbian-characters -in-almost-all-US-movies-or-TV-series.

Rabkin, Yakov M. *What Is Modern Israel?* English ed. London: Pluto Press, 2016.

Racz, Elizabeth. "The Women's Rights Movement in the French Revolution." *SSoc* 16 (1952): 151–74.

Regnerus, Mark. "Does 'Conversion Therapy' Hurt People Who Identify as Transgender? The New *JAMA Psychiatry* Study Cannot Tell Us." *Public Discourse*, September 18, 2019. https://www.thepublicdiscourse.com/2019/09/57145/?fbclid= IwAR0BI7nbxroWWPwwDmIc-EIC1UwlOLLH06yl7GlgGAQr MtpYyRF8KMBCG9g.

Reno, R. R. "Empire of Desire: Outlining the Postmodern Metaphysical Dream." *First Things*, June 2014. https://www.firstthings.com/article/2014/06/empire-of -desire.

Reventlow, Henning G. *History of Biblical Interpretation*. Vol. 1: *From the Old Testament to Origen*. Translated by Leo Perdue. RBS 50. Atlanta: Society of Biblical Literature, 2009.

Rippon, Gina. *The Gendered Brain: The New Neuroscience that Shatters the Myth of the Female Brain*. London: Bodley Head, 2019.

Ritter, Adolf M. "Church and State up to *c*. 300 CE." Pages 524–37 in Mitchell, Young, and Bowie, *Origins to Constantine*.

Robbins, Jane. "The Cracks in the Edifice of Transgender Totalitarianism." *Public Discourse*. July 13, 2019. https://www.thepublicdiscourse.com/2019/07/54272/.

Roberts, Vaughan. *Transgender*. Good Book Company, 2016. Kindle edition.

Rosenwein, Barbara H., ed. *Reading the Middle Ages: Sources from Europe, Byzantium, and the Islamic World*. Toronto: University of Toronto Press, 2013.

Rousseau, Jean-Jacques. *The Social Contract*. Translated by Maurice Cranston. London; Penguin Books, 1968.

Rowe, Peter. "How a Girl Born at 2 Pounds Became a Happy Boy." *San Diego Union Tribune*, April 7, 2016. https://www.sandiegouniontribune.com/lifestyle/people/sdut-transgender-teens-new-life-2016apr07-story.html.

Rowland, Christopher. "A Summary of Sabbath Observance in Judaism at the Beginning of the Christian Era." Pages 44–55 in Carson, *Sabbath*.

Ruether, Rosemary Radford, and Herman J. Ruether. *The Wrath of Jonah: The Crisis of Religious Nationalism in the Israeli-Palestinian Conflict*. 2nd ed. Minneapolis: Fortress, 2002.

Rush, Benjamin. "Letter to Thomas Jefferson, August 22, 1800." Pages 820–21 in *Letters of Benjamin Rush*. Vol. 2. Edited by Lyman H. Butterfield. MAPS 30. Princeton: Princeton University Press, 1951.

Russell, Nicole. "Here's What People Who Used to Be Transgender Are Telling the Supreme Court." *The Federalist*, August 30, 2019. https://thefederalist.com/2019/08/30/heres-people-used-transgender-telling-supreme-court/.

Ruthven, Malise. *Islam: A Very Short Introduction*. New York: Oxford University Press, 1997.

Saleh, Naveed. "Body Integrity Identity Disorder." Verywell Mind, July 26, 2019. https://www.verywellmind.com/amputating-a-healthy-limb-1123848.

Santero, Paul L., Neil E. Whitehead, and Dolores Ballesteros. "Effects of Therapy on Religious Men Who Have Unwanted Same-Sex Attraction." *Linacre Quarterly*, July 23, 2018. DOI: 10.1177/0024363918788559.

Savulescu, Julian. "Conscientious Objection in Medicine." *BMJ (Clinical Research Ed.)* 332, no. 7536 (2006): 294–97.

Schadenberg, Alex. *Exposing Vulnerable People to Euthanasia and Assisted Suicide*. Brisbane: Connor Court, 2014.

Schaeffer, Francis A. *Pollution and the Death of Man: The Christian View of Ecology*. Wheaton, Ill.: Tyndale House, 1970.

Schafer, Peter. *The History of the Jews in the Greco-Roman World: The Jews of Palestine from Alexander the Great to the Arab Conquest*. London: Routledge, 2003.

Schmidt, Thomas E. *Straight and Narrow? Compassion & Clarity in the Homosexuality Debate*. Downers Grove, Ill.: IVP, 1995.

Schramm, Brooks, and Kirsi I. Stjerna, eds. *Martin Luther, the Bible, and the Jewish People*. Minneapolis: Fortress, 2012.

Schreiner, Thomas R. "Paul and Gender: A Review Article." *Them* 43 (2018): 178–92.

Schwartz, Mel. "Who Am I?" *Psychology Today*, June 20, 2010. https://www.psychology today.com/ca/blog/shift-mind/201006/who-am-i.

Scofield, Cyrus I. *Scofield Bible Correspondence Course*. Chicago: Moody Bible Institute, n.d.

Scott, S. P., ed. *The Civil Law: Including the Twelve Tables, the Institutes of Gaius, the Rules of Ulpian, the Opinions of Paulus, the Enactments of Justinian, and the Constitutions of Leo*. Vol. 12. Cincinnati: Central Trust, 1932.

Scruton, Roger. "The Failure to Stand Up for Conservative Thinking Is Leading Us into a New Cultural Dark Age." *The Telegraph*, July 20, 2019. https://www .rogerscruton.com/articles/20-latest/619-the-telegraph-20th-july-19.

Seiler, Linda. "Becoming the Woman God Made Me to Be." Focus on the Family, December 6, 2019. https://www.focusonthefamily.com/media/daily-broadcast/ becoming-the-woman-god-made-me-to-be.

Seitz, Christopher R. *The Character of Christian Scripture: The Significance of a Two-Testament Bible*. STI. Grand Rapids: Baker Academic, 2011.

Seneca. *De Ira*. In *Seneca: Moral Essays*. Translated by John W. Basor. Cambridge, Mass.: Harvard University Press, 1923.

Servetus, Michael. *On the Errors of the Trinity* (1531) and *Dialogues on the Trinity* (1532). In *The Two Treatises of Servetus on the Trinity*. Translated by Earl Morse Wilbur. HTS 16. Cambridge, Mass.: Harvard University Press, 1932.

Shalev, Eran. *American Zion: The Old Testament as a Political Text from the Revolution to the Civil War*. New Haven: Yale University Press, 2013.

Shapira, Anita. "Ben-Gurion and the Bible: The Forging of an Historical Narrative?" *Middle Eastern Studies* 33 (1997): 645–74.

———. *Israel: A History*. Waltham, Mass.: Brandeis University Press, 2012.

Shelley, Mary Wollstoncraft. *Frankenstein: Or, The Modern Prometheus*. London: Printed for Lackington, Hughes, Harding, Mavor & Jones, 1818.

Sherwood, Jessie. "Interpretation, Negotiation, and Adaptation: Converting the Jews in Gerhard of Mainz's *Collectio*." Pages 119–29 in *Jews in Early Christian Law: Byzantium and the Latin West, 6th–11th Centuries*. Edited by John Tolan et al. RLMCMS 2. Turnhout: Brepols, 2014.

Shuler, Eric. "Caesarius of Arles and the Development of the Ecclesiastical Tithe: From a Theology of Almsgiving to Practical Obligations." *Traditio* 67 (2012): 43–69.

Shulevitz, Judith. *The Sabbath World: Glimpses of a Different Order of Time*. New York: Random House, 2011.

———. "Why You Never See Your Friends Anymore." *The Atlantic*, November 2019. https://www.theatlantic.com/magazine/archive/2019/11/why-dont-i-see-you-anymore/598336/.

Simonsohn, Shlomo. *The Apostolic See and the Jews: History*. Rome: Pontifical Institute of Mediaeval Studies, 1991.

Sizer, Stephen. "The Bible and Christian Zionism: Roadmap to Armageddon?" *Transf* 27 (2010): 122–32.

Skalko, John. "Why There Are Only Two Sexes." *Public Discourse*, June 5, 2017. https://www.thepublicdiscourse.com/2017/06/19389.

Smith, Gary V. *Isaiah 1–39*. NAC 15A. Nashville: B&H, 2007.

Smith, Robert O. *More Desired than Our Owne Salvation: The Roots of Christian Zionism*. New York: Oxford University Press, 2013.

Soh, Debra W. "CBC's Decision against Airing Transgender Kids Doc Should Leave Everyone Unsettled." CBC News, December 18, 2017. https://www.cbc.ca/news/opinion/transgender-kids-documentary-1.4453667.

Solon, Olivia. "Ex-Facebook President Sean Parker: Site Made to Exploit Human 'Vulnerability.'" *The Guardian*, November 9, 2017. https://www.theguardian.com/technology/2017/nov/09/facebook-sean-parker-vulnerability-brain-psychology.

Somerville, Margaret A. *Death Talk: The Case against Euthanasia and Physician-Assisted Suicide*. 2nd ed. Montreal: McGill-Queen's University Press, 2014.

Spinoza, Benedict de. *Theological-Political Treatise*. Edited by Jonathan Israel. Translated by Michael Silverthorne and Jonathan Israel. CTHP. Cambridge: Cambridge University Press, 2007.

Stackhouse, John. G. Jr. *Making the Best of It: Following Christ in the Real World*. Oxford: Oxford University Press, 2008.

Stanton, Elizabeth Cady, Susan B. Anthony, Matilda Joslyn Gage, and Ida Husted Harper. *History of Woman Suffrage*. Vol. 1. Rochester, N.Y.: S. B. Anthony, 1887.

Stark, Rodney. *God's Battalions: The Case for the Crusades*. New York: HarperOne, 2009.

Stayer, James M. *Anabaptists and the Sword*. Rev. ed. Eugene, Ore.: Wipf & Stock, 1976.

Stearman, Allyn MacLean. "Only Slaves Climb Trees: Revisiting the Myth of the Ecologically Noble Savage in Amazonia." *HN* 5 (1994): 339–57.

Steensma T. D., et al. "Factors Associated with Desistence and Persistence of Childhood Gender Dysphoria: A Quantitative Follow-Up Study." *Journal of the American Academy of Child and Adolescent Psychiatry* 52 (2013): 582–590.

Stein, Leonard. *The Balfour Declaration*. New York: Simon and Schuster, 1961.

Stephenson, Paul. *Constantine: Unconquered Emperor, Christian Victor*. London: Quercus 2011.

Strand, Kenneth A. "Tertullian and the Sabbath." *AUSS* 9 (1971): 129–46.

Sutcliffe, Adam. "The Philosemitic Moment?" Pages 67–90 in Karp and Sutcliffe, *Philosemitism in History*.

Suzuki, David. *The Legacy: An Elder's Vision for Our Sustainable Future*. Vancouver: Greystone Books, 2010.

Suzuki, David, and Peter Knudtson. *Wisdom of the Elders: Honoring Sacred Native Visions of Nature*. Vancouver: Greystone Books, 1992.

Swartley, Willard. M. *Slavery, Sabbath, War, and Women: Case Issues in Biblical Interpretation*. Scottdale, Pa.: Herald, 1983.

Tanner, Norman P., S.J., ed. *Decrees of the Ecumenical Councils*. 2 vols. London: Sheed & Ward, 1990.

Taylor, Bron. *Dark Green Religion: Nature Spirituality and the Planetary Future*. Berkeley: University of California, 2010.

The Teaching of the Twelve Apostles, Commonly Called the Didache. Pages 177–78 in *Early Christian Fathers*. Edited by Cyril Charles Richardson. LCC 1. New York: Macmillan, 1970.

Thibedeau, Hannah. "Ottawa Looking at Criminal Code Reforms to Deter 'Shameful' Conversion Therapy." CBC News, July 9, 2019. https://www.cbc.ca/news/politics/conversion-therapy-criminal-code-1.5204919.

Thiselton, Anthony C. *The First Epistle to the Corinthians*. NIGTC. Grand Rapids: Eerdmans, 2000.

Thompson, C. Bradley, ed. *Anti-Slavery Political Writings, 1833–1860: A Reader*. Armonk, N.Y.: M. E. Sharpe, 2004.

Tiffany, Kaitlyn. "GLAAD on LGBTQ Representation in Film: 'It Is Not Getting Better.'" *The Verge*, May 25, 2017. https://www.theverge.com/2017/5/25/15690404/glaad-lgbtq-representation-film-not-getting-better.

Todd, Douglas. "If Your Child Talks about Being a Different Gender, Take It Slowly." *Vancouver Sun*, https://vancouversun.com/opinion/columnists/douglas-todd-if-your-child-talks-about-being-a-different-gender-take-it-slowly.

Tolstoy, Leo. *War and Peace*. Translated by Anthony Briggs. London: Penguin, 2005.

Trible, Phyllis. *Texts of Terror: Literary-Feminist Readings of Biblical Narratives*. Philadelphia: Fortress, 1984.

Trompf, G. W. "The Concept of the Carolingian Renaissance." *JHI* 34 (1973): 3–26.

Trotter, Geoffrey. "Legal Worldview and the New Coercion," *Christian Legal Journal* 28, no. 2 (2019): 22–27.

Tuffrey-Wijne, Irene, Leopold Curfs, Ilora Finlay, and Sheila Hollins. "'Because of His Intellectual Disability, He Couldn't Cope': Is Euthanasia the Answer?" *Journal of Policy and Practice in Intellectual Disabilities* 16, no. 2 (2019): 113–16.

Turban, Jack L., et al. "Association between Recalled Exposure to Gender Identity Conversion Efforts and Psychological Distress and Suicide Attempts among Transgender Adults." *JAMA Psychiatry*, September 11, 2019. https://jamanetwork.com/journals/jamapsychiatry/article-abstract/2749479?resultClick=1.

UN Conference on Environment and Development (1992). May 23, 1997. https://www.un.org/geninfo/bp/enviro.html.

UN General Assembly. "Resolution Adopted by the Human Rights Council on 30 June, 2016." July 15, 2016. https://www.un.org/en/ga/search/view_doc.asp?symbol=A/HRC/RES/32/2.

UN Human Rights. Office of the High Commissioner. "Vitit Muntarbhorn." https://www.ohchr.org/EN/Issues/SexualOrientationGender/Pages/VititMuntarbhorn.aspx.

U.S. Congress. *French Declaration of the Rights of Man and of the Citizen and the American Bill of Rights: A Bicentennial Commemoration Issued Pursuant to S.J. Res. 317, 100th Congress.* Washington, D.C.: U.S. Congress, Senate, 1989.

Van Gend, David. "Banning Therapy, Banning Liberty." MercatorNet, March 7, 2019. https://www.mercatornet.com/conjugality/view/banning-therapy-banning-liberty/22255.

Vandenberghe, Joris. "Euthanasia in Patients with Intolerable Suffering Due to an Irremediable Psychiatric Illness." Pages 150–72 in Jones et al., *Euthanasia and Assisted Suicide.*

Vermes, Geza. *The Dead Sea Scrolls in English.* 3rd ed. Sheffield: JSOT, 1987.

Walton, John H. *Ancient Near Eastern Thought and the Old Testament: Introducing the Conceptual World of the Hebrew Bible.* Grand Rapids: Baker Academic, 2006.

———, ed. *The Zondervan Illustrated Bible Backgrounds Commentary.* 5 vols. Grand Rapids: Zondervan, 2009.

Walton, John H., and J. Harvey Walton. *The Lost World of the Torah: Laws as Covenant and Wisdom in Ancient Context.* Downers Grove, Ill.: IVP Academic, 2019.

Wanliss, James. *Resisting the Green Dragon: Dominion Not Death.* Burke, Va.: Cornwall Alliance for the Stewardship of Creation, 2010.

Ward, W. R. "Response." Pages 51–56 in Hutchison and Lehmann, *Many Are Chosen.*

Watson, Amy. "Television in Canada—Statistics & Facts." Statista, May 17, 2019, https://www.statista.com/topics/2730/television-in-canada/.

Weiss, Herold. "The Sabbath in the Writings of Josephus." *JSJ* 29 (1998): 363–90.

Wenham, Gordon J. *Genesis 1–15.* WBC 1. Waco: Word, 1987.

Werner, Ernst. "Popular Ideologies in Late Mediaeval Europe: Taborite Chiliasm and Its Antecedents." *CSSH* 2 (1960): 344–63.

Westermarck, Edward. *The Origin and Development of the Moral Ideas.* 2nd ed. 2 vols. London: Macmillan, 1924.

Westfall, Cynthia Long. *Paul and Gender: Reclaiming the Apostle's Vision for Men and Women.* Grand Rapids: Baker Academic, 2016.

Westminster Assembly. *The Confession of Faith, Agreed upon by the Assembly of Divines at Westminster, with the Assistance of Commissioners from the Church of Scotland.* Haverhill, N.H.: Goss, 1821.

Whalen, Brett E. *Dominion of God: Christendom and Apocalypse in the Middle Ages.* Cambridge, Mass.: Harvard University Press, 2009.

White, Lynn. "The Historical Roots of Our Ecologic Crisis." *Science* 155 (1967): 1203–7.

Wickham, Chris. *The Inheritance of Rome: Illuminating the Dark Ages, 400–1000.* PHE 2. New York: Penguin, 2010.

Wilkinson, Loren, ed. *Earthkeeping: Christian Stewardship of Natural Resources.* Grand Rapids: Eerdmans, 1980.

Williams, George H. *The Radical Reformation.* 3rd ed. SCES 15. Kirksville, Mo.: Truman State University Press, 1995.

Williams, Sarah C. *Perfectly Human: Nine Months with Cerian.* Walden, N.Y.: Plough, 2018.

Witte, John, Jr., and Robert M. Kingdon. *Sex, Marriage, and Family in John Calvin's Geneva.* Vol. 1: *Courtship, Engagement, and Marriage.* Grand Rapids: Eerdmans, 2005.

Wolf, Ron. "God, James Watt, and the Public Land." *Audubon* 83 (1981): 58–65.

Wollstonecraft, Mary. *A Vindication of the Rights of Woman: With Strictures on Political and Moral Subjects.* Dublin: Stockdale, 1792.

Wordsworth, William. "The Tables Turned." In *Selected Poetry.* Edited by Mark Van Doren. New York: Modern Library, 1950.

Wright, Colin. "The New Evolution Deniers." Quillette, November 30, 2018. https://quillette.com/2018/11/30/the-new-evolution-deniers/.

Yarhouse, Mark A. *Understanding Gender Dysphoria: Navigating Transgender Issues in a Changing Culture.* Downers Grove, Ill.: IVP Academic, 2015.

Yarhouse, Mark A., and Olya Zaporozhets. *Costly Obedience: What We Can Learn from the Celibate Gay Christian Community.* Grand Rapids: Zondervan, 2019.

Yogyakarta Principles. "About the Yogyakarta Principles." http://yogyakartaprinciples.org/principles-en/about-the-yogyakarta-principles.

Young, Toby. "Why I Want to Start a Free Speech Trade Union." Quillette, August 1, 2019. https://quillette.com/2019/08/01/why-i-want-to-start-a-free-speech-trade-union/.

Younger, K. Lawson, Jr. *Ancient Conquest Accounts: A Study in Ancient Near Eastern and Biblical History Writing.* JSOTS 98. Sheffield: JSOT, 1990.

Yu, Alvin. "Conversion Therapy: What You Need to Know." CBC News, July 13, 2019. https://www.cbc.ca/news/canada/conversion-therapy-what-you-need-to-know-1.5209598.

Zagorin, Perez. *How the Idea of Religious Toleration Came to the West.* Princeton: Princeton University Press, 2003.

Zerzan, John. *Twilight of the Machines.* Port Townsend, Wash.: Feral House, 2008.

Zucker, Kenneth J. "The Myth of Persistence." *International Journal of Transgenderism* 19 (2018): 231–45.

Index of Scripture

EXODUS

LEVITICUS

Index of Authors

Index of Subjects

governance, 190–201; constitutional monarchy, 192; divine kingship, 191–92;
hermeneutics of, 195–201; republicanism, 192–95, 203–8

Hebraic republic, 212–13
Hebrew Roots movement, 29–30, 41–42

icons, veneration of, 75–79
identity: inculcation of, 359–60, 370–73,
375–78; nature of, 325–26

Jerusalem: as apocalyptic reality, 126–29;
hermeneutics of, 100–6; history of the
postbiblical city, 94–96
Jews: in early Christendom, 53–54; from
the Renaissance to the State of Israel,
250–52; in the pagan Roman Empire,
52–53; in the Middle Ages, 247–50;
Israeli Proclamation of Independence,
245–47; Zionism and the State of
Israel, 252–55

liberalism, political, 189–90, 194, 294–95,
301–2, 315, 321, 344–45, 351–52

modern science, 270–72
Münster rebellion, 129–34

Old Testament: as authority in respect
of Christian ethics, 17–28; continuity and discontinuity with the New
Testament, 29–45; heroic reading of,
26–27, 42–43; literal and allegorical
reading of, 23–26; Marcionite views,
21–22; overall shape of its story,
30–34; reading the Bible for ethics,
287–96, 380–82
Old Testament Law/Torah, 34–45;
creational law, 34–36; redundancy in
respect of the New Testament, 40–41;
stiff-neck law, 38–40; Ten Commandments, 18–20, 35–37, 77–78, 113, 134,
173–75, 280, 290

Papacy: its rise to power, 90–93; its troubles in the High Middle Ages, 108–9
Parliament, 145

punishment, the hermeneutics of, 134–41
Puritans: their conflict with Charles I,
145–51; Cromwell's Protectorate,
151–53; early history, 144; in New
England, 163–68

Reformation: John Calvin on civil gov-
ernment, 111–13; in Geneva 114–20;
Martin Luther 109–11
Romanticism, 272–74

same-sex attraction, 337–46
sex and marriage: hermeneutics of,
120–24; in Reformed Geneva, 117–20
slavery: hermeneutics of, 214–21; in the
Bible, 213–14; in North America,
208–13
suffering, 32, 55, 97, 104, 133, 139, 161, 201,
250, 303, 308, 318–21, 327, 330–31, 336,
344, 374, 378, 381
suicide, 316–19, 321–23
Sunday: among the Puritans, 169–71, 186;
history of, 168–69; hermeneutics of,
171–82

television/internet, 370–72
tithing, 79–81
toleration: hermeneutics of, 189–90;
Lactantius to Westphalia, 184–87;
Westphalia to the Enlightenment,
187–89
transgenderism, 326–37

war, hermeneutics of, 153–61
women's rights: activism and debate in
the United States, 223–29; in France,
229–30; hermeneutics of, 231–42